Anonymous

**The advanced book of reading lessons,**

Forming a supplement to the fourth and fifth reading books of the authorized

series

Anonymous

**The advanced book of reading lessons,**
*Forming a supplement to the fourth and fifth reading books of the authorized series*

ISBN/EAN: 9783337808327

Printed in Europe, USA, Canada, Australia, Japan

Cover: Foto ©ninafisch / pixelio.de

More available books at **www.hansebooks.com**

Canadian Series of School Books.

# THE
# ADVANCED BOOK
OF
# READING LESSONS,

FORMING A

SUPPLEMENT TO THE FOURTH AND FIFTH READING
BOOKS OF THE AUTHORIZED SERIES.

Authorized
By the Council of Public Instruction
for Ontario.

TORONTO:
JAMES CAMPBELL & SON.
1871.

Entered according to the Act of the Parliament of Canada, in the year one thousand eight hundred and seventy-one, by the Reverend EGERTON RYERSON, LL.D., Chief Superintendent of Education for Ontario, in the Office of the Minister of Agriculture.

# INTRODUCTION.

The following pages contain a selection of extracts intended to be used as a sequel to the Fourth or Fifth Book of Reading Lessons authorized by the Council of Public Instruction for Ontario, or in some cases as a substitute for them. In this as in the preceding volumes of the series, specimens are given of the best authors in English literature, but many additional writers of high reputation are here introduced. With a view to the wants of those students who desire to ascend to the sources, an Appendix is subjoined, illustrating the origin and progress of the Language.

Education Office,
Toronto, October, 1871.

# CONTENTS.

| | | PAGE |
|---|---|---|
| The Sciences in Ancient Egypt | Wilkinson | 1 |
| Hymn to the Sea | Alford | 4 |
| Nineveh | Layard | 5 |
| Persepolis | Rawlinson | 8 |
| *Assyrian Batt'e Scene* | Atherstone | 11 |
| The Battle of Salamis | Mitford | 12 |
| The Passage of the Red Sea | Heber | 15 |
| Song of Praise | Moore | 18 |
| Hymn of the Hebrew Maid | Scott | 18 |
| Palestine, the Land of Ruins | A. P. Stanley | 19 |
| The Death of Moses | Jessie G. McCartee | 21 |

## CONTENTS.

| | | PAGE |
|---|---|---|
| Socrates | Grote | 23 |
| —Marvels of the Sun—The Zollner Pictures | London Spectator | 26 |
| The Elephant | Baker | 29 |
| Gentle River | Percy | 34 |
| The Rhea, or South American Ostrich | My Feathered Friends | 35 |
| Pelopidas and Epaminondas | Thirlwall | 38 |
| How Sleep the Brave | Collins | 41 |
| The Study of Archæology | Lord Lytton | 41 |
| Honor must be Active | Shakespeare | 43 |
| The Battle of Arbela | Cresy | 44 |
| —Bligh's Boat Voyage | Ballantyne | 49 |
| The Desert | Skinner | 59 |
| Adam | Milton | 60 |
| The Earthquake at Lisbon | Davy | 61 |
| Happy Life | Sir H. Wotton | 71 |
| Death the Leveller | F. Shirley | 72 |
| The Present Age | Channing | 72 |
| The Mediterranean | F. B. Head | 77 |
| Palmyra | Tweedie | 78 |
| Man Fitted for his Position | Pope | 82 |
| The Fossil Elephant | Milner | 83 |
| God of my Life | Cowper | 86 |
| The Mississippi Scheme | Tucker | 86 |
| Harmosan | R. C. Trench | 93 |
| Building and Engineering in Ancient Rome | Liddell | 94 |
| Resignation | Chatterton | 95 |
| —The Ostrich | Livingstone | 95 |
| The Scholar | Southey | 98 |
| Spectrum Analysis | Edinburgh Review | 98 |
| Pompeii | Macaulay | 102 |
| The Giant Trees of California | Cassell's Family Paper | 104 |
| Trajan | Merivale | 107 |
| Marine Views | Crabbe | 109 |
| The Trade Winds | Maury | 114 |
| Youth and Age | Coleridge | 114 |
| The Emily St. Pierre | Kingston | 115 |
| Kirkdale Cavern | Milner | 119 |
| Military Glory | Johnson | 121 |
| The Battle of Cannæ | Arnold | 122 |
| The Antonines | Gibbon | 128 |
| The Spanish Armada | Macaulay | 130 |
| God's Providence Inscrutable | London Daily Telegraph | 132 |
| Corn Fields | Mary Howitt | 135 |
| On Law | Hooker | 136 |
| The Progress of Decay | Gray | 139 |
| The Fall of Montreal | Clarendon | 140 |
| The Second Advent | Milman | 145 |
| Tours | Brougham | 145 |
| The Alhambra | Croly | 146 |
| Merchant Princes | Fyfe | 147 |
| King Alfred | Hume | 149 |
| The Light of Home | Mrs Hale | 151 |
| Inundation | Addison | 152 |
| Messages | Byron | 154 |
| —The Footsteps of the Times | Gibbon | 156 |
| I gave my Mother my a Blade | Magunn | 162 |

## CONTENTS

|   | | PAGE |
|---|---|---|
| The Nubian | Scott | 163 |
| The Spilt Pearls | Trench | 169 |
| Coral Reefs | Hall | 170 |
| The Reaper and the Flowers | Longfellow | 172 |
| Beaver Trapping | Ballantyne | 172 |
| The Battle of Killiecrankie | Macaulay | 174 |
| The Burial March of Dundee | Aytoun | 177 |
| The Pleasures of a Cultivated Imagination | Stewart | 180 |
| The Family Meeting | Sprague | 181 |
| The Plague at Constantinople | Finlay | 182 |
| Song | Hood | 185 |
| Extinct Reptiles | Ansted | 185 |
| Bernardine du Born | Mrs. Sigourney | 188 |
| Snakes and Snake Charmers | Chambers | 189 |
| Thou did'st, O Mighty God, exist | Mrs. Rowe | 192 |
| The Evening Wind | Bryant | 193 |
| Man's Faculties | Ruskin | 194 |
| The River of Life | Campbell | 196 |
| Elihu | Alice Carey | 196 |
| Damascus | Warburton | 198 |
| Sleep | Shakespeare | 201 |
|  |  | 202 |
| Vanity of Power |  |  |
| The Stork | Bishop Stanley | 203 |
| A Survey of the Heavens | Kirke-White | 205 |
| Grecian Mythology | Wordsworth | 207 |
| Wordsworth | DeQuincey | 208 |
| The Spinning Maiden's Cross | Whewell | 210 |
| Killed at the Ford | Longfellow | 213 |
| The Beginning of Commerce | Robertson | 213 |
| From "The Traveller" | Goldsmith | 2.7 |
| The Death of Paul Dombey | Dickens | 218 |
| Woodlark Lane | Miss Mitford | 222 |
| A Name in the Sand | Gould | 226 |
| The Happiness of Animals | Paley | 227 |
| Spring | Wordsworth | 229 |
| On the Death of Wellington | B. Disraeli | 230 |
| The Inn at Terracina | Washington Irving | 234 |
| The Bower of Roses | Moore | 241 |
| Magna Charta | Hallam | 242 |
| The Battle of Morgarten | Mrs. Hemans | 245 |
| Christianity a Sword | Melvill | 247 |
| The Ruined Cottage | L. E. L. (Mrs. Maclean) | 250 |
| The Study of the Natural Sciences | W. B. Rogers | 252 |
| May | Alex. McLachlan | 254 |
| The Last Days of Colonel Newcome | Thackeray | 255 |
| Legend of Strasburg Cathedral | Miss Wilkins | 258 |
| Execution of Counts Egmont and Horn | Motley | 259 |
| The Sea Gull | Griffin | 263 |
| On the General Deficiency of Self-Observation | Foster | 264 |
| The Fall | Ascher | 267 |
| The New Year | Hugh Miller | 267 |
| Another Year | A. Norton | 269 |
| The Power of England | Canning | 270 |
| Competitive Examinations | Lord Palmerston | 271 |
| Richard Arkwright | Smiles | 274 |
| The Shunammite | N. P. Willis | 277 |

## CONTENTS.

| | PAGE |
|---|---|
| The Sword and the Press . . . . Carlyle . . . 279 |
| Childhood and his Visitors . . . Praed . . . . 280 |
| The Tsetse . . . . . . . Livingstone . . 281 |
| Home—A Duet . . . . . . Barry Cornwall (B. W. Procter) . . 283 |
| Reading . . . . . . . . Locke . . . . 284 |
| Lady Care . . . . . . . Tennyson . . . 286 |
| Justice . . . . . . . . Sheridan . . . 288 |
| The Conqueror's Grave . . . . Bryant . . . . 288 |
| Reflections on the French Revolution . Burke . . . . 290 |
| The Hunter . . . . . . . Toronto Maple Leaf . 291 |
| The Battle of Creci . . . . . Lingard . . . 292 |
| Tears . . . . . . . . Bickersteth . . 296 |
| Jerusalem . . . . . . . Kitto . . . . 297 |
| Palestine . . . . . . . Whittier . . . 302 |
| Perils of Ballooning . . . . . Glaisher . . . 303 |
| One by One . . . . . . . Adelaide Procter . 306 |
| Washington . . . . . . . Brougham . . . 307 |
| Night on Lake Couchiching . . . Chapman . . . 309 |
| Rolla's Address to the Peruvians . . Sheridan . . . 311 |
| On the River . . . . . . . E. H. Dewart . . 312 |
| Louis XI and Charles, Duke of Burgundy . Scott . . . . 313 |
| The Souls of Books . . . . . Lord Lytton . . 319 |
| The Origin of Language . . . . Thomson . . . 320 |
| The Presence of God . . . . . Amelia B. Welby . 324 |
| The Vastness of the Universe . . . Whewell . . . 325 |
| Twilight . . . . . . . . Halleck . . . . 328 |
| The Dignity of Labor . . . . . Newman Hall . . 329 |
| My Own Fireside . . . . . . A. A. Watts . . 332 |
| Burns . . . . . . . . Carlyle . . . . 334 |
| The Mother . . . . . . . Swain . . . . 335 |
| The Snow Storm . . . . . . Christopher North . 336 |
| The Coast of 1811 . . . . . . G. Hogg . . . 339 |
| Sharks as Food . . . . . . Kingston . . . 340 |
| The Owl . . . . . . . . Barry Cornwall . 342 |
| Gold Leaf . . . . . . . . Dodd . . . . 342 |
| The Founding of the Bell . . . . C. Mackay . . . 345 |
| A Forest on Fire . . . . . . Audubon . . . 346 |
| The Battle of Agincourt . . . . Nicolas . . . . 349 |
| The Pleasant Days of Old . . . . Frances Browne . 352 |
| Charles James Fox . . . . . Mackintosh . . 353 |
| The City of Yeddo . . . . . Alcock . . . . 356 |
| I. Christabel . . . . . . . Massey . . . . 359 |
| Prejudices and Opinions . . . . Berkeley . . . 360 |
| The Coliseum by Moon-Light . . . Byron . . . . 362 |
| Coal . . . . . . . . . Ansted . . . . 363 |
| T. Miner . . . . . . . . Miss Clephane . . 367 |
| Caves . . . . . . . . Macaulay . . . 368 |
| Corps and Fame . . . . . . Prince . . . . 370 |
| Anne Boleyn's Coronation Pageant . Froude . . . . 371 |
| Charms of the Sea . . . . . Darnell . . . . 374 |
| The Law of Causation . . . . Mill . . . . . 375 |
| Loss of the Royal George . . . . Cowper . . . . 378 |
| To My Mate . . . . . . . Dodd . . . . 379 |
| For Full of Moor . . . . . . Burns . . . . 380 |
| The Study of the Classics . . . . H. N. Coleridge . 382 |

## CONTENTS.

| | PAGE. |
|---|---|
| Youths at an early Age leaving College | |
| The Regatta at Venice | |
| From the East and from the West | |
| The Farmer | |
| The Canadian Farmer's Song | |
| Natural Philosophy | |
| Canadian Christmas Carol | |
| The Telescope and the Microscope | |
| Contentment | |
| Light | |
| Music | |
| The Voice of the Wind | |
| The Spring | |
| The Siege of Gibraltar | |
| Fore-Knowledge | |
| The Use of Adversity | |
| God's Care for man | |
| Machinery | |
| Bernardo and Alphonso | |
| Alonzo de Aguilar | |
| Time | |
| Time | |
| The Infidel and the Angel | |
| The Prayer of Festus | |
| The Girondists | |
| Go, Dream no more | |
| The Young Men of Canada | |
| The Joys of Home | |
| The Three Sister Arts | |
| Insult | |
| The Better Life | |
| The True King | |
| Society | |
| The Death of Theodore | |
| A Voice for the Times | |
| Precious Stones | |
| The Soul's Aspirations | |
| My Mother Dear | |
| Reflections on War | |
| Fame | |
| Repose | |
| The Surrender of the Emperor Napoleon III. | |
| Aufidius and Coriolanus | |
| Samson's Death | |
| Maximilian and Octavio | |
| Adrastus, Crythes and Ion | |

| | |
|---|---|
| Mrs. Butler | 383 |
| Cooper | 384 |
| Bonar | 387 |
| Country Gentleman's Magazine | 388 |
| Dewart | 390 |
| Hogg | 391 |
| Toronto Maple Leaf | 394 |
| Chalmers | 395 |
| Keble | 398 |
| Elliott | 399 |
| Hogarth | 399 |
| Taylor | 402 |
| Barbauld | 402 |
| Lord Mahon | 403 |
| Dryden | 405 |
| Daniel | 405 |
| Spenser | 405 |
| Popular Encyclopedia | 406 |
| Lockhart | 410 |
| Prescott | 411 |
| Spencer | 414 |
| Cowley | 414 |
| Punshon | 415 |
| Bailey | 417 |
| Alison | 418 |
| Mrs. Yule | 420 |
| Dr. Ormiston | 420 |
| Bowring | 421 |
| Cleghorn | 422 |
| Ben Jonson | 425 |
| Massinger | 426 |
| Marston | 425 |
| F. Beaumont | 427 |
| Markham | 427 |
| Miss Haight | 430 |
| Emanuel | 431 |
| Akenside | 433 |
| Lover | 434 |
| Robert Hall | 434 |
| Beattie | 437 |
| Thomson | 437 |
| W. H. Russell | 438 |
| Shakespeare | 442 |
| Milton | 443 |
| Schiller, trans. by Coleridge | 446 |
| Talfourd | 448 |

# APPENDIX.

### I. ANGLO-SAXON PERIOD.

|  |  | PAGE. |
|---|---|---|
| From *The Creation* . . . . . . . Cædmon | . . | 451 |
| From his Translation of Boethius . . . King Alfred | . . | 452 |

### II. SEMI-SAXON PERIOD.

| *King Arthur's Dream* . . . . . . Layamon . | . . | 453 |
|---|---|---|

### III. OLD ENGLISH PERIOD.

| From *Piers Ploughman's Vision* . . . Langlande . | . . | 455 |
|---|---|---|
| *The Temple of Mars* . . . . . . Chaucer | . . | 457 |
| *Caius Fabricius* . . . . . . . Gower | . . | 458 |
| *Freedom* . . . . . . . . Barbour | . . | 459 |
| *Mahomet* . . . . . . . . Mandevil | . . | 460 |
| *Be Merry* . . . . . . . . Dunbar | . . | 461 |
| *Sir Lancelot* . . . . . . . Malory | . . | 462 |
| Letter of Sir Thomas More to his Wife ; . More . | . . | 463 |
| *The Shepherds of Bethlehem* . . . . Latimer | . . | 464 |
| *Blame not my Lute* . . . . . . Wyatt | . . | 464 |
| The first fifteen verses of the eighth Chapter of St. Matthew ; six versions . . . Marsh | . . |  |

# ADVANCED
# READING BOOK.

### THE SCIENCES IN ANCIENT EGYPT.

IN considering the state of agriculture in Egypt, we do not confine its importance to the direct and tangible benefits it annually conferred upon the people, by the improved condition of the productions of the soil; the influence it had on the manners and scientific acquirements of the people is no less obvious, and worthy our contemplation; and to the peculiar nature of the Nile, and the effects of its inundation, has been reasonably attributed the early advancement of the Egyptians in geometry and mensuration.

It is reasonable to suppose that as the inundation subsided, much litigation sometimes occurred between neighbors respecting the limits of their unenclosed fields; and the fall of a portion of the bank, carried away by the stream during the rise of the Nile, frequently made great alterations in the extent of land near the river side; we therefore readily perceive the necessity of determining the quantity which belonged to each individual, whether to settle disputes with a neighbor, or to ascertain the tax due to government. But it is difficult to fix the period when the science of mensuration commenced; if we have ample proofs of its being known in the time of Joseph, this does not carry us far back into the ancient history of Egypt; and there is evidence of geometry and mathematics having already made the same progress at the earliest period of which any monuments remain, as in the later era of the Patriarch, or of the Great Remeses.

Besides the mere measurement of superficial areas, it was of paramount importance to agriculture, and to the interests of the peasant, to distribute the benefits of the inundation in due proportion to each individual, that the lands which were low might not enjoy the exclusive advantages of the fertilising water, by constantly draining it from those of a higher level. For this purpose, the necessity of ascertaining the various elevations of the country, and of constructing accurately levelled canals and dykes, obviously occurred to them; and if it be true, that Menes, their first king, turned the course of the Nile into a new channel he had made for it, we have a proof of their having, long before his time, arrived at considerable knowledge in this branch of science, since so great an undertaking could only have been the result of long experience.

These dykes were succeeded or accompanied by the invention of sluices, and all the mechanism appertaining to them; the regulation of the supply of water admitted into plains of various levels, the report of the exact quantity of land irrigated, the depth of the water and the time it continued upon the surface, which determined the proportionate payment of the taxes, required much scientific skill; and the prices of provisions for the ensuing year were already ascertained by the unerring prognostics of the existing inundations. This naturally led to minute observations respecting the increase of the Nile during the inundation; Nilometers, for measuring its gradual rise or fall, were constructed in various parts of Egypt, and particular persons were appointed to observe each daily change, and to proclaim the favorable or unfavorable state of this important phenomenon. On these reports depended the time chosen for opening the canals, whose mouths were closed until the river rose to a fixed height, upon which occasion grand festivities were proclaimed throughout the country, in order that every person might show his sense of the great benefit vouchsafed by the Gods to the land of Egypt. The introduction of the waters of the Nile into the interior, by means of these canals, was allegorically construed into the union of Osiris and Isis; the instant of cutting away the dam of earth, which separated the bed of the canal from the Nile, was looked forward to with the utmost anxiety; and it is reasonable to suppose that many omens were consulted in order to ascertain the auspicious moment for this important ceremony.

Superstition added greatly to the zeal of a credulous people. The Deity, or presiding Genius, of the river was propitiated by suitable oblations, both during the inundation, and about the period when it was expected; and Seneca tells us, that on a particular fête the priests threw presents, and offerings of gold into the river near Philæ, at a place called the Veins of the Nile, where they first perceived the rise of the inundation. Indeed, we may reasonably suppose that the grand and wonderful spectacle of the inundation excited in them feelings of the deepest awe for the divine power, to which they were indebted for so great a blessing: and a plentiful supply of water was supposed to be the result of the favor of the Gods, as a deficiency was attributed to their displeasure, punishing the sins of an offending people.

On the inundation depended all the hopes of the peasant; it affected the revenue of the government, both by its influence on the scale of taxation, and by the greater or less profits on the exportation of grain and other produce; and it involved the comfort of all classes. For in Upper Egypt no rain fell to irrigate the land; it was a country, as ancient writers state, which did not look for showers to advance its crops; and if, as Proclus says, these fell in Lower Egypt, they were confined to that district, and heavy rain was a prodigy in the Thebaid. There is, however, evidence that heavy rain did occasionally fall in the vicinity of Thebes, from the appearance of the deep ravines worn by water in the hills, about the tombs of the Kings, though probably, as now, after intervals of fifteen or twenty years; and it may be said from modern experience, that slight showers fall there about five or six times a year, in Lower Egypt much more frequently, and at Alexandria almost as often as in the South of Europe.

The result of a favorable inundation was not confined to tangible benefits; it had the greatest effect on the mind of every Egyptian by long anticipation; the happiness arising from it, as the regrets on the appearance of a scanty supply of water, being far more sensibly felt than in countries which depend on rain for their harvest, where future prospects not being so soon foreseen, hope continues longer; the Egyptian, on the other hand, being able to form a just estimate of his crops even before the seed is sown, or the land prepared for its reception.

Other remarkable effects may likewise be partially attributed to the interest excited by the expectation of the rising Nile; and it is probable that the accurate observations required for fixing the seasons, and the period of the annual return of the inundation, which was found to coincide with the heliacal rising of Sothis, or the Dog-star, contributed greatly to the early study of astronomy in the valley of the Nile. The precise time when these and other calculations were first made by the Egyptians, it is impossible now to determine; but from the height of the inundation being already recorded in the reign of Mœris, we may infer that constant observations had been made, and Nilometers constructed, even before that early period; and astronomy, geometry, and other sciences are said to have been known in Egypt in the time of the hierarchy which preceded the accession of their first king, Menes.

—WILKINSON.

## HYMN TO THE SEA.

Who shall declare the secret of thy birth,
Thou old companion of the circling earth?
   And having marked with keen poetic sight
     Ere beast or happy bird
     Through the vast silence stirred,
Roll back the folded darkness of the primal night?

Corruption like, thou teemedst in the graves
Of mouldering systems, with dark weltering waves
   Troubling the peace of the first mother's womb;
     Whose ancient awful form,
     With inly tossing storm,
Unquiet heavings kept—a birth-place and a tomb.

Till the life-giving Spirit moved above
The face of the waters, with creative love
   Warming the hidden seeds of infant light;
     What time the mighty Word
     Through thine abyss was heard,
And swam from out thy deeps the young day heavenly bright.

Sunlight and moonlight minister to thee;—
O'er the broad circle of the shoreless sea
   Heaven's two great lights for ever set and rise;
     While the round vault above,
     In vast and silent love,
Is gazing down upon thee with his hundred eyes.

All night thou utterest forth thy solemn moan,
Counting thy weary minutes all alone ;
  Then in the morning thou dost calmly lie,
    Deep blue ere yet the sun
    His day-work hath begun,
Under the opening windows of the golden sky.

The spirit of the mountain looks on thee
Over an hundred hills ; quaint shadows flee
  Across thy marbled mirror : brooding lie
    Storm-mists of infant cloud,
    With a sight-baffling shroud
Mantling the grey-blue islands in the western sky.

Sometimes thou liftest up thine hands on high
Into the tempest-cloud that blurs the sky,
  Holding rough dalliance with the fitful blast,
    Whose stiff breath, whistling shrill,
    Pierces with deadly chill
The wet crew feebly clinging to their shattered mast.

Foam-white along the border of the shore
Thine onward-leaping billows plunge and roar ;
  While o'er the pebbly ridges slowly glide
    Cloaked figures, dim and grey,
    Through the thick mist of spray,
Watching for some struck vessel in the boiling tide.

Daughter and darling of remotest eld—
Time's childhood and Time's age thou hast beheld ;
  His arm is feeble and his eye is dim—
    He tells old tales again,—
    He wearies of long pain ;—
Thou art as at the first : thou journeyedst not with him.
                        —ALFORD.

## NINEVEH.

WE descend into the principal trench, by a flight of steps rudely cut into the earth, near the western face of the mound ; and, at a depth of about twenty feet, we suddenly find ourselves between a pair of colossal lions, winged and human-headed, forming a portal. Before these wonderful forms, Ezekiel, Jonah, and others of the prophets stood, and Sennacherib bowed ; even the patriarch Abraham himself may possibly have bowed.

    Leaving behind us a small chamber, in which the sculptures

are distinguished by a want of finish in the execution, and considerable rudeness in the design of the ornaments, we issue from between the winged lions, and enter the remnants of the principal hall. On both sides of us are sculptured gigantic winged figures; some with the heads of eagles, others entirely human, and carrying mysterious symbols in their hands. To the left is another portal, also formed by winged lions. One of them has, however, fallen across the entrance, and there is just room to creep beneath it. Beyond this portal is a winged figure, and two slabs with bas-reliefs; but they have been so much injured, that we can scarcely trace the subject upon them. Further on, there are no traces of wall, although a deep trench has been opened. The opposite side of the hall has also disappeared, and we only see a high wall of earth. On examining it attentively, we can detect the marks of masonry; and we soon find that it is a solid structure, built of bricks of unbaked clay, now of the same color as the surrounding soil, and scarcely to be distinguished from it.

The slabs of alabaster, fallen from their original position, have, however, been raised; and we tread in the midst of a maze of small bas-reliefs, representing chariots, horsemen, battles, and sieges. Perhaps the workmen are about to raise a slab for the first time; and we watch with eager curiosity what new event of Assyrian history, or what unknown custom or religious ceremony, may be illustrated by the sculpture beneath.

Having walked about one hundred feet amongst these scattered monuments of ancient history and art, we reach another doorway formed by gigantic winged bulls in yellow limestone. One is still entire, but its companion is fallen, and is broken into several pieces—the great human head is at our feet.

We pass on without turning into the part of the building to which this portal leads. Beyond it we see another winged figure, holding a graceful flower in its hand, and apparently presenting it as an offering to the winged bull. Adjoining this sculpture we find eight fine bas-reliefs. There is the king, hunting and triumphing over the lion and the wild bull; and the siege of the castle, with the battering ram. We have now reached the end of the hall, and find before us an elaborate and beautiful sculpture, representing two kings, standing beneath the emblem of the supreme deity, and attended by winged figures. Between them is the sacred tree. In front of this bas-relief is the great stone platform, upon which, in days of old, may have been placed the thrones of the Assyrian monarch, when he received his captive enemies, or his courtiers.

To the left of us is a fourth outlet from the hall, formed by another pair of lions. We issue from between them, and find ourselves on the edge of a deep ravine, to the north of which rises, high above us, the lofty pyramid. Figures of captives bearing objects of tribute; ear-rings, bracelets, and monkeys, may be seen on walls near this ravine: and two enormous bulls, and two winged figures above fourteen feet high, are lying on its very edge.

As the ravine bounds the ruins on this side, we must return to the yellow bulls. Passing through the entrance formed by them, we enter a large chamber surrounded by eagle-headed figures: at one end of it is a doorway, guarded by two priests or divinities, and in the centre another portal with winged bulls. Whichever way we turn, we find ourselves in the midst of a nest of rooms; and, without an acquaintance with the intricacies of the place, we should soon lose ourselves in this labyrinth. The accumulated rubbish being generally left in the centre of the chambers, the whole excavation consists of a number of narrow passages, panelled on one side with slabs of alabaster; and shut in on the other by a high wall of earth, half-buried in which may here and there be seen a broken vase, or a brick painted with brilliant colours. We may wander through these galleries for an hour or two, examining the marvellous sculptures, or the numerous inscriptions that surround us. Here, we meet long rows of kings, attended by their eunuchs and priests; there, lines of winged figures, carrying fir-cones and religious emblems, and seemingly in adoration before the mystic tree. Other entrances, formed by winged lions and bulls, lead us into new chambers. In every one of them are fresh objects of curiosity and surprise. At length, wearied, we issue from the buried edifice by a trench on the opposite side to that by which we entered, and find ourselves again upon the naked platform. We look around in vain for any traces of the wonderful remains we have just seen, and are half inclined to believe that we have dreamed a dream, or have listened to some tale of Eastern romance.—LAYARD.

# PERSEPOLIS.

WE have now to pass to the most magnificent of the Persepolitan buildings—the Great Pillared Halls—which constitute the glory of Arian architecture, and which, even in their ruins, provoke the wonder and admiration of modern Europeans, familiar with all the triumphs of Western art, with Grecian temples, Roman baths and amphitheatres, Moorish palaces, Turkish mosques, and Christian cathedrals. Of these pillared halls, the Persepolitan platform supports two, slightly differing in their design, but presenting many points of agreement. They bear the character of an earlier and a later building—a first effort in the direction which circumstances compelled the architecture of the Persians to take, and the final achievement of their best artists in this kind of building.

Nearly midway in the platform between its northern and its southern edges, and not very far from the boundary of the rocky mountain on which the platform abuts towards the east, is the vast edifice which has been called with good reason the "Hall of a Hundred Columns," since its roof was in all probability supported by that number of pillars. This building consisted of a single magnificent chamber, with a portico, and probably guard-rooms, in front, of dimensions quite unequalled upon the platform. The portico was 183 feet long by fifty-two feet deep, and was sustained by sixteen pillars, about thirty-five feet high, arranged in two rows of eight. The great chamber behind was a square of 227 feet, and had therefore an area of about 51,000 feet. Over this vast space were distributed, at equal distances from one another, one hundred columns, each thirty-five feet high, arranged in ten rows of ten each, every pillar thus standing at a distance of nearly twenty feet from any other. The four walls which enclosed this great hall had a uniform thickness of ten and a half feet, and were each pierced at equal intervals by two doorways, the doorways being thus exactly opposite to one another, and each looking down an avenue of columns. In the spaces of wall on either side of the doorways, eastward, westward, and southward, were three niches, all square-topped, and bearing the ornamentation which is universal in the case of all niches, windows, and doorways in the Persepolitan ruins. In the northern, or front, wall, the niches were replaced by windows, looking upon the portico, excepting towards the angles of the building, where niches were retained, owing to a peculiarity in the plan of the edifice which has now to be noticed. The portico, instead of being, as in every other Persian instance, of the same width with the building which it fronted, was forty-four feet narrower, its *antæ* projecting from the front wall, not at either extremity, but at the distance of eleven feet from the corner. While the porch was thus contracted so that the pillars had to be eight in each row instead of ten, space was left on either side for a narrow guard-room opening on to the porch, indications of which are seen in the doorways placed at right angles to the front wall, which are ornamented with the usual figures of soldiers armed with spear and shield. It has been suggested that the hall was, like the smaller pillared chambers upon the platform, originally surrounded on three sides by a number of lesser apartments; and this is certainly possible: but no trace remains of any such buildings. The ornamentation which exists seems to show that the building was altogether of a public character. Instead of exhibiting attendants bringing articles for the toilet or the banquet, it shows on its doors the monarch, either engaged in the act of destroying symbolical monsters, or seated on his throne under a canopy, with the tiara on his head, and the golden sceptre in his right hand. The throne representations are of two kinds. On the jambs of the great doors leading out upon the porch, we see in the top compartment the monarch seated under the canopy, accompanied by five attendants, while below him are his guards, arranged in five rows of ten each, some armed with spears and shields, others with spears, short swords, bows and quivers. Thus the two portals together exhibit the figures of two hundred Persian guardsmen in attendance on the person of the King. The doors at the back of the building present us with a still more curious sculpture. On these the throne appears elevated on a lofty platform, the stages of which, three in number, are upheld by figures in different costumes, representing apparently the natives of all the different provinces of the empire. It is a reasonable conjecture that this great hall was intended especially for a throne-room, and that in the representations on these doorways we have figured a structure which actually existed under its roof—a platform reached by steps, whereon in the great ceremonies of state the royal throne was placed, in order that the monarch might be distinctly seen at one and the same time by the whole court.

The question of the lighting of this huge apartment presents some difficulties. On three sides, as already observed, the hall had (so far as appears) no windows—the places where windows might have been expected to occur being occupied by niches. The apparent openings are consequently reduced to some fifteen, viz., the eight doorways, and seven windows, which looked out upon the portico and were therefore overhung and had a north aspect. It is clear that sufficient light could not have entered the apartment from these—the only visible— apertures. We must therefore suppose either that the walls above the niches were pierced with windows, which is quite possible, or else that light was in some way or other admitted from the roof. The latter is the supposition of those most competent to decide. M. Flandin conjectures that the roof had four apertures placed at the points where the lines drawn from the northern to the southern, and those drawn from the eastern to the western, doors would intersect one another. He seems to suppose that these openings were wholly unprotected, in which case they would have admitted, in a very inconvenient way, both the sun and the rain. May we not presume that, if such openings existed, they were guarded by *louvres* such as have been regarded as probably lighting the Assyrian halls?

The portico of the "Hall of a Hundred columns" was flanked on either side by a colossal bull, standing at the inner angle of the *antæ*, and thus in some degree narrowing the entrance. Its columns were fluted, and had in every case the complex capital, which occurs also in the great propylæa and in the Hall of Xerxes. It was built of the same sort of massive blocks as the south-eastern edifice, or Ancient Palace—blocks often ten feet square by seven feet thick, and may be ascribed probably to the same age as that structure. Like that edifice, it is situated somewhat low; it has no staircase, and no inscription. We may fairly suppose it to have been the throne room, or great hall of audience of the early king who built the South-Eastern Palace. —RAWLINSON.

## ASSYRIAN BATTLE SCENE.

O'er all the plain th' Assyrian camp-fires now
Blaze high ; and with the darkness a drear red
Strangely commingle. Like a burning gulf,
Sleeping till stirr'd by winds ; the heaving mass
Of warriors at the mountain's foot appears,
Breast-plates, and shields, and helms, and gonfalons,
Glow blood-red here and there ; but doubly dark
Elsewhere the night. Now, toward the hills all haste ;
If Medes alone, or with Assyrians mixed,
I cannot know ; but rapid is the speed.
The light increases : up the mountain's side,
In the red darkness faintly I discern
The slumbering myriads ; and towards its foot
Onward they come ; like billows of dark fire.
But farther off, in one bright blaze, the camp
Shines out : a countless multitude I see,
In flaming armor pouring o'er the plain.
Like ocean glittering 'neath the ruddy sun,
The wide field flashes ; like the ocean's roar
Their clamors rise.
            Among the trees a crash
I hear,—a heaving of the branches. Lights
Are thickening near the hill. Ha ! now I see
They rend the boughs for torches. In his hand
Each soldier bears a branch of blazing pine.
They speed toward the heights : they shake the torch :
They wave the sword : like running flame they seem.
Now up the steep they urge. A cloud of darts
And arrows from the Medes upon them pours,—
A fiery cloud ; and stones are hurled—and spears ;—
Yet upward still they come. The watch-fires now
Are flaming on the hills : distinctly gleams
The battle forth. Their torches they cast down ;
Not needed now. Ha ! by his star-like helm,
Assyria's king appears. He shouts : he flies :
He points towards the rocks ;—he waves them on.
A warrior meets him : sword with sword they fight—
Arabia's monarch, sure.—But both are lost,—
The waves of fight roll o'er them—

Meantime, along the sapphire bridge of heaven,
Far, far beyond the canopy of cloud
That mantled earth, the day-god's lightning steeds
Through the pure ether rapt his chariot-wheels,
Sounding harmonious thunder. To the height
They had ascended ; and the steep decline
Half-way had measured ; yet the hard-fought field

Still was contested ; for, like men resolved
On that one day to peril all to come—
To die, perchance, but never to submit—
The Assyrian captains strove ; and, with like fire,
Their soldiers' hearts inflamed.  Aid too had come—
Chariots, and horse, and foot ; who, when the scale,
Charged with Assyria's doom, was sinking fast,
Twice had its fall arrested.  Once again,
When seemed that utter ruin hovered nigh,
The chariot of Assyria's beauteous queen
From rank to rank flew on : and, as they saw,
The warriors' breast, as with new soul infused,
Like beacons freshly kindled, burst at once
Into intensest flame.  Unhelmed, unarmed,
Her ebon hair loose flying in the wind,
She raised aloft her arms, her voice uplift,
And bade them on to glory.  As the star
Of morning, while the sun yet sleeps below,
And the grey mist is on the dewy earth,
Her face was pale and radiant.  Like a shape
From heaven descended, and to mortal harm
Impassive, gloriously and fearlessly
Through the death-laden air she flew along.
Her spirit fired the host ; with deafening shouts
Onward they bore ; and, for a time, the Medes
Compelled, though slowly, backward.  —ATHERSTONE.

## THE BATTLE OF SALAMIS.

### (B.C. 480.)

CONFIDENT therefore in their strength, and urged by the common necessity of invaders to push vigorous measures, the Persians were impatient for decision.  Accident seems to have made the Greeks at last the assailants ; and thus perhaps contributed not a little to the greatness of their success.  By daybreak, it is said; on the twentieth of October, in the four hundred and eightieth year before the Christian era, they had formed their fleet in order of battle.  The Athenians, on the right, were opposed to the Phœnician squadron ; the Lacedæmonians, on the left, to the Ionian.  As the sun rose trumpets sounded, pæans were sung, and the Grecian leaders endeavored by all means to excite that animation among their people which their own divided and hesitating counsels had so tended to repress.  A trireme galley returning from Ægina, excluded

## THE BATTLE OF SALAMIS.

from the Grecian fleet by the enemy's line, and nevertheless endeavoring to pass was attacked. An Athenian galley commanded by Aminias, brother of the poet Æschylus, advanced to her rescue: others followed: then the Æginetans moved, and the battle soon became general.

The onset was vigorous on both sides. But space did not suffice for the Persians to bring their whole fleet regularly into action, nor for the Phœnicians, in particular, to profit from the superior swiftness of their galleys and skill of their seamen. The Athenians and Æginetans therefore, after a sharp contest, broke the part of the Persian line first engaged. Numbers of galleys, yet out of action, pressed to its support. Among the various nations who composed the Persian fleet, commanded in chief by Persian officers little versed in naval business, while the vast army which lined the Attic shore, with the sovereign of the East at its head were witnesses of the scene, zeal itself contributed to disorder. Damage and loss of oars, and wounds in the hull from the beaks of their own galleys, ensued; while the Athenians and Æginetans, forgetting their late enmity, or remembering it only as an incentive to generous emulation, with the most animated exertion preserved the steadiest discipline. Shortly the sea itself became scarcely visible for the quantity of wreck and floating bodies. Such is the strong expression of the poet who himself fought in the Athenian squadron. In the meantime the business was easier to the Lacedæmonians and other Greeks in the left wing. Some of the Ionian officers exerted themselves to earn the favor of the monarch whom they served; but others were zealously disposed to the cause of the confederates. The confusion arising, thus and variously otherwise in the Persian fleet, spread and rapidly became general and extreme. All their galleys which could disengage themselves fled. Some were taken; many were sunk; and numbers of the crews, inland men, unpractised in swimming, were drowned. Among those who perished were very many of high rank, who had been forward to distinguish themselves, in this new species of war, under their monarch's eye. According to Herodotus, Ariabignes, brother of Xerxes, and admiral of the fleet, was among the killed; but he is not mentioned by Æschylus. Forty Grecian galleys are said to have been sunk, or otherwise destroyed: but the crews mostly saved themselves aboard other ships, or on the neighboring friendly shore of Salamis. When the rout was become total, Aristides, landing on Psyttalea at the head of a body of Athenians, put all the Persians there to the sword, under the very eye of Xerxes, who, with his immense army around him, could afford them no assistance.

In considering Herodotus's account of this memorable seafight we find not less reason than on former occasions to praise his scrupulous honesty and modesty. His narrative is doubtful and incomplete, as all faithful narratives of great battles must be, unless some eye-witness, very peculiarly qualified by knowledge and situation be the relater. It is therefore matter of regret, not indeed that Æschylus was a poet, but that prose-writing was yet in his age so little common that his poetical sketch of this great transaction is the most authoritative, the clearest and the most consistent of any that has passed to posterity. Concerning a day however so glorious, so singularly interesting to Greece, and particularly to Athens, anecdotes would of course abound and a historian, a few years only later, desirous to shine in description rather than to relate the truth, could not have wanted materials. Anecdotes indeed of particular circumstances in great battles may often be authenticated; and to those Herodotus has chiefly confined himself, avoiding a detail of the battle at large, with an express declaration that he could obtain none upon which he could rely. Among his anecdotes, one is too remarkable and of too much fame to be omitted. The queen of Halicarnassus, after showing extraordinary bravery during the action, being among the last who fled, was closely pursued by the Athenian galley which Aminias commanded. In this extremity, at a loss for other refuge, she suddenly turned against the nearest galley of the Persian fleet, which happened to be that of Damasithymus, prince of Calynda in Lycia, with whom she is said to have been upon terms not of perfect friendship: and taking him totally unprepared for such an attempt, the stroke of the beak of her galley against the side of his was so violent and so well aimed that the vessel instantly sunk, and the Calyndian prince and his crew were at the mercy of the enemy and the waves. Aminias, in the hurry of the moment, without means for enquiry, concluding from what he had seen that Artemisia's galley was either one of the confederate fleet, or one that had deserted to it, turned his pursuit toward other vessels, and the queen of

Halicarnassus escaped. According to Herodotus, though in this instance we may have difficulty to give him entire credit, Xerxes, from the shore where he sat, saw, admired, and applauded the exploit. —MITFORD.

## THE PASSAGE OF THE RED SEA.

With heat o'erlabor'd and the length of way.
On Ethan's beach the bands of Israel lay.
'Twas silence all, the sparkling sands along ;
Save where the locust trill'd her feeble song,
Or blended soft in drowsy cadence fell
The wave's low whisper, or the camel's bell.—
'Twas silence all !—the flocks for shelter fly
Where, waving light, the acacia shadows lie ;
Or where, from far, the flattering vapors make
The noontide semblance of a misty lake :
While the mute swain, in careless safety spread,
With arms enfolded, and dejected head,
Dreams o'er his wondrous call, his lineage high,
And, late reveal'd, his children's destiny.—
For, not in vain, in thraldom's darkest hour,
Had sped from Amram's sons the word of power ;
Nor fail'd, the dreadful wand, whose godlike sway
Could lure the locust from her airy way :
With reptile war assail their proud abodes,
And mar the giant pomp of Egypt's gods.
Oh, helpless gods ! who nought avail'd to shiel
From fiery rain your Zoan's favour'd field !—
Oh, helpless gods, who saw the curdled blood
Taint the pure love of your ancient flood,
And four-fold might the wondering earth enchain,
While Memnon's orient harp was heard in vain !—
Such musings held the tribe, till now the west
With milder influence on their temples prest ;
And that portentous cloud, which all the day
Hung its dark curtain o'er their weary way,
(A cloud by day, a friendly flame by night,)
Roll'd back its misty veil, and kindled into light !—
Soft fell the eve :—But, ere the day was done,
Tall waving banners streak'd the level sun ;
And wide and dark along the horizon red,
In sandy surge the rising desert spread.—
" Mark, Israel, mark !"—On that strange sight intent,
In breathless terror, every eye was bent ;
And busy factions fast-increasing hum,
And female voices shriek, " They come ! they come !"
They come, they come, in scintillating show

O'er the dark mass the brazen lances glow ;
And sandy clouds in countless shapes combine,
As deepens or extends the long tumultuous line ;—
And fancy's keener glance e'en now may trace
The threatening aspects of each mingled race :
For many a coal-black tribe and cany spear,
The hireling guards of Misraim's throne, were there.
From distant Cush they troop'd a warrior train,
Siwah's green isle and Sennaar's marly plain :
On either wing their fiery coursers check
The parch'd and sinewy sons of Amalek :
While close behind, inured to feast on blood,
Deck'd in Behemoth's spoils, the tall Shangalla strode.
'Mid blazing helms and bucklers rough with gold,
Saw ye how swift the scythed chariots roll'd ?
Lo, these are they whom, lords of Afric's fates,
Old Thebes hath pour'd through all her hundred gates,
Mother of armies !—How the emeralds glow'd,
Where, flush'd with power and vengeance, Pharaoh rode !
And stoled in white, those brazen wheels before,
Osiris' ark his swarthy wizards bore ;
And, still responsive to the trumpet's cry,
The priestly sistrum murmur'd—Victory !
Why swell these shouts that rend the desert's gloom ?
Whom come ye forth to combat ?—warriors, whom ?—
These flock and herds—this faint and weary train—
Red from the scourge and recent from the chain ?—
God of the poor, the poor and friendless save !
Giver and Lord of freedom help the slave !—
North, south, and west, the sandy whirlwinds fly,
The circling horns of Egypt's chivalry.
On earth's last margin throng the weeping train :
Their cloudy guide moves on :—" And must we swim the main ?"
'Mid the light spray their snorting camels stood,
Nor bath'd a fetlock in the nauseous flood—
He comes—their leader comes !—the man of God
O'er the wide waters lifts his mighty rod,
And onward treads.—The circling waves retreat,
In hoarse deep murmur, from his holy feet ;
And the chased surges, inly roaring, show
The hard wet sand and coral hills below.

With limbs that falter, and with hearts that ṛw
Down, down they pass—a steep and slippery dell—
Around them rise, in pristine chaos hurl'd,
The ancient rocks, the secrets of the world ;
And flowers that blush beneath the ocean green,
And caves, the sea-calves' low-roof'd haunt, are so n.
Down, safely down the narrow pass they tread ;
The beetling waters storm above their head :
While far behind retires the sinking day,
And fades on Edom's hills its latest ray.

## THE PASSAGE OF THE RED SEA.

Yet not from Israel fled the friendly light,
Or dark to them, or cheerless came the night.
Still in their van, along that dreadful road,
Blazed broad and fierce the brandish'd torch of God,
Its meteor glare a tenfold lustre gave,
On the long mirror of the rosy wave.
While its blest beams a sunlike heat supply,
Warm every cheek, and dance in every eye—
To them alone—for Misraim's wizard train
Invoked for light their monster-gods in vain
Clouds heap'd on clouds their struggling sight confine,
And tenfold darkness broods above their line,
Yet on they fare, by reckless vengeance led,
And range unconscious through the ocean's bed;
Till midway now—that strange and fiery form
Show'd his dread visage lightening through the storm;
With withering splendor blasted all their might,
And broke their chariot-wheels, and marr'd their coursers' flight.
"Fly, Misraim, fly!"—The ravenous floods they see,
And, fiercer than the floods, the Deity.
"Fly, Misraim, fly!"—From Edom's coral strand
Again the prophet stretch'd his dreadful wand :—
With one wild crash the thundering waters sweep,
And all is waves—a dark and lonely deep—
Yet o'er those lonely waves such murmurs past,
As mortal wailing swell'd the nightly blast;
And strange and sad the whispering breezes bore
The groans of Egypt to Arabia's shore.
Oh! welcome came the morn, where Israel stood
In trustless wonder by the avenging flood!
Oh! welcome came the cheerful morn, to show
The drifted wreck of Zoan's pride below;
The mangled limbs of men—the broken car—
A few sad relics of a nation's war;
Alas, how few!—Then, soft as Elim's well,
The precious tears of new-born freedom fell.
And he, whose hardened heart alike had borne
The house of bondage and the oppressor's scorn,
The stubborn salve, by hope's new beams subdued,
In faltering accents sobb'd his gratitude—
Till, kindling into warmer zeal, around
The virgin timbrel waked its silver sound :
And in fierce joy, no more by doubt supprest,
The struggling spirit throbb'd in Miriam's breast.
She, with bare arms, and fixing on the sky
The dark transparence of her lucid eye,
Pour'd on the winds of heaven her wild sweet harmony.
"Where now," she sang, "the tall Egyptian spear?
On's sun-like shield, and Zion's chariot, where?
Above their ranks the whelming waters spread.
Shout, Israel, for the Lord hath triumphed!"

And every pause between as Miriam sang,
From tribe to tribe the martial thunder rang,
And loud and far their stormy chorus spread,—
"Shout, Israel, for the Lord hath triumphed!"         —HEBER.

---

## SONG OF PRAISE.

*Jochebed.* All is lost.
*Miriam.* But what suspends their progress? Something stays them;
Slow, and more slow, their lagging motion seems.
Their chariot wheels drive heavily along
They stop; they're moveless. Now, O extasy!
The refluent waters haste to meet again!
They close above their heads! Egypt, ingulph'd,
Is lost to sight!—the rider and his horse
Together sink—they sink—they rise no more.
*Jochebed.* Can this be realiz'd?
*Miriam.* It can, it will.
'Tis great; but great is HE whose will controls it.
Methinks I hear the shouts of victory,
I hear triumphant Moses' grateful song!
Thou art our strength, O Lord! the work is thine,
Thine is the power, and thine be all the praise;
Pharaoh is sunk—his chariots and his host
Plung'd in the dark abyss! As lead they sank.
To save the favor'd sons of Jacob's race,
The flood, no longer liquid, stood congeal'd.
The crystal wall stood firm, as Israel pass'd:
When Egypt came, the crystal wall dissolv'd.
Thou didst stretch forth Thy hand, and Moses pass'd;
Thou didst stretch forth, and Pharaoh sank.
Lord! who among the Gods is like to Thee?
Fearful in praises, wonderful in power,
Glorious in holiness! thou great I AM!
What mighty marvels Thy right hand has wrought!
Thy hand pre-eminent! Thou art my God!
And all I have is Thine! My father's God!
Thy name I will exalt; 'tis Thou hast conquer'd.
See Pharaoh's captains perish with his host!
The horse and rider meet one common fate.
The depths have cover'd them: they sink together.
Vainly they boasted—"Though the slaves escape,
Yet we will follow them, o'ertake, and crush them."

## HYMN OF THE HEBREW MAID.

When Israel, of the Lord beloved,
   Out from the land of bondage came,
Her fathers' God before her moved,
   An awful guide, in smoke and flame.
By day, along the astonished lands,
   The cloudy pillar glided slow;
By night Arabia's crimsoned sands
   Returned the fiery column's glow.

Then rose the choral hymn of praise,
   And trump and timbrel answered keen;
And Zion's daughters poured their lays,
   With priest's and warrior's voice between.
No portents now our foes amaze,
   Forsaken Israel wanders lone:
Our fathers would not know Thy ways,
   And Thou hast left them to their own.

But,—present still, though now unseen!—
   When brightly shines the prosperous day
Be thoughts of Thee a cloudy screen
   To temper the deceitful ray.
And, O! when stoops on Judah's path
   In shade and storm the frequent night,
Be Thou, long suffering, slow to wrath,
   A burning and a shining light!

Our harps we left by Babel's streams,
   The tyrant's jest, the Gentile's scorn;
No censer round our altar beams,
   And mute are timbrel, harp, and horn.
But Thou hast said, The blood of goat,
   The flesh of rams, I will not prize;
A contrite heart, a humble thought,
   Are mine accepted sacrifice.   —Scott.

## PALESTINE, THE LAND OF RUINS.

This is the most convenient place for noticing a peculiarity of the present aspect of Palestine, which, though not, properly speaking, a physical feature, is so closely connected both with its outward imagery and with its general situation, that it cannot be omitted. Above all other countries in the world, it is a *Land of Ruins*. It is not that the particular ruins are on a scale equal to those of Greece and Italy, still less to those of Egypt. But there is no country in which they are so numerous, none in which they bear so large a proportion to the villages and towns still in existence. In Judæa it is hardly an exaggeration to say that whilst for miles and miles there is no appearance of present life or habitation, except the occasional goat-herd on the hill-side, or gathering of women at the wells, there is yet hardly a hill-top of the many within sight which is not covered by the vestiges of some fortress or city of former ages. Sometimes they are fragments of ancient walls, sometimes mere foundations and piles of stone, but always enough to indicate signs of human habitation and civilisation. Such is the case in Western Palestine. In Eastern Palestine, and still more if we include the Haurân and the Lebanon, the same picture is continued although under a somewhat different aspect. Here the ancient cities remain, in like manner deserted, ruined but standing; not mere masses and heaps of stones, but towns and houses, in amount and in a state of preservation which have no parallel except in the cities of Herculaneum and Pompeii, buried under the eruption of Vesuvius. Not even in Rome or Athens, hardly in Egyptian Thebes, can ancient buildings be found in such magnitude and such profusion as at Baalbec, Jerash, Ammân, and Palmyra. No where else, it is said, can all the details of Roman domestic architecture be seen so clearly as in the hundreds of deserted villages which stand on the red desert of the Haurân. This difference between the ruins of the two regions of Palestine arises no doubt from the circumstance, that, whereas Eastern Syria has been for the last four hundred years entirely, for the last fifteen hundred years nearly, deserted by civilised, almost by barbarian, man, Western Palestine has always been the resort of a population which, however rude and scanty, has been sufficiently numerous and energetic to destroy and to appropriate edifices which in the less frequented parts beyond the Jordan have escaped through neglect and isolation.

But the general fact of the ruins of Palestine, whether erect or fallen, remains common to the whole country; deepens and confirms, if it does not create, the impression of age and decay which belongs to almost every view of Palestine, and invests it with an appearance which can be called by no other name than *venerable.* Moreover, it carries us deep into the historical peculiarities of the country. The ruins we now see are of the most diverse ages; Saracenic, Crusading, Roman, Grecian, Jewish, extending perhaps even to the old Canaanitish remains, before the arrival of Joshua. This variety, this accumulation of destruction, is the natural result of the position which has made Palestine for so many ages the thoroughfare and prize of the world. And although we now see this aspect brought out in a fuller light than ever before, yet, as far back as the history and language of Palestine reach, it was familiar to the inhabitants of the country. In the rich local vocabulary of the Hebrew language, the words for sites of ruined cities occupy a remarkable place. Four separate designations are used for the several stages of decay or of destruction, which were to be seen even during the first vigour of the Israelite conquest and monarchy. There was the rude "cairn," or pile of stones, roughly rolled together. There was the mound or heap of ruin, which, like the Monte Testaccio at Rome, was composed of the rubbish and débris of a fallen city. There were the forsaken villages, such as those in the Hurân, when "the cities were wasted without inhabitant and the houses without man,"—" forsaken, and not a man to dwell therein." There are lastly true ruins, such as those to which we give the name —buildings standing, yet shattered, like those of Baalbec or Palmyra. —A. P. STANLEY.

## THE DEATH OF MOSES.

LED by his God, on Pisgah's height,
 The pilgrim-prophet stood—
When first fair Canaan blessed his sight,
 And Jordan's crystal flood.

Behind him lay the desert ground
 His weary feet had trod;
While Israel's host had camped around,
 Still guarded by their God.

With joy the aged Moses smiled
 On all his wanderings past,
While thus he poured his accents mild
 Upon the mountain-blast:

## THE DEATH OF MOSES.

"I see them all before me now,—
  The city and the plain,
From where bright Jordan's waters flow,
  To yonder boundless main.

"Oh! there the lovely promised land
  With milk and honey flows;
Now, now my weary murmuring band
  Shall find their sweet repose.

"There groves of palm and myrtle spread
  O'er valleys fair and wide;
The lofty cedar rears its head
  On every mountain-side.

"For them the rose of Sharon flings
  Her fragrance on the gale;
And there the golden lily springs,—
  The lily of the vale.

"Amid the olive's fruitful boughs
  Is heard the song of love,
For there doth build and breathe her vows
  The gentle turtle-dove.

"For them shall bloom the clustering vine,
  The fig-tree shed her flowers,
The citron's golden treasures shine
  From out her greenest bowers.

"For them, for them, but not for me—
  Their fruits I may not eat;
Not Jordan's stream, nor yon bright sea,
  Shall lave my pilgrim feet.

"'Tis well, 'tis well, my task is done,
  Since Israel's sons are blest:
Father, receive thy dying one
  To thine eternal rest!"

Alone he bade the world farewell,
  To God his spirit fled.
Now, to your tents, O Israel,
  And mourn your prophet dead!   —JESSIE G. M'CARTER.

## SOCRATES.

(B.C. 468.—399.)

AUTHORS describe the private life and habits of Socrates, his contented poverty, justice, temperance, in the largest sense of the word, and self-sufficing independence of character. On most of these points, too, Aristophanes and the other comic writers, so far as their testimony counts for anything, appear as confirmatory witnesses; for they abound in jests on the coarse fare, shabby and scanty clothing, bare feet and pale face, poor and joyless life of Socrates. Of the circumstances of his life we are almost totally ignorant. He served as an hoplite in Potidæa, at Delium, and Amphipolis, with credit, apparently, in all, though exaggerated encomiums on the part of his friends provoked an equally exaggerated scepticism on the part of Athenæus and others. He seems never to have filled any political office until the year B.C. 406, in which the battle of Arginusæ occurred, in which year he was member of the Senate of Five Hundred, and one of the prytanes of that memorable day, when the proposition of Kallixenus against the six generals was submitted to the public assembly. That during his long life he strictly obeyed the laws, is proved by the fact that none of his numerous enemies ever arraigned him before a court of justice; that he discharged all the duties of an upright man, and a brave as well as a pious citizen, may also be confidently asserted. His friends lay especial stress upon his piety, that is, upon his exact discharge of all the religious duties considered as incumbent upon an Athenian.

At what time Socrates relinquished his profession as a statuary we do not know, but it is certain that all the middle and later part of his life, at least, was devoted exclusively to the self-imposed task of teaching, excluding all other business, public or private, and to the neglect of all means of fortune. We can hardly avoid speaking of him as a teacher, though he himself disclaimed the appellation; his practice was to talk, or converse, or "to prattle without end," if we translate the derisory word by which the enemies of philosophy described dialectic conversation. Early in the morning he frequented the public walks, the gymnasia for bodily training, and the schools where youths were receiving instruction. He was to be seen in the

market-place at the time when it was most crowded, among the
the booths and tables where goods were exposed for sale. His
whole day was usually spent in this manner. He talked with
any one, young or old, rich or poor, who sought to address
him, and in the hearing of all who chose to stand by. Not
only he never either asked or received any reward, but he made
no distinction of persons, never withheld his conversation from
any one, and talked upon the same general topics to all.

This extreme publicity of life and conversation was one,
among the characteristics of Socrates, distinguishing him from
all teachers, both before and after him. Next was his persuasion of a special religious mission, restraints, impulses, and communications sent to him by the gods. Taking the belief in
such natural intervention generally, it was, indeed, no way
peculiar to Socrates; it was that ordinary faith of the ancient
world, in so much that the attempts to resolve phenomena into
general laws were looked upon with a certain disapprobation,
as indirectly setting it aside. He had been accustomed to hear,
even from his childhood, a divine voice, interfering at moments
when he was about to act, in the way of restraint, but never
in the way of instigation. Such prohibitory warning was wont
to come upon him very frequently, not merely on great, but
even on small, occasions, intercepting what he was about to do
or to say. Though later writers speak of this as the demon or
genius of Socrates, he himself does not personify it, but treats
it merely as "a divine sign, a prophetic or supernatural voice."
He was accustomed not only to obey it implicitly, but to speak
of it publicly and familiarly to others, so that the fact was well
known both to his friends and his enemies. It had always forbidden him to enter upon public life; it forbade him, while the
indictment was hanging over him, to take any thought for a
prepared defence; and so completely did he march with a consciousness of this bridle in his mouth, that when he felt no
check, he assumed that the turning he was about to take was
the right one. Though his persuasion on the subject was perfectly sincere, and his obedience constant, yet he never dwelt
upon it himself as anything grand or awful, or entitling him to
peculiar deference, but spoke of it often in his peculiar strain
of familiar playfulness.

Such was the demon or genius of Socrates, as described by
himself, and as conceived in the genuine Platonic dialogues—a

voice always prohibitory, and bearing exclusively on his own personal conduct. That which Plutarch, and other admirers of Socrates, conceived as a demon, or intermediate being between gods and men, was looked upon by the fathers of the Christian Church as a devil, by Le Clerc as one of the fallen angels, by some other modern commentators as mere ironical phraseology on the part of Socrates himself. Without presuming to determine the question raised in the former hypothesis, I believe the last to be untrue, and that the conviction of Socrates on the point was quite sincere. But though this peculiar form of inspiration belonged exclusively to him, there were also other ways in which he believed himself to have received the special mandates of the gods; not simply checking him, but spurring him on, directing and peremptorily exacting from him a positive course of proceeding. Such distinct mission had been imposed upon him by dreams, by oracular intimations, and by every other means which the gods employed for signifying their special will.

To hear of any man, especially of so illustrious a man, being condemned to death on such accusations as those of heresy and alleged corruption of youth, inspires, at the present day, a sentiment of indignant reprobation, the force of which I have no desire to enfeeble. The fact stands eternally recorded as one among the thousand misdeeds of intolerance, religious and political. But since, amid this catalogue, each item has its own peculiar character, grave or light, we are bound to consider at what point of the scale the condemnation of Socrates is to be placed, and what inference it justifies in regard to the character of the Athenians. If we examine the circumstances of the case, we will find them all extenuating, and so powerful, indeed, as to reduce such inferences to their minimum, consistent with the general class to which the inference belongs. Though the mischievous principle of intolerance cannot be denied, yet all the circumstances show that principle was neither irritable nor predominant in the Athenian bosom,—that even a large body of collateral antipathies did not readily call it forth against any individual,—that the more liberal and generous dispositions, which deadened its malignity, were of steady efficacy, not easily overborne; and that the condemnation ought to count as one of the least gloomy items in an essentially gloomy catalogue.

—GROTE.

## MARVELS OF THE SUN—THE ZOLLNER "PICTURES."

ASTRONOMERS have been revealing so many wonders in the vast globe which rules the planetary scheme, that we cannot yet hope to see the startling results of their researches co-ordinated into a consistent whole. On every hand new marvels are being brought to light. At one time Mr. Lockyer surprises us by exhibiting the velocities with which the solar storms rage across the blazing surface of our luminary. At another, the energetic astronomer who presides at the Roman Observatory tells us of water within the fierce tumult of the solar spots. The Kew observers track the strange influences of the planets on the solar atmosphere, watching not only the great tide of spots which sweeps in the ten-year period over the solar storm-zones, and then leaves our sun clear from speck or stain, but also the ripples of spot-formation which come in shorter periods, and seem inextricably blended to ordinary observers with the great periodic disturbances. Lastly, Lockyer, Huggins, Zollner, and Secchi describe the magic changes of forms which pass over tongues of flame, projecting thousands of miles from the solar surface. We have before us as we write, a series of colored prominence-pictures taken by Dr. Zollner, the eminent photometrician. It is impossible to contemplate these strange figures without a sense of the magnificence of the problem which the sun presents to astronomers. Here are vast entities—flames, if we will, but flames unlike all those with which we are familiar. And these vast tongues of fire assume forms which speak to us at once of the action of forces of the utmost violence and intensity. The very aspect of these objects at once teaches this, but it is the rapid changes of place and of figure, to which the spots are subjected, that are most significant on this point. Here is a vast cone-shaped flame, with a mushroom-shaped head of enormous proportions, the whole object standing 16,000 or 17,000 miles from the sun's surface. In the cone-figure we see the uprush of the lately imprisoned gases, in the outspreading head, the sudden diminution of pressure as these gases reach the rarer upper atmosphere. But turn from this object to a series of six pictures placed beside it, and we see the solar forces in action. First, there is a vast flame, some 18,000 miles high, bowed towards the right, as though some fierce wind were blowing upon it. It extends in this direction some four or five thousand miles. The next picture represents the same object ten minutes later. The figure of the prominence has wholly changed. It is now a globe shaped mass, standing on a narrow stalk of light above a row of flame-hillocks. It is bowed towards the left, so that in those short minutes the whole mass of the flame has swept thousands of miles away from its former position. Only two minutes later, and again a complete change of appearance. The stalk and flame-hillocks have vanished, and the globe-shaped mass has become elongated. Three minutes later, the shape of the prominence has altered so completely that one can hardly recognize it for the same. The stalk is again visible, but the upper mass is bowed down on the right so that the whole figure resembles a gigantic A, without the crow-bar, and with the down stroke abnormally thick. This great A is some twenty thousand miles in height, and the whole mass of our earth might be bowled between its legs without touching them! Four minutes pass, and again the figure has changed. The flame-hillocks reappear, the down-stroke of the A begins to raise itself from the sun's surface. Lastly, after yet another interval of four minutes, the figure of the prominence has lost all resemblance to an A., and may now be likened to a camel's head looking towards the right. The whole series of changes has occupied but twenty-three minutes, yet the flame exceeded our earth in volume ten-fold at the least. But Mr. Lockyer has recorded an instance of a yet more marvellous nature. A vast prominence extending seventy or eighty thousand miles from the sun's surface vanished altogether in ten minutes. The very way in which Zöllner's drawings were taken savors of the marvellous. We have spoken of them as colored. They are ruby-red, and so the prominences appeared to the astronomer. The real light of the prominences is not ruby-red, however, but rose-colored, with faint indications of pink, of even bluish tints. The fact is, that, by the new method of observation, the image of a prominence was formed by only a certain part of its light. We may say that out of the several colored images of the same prominence the astronomer selects one only for examination. The explanation of this is worth consideration, as it involves the essence of the method by which the prominences are seen at all. When we analyze light with a simple prism as Newton did, we get instead of a round spot of white—that is, mixed light—a row of overlapping spots of different color. It was only when, instead of a round spot, a fine line of white light was analyzed, that one could detect the absence of images of this line along certain parts of the rainbow-colored streak—in other words, it was thus only that the dark lines of the spectrum could be seen. And it was to see these lines more clearly that the slit of the spectroscope was made so narrow and the rainbow-spectrum made so long by spectroscopists. But the observers of the prominences go back to the old method. If they use a narrow slit, a narrow strip of the prominence would alone form its spectrum, which would consist of a few bright lines. But by having a wide slit the whole prominence form its spectrum, which consists of a few bright pictures of the prominences. There is a green picture corresponding to the bright spectral line called F, a red picture corresponding to the bright spectral line called C, and so on. If the whole set of pictures were formed at once we could see none of them, for there would be side by side with them the blazing solar spectrum which would obliterate them altogether just as in ordinary telescopic observation the bright sun light blots out the prominences from view. But if the observer uses such a battery of prisms that the solar spectrum would be very long indeed, and if he admits to view only that part of the spectrum opposite which one of the prominence-images exists, he can then see that image quite distinctly for the neighboring part of the solar spectrum is so reduced in splendor that it no longer obliterates the prominence figure. In this way, then, the observer selects one or other of the pictures of a prominence, either the red or the green picture, to examine. And strangely enough, it is by no means certain that the two pictures are alike. Rather it is highly probable that they are different, though we have not space here either to indicate reasons for believing this, or to explain the significance of the circumstance should it eventually be established.

It seems to us that when we consider the real dimensions of the solar globe, we appreciate more fully the wonderful nature of these processes of action indicated by recent researches, than when we regard these without direct reference to the sun's

magnitude. How many of us really appreciate the enormous volume of the sun? We read certain figures in books of astronomy, but do we grasp their full significance?
—*London Spectator.*

## THE ELEPHANT.

THE African elephant is not only entirely different from the Indian species in his habits, but he also differs in form.

There are three distinguishing peculiarities. The back of the African elephant is concave, that of the Indian is convex; the ear of the African is enormous, entirely covering the shoulder when thrown back, while the ear of the Indian variety is comparatively small. The head of the African has a convex front, the top of the skull sloping back at a rapid inclination, while the head of the Indian elephant exposes a flat surface a little above the trunk. The average size of the African elephant is larger than those of Ceylon, although I have occasionally shot monster rogues in the latter country, equal to anything that I have seen in Africa. The average height of female elephants in Ceylon is about 7 ft. 10 in. at the shoulder, and that of the males is about 9 ft.; but the usual height of the African variety I have found, by actual measurement of females, to be 9 ft., while that of the bulls is 10 ft. 6 in. Thus the females of the African are equal to the males of Ceylon.

They also differ materially in their habits. In Ceylon, the elephant seeks the shade of thick forests at the rising of the sun, in which he rests until about 5 P.M., when he wanders forth upon the plains. In Africa, the country being generally more open, the elephant remains throughout the day either beneath a solitary tree, or exposed to the sun in the vast prairies, where the thick grass attains a height of from nine to twelve feet. The general food of the African elephant consists of the foliage of trees, especially of mimosas. In Ceylon, although there are many trees that serve as food, the elephant nevertheless is an extensive grass feeder. The African variety, being almost exclusively a tree feeder, requires his tusks to assist him in procuring food. Many of the mimosas are flat-headed, about thirty feet high, and the richer portion of the foliage confined to the crown; thus the elephant, not being able to reach to so great a height, must overturn the tree to procure the coveted food. The destruction caused by a herd of African elephants in a mimosa forest is extraordinary; and I have seen trees uprooted of so large a size, that I am convinced no single elephant could have overturned them. I have measured trees four feet six inches in circumference, and about thirty feet high, uprooted by elephants. The natives have assured me that they mutually assist each other, and that several engage together in the work of overturning a large tree. None of the mimosas have tap-roots; thus the powerful tusks of the elephants, applied as crow-bars at the roots, while others pull at the branches with their trunks, will effect the destruction of a tree so large as to appear invulnerable. The Ceylon elephant, rarely possessing tusks, cannot destroy a tree thicker than the thigh of an ordinary man.

In Ceylon, I have seldom met old bulls in parties—they are generally single or remain in pairs; but, in Africa, large herds are met with, consisting entirely of bulls. I have frequently seen sixteen or twenty splendid bulls together, presenting a show of ivory most exciting to a hunter. The females in Africa congregate in vast herds of many hundreds, while in Ceylon the herd seldom average more than ten.

The elephant is by far the most formidable of all animals, and the African variety is more dangerous than the Indian, as it is next to impossible to kill it by the forehead shot. The head is so peculiarly formed, that the ball either passes over the brain, or lodges in the immensely solid bones and cartilages that contain the roots of the tusks. I have measured certainly a hundred bull tusks, and I have found them buried in the head a depth of 24 inches. One large tusk, that measured 7 ft. 8 in. in length, and 22 inches in girth, was imbedded in the head a depth of 31 inches. This will convey an idea of the enormous size of the head, and of the strength of bone and cartilage required to hold in position so great a weight, and to resist the strain when the tusk is used as a lever to uproot trees.

The brain of an African elephant rests upon a plate of bone exactly above the roots of the upper grinders, it is thus wonderfully protected from a front shot, as it lies so low that the ball passes above it when the elephant raises his head, which he invariably does when in anger, until close to the object of his attack.

## THE ELEPHANT. 31

The character of the country naturally influences the habits of the animals : thus, Africa being more generally open than the forest-clad Ceylon, the elephant is more accustomed to activity, and is much faster than the Ceylon variety. Being an old elephant-hunter, of the latter island, I was exceedingly interested in the question of variety of species, and I had always held the opinion that the African elephant might be killed with the same facility as that of Ceylon, by the forehead shot, provided that a sufficient charge of powder were used to penetrate the extra thickness of the head. I have found, by much experience, that I was entirely wrong, and that, although by *chance* an African elephant may be killed by the front shot, it is the exception to the rule. The danger of the sport is, accordingly, much increased, as it is next to impossible to kill the elephant when in full charge, and the only hope of safety consists in turning him by a continuous fire with heavy guns : this cannot always be effected.

The natives of Central Africa generally hunt the elephant for the sake of the flesh, and prior to the commencement of the White Nile trade by the Arabs, and the discovery of the Upper White Nile to the 5° N. lat. by the expedition sent by Mehemet Ali Pasha, the tusks were considered as worthless, and were treated as bones. The death of an elephant is a grand affair for the natives, as it supplies flesh for an enormous number of people, also fat, which is the great desire of all savages for internal and external purposes. There are various methods of killing them. Pitfalls are the most common, but the wary old bulls are seldom caught in this manner. The position chosen for the pit is, almost without exception, in the vicinity of a drinking-place, and the natives exhibit a great amount of cunning in felling trees across the usual run of the elephants, and sometimes cutting an open pit across the path, so as to direct the elephant by such obstacles into the path of snares. The pits are usually about twelve feet long, and three feet broad, by nine deep ; these are artfully made, decreasing towards the bottom to the breadth of a foot. The general elephant route to the drinking-place being blocked up, the animals are diverted by a treacherous path towards the water, the route intersected by numerous pits, all of which are carefully concealed by sticks and straw, the latter being usually strewn with elephants' dung to create a natural effect.

Should an elephant, during the night, fall through the deceitful surface, his foot becomes jammed in the bottom of the narrow grave, and he labours shoulder deep, with two feet in the pitfall so fixed that extrication is impossible. Should one animal be thus caught, a sudden panic seizes the rest of the herd, and in their hasty retreat one or more are generally victims to the numerous pits in the vicinity. The old bulls never approach a watering-place rapidly, but carefully listen for danger, and then slowly advance with their warning trunks stretched to the path before them; the delicate nerves of the proboscis at once detect the hidden snare, and the victims to pitfalls are the members of large herds who, eager to push forward incautiously, put their "foot into it," like shareholders in bubble companies. Once helpless in the pit, they are easily killed with lances.

The great elephant hunting season is in January, when the high prairies are parched and reduced to straw. At such a time, should a large herd of animals be discovered, the natives of the entire district collect together to the number of perhaps a thousand men; surrounding the elephants by embracing a considerable tract of country, they fire the grass at a given signal. In a few minutes the unconscious elephants are surrounded by a circle of fire, which, however distant, must eventually close in upon them. The men advance with the fire, which rages to the height of twenty or thirty feet. At length the elephants, alarmed by the volumes of smoke and the roaring of the flames, mingled with the shouts of the hunters, attempt an escape. They are hemmed in on every side—wherever they rush, they are met by an impassable barrier of flames and smoke, so stifling, that they are forced to retreat. Meanwhile the fatal circle is decreasing; buffaloes and antelopes, likewise doomed to a horrible fate, crowd panic-stricken to the centre of the encircled ring, and the raging fire sweeps over all. Burnt and blinded by the fire and smoke, the animals are now attacked by the savage crowd of hunters, excited by the helplessness of the unfortunate elephants thus miserably sacrificed, and they fall under countless spears. This destructive method of hunting ruins the game of that part of Africa, and so scarce are the antelopes, that, in a day's journey, a dozen head are seldom seen in the open prairie.

The next method of hunting is perfectly legitimate. Should many elephants be in the neighbourhood, the natives post about a hundred men in as many large trees; these men are armed with heavy lances specially adapted to the sport, with blades about eighteen inches long and three inches broad. The elephants are driven by a great number of men towards the trees in which the spearmen are posted, and those that pass sufficiently near are speared between the shoulders. The spear being driven deep into the animal, creates a frightful wound, as the tough handle, striking against the intervening branches of trees, acts as a lever, and works the long blade of the spear within the elephant, cutting to such an extent that he soon drops from exhaustion.

The best and only really great elephant-hunters of the White Nile are the Bagāra Arabs, on about the 13° N. lat. These men hunt on horseback, and kill the elephant in fair fight with their spears.

The lance is about fourteen feet long, of male bamboo; the blade is about fourteen inches long by nearly three inches broad; this is as sharp as a razor. Two men, thus armed and mounted, form the hunting party. Should they discover a herd, they ride up to the finest tusker and single him from the others. One man now leads the way, and the elephant, finding himself pressed, immediately charges the horse. There is much art required in leading the elephant, who follows the horse with great determination, and the rider adapts his pace so as to keep his horse so near the elephant that his attention is entirely absorbed with the hope of catching him. The other hunter should by this time have followed close to the elephant's heels, and, dismounting when at full gallop with wonderful dexterity, he plunges his spear with both hands into the elephant about two feet below the junction of the tail, and with all his force he drives the spear about eight feet into his abdomen, and withdraws it immediately. Should he be successful in his stab, he remounts his horse and flies, or does his best to escape on foot, should he not have time to mount, as the elephant generally turns to pursue him. His comrade immediately turns his horse, and, dashing at the elephant, in his turn dismounts, and drives his lance deep into his intestines.

Generally, if the first thrust is scientifically given, the bowels protrude to such an extent that the elephant is at once disabled. Two good hunters will frequently kill several out of one herd;

but in this dangerous hand-to-hand fight the hunter is often the victim. Hunting the elephant on horseback is certainly far less dangerous than on foot, but although the speed of the horse is undoubtedly superior, the chase generally takes place upon ground so disadvantageous, that he is liable to fall, in which case there is little chance for either animal or rider.

So savage are the natural instincts of Africans, that they attend only to the destruction of the elephant, and never attempt its domestication. —BAKER.

## GENTLE RIVER.

GENTLE river, gentle river,
    Lo, thy streams are stain'd with gore,
Many a brave and noble captain
    Floats along thy willow'd shore.

All beside thy limpid waters,
    All beside thy sands so bright,
Moorish Chiefs and Christian Warriors
    Join'd in fierce and mortal fight.

Lords, and dukes, and noble princes,
    On thy fatal banks were slain:
Fatal banks, that gave to slaughter
    All the pride and flower of Spain.

There the hero, brave Alonzo,
    Full of wounds and glory, died:
There the fearless Urdiales
    Fell a victim by his side.

Lo! where yonder Don Saavedra
    Through their squadrons slow retires;
Proud Seville, his native city,
    Proud Seville his worth admires.

Close behind, a renegado,
    Loudly shouts with taunting cry:
"Yield thee, yield thee, Don Saavedra;
    Dost thou from the battle fly!

"Well I know thee, haughty Christian,
    Long I liv'd beneath thy roof;
Oft I've in the lists of glory
    Seen thee win the prize of proof.

"Well I know thy aged parents,
    Well thy blooming bride I know;
Seven years I was thy captive,
    Seven years of pain and woe.

"May our Prophet grant my wishes,
    Haughty Chief, thou shalt be mine;
Thou shalt drink that cup of sorrow,
    Which I drank when I was thine."

Like a lion turns the warrior,
    Back he sends an angry glare;
Whizzing came the Moorish javelin,
    Vainly whizzing through the air

Back the hero, full of fury,
    Sent a deep and mortal wound:
Instant sunk the Renegado,
    Mute and lifeless on the ground

With a thousand Moors surrounded,
    Brave Saavedra stands at bay;
Wearied out, but never daunted,
    Cold at length the warrior lay.

Near him fighting, great Alonzo
    Stout resists the Paynim bands;
From his slaughter'd steed dismounted
    Firm intrench'd behind him stands.

Furious press the hostile squadron,
    Furious he repels their rage:
Loss of blood at length enfeebles:
    Who can war with thousands wage!

Where yon rock the plain o'ershadows.
    Close beneath its foot retir'd,
Fainting, sunk the bleeding hero,
    And without a groan expir'd.    —Percy.

---

## THE RHEA, OR SOUTH AMERICAN OSTRICH.

Of the habit of the Rhea, so excellent an account is given by Darwin, that part of the description is here given in his own words.

"This bird is well known to abound on the plains of La

Plata. To the north it is found, according to Azara, in Paraguay, where, however, it is not common; to the south its limit appears to have been from 42° to 43°. It has not crossed the Cordilleras, but I have seen it within the first range of mountains, on the Uspallata plain, elevated between six and seven thousand feet.

"The ordinary habits of the ostrich (rhea) are well known. They feed on vegetable matter, such as roots or grass; but at Bahia Blanca I have repeatedly seen three or four come down at low water to the extensive mud banks, for the sake, as the Gauchos say, of catching small fish.

"Although the ostrich, in its habits is so shy, wary, and solitary, and although so fleet in its pace, it falls a prey, without much difficulty, to the Indian or Gaucho armed with the bolas. When several horsemen appear in a semi-circle, it becomes confounded, and does not know which way to escape. They generally prefer running against the wind, yet at the instant, they expand their wings, and, like a vessel, make all sail.

"On one fine hot day, I saw several ostriches enter a bed of tall rushes, where they squatted, concealed, till quite closely approached.

"It is not generally known that ostriches readily take to the water. Mr. King informs me that at Patagonia, at the Bay of San Blas, and at Port Valdes, he saw these birds swimming several times from island to island. They ran into the water both when driven down to a point, and, likewise, of their own accord, when not frightened. The distance crossed was about two hundred yards. When swimming, very little of their bodies appear above water, and their necks are extended a little forward; their progress is slow. On two occasions I saw some ostriches swimming across the Santa Cruz river, where it was about four hundred yards wide, and the stream rapid.

"The inhabitants of the country readily distinguish, even at a distance, the male bird from the female. The former is larger, and darker colored, and has a larger head.

"The ostrich, I believe the cock, emits a singular, deep toned hissing note. When first I heard it, while standing in the midst of some sand hillocks, I thought it was made by some wild beast, for it is such a sound that one cannot tell from whence it comes, or from how far distant.

"When we were at Bahia Blanca, in the months of September and October, the eggs were found in extraordinary numbers, all over the country. They either lie scattered single, in which case they are never hatched, and are called by the Spaniards ʻhuachos,' or they are collected together into a hollow excavation, which forms the nest. Out of the four nests which I saw, three contained twenty-two eggs each, and the fourth twenty-seven. In one day's hunting on horseback, sixty-four eggs were found; forty-four of these were in two nests, and the remaining twenty scattered ʻhuachos.'

"The Gauchos unanimously affirm—and there is no reason to doubt their statement—that the male bird alone hatches the eggs, and that he for some time afterwards accompanies the young. The cock, when on the nest, lies very close; I have myself almost ridden over one. It is asserted that at such times they are occasionally fierce, and even dangerous, and that they have been known to attack a man on horseback, trying to kick and leap on him. My informant pointed out to me an old man whom he had seen much terrified by one of these birds chasing him."

This account corroborates the assertion respecting the fish-eating habits of the Rhea; and the fact of its swimming so well is very remarkable, for the ostrich, to which it is so nearly allied, does not seem to have any power in the water. Indeed, it would have but little chance of exercising that power, and, as has been already mentioned, is purposely driven into water, whenever practicable, because it can be there easily knocked on the head.

The "bolas" by which this bird is taken, form a terrible weapon in the hands of any one, terrible to the foe in the hands of an experienced hunter, and equally terrible to himself, in those of a tyro, who will be quite as likely to knock out his own brains as those of his enemy; much in the same way that an inexperienced thresher generally fetches himself some severe blows on the top of his head before he learns to strike the corn at his feet.

The form of the bolas is simple enough. Two round, heavy balls, sometimes spherical pebbles, but generally made of iron, are affixed at the ends of a thin but strong rope. This weapon is carried in the hunter's hands, and can be used in various ways. If he comes close up to an antagonist, he holds the rope near the end, and delivers a violent blow with the iron ball, much after the fashion of the "life preserver" of this country. Sometimes he swings it round his head like a lasso, and hurls the loaded end at his adversary, retaining the other end so as to draw back the weapon after the blow has taken effect, or in case of missing.

But when he is chasing game, he employs the bolas in a very different way. Having ridden as near as he judges expedient for his aim, and still whirling the bolas round his head, he launches one of the balls at his intended victim, following it immediately with the other.

The two balls circle through the air, and they are thrown with so excellent an aim that a portion of the cord comes on the creature's back, neck or legs. The weight of the balls instantly wraps the cord round the embarrassed creature, and the more they turn the tighter the cord becomes, so that in most cases the animal is so entangled as to be brought to the ground at once, even if the heavy balls do not stun it, as they twist round the body. But, in any case, the bolas impede the course so much that the hunter easily comes up with his chase. Some hunters use a third ball, attached to one end of a cord, whose other end is fastened to the centre of the chief rope, so that there are three of these terrible weapons revolving at the same time.

The facts that have been ascertained respecting the eggs of the Rhea, and the mode of their maturing, will probably afford a key to the difficulties concerning those of the African ostrich; for their habits are so very similar, that there is good ground for supposing the Rhea may be, as it were, a telescope through which to observe the ostrich. —*My Feathered Friends.*

## PELOPIDAS AND EPAMINONDAS.

(B. C. 379.)

THEBES at this time possessed two great men, not perhaps the first or the last whom she produced, but the only ones whom the course of events permitted to take a prominent part in the affairs of Greece. These two men were not more conspicuous for their personal qualities, than for the mutual attachment by which they were united, notwithstanding a dissimilarity amounting almost to a contrast in their characters and circumstances. Pelopidas was of noble birth, inherited an ample fortune, and enlarged his connections by an honorable marriage. He was wholly possessed with an ardent desire of action and glory, conscious of abilities equal to the loftiness of his aims, and valued the advantages of his rank and wealth only as they might be subservient to a generous ambition, in which his own elevation was not distinguished from his country's greatness. His friend Epaminondas was of a nature formed rather for contemplation than for action, and highly cultivated by philosophical studies; but it was also one which found a sufficient impulse to the most strenuous exertions in the light which his philosophy threw on his duties as a man and a citizen. He was, it seems, of a good family, but was bred and lived in poverty: poverty not merely relative to his birth and station, but real and absolute as that of Socrates. But as it did not exclude him from the best society, nor from any opportunity of serving the State, he appears to have reckoned it as one of the favors of fortune, which kept him free from useless incumbrances. His mind had been chiefly formed by his intercourse with Lysis, one of those Italian Greeks who preserved and unfolded the doctrines of Pythagoras, and who were induced by some causes which are now only matter for conjecture, to fix their residence at Thebes.

The arrival of these learned emigrants would have been an event of no slight importance, if it had produced no other effect that that of moulding the character of Epaminondas. But it seems probable that it was attended with consequences much more extensive, and that it contributed not a little to that great turn in the affairs of Greece, which we are now about to relate. We collect from Plutarch's work on the Genius of Socrates, that these Pythagoreans diffused a general taste for philosophical pursuits among the Theban youth. One tendency of these new intellectual habits may have been to soften the Theban prejudices against Athens, now the central seat of literature and philosophy, and thus to prepare for the hospitable reception of the Athenian exiles, which in its turn may be supposed to have given a fresh impulse to liberal studies at Thebes; and this was an excitement which must have rendered those who shared it the more impatient of Spartan domination, and the more indignant at the treachery by which Thebes had been subjected to it. The violence of Sparta probably united many Thebans in the cause of liberty, whose political sentiments might otherwise have kept them wide apart. There is no reason for thinking that the exiles who took refuge at Athens after the seizure of the Cadmea were in general partizans of democracy. Among them were several men of the highest rank, including almost all who had filled the high office of *hipparchus*, or master of the horse, which at Thebes seems to have been invested by the old aristocratical institutions with somewhat of a religious, as well as a military and civil character. But whatever may have been their previous opinions, they were now naturally led to consider the independence of Thebes as intimately connected with the establishment of popular government.

Pelopidas and Epaminondas were attracted toward each other by the secret sympathy of kindred natures; that it was no accidental cause which cemented their friendship, was proved by the invariable constancy with which it maintained itself through the course of a highly agitated public life, in which less congenial spirits would have found abundant motives for jealousy and discord. They had served together in the Theban division which had been sent to support the Spartan invasion of Mantinea, and had fought side by side in the engagement which has been already mentioned as having taken place before the siege of that city. Their line had partially given way, and they were almost surrounded by the enemy. Pelopidas fell pierced with wounds, and Epaminondas, though he believed him to be dead, continued to shield his body until he himself, having received several wounds, was nearly overpowered by superior numbers, when Agesipolis came up to his relief. But this occurrence might rather be considered as an indication of the friendship established between them, than as its foundation, or as the occasion from which it derived much additional warmth. Epaminondas is said to have been the only one among the friends of Pelopidas, whom he could not prevail on to accept pecuniary assistance from him. Pelopidas, on the other hand, emulated his friend's poverty in the simplicity of his own habits, though he took no interest in his philosophical pursuits, but after the old Theban fashion gave his leisure to field sports and athletic exercises.—THIRLWALL.

## HOW SLEEP THE BRAVE.

How sleep the Brave who sink to rest
By all their Country's wishes blest!
When Spring, with dewy fingers cold,
Returns to deck their hallow'd mould,
She there shall dress a sweeter sod
Than Fancy's feet have ever trod.

By fairy hands their knell is rung,
By forms unseen their dirge is sung:
There Honor comes, a pilgrim grey,
To bless the turf that wraps their clay,
And Freedom shall awhile repair
To dwell a weeping hermit there !           —COLLINS.

## THE STUDY OF ARCHÆOLOGY.

ARCHÆOLOGY has been called the handmaid of history ; and, indeed, without its aid history would as little represent the particular time it endeavours to recall, as the drawing of a skeleton would represent the features and the form by which the individual human being was recognised while in life. It is to the skeleton of a former age that archæology restores the flesh and the sinews and the lineaments that distinguish it from the countless centuries of which it is a link, clothes it in the very garments that it wore, and rebuilds the very home in which it dwelt.

But archæology is not only the handmaid of history, it is also the conservator of art. It disinters from neglected tombs the inventions of departed genius, and bids them serve as studies and sources of inspiration to the genius of a later day. When the Baths of Titus were excavated at Rome, the attention of Raphael was directed by a fellow artist to their faded arabesques. Those arabesques roused his own creative imagination, and under his pencil reappeared on the walls of the Vatican in new and original combinations of form and color. Nay, that discovery and the train of ideas it aroused, may be said to have suggested the delicate tracery and elaborate ornament of that new school of architecture called the *Renaissance*, out of which grew the palaces of Fontainebleau and Heidelberg, and which we have nationalized in England in those noble manorial residences which adorn the reigns of Elizabeth and James.

But it is not only history and the plastic arts which are indebted to the science of the archæologist. It is amongst his labors to guard from oblivion the myths, the traditions, the legends of former days; and critical and severe though his genius and its obligations must be, still it is to his care that we owe the preservation of many a pure and sacred well-spring of poetry and romance,—well-springs from which Spenser and Milton, Dryden, Gray, Wordsworth, and Scott, have drawn each his own special stream of inspiration, to refresh the banks that he cultivated, and nourish the flowers that he reared. Last, and not least, of our obligations to the spirit of archæology, is that it stimulates and deepens in the heart of a people sentiments of pride and affection for the native land. In proportion as we cherish the memories of our ancestors, and revere the heirlooms they have left us, in monuments reared by their piety, or bearing witness of their lives and their deeds, the soil which they trod becomes hallowed ground; and we feel that patriotism is no idle name, but the mainspring of every policy which makes statesmen wise, and the borders of a state secure. Indeed, if we look back to the annals of the world we find that there is no surer sign of the impending downfall of any nation than a cynical contempt for the memorials of its old renown. When Gibbon gives us the mournful picture of Roman corruption and decrepitude, just before the final extinction of the Western Empire and the accession of a barbarian king to the throne of the Cæsars, he tells us "that the monuments of consular or imperial greatness were no longer revered as the glory of the capital; they were only esteemed as an inexhaustible mine of materials cheaper and more convenient than the distant quarry." And with this miserable desecration of objects that attested the majesty of Rome, the very name of the Roman passed away; and, to borrow the expression of a French writer "the descendants of Brutus became the vassals of the Goth."

\* \* \* \* \* \* \*

So long as we keep the past before us as a guide, we are not altogether (speaking humanly, and with due submission to the decrees of Providence), we are not altogether without some power to shape the future so as to preserve, through all its changes, that national spirit without which the unity of a race disappears. It has been vouchsafed to England to diffuse her children and her language amidst realms unknown to the ambition of Alexander, and far beyond the boldest flights of the Roman eagle. Ages hence, from the shores of Australasia and America, pilgrims will visit this land as the birth-place of their ancestors, and venerate every relic of our glorious if chequered past, from the day of the Druid to that in which we now are; for while we speak we ourselves are acting history, and becoming in our turn the ancients to posterity. May no future Gibbon trace to the faults of our time the causes which insure the rise and fall of empires. Century after century may our descendants in those vast new worlds, compared to which Europe itself shrinks to the dimensions of a province or a shire,—century after century may they find still flourishing on these ancestral shores, not ashamed to number the men of our generation among its fathers, a race adorned by the graces of literature, and enriched by the stores of science. May they find still unimpaired, and sacred alike from superstition and unbelief, the altars of Christian faith; may our havens and docks still be animated by vessels fitted for commerce abroad, or armed, in case of need, for defence at home. Still may our institutions and our liberties find the eloquence of freemen and patriots in our legislative halls, and the ermine of Justice be unsullied by a spot in the courts where she adjudicates between man and man. These are the noblest legacies we receive from the past; and while we treasure these at every hazard, and through every change, the soul of England will retain vitality to her form, and no archæologist will seek her grave amidst the nations that have passed away. —LORD LYTTON.

## HONOR MUST BE ACTIVE.

TIME hath, my lord, a wallet at his back,
Wherein he puts alms for oblivion,
A great-sized monster of ingratitudes;
Those scraps are good deeds past, which are devoured
As fast as they are made, forgot as soon
As done. Perseverance, dear my lord,
Keeps honor bright. To have done, is to hang

Quite out of fashion, like a rusty mail,
In monumental mockery. Take the instant way;
For honor travels in a strait so narrow,
Where one but goes abreast; keep then the path;
For emulation hath a thousand sons,
That one by one pursue; if you give way,
Or hedge aside from the direct forthright,
Like to an entered tide, they all rush by,
And leave you hindmost;
Or, like a gallant horse, fallen in the first rank,
Lie there for pavement to the abject rear,
O'errun and trampled on. Then what they do in present
Though less than yours in past, must o'ertop yours;
For time is like a fashionable host,
That slightly shakes his parting guest by the hand,
And with his arms outstretched, as he would fly,
Grasps in the comer. Welcome ever smiles,
And farewell goes out sighing. Let not virtue seek
Remuneration for the thing it was;
For beauty, wit,
High birth, vigor of bone, desert in service,
Love, friendship, charity, are subjects all
To envious and calumniating time.
One touch of nature makes the whole world kin—
That all, with one consent, praise new-born gawds,
Though they are made and moulded of things past,
And give to dust, that is a little gilt,
More laud than gilt o'erdusted.
The present eye praises the present object. —SHAKESPEARE

## THE BATTLE OF ARBELA.

### (B.C. 331.)

GREAT reliance had been placed by the Persian king on the effects of the scythe-bearing chariots. It was designed to launch these against the Macedonian phalanx, and to follow these up by a heavy charge of cavalry, which it was hoped would find the ranks of the spearmen disordered by the rush of the chariots, and easily destroy this most formidable part of Alexander's force. In front, therefore, of the Persian centre, where Darius took his station, and which it was supposed the phalanx would attack, the ground had been carefully levelled and smoothed, so as to allow the chariots to charge over it with their full sweep and speed. As the Macedonian army approached the Persian, Alexander found that the front of his whole line barely equalled the front of the Persian centre, so that he was outflanked on his right by the entire left wing of the enemy, and by their entire right wing on his left. His tactics were to assail some one point of the hostile army, and gain a decisive advantage : while he refused, as far as possible, the encounter along the rest of the line. He therefore inclined his order of march to the right, so as to enable his right wing and centre to come into collision with the enemy on as favourable terms as possible though the manœuvre might in some respect compromise his left.

The effect of this oblique movement was to bring the phalanx and his own wing nearly beyond the limits of the ground which the Persians had prepared for the operations of the chariots : and Darius, fearing to lose the benefit of this arm against the most important parts of the Macedonian force, ordered the Scythian and Bactrian cavalry, who were drawn up in advance on his extreme left, to charge round upon Alexander's right wing, and check its further lateral progress. Against these assailants Alexander sent, from his second line, Menidas's cavalry. As these proved too few to make head against the enemy, he ordered Ariston also from the second line with his light horse, and Cleander with his foot, in support of Menidas. The Bactrians and Scythians now began to give way, but Darius reinforced them by the mass of Bactrian cavalry from his main line, and an obstinate cavalry fight now took place. The Bactrians and Scythians were numerous, and were better armed than the horsemen under Menidas and Ariston ; and the loss at first was heaviest on the Macedonian side. But still the European cavalry stood the charge of the Asiatics, and at last, by their superior discipline, and by acting in squadrons that supported each other, instead of fighting in a confused mass like the barbarians, the Macedonians broke their adversaries, and drove them off the field.

Darius now directed the scythe-armed chariots to be driven against Alexander's horseguards and the phalanx ; and these formidable vehicles were accordingly sent rattling across the plain, against the Macedonian line. When we remember the alarm which the war-chariots of the Britons created among Cæsar's legions, we shall not be prone to deride this arm of ancient warfare as always useless. The object of the chariots was to create unsteadiness in the ranks against which they were driven, and squadrons of cavalry followed close upon them, to profit by such disorder. But the Asiatic chariots were rendered ineffective at Arbela by the light armed troops whom Alexander had specially appointed for the service, and who, wounding the horses and drivers with their missile weapons, and running alongside so as to cut the traces or seize the reins, marred the intended charge ; and the few chariots that reached the phalanx, passed harmlessly through the intervals which the spearmen opened for them, and were easily captured in the rear.

A mass of the Asiatic cavalry was now, for the second time, collected against Alexander's extreme right, and moved round it, with the view of gaining the flank of his army. At the critical moment, Aretes, with his horsemen from Alexander's second line, dashed on the Persian squadrons when their own flanks were exposed by this evolution. While Alexander thus met and baffled all the flanking attacks of the enemy with troops brought up from his second line, he kept his own horseguards and the rest of the front line of his wing fresh, and ready to take advantage of the first opportunity for striking a decisive blow. This soon came. A large body of horse, who were posted on the Persian left wing nearest to the centre, quitted their station and rode off to help their comrades in the cavalry fight that still was going on at the extreme right of Alexander's wing against the detachments from his second line. This made a huge gap in the Persian array, and into this space Alexander instantly dashed with his guard, and then pressing towards his left, he soon began to make havoc in the left flank of the Persian centre. The shield-bearing infantry now charged also among the reeling masses of the Asiatics ; and five of the brigades of the phalanx, with the irresistible might of their sarissas, bore down the Greek mercenaries of Darius, and dug their way through the Persian centre. In the early part of the battle, Darius had showed skill and energy ; and he now for some time encouraged his men, by voice and example, to keep firm. But the lances of Alexander's cavalry, and the pikes of the phalanx now gleamed nearer and nearer to him. His charioteer was struck down by a javelin at his side ; and at last Darius's nerve failed him ; and, descending from his chariot, he mounted on a fleet horse and galloped from the plain, regardless of the state of the battle in other parts of the field where matters were going on much more favorably for his cause, and where his presence might have done much towards gaining a victory.

Alexander's operations with his right and centre had exposed his left to an immensely preponderating force of the enemy. Parmenio kept out of action as long as possible; but Mazæus, who commanded the Persian right wing, advanced against him, completely outflanked him, and pressed him severely with reiterated charges by superior numbers. Seeing the distress of Parmenio's wing, Simmias, who commanded the sixth brigade of the phalanx, which was next to the left wing, did not advance with the other brigades in the great charge upon the Persian centre, but kept back to cover Parmenio's troops on *their* right flank, as otherwise they would have been completely surrounded and cut off from the rest of the Macedonian army. By so doing, Simmias had unavoidably opened a gap in the Macedonian left centre, and a large column of Indian and Persian horse, from the Persian right centre, had galloped forward through the interval, and right through the troops of the Macedonian second line. Instead of then wheeling round upon Parmenio, or upon the rear of Alexander's conquering wing, the Indian and Persian cavalry rode straight on to the Macedonian camp, overpowered the Thracians who were left in charge of it, and began to plunder. This was stopped by the phalangite troops of the second line, who, after the enemy's horsemen had rushed by them, faced about, countermarched upon the camp, killed many of the Indians and Persians in the act of plundering, and forced the rest to ride off again. Just at this crisis. Alexander had been recalled from his pursuit of Darius, by tidings of the distress of Parmenio, and of his inability to bear up any longer against the hot attacks of Mazæus. Taking his horseguards with him, Alexander rode towards the part of the field where his left wing was fighting; but on his way thither he encountered the Persian and Indian cavalry, on their return from his camp.

These men now saw that their only chance of safety was to cut their way through; and in one huge column they charged desperately upon the Macedonians. There was here a close hand-to-hand fight, which lasted some time, and sixty of the royal horseguards fell, and three generals, who fought close to Alexander's side, were wounded. At length the Macedonian discipline and valor again prevailed, and a large number of the Persian and Indian horsemen were cut down, some few only succeeded in breaking through and riding away. Relieved of these obstinate enemies, Alexander again formed his horse-guards, and led them towards Parmenio; but by this time that general also was victorious. Probably the news of Darius's flight had reached Mazæus, and had damped the ardor of the Persian right wing; while the tidings of their comrades' success must have proportionably encouraged the Macedonian forces under Parmenio. His Thessalian cavalry particularly distinguished themselves by their gallantry and persevering good conduct, and by the time that Alexander had ridden up to Parmenio, the whole Persian army was in full flight from the field.

It was of the deepest importance to Alexander to secure the person of Darius, and he now urged on the pursuit. The river Lycus was between the field of battle and the city of Arbela, whither the fugitives directed their course, and the passage of this river was even more destructive to the Persians than the swords and spears of the Macedonians had been in the engagement. The narrow bridge was soon choked up by the flying thousands who rushed towards it, and vast numbers of the Persians threw themselves, or were hurried by others, into the rapid stream, and perished in its waters. Darius had crossed it, and had ridden on through Arbela without halting. Alexander reached that city on the next day, and made himself master of all Darius's treasure and stores; but the Persian king, unfortunately for himself, had fled too fast for his conqueror: he had only escaped to perish by the treachery of his Bactrian satrap, Bessus.

A few days after the battle, Alexander entered Babylon, "the oldest seat of earthly empire" then in existence, as its acknowledged lord and master. There were yet some campaigns of his brief and bright career to be accomplished. Central Asia was yet to witness the march of his phalanx. He was yet to effect that conquest of Affghanistan in which England since has failed. His generalship, as well as his valor, were yet to be signalized on the banks of the Hydaspes, and the field of Chilianwallah; and he was yet to precede the Queen of England in annexing the Punjaub to the dominions of an European sovereign. But the crisis of his career was reached; the great object of his mission was accomplished ; and the ancient Persian empire, which once menaced all the nations of the earth with subjection, was irreparably crushed, when Alexander had won his crowning victory at Arbela. —CREASY.

## BLIGH'S BOAT VOYAGE.

WHEN Fletcher Christian and his merciless companions set their commander adrift in the boat, they flung them a small quantity of provisions and a few stores which, together with the crew, sank the boat so deep in the water that one would have expected that the first breeze of wind would have filled and swamped it.

The boat, in which these nineteen men found themselves floating in the midst of the Pacific Ocean, was the launch. Its length was 23 feet ; its breadth 6 feet 9 inches. In this, without awning or covering of any kind and with a small allowance of food—scarce enough to sustain life, they encountered heavy storms and endured the severest privations and sufferings from cold and exposure during a voyage of several thousands of miles.

The names of the men thus cast away are as follows:— Lieutenant Bligh ; John Fryer, master ; William Elphinstone, master's mate ; John Hallet, midshipman ; Thomas Hayward, midshipman ; William Peckover, gunner ; William Cole, boatswain ; William Purcell, carpenter ; Thomas Ledward, surgeon's-mate ; John Samuel, clerk and steward ; David Nelson, botanist ; Lawrence Labogue, sailmaker ; Peter Linkletter, quarter-master ; John Norton, quarter-master ; George Simpson, quarter-master's mate ; Thomas Hall, ship's cook ; John Smith, commander's cook ; Robert Lamb, butcher ; and Robert Tinkler, a boy.

None but a man of decided firmness and energy of character could have carried himself and his companions through the dangers and trials of that voyage in safety. Lieutenant Bligh proved himself fully equal to the emergency.

His first care after the *Bounty* left them was to examine the condition of his boat and the amount of his provisions. These last were very meagre. They consisted of one hundred and fifty pounds of biscuit, thirty pounds of pork, six quarts of rum, six bottles of wine, and twenty-eight gallons of water. Of stores they had a few pieces of canvas, some twine and cordage, four cutlasses, a quadrant, and a compass.

The condition of the launch and her crew is beautifully and forcibly expressed in the following lines :—

> "The boat is lowered with all the haste of hate,
> With its slight plank between thee and thy fate;
> Her only cargo such a scant supply
> As promises the death their hands deny ;
> And just enough of water and of bread
> To keep, some days, the dying from the dead.
> Some cordage, canvas, sails, and lines, and twine,
> But treasures all to hermits of the brine,
> Were added after, to the earnest prayer
> Of those who saw no hope save sea and air ;
> And last, that trembling vassal of the Pole,
> The feeling compass, navigators' soul.
> \* \* \* \*
>
> The launch is crowded with the faithful few
> That wait their chief—a melancholy crew,
> But some remained reluctant on the deck
> Of that proud vessel, now a moral wreck—
> And viewed their captain's fate with piteous eyes ;
> While others scoffed his augured miseries,
> Sneered at the prospect of his pigmy sail,
> And the slight bark, so laden and so frail."

Being within about thirty miles of the island of Tofoa, Bligh resolved in the first instance to proceed thither in order to procure, if possible, bread-fruit and water. But the natives who lined the beach turned out to be of exceedingly treacherous and fierce disposition. One of the chiefs earnestly entreated Bligh to spend the night there, and upon his refusing to do so, he exclaimed angrily, " Then we will kill you." Thereupon he gave a signal, and immediately about two hundred savages rushed upon the sailors and attacked them with stones, which flew about their heads like a shower of shot. Fortunately none were seriously hit, and they all succeeded in getting safely into the boat with the exception of John Norton, the quartermaster, who boldly ran up the beach to cast off the stern fast. Upon this brave but unfortunate man the natives rushed, and in a few minutes stoned him to death.

The crew of the launch pushed hastily off to sea, but were

followed by several canoes, laden with stones from which the attack was continued. Having no fire-arms, the only defence they could make was to throw back the stones which happened to lodge in the boat, but in this mode of warfare the savages were much more expert, and it is probable the Europeans would have been murdered had they not hit upon the ruse of throwing part of their clothing into the sea. As they expected, the natives stopped to pick up the garments, and the crew of the boat pulled lustily till beyond the reach of stones. Soon after, night coming on, the pursuit was abandoned.

Before this occurred, however, one or two bread-fruits and a few small cocoa-nuts had been gathered, and added to their slender stock of provisions.

The eyes of the wretched men in the launch were now turned anxiously towards their commander, in whose energy and knowledge they felt their hope of deliverance depended. It is to be hoped that, among men in such desperate circumstances, there were some who earnestly looked to a higher Power for deliverance. The commander now informed his men that he meant to steer straight for a Dutch settlement on the island of Timor, distant above three thousand six hundred miles, and added that the only chance they had of accomplishing such a voyage successfully was to place themselves voluntarily on a fixed allowance of food, which, on careful calculation, he said, would afford each man one ounce of bread and quarter of a pint of water per day !

To this the men readily agreed, and that night, it may be said, the perilous voyage began. They gave up all idea of steering for any of the islands of the Pacific, knowing full well that the natives, seeing their helpless condition, would slay and devour them.

" We bore away," says Bligh, " across a sea where the navigation is but little known, in a small boat, twenty-three feet long from stem to stern, deeply laden with eighteen men. I was happy, however, to see that every one seemed better satisfied with our situation than myself. It was about eight o'clock at night on the 2d of May, 1789, when we bore away under a reefed lug-foresail, and having divided the people into watches, and got the boat into a little order, we returned thanks to God for our miraculous preservation, and, in full confidence of his gracious support, I found my mind more at ease than it had been for some days past."

But this happy frame of mind was not to last long. At dawn of the following day the sun arose red and fiery—a sure indication of coming storms—and ere the day had far advanced the gale burst upon them in all its fury ; so fierce was it that, we are told, the sail of the boat was actually *becalmed* when between the heavy billows, while, when on the top of the seas, it proved almost more than they could carry, yet they did not dare to take it in. The sea curled constantly over the gunwale, and incessant baling was necessary to keep them afloat.

In order to lighten the boat, all their superfluous clothing, with some spare sails and cordage were thrown overboard, and the biscuit was stowed in the carpenter's chest to preserve it from the spray that lashed over them.

Bligh had apportioned the provisions so as to last eight weeks, that being the time that would be probably required under ordinary circumstances to complete the voyage ; and being a man of firm character he resolved to enforce the rules as to food at the risk of his life if need be. As the men were exhausted with baling, and thoroughly wet, a teaspoonful of rum and quarter of a bread-fruit were served out to each. but, in spite of this, their limbs were so benumbed with cold when day-light came, that they could scarcely continue the work of baling, upon which, under God, the lives of all depended ; another teaspoonful of rum was therefore served out, by which they felt much revived.

That day the boat was kept running before the wind. Five small cocoa-nuts were served out for dinner, and in the evening a few pieces of bread-fruit were distributed for supper, after which they commended themselves to God in prayer.

The gale continued till the morning of the 5th, when it began to abate, and now Bligh prepared a small log-line with which he afterwards marked more correctly than heretofore their progress over the unknown ocean. The sufferings of the poor fellows from fatigue and cold were extreme, for, in addition to their laborious work and exposure, they had not sufficient room in the bottom of the boat to stretch their limbs when they lay down to rest, and usually awoke with severe cramps. To add to their misfortunes, the biscuit, it was found, had been much damaged during the gale, part of it was quite decayed and unfit for food. Nevertheless it was carefully preserved.

On the 6th they came in sight of islands, but, remembering the reception at Tofoa, the sight of land aroused fear instead of joy in their breasts. On the same day they hooked a fish. Circumstanced as they were, such an event created a burst of anxious delight, which, alas, was almost instantly changed into a groan of disappointment, in consequence of the fish escaping while they were endeavoring to get it over the side of the boat. That night each man supped on an ounce of damaged biscuit, and quarter of a pint of water.

Next day they were pursued by two canoes, which, however, failed to overtake them, although they did not give up the chase till the afternoon. Well was it for them that these natives did fail, and that the people in the boat had resolution enough to refrain from attempting to land, for the islands they were passing turned out to be part of the Feejee group, the inhabitants of which are now known to be the fiercest and most addicted to cannibalism, as well as the most cruel and inhospitable, of all the islanders of the South Seas.

Soon after this heavy rain came on, and every effort was made to collect the shower. By this means their stock of fresh water was increased to thirty-four gallons, and their thirst, for the first time since they were turned adrift, was thoroughly quenched. But the consequences of the rain were hurtful in other respects, for everything in the boat and on their persons was soaked, and being compelled to sleep all night in this condition, unable, from want of room, to make any exertion to warm themselves by means of muscular effort, they were seized with severe shiverings. On the 8th, therefore, Bligh deemed it advisable to issue a slightly more substantial breakfast, and served to each man an ounce and a half of pork, half a pint of cocoa-nut milk, an ounce of biscuit, and a teaspoonful of rum, which last though so small in quantity, is said to have been of the greatest service.

During all this time, and, indeed, during the whole voyage, Bligh kept a short journal in a small book which had been used in the *Bounty* for the insertion of signals. He says, in regard to it, " It is with the utmost difficulty that I can open a book to write, and I feel truly sensible I can do no more than point out where these lands are to be found, and give some idea of their extent."

Yet the persevering commander on that forlorn voyage continued to keep the journal to the end, and it, with several other weather-stained relics, is now in possession of his daughters.

Bligh now adopted a more certain method of doling out the scanty allowance. "Hitherto," he says, "I had issued the allowance by guess, but now I made a pair of scales, with two cocoa-nut shells, and having accidentally some pistol balls in the boat, twenty-five of which weighed one pound, or sixteen ounces, I adopted one of these balls as the proportion of weight that each person should receive of bread at the times I served it out. I also amused all hands with describing the situation of New Guinea and New Holland, and gave them every information in my power, that, in case any accident should happen to me, those who survived might have some idea of what they were about, and be able to find their way to Timor, which at present they knew nothing of more than the name, and some not even that. At night I served a quarter of a pint of water and half an ounce of bread for supper."

Bligh entertained his men thus during a brief respite of a few hours' fine weather and sunshine, which they availed themselves of to dry their clothes and sails. But this was scarcely accomplished when another gale, accompanied by thunder, lightning and rain, burst upon them, and again drenched them all to the skin.

On the 10th it was very severe. The sea broke over them so constantly that they were compelled to run before the wind, and to keep two men constantly baling. The allowance, too, was still further reduced, one twenty-fifth part of a pound of biscuit, and a quarter of a pint of water, being the allowance for breakfast, and the same at dinner and supper. Occasionally, when the weather was very bad, half an ounce or so of pork, and a teaspoonful of rum was added.

"In the evening of the 12th," says Bligh, "it still rained hard, and we again experienced a dreadful night. At length the day came, and showed a miserable set of beings, full of wants, without anything to relieve them. Some complained of great pain in the bowels, and every one of having almost lost the use of his limbs. The little sleep we got was in no way refreshing as we were constantly covered with the sea and rain. The weather continuing bad, and no sun affording the least prospect of getting our clothes dried, I recommended to every one to strip and wring them through the sea-water, by which means they received a warmth that. while wet with rain water, they could not have."

The gale continued unabated during several days, and as the nights were intensely dark, not a star being visible, they were often very uncertain as to their steering. Yet, although islands were seen more than once, they held on their miserable course, preferring the chance of being starved to death in an open boat, to the risk of being killed and eaten by the savages.

The night of the 16th was horribly dark and tempestuous, and they expected each moment that the boat would be overwhelmed. That day was also marked by the issue of an ounce of pork in addition to the ordinary allowance. The bad weather continued, and several days later Mr. Bligh speaks of some of his people seeming half dead, while their appearance was "horrible."

"During the whole of the afternoon of the 21st," he says, "we were so covered with rain and salt water that we could scarcely see. We suffered extreme cold, and every one dreaded the approach of night. Sleep, though we longed for it, afforded no comfort, for my own part I almost lived without it. On the 22nd our situation was extremely calamitous. We were obliged to take the course of the sea, running right before it, and watching with the utmost care, as the least error in the helm would in a moment have been our destruction. It continued through the day to blow hard, and the foam of the sea kept running over our stern and quarters.

"The misery we suffered this night exceeded the preceding. The sea flew over us with great force, and kept us baling with horror and anxiety. At dawn of day I found every one in a most distressed condition, and I began to fear that another such night would put an end to the lives of several who seemed no longer able to support their sufferings. I served an allowance of two teaspoonfuls of rum; after drinking which, and having wrung our clothes, and taken our breakfast of bread and water, we became a little refreshed."

Next day the wind moderated, the sun came out to cheer their drooping spirits, and Bligh speaks, for the first time, of seeing "cheerful faces" about him. Wretched as was their condition they experienced some degree of comfort and warmth, —the first they had felt during the previous fifteen days. This moment of breathing time was employed by the commander in examining into the state of the provisions, which he found so reduced that a further reduction in the allowance became absolutely essential. He expected that a mutinous spirit would be roused in the poor fellows when this was announced, but to his surprise they at once agreed to it on the necessity being explained.

It was important that the rate of consumption should be so proportioned that the stock might last six weeks longer. Accordingly it was arranged that the allowance in future should be one twenty-fifth part of a pound of bread for breakfast, and the same quantity for dinner, as usual, but that the proportion for supper should be discontinued !

It seemed as if God, in his mercy, smiled upon this instance of self-denial on the part of those weary and worn-out men, for the very next day, about noon, some noddies—a small species of sea-fowl, about the size of a pigeon—came so near the boat that one of them was caught by the hand.

This little bird was divided, with its entrails, into eighteen portions. Then one of the sailors was made to turn his back upon the feast, while another sailor pointed separately to each portion, saying, "*Who shall have this ?*" Thus every one felt that he had an equal chance with the rest of getting the best portion, and all grumbling at supposed unfairness was avoided. Curiously enough the poor commander fared worst upon this occasion, for, much to the amusement of the men, the beak and claws were included in the share that fell to him !

On the same evening several boobies approached, and one of them was caught and divided in the same manner. It was about the size of a duck. The blood was given to three of the men who had been most distressed for want of food. Of course it was eaten raw. Even had they possessed the means of cooking it, these half famished men would not have delayed their meal for such a trifle. On the 26th another booby was caught.

The heat of the sun now became even more distressing than cold and rain had been before, and some of the people were seized with a languor and faintness that rendered them indifferent to life.

At last, on the 28th, about one in the morning, the sound of breakers was heard by the man at the helm, and soon after they approached the "barrier reef," which runs along the eastern coast of New Holland. The sea broke furiously over this reef, but within the water was as smooth as a pond. Along it they steered until an opening was found, and passing in with a strong stream, they at last found themselves in smooth water, and returned thanks to God who had brought them thus far in safety. But their terrible voyage was not yet done. Here they could only rest and recruit their strength for a few days.

Oysters were found on the rocks in great abundance. Fresh water was also found; but above all, rest—sound, sweet, refreshing repose to their wearied limbs and minds—was obtained.

With returning health, as is too often the case in such circumstances, came a mutinous spirit. Bligh ordered some of the crew to go along the shore to gather supplies. They grumbled at what they considered too severe duty, and one of them told his commander that he was as good a man as himself.

Bligh says, "It was not possible for one to judge where this might have an end if not stopped in time. To prevent, therefore, such disputes in future, I determined either to preserve my command or die in the attempt; and seizing a cutlass, I ordered him to lay hold of another and defend himself; on which he called out that I was going to kill him, and immediately made concessions. I did not allow this to interfere further with the harmony of the boat's crew, and everything soon became quiet."

About this time—June 1st—Nelson, the botanist, became very ill; two of the men also began to show symptoms of sinking under the effects of the exposure and suffering they had endured, notwithstanding their recent rest. But the voyage to the nearest habitable part of the globe could not be delayed on this account; so, on the 3rd, the little boat once more launched out into the open sea.

Soon they were again reduced to the old allowance—the twenty-fifth of an ounce of biscuit, carefully weighed in the cocoa-nut scales, with the pistol bullet; and ere long they were reduced to worse straits than before. The surgeon and one of the stoutest sailors broke down.

"On the morning of the 10th, after a comfortless night," says Bligh, "there was a visible alteration for the worse in many of the people, which gave me great apprehensions. An extreme weakness, swelled legs, hollow and ghastly countenances, a more than common inclination to sleep, with an apparent debility of understanding, seemed to me the melancholy presage of an approaching dissolution. The surgeon and Lobogue, in particular, were most miserable objects. I occasionally gave them a few teaspoonfuls of wine out of the little that remained, which greatly assisted them. The hopes of being able to accomplish the voyage was our principal support. The boatswain very innocently told me that he really thought I looked worse than any in the boat. The simplicity with which he uttered such an opinion amused me, and I returned him a better compliment."

But the suffering of this much enduring crew were soon to terminate; with some in restoration to health and to their native land; with others in the last quiet resting place of man. On the 11th, Mr. Bligh told his companions that they were approaching Timor; and, accordingly, the next day they arrived at that island, where the people received them with the utmost hospitality and kindness; vieing with each other in acts of kindness, while they gazed in horror and pity at the living skeletons who, with tears streaming from their eyes, and words of thankfulness to God upon their lips, landed on their shores.

Two months they remained here to recruit; then they set forth on their return to England. But all of them did not reach it. Of the nineteen who were forced from the *Bounty* by the mutineers, thirteen survived to tell the tale of their wonderful voyage and almost miraculous escape. Besides John Norton, who was stoned by the savages of Tofoa, Nelson, the botanist, perished at Timor. Two others died at Batavia, and another on the passage home. The surgeon, Mr. Ledward, was left behind, and never again heard of.

"Thus happily ended," says Bligh, in conclusion, "through the assistance of Divine Providence, without accident, a voyage of the most extraordinary nature that ever happened in the world."

# THE DESERT.

"I MUST give a description of our equipage, now that we are fairly launched on the great waste. I ride a white camel, with my saddlebags under me, and a pair of water-skins, quite full, beneath them: over the saddle is my bed. A thick cherry-stick, with a cross at the end of it, serves to guide the animal; a gentle tap on the side of his neck, sends him to the left, and one on the opposite makes him turn back again to the right: a knock on the back of his head stops him, and a few blows between the ears bring him to his knees, if accompanied by a guttural sound, resembling, as the Arabs say, the pronunciation of their letter *sche*. To make him move quickly, it is necessary to prick him, with the point of the stick, on the shoulders.

To the north there is a range of bare hills, and at their bases are patches of green; the rude tents of a tribe of Bedouins are pitched, and their cattle enliven the scene. We passed over a perfect level this morning, strewed with flowers and thick with pasture for the camels, where we are now resting. It is not usual here, as in many parts of the East, for the camels to wind in long strings, one after the other. Our numbers, amounting to fifteen hundred, are scattered over the surface in all directions, as far as the eye can trace.

In travelling, the sheiks or chiefs of the caravan, attended by the military part of their equipage, mounted on dromedaries, move in advance, while the loaded camels follow at some distance, in parallel masses, opening out, or changing the form, as the grass renders it necessary. They fall so naturally into military figures, that it is difficult to conceive their doing it without direction.

We have several tents in the caravan. They are pitched so as to permit the camels belonging to each to lie in the intervals, where they are placed in *squads* for the night. They are by no means agreeable neighbors: for, although they are not able to move from their place, they make a most unpleasant gurgling noise; the bales of the merchants always form the windward defence, for the tents have no sides to them, and but flutter over the goods to keep the sun from their owners.

At the usual hours of prayer, a loud call is heard throughout the camp, and parties flock to where the Muezzin takes his stand. At sunset, as the camels draw in from the pasture, all the Arabs are on their knees, in a line of two or three hundred, in two ranks. The priest, like a fugelman, in front, gives the time for bowing their heads, and performing the rest of the enjoined ceremonies. As they rise on the signal, they sink again to their knees, and press their foreheads to the earth with the utmost devotion; the scene is singularly impressive.

The rate at which a loaded camel travels is estimated at two miles and a half an hour by almost every traveller. Our caravan has not, I think, exceeded this; but the variety of its movements has been very tiresome. The Arab drivers, who walk in front of the animals, never miss an opportunity of a piece of pasture; but, however distant it may be from the proper course, lead them towards it, and with the short sticks they carry, beat them into the thickest part of it. The camels are anxious enough for the matter themselves, and huddle so together that their riders' legs are in tolerable danger of being crushed in the contact.

There is so strong a resemblance to a voyage at sea, in a passage across the desert, that I cannot divest myself of the belief that the moving mass is but a collection of small vessels carried into a heap by the tide. Every man is ready with his stick to fend off the animal that approaches him; one push separates the camels as it would separate a couple of boats, and the camels move away quite unconscious of the circumstance, till another movement swings them together again.

—SKINNER.

## ADAM.

As new waked from soundest sleep,
Soft on the flowery herb I found me laid,
In balmy sweat which with his beams the Sun
Soon dried, and on the reeking moisture fed.
Straight toward heaven my wondering eyes I turned,
And gazed a while the ample sky; till, raised
By quick instinctive motion, up I sprung,
As thitherward endeavoring, and upright
Stood on my feet. About me round I saw
Hill, dale, and shady woods, and sunny plains,
And liquid lapse of murmuring streams; by these,
Creatures that lived and moved, and walked or flew;

Birds on the branches warbling. All things smiled;
With fragrance and with joy my heart o'erflowed.
Myself I then perused, and limb by limb
Surveyed, and sometimes went, and sometimes ran
With supple joints, as lively vigor led :
But who I was, or where, or from what cause,
Knew not. To speak 1 tried, and forthwith spake ;
My tongue obeyed, and readily could name
Whate'er I saw. "Thou Sun," said I, "fair light,
And thou enlightened Earth, so fresh and gay,
Ye hills and dales, ye rivers, woods, and plains,
And ye that live and move, fair creatures, tell,
Tell, if you saw, how I came thus, how here ?
Not of myself ! By some great Maker, then,
In goodness and in power pre-eminent :
Tell me how may I know him, how adore,
From whom I have that thus I move, and live,
And feel that I am happier than I know." —MILTON.

## THE EARTHQUAKE AT LISBON.

(A. D. 1755.)

THERE never was a finer morning seen than the first of November ; the sun shone out in its full lustre ; the whole face of the sky was perfectly serene and clear , and not the least signal or warning of that approaching event, which has made this once flourishing, opulent, and populous city, a scene of the utmost horror and desolation, except only such as served to alarm, but scarcely left a moment's time to fly from the general destruction.

It was on the morning of this fatal day, between the hours of nine and ten, that I was set down in my apartment, just finishing a letter, when the papers and table I was writing on, began to tremble with a gentle motion, which rather surprised me, as I could not perceive a breath of wind stirring. Whilst I was reflecting with myself what this could be owing to, but without having the least apprehension of the real cause, the whole house began to shake from the very foundation,which at first I imputed to the rattling of several coaches in the main street, which usually passed that way, at this time, from Belem to the palace ; but on hearkening more attentively, I was soon undeceived, as I found it was owing to a strange frightful kind of noise under ground, resembling the hollow distant rumbling of thunder. All this passed in less than a minute, and I must confess I now began to be alarmed, as it naturally occurred to me that this noise might possibly be the forerunner of an earthquake, as one I remembered, which had happened about six or seven years ago, in the island of Madeira, commenced in the same manner, though it did little or no damage.

Upon this I threw down my pen, and started upon my feet, remaining a moment in suspense, whether I should stay in the apartment or run into the street, as the danger in both places seemed equal; and still flattering myself that this tremor might produce no other effects than such inconsiderable ones as had been felt at Madeira, but in a moment I was roused from my dream, being instantly stunned with a most horrid crash, as if every edifice in the city had tumbled down at once. The house in which I was shook with such violence, that the upper storeys immediately fell, and though my apartment (which was the first floor) did not then share the same fate, yet everything was thrown out of its place, in such a manner that it was with no small difficulty I kept my feet, and expected nothing less than to be soon crushed to death, as the walls continued rocking to and fro in the frightfullest manner, opening in several places; large stones falling down on every side from the cracks, and the ends of most of the rafters starting out from the roof. To add to this terrifying scene, the sky in a moment became so gloomy that I could now distinguish no particular object; it was an Egyptian darkness indeed, such as might be felt, owing, no doubt, to the prodigious clouds of dust and lime raised from so violent a concussion, and, as some reported, to sulphureous exhalations, but this I cannot affirm; however, it is certain I found myself almost choked for near ten minutes.

As soon as the gloom began to disperse, and the violence of the shock seemed pretty much abated, the first object I perceived in the room was a woman sitting on the floor with an infant in her arms, all covered with dust, pale and trembling. I asked her how she got hither, but her consternation was so great she could give me no account of her escape. I suppose that when the tremor first began, she ran out of her own house, and finding herself in such imminent danger from the falling stones, retired into the door of mine, which was almost contiguous to hers, for shelter, and when the shock increased, which filled the door with dust and rubbish, ran upstairs into my apartment, which was then open; be it as it might, this was no time for curiosity. I remember the poor creature asked me, in the utmost agony, if I did not think the world was at an end; at the same time she complained of being choked, and begged, for God's sake, I would procure her a little drink. Upon this I went to a closet where I kept a large jar of water (which you know is sometimes a pretty scarce commodity in Lisbon), but finding it broken into pieces, I told her she must not now think of quenching her thirst but saving her life, as the house was just falling on our heads, and if a second shock came, would certainly bury us both. I bade her take hold of my arm, and that I would endeavor to bring her into some place of security.

I shall always look upon it as a particular providence that I happened on this occasion to be undressed; for had I dressed myself as proposed when I got out of bed, in order to breakfast with a friend, I should, in all probability, have run into the street at the beginning of the shock, as the rest of the people in the house did, and, consequently, have had my brains dashed out, as every one of them had. However, the imminent danger I was in did not hinder me from considering that my present dress, only a gown and slippers, would render my getting over the ruins almost impracticable; I had, therefore, still presence of mind enough left to put on a pair of shoes and a coat, the first that came in my way, which was everything I saved, and in this dress I hurried down stairs, the woman with me, holding by my arm, and made directly to that end of the street which opens to the Tagus. Finding the passage this way entirely blocked up with the fallen houses to the height of their second storeys, I turned back to the other end which led into the main street (the common thoroughfare to the palace), having helped the woman over a vast heap of ruins, with no small hazard to my own life. Just as we were going into this street, as there was one part I could not well climb over without the assistance of my hands as well as feet, I desired her to let go her hold, which she did, remaining two or three feet behind me, at which instant there fell a vast stone from a tottering wall, and crushed both her and the child in pieces. So dismal a spectacle at any other time would have affected me in the highest degree; but the dread I was in of sharing the same fate myself, and the many instances of the same kind which presented themselves all around, were too shocking to make me dwell a moment on this single object.

I had now a long narrow street to pass, with the houses on each side four or five storeys high, all very old, the greater part already thrown down, or continually falling, and threatening the passengers with inevitable death at every step, numbers of whom lay killed before me, or what I thought far more deplorable—so bruised and wounded that they could not stir to help themselves. For my own part, as destruction appeared to me unavoidable, I only wished I might be made an end of at once, and not have my limbs broken, in which case I could expect nothing else but to be left upon the spot, lingering in misery, like those poor unhappy wretches, without receiving the least succor from any person.

As self-preservation, however, is the first law of nature, these sad thoughts did not so prevail as to make me totally despair. I proceeded on as fast as I conveniently could, though with the utmost caution; and having at length got clear of this horrid passage, I found myself safe and unhurt in the large open space before St. Paul's Church, which had been thrown down a few minutes before, and buried a great part of the congregation, that was generally pretty numerous, this being reckoned one of the most populous parishes in Lisbon. Here I stood some time, considering what I should do, and not thinking myself safe in this situation, I came to the resolution of climbing over the ruins of the west end of the church, in order to get to the river's side, that I might be removed as far as possible from the tottering houses, in case of a second shock.

This, with some difficulty, I accomplished; and here I found a prodigious concourse of people of both sexes, and of all ranks and conditions, among whom I observed some of the principal canons of the patriarchal church, in their purple robes and rochets, as these all go in the habits of bishops; several priests who had run from their altars in their sacerdotal vestments in the midst of their celebrating mass; ladies half dressed, and some without shoes; all these, whom their mutual dangers had here assembled as to a place of safety, were on their knees at prayer, with the terrors of death in their countenances, every one striking his breast and crying out incessantly *Miserecordia meu Dios.*

In the midst of these devotions the second great shock came on, little less violent than the first, and completed the ruin of those buildings which had been already much shattered. The consternation now became so universal that the shrieks and cries of *Miserecordia* could be distinctly heard from the top of St. Catherine's Hill, and a considerable distance off, whither a vast number of people had likewise retreated; at the same time we could hear the fall of the parish church there, whereby many persons were killed on the spot and others mortally wounded. You may judge of the force of this shock when I inform you it was so violent that I could scarce keep on my knees, but it was attended with some circumstances still more dreadful than the former. On a sudden I heard a general outcry, "the sea is coming in we shall be all lost." Upon this, turning my eyes toward the river, which in that place is near four miles broad, I could perceive it heaving and swelling in a most unaccountable manner, as no wind was stirring. In an instant there appeared, at some small distance, a large body of water, rising as it were like a mountain. It came on foaming and roaring, and rushing towards the shore with such impetuosity, that we all immediately ran for our lives as fast as possible; many were actually swept away, and the rest above their waist in water at a good distance from the banks. For my own part I had the narrowest escape, and should certainly have been lost, had I not grasped a large beam that lay on the ground, till the water returned to its channel, which it did almost at the same instant with equal rapidity. As there now appeared at least as much danger from the sea as the land, I scarce knew whither to retire for shelter, I took a sudden resolution of turning back, with my clothes all dripping, to the area of St. Paul's. Here I stood some time, and observed the ships tumbling and tossing about as in a violent storm; some had broken their cables, and were carried to the other side of the Tagus, others were whirled round with incredible swiftness; several large boats were turned keel upwards; and all this without any wind, which seemed the more astonishing. It was at the time of which I am now speaking, that the fine new quay built entirely of rough marble, at an immense expense, was entirely swallowed up, with all the people on it who had fled thither for safety, and had reasons to think themselves out of danger in such a place: at the same time, a great number of boats and small vessels anchored near it, all likewise full of people who had retired thither for the same purpose, were all swallowed up as in a whirlpool, and never more appeared.

This last dreadful incident I did not see with my own eyes, as it passed two or three stones throw from the spot where I then was, but I had the account as here given from several masters of ships, who were anchored within two or three hundred yards of the quay, and saw the whole catastrophe. One of them, in particular, informed me, that when the second shock came on, he could perceive the *whole* city waving backwards and forwards, like the sea when the wind first begins to rise; that the agitation of the earth was so great, even under the river, that it threw up his large anchor from the mooring, which swam, as he termed it, on the surface of the water; that immediately upon this extraordinary concussion, the river rose at once near twenty feet and in a moment subsided; at which instant he saw the quay, with the whole concourse of people upon it, sink down, and at the same time every one of the boats and vessels that were near it were drawn into the cavity, which he supposes instantly closed upon them, inasmuch as not the least sign of a wreck was ever seen afterwards. This account you may give full credit to for as to the loss of the vessels, it is confirmed by everybody, and, with regard to the quay, I went myself a few days after to convince myself of the truth, and could not find even the ruins of a place, where I had taken so many agreeable walks, as this was the common rendezvous of the factory in the cool of the evening. I found it all deep water and in some parts scarcely to be fathomed.

This is the only place I could learn which was swallowed up in or about Lisbon though I saw many large cracks and fissures in different parts, and one odd phenomenon I must not omit, which was communicated to me by a friend who has a house and wine-cellars on the other side of the river, viz., that the dwelling house being first terribly shaken, which made all the family run out, there presently fell down a vast high rock near it; that upon this the river rose and subsided in the manner already mentioned, and immediately a great number of small fissures appeared in several contiguous pieces of ground, from whence there spouted out, like a *jet d'eau*, a large quantity of fine white sand to a prodigious height. It is not to be doubted that the bowels of the earth must have been excessively agitated to cause these surprising effects; but whether the shocks were owing to any sudden explosion of various minerals mixing together, or to air pent up, and struggling for vent, or to a collection of subterraneous waters forcing a passage, God only knows. As to the fiery eruptions then talked of, I believe they are without foundation, though it is certain, I heard several complaining of a strong sulphureous smell, a dizziness in their heads, a sickness in their stomachs, and difficulty of respiration, not that I felt any such symptoms myself.

I had not been long in the area of St. Paul's, when I felt the third shock. Though somewhat less violent than the two former, the sea rushed in again, and retired with the same rapidity, and I remained up to my knees in water, though I had gotten upon a small eminence at some distance from the river, with the ruins of several intervening houses to break its force. At this time I took notice the waters retired so impetuously that some vessels were left quite dry, which rode in seven fathoms' water; the river thus continued alternately rushing on and retiring several times together, in such sort, that it was justly dreaded Lisbon would now meet the same fate which a few years before had befallen the city of Lima; and no doubt had this place lain open to the sea, and the force of the waves not been somewhat broken by the winding of the bay, the lower parts of it at least would have been totally destroyed.

I was now in such a situation, that I knew not which way to turn myself; if I remained there, I was in danger from the sea; if I retired further from the shore, the houses threatened certain destruction; and, at last, I resolved to go to the Mint, which being a low and very strong building, had received no considerable damage, except in some of the apartments towards the river. The party of soldiers, which is every day set there on guard, had all deserted the place, and the only person that remained was the commanding officer, a nobleman's son, of about seventeen or eighteen years of age, whom I found standing at the gate. As there was still a continued tremor of the earth, and the place where we now stood (being within twenty or thirty feet of the opposite houses, which were all tottering) appeared too dangerous, the court-yard likewise, being full of water, we both retired inward to a hillock of stones and rubbish; here I entered into conversation with him, and having expressed my admiration that one so young should have the courage to keep his post when every one of his soldiers had deserted theirs, the answer he made was, though he were sure the earth would open and swallow him up, he scorned to think of flying from his post. In short, it was owing to the magnanimity of this young man that the mint, which at this time had upwards of two millions of money in it, was not robbed; and indeed I do him no more than justice in saying, that I never saw any one behave with equal serenity and composure, on occasions much less dreadful than the present. I believe I might remain in conversation with him near five hours, and though I was now grown faint from the constant fatigue I had undergone, and having not yet broken my fast, yet this had not so much effect upon me as the anxiety I was under for a particular friend, with whom I was to have dined that day, and who, lodging at the top of a very high house in the heart of the city, and being a stranger to the language, could not but be in the utmost danger; my concern, therefore, for his preservation, made me determine, at all events, to go and see what had become of him, upon which I took my leave of the officer.

As I thought it would be the height of rashness to venture back through the same narrow street I had so providentially escaped from, I judged it safest to return over the ruins of St. Paul's to the river side, as the water now seemed little agitated. From hence I proceeded, with some hazard to the large space before the Irish convent of Corpo Santo, which had been thrown down, and buried a great number of people who were hearing mass, besides some of the friars; the rest of the community were standing in the area, looking, with dejected countenances, towards the ruins; from this place I took my way to the back street leading to the palace, leaving the ship-yard on one side, but found the further passage, opening into the principal street, stopped up by the ruins of the Opera House, one of the solidest and most magnificent buildings of the kind in Europe, and just finished at a prodigious expense; a vast heap of stones, each of several tons weight, had entirely blocked up the front of Mr. Bristow's house, which was opposite to it, and Mr. Ward, his partner, told me the next day, that he was just that instant going out at the door, and had actually set one foot over the threshold, when the west end of the Opera House fell down, and had he not in the moment started back, he should have been crushed into a thousand pieces.

The nobility, gentry and clergy, who were assisting at divine service when the earthquake began, fled away with the utmost precipitation, every one where his fears carried him, leaving the splendid apparatus of the numerous altars to the mercy of the first comer; but this did not so much affect me, as the distress of the poor animals, who seemed sensible of their hard fate; some few were killed, others wounded, but the greater part, which had received no hurt, were left there to starve.

From this square, the way led to my friend's lodgings through a long, steep, and narrow street, the new scenes of horror I met with here exceed all description; nothing could be heard but sighs and groans; I did not meet with a soul in the passage who was not bewailing the death of his nearest relations and dearest friends, or the loss of all his substance; I could hardly take a single step, without treading on the dead or the dying; in some places lay coaches, with their masters, horses, and riders, *almost* crushed in pieces; here mothers with infants in their arms; there ladies richly dressed, priests, friars, gentlemen, mechanics, either in the same condition or just expiring; some had their backs or thighs broken, others vast stones on their breasts; some lay almost buried in the rubbish, and, crying out in vain to the passengers for succor, were left to perish with the rest.

At length I arrived at the spot opposite to the house where my friend, for whom I was so anxious, resided; and, finding this, as well as the contiguous buildings, thrown down (which made me give him over for lost), I now thought of nothing but saving my own life in the best manner I could, and in less than an hour got to a public house, kept by one Morley, near the English burying ground, about half a mile from the city, where I still remain, with a great number of my countrymen, as well as Portuguese, in the same wretched circumstances, having almost ever since lain on the ground, and never once within doors, with scarcely any covering to defend me from the inclemency of the night air, which, at this time, is exceedingly sharp and piercing.

Perhaps you may think the present doleful subject here concluded; but, alas! the horrors of the 1st of November are sufficient to fill a volume. As soon as it grew dark, another scene presented itself little less shocking than those already described: the whole city appeared in a blaze, which was so bright that I could easily see to read by it. It may be said without exaggeration, it was on fire at least in a hundred different places at once, and thus continued burning for six days together, without intermission, or the least attempt being made to stop its progress.

It went on consuming everything the earthquake had spared, and the people were so dejected and terrified, that few or none had courage enough to venture down to save any part of their substance; every one had his eyes turned towards the flames, and stood looking on with silent grief, which was only interrupted by the cries and shrieks of women and children calling on the saints and angels for succor, whenever the earth began to tremble, which was so often this night, and indeed I may say ever since, that the tremors, more or less, did not cease for a quarter of an hour together.

But what would appear incredible to you, were the fact less public and notorious, is, that a gang of hardened villains, who had been confined, and got out of prison when the wall fell, at the first shock, were busily employed in setting fire to those buildings which stood some chance of escaping the general destruction. I cannot conceive what could have induced them to this hellish work, except to add to the horror and confusion, that they might, by this means, have the better opportunity of plundering with security. But there was no necessity for taking this trouble, as they might certainly have done their business without it, since the whole city was so deserted before night, that I believe not a soul remained in it, except those execrable villains, and others of the same stamp.

The whole number of persons that perished, including those who were burnt, or afterwards crushed to death whilst digging in the ruins, is supposed, on the lowest calculation, to amount to more than sixty thousand; and though the damage in other respects cannot be computed, yet you may form some idea of it, when I assure you that this extensive and opulent city is now nothing but a vast heap of ruins; that the rich and poor are at present upon a level; some thousands of families which but the day before had been easy in their circumstances, being now scattered about in the fields, wanting every conveniency of life, and finding none able to relieve them.

Thus, my dear friend, have I given you a genuine, though imperfect account of this terrible judgment, which has left so deep an impression on my mind, that I shall never wear it off. I have lost all the money I had by me, and have saved no other clothes than what I have on my back: but what I regret most, is the irreparable loss of my books and papers. To add to my present distress, those friends to whom I could have applied on any other occasion, are now in the same wretched circumstances with myself. However, notwithstanding all that I have suffered, I do not think I have reason to despair, but rather to return my gratefullest acknowledgments to the Almighty, who hath so visibly preserved my life amidst such dangers, where so many thousands perished; and the same good Providence, I trust, will still continue to protect me, and point out some means to extricate myself out of these difficulties. —DAVY.

## HAPPY LIFE.

How happy is he born and taught
That serveth not another's will;
Whose armor is his honest thought
And simple truth his utmost skill !

Whose passions not his masters are,
Whoso soul is still prepared for death,
Not tied unto the world with care
Of public fame, or private breath;

Who envies none that chance doth raise
Or vice ; who never understood
How deepest wounds are given by praise ;
Nor rules of state, but rules of good :

Who hath his life from rumors freed,
Whose conscience is his strong retreat ;
Whose state can neither flatterers feed,
Nor ruin make accusers great ;

Who God doth late and early pray
More of his grace and gifts to lend :
And entertains the harmless day
  With a well-chosen book or friend ;

—This man is freed from servile bands
Of hope to rise, or fear to fall;
Lord of himself, though not of lands;
And having nothing, yet hath all.  —Sir H. Wotton.

## DEATH THE LEVELLER.

The glories of our blood and state
    Are shadows, not substantial things;
There is no armor against fate;
    Death lays his icy hand on kings;
      Sceptre and Crown
      Must tumble down,
And in the dust be equal made
With the poor crooked scythe and spade.

Some men with swords may reap the field,
    And plant fresh laurels where they kill;
But their strong nerves at last must yield;
    They tame but one another still:
      Early or late
      They stoop to fate,
And must give up their murmuring breath
When they, pale captives, creep to death.

The garlands wither on your brow;
    Then boast no more your mighty deeds;
Upon Death's purple altar now
    See where the victor-victim bleeds;
      Your heads must come
      To the cold tomb;
Only the actions of the just
Smell sweet, and blossom in their dust.  —F. Shirley.

## THE PRESENT AGE.

In looking at our age, I am struck, immediately, with one commanding characteristic, and that is, the tendency in all its movements to expansion, to diffusion, to universality. To this, I ask your attention. This tendency is directly opposed to the spirit of exclusiveness, restriction, narrowness, monopoly, which has prevailed in past ages. Human action is now freer, more unconfined. All goods, advantages, helps, are more open to all. The privileged, petted individual is becoming less, and the human race are becoming more. The multitude is rising from the dust. Once we heard of the few, now of the many; once of the prerogatives of a part, now of the rights of all. We are looking, as never before, through the disguises, envelopments of ranks and classes, to the common nature which is below them; and are beginning to learn that every being who partakes of it, has noble powers to cultivate, solemn duties to perform, inalienable rights to assert, a vast destiny to accomplish. The grand idea of humanity, of the importance of man as man, is spreading silently, but surely. Not that the worth of the human being is at all understood as it should be; but the truth is glimmering through the darkness. A faint consciousness of it has seized on the public mind. Even the most abject portions of society are visited by some dreams of a better condition, for which they were designed. The grand doctrine, that every human being should have the means of self-culture, of progress in knowledge and virtue, of health, comfort, and happiness, of exercising the powers and affections of a man; this is slowly taking its place, as the highest social truth. That the world was made for all, and not for a few; that society is to care for all; that no human being shall perish but through his own fault; that the great end of government is to spread a shield over the rights of all; these propositions are growing into axioms, and the spirit of them is coming forth in all the departments of life.

If we look at the various movements of our age, we shall see in them this tendency to universality and diffusion. Look, first, at science and literature. Where is science now? Locked up in a few colleges, or royal societies, or inaccessible volumes? Are its experiments mysteries for a few privileged eyes? Are its portals guarded by a dark phraseology, which, to the multitude, is a foreign tongue? No; science has now left her retreats, her shades, her selected company of votaries, and with familiar tone begun the work of instructing the race. Through the press, discoveries and theories, once the monopoly of philosophers, have become the property of the multitude. Its professors, heard, not long ago, in the university or some narrow school, now speak in the Mechanics' Institute. The doctrine that the laborer should understand the principles of his art, should be able to explain the laws and processes which he turns to account; that instead of working as a machine, he should join intelligence to his toil, is no longer listened to as a dream. Science, once the greatest of distinctions, is becoming popular. The characteristic of our age, then, is not the improvement of science, rapid as this is, so much as its extension to all men.

The same characteristic will appear, if we inquire into the use now made of science. Is it simply a matter of speculation? a topic of discourse? an employment of the intellect? In this case, the multitude, with all their means of instruction, would find in it only a hurried gratification. But one of the distinctions of our time is, that science has passed from speculation into life. Indeed, it is not pursued enough for its intellectual and contemplative uses. It is sought as a mighty power, by which nature is not only to be opened to thought, but to be subjected to our needs. It is conferring on us that dominion over earth, sea and air, which was prophesied in the first command given to man by his Maker; and this dominion is now employed, not to exalt a few, but to multiply the comforts and ornaments of life for the multitude of men. Science has become an inexhaustible mechanician; and by her forges, and mills, and steam cars, and printers' presses, is bestowing on millions not only comforts, but luxuries which were once the distinction of a few.

Another illustration of the tendency of science to expansion and universality may be found in its aims and objects. Science has burst all bonds, and is aiming to comprehend the universe. and thus it multiplies fields of enquiry for all orders of minds. There is no province of nature which it does not invade. Not content with exploring the darkest periods of human history, it goes behind the birth of the human race, and studies the stupendous changes which our globe experienced for hundreds of centuries, to become prepared for man's abode. Not content with researches into visible nature, it is putting forth all its energies to detect the laws of invisible and imponderable matter. Difficulties only provoke it to new efforts. It would lay open the secrets of the polar ocean, and of untrodden barbarous lands. Above all, it investigates the laws of social progress, of arts, and institutions of government, and political economy, proposing as its great end the alleviation of all human burdens, the weal of all the members of the human race. In truth, nothing is more characteristic of our age than the vast range of inquiry which is opening more and more to the multitude of men.

Thought frees the old bounds to which men used to confine themselves. It holds nothing too sacred for investigation. It calls the past to account; and treats hoary opinions as if they were of yesterday's growth. No reverence drives it back. No great name terrifies it. The foundations of what seems most settled must be explored. Undoubtedly this is a perilous tendency. Men forget the limits of their powers. They question the infinite, the unsearchable, with an audacious self-reliance. They shock pious and revering minds, and rush into an extravagance of doubt, more unphilosophical and foolish than the weakest credulity. Still, in this dangerous wildness, we see what I am stating, the tendency to expansion in the movements of thought.

I have hitherto spoken of science, and what is true of science is still more true of literature. Books are now placed within reach of all. Works, once too costly except for the opulent, are now to be found on the laborer's shelf. Genius sends its light into cottages. The great names of literature are become household words among the crowd. Every party, religious or political, scatters its sheets on all the winds. We may lament, and too justly, the small comparative benefit as yet accomplished by this agency; but this ought not to surprise or discourage us. In our present stage of improvement, books of little worth, deficient in taste and judgment, and ministering to men's prejudices and passions, will almost certainly be circulated too freely. Men are never very wise and select in the exercise of a new power. Mistake, error, is the discipline through which we advance. It is an undoubted fact, that, silently, books of a higher order are taking the place of the worthless. Happily, the instability of the human mind works sometimes for good, as well as evil: men grow tired at length even of amusements. Works of fiction cease to interest them, and they turn from novels to books, which, having their origin in deep principles of our nature, retain their hold of the human mind for ages. At any rate, we see in the present diffusion of literature the tendency to universality of which I have spoken.

The remarks now made on literature, might be extended to the fine arts. In these we see, too, the tendency to universality. It is said, that the spirit of the great artists has died out; but the taste for their works is spreading. By the improvements of engraving, and the invention of casts, the genius of the great masters is going abroad. Their conceptions are no longer pent up in galleries open to but few, but meet us in our homes, and are the household pleasures of millions. Works, designed for the halls and eyes of emperors, popes, and nobles, find their way, in no poor representations, into humble dwellings, and sometimes give a consciousness of kindred powers to the child of poverty. The art of drawing, which lies at the foundation of most of the fine arts, and is the best education of the eye for nature, is becoming a branch of common education, and in some countries is taught in schools to which all classes are admitted.

I am reminded, by this remark, of the most striking feature of our times and showing its tendency to universality, and that is, the unparalleled and constantly accelerated diffusion of education. This greatest of arts, as yet little understood, is making sure progress, because its principles are more and more sought in the common nature of man; and the great truth is spreading, that every man has a right to its aid. Accordingly, education is becoming the work of nations. Even in the despotic governments of Europe, schools are open for every child without distinction; and not only the elements of reading and writing, but music and drawing are taught, and a foundation is laid for future progress in history, geography, and physical science. The greatest minds are at work on popular education. The revenues of States are applied most liberally, not to the universities of the few, but to the common schools. Undoubtedly, much remains to be done; especially a new rank in society is to be given to the teacher; but even in this respect a revolution has commenced, and we are beginning to look on the guides of the young as the chief benefactors of mankind.

Thus, we see in the intellectual movements of our times, the tendency to expansion, to universality; and this must continue. It is not an accident, or an inexplicable result, or a violence on nature; it is founded in eternal truth. Every mind was made for growth, for knowledge; and its nature is sinned against, when it is doomed to ignorance. The divine gift of intelligence was bestowed for higher uses than bodily labor, than to make hewers of wood, drawers of water, ploughmen, or servants. Every being, so gifted, is intended to acquaint himself with God and his works, and to perform wisely and disinterestedly the duties of life. Accordingly, when we see the multitude of men beginning to thirst for knowledge, for intellectual action, for something more than animal life, we see the great design of Nature about to be accomplished ; and society, having received this impulse, will never rest till it shall have taken such a form as will place within every man's reach the means of intellectual culture. This is the revolution to which we are tending : and without this all outward political changes would be but children's play, leaving the great work of society yet to be done. —CHANNING.

## THE MEDITERRANEAN.

THE Mediterranean forms a curious and beautiful feature in the picture of the commercial world. By dint of money and shipping we laboriously bring to England the produce of the most distant regions, but the commerce of the whole globe seems to have a natural or instinctive tendency to flow, almost of its own accord, into the Mediterranean sea. Beginning with the great Atlantic Ocean, which connects the old world with the new, we know that, over that vast expanse, the prevailing wind is one which blows from America towards Europe ; and, moreover, that the waters of the Atlantic are, without any apparent return, everlastingly flowing into the narrow straits of Gibraltar. When the produce of America, therefore, is shipped for the Mediterranean, in general terms it may be asserted that wind and tide are in its favor.

Across the trackless deserts of Africa caravans from various parts of the interior are constantly toiling through the deep sand towards the waters of this inland sea. The traveller who goes up the Nile is doomed, we all know, to stem its torrent, but the produce of Egypt and the triple harvest of that luxuriant land is no sooner embarked, than of its own accord it glides majestically towards this favored sea ; and there is truth and nothing speculative in still further remarking, that this very harvest is absolutely produced by the slime or earth of Abyssinian and other most remote mountains, which by the laws of nature has calmly floated 1,200 miles through a desert to top-dress or manure Egypt, that garden which eventually supplies so many of the inhabitants of the Mediterranean with corn.

Again, the Red Sea is a passage apparently created to connect Europe with the great Eastern world; and as the power of steam gradually increases in its stride, it is evident that by this gulf or natural canal, much of the produce of India eventually will easily flow into the Mediterranean sea.

Finally, it might likewise be shown, that much of the commerce of Asia Minor and Europe, either by great rivers or otherwise, naturally moves towards this central point: but besides these sources of external wealth, the Mediterranean, as we all know, is most romantically studded with an archipelago and other beautiful islands, the inhabitants of which have the power not only of trading on a large scale with every quarter of the globe, but of carrying on in small open boats a sort of little village commerce of their own. Among the inhabitants of this sea are to be found at this moment the handsomest specimens of the human race; and if a person not satisfied with the present and future tenses of life, should prefer reflecting or rather ruminating on the past, with antiquarian rapture he may wander over these waters from Carthage to Egypt, Tyre, Sidon, Rhodes, Troy, Ephesus, Athens, Corinth, Argos, Syracuse, Rome, &c., until tired of his flight he may rest upon one of the ocean-beaten pillars of Hercules—and seated there, he may most truly declare that the history of the Mediterranean is like the picture of its own waves beneath him, which one after another he sees to rise, break, and sink.

In the history of this little sea, in what melancholy succession has nation and empire risen and fallen, flourished and decayed; and if the magnificent architectural ruins of these departed states mournfully offer to the traveller any political moral at all, is it not that homely one which the most common tombstone of our country church-yard preaches to the rustic peasant who reads it?

"As I am now, so you will be,
Therefore prepare to follow me!"
—F. B. HEAD.

## PALMYRA.

IN 1 Kings ix. 18, and elsewhere in Scripture, we read that Solomon built "Tadmor in the wilderness." The name means Place of Palms. That wise and wide-viewed man saw that the position was favorable as a commercial centre, for at that period the wealth and productions of the East passed through Tadmor or Palmyra, to gratify, enrich, and corrupt the Western nations. Near it there are copious streams—themselves a treasure in the East. The place was about mid-way between the Euphrates and Syria, and the wealth of India and the stores of Mesopotamia hence found an exchange, or an entrepôt at Tadmor. For nearly a thousand years, however, the place is not mentioned in history; and when it became known again, about the commencement of our era, it was a city of importance, of some architectural beauty, and of magnitude enough at least to attract the cupidity of imperial Rome.

About A.D. 130 it submitted to the Emperor Adrian, who made it a Roman colony, and adorned it with some of the stately colonnades which still amaze and awe every visitor, even in their decay. Prior to that time, however, the Palmyrenes themselves had erected some magnificent structures, as if they would make the grandeur of their city compensate for the sterility of its environment. But from about the time of Adrian, who died A.D. 138, Tadmor rapidly grew in wealth and beauty. It was self-governed, and raised to the rank of a capital; and for nearly a hundred and fifty years its opulence increased, while its pride became proportionally inflated. But this is not the place to detail the ambitious projects, the martial achievements, or the massacres of the Palmyrenes; and we proceed at once to the times of Zenobia—a woman of extraordinary sagacity, virtue and power. As the widow of Odenathus, the associate of Gallienus in the empire of Rome, she was more than royal; and when her husband was murdered by a nephew, she assumed the title of "Queen of the East." By conquest, she added Egypt, Mesopotamia, and Asia Minor to her empire; but having incurred the displeasure of Rome, Aurelian marched against Zenobia A.D. 270, defeated her in several battles, laid siege to Palmyra, and took it after a protracted and bloody struggle. The queen was captured on the banks of the Euphrates, and led to grace the emperor's triumph at Rome (A D. 272), where she appeared bound to his chariot by chains made of her own gold. Her subjects rose and massacred the garrison left in Palmyra by the emperor; but, in revenge, the city was pillaged and in great measure destroyed. The Temple of the Sun was rebuilt, but the place never recovered its former glory, though successive emperors attempted to arrest its decline. Palmyra became the seat of a bishop. The Saracens took early possession of it; a large colony of Jews made it their home; but it gradually dwindled down to a village, and in our day a few miserable huts, clinging like parasitic insects to the noble ruins of Palmyra, are all that remain of the city of Solomon and Zenobia, of Adrian, of Aurelian, of Diocletian, and Constantius. Caravans halt there, and the Bedawin prowl around it for plunder; but Palmyra is a city of the dead rather than of the living,—a grave for ambition,—an antidote, one would think, to pride.

But we are to speak of the ruins themselves, situated in the great desert, about four days' journey east from Damascus. On approaching the place from the west, numbers of tower-like tombs are seen in the valley and along the slopes of the neighboring hills; but all else fades into insignificance when Tadmor in the desert first flashes on the view. The remains stretch from the base of the adjoining mountains to the Temple of the Sun, all as white as marble, and unshaded by a single tree or twig. The ruin is unutterable,—columns and colonnades, porticoes and temples, mouldering capitals, shivered shafts, triumphal arches, and monuments of the illustrious forgotten,—all, all in architecture that can indicate man's mingled littleness and greatness, there meet the eye of the visitor, while at the same time all is still and lifeless as the limestone of the pillars.

Among the ruins, the Temple of the Sun is generally the first that is visited, as it is the most gigantic; but we give an account of another portion, which must nearly suffice for the whole. At the north-west angle of the walls of Palmyra stood a peripteral temple. The door-way was surrounded by a broad border of festooning vine branches and grapes, all exquisitely sculptured in *alto-relievo*. A Corinthian capital, with a monolithic shaft is all that remains of the front row of the portico. But the delicate workmanship and decorations of that capital, the rich scroll-work of the frieze, and the other beauties of these lovely fragments, all proclaim how exquisite the structure in its entireness was. The original plan of the temple was this: It had a portico of four columns in front, with a portico on each side of twenty columns. Near that fabric is a smaller temple, where fragments of fluted columns are still standing;

and at a little distance to the south-east, a mausoleum, with a portico still nearly perfect, formed by six columns, all monoliths, and exquisitely proportioned, enhances the beauty of the spot.

But we feel that *words* can give no adequate idea of this scene. It is a chaos of ruins— of rifled sarcophagi, of subterranean tombs, of shattered columns ; a blending of modern Vandalism and ancient art,—a forest in stone,—a tomb worthy indeed to contain the dust of an empire rather than to encircle or shade the miserable huts of the modern Palmyrenes. The decorations, criticised in detail, are inferior to those at Ba'albek, and cannot rival those of Athens or Rome ; but viewed in their grandeur and their mass, even the ruthless bands of the Bedawin who demolish columns for the sake of the iron clamps, the waste of centuries, and the devastations of war, have not been able to efface the beauty of this wondrous scene. While we gaze upon such magnificent sights as those of Tadmor, or of Ba'albek, the mind feels over-informed. The blending of beauty and decay flashes upon us the truth of a hundred texts, and no adequate vent is found for the emotions which arise.

> " O think who once were blooming there,
> The incense-vase with odor flowing,
> The silver lamp its softness throwing
> O'er cheeks as beautiful and bright
> As roses bathed in summer light,"

—all gone !—all a dream !—all a mirage, a mockery of man, if earth were all !

Of the great colonnade of Palmyra we can only say that it consisted of four rows of columns, forming a central and two side avenues, about 4000 feet in length : and who can tell the more than magical effect of one thousand five hundred columns all gleaming in the brilliance of an Eastern sun ? Only about a hundred and fifty columns, each 57 feet high, now remain ; but even these daguerreotype themselves, by their imposing loveliness, in the minds of all who resort to the scene.

Yet the Temple of the Sun, already mentioned, outrivals even this colonnade. It occupies a square of 740 feet on each side, and the height of the edifice is about 70 feet. A double colonnade lined the interior on three sides, and the shrine, the cell, and other parts of the temple, were all decorated with an art and a beauty such as prompt the thought, How much men have done to honor their false gods, how little to glorify the true! The Ionic and Corinthian decorations which are there,—the pillars and pilasters,—the sculptured eagles, flowers, festoons, and endless ornaments,—all proclaim what Palmyra once was; and though its ruin was no doubt a stage in the world's development, one marvels here at the sad law to which fallen man is subject—to work out all good by suffering, sorrow, and decay. —TWEEDIE.

## MAN FITTED FOR HIS POSITION.

Respecting Man, whatever wrong we call,
May, must be right, as relative to all.
In human works, tho' labor'd on with pain,
A thousand movements scarce one purpose gain;
In God's, one single can its end produce,
Yet serves to second too some other use;
So Man, who here seems principal alone,
Perhaps acts second to some sphere unknown,
Touches some wheel, or verges to some goal;
'Tis but a part we see, and not a whole.
When the proud Steed shall know why man restrains
His fiery course, or drives him o'er the plains;
When the dull Ox, why now he breaks the clod,
Is now a victim, and now Ægypt's God;
Then shall Man's pride and dullness comprehend
His actions', passions', being's, use and end;
Why doing, suff'ring, check'd, impell'd, and why
This hour a slave, the next a deity.

Then say not Man's imperfect, Heaven in fault;
Say rather, Man's as perfect as he ought:
His knowledge measur'd to his state and place;
His time a moment, and a point his space.
Heaven from all creatures hides the book of Fate,
All but the page prescrib'd, their present state;
From brutes what men, from men what spirits know;
Or who could suffer being here below?
The lamb thy riot dooms to bleed to-day;
Had he thy Reason, would he skip and play?
Pleas'd to the last, he crops the flow'ry food,
And licks the hand just rais'd to shed his blood.
Oh blindness to the future! kindly given,
That each may fill the circle mark'd by Heaven;
Who sees with equal eye, as God of all,
A hero perish, or a sparrow fall;
Atoms or systems into ruin hurl'd;
And now a bubble burst, and now a world,

Hope humbly then ; with trembling pinions soar ;
Wait the great teacher Death, and God adore.
What future bliss he gives not thee to know,
But gives that Hope to be thy blessing now.
Hope springs eternal in the human breast :
Man never Is, but always To be, blest.
The soul, uneasy, and confin'd from home,
Rests and expatiates in a life to come.
—POPE.

## THE FOSSIL ELEPHANT.

THERE are two species of the living elephant ; the Indian, inhabiting the warm countries of Asia, below 30° of north latitude, but flourishing the most, near to the equator ; and the African, ranging from Senegal to the Cape of Good Hope. The fossil elephant is a distinct species, but agrees more nearly with its Asiatic than with its African congener, its remains being very widely distributed, and found in very high northern latitudes. Several species have been indicated from differences of form in the molar teeth ; but the living animal will suffice for a general description of the extinct race, only supposing more colossal dimensions, a mane, and a clothing of long hair. Teeth, tusks, and bones of prodigious size have been met with in different parts of our own island, in the county of Northampton, at Gloucester, at Trenton, near Stafford, and Harwich, in the valleys of the Thames and Medway, in Salisbury Plain, and in Holderness, never occurring in the regular strata, but in the overlying drift. They were noticed in the early periods of British history, and occupy a place in the old chronicles. By antiquaries they were once supposed to be the remains of elephants brought over by the armies of Rome—an idea which comparative anatomy refuted, by showing their discordance with the living species of the genus, and which was seen to be untenable by bones of hippopotami being found in connection with them—animals which never could have travelled in the train of the Roman legions. Fossil elephantine remains have been dug up in Ireland and Scotland, in Iceland and Sweden ; and with probability Cuvier conjectured that the bones of supposed giants, mentioned by Pontoppidan as having been found in Norway, were relics of these ancient animals. They have been repeatedly exhumed in North and South America, from the plain of Quito, from Mexico, and the United States; and throughout Europe they are very generally distributed, appearing in abundance in some localities. Those particular spots, rich in elephantine remains, are at Seilberg, near Cronstadt, on the Necker; at the village of Theide, near Brunswick; in the valley of the Arno, near Florence; and at Bielbecks, near Market Weighton in Yorkshire, in a gravel bed of very limited extent, occupying a hollow of the new red sandstone. Blumenbach states, writing in 1803, that within his knowledge more than two hundred elephants had been found in Germany. It is, however, particularly in the severer latitudes of Asiatic Russia that the fossil elephant is common; and there the ivory of the tusks is so far uninjured as to be used for ornamental purposes, and sought as an article of profit. To the natives of Siberia the animal is known as the mammoth, signifying an animal of the earth, from the presumption that it was unable to endure the light of day, and actually lived beneath the surface of the soil, like the existing mole. According to Pallas, from the river Don to the promontory of Tchutskoinoss—the most easterly point of Asia—there is scarcely a stream the banks of which do not afford remains of the mammoth; and one remarkable case in which the animal was found preserved—both the entire skeleton and fleshy parts—and inspected by Mr. Adams, an academician of Petersburg, has attracted great attention.

In the year 1799 a Tungusian fisherman named Schumachoff, who generally went to hunt and fish at the peninsula of Tamut, after the fishing season of the Lena was over, had constructed for his wife some cabins on the banks of the lake Oncoul, and had embarked to seek along the coast for mammoth tusks. During this expedition, he one day observed a strange shapeless mass projecting from a bank, the nature of which he did not understand, and which was at such an elevation as to be beyond his reach. The bank consisted of frozen earth covered with ice partially thawing in the summer season. Returning to the same spot the succeeding year, 1800, he observed the object rather more disengaged, but still could not determine what it was; but towards the end of the summer of 1801, he could distinctly see that it was the frozen carcase of an enormous animal the entire flank of which, and one of the tusks, had become exposed. The summer of 1802 was cold, and the animal remained in much the same state; but that of 1803 was warmer than usual; and, the ice melting largely, the carcase became entirely disengaged, and fell down from the crag on a sand-bank forming part of the coast of the Arctic Ocean. In March, 1804, Schumachoff came to the mammoth, carried off the tusks, which he sold to a merchant for the value of fifty rubles. In 1806—the seventh year from the discovery—Mr. Adams, travelling in that distant and desert region, on an embassy to China with Count Golovkin, examined the animal, which still remained on the sand-bank where it had fallen, but in a greatly mutilated condition. The wandering fishermen had taken away large quantities of the flesh to feed their dogs; the wild animals, white bears, wolves, wolverines, and foxes had also feasted on the carcase; but the skeleton remained quite entire, with the exception of one of the fore-legs. The entire spine, the pelvis, one shoulder blade, and three legs were still held together by their ligaments, and by some remains of the skin; the pupils of the eye were still distinguishable; the brain remained within the skull, but a good deal shrunk and dried; and one of the ears was in excellent preservation, still retaining a tuft of strong bristly hair. The animal was a male, and had a long mane on the neck, but was not one of the largest size. The skin was extremely thick and heavy, and as much was undestroyed as required the exertions of ten men to remove, which they accomplished with difficulty. Mr. Adams had the good fortune to re-purchase the tusks from the merchant to whom they had been sold, and finally transported the whole skeleton to Petersburgh, where it now is, in the museum of the Academy, exhibiting the following dimensions,—9 feet 4 inches high, 16 feet 4 inches long, exclusive of the tusks which are 9 feet 6 inches, measuring along the curve. The hair of the mammoth appears to have consisted of strong bristles, a foot or more in length, with another kind, more flexible, and a third, a reddish brown wool, growing among the roots of the long hair. Cuvier remarks upon this fact, as an undeniable proof that the animal belonged to a race of elephants with which we are now unacquainted, by no means adapted to dwell in the torrid zone, but adapted to a temperature which would soon be fatal to the existing Asiatic and African races from its cold. We shall, subsequently, notice this consideration of climate, merely remarking, that the high latitudes now abounding with the "thick-ribbed ice" appear to have sustained an immense number of these colossal quadrupeds. There are islands in the Arctic Ocean, where the bones of the mammoth occur in prodigious abundance, which show no marks of detrition by a far transportation, and prove the exuberance of the race in the localities where their remains are found. —MILNER.

## GOD OF MY LIFE.

God of my life, to Thee I call;
Afflicted, at Thy feet I fall;
When the great water-floods prevail,
Leave not my trembling heart to fail!

Friend of the friendless and the faint,
Where should I lodge my deep complaint?
Where but with Thee, whose open door
Invites the helpless and the poor?

Did ever mourner plead with Thee,
And Thou refuse that mourner's plea?
Does not the word still fixed remain,
That none shall seek Thy face in vain?

That were a grief I could not bear,
Didst Thou not hear and answer prayer;
But a prayer-hearing, answering God,
Supports me under every load.

Fair is the lot that's cast for me;
I have an Advocate with Thee;
They whom the world caresses most
Have no such privilege to boast.

Poor though I am, despised, forgot,
Yet God, my God, forgets me not;
And he is safe, and must succeed,
For whom the Lord vouchsafes to plead.
—COWPER.

## THE MISSISSIPPI SCHEME.

THE first bank of circulation in France was established two-and twenty years after the bank of England, and, though it lived little more than four years, it became more memorable than any other, from its connexion with the most extensive and ruinous scheme of speculation which history records.

This bank, which has given celebrity to its founder, John Law, a Scotchman, was established in 1716, under the auspices of the Duke of Orleans, then Regent of France, for the express purpose, as some suppose, of wholly or partially paying off the public debt—then amounting to 2,000,000,000 of livres, and of which the government was unable to pay the interest.

Law had, before he left Scotland, written a book on the subject of money and trade; and the principles he therein maintained no doubt influenced him in the execution of his great financial schemes, and thus contributed to the wide-spread ruin that attended their failure. With some just theory, expressed with shrewdness and force, he mixed up the following untenable positions:—That money owes its value to the public confidence; and that paper, or anything else, may answer this purpose as well as the precious metals; (the first, as well as the last, he regarded as the mere signs of wealth:) that land was a better commodity for money than silver, and that the currency of a country might be increased to the whole value of its lands: that the effect of such an increase would not be depreciation, but merely a lowering of interest, by which trade would be encouraged and wealth augmented. The great number of persons, who, from that day to this, have supported similar fallacies, would seem to show that they are as plausible as they are dangerous.

The capital of Law's bank was 6,000,000 of livres, divided into twelve hundred shares of one thousand crowns each; and its notes soon obtained a general credit and currency. Two circumstances mainly contributed to their early success. One was, that the government, according to an habitual abuse of the royal privilege, was then calling in the gold currency for a recoinage; and the louis d'or, which, when restamped, the government meant to pass for twenty livres, it received at no more than sixteen. The bank gave a higher price for these coins than the government, and thus received many in exchange for its notes. The other favorable circumstance also grew out of an abuse of the royal prerogative. The marc of silver, a determinate quantity, had been sometimes made equivalent to a greater and sometimes to a less number of livres, at the pleasure of the crown; so that all contracts in livres (the general money of account) were exposed to the risk of these alterations in their value. Law therefore prudently made the notes of his bank payable in livres *of the same weight and fineness* as the current coin at the date of the note.

These judicious measures, added to the intrinsic recommendations of paper currency, when not used to excess, soon brought the notes of the bank into such general request, that, out of Paris, they commanded a premium of from one to one and a half per cent.

In the following year (1717) the rights of a company, long before incorporated for the purposes of trading to Louisiana and Canada, and which were alleged to have been forfeited, were transferred to Law, to erect a new company; and then, if not before, the plan was formed of paying off the national debt by the joint aid of the company and the bank.

Books were immediately opened for subscriptions to this *Company of the West*, or *Mississippi Company*, to the amount of 100,000,000,000 of livres, in shares of 500 livres, payable in a part of the public debt, which was then passing at about thirty per cent. of its nominal amount. The shares were soon subscribed; and, as the government then punctually paid to the company the interest (four per cent.) on these 100,000,000,000, the company was able to make a correspondent dividend on its capital; that is, four per cent. on its nominal amount; by reason of which, the shares, which had cost in the market but 160 or 170 livres, now rose to par, or 500 livres; and the rise was imputed, by an indiscriminating public, to Law's financial skill, and the operation of his bank.

About the close of the succeeding year, the regent, by way of giving greater credit to the bank, and of enlarging the sphere of its operations, paid off the original shareholders, and converted it into a royal bank. The notes it had then circulated amounted to 59,000,000—near twelve times its capital, but not quite a twentieth of the current coin of the kingdom, which was then estimated at 1,200,000,000.

It would seem that the regent already anticipated inconvenience from the tenor of the notes first issued; and, in those issued by him it was changed to a simple promise to pay the bearer the stated number of livres *in silver coin*. The reason assigned for this change (for governments rightly think that, with the mass of mankind, a bad reason is better than none) was, that the bank money, instead of being liable to perpetual fluctuations, as it had been, when compared with the livre, should be hereafter fixed. It is said by Stewart, Law's apologist, that he strenuously opposed this change.

Although this alteration in the tenor of the note was calculated to excite distrust, it seems not to have had that effect; but the bank paper retained its credit, notwithstanding the large additions which the regent made to its amount. It is even asserted by contemporary writers, that their credit seemed unimpaired throughout the year 1719, though the issues of the bank then amounted to 1,000,000,000 !

The first project of the regent and Law is supposed to have been to pay off portions of the public debt with the coin which was constantly flowing into the bank, in consequence of the premium it bore over coin; and in this way the regent might obtain the use of the whole coin of the kingdom; and that the money thus paid to the public creditors would gradually return to the bank, in the payment of the public revenues—or, at least, enough of it to redeem such notes as should be returned to the bank.

It was not foreseen by them, that no considerable addition could be made to the currency without depreciating it ; and that such large issues of paper as their plan contemplated must necessarily drive gold and silver out of the country. Accordingly it was found, soon after the regent took charge of the bank, that coin did not continue to flow into the bank as at first; and it became therefore necessary to change their plan, and to adopt one by which they might use the notes of the bank to discharge the public debt, without raising a suspicion of their credit. To effect this purpose, their plan was, for the regent to purchase shares of the Mississippi Company with the notes of the bank; then borrow of the company at a low interest, and with them, when thus endowed with a false credit, pay off the public creditors. By throwing the shares into the market, the regent might withdraw the notes from circulation. The result of these operations would be, that the public creditors would find themselves transformed into shareholders in the Mississippi Company; the government would have transferred a part of its revenues to the company, instead of owing all of them to its creditors, and be a gainer, first, by the lower interest paid to the company, and secondly, by the advance the shares would naturally experience, when so large an addition had been made to the currency, by paying off the national debt.

In the execution of this vast scheme, which it seems as difficult to reconcile with uprightness of intention as soundness of judgment, the bank proceeded to make new notes, and the company to create new shares, to raise the value of which every expedient was resorted to. In May, 1719, Law's company was incorporated with the East India Company. In June the mint was transferred to it for 50,000,000; and, to give it a supply of cash, fifty thousand shares were sold for 550 livres a share. A few ships were then purchased, to aid in deluding the credulous public with the hope of gain from traffic; and, in the succeeding month, 50,000 additional shares were sold at the advanced price of 1,000 livres a share.

The spirit of speculation being now called into existence, no time was lost in profiting by it. In August, the company farmed all the public revenues, and it agreed to lend to the government 1,600,000,000 at three per cent. On the faith of this arrangement, it publicly declared itself able to make an annual dividend of 200 livres a share. As interest was then four per cent., the shares, with such a dividend, would be worth 5,000 livres; and they immediately rose to that price.

The bank continued to fabricate more notes, as the company had continued to create more shares, until, in October, 1719, the shares amounted to 624,000, and by the 1st of May following, the notes amounted to 2,696,400,000 livres! The scheme that had been previously concerted being now ripe for execution, the regent became the purchaser of the new shares with the notes of his bank, and then borrowing back the same notes of the company, he with them paid off the public debt. The great object being thus effected, he, in February, 1720, reunited the bank with the company.

The effect of these financial operations on the community was immense. The large fortunes which had been made by the first subscribers to the Mississippi Company, whose shares had, in the course of a single year (from September, 1718 to 1719), risen from 170 livres to 5,000, produced a mania for speculation and stock-jobbing that was without example, and which attracted men of capital and adventurers from all parts of Europe, to Paris, to share in its enormous profits. This real accession of wealth, added to the redundancy of the paper in circulation, raised the price of every species of property, and thus deluded the public with the belief of extraordinary national prosperity. Among other consequences of the depreciation of money, land sold at fifty years' purchase; and consequently, as so large a part of the national capital yielded but two per cent., that became the market rate of interest for large sums, and the shares of the company, which the credulous public estimated at 200 livres a year, accordingly now rose to 10,000 livres a share.

But this state of things could not last. The depreciation of money, necessarily tending to expel gold and silver from the kingdom, soon began to be felt at the bank. To counteract the apprehended diminution of these metals, every device which Law's ingenuity could suggest, or the power of an arbitrary government could enforce, was resorted to for the purpose of retaining the coin in the bank, and of replenishing its coffers. Bills of exchange were required to be paid solely in bank notes. Public officers were to receive them in preference to coin. The value of the livre was greatly reduced in value, then raised, and lowered again to induce persons to deposit their specie (the value of which was thus suddenly and capriciously changed) in the bank, as a place of safety. These expedients proving insufficient, it was at length declared penal for any one to have more than 500 livres in his possession, or any articles of gold or silver, or to make any payment for more than 100 livres, except in bank notes; and domiciliary visits were enjoined on all public officers, for the purpose of enforcing these tyrannical edicts. If we had no other data for estimating the motives of the authors of the scheme, we may judge of the probity of their intentions by the means they adopted for their execution.

Those harsh measures brought some coin to the bank, but not enough to counterbalance the previous drain, and that which was still going on by the conversion of small notes into specie. Nor was this all the difficulty in the execution of the plan. After the shares rose to 5,000 livres, and yet more, to 10,000 livres, many of the original holders were tempted to sell out, and the number thus thrown on the market at once, interfered with the sales of those belonging to the government, and tended to lower their prices. Money, too, would recover somewhat from its extreme depreciation, both by the export of coin, and by the withdrawal from circulation of those notes which were paid to the regent for shares; and as money rose in value, the market prices of shares would fall. Had the project, then, been an honest one, these inherent and insuperable defects must have prevented its complete execution. Accordingly, in May, 1720, its authors, finding it impracticable either to sustain a paper currency, which then amounted to 2,235,000,000, or to withdraw it from circulation, reduced its value one-half, by seven successive reductions, to take place between May and December. This royal edict broke the spell which had hitherto bound the people of France, and the day after its promulgation bank notes ceased to have circulation.

The government, seeing the fatal consequences of its last decree, repealed it six days afterwards; but the credit of the notes had received its death-blow, and could not be revived. After several ineffectual attempts to restore it, their circulation was formally suppressed in October.

On the winding up of this colossal scheme of stock-jobbing and fraud, it appeared that, of the 2,696,000,000 of notes struck off, 700,000,000 were found in the bank, and the rest were in circulation. The cash in the bank amounted to 90,000,000, which were used to pay off notes to the same amount; and the greater part of the residue were funded by the government, at an interest of from two and a half to two per cent., and a part remained a *caput mortuum* in the hands of its owners. The holders of the notes thus lost about one-half of their nominal value by the bankruptcy.

The loss sustained by the shareholders of the company was much greater. Of these shares, 200,000 were in the hands of the community, and the remaining 424 were found to be in the possession of the regent. The affairs of the company were in utter confusion after the explosion of the scheme; but when they were brought to a final adjustment with the government, in 1725, their whole capital—all that remained from the wreck of their splendid hopes—amounted only to 137,000,000; so that, if we estimate the 200,000 shares at the price they had actually borne a short time before, the loss of their holders amounted to 1,863,000,000 ! Besides the thousands and tens of thousands who were thus reduced from affluence to penury, 500,000,000 of coin are computed to have found their way to foreign countries; the government was penniless; confidence between man and man was destroyed; in the unsettled value of money, no one knew in his dealings what to ask or what to give; and France, lately thought to be overflowing with wealth, now presented one general scene of poverty, distrust and wretchedness.

The gambling spirit which the Mississippi scheme had engendered in France, extended soon after to England, and manifested itself in the South Sea scheme, and a thousand projects yet more visionary. —TUCKER.

## HARMOSAN.

Now the third and fatal conflict of the Persian throne was done,
And the Moslem's fiery valor had the crowning victory won.
Harmosan, the last and boldest the invader to defy,
Captive overborne by numbers, they were bringing forth to die.
Then exclaimed that noble captive—" Lo! I perish in my thirst,
Give me but one drink of water, and let then arrive the worst."
In his hand he took the goblet, but awhile the draught forbore,
Seeming doubtfully the purpose of the foemen to explore.
Well might then have paused the bravest—for around him angry foes,
With an hedge of naked weapons did that lonely man enclose.
"But what fear'st thou?" cried the Caliph : " is it, friend, a secret blow?
Fear it not—our gallant Moslem no such treacherous dealing know :
Thou may'st quench thy thirst securely, for thou shalt not die before
Thou hast drunk that cup of water—this reprieve is thine—no more."
Quick the Satrap dashed the goblet down to earth with ready hand,
And the liquid sank for ever, lost amid the burning sand.
" Thou hast said that mine my life is, till the water of that cup
I have drained—then bid thy servants that spilled water gather up.'
For a moment stood the Caliph, as by doubtful passions stirred,
Then exclaimed, " For ever sacred must remain a monarch's word !
Bring another cup, and straightway to the noble Persian give :
Drink, I said before, and perish—now I bid thee drink and live."

—R. C. TRENCH.

## BUILDING AND ENGINEERING IN ANCIENT ROME.

THE Arts also of the Builder and Engineer grew with the growing wealth of Rome. It was one of the chief and favorite occupations of C. Gracchus, during his brief reign, to improve the roads and bridges. The great Dictator Cæsar had many projects in view when he was cut off,—as, for instance, the draining of the mountain lakes by tunnels, of the Pontine marshes by canal. Many of these works were afterwards executed by Agrippa, who also constructed the Julian harbor, by uniting the Lucrine and Avernian Lakes with the sea. In the year 33 B.C. he condescended to act as Ædile, and signalized his Magistracy by a complete repair of the aqueducts and sewers.

Before this time, also, had begun the adornment of the City with noble buildings of public use. A vast Basilica was laid out and begun by M. Æmilius Paullus, Consul in 50 B.C. This magnificent work was said to have been erected with money received from Cæsar as the price of the Consul's good services. But the Basilica Æmilia was eclipsed by the splendid plans of the Dictator Cæsar. A great space had lately been cleared by the fire kindled at the funeral of Clodius. Other buildings were pulled down, and the Basilica Julia extended on the south of the Forum along the frontage formerly occupied by the Tabernæ Veteres. The great work was completed by Octavian. A still more magnificent edifice were the Thermæ or Hot-baths of Agrippa, and the noble Temple erected by the same great builder, which still remains under the name of the Pantheon. In this structure the Arch, that instrument by which Rome was enabled to give that combination of stability and magnitude which distinguishes all her works, achieved its greatest triumph, and here was seen the first of those great vaulted domes which became the distinctive attribute of the Christian Architecture of modern Italy. By these and many other works,—politic both because they increased the magnificence and the health of the capital, and also gave constant employment to workmen who might otherwise have been turbulent, —the Emperor Augustus was enabled to boast that he had "found Rome of brick, and left it of marble."

—LIDDELL.

## RESIGNATION.

O God, whose thunder shakes the sky;
   Whose eye this atom-globe surveys;
To Thee, my only rock, I fly,
   Thy mercy in Thy justice praise.

The mystic mazes of Thy will,
   The shadows of celestial light,
Are past the power of human skill—
   But what the Eternal acts is right.

O teach me in the trying hour
   When anguish swells the dewy tear,
To still my sorrows, own Thy power,
   Thy goodness love, Thy justice fear.

If in this bosom aught but Thee,
   Encroaching sought a boundless way,
Omniscience could the danger see,
   And Mercy look the cause away.

Then why, my soul, dost thou complain?
   Why, drooping, seek the dark recess?
Shake off the melancholy chain,
   For God created all to bless.

The gloomy mantle of the night,
   Which on my sinking spirit steals,
Will vanish at the morning light,
   Which God, my East, my Sun, reveals.

                  —Chatterton.

## THE OSTRICH.

The ostrich is generally seen quietly feeding on some spot where no one can approach him without being detected by his wary eye. As the waggon moves along far to the windward he thinks it is intending to circumvent him, so he rushes up a mile or so from the leeward, and so near to the front oxen that one sometimes gets a shot at the silly bird. When he begins to run all the game in sight follow his example. I have seen this folly taken advantage of when he was quietly feeding in a valley open at both ends. A number of men would commence running, as if to cut off his retreat from the end through which the wind came; and although he had the whole country hundreds of miles before him by going to the other end, on he madly rushed to get past the men, and so was speared. He never swerves from the course he once adopts, but only increases his speed.

When the ostrich is feeding his pace is from twenty to twenty-two inches; when walking, but not feeding, it is twenty-six inches; and when terrified, as in the case noticed, it is from eleven and a half to thirteen and even fourteen feet in length. Only in one case was I at all satisfied of being able to count the rate of speed by a stop watch, and, if I am not mistaken, there were thirty in ten seconds; generally one's eye can no more follow the legs than it can the spokes of a carriage-wheel in rapid motion. If we take the above number, and twelve feet stride as the average pace, we have a speed of twenty-six miles an hour. It cannot be very much above that, and is therefore slower than a railway locomotive. They are sometimes shot by the horseman making a cross cut to their undeviating course, but few Englishmen ever succeed in killing them.

The ostrich begins to lay her eggs before she has fixed on a spot for a nest, which is only a hollow a few inches deep in the sand, and about a yard in diameter. Solitary eggs, named by the Bechuanas "lesetla," are thus found lying forsaken all over the country, and become a prey to the jackal. She seems averse to risking a spot for a nest, and often lays her eggs in that of another ostrich, so that as many as forty-five have been found in one nest. Some eggs contain small concretions of the matter which forms the shell, as occurs also in the egg of the common fowl; this has given rise to the idea of stones in the eggs. Both male and female assist in the incubations; but the numbers of females being always greatest, it is probable that cases occur in which the females have the entire charge. Several eggs lie out of the nest, and are thought to be intended as food for the first of the newly-hatched brood till the rest come out and enable the whole to start in quest of food. I have several times seen newly hatched young in charge of the cock, who made a very good attempt at appearing lame in the plover fashion, in order to draw off the attention of pursuers. The young squat down and remain immovable when too small to run far, but attain a wonderful degree of speed when about the size of common fowls. When caught they are easily tamed, but are of no use in their domesticated state.

The egg is possessed of very great vital power. One kept in a room during more than three months, in a temperature about 60°, when broken was found to have a partially developed live chick in it. The Bushmen carefully avoid touching the eggs, or leaving marks of human feet near them, when they find a nest. They go up the wind to the spot, and with a long stick remove some of them occasionally, and, by preventing any suspicion, keep the hen laying on for months, as we do with fowls. The eggs have a strong disagreeable flavor, which only the keen appetite of the Desert can reconcile one to. The Hottentots use their trousers to carry home the twenty or twenty-five eggs usually found in a nest; and it has happened that an Englishman, intending to imitate this knowing dodge, comes to the waggons with blistered legs, and, after great toil, finds all the eggs uneatable, from having been some time sat upon. Our countrymen invariably do best when they continue to think, speak, and act in their own proper character.

The food of the ostrich consists of pods and seeds of different kinds of leguminous plants, with leaves of various plants; and, as these are often hard and dry, he picks up a great quantity of pebbles, many of which are as large as marbles. He picks up also some small bulbs, and occasionally a wild melon to afford moisture, for one was found with a melon which had choked him by sticking in his throat. It requires the utmost address of the Bushmen, crawling for miles on their stomachs, to stalk them successfully; yet the quantity of feathers collected annually shows that the numbers slain must be considerable, as each bird has only a few in the wings and tail. The male bird is of a jet black glossy color, with the single exception of the white feathers, which are objects of trade. Nothing can be finer than the adaptation of these flossy feathers for the climate of the Kalahari, where these birds abound; for they afford a perfect shade to the body, with free ventilation beneath them. The hen ostrich is of a dark brownish-grey color, and so are the half-grown cocks.

The organs of vision in this bird are placed so high that he can detect an enemy at a great distance, but the lion sometimes

kills him. The flesh is white and coarse, though, when in good condition, it resembles in some degree that of a tough turkey, It seeks safety in flight; but when pursued by dogs it may be seen to turn upon them and inflict a kick, which is vigorously applied, and sometimes breaks the dog's back.
—LIVINGSTONE.

## THE SCHOLAR.

My days among the dead are past;
Around me I behold,
Where'er these casual eyes are cast,
The mighty minds of old;
My never failing friends are they,
With whom I converse day by day.

With them I take delight in weal
And seek relief in woe,
And while I understand and feel
How much to them I owe,
My cheeks have often been bedew'd
With tears of thoughtful gratitude

My thoughts are with the Dead; with them
I live in long past years,
Their virtues love, their faults condemn
Partake their hopes and fears,
And from their lessons seek and find
Instruction with an humble mind.

My hopes are with the Dead; anon
My place with them will be,
And I with them shall travel on
Through all futurity;
Yet leaving here a name, I trust,
That will not perish in the dust.
—SOUTHEY.

## SPECTRUM ANALYSIS.

THE field of spectrum analysis was not wholly untrodden until it was explored by the two German professors. Even so long ago as 1826, Mr Fox Talbot, a gentleman whose name is honorably associated with discoveries in that most beautiful of the modern applications of science to art—Photography—made some experiments upon the spectra of colored flames.

and pointed out the advantages which such a method of analysis would possess. Professor Wheatstone, Mr. Swan, Sir David Brewster, and Professor W. Allen Miller in our own country, and Ångström, Plücker, Masson and others on the Continent, have likewise contributed to our knowledge of this subject; but whatever may have been done by others for the establishment of the new method, it must be admitted that the names of Bunsen and Kirchhoff will justly go down to posterity as the founders of the Science of Spectrum Analysis; for they established it on a firm scientific basis, by applying to it the modern methods of exact research.

For the purpose of obtaining the peculiar spectra of iron, platinum, copper, and most of the other metals, these metals must be exposed to a much higher temperature than that of the gas flame, to which they impart no color. This high temperature is best attained by the use of the electric spark. So great, indeed, is the heat developed by this agent, that a single electric discharge passed through a gold wire dissipates the metal at once in vapor. Our illustrious Faraday—the founder of so many branches of electrical science—first showed that the electric spark was produced by the intense ignition of the particles composing the poles; and Professor Wheatstone proved that if we look at the spark proceeding from two metallic poles, through a prism, we see spectra containing bright lines which differ according to the kind of metal employed. "These differences," said Wheatstone, writing in 1834, "are so obvious, that any one metal may instantly be distinguished from others by the appearance of its spark; and we have here a mode of discriminating metallic bodies more ready than a chemical examination, and which may hereafter be employed for useful purposes." This has, indeed, turned out to be a true prediction.

The large number of bright lines which are seen in the spark spectrum are not all caused by the glowing vapor of the metal forming the poles; a portion of them proceed, as Ångström first pointed out, from the particles of gas or air, through which the spark passes, becoming luminous also, and emitting their own peculiar light. Thus, if we examine the spectrum of an electric spark passing from two iron poles in the air, we see at least three superimposed spectra, one of the iron, one of the oxygen, and a third of the nitrogen of the air. By help of a little mechanical device, it is easy to distinguish between the air lines and the true metallic lines, and in this way to detect the various metals. So certain and accurate is this method that Professor Kirchhoff has, without difficulty, been able to detect and distinguish the presence of minute traces of the rare metals Erbium and Terbium, as well as Cerium, Lanthanum, and Didymium, when they are mixed together; a feat which the most experienced analyst would find it almost impossible, even after the most lengthened and careful investigation, to accomplish with the older methods.

In endeavouring to form an idea of the present and future bearings of the science of spectrum analysis as applied to the investigation of terrestrial matter, we must remember that the whole subject is as yet in its earliest infancy; that the methods of research are scarcely known; and that speculations, as to the results which further experiments will bring forth, are therefore, for the most part, idle and premature.

So long ago as 1815, Fraunhofer made the important observation, that the two bright yellow lines, which we now know to be the sodium lines, were coincident with, or possessed the same degree of refrangibility as, two dark lines in the solar spectrum, called by Fraunhofer the lines D. A similar coincidence was observed by Sir David Brewster, in 1842, by the bright red line of potassium and a dark line in the solar spectrum called Fraunhofer's A. The fact of the coincidence of these lines is easily rendered visible if the solar spectrum is allowed to fall into the upper half of the field of our telescope whilst the sodium or potassium spectrum occupies the lower half. The bright lines produced by the metal, as fine as the finest spider's web, are then seen to be exact prolongations, as it were, of the corresponding dark solar lines.

We do not think we can give our readers a more clear and succinct account of the development of this great discovery than by quoting from Kirchhoff's admirable memoir the following passage:—

"As soon as the presence of *one* terrestrial element in the solar atmosphere was thus determined, and thereby the existence of a large number of Fraunhofer's lines explained, it seemed reasonable to suppose that other terrestrial bodies occur there, and that, by exerting their absorptive power, they may cause the production of other Fraunhofer's lines. For it is very probable that elementary bodies which occur in large quantities on the earth, and are likewise distinguished by special bright lines in their spectra, will, like iron, be visible in the solar atmosphere. This is found to be the case with calcium, magnesium, and sodium. The number of bright lines in the spectrum of each of these metals is indeed small, but those lines, as well as the dark lines in the solar spectrum with which they coincide, are so uncommonly distinct that the coincidence can be observed with great accuracy. In addition to this, the circumstance that these lines occur in groups renders the observation of the coincidence of these spectra more exact than is the case with those composed of single lines. The lines produced by chromium, also form a very characteristic group, which likewise coincides with a remarkable group of Fraunhofer's lines; hence, I believe that I am justified in affirming the presence of chromium in the solar atmosphere. It appeared of great interest to determine whether the solar atmosphere contains nickel and cobalt, elements which invariably accompany iron in meteoric masses. The spectra of these metals, like that of iron, are distinguished by the large number of their lines, but the lines of nickel, and still more those of cobalt, are much less bright than the iron lines, and I was therefore unable to observe their position with the same degree of accuracy with which I determined the position of the iron lines. All the brighter lines of nickel appear to coincide with dark solar lines; the same was observed with respect to some of the cobalt lines, but was not seen to be the case with other equally bright lines of this metal. From my observations I consider that I am entitled to conclude that nickel is visible in the solar atmosphere; I do not, however, yet express an opinion as to the presence of cobalt. Carium, copper and zinc appear to be present in the solar atmosphere, but only in small quantities; the brightest of the lines of these metals correspond to distinct lines in the solar spectrum, but the weaker lines are not noticeable. The remaining metals which I have examined— viz., gold, silver, mercury, aluminium, cadmium, tin, lead, antimony, arsenic, strontium, and lithium—are, according to my observations, not visible in the solar atmosphere."

—*Edinburgh Review.*

# POMPEII.
## (A.D. 79.)
### *(From a Cambridge Prize Poem, 1819.)*

The hour is come. E'en now the sulph'rous cloud
Involves the City in its fun'ral shroud,
And far along Campania's azure sky
Expands its dark and boundless canopy.
The Sun, tho' throng'd on heaven's meridian height,
Burns red and rayless thro' that sickly night.
Each bosom felt at once the shudd'ring thrill—
At once the music stopp'd—the song was still.
None in that cloud's portentous shade might trace
The fearful changes of another's face:
But thro' that horrid stillness each could hear
His neighbor's throbbing heart beat high with fear.

A moment's pause succeeds. Then wildly rise
Grief's sobbing plaints and terror's frantic cries.
The gates recoil; and tow'rds the narrow pass
In wild confusion rolls the living mass.
Death,—when thy shadowy sceptre waves away
From his sad couch the pris'ner of decay
Tho' friendship view the close with glist'ning eye,
And love's fond lips imbibe the parting sigh,
By torture rack'd, by kindness soothed in vain,
The soul still clings to being and to pain:
But when have wilder terrors clothed thy brow,
Or keener torments edged thy dart than now,
When with thy regal horrors vainly strove
The laws of Nature and the power of Love?
On mothers, babes in vain for mercy call,
Beneath the feet of brothers, brothers fall.
Behold the dying wretch in vain upraise
Tow'rds yonder well-known face the accusing gaze;
See, trampled to the earth, the expiring maid
Clings round her lover's feet, and shrieks for aid.
Vain is the imploring glance, the frenzied cry;
All, all is fear;—To succor is to die—
Say ye how wild, how red, how broad a light
Burst on the darkness of that mid-day night,
As fierce Vesuvius scatter'd o'er the vale
His drifted flames and sheets of burning hail,
Shook hell's wan light'nings from his blazing cone,
And gilded heaven with meteors not its own?

The morn all blushing rose; but sought in vain
The snowy villas and the flow'ry plain,
The purple hills with marshall'd vineyards gay,
The domes that sparkled in the sunny ray.
Where art or nature late had deck'd the scene

## POMPEII.

With blazing marble or with spangled green,
There, streak'd by many a fiery torrent's bed,
A boundless waste of hoary ashes spread.
  Along that dreary waste where lately rung
The festal lay which smiling virgins sung,
Where rapture echoed from the warbling lute,
And the gay dance resounded, all is mute.—
Mute!—Is it Fancy shapes that wailing sound
Which faintly murmurs from the blasted ground?
Or live there still, who, breathing in the tomb,
Curse the dark refuge which delays their doom,
In massive vaults, on which th' incumbent plain
And ruin'd City heap their weight in vain?
Oh! who may sing that hour of mortal strife,
When Nature calls on Death, yet clings to life?
Who paint the wretch that draws sepulchral breath,
A living pris'ner in the house of Death?
Pale as the corpse which loads the fun'ral pile,
With face convulsed that writhes a ghastly smile,
Behold him speechless move with hurried pace,
Incessant, round his dungeon's cavern'd space,
Now shriek in terror, and now groan in pain,
Gnaw his white lips, and strike his burning brain,
Till Fear o'erstrain'd in stupor dies away,
And Madness wrests her victim from dismay.
His arms sink down: his wild and stony eye
Glares without sight on blackest vacancy.
He feels not, sees not; wrapp'd in senseless trance
His soul is still and listless as his glance.
One cheerless blank, one rayless mist is there,
Thoughts, senses, passions, live not with despair.
  Haste, Famine, haste, to urge the destined close,
And lull the horrid scene to stern repose.
Yet ere, dire Fiend, thy ling'ring tortures cease,
And all be hush'd in still sepulchral peace,
Those caves shall wilder, darker deeds behold
Than e'er the voice of song or fable told,
Whate'er dismay may prompt, or madness dare,
Feasts of the grave, and banquets of despair.—
Hide, hide the scene! and o'er the blasting sight
Fling the dark veil of ages and of night.
  Go, seek Pompeii now—with pensive tread
Roam thro' the silent city of the dead.
Explore each spot, where still, in ruin grand,
Her shapeless piles and tott'ring columns stand;
Where the pale ivy's clasping wreaths o'ershade
The ruin'd temple's moss-clad colonnade,
Or violets on the hearth's cold marble wave,
And muse in silence on a people's grave.
                    —T. B. (Lord) Macaulay.

## THE GIANT TREES OF CALIFORNIA.

AMONG the more remarkable natural curiosities of California, not the least is that solitary group of gigantic pines known as the "Big Trees of Calaveras County."

The group are solitary specimens of their race. There are no other of their kind or size on the known globe. It is a singular fact that the group, consisting of ninety-two trees, is contained in a valley only one hundred and sixty acres in extent. Beyond the limits of this little amphitheatre the pines and cedars of the country shrink into the Lilliputian dimensions of the common New England pine—say a hundred and fifty feet or thereabout. They are situated in Calaveras county, about two hundred and forty miles from San Francisco, but may be reached in a couple of days by railroad and stage coach.

A few hunters, in 1850, were pushing their way into the then unexplored forest, when one of them, who was in advance, broke into this space, and the giants were then first seen by white men. Their colossal proportions, and the impressive silence of the surrounding woods, created a feeling of awe among the hunters; and after walking around the great trunks, and gazing reverently up at their grand proportions, they returned to the nearest settlements and gave an account of what they had seen. Their statements, however, were considered fabulous until confirmed by actual measurement. The trees have been appropriately named *Washingtonia Gigantea*, though some of the savans of San Francisco have endeavored to have the *Washingtonia* changed to *Wellingtonia*, because some patriotic botanist, availing himself of this discovery by American frontier men, hastened to appropriate the name for our own hero. The basin or valley in which they stand is very damp, and retains here and there pools of water. Some of the largest trees extend their roots directly into the stagnant water, or into the brooks. Arriving at "Murphy's Diggings" by one of the daily lines of stages, either from Sacramento or Stockton, or by the Sonora coach, you are within fifteen miles of the celebrated grove; and from here it is a pretty ride to the "Mammoth Tree Hotel." This has been erected within a year or two to accommodate the many visitors; for the big trees have now become objects of general interest.

Adjoining the hotel, with which it is connected by a floor, stands the stump of the "Big Tree," which was cut down three years since. It measures ninety-six feet in circumference. Its surface is smooth, and offers ample space for thirty-two persons to dance, shewing seventy-five feet of circumference of solid timber. Theatrical performances were once given upon it by the Chapman family and Robinson family, in May, 1855. This monster was cut down by boring with long and powerful augers, and sawing the spaces between—an achievement of vandalism as ingenious as the Chinese refinement in cruelty, in pulling out the nails of criminals with pincers. It required the labor of five men twenty-five days to effect its fall, the tree standing so nearly perpendicular that the aid of wedges and a battering ram was necessary to complete the destruction. But even then the immense mass resisted all efforts to overthrow it, until in the dead of a tempestuous night it began to groan and sway in the storm like an expiring giant, and it succumbed at last to the element, which alone could complete from above what the human ants had commenced below. Its fall was like the shock of an earthquake, and was heard fifteen miles away at "Murphy's Diggings." There fell in this great trunk some thousands of cords of wood, and it buried itself twelve feet deep in the mire that bordered the little creek hard by. Not far from where it struck stand two colossal members of this family, called "The Guardsmen," the mud splashing nearly a hundred feet high upon their trunks. As it lay on the ground it measured three hundred and two feet clear of the stump and broken top. Large trees had been snapped asunder like pipe-stems, and the woods around were splintered and crushed to the earth. On its levelled surface are now situated the bar-room and two bowling alleys of the hotel, the latter running parallel a distance of eighty-one feet.

One of the most interesting of the group is that called the "Mother of the Forest." It is now the loftiest of the grove, rising to the height of three hundred and twenty-seven feet, straight and beautifully proportioned, and at this moment the largest living tree in the world. It is ninety feet in circumference. Into this trunk could be cut an apartment as large as a common sized parlor, and as high as an architect chose to make it, without endangering the tree, or injuring its outward appearance.

A scaffolding was built around this tree for the purpose of stripping off its bark for exhibition abroad. This was accomplished in 1854, for a distance of something over one hundred feet from the ground, and was effected with as much neatness and industry as a troop of jackals would display in cleaning the bones of a dead lion. Such was its vitality, that, although completely girdled and deprived of its means of sustenance, it annually put forth green leaves until the past year, when its blanched and withered limbs shewed that nature was exhausted.

But the dimensions of the whole group pale before those of the prostrate giant known as "the *Father of the Forest.*" This monster has long since bowed his head in the dust; but how stupendous in his ruin! The tree measures one hundred and twelve feet in circumference at the base, and forty-two feet in circumference at a distance of three hundred feet from the roots, at which point it was broken short off in its fall. The upper portion, beyond this break, is greatly decayed; but judging from the average size of the others, this tree must have towered to the prodigious height of at least four hundred and fifty feet! A chamber, or burned cavity, extends through the trunk two hundred feet, broad and high enough for a person to ride through on horseback; and a pond deep enough to float a common river steamboat stands in this great excavation during the rainy season. Walking on the trunk, and looking from its uprooted base, the mind can scarce conceive its astounding dimensions. Language fails to give an adequate idea of it. It was, when standing, a pillar of timber that overtopped all other trees on the globe. "To read simply of a tree four hundred and fifty feet high," observes a contemporary, "we are struck with large figures; but we can hardly appreciate the height without some comparison. Such a one as this would stretch across a field twenty-seven rods wide. If standing in the Niagara chasm at Suspension Bridge, it would tower two hundred feet above the top of the bridge, and would be ninety feet above the top of the cross of St. Paul's, and two hundred and thirty-eight feet above the Monument. If cut up for fuel, it would make at least three thousand cords, or as much as would be yielded by sixty acres of good wood land. If sawed into two inch boards, it would yield about two million feet, and furnish enough three inch plank for thirty miles of plank road.

This will do for the product of one little seed, less in size than a grain of wheat."

These trees are not the California red-wood, as has been affirmed of them. They are a species of cedar peculiar to the western slopes of the Sierra Nevada. The growth, bark, and leaf are different from those of any other tree. Botanists class them, and probably correctly, among the *Taxodiums*. Visitors will doubtless continue to re-christen them after this or that national celebrity; but all who write or speak of them should avoid being thus led, and perpetuate the appropriate name given them shortly after their discovery—*Washingtonia Gigantea*. —*Cassell's Family Paper*.

---

## TRAJAN.
### (Emperor A. D. 97—117.)

THE princely prodigality of Trajan's taste was defrayed by the plunder or tribute of conquered enemies, and seems to have laid at least no extraordinary burdens on his subjects. His rage for building had the further merit of being directed for the most part to works of public interest and utility. He built for the gods, the senate, and the people, not for himself; he restored the temples, enlarged the halls and places of public resort; but he was content himself with the palaces of his predecessors. Not in Rome only, but in innumerable places throughout Italy and the provinces, the hand of Trajan was conspicuous in the structures he executed, some of which still attest the splendor of the epoch, and the large-minded patriotism of their author. An arch at Ancona still reminds us that here he constructed a haven for his navy on the upper sea; and the port of Civita Vecchia is still sheltered by the mole he cast into the waters to defend the roadstead of Centumcellæ. The bridge over the Tagus at Alcantara affirms, by an inscription still legible upon it, that it was built by Julius Lacer, one of Trajan's favourite architects, though the cost was defrayed, according to the same interesting record, by the local contributions of some rich and spirited communities. A writer three centuries later declares of Trajan that he *built the world over;* and the wide diffusion and long continuance of his fame, beyond that of so many others of the imperial series, may be partly attributed to the constant recurrence of his name conspicuously inscribed on the most solid and best known monuments of the empire. The greatest of his successors, the illustrious Constantine, full of admiration for his genius, and touched perhaps with some envy of his glory, compared him pleasantly to a wallflower, which clings for support to the stones on which it flourishes so luxuriantly.

The care of this wise and liberal ruler extended from the harbors, aqueducts and bridges, to the general repair of the highways of the empire. Nor was it only as the restorer of military discipline or the reviver of the old tradition of conquest, that he took in charge the communications which were originally designed chiefly for military purposes. He was the great improver, though not the inventor, of the system of posts upon the chief roads, which formed a striking feature of Roman civilization as an instrument for combining the remotest provinces under a centralized administration. The extent to which the domestic concerns of every distant municipium were subjected to the prince's supervision is curiously portrayed in the letters of Pliny, who appears as governor of Bithynia, to have felt it incumbent upon him to consult his master on the answer he should return to every petition of the provincials, whether they wanted to construct an aqueduct, to erect a gymnasium, or to cover a common sewer. It is possible indeed that the courtly prefect may, in this instance, have been over obsequious, and Trajan himself seems almost to resent the importunity with which he begs to have an architect sent him from Rome. *Are there no such artists in your province or elsewhere?* asks the emperor. *It is from Greece that the architects come to Rome, and Greece is nearer to you than Italy.* These works, whether of convenience or splendor were, it seems, generally constructed by the governing bodies in the provinces themselves and by local taxation, though assisted not uncommonly by imperial munificence. Wealthy citizens might continue, as of old, thus to gratify their own vanity, taste, or generosity, of which Pliny is himself an example; but the days of the splendid magnates, who pretended to rival the prince in their lavish expenditure, had passed away, and it was upon the master of the empire and proprietor of the fiscus, that the burden continued more and more to fall. MERIVALE.

## MARINE VIEWS.

Be it the Summer-noon : a sandy space
The ebbing tide has left upon its place ;
Then just the hot and stony beach above,
Light twinkling streams in bright confusion move ;
(For heated thus, the warmer air ascends,
And with the cooler in its fall contends)—
Then the broad bosom of the ocean keeps
An equal motion ; swelling as it sleeps,
Then slowly sinking ; curling to the strand,
Faint, lazy waves o'ercreep the rigid sand,
Or tap the tarry boat with gentle blow,
And back return in silence, smooth and slow.
Ships in the calm seem anchor'd ; for they glide
On the still sea, urg'd solely by the tide :
Art thou not present, this calm scene before,
Where all beside is pebbly length of shore,
And far as eye can reach, it can discern no more ?
   Yet sometimes comes a ruffling cloud to make
The quiet surface of the ocean shake ;
As an awaken'd giant with a frown
Might show his wrath, and then to sleep sink down.
   View now the Winter-storm ! above one cloud,
Black and unbroken, all the skies o'ershroud :
Th' unwieldly porpoise through the day before,
Had roll'd in view of boding men on shore ;
And sometimes hid and sometimes show'd his form,
Dark as the cloud, and furious as the storm.
   All where the eye delights, yet dreads, to roam,
The breaking billows cast the flying foam
Upon the billows rising—all the deep
Is restless change ; the waves so swell'd and steep,
Breaking and sinking, and the sunken swells,
Nor one, one moment, in its station dwells :
But nearer land you may the billows trace,
As if contending in their watery chase ;
May watch the mightiest till the shoal they reach,
Then break and hurry to their utmost stretch ;
Curl'd as they come, they strike with furious force,
And then, re-flowing, take their grating course,
Raking the rounded flints, which ages past
Roll'd by their rage, and shall to ages last.
   Far off the Petrel in the troubled way
Swims with her brood, or flutters in the spray ;
She rises often, often drops again,
And sports at ease on the tempestuous main.
   High o'er the restless deep, above the reach
Of gunner's hope, vast flocks of Wild-ducks stretch ;
Far as the eye can glance on either side,

## MARINE VIEWS.

In a broad space and level line they glide;
All in their wedge-like figures from the north,
Day after day, flight after flight, go forth.
 In-shore their passage tribes of sea-gulls urge,
And drop for prey within the sweeping surge;
Oft in the rough opposing blast they fly
Far back, then turn, and all their force apply,
While to the storm they give their weak complaining cry;
Or clap the sleek white pinion to the breast,
And in the restless ocean dip for rest.
 Darkness begins to reign; the louder wind
Appals the weak, and awes the firmer mind;
But frights not him whom evening and the spray
In part conceal—yon Prowler on his way;
Lo, he has something seen; he runs apace,
As if he fear'd companion in the chase;
He sees his prize, and now he turns again,
Slowly and sorrowing—"Was your search in vain?"
Gruffly he answers, "'Tis a sorry sight!—
A seaman's body: there'll be more to night!"
Hark to those sounds! they're from distress at sea:
How quick they come! What terrors may there be!
Yes, 'tis a driven vessel: I discern
Lights, signs of terror, gleaming from the stern.
Others behold them too, and from the town
In various parties seamen hurry down;
Their wives pursue, and damsels, urged by dread,
Lest men so dear be into danger led;
Their head the gown has hooded, and their call
In this sad night is piercing like the squall;
They feel their kinds of power, and when they meet,
Chide, fondle, weep, dare, threaten, or entreat.
 See one poor girl all terror and alarm,
Has fondly seiz'd upon her lover's arm;
"Thou shalt not venture;" and he answers "No!
I will not,"—still she cries, "Thou shalt not go."
 No need of this; not here the stoutest boat
Can through such breakers, o'er such billows float;
Yet may they view these lights upon the beach,
Which yield them hope whom help can never reach.
 From parted clouds the moon her radiance throws
On the wild waves, and all the danger shows;
But shows them beaming in her shining vest
Terrific splendor! gloom in glory dress'd!
This for a moment, and then clouds again
Hide every beam, and fear and darkness reign.
 But hear we not those sounds? Do lights appear?
I see them not! the storm alone I hear:
And lo! the sailors homeward take their way;
Man must endure—let us submit and pray.

— CRABBE.

## THE TRADE WINDS.

From the parellel of about 30° north and south, nearly to the equator, we have two zones of perpetual winds, viz. : the zones of northeast trades on this side, and of southeast on that. They blow perpetually, and are as steady and as constant as the currents of the Mississippi River—always moving in the same direction. As these two currents of air are constantly flowing from the poles towards the equator, we are safe in assuming that the air which they keep in motion must return by some channel to the place near the poles, whence it came in order to supply the trades. If this were not so, these winds would soon exhaust the polar regions of atmosphere, and pile it up about the equator, and then cease to blow for the want of air to make more wind of.

This return current, therefore, must be in the upper regions of the atmosphere, at least until it passes over these parallels between which the trade-winds are always blowing on the surface. The return current must also move in the direction opposite to the direction of that wind which it is intended to supply. These direct and counter-currents are also made to move in a sort of spiral curve, turning to the west as they go from the poles to the equator, and in the opposite direction as they move from the equator toward the poles.

This turning is caused by the rotation of the earth on its axis. The earth, we know, moves from west to east. Now if we imagine a particle of atmosphere at the north pole, where it is at rest, to be put in motion in a straight line toward the equator, we can easily see how this particle of air, coming from the pole, where it did not partake of the diurnal motion of the earth, would, in consequence of its *vis inertiæ*, find, as it travels south, the earth slipping under it, as it were, and thus it would appear to be coming from the northeast and going toward the southwest: in other words, it would be a northeast wind.

On the other hand, we can perceive how a little particle of atmosphere that starts from the equator, to take the place of the other at the pole, would, as it travels north, in consequence of its *vis inertiæ*, be going toward the east faster than the earth. It would, therefore, appear to be blowing from the southwest, and going toward the north-east, and exactly in the opposite direction to the other. Writing south for north, the same takes place between the south pole and the equator. Now this is the process which is actually going on in Nature; and if we take the motions of these two particles as the type of the motion of all, we shall have an illustration of the great currents in the air, the equator being near one of the nodes, and there being two systems of currents—an upper and an under—between it and each pole.

Let us return now to our northern particle, and follow it in a round from the north pole to the equator and back again, supposing it, for the present to turn back toward the pole after reaching the equator. Setting off from the polar regions, this particle of air, for some reason, which does not appear to have been satisfactorily explained by philosophers, travels in the upper regions of the atmosphere, until it gets near the parallel of 30°. Here it meets, also in the clouds, the hypothetical particle that is going from the equator to take its place toward the pole.

About this parallel of 30°, then, these two particles meet, press against each other with the whole amount of their motive power, produce a calm and an accumulation of atmosphere sufficient to balance the pressure from the two winds north and south. From under this bank of calms, two surface currents of wind are ejected: one toward the equator, as the north-east trades—the other toward the pole, as the south-west passage winds—supposing that we are now considering what takes place in the northern hemisphere only.

These winds come out at the lower surface of the calm region, and consequently the place of the air borne away in this manner must be supplied, we may infer, by downward currents from the superincumbent air of the calm region. Like the case of a vessel of water which has two streams from opposite directions running in at the top and two of equal capacity discharging in opposite directions at the bottom—the motion of water in the vessel would be downward; so is the motion of air in this calm zone. The barometer, in this calm region is said by Humboldt and others to stand higher than it does either to the north or to the south of it; and this is another proof as to the banking up here of the atmosphere and pressure from its downward motion.

## THE TRADE WINDS.

Following our imaginary particle of air from the north across this calm belt we now feel it moving on the surface of the earth as the north-east trade-wind, and as such it continues till it arrives near the equator, where it meets a like hypothetical particle, which has blown as the south-east trade wind. Here, at this equatorial place of meeting, there is another conflict of winds, and another calm region, for a north-east and south-east wind can not blow at the same time in the same place. The two particles have been put in motion by the same power; they meet with equal force, and, therefore, at their place of meeting, are stopped in their course. Here, therefore, there is also a calm belt.

Warmed by the heat of the sun and pressed on each side by the whole force of the north-east and south-east trades, these two hypothetical particles, taken as the type of the whole, ascend. This operation is the reverse of that which took place at the other meeting near the parallel of 30°. This imaginary particle now returns to the upper regions of the atmosphere again, and travels there until it meets, near the calm belt of Cancer, its fellow particle from the north, where it descends as before, and continues to flow toward the pole as a surface wind from south-west. Entering the polar regions obliquely, it is pressed upon by similar currents coming from every meridian; here our imaginary particle approaches the higher parallels more and more obliquely, until it with all the rest, is whirled about the pole in a continued circular gale: finally reaching the vortex, it is carried upward to the regions of atmosphere above, whence it commences again its circuit to the south as an upper current.

Nothing excited the wonder of the early navigators so much as the east wind which blows regularly within the tropics. The companions of Columbus were terrified when they found themselves driven on by continuous east winds, which seemed to forewarn them that they would never return to their country. Fortunately for the fame of the great navigator, and for the world, he firmly held on his course, and made the discovery of a new continent.

The trade-winds serve important uses to navigators, in facilitating the passage of ships round the world. In passing from the Canaries to Cumana, on the north coast of South America, it is scarcely ever necessary to touch the sails of a ship; and with equal facility a passage is made across the Pacific, from Acapulco, on the west coast of Mexico, to the Philippine Islands. The customary route of vessels on their outward voyage from New York to Canton is by the way of Cape Horn, and thence westwardly through the Pacific: the return voyage is by the way of the Cape of Good Hope. If a channel were cut through the Isthmus of Panama, the voyage to China would be more speedy, agreeable and safe than the usual route by Cape Horn.

All mariners and passengers have spoken with delight of the region of the trade winds. It is noted for the favoring gales, the transparent atmosphere, the splendid sunsets, and the brilliancy of the unclouded heavens, day and night. Columbus, in recording his first voyage into their territory, compares the air, soft and refreshing without being cool, to that of the pure and balmy April mornings he had experienced in Andalusia. Humboldt, in describing the tropical regions, remarks upon the mildness of the climate and the beauty of the southern sky. He observed stars seen from infancy progressively sinking and finally disappearing below the horizon, an unknown firmament unfolding its aspect, and scattered nebulæ rivaling in splendor the milky way. The Spaniards gave to the zone in which the trade winds are constant the title *el Galpo de las Damas*, the Sea of the Ladies, on account of the ease with which it may be navigated, the uniform temperature prevalent night and day, and its pacific aspect. —MAURY.

---

## YOUTH AND AGE.

Verse, a breeze 'mid blossoms straying,
Where Hope clung feeding, like a bee—
Both were mine! Life went a-maying
   With Nature, Hope, and Poesy,
    When I was young!
When I was young?—Ah, woful when!
Ah! for the change 'twixt Now and Then:
This breathing house not built with hands,
This body that does me grievous wrong,
O'er aery cliffs and glittering sands
How lightly then it flash'd along:
Like those trim skiffs, unknown of yore,
On winding lakes and rivers wide,

That ask no aid of sail or oar,
That fear no spite of wind or tide !
Nought cared this body for wind or weather
When Youth and I lived in't together.

Flowers are lovely ; Love is flower-like ;
Friendship is a sheltering tree ;
O ! the joys, that came down shower-like,
Of Friendship, Love, and Liberty,
     Ere I was old !
Ere I was old ? Ah woful Ere,
Which tells me, Youth's no longer here !
O Youth ! for years so many and sweet
'Tis known that Thou and I were one,
I'll think it but a fond conceit—
It cannot be, that Thou art gone !
Thy vesper-bell hath not yet toll'd : —
And Thou wert aye a masker bold !
What strange disguise hast now put on
To make believe that Thou art gone ?
I see these locks in silvery slips,
This drooping gait, this alter'd size :
But Springtide blossoms on thy lips,
And tears take sunshine from thine eyes !
Life is but Thought : so think I will
That Youth and I are housemates still.

Dew-drops are the gems of morning,
But the tears of mournful eve !
Where no hope is, life's a warning
That only serves to make us grieve
    When we are old :
—That only serves to make us grieve
With oft and tedious taking-leave,
Like some poor nigh-related guest
That may not rudely be dismist,
Yet hath out-stay'd his welcome while,
And tells the jest without the smile.
      —S. T. COLERIDGE.

## THE EMILY ST. PIERRE.

THE recapture of the " Emily St. Pierre" reminds us of the fighting days of the wars with France and America, when several similar events took place ; but during the whole course of English Naval history we find no deed more gallant or more worthy of record. The " Emily St. Pierre" was a large Liverpool East India trader, commanded by Captain William Wilson.

She left Calcutta on the 27th of November 1861, with orders to make the coast of South Carolina, to ascertain whether there was peace or war. If peace had been declared, Captain Wilson was to take a pilot and enter the port of Charleston ; if there was a blockade, he was to proceed to St. John, New Brunswick.

On the 8th of March 1862, he considered his vessel to be about twelve miles off the land, when a steamer was made out approaching. When the steamer, which proved to be a Federal vessel of war, the "James Adger," came within hail, the "Emily St. Pierre" was ordered to heave-to, and was soon afterwards boarded by two boats, whose officers and crews took possession of her. Filling on the main-yard, they steered for the Federal squadron. Captain Wilson was now ordered into the boat, and carried on board the flagship, when he was informed by Flag Officer Goldboursh that his vessel had saltpetre on board, and that consequently she was a lawful prize to the Federal Government, but that he might take a passage on board her to Philadelphia. He replied that his cargo was not saltpetre, that his ship was British property, and that he could not acknowledge her a lawful prize.

On returning to his ship in about an hour, he found that all his crew had been taken away except the cook and steward, and that a fresh ship's company had been placed on board, consisting of Lieutenant Stone, a master's mate, twelve men, and an engineer, a passenger, fifteen in all. Having weighed anchor, they proceeded to sea. Captain Wilson felt confident of the illegality of the capture, and that if he could regain possession of his ship, he was justified in making the attempt. He had studied the characters of his cook and steward, and knew that he could trust them. He waited his opportunity. There was, however, not much time to spare. The 21st of March arrived. The commanding officer, Lieutenant Stone, had the watch on deck. It was about half-past four, and still dark, when Captain Wilson called his steward and cook into his stateroom, and told them that he was resolved to regain his ship or lose his life. He asked their assistance, which they at once promised to afford. He then gave them each a pair of irons, which he had secured, and a sheet, and told them to follow him, as the moment for action had arrived. The master's mate was asleep in his berth. Captain Wilson opened the door, and walked in. After handing out his revolver and sword, he grasped the mate's hands. In an instant the gag was in his mouth, and the irons were fixed. The brave captain, with his two followers, then went to the passenger's cabin, and having taken the arms from his berth, secured him in the way they had the mate. The most difficult part of the undertaking was now to overcome the commanding officer, who, unsuspicious of danger, was walking the deck of his prize. However, retaining wonderful coolness, and undaunted by the hazard he ran, Captain Wilson went on deck as if he had just turned out, and joined Lieutenant Stone in his walk, making some remarks as to the state of the weather. After walking for about ten minutes, he induced him to go down into the cabin to look at the chart which he had himself been examining, taking up on his way, as he followed, a belaying pin. Now was the critical moment—the cook and steward stood in ambush behind the door. They reached the door of the after-cabin where the chart was spread out, when, lifting up the belaying pin, Captain Wilson told the lieutenant that if he moved he was a dead man, and that the ship should never go to Philadelphia ; when the cook and steward, springing on him, had in a moment the irons on his wrists and the gag in his mouth, and he was pitched without ceremony into a cabin, and the door locked upon him. The crew had next to be mastered. Three were walking the deck, another was at the helm, and a fifth was on the look-out forward.

With truly wonderful nerve and command of voice, Captain Wilson called the three men aft, and pointing to the hatchway of the store-room, near the helm, told them that a coil of rope was wanted up. He then shoved off the hatch, and pointing to a corner where it was, they all three jumped down. Quick as lightning he replaced the hatch, which his followers secured, while he warned the man at the helm that his life would pay the penalty if he moved or uttered a word. The look-out was then called aft, and being seized, was asked if he would assist in navigating the ship to a British port. On his declining to do so, he was hand-cuffed and secured in a cabin. Captain Wilson then called the watch, knowing well that they would not all come on deck together. He was consequently able to secure two before the suspicions of the rest were aroused. The third, however, drew his knife as the steward was about to seize him, when the latter shot him in the shoulder with his pistol, and he was seized. The remaining men jumping on deck were knocked over and secured.

Once more Captain Wilson had entire command of his ship, but with a crew of two men, neither of whom could even steer, nor were they accustomed to go aloft; while he had fifteen prisoners below, who would naturally lose no opportunity of retaking the ship. His greatest difficulties were only now beginning. What consciousness of his superlative seaman-like qualities, what perfect and just self-reliance he must have possessed, to have undertaken the task of navigating a ship completely across the Atlantic, with such means at his disposal! Considerate and generous, as well as brave, as soon as he had shaped a course for England, he went below, and announced to Lieutenant Stone that the ship was his own again, but offered to take the gag out of his mouth, and the irons off his wrists, if he would consent to remain a prisoner in his berth, and make no attempt to regain possession of the ship.

To this Lieutenant Stone consented, and dined at table every day under guard, while the crew were supplied with an ample allowance of bread, beef and water. Four of their number, after some consideration, volunteered, rather than remain prisoners, to lend a hand in working the ship; but as they were landsmen, they were of no use aloft. It seems surprising that Captain Wilson should have trusted them; but undoubtedly his bravery must have inspired them with such awe that they dared not prove treacherous.

But few days had passed, after he had commenced his homeward passage with his crew of six landsmen, than it came on to blow so hard that he had to close-reef the topsails. Placing his cook and steward at the helm, he made the other men take the reef tackles to the capstern, while he went alone aloft, lay out on the yard, passed the earings, and tied the reef-points, keeping an eye all the time at the helm, and directing his two faithful men by signs how to steer. The wind increased till it blew a heavy gale and the sea getting up, the tiller by a sudden jerk was carried away. He now began for the first time perhaps, to have fears that he might not after all make his passage, but, undaunted, he set to work to repair the mischief as well as he was able. His strength and energies, as well as those of his brave companions were tried to the utmost. They had both to navigate the ship, to watch the four men who had been liberated, and to feed and attend to their prisoners.

Providence favoured them; the weather moderated, the wind was fair, and without accident Captain Wilson brought the "Emily St. Pierre," into the Mersey, thirty days after he had retaken her, having accomplished a passage of nearly 3,000 miles. As an act of individual courage, forethought, coolness, nerve, and the highest seaman-like qualities, the recapture of the "Emily St. Pierre" stands unsurpassed by any performed by seamen of any period, rank, or country.

Captain Wilson received the welcome he so richly deserved, on his arrival at Liverpool, from the mercantile as well as all other classes. The Council of the Mercantile Marine Service presented him with a gold medal, and silver medals with suitable inscriptions to the steward and cook; they also each of them received a purse with twenty guineas, and 170 merchants of Liverpool bestowed on Captain Wilson the sum of 2000 guineas; while numerous other presents were made by various companies, eager to show him in what high estimation his gallantry was held. His officers and crew who had been made prisoners by the Federals, on their arrival at Liverpool after their release, presented to him a valuable sextant, to show their sense of his kindness to them during the voyage from India, and of his noble conduct.

Captain Wilson's conduct adds another to many proofs that true bravery, humanity, and generosity are ever united.

—Kingston.

## KIRKDALE CAVERN.

There is another circumstance of high interest disclosed by the interior of many caverns, the occurrence of extinct animals of the ancient earth; on which account these receptacles have obtained the name of zoolithes or bone caverns. This phenomenon prevails in almost every country of Europe, and also of America, and has obtained of late years, particularly by the investigations of Dr. Buckland, who has made it the subject of his peculiar study, a high degree of importance, on account of the light which it throws upon the ancient condition of the earth, and the changes which the surface has undergone. His researches into the condition of a cave discovered in 1821 at

Kirkdale in Yorkshire are highly valuable, and deserve a notice here. Its mouth has long been choked up with rubbish, and overgrown with grass and bushes, but was accidentally found by some workmen. The cave is situated on the older portion of the oolite formation (in the coral rag and Oxford clay) on the declivity of a valley. It extends as an irregular narrow passage 250 feet into the hill. There are a few expansions, but scarcely high enough to allow a man to stand upright. The sides and floor were found covered with a deposit of stalagmite, beneath which there was a bed of from two to three feet of fine sandy and micaceous loam, the lower portion of which in particular contained an innumerable quantity of bones, with which the floor was completely strewn. The greatest part of them were very well preserved, and still retained a great portion of their natural gluten, in consequence of the peculiar nature of their investiture. The animals to which they belonged were the hyæna, bear, tiger and lion, elephant, rhinoceros, hippopotamus, horse, ox, deer of three species, water-rat, and mouse, belonging wholly to extinct species, and the same with those with which we are acquainted in the steppes of Asia. The most plentiful of all were the remains of the hyæna, and from the amount which he saw, Buckland estimated the number of the individuals interred here to be between two and three hundred. The animal must have been one half larger than the living species, in its structure resembling the hyæna of the Cape. The bears, which were less abundant, belonged to the large cavern species, which, according to Cuvier, was of the size of a large white horse and about eighteen feet in length. The elephants were the Siberian mammoth. Of the stags the largest was of the size of the moose deer. Of the ox two species were distinguished, and its bones were most frequent next to those of the hyæna. All these bones lay irregularly strewed one with another, but those of the largest animals were in the most remote and narrowest corners, into which they could never have penetrated while living. The teeth, and the hard marrowless bones of the extremities, as well as those of the fore and hind feet, were uninjured: these were so numerous that they must have belonged to a much greater number of individuals than could be estimated as belonging to the other bones. Many of the bones bore marks which exactly corresponded with the form of the incisor teeth of the hyæna, and the broken horns of the stag were evidently marked by gnawing. These facts warranted the conclusion, that the hyænas must have lived for a long time in this cave, and have dragged the bones of the larger animals, particularly the oxen, into this den, as their prey. The supposition was confirmed in a most striking manner by a variety of other facts. Dr. Buckland found that bones which he caused to be gnawed by living hyænas had exactly the same appearance as those found in the cavern, and the teeth and harder bones were thrown aside by them. He even found in great abundance excrements of the hyæna, which offered the closest resemblance to those of the living animal. From the facts described, it appears that the Kirkdale cave was for a long series of years a den inhabited by hyænas, who dragged into its recesses the other animal bodies whose remains are there commingled with their own,—some great catastrophe causing an inundation in this region which destroyed the whole race. —MILNER.

## MILITARY GLORY.

The festal blazes, the triumphal show,
The ravish'd standard, and the captive foe,
The senate's thanks, the gazette's pompous tale,
With force resistless o'er the brave prevail.
Such bribes the rapid Greek o'er Asia whirl'd,
For such the steady Romans shook the world ;
For such in distant lands the Britons shine,
And stain with blood the Danube or the Rhine ;
This pow'r has praise, that virtue scarce can warm
Till fame supplies the universal charm.
Yet Reason frowns on War's unequal game,
Where wasted nations raise a single name,
And mortgag'd states their grandsires' wreaths regret,
From age to age in everlasting debt ;
Wreaths which at last the dear-bought right convey
To rust on medals, or on stones decay.
   On what foundation stands the warrior's pride,
How just his hopes, let Swedish Charles decide ;
A frame of adamant, a soul of fire,
No dangers fright him, and no labors tire ;
O'er love, o'er fear, extends his wide domain,
Unconquer'd lord of pleasure and of pain ;
No joys to him pacific sceptres yield,
War sounds the trump, he rushes to the field ;

> Behold surrounding kings their pow'r combine,
> And one capitulate, and one resign;
> Peace courts his hand, but spreads her charms in vain;
> "Think nothing gain'd, he cries, till nought remain,
> "On Moscow's walls till Gothic standards fly,
> "And all be mine beneath the polar sky."
> The march begins in military state,
> And nations on his eye suspended wait;
> Stern Famine guards the solitary coast,
> And Winter barricades the realms of Frost;
> He comes, nor want nor cold his course delay;—
> Hide, blushing Glory, hide Pultowa's day:
> The vanquish'd hero leaves his broken bands,
> And shews his miseries in distant lands;
> Condemn'd a needy supplicant to wait,
> While ladies interpose, and slaves debate.
> But did not Chance at length her error mend?
> Did no subverted empire mark his end?
> Did rival monarchs give the fatal wound?
> Or hostile millions press him to the ground?
> His fall was destin'd to a barren strand,
> A petty fortress, and a dubious hand;
> He left the name, at which the world grew pale,
> To point a moral, or adorn a tale.
> — JOHNSON.

## THE BATTLE OF CANNÆ.

### (B.C. 216.)

IT appears that the Romans, till the arrival of the new consuls, had not ventured to follow Hannibal closely; for when they did follow him, it took them two days' march to arrive in his neighborhood, where they encamped at about six miles distance from him. They found him on the left bank of the Aufidus, about eight or nine miles from the sea, and busied, probably, in collecting the corn from the early district on the coast, the season being about the middle of June. The country here was so level and open that the consul, L. Æmilius, was unwilling to approach the enemy more closely, but wished to take a position on the hilly ground further from the sea, and to bring on the action there. But Varro, impatient for battle, and having the supreme command of the whole army alternately with Æmilius every other day, decided the question irrevocably on the very next day, by interposing himself between the enemy and the sea, with his left resting on the Aufidus, and his right communicating with the town of Salapia.

From this position Æmilius, when he again took the command in chief, found it impossible to withdraw. But availing himself of his great superiority in numbers, he threw a part of his army across the river, and posted them in a separate camp on the right bank, to have the supplies of the country south of the Aufidus at command, and to restrain the enemy's parties who might attempt to forage in that direction. When Hannibal saw the Romans in this situation, he also advanced nearer to them, descending the left bank of the Aufidus, and encamped over against the main army of the enemy, with his right resting on the river.

The next day, which, according to the Roman calendar, was the last of the month Quinctilis, or July, the Roman reckoning being six or seven weeks in advance of the true season, Hannibal was making his preparations for battle, and did not stir from his camp; so that Varro, whose command it was, could not bring on an action. But on the first of Sextilis, or August, Hannibal being now quite ready, drew out his army in front of his camp and offered battle. Æmilius, however, remained quiet, resolved not to fight on such ground, and hoping that Hannibal would soon be obliged to fall back nearer the hills, when he found that he could no longer forage freely in the country near the sea. Hannibal, seeing that the enemy did not move, marched back his infantry into his camp, but sent his Numidian cavalry across the river to attack the Romans on that side, as they were coming down in straggling parties to the bank to get water. For the Aufidus, though its bed is deep and wide to hold its winter floods, is a shallow or a narrow stream in summer, with many points easily fordable, not by horse only, but by infantry. The watering parties were driven in with some loss, and the Numidians followed them to the very gates of the camp, and obliged the Romans, on the right bank, to pass the summer night in the burning Apulian plain without water.

At daybreak on the next morning, the red ensign, which was the well-known signal for battle, was seen flying over Varro's head-quarters; and he issued orders, it being his day of command, for the main army to cross the river, and form in order of battle on the right bank. Whether he had any further object in crossing to the right bank, than to enable the soldiers on that side to get water in security, we do not know; but Hannibal, it seems, thought that the ground on either bank suited him equally; and he too forded the stream at two separate points, and drew out his army opposite to the enemy. The strong town of Canusium was scarcely three miles off in his rear; he had left his camp on the other side of the river; if he were defeated, escape seemed hopeless. But when he saw the wide, open plain around him, and looked at his numerous and irresistible cavalry, and knew that his infantry, however inferior in numbers, were far better and older soldiers than the great mass of their opponents, he felt that defeat was impossible. In this confidence his spirits were not cheerful merely, but even mirthful; he rallied one of his officers jestingly, who noticed the overwhelming numbers of the Romans; those near him laughed; and as any feeling at such a moment is contagious, the laugh was echoed by others; and the soldiers, seeing their great general in such a mood, were satisfied that he was sure of victory.

The Carthaginian army faced the north, so that the early sun shone on their right flank, while the wind, which blew strong from the south, but without a drop of rain, swept its clouds of dust over their backs, and carried them full into the faces of the enemy. On their left, resting on the river, were the Spanish and Gaulish horse; next in the line, but thrown back a little, were half of the African infantry armed like the Romans; on their right, somewhat in advance, were the Gauls and Spaniards, with their companies intermixed; then came the rest of the African foot, again thrown back like their comrades; and on the right of the whole line were the Numidian light horsemen. The right of the army rested, so far as appears, on nothing; the ground was open and level; but at some distance were hills overgrown with copsewood, and furrowed with deep ravines, in which, according to one account of the battle, a body of horsemen and of light infantry lay in ambush. The rest of the light troops, and the Balearian slingers, skirmished as usual in front of the whole line.

Meanwhile the masses of the Roman infantry were forming their line opposite. The sun on their left flashed obliquely on their brazen helmets, now uncovered for battle, and lit up the waving forest of their red and black plumes, which rose upright from their helmets a foot and a half high.

They stood brandishing their formidable pila, covered with their long shields, and bearing on their right thigh their peculiar and fatal weapon, the heavy sword, fitted alike to cut and to stab. On the right of the line were the Roman legions; on the left the infantry of the allies; while between the Roman right and the river were the Roman horsemen, all of them of wealthy or noble families; and on the left, opposed to the Numidians, were the horsemen of the Italians and of the Latin name. The velites or light infantry covered the front, and were ready to skirmish with the light troops and slingers of the enemy.

For some reason or other, which is not explained in any account of the battle, the Roman infantry were formed into columns rather than in line, the files of the maniples containing many more than their ranks. This seems an extraordinary tactic to be adopted in a plain by an army inferior in cavalry, but very superior in infantry. Whether the Romans relied on the river as a protection to their right flank, and their left was covered in some manner not mentioned,—one account would lead us to suppose that it reached nearly to the sea,—or whether the great proportion of the new levies obliged the Romans to adopt the system of the phalanx, and to place their raw soldiers in the rear, as incapable of fighting in the front ranks with Hannibal's veterans, it appears at any rate that the Roman infantry, though nearly double the number of the enemy, yet formed a line of only equal length with Hannibal's.

The skirmishing of the light-armed troops preluded as usual to the battle: the Balearian slingers slung their stones like hail into the ranks of the Roman line, and severely wounded the consul Æmilius himself. Then the Spanish and Gaulish horse charged the Romans front to front, and maintained a standing fight with them, many leaping off their horses and fighting on foot, till the Romans, outnumbered and badly armed, without cuirasses, with light and brittle spears, and with shields made only with ox-hide, were totally routed, and driven off the field. Hasdrubal, who commanded the Gauls and Spaniards, followed up his work effectually; he chased the Romans along the river till he had almost destroyed them; and then, riding off to the right, he came up to aid the Numidians, who, after their manner, had been skirmishing indecisively with the cavalry of the Italian allies. These, on seeing the Gauls and Spaniards advancing, broke away and fled; the Numidians, most effective in pursuing a flying enemy, chased them with unweariable speed, and slaughtered them unsparingly; while Hasdrubal, to complete his signal services on this day, charged fiercely upon the rear of the Roman infantry.

He found its huge masses already weltering in helpless confusion, crowded upon one another, totally disorganized, and fighting each man as he best could, but struggling on against all hope by mere indomitable courage. For the Roman columns on the right and left, finding the Gaulish and Spanish foot advancing in a convex line or wedge, pressed forwards to assail what seemed the flanks of the enemy's column; so that, being already drawn up with too narrow a front by their original formation, they now became compressed still more by their own movements, the right and left converging towards the centre, till the whole army became one dense column, which forced its way onwards by the weight of its charge, and drove back the Gauls and Spaniards into the rear of their own line. Meanwhile its victorious advance had carried it, like the English column at Fontenoy, into the midst of Hannibal's army; it had passed between the African infantry on its right and left; and now, whilst its head was struggling against the Gauls and Spaniards, its long flanks were fiercely assailed by the Africans, who, facing about to the right and left, charged it home, and threw it into utter disorder. In this state, when they were forced together into one unwieldy crowd, and already falling by thousands, whilst the Gauls and Spaniards, now advancing in their turn, were barring further progress in front, and whilst the Africans were tearing their mass to pieces on both flanks, Hasdrubal with his victorious Gaulish and Spanish horsemen broke with thundering fury upon their rear. Then followed a butchery such as has no recorded equal, except the slaughter of the Persians in their camp, when the Greeks forced it after the battle of Platæa. Unable to fight or fly, with no quarter asked or given, the Romans and Italians fell before the swords of their enemies, till, when the sun set upon the field, there were left out of that vast multitude no more than three thousand men alive and unwounded; and these fled in straggling parties, under cover of the darkness, and found a refuge in the neighboring towns. The consul Æmilius, the pro consul Cn. Servilius, the late master of the horse M. Minucius, two quæstors. twenty-one military tribunes, and eighty senators, lay dead amidst the carnage; Varro with seventy horsemen had escaped from the rout of the allied cavalry on the right of the army, and made his way safely to Venusia.

But the Roman loss was not yet completed. A large force had been left in the camp on the bank of the Aufidus, to attack Hannibal's camp during the action, which it is supposed that, with his inferior numbers, he could not leave adequately guarded. But it was defended so obstinately, that the Romans were still besieging it in vain, when Hannibal, now completely victorious in the battle, crossed the river to its relief. Then the besiegers fled in their turn to their own camp, and there, cut off from all succor, they presently surrendered. A few resolute men had forced their way out of the smaller camp on the right bank, and had escaped to Canusium; the rest who were in it followed the example of their comrades on the left bank, and surrendered to the conqueror.

Less than six thousand men of Hannibal's army had fallen: no greater price had he paid for the total destruction of more than eighty thousand of the enemy, for the capture of their two camps, for the utter annihilation, as it seemed, of all their means for offensive warfare. It is no wonder that the spirits of the Carthaginian officers were elated by this unequalled victory. Maharbal, seeing what his cavalry had done, said to Hannibal, "Let me advance instantly with the horse, and do thou follow to support me; in four days from this time thou shalt sup in the capitol." There are moments when rashness is wisdom; and it may be that this is one of them. The statue of the goddess Victory in the capitol may well have trembled in every limb on that day, and have dropped her wings, as if forever, but Hannibal came not; and if panic had for one moment unnerved the iron courage of the Roman aristocracy, on the next their inborn spirit revived; and their resolute will, striving beyond its present power, created, as is the law of our nature, the power which it required. —ARNOLD.

## THE ANTONINES.

(A. D. 138—180.)

THE two Antonines governed the Roman world forty-two years with the same invariable spirit of wisdom and virtue. Although Pius had two sons, he preferred the welfare of Rome to the interest of his family, gave his daughter Faustina in marriage to young Marcus, obtained from the senate the tribunitian and proconsular powers, and with a noble disdain, or rather ignorance of jealousy, associated him in all the labors of government. Marcus, on the other hand, revered the character of his benefactor, loved him as a parent, obeyed him as his sovereign, and, after he was no more, regulated his own administration by the example and maxims of his predecessor. Their united reigns are possibly the only period of history in which the happiness of a great people was the sole object of government.

Titus Antoninus Pius has been justly denominated a second Numa. The same love of religion, justice and peace, was the distinguishing characteristic of both princes. But the situation of the latter opened a much larger field for the exercise of those virtues. Numa could only prevent a few neighboring villages from plundering each other's harvests. Antoninus diffused order and tranquillity over the greatest part of the earth. His reign is marked by the rare advantage of furnishing very few materials for history; which is, indeed, little more than the register of the crimes, follies and misfortunes of mankind. In private life he was an amiable as well as a good man. The native simplicity of his virtue was a stranger to vanity or affectation. He enjoyed with moderation the conveniences of his fortune and the innocent pleasures of society; and the benevolence of his soul displayed itself in a cheerful serenity of temper.

The virtue of Marcus Aurelius Antoninus was of a severer and more laborious kind. It was the well-earned harvest of many a learned conference, of many a patient lecture, and many a midnight lucubration. At the age of twelve years he embraced the rigid system of the Stoics, which taught him to "submit his body to his mind, his passions to his reason; to consider virtue as the only good, vice as the only evil, all things external as things indifferent." His Meditations, composed in the tumult of a camp, are still extant; and he even condescended to give lessons of philosophy, in a more public manner than was perhaps consistent with the modesty of a sage or the dignity of an emperor. But his life was the noblest commentary on the precepts of Zeno. He was severe to himself, indulgent to the imperfection of others, just and beneficent to all mankind. He regretted that Avidius Cassius, who excited a rebellion in Syria, had disappointed him, by a voluntary death, of the pleasure of converting an enemy into a friend; and he justified the sincerity of that sentiment, by moderating the zeal of the senate against the adherents of the traitor. War he detested, as the disgrace and calamity of human nature; but when the necessity of a just defence called upon him to take up arms, he readily exposed his person to eight winter campaigns on the frozen banks of the Danube, the severity of which was at last fatal to the weakness of his constitution. His memory was revered by a grateful posterity, and, above a century after his death, many persons preserved the image of Marcus Antoninus among those of their household gods.

If a man were called to fix the period in the history of the world during which the condition of the human race was most happy and prosperous, he would, without hesitation, name that which elapsed from the death of Domitian to the accession of Commodus. The vast extent of the Roman empire was governed by absolute power, under the guidance of virtue and wisdom. The armies were restrained by the firm but gentle hand of four successive emperors whose character and authority commanded involuntary respect. The forms of the civil administration were carefully preserved by Nerva, Trajan, Hadrian, and the Antonines, who delighted in the image of liberty, and were pleased with considering themselves as the accountable ministers of the laws. Such princes deserved the honor of restoring the republic, had the Romans of their days been capable of enjoying a rational freedom.

The labors of these monarchs were overpaid by the immense reward that inseparably waited on their success; by the honest pride of virtue, and by the exquisite delight of beholding the general happiness of which they were the authors. A just but melancholy reflection embittered, however, the noblest of human enjoyments. They must often have recollected the instability of a happiness which depended on the character of a single man. The fatal moment was perhaps approaching, when some licentious youth, or some jealous tyrant, would abuse, to the destruction, that absolute power which they had exerted for the benefit of their people. The ideal restraints of the senate and the laws might serve to display the virtues, but could never correct the vices of the emperor. The military force was a blind and irresistible instrument of oppression; and the corruption of Roman manners would always supply flatterers eager to applaud, and ministers prepared to serve, the fear or the avarice, the lust or the cruelty, of their masters.

These gloomy apprehensions had been already justified by the experience of the Romans. The annals of the emperors exhibit a strong and various picture of human nature, which we should vainly seek amongst the mixed and doubtful characters of modern history. In the conduct of those monarchs we may trace the utmost lines of vice and virtue; the most exalted perfection and the meanest degeneracy of our own species. The golden age of Trajan and the Antonines had been preceded by an age of iron. It is almost superfluous to enumerate the unworthy successors of Augustus. Their unparalled vices and the splendid theatre on which they were acted, have saved them from oblivion. The dark unrelenting Tiberius, the furious Caligula, the feeble Claudius, the profligate and cruel Nero, the beastly Vitellius, and the timid, inhuman Domitian, are condemned to everlasting infamy. During fourscore years (excepting only the short and doubtful respite of Vespasian's reign) Rome groaned beneath an unremitting tyranny, which exterminated the ancient families of the republic, and was fatal to almost every virtue and every talent that arose in that unhappy period. —GIBBON.

## THE SPANISH ARMADA.
### (A. D. 1588.)

ATTEND, all ye who list to hear our noble England's praise;
I tell of the thrice famous deeds she wrought in ancient days,
When that great Fleet Invincible against her bore in vain
The richest spoils of Mexico, the stoutest hearts of Spain.
It was about the lovely close of a warm summer day,

## THE SPANISH ARMADA.

There came a gallant merchant-ship full sail to Plymouth Bay ;
Her crew hath seen Castile's black fleet, beyond Aurigny's isle,
At earliest twilight on the waves lie heaving many a mile ;
At sunrise she escaped their van, by God's especial grace,
And the tall Pinta, till the noon, had held her close in chase.
Forthwith a guard at every gun was placed along the wall ;
The beacon blazed upon the roof of Edgecombe's lofty hall ;
Many a light fishing-bark put out to pry along the coast ;
And with loose rein and bloody spur rode inland many a post,
With his white hair unbonneted, the stout old sheriff comes ;
Behind him march the halberdiers, before him sound the drums ;
His yeomen round the market cross make clear an ample space,
For there behoves him to set up the standard of Her Grace.
And haughtily the trumpets peal, and gaily dance the bells,
As slow upon the laboring wind the royal blazon swells.
Look how the Lion of the sea lifts up his ancient crown,
And underneath his deadly paw treads the gay lilies down.
So stalked he when he turned to flight, on that famed Picard field,
Bohemia's plume, and Genoa's bow, and Cæsar's eagle shield :
So glared he when at Agincourt in wrath he turned to bay,
And crushed and torn beneath his claws the princely hunters lay.
Ho! strike the flagstaff deep, Sir Knight; ho! scatter flowers, fair maids;
Ho! gunners, fire a loud salute ; ho ! gallants, draw your blades ;
Thou sun, shine on her joyously—ye breezes, waft her wide ;
Our glorious SEMPER EADEM, the banner of our pride.
   The freshening breeze of eve unfurl'd that banner's massy fold,—
The parting gleam of sunshine kissed that haughty scroll of gold ;
Night sunk upon the dusky beach, and on the purple sea,
Such night in England ne'er had been, nor e'er again shall be.
From Eddystone to Berwick bounds, from Lynn to Milford Bay,
That time of slumber was as bright and busy as the day ;
For swift to east and swift to west the ghastly war-flame spread ;
High on St. Michael's Mount it shone, it shone on Beachy Head.
Far on the deep the Spaniard saw, along each southern shire,
Cape beyond cape, in endless range, those twinkling points of fire ;
The fisher left his skiff to rock on Tamar's glittering waves ;
The rugged miners poured to war from Mendip's sunless caves ;
O'er Longleat's towers, o'er Cranbourne's oaks, the fiery herald flew ;
He roused the shepherds of Stonehenge, the rangers of Beaulieu ;
Right sharp and quick the bells all night rang out from Bristol town,
And ere the day three hundred horse had met on Clifton Down ;
The sentinel at Whitehall Gate looked forth into the night,
And saw o'erhanging Richmond Hill the streak of blood-red light.
Then bugle's note and cannon's roar the death-like silence broke,
And with one start, and with one cry, the royal city woke.
At once on all her stately gates arose the answering fires ;
At once the wild alarum clashed from all her reeling spires ;
From all the batteries of the Tower pealed loud the voice of fear ;
And all the thousand masts of Thames sent back a louder cheer ;
And from the farthest wards was heard the rush of hurrying feet,
And the broad streams of flags and pikes dashed down each roaring street,

And broader still became the blaze, and louder still the din,
As fast from every village round the horse came spurring in :
And eastward straight from wild Blackheath the warlike errand went,
And roused in many an ancient hall the gallant squires of Kent.
Southward from Surrey's pleasant hills flew those bright couriers forth ;
High on bleak Hampstead's swarthy moor they started for the north ;
And on, and on, without a pause, untired they bounded still,—
All night from tower to tower they sprang; they sprang from hill to hill;
Till the proud peak unfurl'd the flag o'er Darwin's rocky dales,
Till like volcanoes flared to heaven the stormy hills of Wales,
Till twelve fair counties saw the blaze on Malvern's lonely height,
Till streamed in crimson on the wind the Wrekin's crest of light,
Till broad and fierce the star came forth on Ely's stately fane,
And tower and hamlet rose in arms o'er all the boundless plain ;
Till Belvoir's lordly terraces the sign to Lincoln sent,
And Lincoln sped the message on o'er the wide vale of Trent ;
Till Skiddaw saw the fire that burned on Gaunt's embattled pile,
And the red glare on Skiddaw roused the burghers of Carlisle.
—LORD MACAULAY.

## GOD'S PROVIDENCE INSCRUTABLE.

A SHIP, bound for Dublin, sailed once from Chester across the stormy Irish Channel, which has washed so many stout vessels away. A "fatal and perfidious bark, built in the eclipse, and rigged with curses dark"—such it is called in the immortal poem which commemorates the voyage. Was it? The old sailors at Holyhead and the Howthburn boatmen wouldn't have said so: they might have thought a lubber commanded her, or that she would have been the better for some good ground-tackle, or that she was the prey of the nor'-easter, or that she fared as many a better bark had fared before; but as to the moon having to do with her fate, except by way of tides, or as to "curses dark" being at the bottom of the mischief—unless the English riggers swore a great deal too much when fastening the shrouds to the mast-head—they would have shifted their quids and laughed at the notion. But this particular vessel happening to hold Mr. Edward King, son of his Honor the Secretary for Ireland, Sir John King, the time of the shipwreck chanced to be the year of grace 1637, when another John, whose surname was Milton, was living ; and, further, it occurred that between Mr. Edward King and Mr. John Milton there existed a college friendship, which, as friendships go, is generally made of sincere stuff. So when the "perfidious bark," either by bad seamanship or stress of weather, went to the bottom of the Irish Channel, carrying his Honor the Secretary's son along with it, and all the other souls on board, the poet, hearing of the news in the little chamber at Cambridge, straightway gave to the world "Lycidas;" and as long as English shall be a language, living or dead, everybody will remember Mr. Edward King. That stately and noble poem of half-a-dozen pages is his monument, truly more enduring than any pyramid or pile of bronze and marble. But the unlucky ship in which Lycidas paid for his passage was not the only one that went down; and, for the matter of that, there were doubtless lives lost in the "perfidious bark" as dear to others as Edward King's to the poet. Of the others, however, some stonemason's poetry in Chester churchyard was the only epitaph; Lycidas came in for the glorious lyrics that burn with real religion and human affection, and noble images of sorrow fetched from classic treasuries to "strew the laureate hearse where Lycid lies." The wreckers and coastmen that brought the bodies up through the surf, ransacked their pockets, gave the dead a rough burial in the sands, and saw no difference whatever between Lycidas and the captain's cook. A poet did, and made his friend famous and renowned for ever, though perhaps there was a widow in Chester or Dublin who felt as much or more, and said it with the sad prose of sighs, even for that same lowly captain's cook. Which is verse and which is prose—which life is priceless, and which insignificant? Does an accident of acquaintance or information make all the difference; or is not life and death alike a book of equally tragic mystery, from which these poets tear pages, cut and select pictures, till we forget that the thousand volumes from which they came are all of the same kind?

There is a Lycidas, for instance, just lost at Cambridge, only there happens to be no Milton among his friends. Otherwise, Mr. Henry John Purkiss would be as good a theme for a poet as Mr. Edward King. If the story were told in verse, we might have again the portrait in classical outline of a Lycidas "dead, dead ere his prime," and the melodious rhymer would demand again where the nymphs were when "the remorseless wave closed o'er the head of your loved Lycidas." The poet would ask, too, "what boots it" to study, and pore, and "strictly meditate the thankless muse," and be Senior Wrangler, only to be drowned at the end of it in that little ditch which calls itself a river—the Cam? By the Milton of Mr. John Purkiss, indeed, that modest stream would be hight "reverend Camus, footing slow, his mantle hairy and his bonnet sedge;" and he would paint the river god incensed with his Nereids for letting the weeds catch the feet of the young Cambridge scholar and drag him to his death.

As it is, we must be content to have the story in prose, and have only hazarded these views to show that human life, however unconsciously, talks and acts poetry. And, indeed, the prose of the tale is full enough of sorrow without being put into elegiacs. Mr. Purkiss was a boy at the City of London School, when he gained the first Queen's Prize given at South Kensington. Then he carried off scholarships at the University of London and at Cambridge; and, going up to Trinity College, at the latter university he came out in 1864 Senior Wrangler and first Smith's Prizeman—illustrious triumphs that seldom go together; while the feats were capped by his gaining the three Mathematical Scholarships at the London University, and the gold medal. Attracted by such parts, Lord Granville offered the young Cambridge bachelor the vice-principalship of the new Royal College of Naval Architecture; and, after one session—his first and last—he was promoted to the principalship at twenty-three years, the youngest "principal" ever yet installed in the ranks of education. Here was a young recruit of Science, destined most assuredly to fight his way under her banner to new discoveries, new helps for mankind. Such a man could not have failed to become famous; faculties so admirable in youth must have borne noble fruitage in maturity. He repairs, however, to Cambridge to read for his degree, and walks from Grantchester along the Cam, to the bathing-sheds. His companions, inclined to have a swim, undress and plunge in, inviting him to follow. They hear the splash of his header, and think "it's all right;" but when they return down the stream again there are his clothes and hat in the bathing-shed, but nothing else. They scour the banks, they poke about with poles, they drag with hooks; by-and-by the weeds move unnaturally in one place, and the body of the young scholar is fished out. Who can understand these mysterious dispensations of Him who does not judge as we judge, nor spare what we value?—who cuts down the young and splendid scholar in the bloom of his mental power? Perhaps none so well as those who know that nothing is so vain as to demand a solution of the mystery. We are sure only of Providence; we must remain ignorant of its reasons and righteousness.

— *London Daily Telegraph.*

## CORN FIELDS.

In the young merry time of spring,
   When clover 'gins to burst;
When blue-bells nod within the wood,
   And sweet May whitens first—
When merle and mavis sing their fill,
Green is the young corn on the hill.

But when the merry spring is past,
   And summer groweth bold,
And in the garden and the field,
   A thousand flowers unfold;
Before a green leaf yet is sere,
The young corn shoots into the ear.

But then as day and night succeed,
   And summer weareth on,
And in the flowry garden-beds
   The red-rose groweth wan,
And hollyhocks and sun-flowers tall
O'ertop the mossy garden wall.

When on the breath of autumn's breeze,
   From pastures dry and brown,
Goes floating, like an idle thought,
   The fair, white thistledown;
O, then what joy to walk at will,
Upon the golden harvest-hill!

What joy in dreaming ease to lie
   Amid a field new shorn,
And see all round on sunlit slope,
   The piled-up stacks of corn,
And send the fancy wandering o'er
All pleasant harvest-fields of yore.

I feel the day; I see the field;
   The quivering of the leaves;
And good old Jacob, and his house
   Binding the yellow sheaves;
And at the very hour I seem
To be with Joseph in his dream

I see the fields of Bethlehem,
   And reapers many a one,
Bending with their sickles' stroke,
   And Boaz looking on;
And Ruth, the Moabitess fair,
Among the gleaners stooping there

Again, I see a little child,
   His mother's sole delight;
God's living gift of love unto
   The kind, good Shunammite;
To mortal pangs I see him yield,
And the lad bears him from the field.

The sun-bathed quiet of the hills,
   The fields of Galilee,
That eighteen hundred years' agone,
   Were full of corn, I see;
And the dear Saviour take his way
'Mid ripe ears on the sabbath-day.

O golden fields of bending corn,
   How beautiful they seem!—
The reaper-folk, the piled-up sheaves,
   To me are like a dream;
The sunshine and the very air
Seem of old time, and take me there.

               —Mary Howitt.

## ON LAW.

THE stateliness of houses, the goodliness of trees, when we behold them, delighteth the eye; but that foundation which beareth up the one, that root which ministereth unto the other nourishment and life, is in the bosom of the earth concealed; and if there be at any time occasion to search into it, such labor is then more necessary than pleasant, both to them which undertake it, and for the lookers on. In like manner the use and benefit of good laws all that live under them may enjoy with delight and comfort, albeit the grounds and first original causes from whence they have sprung be unknown, as to the greatest part of men they are. But when they who withdraw their obedience pretend that the laws which they should obey are corrupt and vicious, for better examination of their quality, it **behoveth** the very foundation and root, the highest well-spring and fountain of them, to be discovered. Which because we are not oftentimes accustomed to do, when we do it, the pains we take are more needful a great deal than acceptable; and the matters which we handle seem, by reason of newness (till the mind grow better acquainted with them), dark, intricate, and unfamiliar.

And because the point about which we strive is the quality of our laws, our first entrance hereinto cannot better be made than with consideration of the nature of law in general.

All things that are have some operation not violent or casual. Neither doth anything ever begin to exercise the same without some fore-conceived end for which it worketh. And the end which it worketh for is not obtained, unless the work be also fit to obtain it by. For unto every end every operation will not serve. That which doth assign unto each thing the kind, that which doth moderate the force and power, that which doth appoint the form and measure of working, the same we term a *Law*. So that no certain end could ever be obtained unless the actions whereby it is obtained were regular, that is to say, made suitable, fit, and correspondent unto their end by some canon, rule, or law.

Moses, in describing the work of creation, attributeth speech unto God : "God said, let there be light ; let there be a firmament ; let the waters under the heaven be gathered together into one place ; let the earth bring forth ; let there be lights in the firmament of heaven." Was this only the intent of Moses, to signify the infinite greatness of God's power by the easiness of His accomplishing such effects, without travail, pain, or labor ? Surely it seemeth that Moses had herein besides this a further purpose, namely, first to teach that God did not work as a necessary, but a voluntary Agent, intending beforehand and decreeing with Himself that which did outwardly proceed from Him ; secondly, to shew that God did then institute a law natural to be observed by creatures, and therefore, according to the manner of laws, the institution thereof is described as being established by solemn injunction. His commanding those things to be which are, and to be in such sort as they are, to keep that tenure and course which they do, importeth the establishment of nature's law. This world's first creation, and the preservation since of things created, what is it but only so far forth a manifestation by execution, what the eternal law of

God is concerning things natural? And as it cometh to pass in a kingdom rightly ordered, that after a law is once published it presently takes effect far and wide, all states framing themselves thereunto; even so let us think it fareth in the natural course of the world: since the time that God did first proclaim the edicts of His law upon it, heaven and earth have hearkened unto His voice, and their labor hath been to do His will. "He made a law for the rain, he gave his decree unto the sea, that the waters should not pass his commandment." Now, if nature should intermit her course, and leave altogether, though it were but for a while, the observation of her own laws; if those principal and mother elements of the world, whereof all things in this lower world are made, should lose the qualities which now they have; if the frame of that heavenly arch erected over our heads should loosen and dissolve itself; if celestial spheres should forget their wonted motions, and by irregular volubilities turn themselves any way as it might happen; if the prince of the lights of heaven, which now as a giant doth run its unwearied course, should, as it were through a languishing faintness, begin to stand and to rest himself; if the moon should wander from her beaten way; the times and seasons of the year blend themselves by disordered and confused mixture; the winds breathe out their last gasp; the clouds yield no rain; the earth be defeated of heavenly influence; the fruits of the earth pine away as children at the withered breasts of their mother, no longer able to yield them relief; what would become of man himself, whom these things now do all serve? See we not plainly that obedience of creatures unto the law of nature is the stay of the whole world?

Of Law there can be no less acknowledged than that her seat is the bosom of God; her voice the harmony of the world. All things in heaven and earth do her homage; the very least as feeling her care, and the greatest as not exempted from her power. Both angels and men, and creatures of what condition soever, though each in different sort and manner, yet all with uniform consent, admiring her as the mother of their peace and joy. —HOOKER.

## THE PROGRESS OF POESY.

Awake, Æolian lyre, awake,
And give to rapture all thy trembling strings.
From Helicon's harmonious springs
A thousand rills their mazy progress take:
The laughing flowers that round them blow
Drink life and fragrance as they flow.
Now the rich stream of Music winds along
Deep, majestic, smooth, and strong,
Through verdant vales, and Ceres' golden reign;
Now rolling down the steep amain
Headlong, impetuous, see it pour:
The rocks and nodding groves re-bellow to the roar.

O Sovereign of the willing soul,
Parent of sweet and solemn-breathing airs,
Enchanting shell! the sullen Cares
  And frantic Passions hear thy soft control.
On Thracia's hills the Lord of War
Has curb'd the fury of his car
And dropped his thirsty lance at thy command.
Perching on the sceptred hand
Of Jove, thy magic lulls the feather'd king
With ruffled plumes, and flagging wing:
Quench'd in dark clouds of slumber lie
The terror of his beak, and lightnings of his eye.

\* \* \* \* \* \*

Woods, that wave o'er Delphi's steep,
Isles, that crown th' Ægean deep,
Fields that cool Ilissus laves
Or where Maeander's amber waves
In lingering lab'rinths creep,
How do your tuneful echoes languish,
Mute, but to the voice of anguish!
Where each old poetic mountain
  Inspiration breathed around;
Every shade and hallow'd fountain
  Murmur'd deep a solemn sound:
Till the sad Nine in Greece's evil hour
  Left their Parnassus for the Latian plains.
Alike they scorn the pomp of tyrant Power,
  And coward Vice, that revels in her chains.
When Latium had her lofty spirit lost,
They sought, O Albion! next, thy sea-encircled coast.

Far from the sun and summer-gale
In thy green lap was Nature's Darling laid,
What time, where lucid Avon stray'd,
  To him the mighty Mother did unveil

Her awful face: the dauntless Child
Stretch'd forth his little arms, and smiled.
This pencil take (she said), whose colors clear
Richly paint the vernal year:
Thine, too, these golden keys, immortal Boy!
This can unlock the gates of Joy;
Of Horror that, and thrilling Fears,
Or ope the sacred source of sympathetic Tears.

Nor second He, that rode sublime
Upon the seraph-wings of Ecstasy
The secrets of the Abyss to spy:
He pass'd the flaming bounds of Place and Time:
The living Throne, the sapphire-blaze
Where Angels tremble while they gaze,
He saw; but blasted with excess of light,
Closed his eyes in endless night.
Behold where Dryden's less presumptuous car
Wide o'er the fields of Glory bear
Two coursers of ethereal race
With necks in thunder clothed, and long-resounding pace.

Hark, his hands the lyre explore!
Bright-eyed Fancy, hovering o'er,
Scatters from her pictured urn
Thoughts that breathe, and words that burn.
But ah! 'tis heard no more—
O! Lyre divine, what daring Spirit
Wakes thee now! Tho' he inherit
Nor the pride, nor ample pinion,
  That the Theban Eagle bear,
Sailing with supreme dominion
  Thro' the azure deep of air:
Yet oft before his infant eyes would run
  Such forms as glitter in the Muse's ray
With orient hues, unborrow'd of the sun:
Yet shall he mount, and keep his distant way
Beyond the limits of a vulgar fate:
Beneath the Good Low far—but far above the Great.
—Gray.

## FALL OF MONTROSE.
### (*Executed A.D.* 1650.)

THE Marquis of Argyle was vigilant enough to observe the motion of an enemy that was so formidable to him; and had present information of his arrival in the Highlands, and of the small forces which he had brought with him. The Parlia ment was then sitting at Edinburgh, their messenger being returned to them from Jersey, with an account, "that the king would treat with their commissioners at Breda;" for whom they were preparing their instructions.

The alarm of Montrose's being landed startled them all, and gave them no leisure to think of anything else than of sending forces to hinder the recourse of others to join with him. They immediately sent Colonel Straghan, a diligent and active officer, with a choice party of the best horse they had, to make all possible haste towards him, and to prevent the insurrections, which they feared would be in several parts of the Highlands. And within few days after, David Lesley followed with a stronger party of horse and foot. The encouragement the Marquis of Montrose received from his friends, and the unpleasantness of the quarters in which he was, prevailed with him to march, with these few troops, more into the land. And the Highlanders flocking to him from all quarters, though ill armed, and worse disciplined, made him undervalue any enemy who, he thought, was yet like to encounter him. Straghan made such haste, that the Earl of Sutherland, who at least pretended to have gathered together a body of fifteen hundred men to meet Montrose, chose rather to join with Straghan: others did the like, who had made the same promises, or stayed at home to expect the event of the first encounter. The marquis was without any body of horse to discover the motion of an enemy, but depended upon all necessary intelligence from the affection of the people; which he believed to be the same it was when he left them. But they were much degenerated; the tyranny of Argyle, and his having caused very many to be barbarously murdered, without any form of law or justice, who had been in arms with Montrose, notwithstanding all acts of pardon and indemnity, had so broken their hearts, that they were ready to do all offices that might gratify and oblige him. So that Straghan was within a small distance of him, before he heard of his approach; and those Highlanders, who had seemed to come with much zeal to him, whether terrified or corrupted, left him on a sudden, or threw down their arms; so that he had none left, but a company of good officers, and five or six hundred foreigners, Dutch and Germans, who had been acquainted with their officers. With these, he betook himself to a place of some advantage by the inequality of the ground, and the bushes and small shrubs which filled it: and there they made a defence for some time with notable courage.

But the enemy being so much superior in number, the common soldiers, being all foreigners, after about a hundred of them were killed upon the place, threw down their arms; and the marquis seeing all lost, threw away his ribbon and George (for he was a knight of the garter), and found means to change his clothes with a fellow of the country, and so after having gone on foot two or three miles, he got into a house of a gentleman, where he remained concealed about two days: most of the other officers were shortly after taken prisoners, all the country desiring to merit from Argyle by betraying all those into his hands which they believed to be his enemies. And thus, whether by the owner of the house, or any other way, the marquis himself became their prisoner. The strangers who were taken were set at liberty, and transported themselves into their own countries; and the castle, in which there was a little garrison, presently rendered itself; so that there was no fear of an enemy in those parts.

The Marquis of Montrose, and the rest of the prisoners, were the next day, or soon after, delivered to David Lesley; who was come up with his forces, and had now nothing left to do but to carry them in triumph to Edinburgh; whither notice was quickly sent of their great victory; which was received there with wonderful joy and acclamation. David Lesley treated the marquis with great insolence, and for some days carried him in the same clothes, and habit, in which he was taken; but at last permitted him to buy better. His behavior was, in the whole time, such as became a great man; his countenance serene and cheerful, as one that was superior to all those reproaches, which they had prepared the people to pour out upon him in all the places through which he was to pass.

When he came to one of the gates of Edinburgh, he was met by some of the magistrates, to whom he was delivered, and by them presently put into a new cart, purposely made, in which there was a high chair, or bench, upon which he sat, that the people might have a full view of him, being bound with a cord drawn over his breast and shoulders, and fastened through holes made in the cart. When he was in this posture, the hangman took off his hat, and rode himself before the cart in his livery, and with his bonnet on; the other officers, who were taken prisoners with him, walking two and two before, the cart; the streets and windows being full of people to behold the triumph over a person whose name had made them tremble some few years before, and into whose hands the magistrates of that place had, upon their knees, delivered the keys of that city. In this manner he was carried to the common gaol, where he was received and treated as a common malefactor. Within two days after, he was brought before the Parliament, where the Earl of Lowden, the chancellor, made a very bitter and virulent declamation against him: told him, "he had broken all the covenants by which that whole nation stood obliged; and had impiously rebelled against God, the king and the kingdom; that he had committed many horrible murders, treasons and impieties, for all which he was now brought to suffer condign punishment;" with all those insolent reproaches upon his person, and his actions, which the liberty of that place gave him leave to use.

Permission was then given him to speak; and without the least trouble in his countenance, or disorder, upon all the indignities he had suffered, he told them, "he was now again entered into the kingdom by his majesty's command, and with his authority; and what success soever it might have pleased God to have given him, he would always have obeyed any commands he should have received from him." He advised them "to consider well of the consequence before they proceeded against him, and that all his actions might be examined and judged by the laws of the land, or those of nations."

As soon as he had ended his discourse, he was ordered to withdraw; and, after a short space, was again brought in; and told by the chancellor, "that he was, on the morrow, being the one and twentieth of May, 1650, to be carried to Edinburgh cross, and there to be hanged upon a gallows thirty foot high, for the space of three hours, and then to be taken down, and his head to be cut off upon a scaffold, and hanged on Edinburgh tollbooth; his legs and arms to be hanged up in other public towns of the kingdom, and his body to be buried at the place where he was to be executed, except the kirk should take off his excommunication; and then his body might be buried in the common place of burial." He desired, "that he might say somewhat to them;" but was not suffered, and so was carried back to the prison.

The next day, they executed every part and circumstance of that barbarous sentence, with all the inhumanity imaginable; and he bore it with all the courage and magnanimity, and the greatest piety, that a good Christian could manifest. He magnified the virtue, courage, and religion of the last king, exceedingly commended the justice, and goodness, and understanding of the present king; and prayed, "that they might not betray him as they had done his father." When he had ended all he meant to say, and was expecting to expire, they had yet one scene more to act of their tyranny. The hangman brought the book that had been published of his truly heroic actions, whilst he had commanded in that kingdom, which book was tied in a small cord that was put about his neck. The marquis smiled at this new instance of their malice, and thanked them for it; and said, "he was pleased that it should be here; and was prouder of wearing it, than ever he had been of the garter;" and so renewing some devout ejaculations, he patiently endured the last act of the executioner.

Thus died the gallant Marquis of Montrose, after he had given as great a testimony of loyalty and courage, as a subject can do, and performed as wonderful actions in several battles, upon as great inequality of numbers, and as great disadvantages in respect of arms, and other preparations for war, as have been performed in this age. He was a gentleman of a very ancient extraction, many of whose ancestors had exercised the highest charges under the king in that kingdom, and had been allied to the crown itself. He was of very good parts, which were improved by a good education: he had always a great emulation, or rather a great contempt for the Marquis of Argyle, (as he was too apt to contemn those he did not love), who wanted nothing but honesty and courage to be a very extraordinary man, having all other good talents in a very great degree. Montrose was in his nature fearless of danger, and never declined any enterprise for the difficulty of going through with it, but exceedingly affected those which seemed desperate to other men, and did believe somewhat to be in himself above other men, which made him live more easily towards those who were, or were willing to be, inferior to him, (towards whom he exercised wonderful civility and generosity,) than with his superiors or equals. He was naturally jealous, and suspected those who did not concur with him in the way, not to mean so well as he. He was not without vanity, but his virtues were much superior, and he well deserved to have his memory preserved, and celebrated amongst the most illustrious persons of the age in which he lived. —EARL OF CLARENDON.

## THE SECOND ADVENT.

The chariot! the chariot! its wheels roll on fire
As the Lord cometh down in the pomp of His ire;
Self-moving, it drives on its pathway of cloud,
And the heavens with the burden of Godhead are bow'd.

The glory! the glory! By myriads are pour'd
The hosts of the angels to wait on their Lord;
And the glorified saints, and the martyrs are there,
And all who the palm-wreath of victory wear.

The trumpet! the trumpet! The dead have all heard.
Lo! the depths of the stone-cover'd charnels are stirr'd;
From the sea, from the land, from the south and the north,
The vast generations of man are come forth!

The judgment! the judgment! The thrones are all set,
Where the Lamb and the white-vested elders are met:
All flesh is at once in the sight of the Lord,
And the doom of eternity hangs on his word!

Oh mercy! oh mercy! look down from above,
Creator! on us, Thy sad children, with love;
When beneath to their darkness the wicked are driven,
May our sanctified souls find a mansion in heaven.
—MILMAN.

## TAXES.

PERMIT me to inform you, my friends, what are the inevitable consequences of being too fond of glory:—Taxes—upon every article which enters into the mouth, or covers the back, or is placed under the foot—taxes upon everything which it is pleasant to see, hear, feel, smell, or taste—taxes upon warmth, light, and locomotion—taxes on everything on earth, and the waters under the earth, on everything that comes from abroad or is grown at home—taxes upon the raw material—taxes on every fresh value that is added to it by the industry of man—

taxes on the sauce which pampers man's appetite, and the drug that restores him to health—on the ermine which decorates the judge, and the rope which hangs the criminal—on the poor man's salt, and the rich man's spice—on the brass nails of the coffin, and the ribbons of the bride—at bed or board we must pay taxes.

The school-boy whips his taxed top—the beardless youth manages his taxed horse, with a taxed bridle on a taxed road—and the dying Englishman, pouring his medicine which has paid seven per cent. into a spoon that has paid fifteen per cent., flings himself back upon his chintz bed which has paid twenty-two per cent., makes his will on an eight pound stamp, and expires in the arms of an apothecary, who has paid a license of a hundred pounds for the privilege of putting him to death. His whole property is then immediately taxed from two to ten per cent. Besides the probate, large fees are demanded for burying him in the chancel; his virtues are handed down to posterity on taxed marble; and he is then gathered to his fathers—to be taxed no more.

—LORD BROUGHAM.

## THE ALHAMBRA.

PALACE of Beauty! where the Moorish Lord,
King of the bow, the bridle, and the sword,
Sat like a Genie in the diamond's blaze.
Oh! to have seen thee in the ancient days,
When at thy morning gates the coursers stood,
The "thousand" milk-white, Yemen's fiery blood,
In pearl and ruby harness'd for the King;
And through thy portals pour'd the gorgeous flood
Of jewell'd Sheik and Emir, hastening,
Before the sky the dawning purple show'd,
Their turbans at the Caliph's feet to fling.
Lovely thy morn—thy evening lovelier still,
When at the waking of the first blue star
That trembled on the Atalaya hill,
The splendors of the trumpet's voice arose,
Brilliant and bold, and yet no sound of war;
But summoning thy beauty from repose,
The shaded slumber of the burning noon.
Then in the slant sun all thy fountains shone,
Shooting the sparkling column from the vase
Of crystal cool, and falling in a haze

Of rainbow hues on floors of porphyry,
And the rich bordering beds of every bloom
That breathes to African or Indian sky,
Carnation, tuberose, thick anemone;
Then was the harping of the minstrels heard,
In the deep arbors, or the regal hall,
Hushing the tumult of the festival,
When the pale bard his kindling eye-ball rear'd,
And told of Eastern glories, silken hosts,
Tower'd elephants, and chiefs in topaz arm'd;
Or of the myriads from the cloudy coasts
Of the far Western sea,—the sons of blood,
The iron men of tournament and feud,
That round the bulwarks of their fathers swarm'd,
Doom'd by the Moslem scimitar to fall,
Till the Red Cross was hurl'd from Salem's wall

Where are thy pomps, Alhambra, earthly sun,
That had no rival, and no second?—gone!
Thy glory down the arch of time has roll'd,
Like the great day-star to the ocean dim,
The billows of the ages o'er thee swim,
Gloomy and fathomless; thy tale is told.
Where is thy horn of battle? that, but blown,
Brought every chief of Afric from his throne;
Brought every spear of Afric from the wall;
Brought every charger barbed from the stall,
Till all its tribes sat mounted on the shore;
Waiting the waving of the torch to pour
The living deluge on the fields of Spain.
Queen of Earth's loveliness, there was a stain
Upon thy brow—the stain of guilt and gore;
Thy course was bright, bold, treach'rous—and 'tis o'er.
The spear and diadem are from thee gone;
Silence is now sole monarch of thy throne!  —CROLY.

## MERCHANT PRINCES.

WAR has always had such a fascination for the writers of history, that they have occupied themselves with it almost exclusively, and have left scarcely any space in their chronicles for the deeds of Peace. While the military commanders are usually painted at full length, sometimes even to the exclusion of their armies, it is but rarely that we are introduced to any of the great leaders of industry or commerce, who, when they are not disregarded altogether, appear merely as vague shadows in the background. In the fifteenth century, however, flourished an illustrious group of merchants, who, by their dealings with kings and princes, have found a place in the annals of their time.

Foremost among the number were the Fuggers of Augsburg. That city was then not only the seat of an important linen manufacture, but the staple place of the trade between Northern Europe, Italy, and the Levant. From its gates ran the chief highway to Venice, across the Brenner Alps and through the Tyrol. The merchants of Augsburg, however, were not mere agents. They also carried on a direct import trade, either in association with Venetian and Genoese firms, or through establishments of their own in Italy and the Netherlands. Jean, the first of the Fuggers, commenced business as a linen manufacturer, and thus laid the foundation of an enormous fortune and an illustrious family. Without abandoning the factory, he gradually extended his operations into all the fields of commerce and finance. His sons inherited his enterprise and talent. They speculated in all kinds of merchandise—they worked the mines of gold which enriched the valley of the Inn, and the silver of Falkenstein and Schwartz—they had branches in Antwerp, Genoa, and Venice—they dispatched vessels to the Baltic, where the Hanseatic League, indignant at the invasion of its monopoly, once captured nearly a score of them—they also maintained direct relations with both the Indies. In 1506 they took part in a Portuguese expedition to the Indies, which brought home a cargo worth 175,000 ducats. More than once they replenished from their private coffers the exhausted treasuries of the Emperors Maximilian and Charles V. In 1506 they raised a loan of 170,000 ducats to the former in eight weeks. Some thirty years later, when Charles returned from his campaign against Tunis, he was entertained at Augsburg in magnificent style by Anthony Fugger. "I feel myself," said the host, "so amply repaid by the honor of this visit, that this bond now becomes useless;" and suiting the action to the word, he burned in a fire of cinnamon the document which he held as security from the Emperor for a heavy loan of 800,000 florins in aid of the war. Well might Charles afterwards exclaim, when he was shown the crown jewels at Paris, "I know a weaver in Augsburg that could buy all that!" The merchant, however, lost nothing by his princely liberality, for he received in return the privilege of working several rich mines of mercury and silver. The Fuggers were also empowered to coin and issue money of their own. Maximilian granted them patents of nobility; and in the beginning of the seventeenth century the family numbered, in its five branches, forty-seven counts and countesses of the empire, all tracing their origin to the honest linen manufacturer, who had been dead scarcely half a century. The name and family, it is said, are still to be found among the German noblesse; but the living descendants of the patrician stock are reduced in fortune and influence proportionately with the city from which they sprang. The old family mansion in the High Street of Augsburg is still standing, and exhibits on its front brilliant modern frescoes, representing the visits of the Emperors Maximilian and Charles V., who were entertained within its walls. The Fuggers were a liberal, high-souled race, who did not value money merely for its own sake. They were exceedingly charitable, and founded several hospitals and alms-houses. An entire quarter of their native city was built by them for the accommodation of poor people at low rents, and still bears their name. They also did all they could to keep down the price of corn to its minimum point, in order that bread might be cheap. Valuable libraries were founded by several members of the family; and Anthony the Rich was the friend of Erasmus and one of the patrons of Titian. —FYFE.

## KING ALFRED.
### (A.D. 849—901.)

A PRINCE who gave very early marks of those great virtues and shining talents by which, during the most difficult times, he saved his country from utter ruin and subversion. Ethelwolf his father, the year after his return with Alfred from Rome, had again sent the young prince thither with a numerous retinue; and a report being spread of the king's death, Leo III. gave Alfred the royal unction,—whether prognosticating his future greatness from the appearances of his pregnant genius, or willing to pretend, even in that age, to the right of conferring kingdoms. Alfred on his return home became every day more the object of his father's affection; but being indulged in all youthful pleasures, he was much neglected in his education, and he had already reached his twelfth year, when he was yet totally ignorant of the lowest elements of literature. His

genius was first roused by the recital of Saxon
the queen took great delight, and this spec
which is sometimes able to make a considerab
among barbarians, expanded those noble an
ments which he had received from nature.  E
queen, and stimulated by his own ardent inc
learned to read these compositions, and pre
acquire the knowledge of the Latin tongue,
with authors that better prompted his heroic sp
his generous views.

Absorbed in these elegant pursuits, he regar
to royalty rather as an object of regret than
being called to the throne in preference to his b
as well by the will of his father,—a circums
great authority with the Anglo-Saxons,—as b
whole nation and the urgency of public affairs
literary indolence and exerted himself in th
people.

The merit of this great prince, both in p
life, may with advantage be set in oppositior
monarch or citizen which the annals of any
can present to us.  He seems, indeed, to be t
perfect character, which, under the denomina
wise man, philosophers have been fond of deli
a fiction of their imagination than in hopes
really existing—so happily were all his virtue
ther, so justly were they blended, and so pov
prevent the other from exceeding its proper
knew how to reconcile the most enterprisin
coolest moderation, the most obstinate perse
easiest flexibility, the most severe justice
lenity, the greatest vigor in commanding wi
fect affability of deportment, the highest ca
nation for science with the most shining talen
civil and military virtues are almost equally t
admiration, excepting only that the former,
among princes as well as more useful, seem cl
our applause.  Nature also, as if desirous tha
duction of her skill should be set in the fai
stowed on him every bodily accomplishment,
dignity of shape and air, with a pleasing, en

countenance. Fortune alone, by throwing him into that barbarous age, deprived him of historians worthy to transmit his fate to posterity; and we wish to see him delineated in more lively colors, and with more particular strokes, that we may at least discover some of those small specks and blemishes, from which, as a man, it is impossible he could be entirely exempted.

But we should give but an imperfect idea of Alfred's merit were we to confine our narrative to his military exploits, and were not more particular in our account of his institutions for the execution of justice, and of his zeal for the encouragement of arts and sciences. The most effectual expedient employed by Alfred for the encouragement of learning was his own example, and the constant assiduity with which, notwithstanding the multiplicity and urgency of his affairs, he employed himself in the pursuits of knowledge. He usually divided his time into three equal portions: one was employed in sleep and the refection of his body by diet and exercise; another in the despatch of business; a third in study and devotion; and that he might more exactly measure the hours, he made use of burning tapers of equal length, which he fixed in lanterns—an expedient suited to that rude age, when the geometry of dialling, and the mechanism of clocks and watches were entirely unknown. And by such a regular distribution of his time, though he often labored under great bodily infirmities, this martial hero, who fought in person fifty-six battles by sea and land, was able, during a life of no extraordinary length, to acquire more knowledge, and even to compose more books, than most studious men, though blessed with the greatest leisure and application, have in more fortunate ages made the object of their uninterrupted industry. Both living and dead, Alfred was regarded by foreigners, no less than by his own subjects, as the greatest prince after Charlemagne that had appeared in Europe during several ages, and as one of the wisest and best that ever adorned the annals of any nation. —HUME.

## THE LIGHT OF HOME.

My boy, thou wilt dream the world is fair,
And thy spirit will sigh to roam,
And thou must go, but never when there
Forget the light of Home.

Though pleasure may smile with a ray more bright,
　　It dazzles to lead astray;
Like the meteor's flash 't will deepen the night,
　　When thou treadest the lonely way.

But the hearth of Home has a constant flame,
　　And pure as vestal fire:
'T will burn, 't will burn for ever the same,
　　For nature feeds the pyre.

The sea of ambition is tempest-tost,
　　And thy hopes may vanish like foam;
But when sails are shivered, and rudder lost,
　　Then look to the light of Home:—

And then like a star through the midnight cloud,
　　Thou shalt see the beacon bright,
For never, till shining on thy shroud,
　　Can be quenched its holy light.

The sun of fame?—'t will gild the name,
　　But the heart ne'er felt its ray;
And fashion's smiles that rich ones claim,
　　Are but beams of a wintry day.

And how cold and dim these beams must be,
　　Should life's wretched wanderer come!
But my boy, when the world is dark to thee,
　　Then turn to the light of Home.　　—Mrs. Hale.

## DISCRETION.

There are many more shining qualities in the mind of man, but there is none so useful as discretion; it is this, indeed, which gives a value to all the rest, which sets them at work in their proper times and places, and turns them to the advantage of the person who is possessed of them. Though a man has all other perfections, and wants this one, he will be of no great consequence in the world; but, if he has this single talent in perfection, and but a common share of others, he may do what he pleases in his particular station of life. At the same time that I think discretion the most useful talent a man can be master of, I look upon cunning to be the accomplishment of little, mean, ungenerous minds. Discretion points out the noblest ends to us, and pursues the most proper and laudable means of attaining them; cunning has only private, selfish aims, and sticks at nothing which may make them succeed. Discretion has large and extended views, and, like a well-formed eye, commands a whole horizon; cunning is a kind of shortsightedness that discovers the minutest objects which are near at hand, but is not able to discern things at a distance.

Discretion, the more it is discovered, gives a greater authority to the person who possesses it; cunning, when it is once detected, loses its force, and makes a man incapable of bringing about even those events which he might have done had he passed only for a plain man. Discretion is the perfection of reason, and a guide to us in all the duties of life: cunning is a kind of instinct that only looks after our immediate interest and welfare. Discretion is only found in men of strong sense and good understanding: cunning is often to be met with in brutes themselves, and in persons who are but the fewest removes from them. In short, cunning is only the mimic of discretion, and may pass upon weak men, in the same manner as vivacity is often mistaken for wit, and gravity for wisdom.

The cast of mind which is natural to a discreet man, makes him look forward into futurity, and consider what will be his condition millions of ages hence, as well as what it is at present. He knows that the misery or happiness which are reserved for him in another world, lose nothing of their reality by being placed at so great a distance from him. The objects do not appear little to him because they are remote. He considers that those pleasures and pains which lie hid in eternity, approach nearer to him every moment, and will be present with him in their full weight and measure, as much as those pains and pleasures which he feels at this very instant. For this reason he is careful to secure to himself that which is the proper business of his nature, and the ultimate design of his being. He carries his thoughts to the end of every action, and considers the most distant, as well as the most immediate, effects of it. He supersedes every little prospect of gain and advantage which offers itself here, if he does not find it consistent with the views of a hereafter. In a ord, his hopes are full of immortality, his schemes are large and glorious, and his conduct suitable to one who knows his true interests, and how to pursue it by proper methods. I have, in this essay upon discretion, considered it both as an accomplishment and as a virtue, and have therefore described it in its full extent, not only as it is the guide of a mortal creature, but as it is in general the director of a reasonable being. It is in this light that discretion is represented by the wise man, who sometimes mentions it under the name of discretion, and sometimes under that of wisdom. It is, indeed, as described in the latter part of this paper, the greatest wisdom, but, at the same time, in the power of every one to attain. Its advantages are infinite, but its acquisition is easy.

—ADDISON.

## MAZEPPA.

"BRING forth the horse!"—The horse was brought:
  In truth he was a noble steed,
  A Tartar of the Ukraine breed,
Who look'd as though the speed of thought
Were in his limbs; but he was wild,
  Wild as the wild deer, and untaught.
With spur and bridle undefil'd—
  'Twas but a day he had been caught;
And snorting with erected mane,
And struggling fiercely but in vain;
In the full foam of wrath and dread
To me the desert-born was led;
They bound me on, that menial throng,
Upon his back with many a thong;
Then loosed him with a sudden lash—
Away!—away!—and on we dash!
Torrents less rapid and less rash.

Away!—away!—my breath was gone,
I saw not where he hurried on:
'Twas scarcely yet the break of day,
And on he foam'd—away!—away!
The last of human sounds that rose,
As I was darting from my foes,
Was the wild shout of savage laughter,
Which on the wind came roaring after
A moment from that rabble rout:
With sudden wrath I wrench'd my head,
  And snapp'd the cord, which to the mane
Had bound my neck in lieu of rein;
And, writhing half my form about,
Hurl'd back my curse; but 'midst the tread,
The thunder of my courser's speed,
Perchance they did not hear nor heed;
It vexes me—for I would fain
Have paid their insult back again.

Away, away, my steed and I,
  Upon the pinions of the wind,

All human dwellings left behind,
We speed like meteors through the sky,
Town—village—none were on our track,
  But a wild plain of far extent,
And bounded by a forest black.
The sky was dull, and dim, and grey,
  And a low breeze crept moaning by—
  I could have answer'd with a sigh—
But fast we fled away, away—
And I could neither sigh nor pray;
And my cold sweat-drops fell like rain
Upon the courser's bristling mane;
But snorting still with rage and fear
He flew upon his far career,
At times I almost thought, indeed,
He must have slackened in his speed;
But no, my bound and slender frame
  Was nothing to his angry might,
And merely like a spur became:
Each motion which I made to free
My swoll'n limbs from agony
  Increased his fury and affright;
I tried my voice—'twas faint and low,
But yet it swerved as from a blow;
And, starting to each accent, sprang
As from a sudden trumpet's clang:
Meantime my cords were wet with gore,
Which, oozing through my limbs, ran o'er;
And in my tongue the thirst became
A something fiercer far than flame.

We near the wild wood—'twas so wide,
I saw no bounds on either side;
'Twas studded with old sturdy trees,
That bent not to the roughest breeze;
But these were few, and far between,
Set thick with shrubs more young and green;
'Twas a wild waste of underwood,
And here and there a chestnut stood,
The strong oak and the hardy pine;
  But far apart—and well it were,
Or else a different lot were mine—
  The boughs gave way, and did not tear
  My limbs; and I found strength to bear
My wounds already scarr'd with cold—
My bonds forbore to loose their hold.

We rustled through the leaves like wind,
Left shrubs, and trees, and wolves behind;
By night I heard them on the track,
Their troop came hard upon our back,
With their long gallop which can tire

The hound's deep hate and hunter's fire:
Wherev'er we flew they follow'd on,
Nor left us with the morning sun;
Behind I saw them, scarce a rood,
At daybreak winding through the wood,
And through the night had heard their feet
Their stealing, rustling step repeat.

Oh! how I wished for spear or sword,
At least to die amidst the horde,
And perish—if it must be so—
At bay, destroying many a foe.
When first my courser' race begun,
I wish'd the goal already won;
But now I doubted strength and speed—
Vain doubt! his swift and savage breed
Had nerv'd him like the mountain roe:
Nor faster falls the blinding snow
Which whelms the peasant near the door,
Whose threshold he shall cross no more,
Bewilder'd by the dazzling blast,
Than through the forest-paths he passed.

   The wood was past: 'twas more than noon,
But chill the air, although in June;
Or it might be my veins ran cold—
Prolong'd endurance tames the bold;
What marvel if this worn-out trunk
Beneath its woes a moment sunk?
The earth gave way, the skies roll'd round,
I seem'd to sink upon the ground:
But err'd, for I was fastly bound.

   My heart turn'd sick, my brain grew sore,
And throbb'd awhile, and beat no more;
The skies spun like a mighty wheel;
I saw the trees like drunkards reel,
And a slight flash sprung o'er my eyes,
Which saw no farther; he who dies
Can die no more than then I died,
O'ertortur'd by that ghastly ride.   —LORD BYRON.

---

## THE FACTIONS OF THE CIRCUS.
### (A.D. 532.)

A MATERIAL difference may be observed in the games of antiquity: the most eminent of the Greeks were actors, the Romans were merely spectators. The Olympic stadium was open to wealth, merit, and ambition; and if the candidates could depend on their personal skill and activity, they might pursue the footsteps of Diomede and Menelaus, and conduct their own horses in the rapid career. Ten, twenty, forty chariots, were allowed to start at the same instant; a crown of leaves was the reward of the victor, and his fame, with that of his family and country, was chanted in lyric strains more durable than monuments of brass and marble. But a senator, or even a citizen, conscious of his dignity, would have blushed to expose his person or his horses in the circus of Rome. The games were exhibited at the expense of the republic, the magistrates or the emperors; but the reins were abandoned to servile hands; and if the profits of a favorite charioteer sometimes exceeded those of an advocate, they must be considered as the effects of popular extravagance, and the high wages of a disgraceful profession. The race, in its first institution, was a simple contest of two chariots, whose drivers were distinguished by *white* and *red* liveries: two additional colors, a light *green* and a cœrulean *blue*, were afterwards introduced; and as the races were repeated twenty-five times, one hundred chariots contributed in the same day to the pomp of the circus. The four *factions* soon acquired a legal establishment and a mysterious origin, and their fanciful colors were derived from the various appearances of nature in the four seasons of the year; the red dog-star of summer, the snows of winter, the deep shades of autumn, and the cheerful verdure of the spring. Another interpretation preferred the elements to the seasons, and the struggle of the green and blue was supposed to represent the conflict of the earth and sea. Their respective victories announced either a plentiful harvest or a prosperous navigation, and the hostility of the husbandmen and mariners was somewhat less absurd than the blind ardor of the Roman people, who devoted their lives and fortunes to the color which they had espoused. Such folly was disdained and indulged by the wisest princes; but the names of Caligula, Nero, Vitellius, Verus, Commodus, Caracalla, and Elagabalus, were enrolled in the blue or green factions of the circus: they frequented their stables, applauded their favorites, chastised their antagonists, and deserved the esteem of the populace by the natural or affected imitation of their manners. The bloody and tumultuous contest continued to disturb the public festivity till the last one of the spectacles of Rome; and Theodoric, from a motive of justice or affection, interposed his authoriy to protect the greens against the violence of a consul and a patrician who were passionately addicted to the blue faction of the circus.

Constantinople adopted the follies, though not the virtues, of ancient Rome; and the same factions which had agitated the circus raged with redoubled fury in the hippodrome. Under the reign of Anastasius, this popular frenzy was inflamed by religious zeal; and the greens, who had treacherously concealed stones and daggers under baskets of fruit, massacred at a solemn festival three thousand of their blue adversaries. From the capital this pestilence was diffused into the provinces and cities of the East, and the sportive distinction of two colors produced two strong and irreconcileable factions, which shook the foundations of a feeble government. The popular dissensions, founded on the most serious interest of holy pretence, have scarcely equalled the obstinacy of this wanton discord, which invaded the peace of families, divided friends and brothers, and tempted the female sex though seldom seen in the circus, to espouse the inclinations of their lovers, or to contradict the wishes of their husbands. Every law, either human or divine, was trampled under foot; and as long as the party was successful, its deluded followers appeared careless of private distress or public calamity. The licence, without the freedom of democracy, was revived at Antioch and Constantinople, and the support of a faction became necessary to every candidate for civil or ecclesiastical honours.

A sedition, which almost laid Constantinople in ashes, was excited by the mutual hatred and momentary reconciliation of the two factions. In the fifth year of his reign Justinian celebrated the festival of the ides of January: the games were incessantly disturbed by the clamorous discontent of the greens; till the twenty-second race the emperor maintained his silent gravity; at length, yielding to his impatience, he condescended to hold, in abrupt sentences, and by the voice of a crier, the most singular dialogue that ever passed between a prince and his subjects. Their first complaints were respectful and modest; they accused the subordinate ministers of oppression, and proclaimed their wishes for the long life and victory of the emperor. "Be patient and attentive, ye insolent railers!" exclaimed Justinian; "be mute, ye Jews, Samaritans, and Manichæans!" The greens still attempted to awaken his compassion. "We are poor, we are innocent, we are injured, we dare not pass through the streets: a general persecution is exercised against our name and color. Let us die, O emperor! but let us die by your command, and for your service." But the repetition of partial and passionate invectives degraded, in their eyes, the majesty of the purple; they renounced allegiance to the prince who refused justice to his people, lamented that the father of Justinian had been born, and branded his son with the opprobrious names of an homicide, an ass, and a perjured tyrant. "Do you despise your lives?" cried the indignant monarch. The blues rose with fury from their seats, their hostile clamors thundered in the hippodrome, and their adversaries, deserting the unequal contest, spread terror and despair through the streets of Constantinople. At this dangerous moment, seven notorious assassins of both factions, who had been condemned by the præfect, were carried round the city, and afterwards transported to the place of execution in the suburb of Pera. Four were immediately beheaded; a fifth was hanged; but, when the same punishment was inflicted on the remaining two, the rope broke, they fell alive to the ground, the populace applauded their escape, and the monks of St. Conon, issuing from the neighboring convent, conveyed them in a boat to the sanctuary of the church. As one of these criminals was of the blue, and the other of the green, livery, the two factions were equally provoked by the cruelty of their oppressor or the ingratitude of their patron, and a short truce was concluded till they had delivered their prisoners and satisfied their revenge. The palace of the præfect, who withstood the seditious torrent, was instantly burnt, his officers and guards were massacred, the prisons were forced open, and freedom was restored to those who could only use it for the public destruction. A military force which had been despatched to the aid of the civil magistrate was fiercely encountered by an armed multitude, whose numbers and boldness continually increased: and the Heruli, the wildest barbarians in the service of the empire, overturned the priests and their relics, which, from a pious motive, had been rashly interposed to separate the bloody conflict. The tumult was exasperated by this sacrilege; the people fought with enthusiasm in the cause of God; the women, from the roofs and windows, showered stones on the heads of the soldiers, who darted firebrands against the houses; and the various flames, which had been kindled by the hands of citizens and strangers, spread without control over the face of the city. The conflagration involved the cathedral of St. Sophia, the baths of Zeuxippus, a part of the palace from the first entrance to the altar of Mars, and the long portico from the palace to the forum of Constantine: a large hospital, with the sick patients, was consumed; many churches and stately edifices were destroyed; and an immense treasure of gold and silver was either melted or lost. From such scenes of horror and distress the wise and wealthy citizens escaped over the Bosphorus to the Asiatic side, and during five days Constantinople was abandoned to the factions, whose watchword, NIKA *vanquish*! has given a name to this memorable sedition.

As long as the factions were divided, the triumphant blues and desponding greens appeared to behold with the same indifference the disorders of the state. They agreed to censure the corrupt management of justice and the finance; and the two responsible ministers, the artful Tribonian and the rapacious John of Cappadocia, were loudly arraigned as the authors of the public misery. The peaceful murmurs of the people would have been disregarded: they were heard with respect when the city was in flames; the questor and the præfect were instantly removed, and their offices were filled by two senators of blameless integrity. After this popular concession Justinian proceeded to the Hippodrome to confess his own errors, and to accept the repentance of his grateful subjects; but they distrusted his assurances, though solemnly pronounced in the presence of the holy gospels; and the emperor, alarmed by their distrust, retreated with precipitation to the strong fortress of the palace. The obstinacy of the tumult was now imputed to a secret and ambitious conspiracy, and a suspicion was entertained that the insurgents, more especially the green faction, had been supplied with arms and money by Hypatius and Pompey, two patricians who could neither forget with honor nor remember with safety, that they were the nephews of the emperor Anastasius. Capriciously trusted, disgraced, and pardoned by the jealous levity of the monarch, they had appeared as loyal servants before the throne, and, during five days of the tumult, they were detained as important hostages; till at length, the fears of Justinian prevailing over his prudence, he viewed the two brothers in the light of spies, perhaps of assassins, and sternly commanded them to depart from the palace. After a fruitless representation that obedience might lead to involuntary treason, they retired to their houses, and in the morning of the sixth day Hypatius was surrounded and seized by the people, who, regardless of his virtuous resistance and the tears of his wife, transported their favorite to the forum of Constantine, and, instead of a diadem, placed a rich collar on his head. If the usurper, who afterwards pleaded the merit of his delay, had complied with the advice of his senate, and urged the fury of the multitude, their first irresistible effort might have oppressed or expelled his trembling competitor. The Byzantine palace enjoyed a free communication with the sea, vessels lay ready at the garden-stairs, and a secret resolution was already formed to convey the emperor with his family and treasures to a safe retreat at some distance from the capital.

Justinian was lost, if Theodora had not renounced the timidity as well as the virtues of her sex. In the midst of a council where Belisarius was present, she alone displayed the spirit of an hero, and she alone, without apprehending his future hatred, could save the emperor from the imminent danger and his unworthy fears. "If flight," said the consort of Justinian, "were the only means of safety, yet I should disdain to fly. Death is the condition of our birth, but they who have reigned should never survive the loss of dignity and dominion. I implore Heaven that I may never be seen, not a day, without my diadem and purple; that I may no longer behold the light when I cease to be saluted with the name of queen. If you resolve, O Cæsar! to fly, you have treasures; behold the sea, you have ships; but tremble lest the desire of life should expose you to wretched exile and ignominious death. For my own part, I adhere to the maxim of antiquity, that the throne is a glorious sepulchre." The firmness of a woman restored the courage to deliberate and act, and courage soon discovers the resources of the most desperate situation. It was an easy and a decisive measure to revive the animosity of the factions. The blues were astonished at their own guilt and folly, that a trifling injury should provoke them to conspire with their implacable enemies against a gracious and liberal benefactor; they again proclaimed the majesty of Justinian; and the greens, with their upstart em, peror, were left alone in the hippodrome. The fidelity of the guards was doubtful; but the military force of Justinian consisted in three thousand veterans, who had been trained to valor and discipline in the Persian and Illyrian wars. Under the command of Belisarius and Mundus, they silently marched in two divisions from the palace, forced their obscure way through narrow passages, expiring flames, and falling edifices, and burst open at the same moment the two opposite gates of the hippodrome. In this narrow space the disorderly and affrighted crowd was incapable of resisting on either side a firm and regular attack; the blues signalized the fury of their repentance, and it is computed that above thirty thousand persons were slain in the merciless and promiscuous carnage of the day. Hypatius was dragged from his throne, and conducted with his brother Pompey to the feet of the emperor; they implored his clemency, but their crime was manifest, their innocence uncertain, and Justinian had been too much terrified to forgive. The next morning, the two nephews of Anastasius, with eighteen *illustrious* accomplices, of patrician or consular rank, were privately executed by the soldiers, their bodies were thrown into the sea, their palaces razed, and their fortunes confiscated. The hippodrome itself was condemned, during several years, to a mournful silence; with the restoration of the games the same disorders revived, and the blue and green factions continued to afflict the reign of Justinian, and to disturb the tranquillity of the Eastern empire. —GIBBON.

## I GIVE MY SOLDIER BOY A BLADE.

I give my soldier boy a blade,
  In fair Damascus fashion'd well;
Who first the glitt'ring falchion sway'd,
  Who first beneath its fury fell,
I know not, but I hope to know
  That for no mean or hireling trade,
To guard no feeling, base or low,
  I give my soldier boy a blade.

Cool, calm, and clear, the lucid flood
  In which its tempering work was done,
As calm, as clear, as cool of mood,
  Be thou whene'er it sees the sun;
For country's claim, at honor's call,
  For outraged friend, insulted maid,
At mercy's voice to bid it fall,
  I give my soldier boy a blade.

## THE NUBIAN.

The eye which mark'd its peerless edge,
　The hand that weigh'd its balanced poise,
Anvil and pinchers, forge and wedge,
　Are gone, with all their flame and noise—
And still the gleaming sword remains ;
　So, when in dust I lie with land,
Remember, by those heartfelt strains,
　I gave my soldier boy a blade. —MAGINN.

## THE NUBIAN.

*(The scene is laid in the English quarter of the Camp of the Crusaders.)*

RICHARD surveyed the Nubian in silence as he stood before him, his looks bent upon the ground, his arms folded on his bosom, with the appearance of a black marble statue of the most exquisite workmanship, waiting life from the touch of a Promethean. The king of England, who, as is well known, emphatically said of himself, "I am that I am," looked long upon him ; and A MAN, was well pleased with the thews, sinews, and symmetry of him whom he surveyed, and questioned him in the lingua Franca, "Art thou a pagan ?"

The slave shook his head, and raising his finger to his brow, crossed himself in token of his Christianity, then resumed his posture of motionless humility.

"A Nubian Christian, doubtless," said Richard, " and mutilated of the organ of speech by these heathen dogs ?"

The mute again slowly shook his head, in token of negative, pointed with his forefinger to Heaven, and then laid it upon his own lips.

"I understand thee," said Richard ; " thou dost suffer under the infliction of God, not by the cruelty of man. Canst thou clean an armour and belt, and buckle it in time of need ?"

The mute nodded, and stepping towards the coat of mail, which hung with the shield and helmet of the chivalrous monarch, upon the pillar of the tent, he handled it with such nicety of address, as sufficiently to show that he fully understood the business of the armor-bearer.

" Thou art an apt, and wilt doubtless be a useful knave—thou shall wait in my chamber, and on my person," said the King, " to show how much I value the gift of the royal Soldan. If thou hast no tongue, it follows thou canst carry no tales, neither provoke me to be sudden by any unfit reply."

The Nubian again prostrated himself till his brow touched the earth, then stood erect, at some paces distant, as waiting for his new master's commands.

"Nay, thou shalt commence thy office presently," said Richard, " for I see a speck of rust darkening on that shield ; and when I shake it in the face of Saladin, it should be bright and unsullied as the Soldan's honor and mine own."

A horn was winded without, and presently Sir Henry Neville entered with a packet of despatches.—" From England, my lord," he said, as he delivered it.

" From England—our own England !" repeated Richard, in a tone of melancholy enthusiasm—"Alas ! they little think how hard their Sovereign has been beset by sickness and sorrow—faint friends and forward enemies." Then opening the despatches, he said, hastily, " Ha ! this comes from no peaceful land—they too have their feuds.—Neville, begone—I must peruse these tidings alone, and at leisure."

Neville withdrew accordingly, and Richard was soon absorbed in the melancholy details which had been conveyed to him from England, concerning the factions that were tearing to pieces his native dominions—the disunion of his brothers, John and Geoffrey, and the quarrels of both with the High Justiciary Longchamp, Bishop of Ely,—the oppressions practised by the nobles upon the peasantry, and rebellion of the latter against their masters, which had produced every where scenes of discord, and in some instances the effusion of blood. Details of incidents mortifying to his pride, and derogatory from his authority, were intermingled with the earnest advice of his wisest and most attached counsellors, that he should presently return to England, as his presence offered the only hope of saving the kingdom from all the horrors of civil discord, of which France and Scotland were likely to avail themselves. Filled with the most painful anxiety, Richard read, and again read, the ill-omened letters, compared the intelligence which some of them contained with the same facts as differently stated in others, and soon became totally insensible to whatever was passing around him, although seated, for the sake of coolness, close to the entrance of his tent, and having the curtains withdrawn, so that he could see and be seen by the guards and others who were stationed without.

Deeper in the shadow of the pavilion, and busied with the

task his new master had imposed, sat the Nubian slave, with his back rather turned towards the King. He had finished adjusting and cleaning the hauberk and brigandine, and was now busily employed on a broad pavesse, or buckler, of unusual size, and covered with steel-plating, which Richard often used in reconnoitring, or actually storming, fortified places, as a more effectual protection against missile weapons, than the narrow triangular shield used on horseback. This pavesse bore neither the royal lions of England, nor any other device, to attract the observation of the defenders of the walls against which it was advanced; the care, therefore, of the armorer was addressed to causing its surface to shine as bright as crystal, in which he seemed to be peculiarly successful. Beyond the Nubian, and scarce visible from without, lay the large dog, which might be termed his brother slave, and which, as if he felt awed by being transferred to a royal owner, was couched close to the side of the mute, with head and ears on the ground, and his limbs and tail drawn close around and under him.

While the Monarch and his new attendant were thus occupied, another actor crept upon the scene, and mingled among the group of English yeomen, about a score of whom, respecting the unusually pensive posture and close occupation of their sovereign, were, contrary to their wont, keeping a silent guard in front of his tent. It was not, however, more vigilant than usual. Some were playing at games of hazard with small pebbles, others spoke together in whispers of the approaching day of battle, and several lay asleep, their bulky limbs folded in their green mantles.

Amid these careless warders glided the puny form of a little old Turk, poorly dressed like a marabout or santon of the desert, a sort of enthusiasts, who sometimes ventured into the camp of the Crusaders, though treated always with contumely, and often with violence. Indeed, the luxury and profligate indulgence of the Christian leaders had occasioned a motley concourse in their tents, of musicians, Jewish merchants, Copts, Turks, and all the varied refuse of the Eastern nations; so that the caftan and turban, though to drive both from the Holy Land was the professed object of the expedition, were nevertheless neither an uncommon nor an alarming sight in the camp of the Crusaders. When, however, the little insignificant figure we have described approached so nigh as to receive some interruption from the warders, he dashed his dusky green turban from his head, showed that his beard and eyebrows were shaved like those of a professed buffoon, and that the expression of his fantastic and writhen features, as well as of his little black eyes, which glittered like jet, was that of a crazed imagination.

"Dance, marabout," cried the soldiers, acquainted with the manners of these wandering enthusiasts—"dance, or we will scourge thee with our bow-strings, till thou spin as never top did under school-boy's lash."—Thus shouted the reckless warders, as much delighted at having a subject to tease, as a child when he catches a butterfly, or a schoolboy upon discovering a bird's nest.

The marabout, as if happy to do their behests, bounded from the earth, and spun his giddy round before them with singular agility, which, when contrasted with his slight and wasted figure, and diminutive appearance, made him resemble a withered leaf twirled round and around at the pleasure of the winter's breeze. His single lock of hair streamed upwards from his bald and shaven head, as if some genie upheld him by it; and indeed it seemed as if supernatural art were necessary to the execution of the wild whirling dance, in which scarce the tiptoe of the performer was seen to touch the ground. Amid the vagaries of his performance, he flew here and there, from one spot to another, still approaching, however, though almost imperceptibly, to the entrance of the royal tent; so that, when at length he sunk exhausted on the earth, after two or three bounds still higher than those which he had yet executed, he was not above thirty yards from the King's person.

For the space of a quarter of an hour, or longer, after the incident related, all remained perfectly quiet in the front of the royal habitation. The King read, and mused in the entrance of his pavilion behind, and with his back turned to the same entrance, the Nubian slave still lay, as had the triple pass——— in front of all, at an hundred paces distant, the y——— men of the sword stood, sat, or lay stretched on the grass, attentive to their own posts, but pursuing them in silence, only on the esplanade between them and the front of the tent, lay, ———, to be distinguished from a bundle of rags, the ——— form of the marabout.

But the Nubian had the advantage of a mirror, from the brilliant reflection which the surface of the highly polished shield now afforded, by means of which he beheld, to his alarm and surprise, that the marabout raised his head gently from the ground, so as to survey all around him, moving with a well-adjusted precaution, which seemed entirely inconsistent with a state of ebriety. He couched his head instantly, as if satisfied he was unobserved, and began, with the slightest possible appearance of voluntary effort, to drag himself, as if by chance, ever nearer and nearer to the King, but stopping, and remaining fixed at intervals, like the spider, which, moving towards her object, collapses into apparent lifelessness, when she thinks she is the subject of observation. This species of movement appeared suspicious to the Ethiopian, who, on his part, prepared himself, as quietly as possible, to interfere, the instant that interference should seem to be necessary.

The marabout meanwhile glided on gradually and imperceptibly, serpent-like, or rather snail-like, till he was about ten yards' distance from Richard's person, when, starting on his feet, he sprung forward with the bound of a tiger, stood at the King's back in less than an instant, and brandished aloft the cangiar, or poniard, which he had hidden in his sleeve. Not the presence of his whole army could have saved their heroic Monarch—but the motions of the Nubian had been as well calculated as those of the enthusiast, and ere the latter could strike, the former caught his uplifted arm. Turning his fanatical wrath upon what thus unexpectedly interposed betwixt him and his object, the Charegite, for such was the seeming marabout, dealt the Nubian a blow with the dagger, which, however, only grazed his arm, while the far superior strength of the Ethiopian easily dashed him to the ground. Aware of what had passed, Richard had now arisen, and with little more of surprise, anger, or interest of any kind in his countenance, than an ordinary man would show in brushing off and crushing an intrusive wasp, caught up the stool on which he had been sitting, and exclaiming only, "Ha, dog!" dashed almost to pieces the skull of the assassin, who uttered twice, once in a loud, and once in a broken tone, the words "Allah ackbar!" —God is victorious—and expired at the King's feet.

"Ye are careful warders," said Richard to his archers, in a tone of scornful reproach, as, aroused by the bustle of what had passed, in terror and tumult they now rushed into his tent;—" watchful sentinels ye are, to leave me to do such hangman's work with my own hand.—Be silent all of you, and cease your senseless clamor! saw ye never a dead Turk before?—Here—cast that carrion out of the camp, strike the head from the trunk, and stick it on a lance, taking care to turn the face to Mecca, that he may the easier tell the foul impostor, on whose inspiration he came hither, how he has sped on his errand.—For thee, my swart and silent friend," he added, turning to the Ethiopian—" But how's this?—thou art wounded—and with a poisoned weapon, I warrant me, for by force of stab so weak an animal as that could scarce hope to do more than raze the lion's hide.—Suck the poison from his wound one of you—the venom is harmless on the lips, though fatal when it mingles with the blood."

The yeomen looked on each other confusedly and with hesitation, the apprehension of so strange a danger prevailing with those who feared no other.

"How now, sirrahs," continued the King, "are you dainty-lipped, or do you fear death, that you dally thus?"

"Not the death of a man," said Long Allan, to whom the King looked as he spoke; "but methinks I would not die like a poisoned rat for the sake of a black chattel there, that is bought and sold in a market like a Martlemas ox."

"His Grace speaks to men of sucking poison," muttered another yeoman, "as if he said, Go to, swallow a gooseberry!"

"Nay," said Richard, "I never bade man do that which I would not do myself."

And, without farther ceremony, and in spite of the general expostulations of those around, and the respectful opposition of the Nubian himself, the King of England applied his lips to the wound of the black slave, treating with ridicule all remonstrances, and overpowering all resistance. He had no sooner intermitted his singular occupation, than the Nubian started from him, and, casting a scarf over his arm, intimated by gestures, as firm in purpose as they were respectful in manner, his determination not to permit the Monarch to renew so degrading an employment. Long Allan also interposed, saying, that if it were necessary to prevent the King engaging again in a treatment of this kind, his own lips, tongue and teeth, were at the service of the negro, (as he called the

Ethiopian,) and that he would eat him up bodily, rather than King Richard's mouth should again approach him.

Neville, who entered with other officers, added his remonstrances.

"Nay, nay, make not a needless halloo about a hart that the hounds have lost, or a danger when it is over," said the King—"the wound will be a trifle, for the blood is scarce drawn—an angry cat had dealt a deeper scratch—and for me, I have but to take a drachm of orvietan by way of precaution, though it is needless."

Thus spoke Richard, a little ashamed, perhaps, of his own condescension, though sanctioned both by humanity and gratitude. But when Neville continued to make remonstrances on the peril to his royal person, the King imposed silence on him.

"Peace, I prithee—make no more of it—I did it but to show these ignorant prejudiced knaves how they might help each other when these cowardly caitiffs come against us with sarbacanes and poisoned shafts. —SCOTT.

## THE SPILT PEARLS.

His courtiers of the Caliph crave,—
"Oh, say how this may be,
That of thy slaves, this Ethiop slave
Is best beloved by thee?

"For he is ugly as the Night;
But when has ever chose
A nightingale, for its delight,
A hueless, scentless rose?"

The Caliph, then :—"No features fair,
Nor comely mien, are his;
Love is the beauty he doth wear,
And Love his glory is.

"When once a camel of my train
There fell in narrow street,
From broken casket roll'd amain
Rich pearls before my feet.

"I winking to the slaves that I
Would freely give them these,
At once upon the spoil they fly,
The costly boon to seize.

"One only at my side remained—
Beside this Ethiop none :
He, moveless as the steed he reined,
Behind me sat alone.

"'What will thy gain, good fellow, be,
  Thus lingering at my side?'
'My king, that I shall faithfully
  Have guarded thee,' he cried.

"True servant's title he may wear
  He only who has not,
For his Lord's gifts, how rich soe'er,
  His Lord himself forgot."

So thou alone dost walk before
  Thy God with perfect aim,
From Him desiring nothing more
  Besides Himself to claim.

For if thou not to Him aspire,
  But to His gifts alone,
Not Love, but covetous desire,
  Has brought thee to His throne.

While such thy prayer, it climbs above
  In vain—the golden key
Of God's rich treasure-house of love,
  Thine own will never be.           —TRENCH.

## CORAL REEF.

THE examination of a coral reef during the different stages of one tide is particularly interesting. When the sea has left it for some time, it becomes dry, and appears to be a compact rock exceedingly hard and ragged; but no sooner does the tide rise again, and the waves begin to wash over it, than millions of coral worms protrude themselves from holes on the surface which were before quite invisible. These animals are of a great variety of shapes and sizes, and in such prodigious numbers, that in a short time the whole surface of the rock appears to be alive and in motion.

The most common of the worms at Loo Choo (an island in the Pacific ocean near China), has the form of a star, with arms from four to six inches long, which it moves about with a rapid motion in all directions, probably in search of food. Others were also seen, but they are often mistaken for pieces of the rock; for a few moments, of a darker color, and from four to five inches long, are not uncommon. When the rock was completely under water, or rather at the level of high water, it was difficult to find any alive ones; but if any part of it were deep pool of salt water which the tide reached over, day, it was discovered to be full of worms, all of different lengths and colors, some being three or four inches and several feet long, one really of a very bright yellow, and sometimes of a blue color;

while others resembled snails, and some were not unlike lobsters and prawns in shape, but soft, and not above two inches long.

The growth of coral ceases when the worm which creates it is no longer exposed to the washing of the tide. Thus a reef rises in the form of a gigantic cauliflower, till its top has gained the level of the highest tides, above which the worm has no power to carry its operations, and the reef, consequently, no longer extends itself upward. The surrounding parts, however, advance in succession till they reach the surface, where they also must stop. Thus, as the level of the highest tide is the eventual limit to every part of the reef, a horizontal field comes to be formed coincident with that plane, and perpendicular on all sides. The reef, however, continually increases, and being prevented from going higher, must extend itself laterally in all directions; and this growth being probably as rapid at the upper edge as it is lower down, the steepness of the face of the reef is preserved; and it is this circumstance which renders this species of rock so dangerous to navigation. In the first place, they are seldom seen above the water; and in the next, their sides are so abrupt that a ship's bows may strike against the rock before any change of soundings indicates the approach of danger.

For a long time it was supposed that the coral formations were raised from the floor of the fathomless ocean by the unaided efforts of these little creatures, but more accurate observations have proved that the animals cease to live at a greater depth than twenty or thirty fathoms. As some of these islands are elevated 200 and 300 feet above the sea level, it is evident that they must have been raised by submarine forces; in short that the volcano and the earthquake must have been employed in rearing them to their present elevation. Mr. Darwin has traced those regions throughout the Pacific, in which upheaval and depression alternately prevail. Thus a band of *atolls*, and encircled islands, including the Dangerous and Society archipelagoes, constitutes an area of subsidence more than 4,000 miles long and 600 broad. To the westward, the chain of *fringing reefs*, embracing the islands of the New Hebrides, Solomon, and New Ireland, form an area of elevated coral. Farther westward, another area of subsidence is met with, including the islands of New Caledonia, and the Australian barrier.  —HALL,

## THE REAPER AND THE FLOWERS.

There is a Reaper, whose name is Death,
   And, with his sickle keen,
He reaps the bearded grain at a breath,
   And the flowers that grow between.

"Shall I have nought that is fair?" saith he;
   "Have nought but the bearded grain?
Though the breath of these flowers is sweet to me,
   I will give them all back again."

He gazed at the flowers with tearful eyes.
   He kissed their drooping leaves;
It was for the Lord of Paradise
   He bound them in his sheaves.

"My Lord has need of these flowerets gay,"
   The Reaper said, and smiled;
"Dear tokens of the earth are they,
   Where he was once a child.

"They shall all bloom in fields of light,
   Transplanted by my care,
And saints upon their garments white,
   These sacred blossoms wear."

And the mother gave, in tears and pain,
   The flowers she most did love;
She knew she should find them all again
   In the fields of light above.

Oh, not in cruelty, not in wrath,
   The Reaper came that day;
'Twas an angel visited the green earth,
   And took the flowers away.   —Longfellow.

## BEAVER TRAPPING.

It is now day. The upper edge of the sun has just risen, r[ed] and frosty looking, in the east, and countless myriads of i[ce] particles glitter on every tree and bush in its red rays; whi[le] the white tops of the snow drifts, which dot the surface of t[he] small lake at which we have just arrived, are tipped with t[he] same rosy hue. The lake is of considerable breadth, and t[he] woods on its opposite shore are barely visible. An unbroke[n] coat of pure white snow covers its entire surface, while [here] and there a small islet, covered with luxuriant evergreen[s] attracts the eye, and breaks the sameness of the scene. At the extreme left of the lake, where the points of a few bulrushes and sedgy plants appear above the snow, are seen a number of small earthy mounds, in the immediate vicinity of which the trees and bushes are cut and barked in many places, while some of them are nearly cut down. This is a colony of beaver. In the warm months of summer and autumn, this spot is a lively stirring place, as the beavers are then employed *nibbling* down trees and bushes for the purpose of repairing their dams, and supplying their store-houses with food. The bark of willows is their chief food, and all the bushes in the vicinity are more or less cut through by these persevering little animals. Their dams, however, (which are made for the purpose of securing to themselves a constant sufficiency of water) are made with large trees; and stumps will be found, if you choose to look for them, as thick as a man's leg, which the beavers have entirely nibbled through, and dragged by their united efforts many yards from where they grew.

Now, however, no sign of animal life is to be seen, as the beaver keeps within doors all winter: yet I venture to state that there are many now asleep under the snow before us. It is not, reader, merely for the purpose of showing you the outside of a beaver lodge that I have brought you such a distance from human habitations. Be patient and you shall soon see more. Do you observe that small black speck moving over the white surface of the lake, far away on the horizon? It looks like a crow, but the forward motion is much too steady and constant for that. As it approaches it assumes the form of a man, and at last the figure of an Indian, dragging his empty sleigh behind him, becomes clearly distinguishable through the dreamy haze of the cold wintry morning. He arrives at the beaver-lodges, and, I warrant, will soon create some havoc among the inmates.

His first proceeding is to cut down several stakes, which he points at the ends. These are driven, after he has cut away a good deal of ice from around the beaver-lodge, into the ground between it and the shore. The reason of this is to prevent the beaver from running along the passage which they always have from their lodges to the shore, where their store-house is kept, which would make it necessary to excavate the whole passage. The beaver, if there are any, being thus imprisoned in the lodge, the hunter next proceeds to stake up the opening into the storehouse on shore, and so imprison those that may have fled there for shelter on hearing the noise of his axe at the other house. Things being thus arranged to his entire satisfaction, he takes an instrument called an i------, which is ......... about a foot long, by one inch broad, fastened to the end of a stout pole, wherewith he proceeds to dig through ........ This is by no means an easy operation; en........ ........ covered the snow around him with a great quantity of ....... and sticks, yet his work is not half finished. In ......... of time, however, the interior of the hut is laid bare, and ........... stooping down, gives a great pull when ........ ........ ....... heaver, which he flings sprawling on ............ being thus unceremoniously awakened from his ............. ........ ....... animal looks long half round, and even ......... ........ of making a face at his captor by way of ........ ........ ........ with it is rewarded with a blow on the head from the pole of the poleaxe, which puts an end to it. In this way several more are killed, and packed on the sleigh. The hunter then turns his face towards his encampment, and goes off at a tremendous pace, dashing the snow in clouds from his snow-shoes, as he hurries over the trackless wilderness to his forest home.

—BALLANTYNE.

---

## THE BATTLE OF KILLIECRANKIE.

### (A. D. 1689.)

EARLY in the morning of Saturday, the 27th of July, Dundee arrived at Blair Castle. There he learned that Mackay's troops were already in the ravine of Killiecrankie. It was necessary to come to a prompt decision. A council of war was held. The Saxon officers were generally against hazarding a battle. The Celtic chiefs were of a different opinion. Glengarry and Lochiel were now both of a mind. "Fight, my Lord," said Lochiel with his usual energy; "fight immediately: fight, if you have only one to three. Our men are in heart. Their only fear is that the enemy should escape. Give them their way; and be assured that they will either perish or gain a complete victory. But if you restrain them, if you force them to remain on the defensive, I answer for nothing. If we do not fight, we had better break up and retire to our mountains."

Dundee's countenance brightened. "You hear, gentlemen," he said to his lowland officers; "you hear the opinion of one who understands Highland war better than any of us." No voice was raised on the other side. It was determined to fight; and the order was given to the Highlanders to advance to encounter the enemy.

The enemy meanwhile had made his way up the pass. The ascent had, in one place, been so steep that for every three soldiers to climb by trees and bushes; and the baggage horses, two hundred in number, could mount only one at a time. No vehicle carriage had ever been tugged up that rugged path. The head of the column had emerged and was on the table land, while the rear guard was still in the plain below. Yet, looking at the passes was effected, and it took the best of the day to a valley of no great extent. Their right was flanked by a rising ground, their left by the Garry. Weary with their long march work, they threw themselves on the grass to take some refreshments.

Early in the afternoon they were roused by an alarm that the Highlanders were approaching. Regiment after regiment started up and got into order. In a little while the summit of an ascent which was about a musket shot before them was covered with bonnets and plaids. Dundee rode forward for the purpose of surveying the force with which he was to contend, and then drew up his own men with as much skill as their peculiar character permitted him to exert.

Meanwhile a fire of musketry was kept up on both sides, but more skilfully and more steadily by the regular soldiers than by the mountaineers. The space between the armies was one cloud of smoke. Not a few Highlanders dropped, and the clans grew impatient. The sun, however, was low in the west before Dundee gave the order to prepare for action. His men raised a great shout. The enemy, probably exhausted by the toil of the day, returned a feeble and wavering cheer. "We shall do it now," said Lochiel: "that is not the cry of men who are going to win." He had walked through all his ranks, had addressed a few words to every Cameron, and had taken from every Cameron a promise to conquer or die.

It was past seven o'clock. Dundee gave the word. The Highlanders dropped their plaids. The few who were so luxurious as to wear rude socks of untanned hide spurned them away. It was long remembered in Lochaber that Lochiel took off what probably was the only pair of shoes in his clan, and charged barefoot at the head of his men. The whole line advanced firing. The enemy returned the fire and did much execution. When only a small space was left between the armies, the Highlanders suddenly flung away their firelocks, drew their broadswords, and rushed forward with a fearful yell. The Lowlanders prepared to receive the shock; but this was then a long and awkward process; and the soldiers were still fumbling with the muzzles of their guns and the handles of their bayonets when the whole flood of Macleans, Macdonalds, and Camerons came down. In two minutes the battle was lost and won. The ranks of Balfour's regiment broke. He was cloven down while struggling in the press. Ramsay's men turned their backs and dropped their arms. Mackay's own foot were swept away by the furious onset of the Camerons. His brother and nephew exerted themselves in vain to rally the men. The former was laid dead on the ground by a stroke from a claymore. The latter, with eight wounds on his body, made his way through the tumult and carnage to his uncle's side. Even in that extremity Mackay retained all his self-possession. He had still one hope. A charge of horse might recover the day; for of horse the bravest Highlanders were supposed to stand in awe. But he called on the horse in vain. Belhaven indeed behaved like a gallant gentleman; but his troopers, appalled by the rout of the infantry, galloped off in disorder: Annandale's men followed: all was over; and the mingled torrent of red-coats and tartans went raving down the valley to the gorge of Killiecrankie.

Mackay, accompanied by one trusty servant, spurred bravely through the thickest of the claymores and targets, and reached a point from which he had a view of the field. His whole army had disappeared, with the exception of some Borderers whom Leven had kept together, and of Hastings' regiment, which had poured a murderous fire into the Celtic ranks, and which still kept unbroken order. All the men that could be collected were only a few hundreds. The general made haste to lead them across the Garry, and, having put that river between them and the enemy, paused for a moment to meditate on his situation.

He could hardly understand how the conquerors could be so

unwise as to allow him even that moment for deliberation. They might with ease have killed or taken all who were with him before the night closed in. But the energy of the Celtic warriors had spent itself in one furious rush and one short struggle. The pass was choked by the twelve hundred beasts of burden which carried the provisions and baggage of the vanquished army. Such a booty was irresistibly tempting to men who were impelled to war quite as much by the desire of rapine as by the desire of glory. It is probable that few even of the chiefs were disposed to leave so rich a prize for the sake of King James. Dundee himself might at that moment have been unable to persuade his followers to quit the heaps of spoil, and to complete the great work of the day; but Dundee was no more.

At the beginning of the action he had taken his place in front of his little band of cavalry. He bade them follow him, and rode forward. But it seemed to be decreed that, on that day, the Lowland Scotch should in both armies appear to disadvantage. The horse hesitated. Dundee turned round, stood up in his stirrups, and, waving his hat, invited them to come on. As he lifted his arm, his cuirass rose, and exposed the lower part of his left side. A musket ball struck him; his horse sprang forward and plunged into a cloud of smoke and dust, which hid from both armies the fall of the victorious general. A person named Johnstone was near him and caught him as he sunk down from the saddle. "How goes the day?" said Dundee. "Well for King James," answered Johnstone: "but I am sorry for your Lordship." "If it is well for him," answered the dying man, "it matters the less for me." He never spoke again; but when, half an hour later, Lord Dunfermline and some other friends came to the spot, they thought that they could still discern some faint remains of life. The body, wrapped in two plaids, was carried to the Castle of Blair. —MACAULAY.

## THE BURIAL MARCH OF DUNDEE.

### I.

SOUND the fife, and cry the slogan—
Let the pibroch shake the air
With its wild triumphal music,
Worthy of the freight we bear.
Let the ancient hills of Scotland
Hear once more the battle song

Swell within their glens and valleys
  As the clansmen march along!
Never from the field of combat,
  Never from the deadly fray,
Was a nobler trophy carried
  Than we bring with us to-day;
Never since the valiant Douglas
  On his dauntless bosom bore
Good King Robert's heart—the priceless—
  To our dear Redeemer's shore!
Lo! we bring with us the hero—
  Lo! we bring the conquering Græme,
Crowned as best beseems a victor
  From the altar of his fame;
Fresh and bleeding from the battle
  Whence his spirit took its flight,
Midst the crashing charge of squadrons,
  And the thunder of the fight!
Strike, I say, the notes of triumph,
  As we march o'er moor and lea!
Is there any here will venture
  To bewail our dead Dundee?
Let the widows of the traitors
  Weep until their eyes are dim!
Wail ye may full well for Scotland—
  Let none dare to mourn for him!
See! above his glorious body
  Lies the royal banner's fold—
See! his valiant blood is mingled
  With its crimson and its gold.
See how calm he looks and stately
  Like a warrior on his shield,
Waiting till the flush of morning
  Breaks along the battle-field!
See—Oh never more, my comrades,
  Shall we see that falcon eye
Redden with its inward lightning,
  As the hour of fight drew nigh!
Never shall we hear the voice that,
  Clearer than the trumpet's call,
Bade us strike for King and Country,
  Bade us win the field, or fall!

II.

On the heights of Killiecrankie
  Yestermorn our army lay:
Slowly rose the mist in columns
  From the river's broken way;
Hoarsely roared the swollen torrent,
  And the Pass was wrapped in gloom,
When the clansmen rose together
  From their lair amidst the broom.
Then we belted on our tartans,
  And our bonnets down we drew,
And we felt our broadswords' edges,
  And we proved them to be true;

And we prayed the prayer of soldiers,
 And we cried the gathering-cry,
And we clasped the hands of kinsmen,
 And we swore to do or die!
　　*　　*　.　*　　*　　*

Soon we heard a challenge-trumpet
 Sounding in the Pass below,
And the distant tramp of horses,
 And the voices of the foe;
Down we crouched amid the bracken,
 Till the Lowland ranks drew near,
Panting like the hounds in summer,
 When they scent the stately deer.
From the dark defile emerging,
 Next we saw the squadrons come,
Leslie's foot and Leven's troopers
 Marching to the tuck of drum;
Through the scattered wood of birches,
 O'er the broken ground and heath.
Wound the long battalions slowly,
 Till they gained the field beneath;
Then we bounded from our covert.—
 Judge how looked the Saxons then,
When they saw the rugged mountain
 Start to life with armed men!
Like a tempest down the ridges
 Swept the hurricane of steel,
Rose the slogan of Macdonald—
 Flashed the broadsword of Locheill!
Vainly sped the withering volley
 'Mongst the foremost of our band—
On we poured until me met them,
 Foot to foot, and hand to hand.
Horse and man went down like drift-wood
 When the floods are black at Yule,
And their carcasses are whirling
 In the Garry's deepest pool.
Horse and man went down before us—
 Living foe there tarried none
On the field of Killiecrankie,
 When that stubborn fight was done!

### IV.

And the evening star was shining
 On Schehallion's distant head,
When we wiped our bloody broadswords,
 And returned to count the dead.
There we found him gashed and gory,
 Stretched upon the cumbered plain,
As he told us where to seek him,
 In the thickest of the slain.
And a smile was on his visage,
 For within his dying ear
Pealed the joyful note of triumph,
 And the clansmen's clamorous cheer;

So, amidst the battle's thunder,
  Shot, and steel, and scorching flame,
In the glory of his manhood
  Passed the spirit of the Græme!

V.

Open wide the vaults of Athol,
  Where the bones of heroes rest—
Open wide the hallowed portals
  To receive another guest!
Last of Scots, and last of freemen—
  Last of all that dauntless race
Who would rather die unsullied
  Than outlive the land's disgrace.
O thou lion-hearted warrior!
  Reck not of the after-time:
Honor may be deemed dishonor,
  Loyalty be called a crime.
Sleep in peace with kindred ashes
  Of the noble and the true,
Hands that never failed their country,
  Hearts that never baseness knew.
Sleep!—and till the latest trumpet
  Wakes the dead from earth and sea,
Scotland shall not boast a braver
  Chieftain than our own Dundee!

—AYTOUN.

## THE PLEASURES OF A CULTIVATED IMAGINATION

THE attention of young persons may be led, by well selected works of fiction, from the present objects of the sense and the thoughts accustomed to dwell on the past, the distant or the future; and in the same proportion in which this effect is, in any instance, accomplished, "the man," as Dr. Johnson has justly remarked, "is exalted in the scale of intellectual being." The tale of fiction will probably be soon laid aside with the toys and rattles of infancy; but the habits which it has contributed to fix, and the powers which it has brought into a state of activity, will remain with the possessor, permanent and inestimable treasures, to his latest hour.

Nor is it to the young alone that these observations are to be exclusively applied. Instances have frequently occurred of individuals in whom the power of imagination has, at a more advanced period of life, been found susceptible of culture to a wonderful degree. In such men, what an accession is gained to their most refined pleasures! What enchantments are added to their most ordinary perceptions! The mind, awakening, as if from a trance, to a new existence, becomes habituated to the most interesting aspects of life and of nature; the intellectual eye "is purged of its film;" and things the most familiar and unnoticed disclose charms invisible before.

The same objects and events, which were lately beheld with indifference, occupy now all the powers and capacities of the soul: the contrast between the present and the past serving only to enhance and to endear so unlooked-for an acquisition. What Gray has so finely said of the *pleasures of vicissitude* conveys but a faint image of what is experienced by the man who, after having lost, in vulgar occupations and vulgar amusements, his earliest and most precious years, is thus introduced at last to a new heaven and a new earth:

> "The meanest floweret of the vale,
> The simplest note that swells the gale,
> The common sun, the air, the skies,
> To him are opening Paradise."

The effects of foreign travel have been often remarked, not only in rousing the curiosity of the traveller while abroad, but in correcting, after his return, whatever habits of inattention he had contracted to the institutions and manners among which he was bred. It is in a way somewhat analogous that our occasional excursions into the regions of imagination increase our interest in those familiar realities, from which the stores of imagination are borrowed. We learn insensibly to view nature with the eye of the painter and the poet, and to seize those "happy attitudes of things," which their taste at first selected; while, enriched with the accumulations of ages and with "the spoils of time," we unconsciously combine with what we see all that we know and all that we feel; and sublime the organical beauties of the material world, by blending with them the inexhaustible delights of the heart and of the fancy.—STEWART.

---

## THE FAMILY MEETING.

> We are all here!
> Father, Mother,
> Sister, Brother,
> All who hold each other dear.
> Each chair is fill'd—we're all *at home:*
> To-night let no cold stranger come;
> It is not often thus around
> Our old familiar hearth we're found:
> Bless, then, the meeting and the spot;
> For once be every care forgot;

Let gentle peace assert her power,
And kind affection rule the hour ;
    We're all—all here.

    We're *not* all here !
Some are away—the dead ones dear,
Who throng'd with us this ancient hearth,
And gave the hour to guiltless mirth,
Fate, with a stern, relentless hand,
Look'd in and thinn'd our little band :
Some like a night-flash pass'd away,
And some sank, lingering, day by day ;
The quiet grave-yard some lie there—
And cruel Ocean has his share—
    We're *not* all here.

    We *are* all here !
Even they—the dead—though dead, so dear,
Fond Memory, to her duty true,
Brings back their faded forms to view.
How life-like, through the mist of years,
Each well remember'd face appears !
We see them, as in times long past,
From each to each kind looks are cast ;
We hear their words, their smiles behold,
They're round us, as they were of old—
    We *are* all here.

    We are all here !
    Father, Mother,
    Sister, Brother,
You that I love with love so dear.
*This* may not long of us be said ;
Soon we must join the gather'd dead ;
And by the hearth we now sit round,
Some other circle will be found.
Oh ! then, that wisdom may we know,
Which yields a life of peace below ;
So, in the world to follow this,
May each repeat, in words of bliss,
    We're all—all *here !*
                                                        —SPRAGUE.

## THE PLAGUE AT CONSTANTINOPLE.
### (A.D. 745.)

ONE great calamity in the age of Constantine appears to have travelled over the whole habitable world ; this was the great pestilence, which made its appearance in the Byzantine empire as early as 745. It had previously carried off a considerable portion of the population of Syria, and the Caliph Yezid II perished of the disease in 744. From Syria it visited Egypt and Africa, from whence it passed into Sicily. After making great ravages in Sicily and Calabria, it spread to Greece ; and at last, in the year 749, it broke out with terrible violence

Constantinople, then probably the most populous city in the universe. It was supposed to have been introduced, and dispersed through Christian countries, by the Venetian and Greek ships employed in carrying on a contraband trade in slaves with the Mohammedan nations, and it spread wherever commerce extended. Monemvasia, one of the great commercial cities at the time, received the contagion with the return of its trading vessels, and disseminated the disease over all Greece, and the islands of the Archipelago. On the continent, this plague threatened to exterminate the Hellenic race.

Historians have left us a vivid picture of the horrors of this fearful visitation, which show us that the terror it inspired disturbed the fabric of society. Strange superstitions preoccupied men's minds, and annihilated every sense of duty. Some appeared to be urged by a demoniacal impulse to commit heinous but useless crimes, with the wildest recklessness. Small crosses of unctuous matter were supposed to appear suddenly, traced by an invisible hand on the clothes of persons as they were engaged in their ordinary pursuits; examples were narrated of their having appeared suddenly visible to the eyes of the assembled congregation on the vestments of the priest as he officiated at the altar. The individual thus marked out was invariably assailed by the disease on his return home, and soon died. Crosses were constantly found traced on the doors and outer walls of buildings; houses, palaces, huts, and monasteries were alike marked. This was considered as an intimation that some of the inmates were ordered to prepare for immediate death. In the delirium of fear and the first paroxysms of the plague, many declared that they beheld hideous spectres wandering about; these apparitions were seen flitting through the crowded streets of the city, at times questioning the passengers, at times, walking into houses before the inmates, and then driving the proprietors from the door. At times it was said that these spectres had even attacked the citizens with naked swords. That these things were not reported solely on the delusion of the fancy of persons rendered insane by attacks of disease, is asserted by a historian who was born about ten years later, and who certainly passed his youth at Constantinople. The testimony of Theophanes is confirmed by the records of similar diseases in other populous cities. The uncertainty of life offers additional chances of impunity to crime, and thus relaxes the power of the law, and weakens the bonds of moral restraint. Danger is generally what man fears little, when there are several chances of escape. The bold and wicked, deriding the general panic, frequently make periods of pestilence times of revelry and plunder; the very individuals charged as policemen to preserve order in society, finding themselves free from control, have been known to assume the disguise of demons, in order to plunder the terrified and superstitious with impunity. The predominant passions of all find full scope when the feeling of responsibility is removed; shame is thrown aside, the most unfeeling avarice and the wildest debauchery are displayed. But, at the same time, it is on such fearful occasions that we see examples of the noblest courage, the most devoted self-sacrifice and the purest charity. Boccaccio and Defoe, in describing the scenes which occurred at Florence in 1348, and at London in 1665, afford a correct picture of what happened at Constantinople in 747.

The number of dead was so great, that when the ordinary means of transporting the bodies to interment were insufficient, boxes were slung over the pack-saddles of mules, into which the dead were cast without distinction of rank. When the mules became insufficient, low chariots were constructed to receive piles of human bodies, and these frightful hearses were drawn through the streets to receive their loads, by a crowd of men who received a fixed sum of money with each body. Long trenches were prepared without the walls, to serve as graves for hundreds of bodies, and into these the aged beggar and the youthful noble were precipitated side by side. When all the cemeteries around the capital were filled, and the panic kept the mass of the population shut up in their dwellings, bodies were interred in the fields and vineyards nearest to the city gates, or they were cast into vacant houses and empty cisterns. The disease prevailed for a year, and left whole houses tenantless, having exterminated many families. We possess no record of the number of deaths it caused, but if we suppose the population of Constantinople at the time to have exceeded a million, we may form an estimate of the probable loss it sustained, by observing that, during the great plague at Milan, in 1630, about eighty-six thousand persons perished in the course of a year, in a population hardly exceeding one hundred and fifty thousand souls. —FINLAY.

## SONG.

Song should breathe of scent and flowers,
  Song should like a river flow :
Song should bring back scenes and hours,
  That we loved—ah, long ago !

Song from baser thoughts should win us,
  Song should charm us out of woe ;
Song should stir the heart within us,
  Like a patriot's friendly blow.

Pains and pleasures, all man doeth,
  War and peace, and ill and wrong;
All things that the soul subdueth,
  Should be vanquished too by song.

Song should spur the mind to duty,
  Nerve the weak and stir the strong :
Every deed of truth and beauty
  Should be crowned by starry song.
      —Hood.

## EXTINCT REPTILES.

At a comparatively early period in the earth's history, reptiles inhabited the air like birds, some of them only occasionally, perhaps, touching the earth. The bones of such creatures, as we have said, indicate dimensions of the largest size, as compared with winged birds adapted for flight. The greatest width across the expanded wing-membrane, from tip to tip, amounts, in some cases, to more than twenty feet, and the head was exceedingly large and long in proportion to the body. No remains of these creatures have been found in the sandstones with footmarks, but they are common in all newer deposits as far as the chalk. They seem to have been able to swim, and perhaps to dive, and they were certainly reptiles of prey.

In addition to the land and air species, we also find fossil a considerable and interesting group of marine reptiles. These, too, were some of them very gigantic, approaching even the whales in this respect, while there is every probability that they were much more fierce. Unlike the ordinary hard coat of mail that we find covering most known reptiles, and that appears also to have belonged to those in a fossil state, the marine species were soft-skinned, and exhibit strength rather for attack than defence. There are two principal groups, one approaching much more nearly to the true fishes than the other. The one well known as the *Ichthyosaur*, or fish-lizard, has been handed down to us in unusual perfection, many complete skeletons having been worked out of their stony beds, and numerous indications given even of the skin and the contents of the stomach.

The *Plesiosaur*, although more nearly a lizard, as its name implies, would seem to have been even less like any existing animal than its companion. It has been compared to a serpent in a turtle's shell; but in truth, though the neck was exceedingly long and the head that of a lizard, the body was smooth and naked, the tail not very long, and the extremities like the paddles of a whale. Some of the specimens seem to indicate an animal as much as thirty feet long, and the entire and undisturbed skeletons of many individuals, of various sizes and different proportions, are to be found in museums.

At present almost all the common fishes are provided with moderately hard complete skeletons, and are covered with scales usually small and thin. Most of the fish whose remains are found fossil are, however, remarkable for having had cartilaginous instead of bony skeletons. They were enclosed in a bony box, coated with enamel, by means of which the whole animal was defended against powerful enemies. Few fishes of this kind have been found in modern waters; but the "bony pike" of the North American lakes and rivers is a fair illustration of these knights of ancient times. The fishes whose remains are found fossil offer nothing remarkable in regard to size, many existing species being larger than any known extinct kinds. But in strangeness of form, amongst those enclosed in a coat of mail, the oldest species have hardly since been rivalled. The bony plates are very large, and their shapes such as accurately to adapt them to enclose the small body of the animal between back-plate and breast-plate. One kind, called *Pterichthys* (the wing-fish), had strong spines, like arms, placed near the head, and a very curious tail, tapering and flattened, almost like that of a beaver. The head was defended by a kind of helmet joining on to the back.

Exceedingly abundant in the old rocks, these fishes seem gradually to have become fewer and less important, being replaced latterly by the scale-covered fish of modern times. Sharks and Rays, however, seem always to have existed, and were generally common. They left behind them not only teeth, but bony and enamelled spines, and even scales—these being more permanent than modern scales, though often quite detached, and never connecting into complete armor.

There are several curious animals now living, large and strong enough to prey even upon fish, but belonging to a group whose nervous structure places them in a lower position in the series of animals. The cuttle-fish, of which there are many kinds round our own shores and in the Mediterranean, often attain a very large size. Some of them possess, when living, a curious oval flattened plate, called (not very improperly) the "bone," which is constantly found washed up on the seashore, quite detached from the animal. Many of them have a black fluid, which they are able to throw out and thereby darken the water, when they wish either to escape or to confuse their prey.

The Nautilus occupies a shell divided into many small compartments, each of which is pierced with a hole of moderate size, and all of which are crossed by a tube. The animal belonging to this shell is a kind of cuttle-fish, and the whole shell serves as a float to the creature, which inhabits only the outermost chamber, the rest being full of air.

It is not a little interesting to find that of animals covered with shells, these cuttle-fish seem to have been at all times the most characteristic. They have perhaps been more readily preserved than others, owing to various causes; but at any rate, it is certain that in the older rocks, shells, built upon a principle almost the same as that of the nautilus, are so incredibly abundant and so wonderfully varied, as to make it certain that their owners played a very important part in their day. Whether they were accompanied by the commoner kind of shells, which have not been preserved, or whether the conditions of deposit were unfavorable for these latter, we cannot now tell. The geological record is imperfect. The illustrations of particular kinds of animals are numerous and minute, while there are few indications of the existence of the others. The *Ammonites* of geologists include a wonderful variety of curious shells, nearly resembling the nautilus in having a multitude of chambers. They have been found of all sizes, from a coach-wheel down to a pin's head; and where the ordinary forms are absent there are other shells evidently of the same kind, and differing only in matters of detail. So also the *Belemnite*—the hard part or bone of another extinct species of cuttle-fish—though very different from the corresponding part of known living specimens, evidently answered a similar purpose. It is therefore clear, that these curious and, for the most part, powerful representatives of a class of animals which we now think very little of, and of which we speak slightingly—identifying them with the snails, oysters, and limpets—really at one time played a part hardly subordinate to fishes, being quite as active and perhaps almost as intelligent. Certainly no one now can watch them in the sea, and notice their restless activity—their long arms covered with suckers, their large bright eyes always on the look-out, their powerful jaws, and perfect means of helping themselves and supplying every important want—without feeling satisfied that they are well able to perform their part in Nature. —ANSTED.

## BERNARDINE DU BORN.

KING HENRY sat upon his throne,
  And full of wrath and scorn,
His eye a recreant knight survey'd –
  Sir Bernardine du Born.
And he that haughty glance return'd,
  Like lion in his lair,
While loftily his unchanged brow
  Gleam'd through his crispèd hair.

" Thou art a traitor to the realm.
  Lord of a lawless band,
The bold in speech, the fierce in broil.
  The troubler of our land.
Thy castles and thy rebel-towers
  Are forfeit to the crown,
And thou beneath the Norman axe
  Shalt end thy base renown

" Deign'st thou no word to bar thy doom,
  Thou with strange madness fired?
Hath reason quite forsook thy breast?"
  Plantagenet inquired.
Sir Bernard turn'd him toward the king,
  He blench'd not in his pride,
" My reason fail'd, my gracious liege,
  The year Prince Henry died."

Quick at that name a cloud of woe
  Pass'd o'er the monarch's brow;
Touch'd was that bleeding chord of love,
  To which the mightiest bow.

Again swept back the tide of years,
  Again his first-born moved,—
The fair, the graceful, the sublime,
  The erring, yet beloved.

And ever cherish'd by his side,
  One chosen friend was near,
To share in boyhood's ardent sport,
  Or youth's untamed career.
With him the merry chase he sought,
  Beneath the dewy morn;
With him in knightly tourney rode,
  This Bernardine du Born.

Then in the mourning father's soul,
  Each trace of ire grew dim;
And what his buried idol loved
  Seem'd cleansed of guilt to him.
And faintly through his tears he spake,
  "God send his grace to thee,
And, for the dear sake of the dead,
  Go forth—unscathed and free."

—Mrs. Sigourney.

## SNAKES AND SNAKE CHARMERS.

To new-comers in Hindostan, and particularly those of nervous temperament, snakes of various kinds constitute a source of perpetual alarm. Their numbers are immense, and no place is sacred from their visitations. Just fancy the agreeable surprise resulting from such little occurrences as the following, which are far from being rare. You get up in a morning, after a feverish night perhaps; languidly you reach for your boots, and upon pulling on one, feel something soft before your toes, and on turning it upside down, and giving it a shake, out pops a small snake of the carpet tribe—as they are called, probably from their domestic propensities—wondering what can be the cause of his being thus rudely ejected from his night's quarters. Or suppose, at any time during the day, you should be musically inclined, you take your flute from its resting place, and proceed to screw it together, but find, on making an attempt to play, that something is the matter, and on peeping into it, discover that a little serpentine gentleman has there sought and found a snug lodgment. Perhaps your endeavor to give it breath with your mouth, makes Mr Snake feel his habitation in the instrument uncomfortably cold, and, ere you are aware of his presence, he is out, and wriggling among your fingers.

Such incidents as these cause rather unpleasant starts to those who are new to Hindostanic matters, though the natives of the land, or persons who have been long resident in it, might only smile at the new comer's uneasiness, and tell him that these little intruders were perfectly harmless. But even with the assurance of this fact, it is long ere most Europeans can tolerate the sight and presence of these snakes, much less feel comfortable under their cold touch. Besides, it is but too well known that all these creatures are not innoxious. Well do I remember the fright that one poor fellow got in the barracks at Madras. He had possibly been indulging too freely overnight; at least, when he rose in the morning in question, he felt thirsty in the extreme. Yawning most volcanically, he made up to one of the room windows, were stood a large water-bottle or jar, one of those long-necked clay things in which they usually keep fluids in the East. Upon taking this inviting vessel into his hands, he observed that there seemed to be but little water in it, yet enough, as he thought, to cool his parched throat; and he had just applied it to his lips, when something touched them—certainly not water, whatever else it might be He hastily withdrew the vessel from his mouth, though still retaining it in his hands, when, to his amazement and horror, a regular cobra, the most deadly and dangerous of all the common serpents of India, reared its hideously distended and spectacled head from the jar, not a foot from its disturber's nose. "O murder!" cried the poor fellow, who was a son of Erin; and as he uttered the exclamation, he dashed bottle, snake, and all to the ground, and took to his heels, nor stopped until he was a full hundred yards from the spot. Here he told his story in safety, and the intruder was in good time got rid of by the cautious use of fire-arms.

The Hindoos, or at least the serpent-charmers among them, pretend, as is well known, to handle all sorts of snakes with impunity, to make them come and go at a call, and in short, to have a cabalistic authority over the whole race. These pretensions are necessary to the exercise of their profession, which consists, in part, in ridding private houses of troublesome visitants of this description. One of these serpent-charmers will assert to a householder that there are snakes about his premises, and, partly from motives of fear, and partly from curiosity, the householder promises the man a reward, if he succeed in showing and removing them. The juggler goes to work, and soon snakes are seen to issue from some corner or another, obedient to his call. The performer takes them up fearlessly, and they meet like old friends. In fact, the opinion of the more enlightened residents in India is, that the snakes and their charmers *are* old friends; that he hid them there, and of course knew where to find them; and, moreover, that having long ago extracted the poisonous fangs, he may well handle them without alarm. Still, a large portion of the community, European as well as natives, believe that these charmers have strange powers over the snake tribe.

Snake-charming is not confined to India. There are some of the natives of Africa and America, who possess the power of what is called " charming," or producing a benumbing or stupifying effect on poisonous serpents and scorpions, by handling them. This power is, in some, natural and hereditary, while in others it is acquired by chewing the roots or other parts of certain plants, rubbing them in their hands, or bathing their bodies in water containing an infusion of them. In that part of Africa which lies northward of the great desert of Sahara, there was formerly a tribe called the Psylli, who seem to have possessed this power, either from nature or art, in a degree that occasioned the name of Psylli to be given to all persons capable of producing similar effects. Plutarch informs us that Cato, in his march through the desert, took with him a number of these Psylli, to suck out the poisons from the wounds of such of his soldiers as might be bitten by the numerous serpents which infested that region. It was then ignorantly believed that this power of subduing the poison was the effect of magic, and the Psylli, to confirm this belief, always, when in the exercise of this fascination, muttered spells or chanted verses over the person whom they were in the act of curing. Many have ventured to doubt the existence of this power being possessed by any class of people, but the concurrent testimony of the best accredited travellers seems to confirm the fact. Mr. Bruce distinctly states, from minute personal observation, that *all* the blacks in the kingdom of Sennaar are perfectly armed by nature against the bite of either scorpion or viper. They take the horned snake—there the most common, and one of the most fatal of the viper tribe—in their hands at all times, put them in their bosoms, and throw them at each other, as children do apples and balls, during which sport the serpents are seldom irritated to bite, and if they do, no mischief ensues from the wound. The Arabs of the same country, he also observes, have not by nature this protective power, but generally acquire it by the use of certain plants. The artificial means of rendering the person invulnerable to the bite of snakes seems also to be practised in South America.

It is said that the cobra is fond of milk, and that a knowledge of this fact has sometimes saved the lives of persons who were on the point of being bitten. An anecdote is related of a party of gentlemen sitting at table in India, when one of them felt a cobra coiling itself round his leg. Appalled at his situation, he desired his companions, in a whisper, not to speak or make any noise, if they would save his life. All were immediately silent. He next, in a low tone, requested a servant to bring a jug of milk, and pour it cautiously on the floor, near his foot. This being done, the cobra, in a short time, uncoiled itself, and descended to partake of the milk, when, as may be supposed, little ceremony was used in despatching it. An exemption from reptiles of this deadly class is surely one of England's greatest blessings. —CHAMBERS.

## THOU DIDST, O MIGHTY GOD, EXIST.

Thou didst, O mighty God, exist
  Ere time begun its race;
Before the ample elements
  Fill'd up the voids of space.

Before the pond'rous earthly globe
  In fluid air was stayed
Before the ocean's mighty springs
  Their liquid stores display'd.

Ere through the gloom of ancient night
  The streaks of light appear'd,
Before the high celestial arch
  On starry poles was rear'd.

Before the loud, melodious spheres
  Their tuneful round begun;
Before the shining robes of heav'n
  Were measur'd by the sun.

Ere through the empyrean courts
  One hallelujah rung;
Or to their harps the sons of light
  Ecstatic anthems sung.

Ere men ador'd, or angels knew,
  Or prais'd Thy wondrous name;
Thy bliss, O sacred spring of life!
  And glory was the same.

And when the pillars of the world
  With sudden ruin break,
And all this vast and goodly frame,
  Sinks in the mighty wreck;

When from her orb the moon shall start,
  The astonish'd sun roll back;
And all the trembling starry lamps
  Their ancient course forsake;

For ever permanent and fix'd,
  From agitation free,
Unchanged in everlasting years
  Shall Thy existence be. —Mrs. Rowe.

## THE EVENING WIND.

Spirit that breathest through my lattice—thou
  That cool'st the twilight of the sultry day—
Gratefully flows thy freshness round my brow:
  Thou hast been out upon the deep at play,
Riding all day the wild blue wave till now,
  Roughening their crests, and scattering high their spray,
And swelling the white sail. I welcome thee
To the scorch'd land, thou wanderer of the sea!

Nor I alone: a thousand bosoms round
  Inhale thee in the fulness of delight,
And languid forms rise up, and pulses bound
  Livelier, at coming of the wind of night;
And, languishing to hear thy grateful sound,
  Lies the vast inland, stretch'd beyond the sight,
Go forth into the gathering shade—go forth,
God's blessing breathed upon the fainting earth!

Go, rock the little wood-bird in his nest,
  Curl the still waters, bright with stars, and rouse
The wide old wood from his majestic rest,
  Summoning from the innumerable boughs
The strange, deep harmonies that haunt his breast;
  Pleasant shall be thy way where meekly bows
The shutting flower, and darkling waters pass,
  And 'twixt the o'ershadowing branches and the grass.

The faint old man shall lean his silver head
  To feel thee; thou shalt kiss the child asleep,
And dry the moisten'd curls that overspread
  His temples, while his breathing grows more deep;
And they who stand about the sick man's bed
  Shall joy to listen to thy distant sweep,
And softly part his curtains to allow
Thy visit, grateful to his burning brow.

> Go;—but the circle of eternal change,
>   Which is the life of nature, shall restore,
> With sounds and scents from all thy mighty range,
>   Thee to thy birth place of the deep once more;
> Sweet odors in the sea air, sweet and strange,
>   Shall tell the home-sick mariner of the shore;
> And, listening to thy murmur, he shall deem
> He hears the rustling leaf and running stream.
>
> —Bryant.

## MAN'S FACULTIES.

The modern English mind has this much in common with that of the Greek, that it intensely desires, in all things, the utmost completion or perfection compatible with their nature. This is a noble character in the abstract, but becomes ignoble when it causes us to forget the relative dignities of that nature itself, and to prefer the perfectness of the lower nature to the imperfection of the higher; not considering that as, judged by such a rule, all the brute animals would be preferable to man, because more perfect in their functions and kind, and yet are always held inferior to him, so also in the works of man, those which are more perfect in their kind are always inferior to those which are, in their nature, liable to more faults and shortcomings. For the finer the nature, the more flaws it will show through the clearness of it; and it is a law of this universe, that the best things shall be the seldomest seen in their best form. The wild grass grows well and strongly, one year with another; but the wheat is, according to the greater nobleness of its nature, liable to the bitterer blight. And, therefore, while in all things that we see, or do, we are to desire perfection, and strive for it, we are nevertheless not to set the meaner thing, in its narrow accomplishment, above the nobler thing, in its mighty progress; not to esteem smooth minuteness above shattered majesty; not to prefer mean victory to honorable defeat, to lower the level of our aim, that we may the more surely enjoy the complacency of success. But, above all, in our dealings with the souls of other men, we are to take care how we check, by severe requirement or narrow caution, efforts which might otherwise lead to a noble issue; and, still more, how we withhold our admiration from great excellencies, because they are mingled with rough faults. Now, in the make and nature of every man, however rude or simple, whom we employ in manual labour, there are some powers for better things: some tardy imagination, torpid capacity of emotion, tottering steps of thought, there are, even at the worst; and in most cases it is all our own fault that they *are* tardy or torpid. But they cannot be strengthened, unless we are content to take them in their feebleness, and unless we prize and honor them in their imperfection above the best and most perfect manual skill. And this is what we have to do with all our laborers; to look for the *thoughtful* part of them, and get that out of them, whatever we lose for it, whatever faults and errors we are obliged to take with it. For the best that is in them cannot manifest itself but in company with much error. Understand this clearly: You can teach a man to draw a straight line, and to cut one; to strike a curved line, and to carve it; and to copy and carve any number of given lines or forms, with admirable speed and perfect precision; and you find his work perfect of its kind: but if you ask him to think about any of those forms, to consider if he cannot find any better in his own head, he stops; his execution becomes hesitating; he thinks, and ten to one he thinks wrong; ten to one he makes a mistake in the first touch he gives to his work as a thinking being. But you have made a man of him for all that. He was only a machine before, an animated tool.

And observe, you are put to stern choice in this matter. You must either make a tool of the creature, or a man of him. You cannot make both. Men were not intended to work with the accuracy of tools, to be precise and perfect in all their actions. If you will have that precision out of them, and make their fingers measure degrees like cog-wheels, and their arms strike curves like compasses, you must unhumanize them. All the energy of their spirits must be given to make cogs and compasses of themselves. All their attention and strength must go to the accomplishment of the mean act. The eye of the soul must be bent upon the finger-point, and the soul's force must fill all the invisible nerves that guide it, ten hours a day, that it may not err from its steely precision, and so soul and sight be worn away, and the whole human being be lost at last—a heap of sawdust, so far as its intellectual work in this world is concerned; saved only by its Heart, which cannot go into the form of cogs and compasses, but expands, after the ten hours are over, into fireside humanity. On the other hand, if you will make a man of the working creature, you cannot make a tool. Let him but begin to imagine, to think, to try to do anything worth doing; and the engine-turned precision is lost at once. Out come all his roughness, all his dullness, all his incapability; shame upon shame, failure upon failure, pause after pause: but out comes the whole majesty of him also; and we know the height of it only when we see the clouds settling upon him. And, whether the clouds be bright or dark, there will be transfiguration behind and within them.—RUSKIN.

## THE RIVER OF LIFE.

THE more we live, more brief appear
 Our life's succeeding stages:
A day to childhood seems a year,
 And years like passing ages.

The gladsome current of our youth
 Ere passion yet disorders,
Steals lingering like a river smooth
 Along its grassy borders.

But as the careworn cheek grows wan,
 And sorrow's shafts fly thicker,
Ye Stars, that measure life to man,
 Why seem your courses quicker?

When joys have lost their bloom and breath
 And life itself is vapid,
Why, as we reach the Falls of Death,
 Feel we its tide more rapid?

It may be strange—yet who would change
 Time's course to slower speeding,
When one by one our friends have gone
 And left our bosoms bleeding?

Heaven gives our years of fading strength
 Indemnifying fleetness;
And those of youth, a seeming length,
 Proportion'd to their sweetness. —CAMPBELL.

## ELIHU.

"O SAILOR, tell me, tell me true,
 Is my little lad—my Elihu—
 A sailing in your ship?"
The sailor's eyes were dimmed with dew.
 "Your little lad? your Elihu?"
 He said with trembling lip;
 "What little lad—what ship?"

What little lad ?—as if there could be
Another such a one as he !
  " What little lad, do you say ?"
" Why, Elihu, that took to the sea
The moment I put him off my knee.
  It was just the other day
  The *Gray Swan* sailed away."

The other day ?  The sailor's eyes
Stood wide open with surprise.
  " The other day ?—the *Swan* ?"
His heart began in his throat to rise.
" Ay, ay, sir ;  here in the cupboard lies
  The jacket he had on."
  " And so your lad is gone !—

Gone with the *Swan*."  " And did she stand
With her anchor clutching hold of the sand,
  For a month, and never stir ?"
" Why, to be sure !  I've seen from the land,
Like a lover kissing his lady's hand,
  The wild sea kissing her—
  A sight to remember, sir."

" But, my good mother, do you know,
All this was twenty years ago ?
  I stood on the *Gray Swan's* deck,
And to that lad I saw you throw—
Taking it off, as it might be so—
  The kerchief from your neck ;
  Ay, and he'll bring it back.

" And did the little lawless lad,
That has made you sick, and made you sad,
  Sail with the *Gray Swan's* crew ?"
" Lawless !  the man is going mad ;
The best boy mother ever had ;
  Be sure, he sailed with the crew—
  What would you have him do ?"

" And he has never written line,
Nor sent you word, nor made you sign,
  To say he was alive ?"
" Hold—if 'twas wrong, the wrong is mine ;
Besides, he may be in the brine ;
  And could he write from the grave ?
  Tut, man !  what would you have ?"

" Gone twenty years !  a long, long cruise ;
'Twas wicked thus your love to abuse ;
  But if the lad still lives,
And come back home, think you, you can
Forgive him ?"  " Miserable man !
  You're mad as the sea ;  you rave—
  What have I to forgive ?"

> The sailor twitched his shirt so blue,
> And from within his bosom drew
>   The kerchief. She was wild:
> "My God!—my Father!—is it true?
> My little lad—my Elihu?
> And is it?—is it?—is it you?
>   My blessed boy—my child—
>   My dead—my living child!"
>
> —ALICE CAREY.

---

## DAMASCUS.

WE had been sleeping under our horses, and they had never stirred a limb for fear of hurting us. The evening before, our path had lain among bosomy hills and quiet-looking drab-colored valleys. This scenery, if not attractive, was at least not offensive; and when daylight came, and we found where we had wandered, the change was great indeed. It seemed as if some great battle of the elements had taken place during the night, the rocks been rent asunder in the struggle, and Nature frightfully wounded in the fray. Wildly distorted as the scenery seemed when the sun shone over it, there was a fearful silence and want of stir that enhanced its effect. Cliffs nodded over us, as if they had been awake all night, and could stand it no longer; precipices and dark ravines yawned beneath us, fixed, as it were, in some spasm of the nightmare. Not a living thing was to be seen around—no drop of water, no leaf of tree, nothing but a calm, terrible sunshine above, and blackened rocks and burned soil below.

We emerged from these savage gorges into a wide, disheartening plain, bounded by an amphitheatre of dreary mountains. Our horses had had no water for twenty-four hours, and we no refreshment of any kind for twenty. Finding there was still a gallop in my steed's elastic limbs, I pushed on for Damascus, leaving my people to follow more slowly. After a couple of hours' hard riding, I came to another range of mountains, from beyond which opened the view of Damascus, that the Prophet abstained from as too delightful for this probationary world. It is said that after many days of toilsome travel, beholding the city thus lying at his feet, he exclaimed, "Only one paradise is allowed to man; I will not take mine in this world." And so he turned away his horse's head from Damascus, and pitched his tent in the desert.

I reined up my steed with difficulty on the side of the mountain; he had already, perhaps, heard the murmur of the distant waters, or instinct told him that Nature's life-streams flowed beneath that bright-green foliage. For miles around us lay the dead desert, whose sands appear to quiver under the shower of sunbeams: far away to the south and east it spread like a boundless ocean; but there, beneath our feet, lay such an island of verdure as nowhere else perhaps exists. Mass upon mass of dark, delicious foliage rolled like waves among garden tracks of brilliant emerald green. Here and there, the clustering blossoms of the orange or the nectarine lay like foam upon that verdant sea. Minarets, white as ivory, shot up their fairy towers among the groves; and purple mosque domes, tipped with the golden crescent, gave the only sign that a city lay bowered beneath those rich plantations.

One hour's gallop brought me to the suburban gates of Mezzé, and thenceforth I rode on through streets, or rather lanes, of pleasant shadow. For many an hour we had seen no water: now it gushed, and gleamed, and sparkled all around us: from aqueduct above, and rivulet below, and marble fountain in the walls—every where it poured forth its rich abundance; and my horse and I soon quenched our burning thirst in Abana and Pharpar.

On we went, among gardens, and fountains, and odors, and cool shade, absorbed in sensations of delight, like the knights of old, who had just passed from some ordeal to its reward. Fruits of every delicate shape and hue bended the boughs hospitably over our heads; flowers hung in canopy upon the trees, and lay in variegated carpet on the ground; the lanes through which we went were long arcades of arching boughs; the walls were composed of large, square blocks of dried mud, which in that bright, dazzling light somewhat resembled Cyclopean architecture, and gave, I know not what, of simplicity and primitiveness to the scene. At length I entered the city, and thenceforth lost the sun while I remained there. The luxurious people of Damascus exclude all sunshine from their bazaars by awnings of thick mat, wherever vine trellises or vaulted roofs do not render this precaution unnecessary.

The effect of this pleasant gloom, the cool currents of air created by the narrow streets, the vividness of the bazaars, the variety and beauty of the Oriental dress, the fragrant smell of the spice shops, the tinkle of the brass cups of the seller of sherbets—all this affords a pleasant but bewildering change from the silent desert and the glare of sunshine. And then the glimpses of places strange to your eye, yet familiar to your imagination, that you catch as you pass along! Here is the portal of a large khan, with a fountain and cistern in the midst. Camels, and bales of merchandise, and turbaned negroes are scattered over its wide quadrangle, and an arcade of shops or offices surrounds it, above and below, like the streets of Chester. Another portal opens into a public bath, with its fountains, its reservoirs, its gay carpets, and its luxurious inmates, clothed in white linen, and reclining upon cushions as they smoke their chibouques.

Damascus is all of a bubble with nargilehs and fountains; the former are in every mouth, and the latter gush from every corner of the street. These fountains are in themselves very characteristic, beautifully carved with fanciful designs, that seem ever striving to evade the Moslems' law against imitating any thing in creation. The heat of the climate is turned into a source of pleasure by the cool currents of air that are ingeniously cultivated, and the profusion of ices, creams, and juicy fruits that everywhere present themselves. Many of the shopkeepers have large feather fans, which are in constant flutter; and even the jewellers, as they work in public, turn aside from the little crucibles, in which ingots of silver or gold are learning ductility and obedience to art, to fan their pallid cheeks, and agitate their perfumed beards with these wide-spread fans. I was never tired of roaming through the bazaars of Damascus; I strolled about them by the hour, watching the life and little interests of the pale people who live and die in their shadowy arcades.

The merchants sit on their counters; you stand in the street; there is no house to enter, but the whole bazaar is like one great shop, with a number of shelves ranged along its sides in little niches. On each shelf is a man or a boy, whose long draperies are arranged gracefully round them; immense turbans, of some costly material and very vivid colors, on their heads. Here is a pale boy, with a brilliantly gay shawl folded round his brow, working lace in a hand loom, and watching the shop at the same time; there is a man of seventy, with snowy beard, and cashmere shawl, and mulberry-colored mantle.

Here a handsome young Turk is measuring English chintz to a woman veiled from head to foot in a white, shroud-like sheet, with a dark-colored handkerchief over her face; there a water carrier walks swiftly by, jingling his brazen cups together; he has an immense glass jar, full of iced sherbet, slung under his arm; its long neck is tipped with a lump of snow and a bunch of flowers; you drink a deep draught of the nectar, your servant pays four paras (about half a farthing), and he moves on. Here a speculator in smoke is walking about with a sheaf of nargilehs, which he puts unasked into his customers' mouths. They smoke apparently unconsciously; and, when the proprietor returns, he receives about a farthing for his fee.

There is a man selling colored ices at a halfpenny a saucer full. Their trays of fruit attract your eye—plums, apricots, and enormous watermelons that melt in the mouth like snow; here comes a donkey laden with cucumbers, apparently the favorite refreshment, for almost every one stops him; here a string of tall, awkward camels fills the narrow street; there, seated on his shop board, is an old man drowsily nodding among the silks of India and Syria; and there are two pale boys playing dominos in an armorer's shop, from the roof of which daggers hang like the sword of Damocles, and quantities of ivory-handled knives, that make the niche look like a cave of stalactites. On the whole, the bazaars are much better and more striking than those of Cairo, though still rather mean and contemptible when you come to examine and value them. Many of the shopkeepers are mere amateurs—men who have land or houses, but who amuse themselves by sitting cross-legged from morning till night, and selling their quaint commodities in the cool shade. —WARBURTON.

## SLEEP.

——O GENTLE sleep,
Nature's soft nurse, how have I frighted thee,
That thou no more wilt weigh my eye-lids down,
And steep my senses in forgetfulness?
Why rather, sleep, liest thou in smoky cribs,
Upon uneasy pallets stretching thee,
And hush'd with buzzing night-flies to thy slumber;
Than in the perfum'd chambers of the great,
Under the canopies of costly state,
And lull'd with sounds of sweetest melody?
O thou dull god, why liest thou with the vile,
In loathsome beds; and leav'st the kingly couch,

A watch-case, or a common larum-bell?
Wilt thou, upon the high and giddy mast,
Seal up the ship-boy's eyes, and rock his brains
In cradle of the rude imperious surge;
And in the visitation of the winds,
Who take the ruffian billows by the top,
Curling their monstrous heads, and hanging them
With deaf'ning clamors in the slipp'ry clouds,
That, with the hurly, death itself awakes?
Canst thou, O partial sleep! give thy repose
To the wet sea-boy in an hour so rude;
And, in the calmest and most stillest night,
With all appliances and means to boot,
Deny it to a king?
—SHAKESPEARE.

## VANITY OF POWER.

No matter where; of comfort no man speak;
Let's talk of graves, of worms, and epitaphs;
Make dust our paper, and with rainy eyes
Write sorrow on the bosom of the earth.
Let's choose executors, and talk of wills;
And yet not so—for what can we bequeath,
Save our deposed bodies to the ground?
Our lands, our lives, and all, are Bolingbroke's,
And nothing can we call our own, but death;
And that small model of the barren earth,
Which serves as paste and cover to our bones.
For heaven's sake, let us sit upon the ground,
And tell sad stories of the death of kings:
How some have been depos'd, some slain in war;
Some haunted by the ghosts they have depos'd;
Some poison'd by their wives, some sleeping kill'd;
All murder'd:—For within the hollow crown
That rounds the mortal temples of a king,
Keeps Death his court: and there the antic sits,
Scoffing his state, and grinning at his pomp;
Allowing him a breath, a little scene
To monarchise, be fear'd, and kill with looks;
Infusing him with self and vain conceit;
As if this flesh, which walls about our life,
Were brass impregnable: and, humor'd thus,
Comes at the last, and with a little pin
Bores through his castle walls, and—farewell king!
Cover your heads, and mock not flesh and blood
With solemn rev'rence; throw away respect,
Tradition, form, and ceremonious duty.
For you have but mistook me all this while:
I live with bread like you, feel want, taste grief,
Need friends: subjected thus,
How can you say to me—I am a king?
—SHAKESPEARE.

## THE STORK.

So punctual is the arrival and departure of the various migratory birds, that to this day the Persians, as well as ancient Arabs, often form their almanacs on their movements. Thus, the beginning of the singing of the Nightingales was the commencement of a festival, welcoming the return of warm weather; while the coming of the Storks was the period of another, announcing their joy at the departure of Winter. The expression, " the Stork in the Heaven," is more applicable than at first appears, for even when out of sight, its pathway may be traced by the loud and piercing cries, peculiar to those of the New as well as of the Old World. In America too its migrations are equally regular, passing its immense periodical journeys at such a prodigious height as to be seldom observed. It is satisfactory thus to strengthen the authority of a Scriptural passage from so distinct a source, though amply borne out by witnesses in the very country in which the prophet dwelt.

" In the middle of April," says a traveller in the Holy Land, " while our ship was riding at anchor under Mount Carmel, we saw three flights of these birds, each of which took up more than three hours in passing us, extending itself, at the same time, more than half a mile in breadth." They were then leaving Egypt, and steering towards the north-east of Palestine, where it seems, from the account of another eye-witness, they abound in the month of May. " Returning from Cana to Nazareth," he observes, " I saw the fields so filled with flocks of Storks, that they appeared quite white with them; and when they rose and hovered in the air, they seemed like clouds. The respect paid in former times to these birds is still shown; for the Turks, notwithstanding their recklessness in shedding human blood, have a more than ordinary regard for Storks, looking upon them with an almost reverential affection."

In the neighborhood of Smyrna, and indeed throughout the whole of the Ottoman dominions, wherever the bird abides during his summer visits, he is welcomed. They call him their friend and their brother, the friend and brother exclusively of the Moslem race, entertaining a belief that wherever the influence of their religion prevailed, he would still bear them company, and it might seem that these sagacious birds are well aware of this predilection ; for singularly enough, a recent traveller, who met with them in incredible numbers in Asia Minor, observed that, although they built on the mosques, minarets, and Turkish houses, their nests were never erected on a Christian roof. In the Turkish quarters they were met in all directions, strutting about most familiarly, mixing with the people in the streets, but rarely entering the parts of the town inhabited by the Greeks or Armenians, by whom, possibly, they may be occasionally disturbed. Nothing can be more interesting than the view of an assemblage of their nests. Divided as they always are, into pairs, sometimes only the long elastic neck of one of them is to be seen peering from its cradle of nestlings, the mate standing by on one of his long slim legs, and watching with every sign of the closest affection. While other couples on the adjacent walls are fondly entwining their pliant necks, and mixing their long bills, the one sometimes bending her neck over her back, and burying her bill in the soft plumage, while her companion, clacking his hook beak with a peculiar sharp and monotonous sound, raises her head and embraces it with a quivering delight ; while from the holes and crannies of the walls, below the Stork's nest, thousands of little blue Turtle-Doves flit in all directions, keeping up an incessant cooing by day and night.

At another Mohammedan town, Fez, on the coast of Barbary, there is a rich hospital, expressly built, and supported by large funds, for the sole purpose of assisting and nursing sick Cranes and Storks, and of burying them when dead ! This respect arises from a strange belief, handed down from time immemorial, that the Storks are human beings in that form, men from some distant islands, who, at certain seasons of the year, assume the shape of these birds, that they may visit Barbary, and return at a fixed time to their own country, where they resume the human form. It has been conjectured that the tradition came originally from Egypt, where the Storks are held in equal respect, as we shall see, when we speak of their sacred bird, the Ibis. By the Jews, the former was also respected, though for a different reason ; they called it Chaseda,—which in Hebrew signifies piety or mercy,--from the tenderness shown by the young to the older birds, who, when the latter were feeble or sick, would bring them food.

This affection, however, appears to be mutual, for the parent birds have a more than ordinary degree of affection for their young, and have been known to perish rather than desert them. An attachment of this sort once occasioned the death of an old Stork, at the burning of the city of Delft, in Holland. When the flames approached her nest, situated on a house-top, she exerted herself to the utmost to save her young; but finding every effort useless, she remained and perished with them. Besides the Jews, other ancient nations held these birds in veneration. A law among the Greeks, obliging children to support their parents, even received its name from a reference to these birds. By the Romans it was called the pious bird, and was also an emblem on the medals of such Roman princes as merited the title of *Pius*. Of their attachment towards each other, we can give another instance, which occurred in this country.

A gentleman had for some years been possessed of two brown Cranes (*Ardea pavonia*); one of them at length died, and the survivor became disconsolate. He was apparently following his companion, when his master introduced a large looking-glass into the aviary. The bird no sooner beheld his reflected image, than he fancied she for whom he mourned had returned to him; he placed himself close to the mirror, plumed his feathers, and showed every sign of happiness. The scheme answered completely: the Crane recovered his health and spirits, passed almost all his time before the looking-glass, and lived many years after, dying at length of an accidental injury.

—Bishop Stanley.

## A SURVEY OF THE HEAVENS.

Ye many twinkling stars, who yet do hold
Your brilliant places in the sable vault
Of night's dominions!—Planets, and central orbs
Of other systems;—big as the burning sun
Which lights this nether globe,—yet to our eye
Small as the glow-worm's lamp!—To you I raise
My lowly orisons, while, all bewildered,
My vision strays o'er your ethereal hosts;
Too vast, too boundless for our narrow mind,
Warped with low prejudices, to unfold,
And sagely comprehend. Thence higher soaring,
Through ye I raise my solemn thoughts to Him,
The mighty Founder of this wond'rous maze,
The great Creator! Him! who now sublime,

## A SURVEY OF THE HEAVENS.

Wrapt in the solitary amplitude
Of boundless space, above the rolling spheres
Sits on his silent throne, and meditates.

The angelic hosts, in their inferior Heaven,
Hymn to the golden harps his praise sublime,
Repeating loud, "The Lord our God is great,"
In varied harmonies. The glorious sounds
Roll o'er the air serene. The Æolian spheres,
Harping along their viewless boundaries,
Catch the full note, and cry, "The Lord is great,"
Responding to the Seraphim. O'er all,
From orb to orb, to the remotest verge
Of the created world, the sound is borne,
Till the whole universe is full of Him.

Oh! 'tis this heavenly harmony which now
In fancy strikes upon my listening ear,
And thrills my inmost soul. It bids me smile
On the vain world and all its bustling cares,
And gives a shadowy glimpse of future bliss.
Oh! what is man, when at ambition's height?
What even are kings, when balanced in the scale
Of these stupendous worlds? Almighty God!
Thou, the dread Author of these wondrous works,
Say, canst thou cast on me, poor passing worm,
One look of kind benevolence? Thou canst;
For Thou art full of universal love,
And in thy boundless goodness wilt impart
Thy beams as well to me as to the proud,
The pageant insects of a glittering hour.

Oh! when reflecting on these truths sublime,
How insignificant do all the joys,
The gauds, and honors of the world appear!
How vain ambition! Why has my wakeful lamp
Outwatched the slow-paced night?— Why on the page,
The schoolman's labored page, have I employed
The hours devoted by the world to rest,
And needful to recruit exhausted nature?
Say, can the voice of narrow Fame repay
The loss of health? or can the hope of glory
Lend a new throb unto my languid heart,
Cool, even now, my feverish aching brow,
Relume the fires of this deep-sunken eye,
Or paint new colors on this pallid cheek?
Say, foolish one, can that unbodied frame,
For which thou barterest health and happiness,
Say, can it sooth the slumbers of the grave?
Give a new zest to bliss, or chase the pangs
Of everlasting punishment condign?
Alas! how vain are mortal man's desires!
How fruitless his pursuits! Eternal God!
Guide Thou my footsteps in the way of truth,
And, oh! assist me so to live on earth,
That I may die in peace, and claim a place
In thy high dwelling. All but this is folly,
The vain illusions of deceitful life.
—KIRKE-WHITE.

# GRECIAN MYTHOLOGY.

The lively Grecian, in a land of hills,
Rivers, fertile plains, and sounding shores,
Under a cope of sky more variable,
Could find commodious place for every god,
Promptly received, as prodigally brought,
From the surrounding countries, at the choice
Of all adventurers. With unrivalled skill,
As nicest observation furnished hints
For studious fancy, his quick hand bestowed
On fluent operations a fixed shape;
Metal or stone, idolatrously served.
And yet—triumphant o'er this pompous show
Of art, this palpable array of sense,
On every side encountered; in despite
Of the gross fictions chanted in the streets
By wandering rhapsodists; and in contempt
Of doubt, and bold denial hourly urged
Amid the wrangling schools—a spirit hung,
Beautiful region, o'er thy towns and farms,
Statues and temples, and memorial tombs.

\* \* \* \* \*

In that fair clime, the lonely herdsman, stretched
On the soft grass through half a summer's day,
With music lulled his indolent repose;
And in some fit of weariness, if he,
When his own breath was silent, chanced to hear
A distant strain, far sweeter than the sounds
Which his poor skill could make, his fancy fetched
Even from the blazing chariot of the sun
A beardless youth, who touched a golden lute,
And filled the illumined groves with ravishment.
The nightly hunter, lifting a bright eye
Up towards the crescent moon, with grateful heart
Called on the lovely wanderer who bestowed
That timely light, to share his joyous sport.
And hence a beaming goddess, with her nymphs,
Across the lawn, and through the darksome grove
(Not unaccompanied with tuneful notes
By echo multiplied from rock or cave)
Swept in the storm of chase; as moon and stars
Glance rapidly along the clouded heaven,
When winds are blowing strong. The traveller slaked
His thirst from rill or gushing fount, and thanked
The Naiad. Sunbeams, upon distant hills
Gliding apace, with shadows in their train,
Might, with some help from fancy, be transformed
Into fleet Oreads sporting visibly.
The Zephyrs fanning, as they passed, their wings,
Lacked not for love fair objects, whom they wooed
With gentle whisper. Withered boughs grotesque,
Stripped of their leaves and twigs of hoary age,
From depth of shaggy covert peeping forth

> In the low vale, or on steep mountain side;
> And sometimes intermixed with stirring horns
> Of the live deer, or goat's depending beard,—
> These were the lurking satyrs, a wild brood
> Of gamesome deities; or Pan himself,
> The simple shepherd's awe-aspiring God.      —WORDSWORTH.

## WORDSWORTH.

### (A.D. 1770—1850.)

AT length, as the eighteenth century was winding up its accounts, forth stept William Wordsworth, of whom, as a reader of all pages of nature, it may said that, if we except Dampier, the admirable buccaneer, the gentle *flibustier*, and some few professional naturalists, he first and he last looked at natural objects with the eye that neither will be dazzled from without, nor cheated by preconceptions from within. Most men look at nature in the hurry of a confusion that distinguishes nothing; their error is from without. Pope, again, and many who live in towns, make such blunders as that of supposing the moon to tip with silver the hills behind which she is rising; not by erroneous use of their eyes—for they use them not at all—but by inveterate preconceptions. Scarcely has there been a poet with what could be called a learned eye, or an eye extensively learned, before Wordsworth. Much affectation there has been of that sort since his rise, and at all times much counterfeit enthusiasm; but the sum of the matter is this, that Wordsworth had his passion for nature fixed in his blood; it was a necessity, like that of the mulberry leaf to the silkworm; and through his commerce with nature did he live and breathe. Hence it was, viz., from the truth of his love, that his knowledge grew; whilst most others, being merely hypocrites in their love, have turned out merely sciolists in their knowledge.

A volume might be filled with such glimpses of novelty as Wordsworth has first laid bare, even to the apprehension of the senses. For the understanding, when moving in the same track of human sensibilities, he has done only not so much. How often, to give an instance or two, must the human heart have felt the case, and yearned for an expression of the case, when there are sorrows which descend far below the region in which tears gather ; and yet, who has ever given utterance to this feeling until Wordsworth came with his immortal line—

> "Thoughts that do often lie too deep for tears."

This sentiment, and others that might be adduced, such as "The child is father of the man," have even passed into the popular heart, and are often quoted by those who know not whom they are quoting. Magnificent, again, is the sentiment, and yet an echo to one which lurks amongst all hearts, in relation to the frailty of merely human schemes for working good, which so often droop and collapse through the unsteadiness of human energies,—

> "Foundations must be laid
> In Heaven."

How ? Foundations laid in realms that are above ? But that is impossible ; that is at war with elementary physics ; foundations must be laid below. Yes ; and even so the poet throws the mind yet more forcibly upon the hyperphysical character, on the grandeur transcending all physics, of those spiritual and shadowy foundations which alone are enduring.

But the great distinction of Wordsworth, and the pledge of his increasing popularity is the extent of his sympathy with what is really permanent in human feelings, and also the depth of this sympathy. Young and Cowper, the two earlier leaders in the province of meditative poetry, are too circumscribed in the range of their sympathies, too narrow, too illiberal, and too exclusive. Both these poets manifested the quality of their strength in the quality of their public reception. Popular in some degree from the first, they entered upon the inheritance of their fame almost at once. Far different was the fate of Wordsworth ; for in poetry of this class, which appeals to what lies deepest in man, in proportion to the native power of the poet, and his fitness for permanent life, is the strength of resistance in the public taste. Whatever is too original will be hated at the first. It must slowly mould a public for itself, and the resistance of the early thoughtless judgments must be overcome by a counter-resistance to itself in a better audience, slowly mustering against the first. Forty and seven years (written in 1845) it is since William Wordsworth first appeared as an author. Twenty of those years he was the scoff of the world, and his poetry a by-word of scorn. Since then, and more than once, senates have rung with acclamations to the echo of his name. Now, at this moment, whilst we are talking about him, he has entered upon his seventy-sixth year. For himself, according to the course of nature, he cannot be far from his setting; but his poetry is only now clearing the clouds that gathered about its rising. Meditative poetry is perhaps that province of literature which will ultimately maintain most power amongst the generations which are coming ; but in this department at least there is little competition to be apprehended by Wordsworth, from anything that has appeared since the death of Shakespeare. —DE QUINCEY.

## THE SPINNING MAIDEN'S CROSS.

BENEATH Vienna's ancient wall
  Lie level plains of sand,
And there the pathway runs of all
  That seek the Holy Land.

And from the wall a little space,
  And by the trodden line,
Stands, seen from many a distant place,
  A tall and slender shrine.

It seems, so standing there alone,
  To those who come and go,
No pile of dull unconscious stone,
  But touch'd with joy or woe;

Seems to the stranger on his way,
  A friend that forth hath set,
The parting moment to delay,
  And stands and lingers yet.

While to the long-gone traveller
  Returning to his home,
It seems with doubtful greeting there
  Of joy and sorrow come.

Smiles have been there of beaming joy,
  And tears of bitter loss,
As friends have met and parted by
  The Spinning Maiden's Cross.

Young Margaret had the gentlest heart
  Of all the maidens there,
Nor ever fail'd her constant part
  Of daily toil and prayer.

But when the Sabbath-morn had smiled,
    And early prayer was o'er,
Then Marg'ret, gentle, still, and mild,
    Had happiness in store.

For then with Wenzel side by side
    In calm delight she stray'd,
Amid the Prater's flowery pride,
    Or in the Augarten's shade.

"Gretchen beloved! Gretchen dear!
    Bright days we soon shall see;
My master, lord of Lowethier,
    Will link my lot with thee.

And there, upon the Kahlen's swell,
    Where distant Donau shines,
He gives a cot where we shall dwell,
    And tend his spreading vines."

Though joy through Margaret sent a thrill,
    And at her eyes ran o'er,
Few words she spoke for good or ill,
    Nor Wenzel needed more.

But when again the Sabbath-bell
    Had struck on Wenzel's ear,
A sadder tale had he to tell,
    And Margaret to hear.

"Gretchen beloved! Gretchen dear!
    Joy yet;—but patience now;
My master, lord of Lowethier,
    Has bound him with a vow;

And he must to the Holy Land,
    Our Saviour's tomb to free;
And I and all his faithful band
    Must with him o'er the sea."

A swelling heart did Margaret press,
    But calm was she to view;
Meekly she bore her happiness,
    Her sorrow meekly too.

Her solitary Sabbaths brought
    A prayer, a patient sigh,
As on the Holy Land she thought,
    Where saints did live and die.

But from the Holy Land soon came
    Returning pilgrims there,
And heavy tidings brought with them
    For Margaret's anxious ear.

For Wenzel is a captive made
 In Paynim dungeon cold,
And there must lie till ransom paid
 A hundred coins of gold.

Alas for Margaret! should she spin,
 And all her store be sold,
In one long year she scarce could win
 A single piece of gold.

Yet love can hope through good and ill,
 When other hope is gone;
Shall she who loves so well be still,
 And he in prison groan?

She felt within her inmost heart
 A strange bewilder'd swell,
Too soft to break with sudden start,
 Too gentle to rebel.

And what she hoped or thought to earn
 Poor Margaret never knew,
But on her distaff oft she'd turn
 A thoughtful, hopeful view.

And by the stone where last they met,
 Each day she took her stand;
And twirl'd the thread till daylight set,
 With unremitting hand.

Her little store upon the stone
 She spread to passers-by;
And oft they paused and gazed upon
 Her meek and mournful eye.

And e'en from those who had but few,
 Full oft a coin she won,
And faster far her treasure grew
 Than e'er her hopes had done.

Through shine and rain, through heat and snow,
 Her daily task she plied;
And wrought for two long twelvemonths so,
 And then she gently died.

They took the treasure she had won,
 Full many a varied coin,
And o'er the stone where she had spun,
 They raised that shapely shrine.

And still Vienna's maids recall
 Her meekly suffer'd loss,
And point the fane beneath the wall—
 THE SPINNING MAIDEN'S CROSS.

—WHEWELL.

## KILLED AT THE FORD.

He is dead, the beautiful youth,
The heart of honor, the tongue of truth,—
He, the life and light of us all,
Whose voice was blithe as a bugle call.
Whom all eyes followed with one consent,
The cheer of whose laugh, and whose pleasant word,
Hushed all murmurs of discontent.

Only last night as we rode along,
Down the dark of the mountain gap,
To visit the picket-guard at the ford,
Little dreaming of any mishap,
He was humming the words of some old song:
"Two red roses he had on his cap,
And another he bore at the point of his sword"

Sudden and swift a whistling ball
Came out of a wood, and the voice was still,
Something I heard in the darkness fall,
And for a moment my blood grew chill;
I spake in a whisper, as he who speaks.
In a room where some one is lying dead;
But he made no answer to what I said.

We lifted him up on his saddle again,
And through the mire, and the mist, and the rain,
Carried him back to the silent camp,
And laid him as if asleep on his bed;
And I saw by the light of the surgeon's lamp
Two white roses upon his cheeks,
And one just over his heart blood red!

And I saw in a vision how far and fleet
That fatal bullet went speeding forth,
Till it reached a town in the distant North,
Till it reached a house in a sunny street,
Till it reached a heart that ceased to beat
Without a murmur, without a cry;
And a bell was tolled in that far-off town,
For one who had passed from cross to crown,—
And the neighbors wondered that she should die.
—LONGFELLOW.

## THE BEGINNINGS OF COMMERCE.

THE original station allotted to man by his Creator was in the mild and fertile regions of the East. There the human race began its career of improvement; and from the remains of sciences which were anciently cultivated, as well as of arts which were anciently exercised in India, we may conclude it to be one of the first countries in which men made any considerable progress in that career. The wisdom of the East was early celebrated, and its productions were early in request among distant nations. The intercourse, however, between different countries was carried on, at first, entirely by land. As the people of the East appear soon to have acquired complete dominion over the useful animals, they could early undertake the long and tiresome journeys which it was necessary to make, in order to maintain their intercourse, and by the provident bounty of Heaven they were furnished with a beast of burden, without whose aid it would have been impossible to accomplish them. The camel, by its persevering strength, by its moderation in the use of food, and the singularity of its internal structure, which enables it to lay in a stock of water sufficient for several days, put it in their power to convey bulky commodities through those deserts which must be traversed by all who travel from any of the countries west of the Euphrates, towards India. Trade was carried on in this manner, particularly by the nations near to the Arabian Gulf, from the earliest period to which historical information reaches. Distant journeys, however, would be undertaken at first only occasionally, and by a few adventurers. But by degrees, from attention to their mutual safety and comfort, numerous bodies of merchants assembled at stated times, and formed a temporary association, known afterwards by the name of a Caravan, governed by officers of their own choice, and subject to regulations, of which experience had taught them the utility; they performed journeys of such extent and duration, as appear astonishing to nations not accustomed to this mode of carrying on commerce.

But notwithstanding every improvement that could be made in the manner of conveying the productions of one country to another by land, the inconveniences which attended it were obvious and unavoidable. It was often dangerous, always expensive, and tedious and fatiguing. A method of communication more easy and expeditious was sought, and the ingenuity of man gradually discovered that the rivers, the arms of the sea, and even the ocean itself, were destined to open and facilitate intercourse with the various regions of the earth, between which they appear, at first view, to be placed as insuperable barriers. Navigation, however, and shipbuilding, as I have observed in another work, are arts so nice and complicated, that they require the talents, as well as experience, of many successive ages to bring them to any degree of perfection. From the raft or canoe which first served to carry a savage over the river that obstructed him in the chase, to the construction of a vessel capable of conveying a numerous crew or a considerable cargo of goods to a distant coast, the progress of improvement is immense. Many efforts would be made, many experiments would be tried, and much labour as well as ingenuity would be employed, before this arduous and important undertaking could be accomplished.

Even after some improvement was made in shipbuilding, the intercourse of nations with each other by sea was far from being extensive. From the accounts of the earliest historians, we learn that navigation made its first efforts in the Mediterranean and the Arabian Gulf; and in them the first active operations of commerce were carried on. From an attentive inspection of the position and form of these two great inland seas, these accounts appear to be highly probable. These seas lay open the continents of Europe, Asia, and Africa, and spreading to a great extent along the coasts of most fertile and most early civilized countries in each, seem to have been destined by nature to facilitate their communication with one another. We find, accordingly, that the first voyages of the Egyptians and Phœnicians, the most ancient navigators mentioned in history, were made in the Mediterranean. Their trade, however, was not long confined to the countries bordering upon it. By acquiring early possession of ports on the Arabian Gulf, they extended the sphere of their commerce, and are represented as the first people of the west who opened a communication by sea with India.

In that account of the progress of navigation and discovery, which I prefixed to the history of America, I considered with attention the maritime operations of the Egyptians and Phœnicians; a brief review of them here, as far as they relate to their connexion with India, is all that is requisite for illustrating the subject of my present inquiries. With respect to the former of these people, the information which history affords is slender, and of doubtful authority. The fertile soil and mild climate of Egypt produced the necessaries and comforts of life in such profusion as to render its inhabitants so independent of other countries, that it became early an established maxim in their policy to renounce all intercourse with foreigners. In consequence of this, they held all seafaring persons in detestation, as impious and profane, and fortifying their harbors, they denied strangers admission into them.

The enterprising ambition of Sesostris disdained the restraints imposed upon it by these contracted ideas of his subjects, and prompted him to render the Egyptians a commercial people; and in the course of his reign he so completely accomplished this, that if we may give credit to some historians, he was able to fit out a fleet of four hundred ships in the Arabian Gulf, which conquered all the countries stretching along the Erythrean sea to India. At the same time his army, led by himself, marched through Asia, and subjected to his dominion every port of it as far as to the banks of the Ganges; and crossing that river, advanced to the Eastern Ocean. But these efforts produced no permanent effect, and appear to have been so contrary to the genius and habits of the Egyptians, that, on the death of Sesostris, they resumed their ancient maxims, and many ages elapsed before the commercial connexion of Egypt with India came to be of such importance as to merit any notice in this Disquisition.

The history of the early maritime operations of Phœnicia is not involved in the same obscurity with those of Egypt. Every circumstance in the character and situation of the Phœnicians was favourable to the commercial spirit. The territory which they possessed was neither large nor fertile; it was from commerce only that they could derive either opulence or power. Accordingly, the trade carried on by the Phœnicians of Sidon and Tyre was extensive and adventurous; and, both in their manners and policy, they resemble the great commercial states of modern times more than any people in the ancient world. Among the various branches of their commerce, that with India may be regarded as one of the most considerable and most lucrative. As by their situation on the Mediterranean, and the imperfect state of navigation, they could not attempt to open a direct communication with India by sea, the enterprising spirit of commerce prompted them to wrest from the Idumæans some commodious harbors towards the bottom of the Arabian Gulf.

From these they held a regular intercourse with India, on the one hand, and with the eastern and southern coasts of Africa on the other. The distance, however, from the Arabian Gulf to Tyre was considerable, and rendered the conveyance of goods to it by land-carriage so tedious and expensive that it became necessary for them to take possession of Rhinocolura, the nearest port in the Mediterranean to the Arabian Gulf. Thither all the commodities brought from India were conveyed overland, by a route much shorter and more practicable than that by which the productions of the East were carried, at a subsequent period, from the opposite shore of the Arabian Gulf to the Nile. At Rhinocolura they were re-shipped and transported, by an easy navigation, to Tyre, and distributed through the world. This, as it is the earliest route of communication with India of which we have any authentic description, had so many advantages over any ever known before the modern discovery of a new course of navigation to the East, that the Phœnicians could supply other nations with the productions of India in greater abundance, and at a cheaper rate, than any people of antiquity. To this circumstance, which, for a considerable time, secured to them a monopoly of that trade, was owing, not only the extraordinary wealth of individuals, which rendered the "merchants of Tyre princes, and her traffickers the honorable of the earth;" but the extensive power of the state itself, which first taught mankind to conceive what vast resources a commercial people possess, and what great exertions they are capable of making. — ROBERTSON.

## FROM THE TRAVELLER.

WHERE'ER I roam, whatever realms to see,
My heart untravell'd fondly turns to thee:
Still to my brother turns, with ceaseless pain,
And drags at each remove a lengthened chain.

Eternal blessings crown my earliest friend,
And round his dwelling guardian saints attend;
Blest be that spot where cheerful guests retire
To pause from toil, and trim their evening fire:
Blest that abode, where want and pain repair,
And every stranger finds a ready chair:
Blest be those feasts with simple plenty crown'd,
Where all the ruddy family round
Laugh at the jests or pranks that never fail,
Or sigh with pity at some mournful tale :
Or press the bashful stranger to his food,
And learn the luxury of doing good.

But me not destin'd such delights to share,
My prime of life in wandering spent and care:

    Impelled, with steps unceasing, to pursue
Some fleeting good, that mocks me with the view;
That, like the circle bounding earth and skies,
Allures from far, yet, as I follow, flies;
My fortune leads to traverse realms alone,
And find no spot of all the world my own.

    Ev'n now where Alpine solitudes ascend,
I sit me down a pensive hour to spend;
And placed on high above the storm's career,
Look downward where an hundred realms appear;
Lakes, forests, cities, plains extending wide,
The pomp of kings, the shepherd's humbler pride.

    When thus Creation's charms around combine,
Amidst the store, should thankless pride repine;
Say, should the philosophic mind disdain
That good which makes each humbler bosom vain?
Let school-taught pride dissemble all it can,
These little things are great to little man;
And wiser he, whose sympathetic mind
Exults in all the good of all mankind.
Ye glittering towns with wealth and splendor crown'd,
Ye fields, where summer spreads profusion round;
Ye lakes, whose vessels catch the busy gale;
Ye bending swains, that dress the flowery vale;
For me your tributary stores combine:
Creation's heir, the world, the world is mine.

    As some lone miser, visiting his store,
Bends at his treasure, counts, recounts it o'er;
Hoards after hoards his rising raptures fill,
Yet still he sighs for hoards are wanting still:
Thus to my breast alternate passions rise,
Pleas'd with each good that heaven to man supplies:
Yet oft a sigh prevails, and sorrows fall,
To see the hoard of human bliss so small;
And oft I wish, amidst the scene to find
Some spot to real happiness consign'd,
Where my worn soul, each wandering hope at rest,
May gather bliss to see my fellows blest.
                                 – GOLDSMITH.

## THE DEATH OF PAUL DOMBEY.

PAUL had never risen from his little bed. He lay there, listening to the noises in the street, quite tranquilly; not caring much how the time went, but watching it, and watching everything about him with observing eyes. When the sunbeams struck into his room through the rustling blinds, and quivered on the opposite wall like golden water, he knew that evening was coming on, and that the sky was red and beautiful. As the reflection died away, and a gloom went creeping up the wall, he watched it deepen, deepen, deepen into night. Then he thought how the long streets were dotted with lamps, and how the peaceful stars were shining overhead. His fancy had a strange tendency to wander to the river, which he knew was flowing through the great city; and now he thought how black it was, and how deep it would look, reflecting the hosts of stars—and more than all, how steadily it rolled away to meet the sea.

As it grew later in the night, and footsteps in the streets became so rare that he could hear them coming, count them as they passed, and lose them in the hollow distance, he would lie and watch the many-coloured ring about the candle, and wait patiently for day. His only trouble was, the swift and rapid river. He felt forced, sometimes, to try to stop it—to stem it with his childish hands—or choke its way with sand— and when he saw it coming on resistless, he cried out. But a word from Florence, who was always at his side, restored him to himself; and leaning his poor head upon her breast, he told Floy of his dream, and smiled.

When day began to dawn again, he watched for the sun; and when its cheerful light began to sparkle in the room, he pictured to himself—pictured?—he saw the high church towers rising up into the morning sky, the town reviving, waking, starting into life once more, the river glistening as it rolled (but rolling fast as ever), and the country bright with dew. Familiar sounds and cries came by degrees into the street below; the servants in the house were roused and busy; faces looked in at the door, and voices asked his attendants softly how he was. Paul always answered for himself, "I am better. I am a great deal better, thank you! Tell papa so!" By little and little, he got tired of the bustle of the day, the noise of carriages and carts, and people passing and repassing; and would fall asleep, or be troubled with a restless and uneasy sense again—the child could hardly tell whether this were in his sleeping or his waking moments—of that rushing river. "Why, will it never stop, Floy?" he would sometimes ask her. "It is bearing me away, I think."

But Floy could always soothe and reassure him; and it was his daily delight to make her lay her head down on his pillow, and take some rest. "You are always watching me, Floy. Let me watch you now!" They would prop him up with cushions in a corner of his bed, and there he would recline the while she lay beside him; bending forwards oftentimes to kiss her, and whispering to those who were near that she was tired, and how she had sat up so many nights beside him. Thus the flush of the day, in its heat and light, would gradually decline; and again the golden water would be dancing on the wall.

He was visited by as many as three grave doctors—they used to assemble down-stairs, and come up together—and the room was so quiet, and Paul was so observant of them (though he never asked of anybody what they said), that he even knew the difference in the sound of their watches. But his interest centred in Sir Parker Peps, who always took his seat on the side of the bed. For Paul had heard them say long ago, that that gentleman had been with his mamma when she clasped Florence in her arms, and died. And he could not forget it now. He liked him for it. He was not afraid. The people round him changed as unaccountably as on that first night at Dr. Blimber's—except Florence; Florence never changed—and what had been Sir Parker Peps was now his father, sitting with his head upon his hand. Old Mrs. Pipchin, dozing on an easy-chair, often changed to Miss Fox, or his aunt; and Paul was quite content to shut his eyes again, and see what happened next without emotion. But this figure with its head upon its hand returned so often, and remained so long, and sat so still and solemn, never speaking, never being spoken to, and rarely lifting up its face, that Paul began to wonder languidly if it were real; and in the night-time saw it sitting there with fear.

"Floy," he said, "what is that?" "Where, dearest?" "There! at the bottom of the bed." "There's nothing there, except papa!" The figure lifted up its head, and rose, and coming to the bedside, said—"My own boy, don't you know me?" Paul looked it in the face, and thought, was this his father! But the face, so altered to his thinking, thrilled while he gazed, as if it were in pain; and before he could reach out both his hands to take it between them, and draw it towards him, the figure turned away quickly from the little bed, and went out at the door. Paul looked at Florence with a fluttering heart, but he knew what she was going to say, and stopped her with his face against her lips. The next time he observed the figure sitting at the bottom of the bed, he called to it, "Don't be so sorry for me, dear papa; indeed I am quite happy!" His father coming, and bending down to him—which he did quickly, and without first pausing by the bedside—Paul held him round the neck, and repeated these words to him several times, and very earnestly; and Paul never saw him again in his room at any time, whether it were day or night, but he called out, "Don't be so sorry for me; indeed I am quite happy." This was the beginning of his always saying in the morning that he was a great deal better, and that they were to tell his father so.

How many times the golden water danced upon the wall; how many nights the dark river rolled towards the sea in spite of him; Paul never counted, never sought to know. If their kindness, or his sense of it, could have increased, they were more kind, and he more grateful every day; but whether they were many days, or few, appeared of little moment now to the gentle boy. One night he had been thinking of his mother, and her picture in the drawing-room down-stairs, and had thought she must have loved sweet Florence better than his father did, to have held her in her arms when she felt that she was dying; for even he, her brother, who had such dear love for her, could have no greater wish than that. The train of thought suggested to him to inquire if he had ever seen his mother; for he could not remember whether they had told him yes or no, the river running very fast, and confusing his mind. "Floy, did I ever see mamma?" "No, darling; why?" "Did I never see any kind face, like mamma's looking at me when I was a baby, Floy?" he asked, incredulously, as if he had some vision of a face before him. "Oh yes, dear!" "Whose, Floy?" "Your old nurse's; often." "And where is my old nurse?" said Paul. "Is she dead too? Floy, are we *all* dead, except you?"

There was a hurry in the room, for an instant—longer, perhaps; but it seemed no more—then all was still again; and Florence, with her face quite colourless, but smiling, held his head upon her arm. Her arm trembled very much. "Show me that old nurse, Floy, if you please?" "She is not here, darling. She shall come to-morrow."—"Thank you, Floy!"

"And who is this? Is this my old nurse?" said the child, regarding with a radiant smile a figure coming in. Yes, yes! No other stranger would have shed those tears at sight of him, and called him her dear boy, her pretty boy, her own poor blighted child. No other woman would have stooped down by his bed, and taken up his wasted hand and put it to her lips and breast, as one who had some right to fondle it. No other woman would have so forgotten everybody there but him and Floy, and been so full of tenderness and pity. "Floy, this is a kind good face," said Paul. "I am glad to see it again. Don't go away, old nurse! Stay here!"

"Now lay me down," he said; "and, Floy, come close to me, and let me see you!" Sister and brother wound their arms around each other, and the golden light came streaming in, and fell upon them, locked together. "How fast the river runs, between its green banks and the rushes, Floy! But it's very near the sea. I hear the waves! They always said so." Presently he told her that the motion of the boat upon the stream was lulling him to rest. How green the banks were now, how bright the flowers growing on them, and how tall the rushes! Now the boat was out at sea, but gliding smoothly on; and now there was a shore before them. Who stood on the bank? He put his hands together, as he had been used to do at his prayers. He did not remove his arms to do it; but they saw him fold them so behind her neck. "Mamma is like you, Floy; I know her by the face! But tell them that the print upon the stairs at school is not divine enough. The light about the head is shining on me as I go!"

The golden ripple on the wall came back again, and nothing else stirred in the room. The old, old fashion! The fashion that came in with our first garments, and will last unchanged until our race has run its course, and the wide firmament is rolled up like a scroll. The old, old fashion—Death! Oh, thank God, all who see it, for that older fashion yet, of Immortality! And look upon us, angels of young children, with regard not quite estranged, when the swift river bears us to the ocean! —DICKENS.

## WOODLARK LANE.

THERE are some places that seem formed by nature for doubling and redoubling the delight of reading and dreaming over the greater poets. Their works never seem to me half so delightful as when I pore over them in the silence and solitude of a certain green lane, about half a mile from home; sometimes seated on the roots of an old fantastic beech, sometimes on the trunk of a felled oak, or sometimes on the ground itself, with my back propped lazily against a rugged elm.

In that very lane am I writing on this sultry June day, luxuriating in the shade, the verdure, the fragrance of hay-field and of bean-field, and the absence of all noise, except the song of birds, and that strange mingling of many sounds, the whiz of a thousand forms of insect life, so often heard among the general hush of a summer noon.

Woodlark Lane is so called, not after the migratory bird so dear to sportsmen and epicure, but from the name of a family, who, three centuries ago, owned the old manor-house, a part of which still adjoins it, just as the neighboring eminence of Beech Hill is called after the ancient family of De la Beeche, rather than from the three splendid beech-trees that still crown its summit; and this lane would probably be accounted beautiful by any one who loved the close recesses of English scenery, even though the person in question should happen not to have haunted it these fifty years as I have done.

It is a grassy lane, edging off from the high road, nearly two miles in length, and varying from fifty to one hundred yards in width. The hedge rows on either side are so thickly planted with tall elms as almost to form a verdant wall, for the greater part doubly screened by rows of the same stately tree, the down-dropping branches forming close shady footpaths on either side, and leaving in the centre a broad level strip of the finest turf, just broken, here and there, by cart tracks, and crossed by slender rills. The effect of these tall solemn trees, so equal in height, so unbroken, and so continuous, is quite grand and imposing as twilight comes on; especially when some slight bend in the lane gives to the outline almost the look of an amphitheatre.

On the southern side, the fields slope with more or less abruptness to the higher lands above, and winding foot paths and close woody lanes lead up the hill to the breezy common. To the north, the fields are generally of pasture-land, broken by two or three picturesque farm-houses, with their gable ends, their tall chimneys, their trim gardens, and their flowery orchards; and varied by a short avenue, leading to the equally picturesque old manor-house, of darkest brick and quaintest architecture. Over the gates, too, we catch glimpses of more distant objects. The large white mansion where my youth was spent, rising from its plantations, and the small church embowered in trees, whose bell is heard at the close of day, breathing of peace and holiness.

Toward the end of the lane, a bright clear brook comes dancing over a pebbly bed, bringing with it all that water is wont to bring of life, of music, of color. Gayly it bubbles through banks adorned by the yellow flag, the flowering rush, the willow-herb, the meadow-sweet, and the forget-me-not; now expanding into a wide quiet pool, now contracted into a mimic rapid between banks that almost meet; and so the little stream keeps us company, giving, on this sunny day, an indescribable feeling of refreshment and coolness, until we arrive at the end of the lane, where it slants away to the right amid a long stretch of water meadows; while we pause to gaze at the lovely scenery on the other hand, where a bit of marshy ground leads to the park paling and grand old trees of the Great House at Beech Hill, through an open grove of oaks, terminated by a piece of wild woodland, so wild, that Robin-hood might have taken it for a glade in his own Forest of Merry Sherwood.

Except about half a mile of gravelly road, leading from the gate of the manor-house to one of the smaller farms, and giving by its warm orange tint, much of richness to the picture, there is nothing like a passable carriage way in the whole length of the lane, so that the quiet is perfect.

Occasional passengers there are, however, gentle and simple; my friend, Mr. B., for instance, has just cantered past on his blood-horse, with a nod and a smile, saying nothing, but apparently a good deal amused with my arrangements. And here comes a procession of cows going to milking, with an old attendant, still called the cow-boy, who, although they have seen me often enough, one should think, sitting underneath a tree writing, with my little maid close by hemming flounces, and my dog, Fanchon, nestled at my feet—still *will* start, as if they had never seen a woman before in their lives. Back they start, and then they rush forward, and then the old drover emits certain sounds, which it is to be presumed the cows understand; sounds so horribly discordant that little Fanchon although to her, too, they ought to be familiar, if not comprehensible— starts up in a fright on her feet, deranging all the economy of my extempore desk, and well-nigh upsetting the inkstand. Very much frightened is my pretty pet, the arrantest coward that ever walked upon four legs! And so she avenges herself, as cowards are wont to do, by following the cows, at a safe distance, as soon as they are fairly past, and beginning to bark amain when they are nearly out of sight. Then follows a motley group of the same nature, colts, yearlings, calves, heifers, with a shouting boy and his poor shabby mongrel cur for driver. The poor cur wants to play with Fanchon, but Fanchon, besides being a coward, is also a beauty, and holds her state; although, I think, if he could but stay long enough, that the good humor of the poor merry creature would prove infectious, and beguile the little lady into a game of romps. Lastly appears the most solemn troop of all, a grave company of geese and goslings, with the gander at their head, marching with the decorum and dignity proper to the birds who saved Rome. Fanchon, who once had an affair with a gander, in which she was notably worsted, retreats out of sight, and ensconces herself between me and the trees.

Besides these mere passing droves, we have a scattered little flock of ewes and lambs belonging to an industrious widow, on the hill, and tended by two sunburnt smiling children, her son and daughter; a pretty pair, as innocent as the poor sheep they watch beside, never seen apart. And peasants returning from their work, and a stray urchin bird's nesting; and that will make a complete catalogue of the frequenters of our lane—except, indeed, that now and then a village youth and village maiden will steal along the sheltered path. Perhaps they came to listen to the nightingales, for which the place is famous, perhaps they came to listen to the voice which each prefers to all the nightingales that ever sang—who knows?

Such are our passers-by. Sometimes, however, we have what I was about to call settled inhabitants, in the shape of a camp of gipsies.

Just where the lane, enlivened by a rustic bridge, suddenly expands to nearly double its proper width, a nook appears, so dry, so snug, so shady, so cozy, that it is almost worth while to be a gipsy to live in it. Here, at almost every season, between May and November, may be seen two or three low tents, with a cart or so drawn up under the hedge, an old horse and sundry donkeys grazing round about. At a safe distance from the encampment appears a fire, glimmering and vapory by day, glowing into an intensity of blaze and comfort in the twilight. Sometimes a pot is hung on by the primitive contrivance of three sticks united at the top; sometimes a copper kettle dazzling bright and clean, and around it the usual group of picturesque women and children. The men, who carry on a small trade in forest ponies, are seldom visible at the camp; the children make baskets, and the women sell them and tell fortunes; the former calling affording an excuse and an introduction to the less ostensible, but not less profitable, craft.

Baskets they make, and baskets they sell, at about double the price at which they might be bought at the dearest shop in the good town of Belford Regis; of this I am myself a living instance, having been talked into buying a pair at that rate only the last Saturday that ever fell.

I confess to liking the gipsies; strange, wild, peculiar people, whose origin, whose history, whose very language is a mystery! I do not like them the less that I have never experienced at their hands the slightest incivility, or the most trifling wrong, for this affair of the baskets can hardly be called such, it being wholly at my option to buy or to refuse.

—MARY R. MITFORD.

## A NAME IN THE SAND.

ALONE I walk'd the ocean strand;
A pearly shell was in my hand;
I stoop'd and wrote upon the sand
    My name—the year—the day.
As onward from the spot I pass'd
One lingering look behind I cast,
A wave came rolling high and fast
    And wash'd my lines away.

And so, methought, 'twill shortly be
With every mark on earth from me;
A wave of dark oblivion's sea
    Will sweep across the place,
Where I have trod the sandy shore
Of time, and been to be no more,
Of me—my day—the name I bore,
    To leave nor track nor trace.

And yet, with Him who counts the sands,
And holds the waters in his hands,
I know the lasting record stands
    Inscribed against my name,
Of all this mortal part has wrought
Of all this thinking soul has thought,
And from all these fleeting moments caught
    For glory, or for shame.

—GOULD.

## THE HAPPINESS OF ANIMALS.

THE air, the earth, the water, teem with delighted existence. In a spring noon or a summer evening, on whichever side we turn our eyes, myriads of happy beings crowd upon our view. "The insect youth are on the wing." Swarms of new-born flies are trying their pinions in the air. Their sportive motions, their gratuitous activity, their continual change of place without use or purpose, testify their joy, and the exultation which they feel in their lately-discovered faculties.

A *bee*, amongst the flowers in spring, is one of the most cheerful objects that can be looked upon. Its life appears to be all enjoyment: so busy and so pleased: yet it is only a specimen of insect life, with which, by reason of the animal being half domesticated, we happen to be better acquainted than we are with that of others. The whole winged insect tribe, it is probable, are equally intent upon their proper employments, and under every variety of constitution gratified, and perhaps equally gratified, by the offices which the Author of their nature has assigned to them.

But the atmosphere is not the only scene of their enjoyment. Plants are covered with little insects, greedily sucking their juices, and constantly, as it should seem, in the act of sucking. It cannot be doubted that this is a state of gratification. What else should fix them so closely to the operation, and so long? Other species are running about, with an alacrity in their motions which carries with it every mark of pleasure. Large patches of ground are sometimes half covered with these brisk and sprightly natures.

If we look to what the *waters* produce, shoals of the fry of fish frequent the margins of rivers, of lakes, and of the sea itself. These are so happy that they know not what to do with themselves. Their attitudes, their vivacity, their leaps out of the water, their frolics in it, all conduce to show their excess of spirits, and are simply the effects of that excess. Walking by the seaside, in a calm evening, upon a sandy shore, and with an ebbing tide, I have frequently remarked the appearance of a dark cloud, or, rather, very thick mist, hanging over the edge of the water, to the height, perhaps, of half a yard, and of the breadth of two or three yards, stretching along the coast as far as the eye could reach, and always retiring with the water.

When this cloud came to be examined, it proved to be so much space filled with young *shrimps*, in the act of bounding into the air, from the shallow margin of the water, or from the wet sand. If any motion of a mute animal could express delight, it was this: if they had meant to make signs of their happiness, they could not have done it more intelligibly. Suppose, then, what there is no reason to doubt, each individual of this number to be in a state of positive enjoyment; what a sum, collectively, of gratification and pleasure, have we here before our view!

The *young* of all animals appear to receive pleasure simply from the exercise of their limbs and bodily faculties, without reference to any end to be attained, or any use to be answered, by the exertion. A child, without knowing anything of the use of language, is in a high degree delighted with being able to speak. Its incessant repetition of a few articulate sounds, or, perhaps, of a single word, which it has learned to pronounce, proves this point clearly. Nor is it less pleased with its first successful endeavors to walk, or rather to run (which precedes walking), although entirely ignorant of the importance of the attainment to its future life, and even without applying it to any present purpose. A child is delighted with speaking, without having anything to say; and with walking, without knowing whither to go. And, previously to both these, it is reasonable to believe that the waking hours of infancy are agreeably taken up with the exercise of vision, or perhaps, more properly speaking, with learning to see.

But it is not for youth alone that the great Parent of creation has provided. Happiness is found with the purring cat, no less than with the playful kitten: in the arm-chair of dozing age, as well as in either the sprightliness of the dance or the animation of the chase. To novelty, to acuteness of sensation, to hope, to ardor of pursuit, succeeds, what is, in no inconsiderable degree, an equivalent for them all, "perception of ease." Herein is the exact difference between the young and the old. The young are not happy but when enjoying pleasure; the old are happy when free from pain. And this constitution suits with the degree of animal power, which they respectively possess. The vigor of youth was to be stimulated to action by impatience of rest; whilst to the imbecility of age, quietness and repose become positive gratifications. In one important respect, the advantage is with the old. A state of ease is, generally speaking, more attainable than a state of pleasure. A constitution, therefore, which can enjoy ease, is preferable to that which can taste only pleasure.

This same perception of ease oftentimes renders old age a condition of great comfort; especially when riding at its anchor, after a busy or tempestuous life. It is well described, by Rousseau, to be the interval of repose and enjoyment, between the hurry and the end of life. How far the same cause extends to other animal natures, cannot be judged of with certainty. The appearance of satisfaction with which most animals, as their activity subsides, seek and enjoy rest, affords reason to believe that this source of gratification is appointed to advanced life, under all, or most, of its various forms.

There is a great deal of truth in the following representation, given by Dr. Percival, a very pious writer, as well as excellent man: " To the intelligent and virtuous, old age presents a scene of tranquil enjoyments, of obedient appetites, of well-regulated affections, of maturity in knowledge, and of calm preparation for immortality. In this serene and dignified state, placed, as it were, on the confines of two worlds, the mind of a good man reviews what is past with the complacency of an approving conscience; and looks forward with humble confidence in the mercy of God, and with devout aspirations towards his eternal and ever-increasing favor." —PALEY.

## SPRING.

I HEARD a thousand blended notes
While in a grove I sat reclined,
In that sweet mood when pleasant thoughts
Bring sad thoughts to the mind.

To her fair works did Nature link
The human soul that through me ran;
And much it grieved my heart to think
What Man has made of Man.

Through primrose tufts, in that sweet bower,
The periwinkle trail'd its wreaths;
And 'tis my faith that every flower
Enjoys the air it breathes.

The birds around me hopp'd and play'd,
Their thoughts I cannot measure—
But the least motion which they made
It seem'd a thrill of pleasure.

The budding twigs spread out their fan
To catch the breezy air;
And I must think, do all I can,
That there was pleasure there.

If this belief from heaven be sent,
If such be Nature's holy plan,
Have I not reason to lament
What Man has made of Man?

## ON THE DEATH OF WELLINGTON.
### (A.D. 1769—1852.)

THE Chancellor of the Exchequer rose, and, while the House lent him its deepest attention, spoke as follows:—

"The House of Commons is called upon to-night to fulfil a sorrowful, but a noble duty. It has to recognize, in the face of the country, and of the civilized world, the loss of the most illustrious of our citizens, and to offer to the ashes of the great departed the solemn anguish of a bereaved nation. The princely personage who has left us was born in an age more fertile of great events than any period of recorded time. Of these vast incidents the most conspicuous were his own deeds, and these were performed with the smallest means, and in defiance of the greatest obstacles. He was therefore, not only a great man, but the greatest man of a great age. Amid the chaos and conflagration which attended the end of the last century there rose one of those beings who seem born to master mankind. It is not too much to say that Napoleon combined the imperial ardor of Alexander with the strategy of Hannibal. The kings of the earth fell before his fiery and subtile genius, and at the head of all the power of Europe, he denounced destruction to the only land that dared to be free. The Providential superintendence of this world seems seldom more manifest than in the dispensation which ordained that the French Emperor and Wellesley should be born in the same year; that in the same year they should have embraced the same profession; and that, natives of distant islands, they should both have sought their military education in that illustrious land which each in his turn was destined to subjugate. During the long struggle for our freedom, our glory, I may say our existence, Wellesley fought and won fifteen pitched battles, all of the highest class, concluding with one of those crowning victories which give a color and aspect to history. During this period that can be said of him which can be said of no other captain—that he captured three thousand cannon from the enemy, and never lost a single gun. The greatness of his exploits was only equalled by the difficulties he overcame. He had to encounter at the same time a feeble Government, a factious Opposition, and a distrustful people, scandalous allies, and the most powerful enemy in the world. He gained victories with starving troops, and carried on sieges without tools; and, as if to complete the fatality which in this sense always awaited him, when he had succeeded in creating an army worthy of Roman legions, and of himself, this invincible host was broken up on the eve of the greatest conjuncture of his life, and he entered the field of Waterloo with raw levies and discomfited allies.

"But the star of Wellesley never paled. He has been called fortunate, for fortune is a divinity that ever favors those who are alike sagacious and intrepid, inventive and patient. It was his character that created his career. This alike achieved his exploits and guarded him from vicissitudes. It was his sublime self control that regulated his lofty fate. It has been the fashion of late years to disparage the military character. Forty years of peace have hardly qualified us to be aware how considerable and how complex are the qualities which are necessary for the formation of a great general. It is not enough to say that he must be an engineer, a geographer, learned in human nature, adroit in managing mankind; that he must be able to perform the highest duties of a Minister of State, and sink to the humblest offices of a commissary and a clerk; but he has to display all this knowledge and he must do all these things at the same time, and under extraordinary circumstances. At the same moment he must think of the eve and the morrow— of his flanks and of his reserves; he must carry with him ammunition, provisions, hospitals; he must calculate at the same time the state of the weather and the moral qualities of man; and all these elements, which are perpetually changing, he must combine amid overwhelming cold or overpowering heat: sometimes amid famine, often amid the thunder of artillery. Behind all this, too, is the ever-present image of his country, and the dreadful alternative whether that country is to receive him with cypress or laurel. But all these conflicting ideas must be driven from the mind of the military leader, for he must think—and not only think—he must think with the rapidity of lightning, for on a moment more or less, depends the fate of the finest combination, and on a moment more or less, depends glory or shame. Doubtless all this may be done in an ordinary manner by an ordinary man; as we see every day of our lives ordinary men making successful Ministers of State, successful speakers, successful authors. But to do all this with genius is sublime. Doubtless to think deeply and clearly in the recess of a Cabinet is a fine intellectual demonstration, but to think with equal depth and equal clearness amid bullets is the most complete exercise of the human faculties. Although the military career of the Duke of Wellington fills so large a space in history, it was only a comparatively small section of his prolonged and illustrious life. Only eight years elapsed from Vimiera to Waterloo, and from the date of his first commission to the last cannon-shot on the field of battle scarcely twenty years can be counted. After all his triumphs he was destined for another career, and, if not in the prime, certainly in the perfection of manhood, he commenced a civil career scarcely less eminent than those military achievements which will live for ever in history. Thrice was he the Ambassador of his Sovereign to those great historic congresses that settled the affairs of Europe; twice was he Secretary of State; twice was he Commander-in-Chief; and once he was Prime Minister of England. His labours for his country lasted to the end. A few months ago he favored the present advisers of the Crown with his thoughts on the Burmese War, expressed in a state paper characterized by all his sagacity and experience; and he died the active chieftain of that famous army to which he has left the tradition of his glory.

"There was one passage in the life of the Duke of Wellington which should hardly be passed unnoticed on such an occasion, and in such a scene as this. It is our pride that he was one of ourselves; it is our pride that Sir Arthur Wellesley sat upon these benches. Tested by the ambition and the success of ordinary men, his career here, though brief, was distinguished. He entered Royal Councils, and held a high ministerial post. But his House of Commons success must not be measured by his seat at the Privy Council and his Irish Secretaryship. He achieved a success here which the greatest Ministers and the most brilliant orators can never hope to rival. That was a parliamentary success unequalled when he rose in his seat to receive the thanks of Mr. Speaker for a glorious victory; or, later still, when he appeared at the bar of this House, and received, Sir, from one of your predecessors, in memorable language, the thanks of a grateful country for accumulated triumphs. There is one consolation which all Englishmen must feel under this bereavement. It is, that they were so well and so completely acquainted with this great man. Never did a person of such mark live so long, and so much in the public eye.

"To complete all, that we might have a perfect idea of this sovereign master of duty in all his manifold offices, he himself gave us a collection of administrative and military literature which no age and no country can rival; and, fortunate in all things, Wellesley found in his lifetime an historian whose immortal page already ranks with the classics of that land which Wellesley saved. The Duke of Wellington left to his countrymen a great legacy—greater even than his glory. He left them the contemplation of his character. I will not say his conduct revived the sense of duty in England. I would not say that of our country. But that his conduct inspired public life with a purer and more masculine tone I cannot doubt. His career rebukes restless vanity, and reprimands the irregular ebullitions of a morbid egotism. I doubt not that, among all orders of Englishmen, from those with the highest responsibilities of our society to those who perform the humblest duties, I dare say there is not a man who in his toil and his perplexity has not sometimes thought of the duke and found in his example support and solace.

"Though he lived so much in the hearts and minds of his countrymen—though he occupied such eminent posts and fulfilled such august duties—it was not till he died that we felt what a space he filled in the feelings and thoughts of the people of England. Never was the influence of real greatness more completely asserted than on his decease. In an age whose boast of intellectual equality flatters all our self-complacencies, the world suddenly acknowledged that it had lost the greatest of men; in an age of utility the most industrious and commonsense people in the world could find no vent for their woe and no representative for their sorrow but the solemnity of a pageant; and we—we who have met here for such different purposes—to investigate the sources of the wealth of nations, to enter into statistical research, and to encounter each other in fiscal controversy—we present to the world the most sublime and touching spectacle that human circumstances can well produce—the spectacle of a Senate mourning a Hero!"

—D'ISRAELI.

## THE INN AT TERRACINA.

ANOTHER apparition of the road attracted the attention of mine host and his guests. From the direction of the Pontine Marshes a carriage drawn by half a dozen horses came driving at a furious rate; the postilions smacking their whips like mad, as is the case when conscious of the greatness or of the munificence of their fare. It was a landaulet, with a servant mounted on the dickey. The compact, highly finished, yet proudly simple construction of the carriage, the quantity of neat, well-arranged trunks and conveniences; the loads of box-coats on the dickey; the fresh, burly, bluff-looking face of the master at the window; and the ruddy, round-headed servant, in close-cropped hair, short coat, drab breeches, and long gaiters, all proclaimed at once that this was the equipage of an Englishman.

"Horses to Fondi," said the Englishman, as the landlord came bowing to the carriage door.—"Would not his Eccellenza alight and take some refreshment?"—"No; he did not mean to eat until he got to Fondi."—"But the horses will be some time in getting ready."—"Ah! that's always the way; nothing but delay in this horrid country."—"If his Eccellenza would only walk into the house——"—"No, no, no!—I tell you no! I want nothing but horses, and as quick as possible. John, see that the horses are got ready, and don't let us be kept here an hour or two. Tell him if we're delayed over the time I'll lodge a complaint with the postmaster." John touched his hat, and set off to obey his master's orders with the taciturn obedience of an English servant.

In the mean time, the Englishman got out of the carriage and walked up and down before the inn with his hands in his pockets, taking no notice of the crowd of idlers who were gazing at him and his equipage. He was tall, stout, and well-made; dressed with neatness and precision; wore a travelling cap of the color of gingerbread; and had rather an unhappy expression about the corners of his mouth; partly from not having yet made his dinner, and partly at not having been able to get on at a greater rate than seven miles an hour: not that he had any other cause for haste than an Englishman's usual hurry to get to the end of a journey: or, to use the regular phrase, "to get on." Perhaps too he was a little sore from having been fleeced at every stage of his journey.

After some time, the servant returned from the stable with a look of some perplexity.

"Are the horses ready, John?"—"No, sir—I never saw such a place. There's no getting anything done. I think your honor had better step into the house and get something to eat; it will be a long while before we get to Fundy."—"Not for a minute—it's a mere trick—I'll not eat anything, just to spite them," said the Englishman, still more crusty at the prospect of being so long without his dinner.—"They say your honor's very wrong," said John, "to set off at this late hour. The road's full of highwaymen."—"Mere tales to get custom."— "The estafette which passed us was stopped by a whole gang," said John, increasing his emphasis with each additional piece of information.—"I don't believe a word of it."—"They robbed him of his breeches," said John, giving, at the same time, a hitch to his own waistband.—"All humbug!"

Here the dark handsome young man stepped forward, and addressing the Englishman very politely, in broken English, invited him to partake of a repast he was about to make.

"Thank'ee," said the Englishman, thrusting his hands deeper into his pockets, and casting a slight side glance of suspicion at the young man, as if he thought, from his civility, he must have a design upon his purse.

"We shall be most happy if you will do us that favor," said the lady, in her soft Venetian dialect. There was a sweetness in her accents that was most persuasive. The Englishman cast a look upon her countenance; her beauty was still more eloquent. His features instantly relaxed. He made a polite bow. "With great pleasure, signora," said he.

In short, the eagerness to "get on" was suddenly slackened; the determination to famish himself as far as Fondi, by way of punishing the landlord, was abandoned; John chose an apartment in the inn for his master's reception, and preparations were made to remain there until morning.

The carriage was unpacked of such of its contents as were indispensable for the night. There was the usual parade o trunks and writing desks, and portfolios and dressing-boxes, and those other oppressive conveniences which burden a comfortable man. The observant loiterers about the inn door, wrapped up in great dirt-colored cloaks, with only a hawk's eye uncovered, made many remarks to each other on this quantity of luggage that seemed enough for an army. And the domestics of the inn talked with wonder of the splendid dressing-case with its gold and silver furniture, that was spread out on the toilet table, and the bag of gold that chinked as it was taken out of the trunk. The strange *milord's* wealth, and the treasures he carried about him, were the talk, that evening, over all Terracina.

The Englishman took some time to make his ablutions and arrange his dress for table, and, after considerable labor and effort in putting himself at his ease, made his appearance, with stiff white cravat, his clothes free from the least speck of dust, and adjusted with precision. He made a civil bow on entering, in the unprofessing English way, which the fair Venetian, accustomed to the complimentary salutations of the continent, considered extremely cold.

In the course of the repast, the usual topics of travellers were discussed, and among others, the reports of robbers, which harassed the mind of the fair Venetian. The landlord and waiter dipped into the conversation with that familiarity permitted on the continent, and served up so many bloody tales as they served up the dishes, that they almost frightened away the poor lady's appetite.

The Englishman, who had a national antipathy to everything that is technically called "humbug," listened to them all with a certain screw of the mouth, expressive of incredulity. There was the well-known story of the school of Terracina, captured by the robbers; and one of the students coolly massacred, in order to bring the parents to terms for the ransom of the rest. And another, of a gentleman of Rome, who received his son's ear, in a letter, with information that his son would be remitted to him in this way, by instalments, until he paid the required ransom.

The fair Venetian shuddered as she heard these tales: the landlord, like a true narrator of the terrible, doubled the dose when he saw how it operated. He was just proceeding to relate the misfortunes of a great English lord and his family, when the Englishman, tired of his volubility, interrupted him, and pronounced these accounts to be mere travellers' tales, or the exaggerations of ignorant peasants and designing innkeepers. The landlord was indignant at the doubt levelled at his stories, and the innuendo levelled at his cloth; he cited, in corroboration, half a dozen tales still more terrible.

"I don't believe a word of them," said the Englishman.—"But the robbers have been tried and executed."—"All a farce!"—"But their heads are stuck up along the road!"—"Old skulls accumulated during a century."

The landlord muttered to himself as he went out at the door, "San Gennaro! quanto sono singolari questi Inglesi!"

\* \* \* \* \* \* \* \* \* \*

In the morning, all was bustle in the inn at Terracina. The procaccio had departed at daybreak on its route towards Rome, but the Englishman was yet to start and the departure of an English equipage is always enough to keep an inn in a bustle. On this occasion there was more than usual stir, for the Englishman, having much property about him, and having been convinced of the real danger of the road, had applied to the police, and obtained, by dint of liberal pay, an escort of eight dragoons and twelve foot soldiers, as far as Fondi. Perhaps, too, there might have been a little ostentation at bottom, though, to say the truth, he had nothing of it in his manner. He moved about, taciturn and reserved as usual, among the gaping crowd; gave laconic orders to John, as he packed away the thousand and one indispensable conveniences of the night; double loaded his pistols with great *sang froid*, and deposited them in the pockets of the carriage, taking no notice of a pair of keen eyes gazing on him from among the herd of loitering idlers.

The fair Venetian now came up with a request, made in her dulcet tones, that he would permit their carriage to proceed under protection of his escort. The Englishman, who was busy loading another pair of pistols for his servant, and held the ramrod between his teeth, nodded assent, as a matter of course, but without lifting up his eyes. The fair Venetian was a little piqued at what she supposed indifference; and ejaculated softly, as she retired, "quanto sono insensibili questi Inglesi." At length, off they set in gallant style. The eight dragoons prancing in front, the twelve foot soldiers marching in rear, and the carriage moving slowly in the centre, to enable the infantry to keep pace with them. * * * *

The Venetian carriage had proceeded in advance, and was now loitering along; its passengers looking out from time to time, and expecting the escort every moment to follow. They had gradually turned an angle of the road that shut them out of sight. The little army was again in motion, and made a very picturesque appearance as it wound along at the bottom of the rocks; the morning sunshine beaming upon the weapons of the soldiery.

The Englishman lolled back in his carriage, vexed with himself at what had passed, and consequently out of humor with all the world. As this, however, is no uncommon case with gentlemen who travel for their pleasure, it is hardly worthy of remark. They had wound up from the coast among the hills, and came to a part of the road that admitted of some prospect ahead.

"I see nothing of the lady's carriage, sir," said John, leaning down from the coach box.—"Pshaw!" said the Englishman, testily—"don't plague me about the lady's carriage; must I be continually pestered with the concerns of strangers?" John said not another word, for he understood his master's mood.

The road grew more wild and lonely; they were slowly proceeding on a foot pace up a hill; the dragoons were some distance ahead, and had just reached the summit of the hill, when they uttered an exclamation or rather shout, and galloped forward. The Englishman was roused from his sulky reverie. He stretched his head from the carriage, which had attained the brow of the hill. Before him extended a long hollow defile, commanded on one side by rugged precipitous heights, covered with bushes and a scanty forest. At some distance he beheld the carriage of the Venetians overturned; a numerous gang of desperadoes were rifling it; the young man and his servant were overpowered and partly stripped, and the lady was in the hands of two of the ruffians. The Englishman seized his pistols, sprung from the carriage, and called upon John to follow him.

In the mean time, as the dragoons came forward, the robbers, who were busy with the carriage, quitted their spoil, formed themselves in the middle of the road, and taking a deliberate aim, fired. One of the dragoons fell, another was wounded, and the whole were for a moment checked and thrown in confusion. The robbers loaded again in an instant. The dragoons discharged their carbines, but without apparent effect. They received another volley, which, though none fell, threw them again into confusion. The robbers were loading a second time, when they saw the foot soldiers at hand.—" *Scampa via !*" was the word: they abandoned their prey, and retreated up the rocks, the soldiers after them. They fought from cliff to cliff, and bush to bush, the robbers turning every now and then to fire upon their pursuers; the soldiers scrambling after them, and discharging their muskets whenever they could get a chance. Sometimes a soldier or a robber was shot down, and came tumbling among the cliffs. The dragoons kept firing from below, whenever a robber came in sight.

The Englishman had hastened to the scene of action, and the balls discharged at the dragoons had whistled past him as he advanced. One object, however, engrossed his attention. It was the beautiful Venetian lady in the hands of two of the robbers, who, during the confusion of the fight, carried her shrieking up the mountain. He saw her dress gleaming among the bushes, and he sprang up the rocks to intercept the robbers, as they bore off their prey. The ruggedness of the steep, and the entanglements of the bushes, delayed and impeded him. He lost sight of the lady, but was still guided by her cries, which grew fainter and fainter. They were off to the left, while the reports of muskets showed that the battle was raging to the right. At length he came upon what appeared to be a rugged footpath, faintly worn in a gully of the rocks, and beheld the ruffians at some distance hurrying the lady up the defile. One of them hearing his approach, let go his prey, advanced towards him, and levelling the carabine, which had been slung on his back, fired. The ball whizzed through the Englishman's hat, and carried with it some of his hair. He returned the fire with one of his pistols, and the robber fell. The other brigand now dropped the lady, and drawing a long pistol from his belt, fired on his adversary with deliberate aim. The ball passed between his left arm and his side, slightly wounding the arm. The Englishman advanced, and discharged his remaining pistol, which wounded the robber, but not severely.

The brigand drew a stiletto and rushed upon his adversary, who eluded the blow, receiving merely a slight wound, and defended himself with his pistol, which had a spring bayonet. They closed with one another, and a desperate struggle ensued. The robber was a square-built, thick-set man, powerful, muscular and active. The Englishman, though of larger frame and greater strength, was less active and less accustomed to athletic exercises and feats of hardihood, but he showed himself practised and skilled in the arts of defence. They were on a craggy height, and the Englishman perceived that his antagonist was striving to press him to the edge. A side-glance showed him also the robber whom he had first wounded, scrambling up to the assistance of his comrade, stiletto in hand. He had in fact attained the summit of the cliff, he was within a few steps, and the Englishman felt that his case was desperate, when he heard suddenly the report of a pistol, and the ruffian fell. The shot came from John, who had arrived just in time to save his master.

The remaining robber, exhausted by loss of blood and the violence of the contest, showed signs of faltering. The Englishman pursued his advantage, pressed on him, and as his strength relaxed, dashed him headlong from the precipice. He looked after him, and saw him lying motionless among the rocks below.

The Englishman now sought the fair Venetian. He found her senseless on the ground. With his servant's assistance he bore her down to the road, where her husband was raving like one distracted. He had sought her in vain, and had given her over for lost; and when he beheld her thus brought back in safety, his joy was equally wild and ungovernable. He would have caught her insensible form to his bosom had not the Englishman restrained him. The latter, now really aroused, displayed a true tenderness and manly gallantry, which one would not have expected from his habitual phlegm. His kindness, however, was practical, not wasted in words. He despatched John to the carriage for restoratives of all kinds, and, totally thoughtless of himself, was anxious only about his lovely charge. The occasional discharge of fire-arms along the height showed that a retreating fight was still kept up by the robbers. The lady gave signs of reviving animation. The Englishman, eager to get her from this place of danger, conveyed her to his own carriage, and, committing her to the care of her husband, ordered the dragoons to escort them to Fondi. The Venetian would have insisted on the Englishman's getting into the carriage, but the latter refused. He poured forth a torrent of thanks and benedictions; but the Englishman beckoned to the postilions to drive on.

John now dressed his master's wounds, which were found not to be serious, though he was faint with loss of blood. The Venetian carriage had been righted, and the baggage replaced; and, getting into it, they set out on their way towards Fondi, leaving the foot soldiers still engaged in ferreting out the banditti.

Before arriving at Fondi, the fair Venetian had completely recovered from her swoon. She made the usual question—"Where was she?"—"In the Englishman's carriage."—"How had she escaped from the robbers?"—"The Englishman had rescued her."

Her transports were unbounded; and mingled with them were enthusiastic ejaculations of gratitude to her deliverer. A thousand times did she reproach herself for having accused him of coldness and insensibility. The moment she saw him she rushed into his arms with the vivacity of her nation, and hung about his neck in a speechless transport of gratitude. Never was man more embarrassed by the embraces of a woman.

"Tut—tut!" said the Englishman.—"You are wounded!" shrieked the fair Venetian, as she saw blood upon his clothes. —"Pooh! nothing at all!"—"My deliverer!—my angel!" exclaimed she, clasping him again round the neck, and sobbing on his bosom.—"Pshaw!" said the Englishman, with a good-humored tone, but looking somewhat foolish, "this is all humbug."—The fair Venetian, however, has never since accused the English of insensibility.

—WASHINGTON IRVING.

## THE BOWER OF ROSES.

THERE'S a bower of roses by Bendemeer's stream,
   And the nightingale sings round it all the day long;
In the time of my childhood 'twas like a sweet dream,
   To sit in the roses and hear the bird's song.

That bower and its music I never forget,
  But oft when alone, in the bloom of the year,
    I think—Is the nightingale singing there yet?
    Are the roses still bright by the calm Bendemeer?

No—the roses soon wither'd that hung o'er the wave:
  But some blossoms were gather'd while freshly they shone,
And a dew was distill'd from their flowers, that gave
  All the fragrance of summer, when summer was gone.

Thus memory draws from delight, ere it dies,
  An essence that breathes of it many a year;
Thus bright to my soul, as 'twas then to my eyes,
  Is that bower of roses by calm Bendemeer.   —MOORE.

---

## MAGNA CHARTA.

### (A. D. 1215.)

IN the reign of John, all the rapacious exactions usual to the Norman kings were not only redoubled, but mingled with other outrages of tyranny still more intolerable. These, too, were to be endured at the hands of a prince utterly contemptible for his folly and cowardice. One is surprised at the forbearance displayed by the barons, till they took arms at length in that confederacy which ended in establishing the Great Charter of Liberties. As this was the first effort towards a legal government, so is it beyond comparison the most important event in our history, except that revolution without which its benefits would rapidly have been annihilated. The constitution of England has indeed no single date from which its duration is to be reckoned. The institutions of positive law, the far more important changes which time has wrought in the order of society, during six hundred years subsequent to the Great Charter, have undoubtedly lessened its direct application to our present circumstances. But it is still the key-stone of English liberty. All that has since been obtained is little more than as confirmation or commentary; and if every subsequent law were to be swept away, there would still remain the bold features that distinguish a free from a despotic monarchy. It has been lately the fashion to depreciate the value of Magna Charta, as if it had sprung from the private ambition of a few selfish barons, and redressed only some feudal abuses. It is indeed of little importance by what motives those who obtained it were guided. The real characters of men most distinguished in the transactions of that time are not easily determined at present. Yet if we bring these ungrateful suspicions to the test, they prove destitute of all reasonable foundation. An equal distribution of civil rights to all classes of freemen forms the peculiar beauty of the charter. In this just solicitude for the people, and in the moderation which infringed upon no essential prerogative of the monarchy, we may perceive a liberality and patriotism very unlike the selfishness which is sometimes rashly imputed to those ancient barons. And, as far as we are guided by historical testimony, two great men, the pillars of our church and state, may be considered as entitled beyond all the rest to the glory of this monument; Stephen Langton, Archbishop of Canterbury, and William, Earl of Pembroke. To their temperate zeal for a legal government, England was indebted during that critical period for the two greatest blessings that patriotic statesmen could confer; the establishment of civil liberty upon an immovable basis, and the preservation of national independence under the ancient line of sovereigns, which rasher men were about to exchange for the dominion of France.

By the Magna Charta of John, reliefs were limited to a certain sum, according to the rank of the tenant, the waste committed by guardians in chivalry restrained, the disparagement in matrimony of female wards forbidden, and widows secured from compulsory marriage. These regulations extending to the sub-vassals of the crown, redressed the worst grievances of every military tenant in England. The franchises of the city of London and of all towns and boroughs were declared inviolable. The freedom of commerce was guaranteed to alien merchants. The Court of Common Pleas, instead of following the king's person, was fixed at Westminster. The tyranny exercised in the neighborhood of royal forests met with some check, which was further enforced by the charter of forests under Henry III.

But the essential clauses of Magna Charta are those which protect the personal liberty and property of all freemen, by giving security from arbitrary imprisonment and arbitrary spoliation. "No freeman" (says the twenty-ninth chapter of Henry III's charter, which, as the existing law, I quote in preference to that of John, the variations not being very material), "shall be taken or imprisoned, or be disseised or his freehold, or liberties, or free customs, or be outlawed, or exiled, or any otherwise destroyed; nor will we pass upon him, nor send upon him, but by lawful judgment of his peers, or by the law of the land. We will sell to no man, we will not deny, or delay to any man judgment or right." It is obvious, that these words, interpreted by any honest court of law, convey an ample security for the two main rights of civil society. From the era, therefore, of King John's charter, it must have been a clear principle of our constitution that no man can be detained in prison without trial. Whether courts of justice framed the writ of Habeas Corpus in conformity to the spirit of this clause, or found it already in their register, it became from that era the right of every subject to demand it. That writ, rendered more actively remedial by the statute of Charles II., but founded on the broad basis of Magna Charta, is the principal bulwark of English liberty; and if ever temporary circumstances, or the doubtful plea of political necessity, shall lead men to look on its denial with apathy, the most distinguishing characteristic of our constitution will be effaced.

As the clause recited above protects the subject from any absolute spoliation of his freehold rights, so others restrain the excessive amercements which had an almost equally ruinous operation. The magnitude of his offence, by the fourteenth clause of Henry III.'s charter, must be the measure of his fine; and in every case the *contenement* (a word expressive of chattels necessary to each man's station, as the arms of a gentleman, the merchandise of a trader, the plough and wagons of a peasant) was exempted from seizure. A provision was made in the charter of John, that no aid or escuage should be imposed, except in the three feudal cases of aid, without consent of parliament. And this was extended to aids paid by the City of London. But the clause was omitted in the three charters granted by Henry III., though parliament seems to have acted upon it in most part of his reign. It had, however, no reference to tallages imposed upon towns without their consent. Four score years were yet to elapse before the great principle of parliamentary taxation was explicitly and absolutely recognized.

A law which enacts that justice shall neither be sold,

denied nor delayed, stamps with infamy that government under which it had become necessary. But from the time of the charter, according to Maddox, the disgraceful perversions of right, which are upon record in the rolls of the exchequer, became less frequent.

From this era a new soul was infused into the people of England. Her liberties, at the best long in abeyance, became a tangible possession, and those indefinite aspirations for the laws of Edward the Confessor were changed into a steady regard for the Great Charter. —HALLAM.

---

## THE BATTLE OF MORGARTEN.

THE wine-month shone in its golden prime,
   And the red grapes clustering hung,
But a deeper sound, through the Switzer's clime,
   Than the vintage-music, rung,
     A sound, through vaulted cave,
     A sound, through echoing glen,
   Like the hollow swell of a rushing wave;
    —'Twas the tread of steel-girt men.

And a trumpet, pealing wild and far,
   'Midst the ancient rocks was blown,
Till the Alps replied to that voice of war
   With a thousand of their own.
     And through the forest-glooms
     Flash'd helmets to the day,
   And the winds were tossing knightly plumes,
    Like the larch-boughs in their play.

In Hasli's wilds there was gleaming steel,
   As the host of the Austrian pass'd;
And the Schreckhorn's rocks, with a savage peal,
   Made mirth of his clarion's blast.
     Up 'midst the Righi snows
     The stormy march was heard,
   With the charger's tramp, whence fire-sparks rose,
    And the leader's gathering word.

But a band, the noblest band of all,
   Through the rude Morgarten straight,
With blazon'd streamers, and lances tall
   Moved onwards in princely state.
     They came with heavy chains,
     For the race despised so long—
   But amidst his Alp-domains,
    The herdsman's arm is strong!

## THE BATTLE OF MORGARTEN.

The sun was reddening the clouds of morn
  When they entered the rock-defile,
And shrill as a joyous hunter's horn
  Their bugles rung the while.
    But on the misty height,
      Where the mountain people stood,
    There was stillness, as of night,
      When storms at distance brood.

There was stillness, as of deep dead night,
  And a pause—but not of fear,
While the Switzers gazed on the gathering might
  Of the hostile shield and spear.
    On wound those columns bright
      Between the lake and wood.
    But they look'd not to the misty height
      Where the mountain-people stood.

The pass was fill'd with their serried power,
  All helm'd and mail-array'd,
And their steps had sounds like a thunder-shower
  In the rustling forest-shade.
    There were prince and crested knight,
      Hemm'd in by cliff and flood,
    When a shout arose from the misty height
      Where the mountain people stood.

And the mighty rocks came bounding down,
  Their startled foes among,
With a joyous whirl from the summit thrown—
  —Oh! the herdsman's arm is strong!
    They came like lauwine hurl'd
      From Alp to Alp in play,
    When the echoes shout through the snowy world
      And the pines are borne away.

The fir-woods crash'd on the mountain side,
  And the Switzers rush'd from high,
With a sudden charge, on the flower and pride
  Of the Austrian chivalry:
    Like hunters of the deer,
      They storm'd the narrow dell,
    And first in the shock, with Uri's spear,
      Was the arm of William Tell.

There was tumult in the crowded strait,
  And a cry of wild dismay,
And many a warrior met his fate,
  From a peasant's hand that day!
    And the empire's banner then
      From its place of waving free,

Went down before the shepherd-men,
    The men of the Forest-sea.

With their pikes and massy clubs they brake
  The cuirass and the shield,
And the war-horse dash'd to the reddening lake
  From the reapers of the field !
    The field—but not of sheaves—
    Proud crests and pennons lay,
Strewn o'er it thick as the birch-wood leaves,
    In the autumn tempest's way.

Oh ! the sun in heaven fierce havoc view'd,
  When the Austrian turn'd to fly,
And the brave, in the trampling multitude,
  Had a fearful death to die !
    And the leader of the war
    At eve unhelm'd was seen,
With a hurrying step on the wilds afar,
    And a pale and troubled mien.

But the sons of the land which the freeman tills,
  Went back from the battle-toil,
To their cabin homes 'midst the deep green hills,
  All burden'd with royal spoil.
    There were songs and festal fires
    On the soaring Alps that night,
When children sprung to greet their sires
    From the wild Morgarten fight.   —Mrs. Hemans.

## CHRISTIANITY A SWORD.

It is easy to upbraid our religion, because it hath fulfilled its own prophecies, and proved itself a sword ; but what engine has been so efficient as this sword in accomplishing results which every lover of virtue admires, and every friend of humanity applauds ? What hath banished gross vices from the open stage on which they once walked unblushingly, and forced them, where it failed to exterminate, to hide themselves in the shades of a disgraceful privacy ? We reply, the sword christianity. What hath covered lands with buildings unknown in earlier and much-vaunted days, with hospitals, and infirmaries, and asylums ? We answer, the sword christianity. What is gradually extirpating slavery from the earth, and bringing on a season, too long delayed indeed, but our approaches to which distance incalculably those of the best heathen times, when man shall own universally a brother in man, and dash off every fetter which cruelty hath forged, and cupidity fastened? We answer unhesitatingly, the sword christianity. What hath softened the horrors of war, rendering comparatively unheard of the massacre of the unoffending, and the oppression of captives? What hath raised the female sex from the degraded position which they still occupy in the lands of a false faith? What hath introduced laws, which shield the weakest from injury, protect the wi   in her loneliness, and secure his rights to the orphan   What hath given sacredness to every domestic relation, to the ties which bind together the husband and the wife, the parent and the child, the master and the servant; and thus brought those virtues to our firesides, the exile of which takes all music from that beautiful word *home?* To all such questions we have but one reply, the sword christianity. The determined foe of injustice in its every form; the denouncer of malice, and revenge, and pride, passions which keep the surface of society ever stormy and agitated; the nurse of genuine patriotism, because the enemy of selfishness; the founder and upholder of noble institutions, because the teacher of the largest philanthropy—christianity has lifted our fallen humanity to a moral greatness which seemed wholly out of reach, to   station, which, compared with that occupied under the tyranny of heathenism, is like a new place amongst orders in creation.

And nothing is needed, in proof that we put forth no exaggerated statement, but that Christendom be contrasted with countries which have not yet received christianity. If you are in search of the attributes which give dignity to a state, of the virtues which shed lustre and loveliness over families, of what is magnificent in enterprise, refined in civilization, lofty in ethics, admira   in jurisprudence, you never turn to any but an evangelized territory, in order to obtain the most signal exhibition. And just in proportion as christianity now gains footing on a district of heathenism, there is a distinct improvement in whatever tends to exalt a nation, and bring comfort and respectability into its households. If we could but plant the cross on every mountain, and in every valley, of this globe, prevailing on a thousand tribes to cast away their idols, and hail Jesus Christ as "King of kings and Lord of lords."

who doubts that we should have done infinitely more towards covering our planet with all the dignities and decencies of civilized life than by centuries of endeavor to humanize barbarism without molesting superstition? We are clear as upon a point which needs no argument, because ascertained by experience, and which, if not proved by experience, might be established by irresistible argument, that, in teaching a nation the religion of Christ, we teach it the principles of government, which will give it fixedness as an empire, the sciences which will multiply the comforts, and the truths which will elevate the character, of its population. Thoroughly to christianize would be thoroughly to regenerate a land. And the poor missionary, who, in the simplicity of his faith, and the fervor of his zeal, throws himself into the waste of paganism, and there, with no apparent mechanism at his disposal for altering the condition of a savage community, labors at making Christ known to idolaters—why, we say of this intrepid wrestler with ignorance, that, in toiling to save the souls, he is toiling to develope the intellectual powers, reform the policy, and elevate in every respect the rank of the beings who engage his solicitudes. The day on which a province of Africa hearkened to his summons, started, from its moral debasement, and acknowledged Jesus as its Saviour, would be also the day on which that province overstepped one half the interval by which it had been separated from civilized Europe, and went on, as with a giant's stride, towards its due place amongst nations.

So that however true it be, that, in sending christianity, you send a sword into a land, we will not for a moment harbor the opinion, that christianity is no temporal blessing, if received by the inhabitants as their guide to immortality. It is a sword; and divided families, and clashing parties, will attest the keenness and strength of the weapon. But then it is also a sword, whose bright flash scatters the darkness of ages, and from whose point shrink away the corruption, the cruelty, and the fraud, which flourished in that darkness as their element. It is a sword: and it must pierce to the sundering many close ties, dissect many interests, and lacerate many hearts. But to wave this sword over a land is to break the spell fastened on it by centuries of ignorance; and to disperse, or, at least, to disturb, those brooding spirits which have oppressed its population, and kept down the energies which ennoble our race. And, therefore, are we nothing moved by the accusation, that christianity has caused some portion of misery. We deny not the truth of the charge: to disprove that truth would be to disprove christianity itself. The Founder prophesied that his religion would be a sword, and the accomplishment of the prophecy is one of our evidences that he came forth from God. But when men would go farther, when they would arraign christianity as having increased, on the whole, the sum of human misery, oh, then we have our appeal to the splendid institutions of civilized states, to the bulwarks of liberty which they have bravely thrown up, to the structures which they have reared for the shelter of the suffering, and to their mighty advancings in equity, and science, and good order, and greatness. We show you the desert blossoming as the rose, and all because ploughed by the sword christianity. We show you every chain of oppression flying into shivers, and all because struck by the sword christianity. We show you the coffers of the wealthy bursting open for the succor of the destitute, and all because touched by the sword christianity. We show you the human intellect springing into manhood, reason starting from dwarfishness, and assuming magnificence of stature, and all because roused by the glare of the sword christianity. Ay, if you can show us feuds, and jealousies, and wars, and massacres, and charge them home on christianity as a cause, we can show you whatsoever is confessed to minister most to the welfare, and glory, and strength, and happiness of society, stamped with one broad impress, and that impress the sword christianity: and, therefore, are we bold to declare that the amount of temporal misery has been immeasurably diminished by the propagation of the religion of Jesus; and that this sword, in spite of produced slaughter and divisions, has been, and still is, as a golden sceptre, beneath which the tribes of our race have found a rest which heathenism knew only in its poetry; a freedom, and a security, and a greatness, which philosophy reached only in its dreams. —MELVILLE.

## THE RUINED COTTAGE

None will dwell in that cottage, for they say
Oppression reft it from an honest man,
And that a curse clings to it: hence the vine
Trails its green weight of leaves upon the ground;

## THE RUINED COTTAGE.

Hence weeds are in that garden ; hence the hedge
Once sweet with honeysuckle, is half dead ;
And hence the grey moss on the apple tree.
   One once dwelt there, who had been in his youth
A soldier ; and when many years had pass'd
He sought his native village, and sat down
To end his days in peace.  He had one child—
A little laughing thing, whose large dark eyes,
He said, were like the mother's he had left
Buried in stranger lands ; and time went on
In comfort and content—and that fair girl
Had grown far taller than the red rose tree
Her father planted her first English birth-day ;
And he had train'd it up against an ash
Till it became his pride ;—it was so rich
In blossom and in beauty, it was call'd
The tree of Isabel.  'Twas an appeal
To all the better feelings of the heart
To mark their quiet happiness ; their home,
In truth, a home of love : and more than all,
To see them on the Sabbath, when they came
Among the first to church ; and Isabel,
With her bright color and her clear glad eyes,
Bowed down so meekly in the house of prayer ;
And in the hymn her sweet voice audible :—
Her father look'd so fond of her, and then
From her look'd up so thankfully to Heaven !
And their small cottage was so very neat ;
Their garden filled with fruits, and herbs, and flowers ;
And in the winter there was no fireside
So cheerful as their own.  But other days
And other fortunes came—an evil power !
They bore against it cheerfully, and hoped
For better times, but ruin came at last ;
And the old soldier left his own dear home,
And left it for a prison.  'Twas in June,
One of June's brightest days—the bee, the bird,
The butterfly, were on their brightest wings ;
The fruits had their first tinge of summer light ;
The sunny sky, the very leaves seemed glad,
And the old man look'd back upon his cottage
And wept aloud :—they hurried him away,
And the dear child that would not leave his side.
They led him from the sight of the blue heaven
And the green trees, into a low, dark cell,
The windows shutting out the blessed sun
With iron grating ; and for the first time
He threw him on his bed, and could not hear
His Isabel's " good night !" But the next morn
She was the earliest at the prison gate,
The last on whom it closed ; and her sweet voice,

And sweeter smile, made him forget to pine.
She brought him every morning fresh wild flowers,
But every morning could he see her cheek
Grow paler and more pale, and her low tones
Get fainter and more faint, and a cold dew
Was on the hand he held. One day he saw
The sun shine through the grating of his cell,
Yet Isabel came not: at every sound
His heart-beat took away his breath, yet still
She came not near him. But one sad day
He mark'd the dull street through the iron bars
That shut him from the world;—at length he saw
A coffin carried carelessly along,
And he grew desperate—he forced the bars;
And he stood on the street, free and alone!
He had no aim, no wish for liberty—
He only felt one want, to see the corpse
That had no mourners. When they set it down,
Or e'er 'twas lower'd into the new dug grave,
A rush of passion came upon his soul,
And he tore off the lid, and saw the face
Of Isabel, and knew he had no child
He lay down by the coffin quietly—
His heart was broken! —L. E. L. (Mrs. Maclean.)

## THE STUDY OF THE NATURAL SCIENCES.

But it is not through the allurements of ambition, even of that noble kind which aims at enlarging the boundaries of knowledge, that the cultivators of natural science are led to the purest enjoyment and the truest success in their pursuits. A higher, more spiritual sensibility must nourish their enthusiasm. The love of truth for its own sake; the power of deriving exquisite satisfaction not only from the discovery of new relations among objects, but from contemplating them in the light of known facts as subordinated to harmonies and laws; a loving appreciation of beauty in external characters, and of that subtler beauty of structure and affinities, akin to the most delicate perceptions of the artist and poet, but which discloses itself only to the penetrating eye of the naturalist,— such are some of the impulses and tastes that qualify us for enjoying the pursuits of natural history, and for giving them their highest usefulness.

In speaking of the delights of knowledge as compared with other pleasures, Lord Bacon has eloquently said, "In all other pleasures there is satiety; but of knowledge there is no satiety, but satisfaction and appetite are perpetually interchangeable." Surely of no kind of knowledge can this be more truly said than of that which unfolds to us the characters, structure and mutual dependences of the endless variety of organic and inorganic objects with which natural science has to deal.

It was once the fashion with poets to decry the growth of positive science, as unfriendly to poetical and spiritual conceptions of the material world, and to lament, although we may trust only for the sake of the verse, "the lovely views" which have been forced to "yield their place to" what they please to call "cold, material laws. But, thanks to a juster knowledge of the spirit, object and results of physical inquiries, now generally diffused among scholars, such complaints are no longer likely to find sympathy with them. From the known laws of the intellect, what more certain conclusion can be drawn, than that thought becomes exalted and suggestion quickened in proportion as they embrace a wider and more varied field of objects and relations? Who that, gazing on the vault of the sky, thinks of the innumerable multitude of worlds which the sure demonstrations of astronomy there point out to him,—measures in imagination their dimensions, and the vast distances which separate them,—follows the planets in their stately march, and watches the whole solar system, as, like a majestic fleet of argosies, it moves sublimely on its voyage of circumnavigation among the stars,—and, while witnessing in thought this grandest of Nature's spectacles, reflects on the profound adjustment of forces and motions by which these results are secured,—who, thus looking and reflecting, can see, in the material laws which control and harmonize this universe, aught lower or less spiritual than the thought of infinite wisdom and the handiwork of infinite power? Surely such a meditative gazer on the skies must feel in his soul the inspiration of a far nobler poetry than ever charmed the reveries of him

"To whose passive ken
Those mighty spheres that gem infinity
Are only specks of tinsel fixed in heaven
To light the midnights of his native town."

And what is true of astronomy is not less true of even the obscurest walks of natural history. For it is less in the magnitude and distance of objects than in their mutual activities, their harmonious arrangements, and their adaptation to wise and beneficent ends, that material phenomena become imbued with a spiritual and poetical significance. Let us then rejoice that in our scientific communings with living and inanimate things we are not only able to catch sweet notes from Apollo's lyre, but to gather into our souls the deeper harmonies which are felt to be the echoes of voices from the skies; let us indeed believe that

> "Nature hath her hoarded poetry
> And her hidden spells, and he
> Who is familiar with her mysteries is even as one
> Who, by some secret charm of soul or eye,
> In every clime, beneath the smiling sun,
> Sees where the springs of living waters lie." —ROGERS.

## MAY.

O SING and rejoice!
Give to gladness a voice;
Shout, a welcome to beautiful May;
Rejoice with the flowers,
And the birds 'mong the bowers,
And away to the green woods, away.
O blithe as the fawn,
Let us dance in the dawn
Of this life-giving glorious day.
'Tis bright as the first
Over Eden that burst;
O welcome, young joy-giving May.

The cataract's horn
Has awakened the morn,
Her tresses are dripping with dew;
O hush thee and hark!
'Tis her herald the lark
That is singing afar in the blue;
Its happy heart's rushing,
In strains mildly gushing,
That reach to the revelling earth,
And sink through the depths
Of the soul, till it leaps
Into raptures far deeper than mirth.

All nature's in keeping,
The live streams are leaping,
And laughing in gladness alone;
The great hills are heaving;
The dark clouds are leaving;

The valleys have burst into song.
We'll range through the dells
Of the bonnie blue bells,
And sing with the streams on their way;
We'll lie in the shades
Of the flower-covered glades,
And hear what the primroses say.

O crown me with flowers,
'Neath the green spreading bowers,
With the gems and the jewels May brings;
In the light of her eyes,
And the depth of her dyes,
We'll smile at the purple of kings;
We'll throw off our years,
With their sorrows and tears,
And time will not number the hours
We'll spend in the woods,
Where no sorrow intrudes,
With the streams and the birds, and the flowers.
—ALEX. McLACHLAN.

## THE LAST DAYS OF COLONEL NEWCOME.

CLIVE, and the boy sometimes with him, used to go daily to Grey Friars, where the Colonel still lay ill. After some days, the fever, which had attacked him, left him; but left him so weak and enfeebled that he could only go from his bed to the chair by his fireside. The season was exceedingly bitter; the chamber which he inhabited was warm and spacious; it was considered unadvisable to move him until he had attained greater strength, and till warmer weather. The medical men of the House hoped he might rally in the spring. My friend, Dr. Goodenough, came to him; he hoped too: but not with a hopeful face. A chamber, luckily vacant, hard by the Colonel's, was assigned to his friends, where we sat when we were too many for him. Besides his customary attendant, he had two dear and watchful nurses, who were almost always with him— Ethel and Madame de Florac, who had passed many a faithful year by an old man's bedside; who would have come, as to a work of religion, to any sick couch, much more to this one, where he lay for whose life she would once gladly have given her own.

But our Colonel, we all were obliged to acknowledge, was no more our friend of old days. He knew us again, and was good to every one round him, as his wont was; especially when Boy came, his old eyes lighted up with simple happiness, and, with eager trembling hands, he would seek under his bedclothes, or the pockets of his dressing-gown, for toys or cakes, which he had caused to be purchased for his grandson. There was a little, laughing, red-cheeked, white-headed gown-boy of the school, to whom the old man had taken a great fancy. One of the symptoms of his returning consciousness and recovery, as we hoped, was his calling for this child, who pleased our friend by his archness and merry ways; and who, to the old gentleman's unfailing delight, used to call him "Codd Colonel." "Tell little F—— that Codd Colonel wants to see him!" and the little gown-boy was brought to him; and the Colonel would listen to him for hours, and hear all about his lessons and his play; and prattle, almost as childishly, about Dr. Raine, and his own early school-days. The boys of the school, it must be said, had heard the noble old gentleman's touching history, and had all got to know and love him. They came every day to hear news of him; sent him in books and papers to amuse him; and some benevolent young souls—God's blessing on all honest boys, say I—painted theatrical characters, and sent them in to Codd Colonel's grandson. The little fellow was made free of gown-boys, and once came thence to his grandfather in a little gown, which delighted the old man hugely. Boy said he would like to be a little gown-boy; and I make no doubt, when he is old enough, his father will get him that post, and put him under the tuition of my friend Dr. Senior.

So weeks passed away, during which our dear old friend still remained with us. His mind was gone at intervals, but would rally feebly; and with his consciousness returned his love, his simplicity, his sweetness. He would talk French with Madame de Florac, at which time his memory appeared to awaken with surprising vividness, his cheek flushed, and he was a youth again —a youth all love and hope—a stricken old man, with a beard as white as snow covering the noble careworn face. At such times he called her by her Christian name of Léonore; he addressed courtly old words of regard and kindness to the aged lady; anon he wandered in his talk, and spoke to her as if they still were young. Now, as in those early days, his heart was pure; no anger remained in it; no guile tainted it; only peace and good-will dwelt in it.

The days went on, and our hopes, raised sometimes, began to flicker and fail. One evening the Colonel left his chair for his bed in pretty good spirits, but passed a disturbed night, and the next morning was too weak to rise. Then he remained in his bed, and his friends visited him there. One afternoon he asked for his little gown-boy, and the child was brought to him, and sat by the bed with a very awe-stricken face; and, then gathering courage, tried to amuse him by telling him how it was a half-holiday, and they were having a cricket-match with the St. Peter's boys in the green, and Grey Friars was in and winning. The Colonel quite understood about it; he would like to see the game; he had played many a game on that green when he was a boy. He grew excited; Clive dismissed his father's little friend, and put a sovereign into his hand; and away he ran to say that Codd Colonel had come into a fortune, and to buy tarts, and to see the match out. *I, curre*, little white-haired gown-boy! Heaven speed you, little friend.

After the child had gone, Thomas Newcome began to wander more and more. He talked louder; he gave the word of command, spoke Hindostanee as if to his men. Then he spoke words in French rapidly, seizing a hand that was near him, and crying, "Toujours, toujours!" But it was Ethel's hand which he took. Ethel and Clive and the nurse were in the room with him; the latter came to us who were sitting in the adjoining apartment; Madame de Florac was there, with my wife and Bayham.

At the look in the woman's countenance, Madame de Florac started up. "He is very bad, he wanders a great deal," the nurse whispered. The French lady fell instantly on her knees, and remained rigid in prayer.

Some time afterwards, Ethel came in with a scared face to our pale group. "He is calling for you again, dear lady," she said, going up to Madame de Florac, who was still kneeling; "and just now he said he wanted Pendennis to take care of his boy. He will not know you." She hid her tears as she spoke.

She went into the room, where Clive was at the bed's foot; the old man within it talked on rapidly for awhile: then again he would sigh and be still: once more I heard him say hurriedly: "Take care of him when I'm in India;" and then with a heart-rending voice he called out, "Léonore, Léonore!" She was kneeling by his side now. The patient's voice sank into faint murmurs; only a moan now and then announced that he was not asleep.

At the usual evening hour the chapel bell began to toll, and Thomas Newcome's hands outside the bed feebly beat a time. And just as the last bell struck, a peculiar sweet smile shone over his face, and he lifted up his head a little, and quickly said "Adsum!" and fell back. It was the word we used at school, when names were called; and lo, he, whose heart was as that of a little child, had answered to his name, and stood in the presence of The Master. —THACKERAY.

## LEGEND OF STRASBURG CATHEDRAL.

Out on the quiet midnight air,
  The thrilling summons swells,
As on the eve of loved St. John,
  Peal out the solemn bells;
A city unawakened lies
  Beneath the mournful sound,
Down street and avenue, and lane;
  A silence reigns profound.

But up from vault and mouldering crypt
  Arise a silent band,
Once the true builders of that pile,
  The guardians of their land.
And silently each takes his place;
  Masters, well robed, are there—
Craftsmen, Apprentices and each,
  With gavel, compass, square.

Then the old Masons meet again,
  Where once their work was known,
Where in sweet music petrified,
  Stands each well chiselled stone.
With silent presages of love,
  Each doth his brother cheer:
Time honored salutations pass
  Among Companions dear.

Then on the weird procession moves,
  Through the dim lighted nave,
Adown the long and columned aisles,
  Where mystic banners wave,
Over the gleaming marble floor,
  Past the old Knights that keep
Their watch and ward with cross and sword,
  The shadowy Masons sweep.

But near the spire one female form
  Floats white-robed, pale and cold,
Mallet and chisel, damp with age,
  Her slender fingers hold.
Loved daughter of the Master, she
  Aided each heavy task,
Beside her father, morn and eve,
  No respite did she ask.

Bread for the hungry Craftsman, she
  Duly prepared and wrought,
And words of Faith, and Hope, and Love
  She to the workmen brought.
Thirsting, she cooled their parching lips;
  Wearied, she heard their sighs,
Fevered, she fanned their throbbing brows—
  Dying, she closed their eyes.

Ghost-like and pale, the once strong men
  Glide over each known spot,
And from the memories of the past,
  Awaken scenes forgot.
No mortal being hath caught the sound,
  Or grasped the palsied hand,
Of them who thus fraternally
  Sweep round each column grand.

Thrice round the olden building, then
  They take their mystic way;
"Happy to meet," they converse hold,
  Till the first dawn of day.
Then down in each sepulchral bed,
  The Masons take their rest,
Till next St. John's loud midnight bell,
  Stirs through each phantom breast.

This is the legend; but far down
  A solemn lesson is
For all who would their work should stand
  Before the Master's eyes.
A voice from Heaven strews words of hope
  Round grave, and vault, and sea,
"From labors freed, their works remain,
  They did it unto me." —Miss Wilkins.

---

# EXECUTION OF COUNTS EGMONT AND HORN.
## (A. D. 1568.)

During the night, the necessary preparations for the morning tragedy had been made in the great square of Brussels. It was the intention of government to strike terror to the heart of the people by the exhibition of an impressive and appalling spectacle. The absolute and irresponsible destiny which ruled them was to be made manifest by the immolation of these two men, so elevated by rank, powerful connexion, and distinguished service.

The effect would be heightened by the character of the locality where the gloomy show was to be presented. The great square of Brussels had always a striking and theatrical aspect. Its architectural effects, suggesting in some degree the debased union between Oriental and a corrupt Grecian art, accomplished in the mediæval midnight, have amazed the eyes of many generations. The splendid Hotel de Ville, with its daring spire and elaborate front, ornamented one side of the place; directly opposite was the graceful but incoherent façade of the Brood-huis, now the last earthly resting place of the two distinguished victims, while grouped around these principal buildings rose the fantastic palaces of the Archers, Mariners, and of other guilds, with their festooned walls and toppling gables bedizened profusely with emblems, statues and quaint decorations. The place had been alike the scene of many a brilliant tournament and of many a bloody execution. Gallant knights had contended within its precincts, while bright eyes rained influence from all those picturesque balconies and decorated windows. Martyrs to religious and to political liberty had, upon the same spot, endured agonies which might have roused every stone of its pavement to mutiny or softened them to pity. Here Egmont himself, in happier days, had often borne away the prize of skill or of valor, the cynosure of every eye; and hence, almost in the noon of a life illustrated by many brilliant actions, he was to be sent, by the hand of tyranny, to his great account.

On the morning of the 5th of June, three thousand Spanish troops were drawn up in battle array around a scaffold which had been erected in the centre of the square. Upon this scaffold, which was covered with black cloth, were placed two velvet cushions, two iron spikes, and a small table. Upon the table was a silver crucifix. The provost-marshal, Spelle, sat on horseback below, with his red wand in his hand, little dreaming that for him a darker doom was reserved than that of which he was now the minister. The executioner was concealed beneath the draperies of the scaffold.

At eleven o'clock a company of Spanish soldiers, led by

Julian Romero and Captain Salinas, arrived at Egmont's chamber. The Count was ready for them. They were about to bind his hands, but he warmly protested against the indignity, and, opening the folds of his robe, showed them that he had himself shorn off his collars,.and made preparations for his death. His request was granted. Egmont, with the Bishop at his side, then walked with a steady step the short distance which separated him from the place of execution. Julian Romero and the guard followed him. On his way, he read aloud the fifty-first Psalm: "Hear my cry, O God, and give ear unto my prayer!" He seemed to have selected these scriptural passages as a proof that, notwithstanding the machinations of his enemies, and the cruel punishment to which they had led him, loyalty to his sovereign was as deeply rooted and as religious a sentiment in his bosom as devotion to his God. "Thou wilt prolong the King's life; and his years as many generations. He shall abide before God forever! O prepare mercy and truth which may preserve him." Such was the remarkable prayer of the condemned traitor on his way to the block.

Having ascended the scaffold, he walked across it twice or thrice. He was dressed in a tabard or robe of red damask, over which was thrown a short black mantle, embroidered in gold. He had a black silk hat, with black and white plumes, on his head, and held a handkerchief in his hand. As he strode to and fro, he expressed a bitter regret that he had not been permitted to die, sword in hand, fighting for his country and his king. Sanguine to the last, he passionately asked Romero whether the sentence was really irrevocable, whether a pardon was not even then to be granted. The marshal shrugged his shoulders, murmuring a negative reply. Upon this, Egmont gnashed his teeth together, rather in rage than despair. Shortly afterward commanding himself again, he threw aside his robe and mantle, and took the badge of the Golden Fleece from his neck. Kneeling, then, upon one of the cushions, he said the Lord's Prayer aloud, and requested the bishop, who knelt at his side, to repeat it thrice. After this, the prelate gave him the silver crucifix to kiss, and then pronounced his blessing upon him. This done, the Count rose again to his feet, laid aside his hat and handkerchief, knelt again upon the cushion, drew a little cap over his eyes, and, folding his hands together, cried with a loud voice, "Lord, into thy hands I commit my spirit." The executioner then suddenly appeared, and severed his head from his shoulders at a single blow.

A moment of shuddering silence succeeded the stroke. The whole vast assembly seemed to have felt it in their own hearts. Tears fell from the eyes even of the Spanish soldiery, for they knew and honored Egmont as a valiant general. The French ambassador, Mondoucet, looking upon the scene from a secret place, whispered that he had now seen the head fall before which France had twice trembled. Tears were even seen upon the iron cheek of Alva, as, from a window in a house directly opposite the scaffold, he looked out upon the scene.

A dark cloth was now quickly thrown over the body and the blood, and, within a few minutes, the Admiral was seen advancing through the crowd. His bald head was uncovered, his hands were unbound. He calmly saluted such of his acquaintances as he chanced to recognize upon his path. Under a black cloak, which he threw off when he had ascended the scaffold, he wore a plain, dark doublet, and he did not, like Egmont, wear the insignia of the Fleece. Casting his eyes upon the corpse, which lay covered with the dark cloth, he asked if it were the body of Egmont. Being answered in the affirmative, he muttered a few words in Spanish, which were not distinctly audible. His attention was next caught by the sight of his own coat of arms reversed, and he expressed anger at this indignity to his escutcheon, protesting that he had not deserved the insult. He then spoke a few words to the crowd below, wishing them happiness, and begging them to pray for his soul. He did not kiss the crucifix, but he knelt upon the scaffold to pray, and was assisted in his devotions by the Bishop of Ypres. When they were concluded, he rose again to his feet. Then drawing a Milan cap completely over his face, and uttering, in Latin, the same invocation which Egmont had used, he submitted his neck to the stroke.

Egmont had obtained, as a last favor, that his execution should precede that of his friend. Deeming himself in part to blame for Horn's reappearance in Brussels after the arrival of Alva, and for his death, which was the result, he wished to be spared the pang of seeing him dead. Gemma Frisius, the astrologer who had cast the horoscope of Count Horn at his birth, had come to him in the most solemn manner to warn him against visiting Brussels. The Count had answered stoutly that he placed his trust in God, and that, moreover, his friend Egmont was going thither also, who had engaged that no worse fate should befall the one of them than the other.

The heads of both sufferers were now exposed for two hours upon the iron stakes. Their bodies, placed in coffins, remained during the same interval upon the scaffold. Meantime, notwithstanding the presence of the troops, the populace could not be restrained from tears and from execrations. Many crowded about the scaffold, and dipped their handkerchiefs in the blood, to be preserved afterwards as memorials of the crime, and as ensigns of revenge.

The bodies were afterwards delivered to their friends. A stately procession of the guilds, accompanied by many of the clergy, conveyed their coffins to the church of Saint Gudule. Thence the body of Egmont was carried to the convent of Saint Clara, near the old Brussels gate, where it was embalmed. His escutcheon and banners were hung upon the outward wall of his residence, by order of the Countess. By command of Alva, they were immediately torn down. His remains were afterwards conveyed to his city of Sottegem, in Flanders, where they were interred. Count Horn was entombed at Kempen. The bodies had been removed from the scaffold at two o'clock. The heads remained exposed between burning torches for two hours longer. They were then taken down, enclosed in boxes, and, as it was generally supposed, despatched to Madrid. The King was thus enabled to look upon the dead faces of his victims without the trouble of a journey to the provinces.

- Thus died Philip Montmorency, Count of Horn, and Lamoral of Egmont, Prince of Gaveren. —MOTLEY.

## THE SEA GULL.

WHITE bird of the tempest ! O beautiful thing
With the bosom of snow, and the motionless wing,
Now sweeping the billow, now floating on high,
Now bathing thy plumes in the light of the sky;

Now poising o'er ocean thy delicate form,
Now breasting the surge with thy bosom so warm;
Now darting aloft, with a heavenly scorn,
Now shooting along, like a ray of the morn ;
Now lost in the folds of the cloud-curtained dome,
Now floating abroad like a flake of the foam :
Now silently poised o'er the war of the main,
Like the Spirit of Charity brooding o'er pain ;
Now gliding with pinion all silently furled,
Like an Angel descending to comfort the world !
Thou seem'st to my spirit, as upward I gaze,
And see thee, now clothed in mellowest rays,
Now lost in the storm-driven vapors, that fly
Like hosts that are routed across the broad sky,
Like a pure spirit, true to its virtue and faith,
'Mid the tempests of nature, of passion, and death !
  Rise ! beautiful emblem of purity, rise
On the sweet winds of Heaven, to thine own brilliant skies ;
Still higher ! still higher ! till, lost to our sight,
Thou hidest thy wings in a mantle of light ;
And I think how a pure spirit gazing on thee,
Must long for that moment—the joyous and free—
When the soul, disembodied from Nature, shall spring
Unfettered, at once to her Maker and King ;
When the bright day of service and suffering past,
Shapes, fairer than thine, shall shine round her at last,
While, the standard of battle triumphantly furled,
She smiles like a victor serene on the world !

—Griffin.

## ON THE GENERAL DEFICIENCY OF SELF-OBSERVATION.

One of the greatest difficulties in the way of executing the proposed task (the review of a man's past life) will have been caused by the extreme deficiency of that self-observation, which is of no common habit either of youth or any later age. Men are content to have no more intimate sense of their existence than what they feel in the exercise of their faculties on extraneous objects. The vital being, with all its agency and emotions, is so blended and absorbed in these its exterior interests, that it is very rarely collected and concentrated in the consciousness of its own absolute *self*, so as to be recognised as a thing internal, apart and alone, for its own inspection and knowledge. Men carry their minds as for the most part they carry their watches, content to be ignorant of the constitution and action within, and attentive only to the little exterior circle of things, to which the passions, like indexes, are pointing. It is surprising to see how little self-knowledge a person not watchfully observant of himself may have gained, in the whole course of an active, or even an inquisitive life. He may have lived almost an age, and traversed a continent, minutely examining its curiosities, and interpreting the half-obliterated characters on its monuments, unconscious the while of a process operating on his own mind, to impress or to erase characteristics of much more importance to him than all the figured brass or marble that Europe contains. After having explored many a cavern or dark ruinous avenue, he may have left undetected a darker recess within where there would be much more striking discoveries. He may have conversed with many people, in different languages, on numberless subjects; but, having neglected those conversations with himself by which his whole moral being should have been kept continually disclosed to his view, he is better qualified perhaps to describe the intrigues of a foreign court, or the progress of a foreign trade; to depict the manners of the Italians, or the Turks; to narrate the proceedings of the Jesuits, or the adventures of the gypsies; than to write the history of his own mind.

If we had practised habitual self-observation, we could not have failed to be made aware of much that it had been well for us to know. There have been thousands of feelings, each of which, if strongly seized upon, and made the subject of reflection, would have shewn us what our character was, and what it was likely to become. There have been numerous incidents, which operated on us as tests, and so fully brought out our prevailing quality, that another person, who should have been discriminatively observing us, would speedily have formed a decided estimate. But unfortunately the mind is generally too much occupied by the feeling or the incident itself, to have the slightest care or consciousness that anything *could* be learnt, or *is* disclosed. In very early youth it is almost inevitable for it to be thus lost to itself even amidst its own feelings, and the external objects of attention; but it seems a contemptible thing, and certainly is a criminal and dangerous thing, for a man in mature life to allow himself this thoughtless escape from self-examination.

We have not only neglected to observe what our feelings indicated, but have also in a very great degree ceased to remember what they were. We may wonder how we could pass away successively from so many scenes and conjunctures, each in its time of no trifling moment in our apprehension, and retain so light an impression, that we have now nothing distinctly to tell about what once excited our utmost emotion. As to my own mind, I perceive that it is becoming uncertain of the exact nature of many feelings of considerable interest, even of comparatively recent date; and that the remembrance of what was felt in very early life has nearly faded away. I have just been observing several children of eight or ten years old, in all the active vivacity which enjoys the plenitude of the moment without "looking before or after;" and while observing, I attempted, but without success, to recollect what I was at that age. I can indeed remember the principal events of the period, and the actions and projects to which my feelings impelled me; but the feelings themselves, in their own pure juvenility, cannot be revived so as to be described and placed in comparison with those of later life. What is become of all those vernal fancies which had so much power to touch the heart? What a number of sentiments have lived and revelled in the soul that are now irrevocably gone! They died like the singing-birds of that time, which sing no more. The life we then had, now seems almost as if it could not have been our own. We are like a man returning, after the absence of many years, to visit the imbowered cottage where he passed the morning of his life, and finding only a relic of its ruins.

Thus an oblivious shade is spread over that early tract of our time, where some of the acquired propensities which remain in force to this hour may have had their origin, in a manner of which we had then no thought or consciousness. When we met with the incident, or heard the conversation, or saw the spectacle, or felt the emotion, which were the first causes or occasions of some of the chief permanent tendencies of future life, how little could we think that long afterwards we might be curiously and in vain desirous to investigate those tendencies back to their origin.

—FOSTER.

## THE FALL.

I HEAR the sobbing rain,
    As if the Heavens weep at Autumn's breath;
I see the leaves of summer fall again,
    Their beauty changed in death.

The idle wind is still,
    A spectral vapor haunts the barren earth;
Upon our teeming joys there comes a chill—
    The chill of Winter's dearth.

What if the tinted woods
    With outward loveliness are gay and fair,
As if around them blushing Summer broods,
    Yearning to linger there!

What if their beauteousness
    At death's cold touch is strangely glorified!
Their leaves will crumble soon to nothingness,
    Or else be swept aside.

Their change is type of all,
    The hectic loveliness forebodes decay,
Steeped with a dying glow before they fall
    To mingle with the clay.

All that we love and prize,
    Changeth like leaves upon our toilsome way;
Man's hoarded wealth, but dust before his eyes,
    Passing, like life, away.

O leaves and blossoms, fall!
    An after-life shall rise from out the gloom;
The Autumn mists are but the outward pall,
    That hides perennial bloom.

O children of decay!
    Swept by the blast and trodden by the rain,
Your scattered dust shall eloquently say,
    That naught will fall in vain.
                                —ASCHER.

## THE NEW YEAR.

IN a few hours we shall have entered on a new year. It is barely ninety degrees distant from us at the present moment. It landed on the eastern extremity of Asia just as we were rising from our breakfasts this morning; and it has been gliding westwards towards us, in the character of *one o'clock in the morning*, ever since. In a few hours more it will be striding across the backwoods of America, in its seven-leagued boots, and careering over the Pacific in its canoe.

The past year has witnessed many curious changes, as a dweller in time; the coming year has already looked down on many a curious scene, as a journeyer over space. It has seen Cochin-China, with all its unmapped islands, and the ancient empire of Japan, with its cities and provinces unknown to Europe. It has heard the roar of a busy population amid the thousand streets of Pekin, and the wild dash of the midnight tides as they fret the rocks of the Indian Archipelago. It has been already with our friends in Hindostan; it has been greeted, we doubt not, with the voice of prayer, as the slow iron hand of the city clock indicated its arrival to the missionaries at Madras; it has swept over the fever jungles of the Ganges, where the scaled crocodile startles the thirsty tiger as he stoops to drink, and the exposed corpse of the benighted Hindo floats drearily past. It has travelled over the land of pagodas, and is now entering the land of mosques. Anon it will see the moon in her wane, casting the dark shadows of columned Palmyra over the sands of the desert; and the dim walls of Jerusalem looking out on a silent and solitary land, that has cast forth its interim tenants, and waits unappropriated for the old predestined race, its proper inhabitants. In two short hours it will be voyaging along the cheerful Mediterranean, greeting the rower in his galley among the isles of Greece, and the seaman in his barque embayed in the Adriatic. And then, after marking the red glare of Ætna reflecting in the waves that slumber around the moles of Syracuse,—after glancing on the towers of the Seven-hilled City, and the hoary snows of the Alps,—after speeding over France, over Flanders, over the waves of the German Sea, it will be with ourselves, and the tall ghostly tenements of Dun-Edin will re-echo the shouts of the High Street. Away, and away it will cross the broad Atlantic, and visit watchers in their beacon-towers on the deep, and the emigrant in his log-hut, among the brown woods of the west; it will see the fire of the red man umbering with its gleam tall trunks and giant branches, in some deep glade of the forest; and then mark, on the far shores of the Pacific, the rugged bear stalking sullenly over the snow. Away, and away, and the vast globe shall be girdled by the zone of the new born year.

Many a broad plain shall it have traversed, that is still unbroken from the waste,—many a moral wilderness, on which the Sun of Righteousness has not yet arisen. Nearly eighteen and a-half centuries shall have elapsed since the shepherds first heard the midnight song in Bethlehem,—"Glory to God in the highest, peace on earth, good will to the children of men." And yet the coming year shall pass, in its first visit, over prisons, over gibbets, and penal settlements, and battle-fields on which the festering dead moulder unburied; it will see the shotted gun and the spear, and the murdering tomahawk, slaves in their huts, and captives in their dungeons. But the years shall pass, and a change shall come: the sacrifice on Calvary was not offered up in vain, nor in vain hath the Adorable Saviour conquered, and ascended to reign as King and Lord over the nations. The kingdoms shall become his kingdoms, the people his people. The morning rises slowly and in clouds, but the dawn has broken; and it shall shine forth more and more, until the twilight shadows shall have dispersed, and the sulphurous fogs shall have dissipated, and all shall be peace and gladness amid the blaze of the perfect day. —MILLER.

## ANOTHER YEAR.

Another year! another year!
  The unceasing rush of time sweeps on!
Whelm'd in its surges, disappear
  Man's hopes and fears, for ever gone

O, no! forbear that idle tale!
  The hour demands another strain,
Demands high thoughts that cannot quail,
  And strength to conquer and retain.

'Tis midnight—from the dark-blue sky,
  The stars, which now look down on earth,
Have seen ten thousand centuries fly,
  And given to countless changes birth.

Shine on! shine on! with you I tread
  The march of ages, orbs of light!
A last eclipse o'er you may spread,
  To me, to me, there comes no night.

O! what concerns it him, whose way
  Lies upward to the immortal dead,
That a few hairs are turning gray,
  Or one more year of life has fled?

Swift years! but teach me how to bear,
  To feel and act with strength and skill,
To reason wisely, nobly dare,
  And speed your courses as ye will.

When life's meridian toils are done,
  How calm, how rich the twilight glow!
The morning twilight of a sun
  Which shines not here on things below.

But sorrow, sickness, death, the pain
  To leave, or lose wife, children, friends!
What then—shall we not meet again
  Where parting comes not, sorrow ends?

The fondness of a parent's care,
  The changeless trust which woman gives,
The smile of childhood,—it is there
  That all we love in them still lives.

Press onward through each varying hour:
  Let no weak fears thy course delay;
Immortal being! feel thy power,
  Pursue thy bright and endless way. —A. NORTON.

## THE POWER OF ENGLAND.

LET it not be said that we cultivate peace, either because we fear, or because we are unprepared for war; on the contrary, if eight months ago the Government did not hesitate to proclaim that the country was prepared for war, if war should be unfortunately necessary, every month of peace that has since passed has but made us so much the more capable of exertion. The resources created by peace are means of war. In cherishing those resources, we but accumulate those means. Our present repose is no more a proof of inability to act, than the state of inertness and inactivity in which I have seen those mighty masses that float in the waters above your town, is a proof that they are devoid of strength, and incapable of being fitted out for action. You well know, gentlemen, how soon one of those stupendous masses, now reposing on their shadows in perfect stillness—how soon, upon any call of patriotism or of necessity, it would assume the likeness of an animated thing, instinct with life and motion; how soon it would ruffle, as it were, its swelling plumage, how quickly would it put forth all its beauty and its bravery, collect its scattered elements of strength, and awaken its dormant thunder. Such as is one of these magnificent machines when springing from inaction into a display of its might, such is England herself, while apparently passive and motionless, she silently concentrates the power to be put forth on an adequate occasion. But God forbid that that occasion should arise. After a war sustained for nearly a quarter of a century, sometimes single-handed, and with all Europe arrayed at times against her, or at her side, England needs a period of tranquillity, and may enjoy it without fear of misconstruction. Long may we be enabled, gentlemen, to improve the blessings of our present situation, to cultivate the arts of peace, to give to commerce, now reviving, greater extension, and new spheres of employment, and to confirm the prosperity now generally diffused throughout this island. Of the blessings of peace, gentlemen, I trust that this borough, with which I have now the honor and happiness of being associated, will receive an ample share. I trust the time is not far distant, when that noble structure *(i. e., the breakwater)*, of which, as I learn from your Recorder, the box with which you have honored me, through his hands, formed a part, that gigantic barrier against the fury of the waves that roll into your harbour, will protect a commercial marine not less considerable in its kind, than the warlike marine of which your port has been long so distinguished an asylum; when the town of Plymouth will participate in the commercial prosperity as largely as it has hitherto done in the naval glories of England. —CANNING.

## COMPETITIVE EXAMINATIONS.

THERE is nothing, perhaps, more remarkable in the progress of the country than the advance which of late years has been made in the diffusion and in the quality of education. The advance which England has made in population, in wealth, in everything that constitutes in common opinion the greatness of a country, is well known and most extraordinary. But we should, indeed, have been wanting in our duties as a nation if we had not accompanied that progress in wealth and population by a corresponding progress in the development of the intellectual faculties of the people. There was a time, now long gone by, when envious critics, who wanted to run down the Universities of the land, said they might be likened to hulks moored in a rapid current, where they served only to mark the rapidity of the stream. That has long since ceased to be a true representation of our Universities. They have improved the course, the object, and the direction of their studies, and they may now fearlessly vie with the academical institutions of any country in the world. Certain objections have been made to the system of competitive examinations. Some people say it leads to cramming. It often happens that when mankind seize upon a word they imagine that word to be an argument, and go about repeating it, thinking they have arrived at some great and irresistible conclusion. So, when they pronounce the word "cramming," they think they have utterly discredited the system to which that word is by them applied. Some people seem to imagine that the human mind is like a bottle, and that when you have filled it with anything you pour it out again and it becomes as empty as it was before. That is not the nature of the human mind. The boy who has been crammed, to use the popular word, has, in point of fact learned a great deal, and that learning has accomplished two objects. In the first place, the boy has exercised the faculties of his mind in being crammed, and in the next place, there remains in his mind a great portion of the knowledge so acquired, and which probably forms the basis of future attainment in different branches of education. Depend upon it that the boy who is crammed, if he is crammed successfully, not only may succeed in the examination for which he is preparing, but is from that time forward more intellectual, better informed, and more disposed to push forward the knowledge which by that cramming he has acquired. It is also said that you are teaching young men a great variety of things which will be of no use to them in the career which they are destined to pursue, and that you are pandering to their vanity by making them believe they are wiser than they really are. These objections, also, are in my opinion utterly futile. As to vanity and conceit, those are most vain and conceited who know the least. The more a man knows, the more he acquires a conviction of the extent of that which he does not know. A man ought to know a great deal to acquire a knowledge of the immensity of his ignorance. If competitive examination is not liable to objection upon the score that it tends to raise undue notions of superiority on the part of those who go through it, so also it is a great mistake to imagine that a range of knowledge disqualifies a man for the particular career and profession to which he is destined. Nothing can be more proper than that a young man, having selected a particular profession, should devote the utmost vigour of his mind to qualify himself for it by acquiring the knowledge which is necessary for distinction in that line of life; but it would be a great mistake for him to confine himself to that study alone, and you may be sure that the more a young man knows of a great variety of subjects, and the more he exercises his faculties in acquiring a great range of knowledge, the better he will perform the duties of his particular profession. That sort of general knowledge may be likened to the gymnastic exercises to which soldiers are accustomed. It is not that it can be expected that these particular movements would be of any use to them on the day of battle; but these gymnastic exercises render their muscles flexible, strengthen their limbs, invigorate their health, and make them better able to undergo fatigue, and to adapt themselves to all circumstances. So with a wide range of study; it sharpens the wits; it infuses general knowledge into the mind; it sets a young man thinking; it strengthens the memory and stores it with facts; and in this way makes him a better and more able man in the particular profession which he is intended to pursue. It has been well said that in this happy land there is no barrier between classes, and that the highest positions are attainable by persons starting from the most humble origin. If he has only talent, if he has only acquirements, if he has only perseverance and good conduct, there is nothing within the range of the institutions of the country to which any man may not aspire, and which any man may not obtain. It is the peculiar character of this country as distinguished from many others, that whereas in some countries, unfortunately for them, men strive to raise the level on which they stand by pulling others

R

down, in England men try to raise the level on which they stand, not by pulling others down, but by elevating themselves. Having stated the advantages which the system of competitive examination confers upon those who are successful, I would take leave to say a word of encouragement to those who may have failed to obtain certificates. Let not these young men, and let not their parents, think that they, the unsuccessful competitors, have gained nothing by the struggle in which they have engaged. Depend upon it, that although they may not have succeeded in obtaining the distinction at which they aimed, they have succeeded in acquiring a great deal of useful knowledge; they have succeeded in acquiring habits of mind and powers of thought, and of application, which will be of use to them during the rest of their lives. You all know the old story of the father who upon his deathbed told his sons that he had a treasure buried in a certain field, and that if they dug the whole field through they would find it. The sons, acting upon this advice, dug the field, but no gold was there. In the next year, however, there was that which was to them a treasure— a most abundant and valuable harvest. That was the treasure which the father wished them to seek for and which they found. So it is with the unsuccessful competitors. They have not found the treasure which they sought for—namely, a certificate of attainments from the examiners—but they have gained a treasure which to them will be of infinite value— those habits of mind, those powers of thought, and that amount of knowledge upon which a larger building may be erected; and they therefore will have reason to thank their parents for having sent them to a competitive examination, thus rendering them better able to struggle through life in whatever career they may choose to pursue.

—Lord Palmerston.

---

## RICHARD ARKWRIGHT.

Richard Arkwright, like most of our great mechanicians, sprang from the ranks. He was born in Preston in 1732. His parents were very poor, and he was the youngest of thirteen children. He was never at school; the only education he received he gave to himself; and to the last he was only able to write with difficulty. When a boy he was apprenticed to a barber, and after learning the business he set up for himself in Bolton in 1760, occupying an underground cellar, over which he put up the sign, "Come to the subterraneous barber—he shaves for a penny." The other barbers found their customers leaving them, and reduced their prices to his standard; when Arkwright, determined to push his trade, announced his determination to give "A clean shave for a half-penny." After a few years he quitted his cellar and became an itinerant dealer in hair. At that time wigs were worn, and this was an important branch of the barbering business. He also dealt in a chemical hair dye, which he used adroitly, and thereby secured a considerable trade. Being of a mechanical turn, he devoted a good deal of his spare time to contriving models of machines, and, like many self-taught men of the same bias, he endeavored to invent perpetual motion. He followed his experiments so devotedly that he neglected his business, lost the little money he had saved, and was reduced to great poverty. His wife—for he had by this time married—was impatient at what she conceived to be a wanton waste of time and money, and in a moment of sudden wrath she seized upon and destroyed his models, hoping thus to remove the cause of the family privations. Arkwright was a stubborn and enthusiastic man, and he was provoked beyond measure by this conduct of his wife, which he never forgave; and he, in consequence, separated from her.

In travelling about the country, Arkwright had become acquainted with a person named Kay, a clockmaker at Wartington, who assisted him in constructing some of the parts of his perpetual motion machinery. It is supposed that he was first informed by Kay of the principle of spinning by rollers. The idea at once took firm possession of his mind, and he proceeded to devise the process by which it was to be accomplished, Kay being able to tell him nothing on this point. Arkwright now abandoned his business of hair collecting, and devoted himself to the perfecting of his machine, a model of which, constructed by Kay under his directions, he set up in the parlor of the Free Grammar School at Preston. Being a burgess of the town he voted at the contested election at which General Burgoyne was returned; but such was his poverty, and such the tattered state of his dress, that a number of persons subscribed a sum sufficient to have him put in a state fit to appear in the poll-room. The exhibition of his machine in a town where so many work-people lived by the exercise of manual labour proved a dangerous experiment: there were ominous growlings heard outside from time to time, and Arkwright—remembering the fate of poor Hargreave's spinning-jenny, which had been pulled to pieces only a short time before by a Blackburn mob—wisely determined on packing up his model, and removing to a less dangerous locality. He went accordingly to Nottingham, where he applied to some of the local bankers for pecuniary assistance, and the Messrs. Wright consented to advance him a sum of money on condition of sharing in the profits of the invention. The machine, however, not being perfected so soon as they anticipated, the bankers recommended Arkwright to apply to Messrs. Strutt and Need, the former of whom was the ingenious inventor and patentee of the stocking-frame. Mr. Strutt was quick to perceive the merits of the invention, and a partnership was entered into with Arkwright, whose road to fortune was now clear. The patent was secured in the name of "Richard Arkwright, of Nottingham, clockmaker," and it is a remarkable fact that it was taken out in 1769, the very same year in which Watt secured the patent for his steam engine. A cotton mill was first erected at Nottingham, driven by horses; and another was shortly after built on a much larger scale, at Cromford, in Derbyshire, turned by a water-wheel, from which circumstance the spinning-machine came to be called the water-frame.

Arkwright's labors, however, were, comparatively speaking, only begun. He had still to perfect all the working details of his machine. It was in his hands the subject of constant modification and improvement, until eventually it was rendered practicable and profitable in an eminent degree. But success was only secured by long and patient labour; for some years, indeed, the speculation was disheartening and unprofitable, swallowing up a very large amount of capital without any result. When success began to appear more certain, then the Lancashire manufacturers fell upon Arkwright's patent to pull it in pieces, as the Cornish miners fell upon Boulton and Watt to rob them of the profits of their steam-engine. Arkwright was even denounced as the enemy of the working people, and a mill which he built near Chorley was destroyed by a mob, in the presence of a strong force of police and military. The

Lancashire men refused to buy his materials, though they were confessedly the best in the market. Then they refused to pay patent-right for the use of his machines, and combined to crush him in the courts of law. To the disgust of right-minded people, Arkwright's patent was upset. But, though beaten, he was not subdued. He established large mills in other parts of Lancashire, in Derbyshire, and at New Lanark, in Scotland. The mills at Cromford also came into his own hands at the expiring of his partnership with Strutt, and the amount and the excellence of his products were such that in a short time he obtained so complete a control of the trade that the prices were fixed by him, and he governed the main operations of the other cotton spinners.

Arkwright was a tremendous worker, and a man of marvellous energy, ardor, and application in business. At one period of his life he was usually engaged in the severe and continuous labors involved by the organization and conduct of his numerous manufactories, from four in the morning until nine at night. At fifty years of age he set to work to learn English grammar, and improve himself in writing and orthography. When he travelled, to save time, he went at great speed, drawn by four horses. Be it for good or for evil, Arkwright was the founder in England of the modern factory system, a branch of industry which has unquestionably proved a source of immense wealth to individuals, and to the nation.

—SMILES.

## THE SHUNAMMITE.

CHILDHOOD is restless ever, and the boy,
Stayed not within the shadow of the tree,
But with a joyous industry went forth
Into the reapers' places, and bound up
His tiny sheaves, and plaited cunningly
The pliant withs out of the shining straw—
Cheering their labor on, till they forgot
The heat and weariness of their stooping toil
In the beguiling of his playful mirth.
Presently he was silent, and his eye
Closed as with dizzy pain, and with his hand
Pressed hard upon his forehead, and his breast
Heaving with the suppression of a cry,
He uttered a faint murmur, and fell back
Upon the onloosened sheaf, insensible.

They bore him to his mother, and he lay
Upon her knees till noon, and then he died!
She had watched every breath, and kept her hand
Soft on his forehead, and gazed in upon
The dreamy languor of his listless eye;
And she had laid back all his sunny curls,
And kissed his delicate lip, and lifted him—
Into her bosom, till her heart grew strong—
His beauty was so unlike death! She leaned
Over him now, that she might catch the low
Sweet music of his breath, that had learned
To love when he was slumbering at her side
In his unconscious infancy.

"—So still!
'Tis a soft sleep! How beautiful he lies,
With his fair forehead, and the rosy veins
Playing so freshly in his sunny cheek!
How could they say that he would die! O God!
I could not lose him! I have treasured all
His childhood in my heart; and even now,
As he has slept, my memory has been there,
Counting like treasures all his winning ways—
His unforgotten sweetness.

"Yet so still!
How like this breathless slumber is death!
I could believe that in that bosom now
There were no pulse—it beats so languidly!
I cannot see it stir; but his red lip!
Death would not be so very beautiful!
And that half smile—would death have left *that* there?
And should I not have felt that he would die?
And have I not wept over him? and prayed
Morning and night for him? And *could* he die?
No; God will keep him! He will be my pride
Many long years to come, and his fair hair
Will darken like his father's, and his eye
Be of a deeper blue when he is grown;
And he will be so tall, and I shall look
With such a pride upon him! *He* to die!"
And the fond mother lifted his soft curls,
And smiled, as if 'twere mockery to think
That such fair things could perish.

—Suddenly
Her hand shrank from him, and the color fled
From her fixed lip, and her supporting knees
Were shook beneath her child. Her hand had touched
His forehead, as she dallied with his hair,
And it was cold, like clay! Slow, very slow
Came the misgiving that her child was dead.
She sat a moment, and her eyes were closed
In a dumb prayer for strength; and then she took
His little hand, and pressed it earnestly,
And put her lip to his, and looked again

Fearfully on him; and then, bending low,
She whispered in his ear, "My son! my son!"
And as the echo died, and not a sound
Broke on the stillness, and he lay there still,
Motionless on her knee, the truth *would* come!
And with a sharp, quick cry, as if her heart
Were crushed, she lifted him and held him close
Into her bosom—with a mother's thought—
As if death had no power to touch him there!

\* \* \* \* \*

The man of God came forth, and led the child
Unto his mother, and went on his way.
And he was there—her beautiful, her own—
Living and smiling on her, with his arms
Folded about her neck, and his warm breath
Breathing upon her lips, and in her ear
The music of his gentle voice once more!  —N. P. WILLIS.

## THE SWORD AND THE PRESS.

WHEN Tamerlane had finished building his pyramid of seventy thousand human skulls, and was seen standing at the gate of Damascus, glittering in his steel, with his battle-axe on his shoulder, till his fierce hosts filed out to new victories and carnage, the pale looker-on might have fancied that Nature was in her death-throes; for havoc and despair had taken possession of the earth, and the sun of manhood seemed setting in a sea of blood.

Yet it might be on that very gala-day of Tamerlane that a little boy was playing nine-pins in the streets of Mentz, whose history was more important than that of twenty Tamerlanes. The Khan, with his shaggy demons of the wilderness, "passed away like a whirlwind," to be forgotten forever; and that German artisan had wrought a benefit which is yet immeasurably expanding itself, and will continue to expand itself, through all countries and all times.

What are the conquests and the expeditions of the whole corporation of captains, from Walter the Penniless to Napoleon Bonaparte, compared with those moveable types of Faust? Truly it is a mortifying thing for your conqueror to reflect how perishable is the metal with which he hammers with such violence; how the kind earth will soon shroud up his bloody footprints; and all that he achieved and skilfully piled together will be but like his own canvas city of a camp—this evening loud with life, to-morrow all struck and vanished,—"a few pits and heaps of straw."

For here, as always, it continues true, that the deepest force is the stillest; that, as in the fable, the mild shining of the sun shall silently accomplish what the fierce blustering of the tempest in vain assayed. Above all, it is ever to be kept in mind that not by material but by moral power are men and their actions to be governed. How noiseless is thought! No rolling of drums, no tramp of squadrons, no tumult of innumerable baggage-wagons, attend its movements.

In what obscure and sequestered places may the head be meditating which is one day to be crowned with more than imperial authority! for kings and emperors will be among its ministering servants; it will rule not over but in all heads; and with these solitary combinations of ideas, and with magic formulas, bend the world to its will. The time may come when Napoleon himself will be better known for his laws than his battles, and the victory of Waterloo prove less momentous than the opening of the first Mechanics' Institute.  —CARLYLE.

> Beneath the rule of men entirely great
> The pen is mightier than the sword. Behold
> The arch enchanter's wand!—itself a nothing!
> But taking sorcery from the master hand
> To paralyze the Cæsars, and to strike
> The loud earth breathless! Take away the sword—
> States can be served without it.            —LYTTON.

## CHILDHOOD AND HIS VISITORS.

> ONCE on a time, when sunny May,
>   Was kissing up the April showers,
> I saw fair Childhood hard at play,
>   Upon a bank of blushing flowers;
> Happy—he knew not whence or how;
>   And smiling,—who could choose but love him?
> For not more glad than Childhood's brow
>   Was the blue heaven that beam'd above him.
>
> Old Time, in most appalling wrath,
>   That valley's green repose invaded;
> The brooks grew dry upon his path,
>   The birds were mute, the lilies faded;
> But Time so swiftly wing'd his flight,
>   In haste a Grecian tomb to batter,
> That Childhood watch'd his paper kite,
>   And knew just nothing of the matter.

With circling lip and glancing eye,
  Guilt gazed upon the scene a minute;
But Childhood's glance of purity
  Had such a holy spell within it,
That the dark demon of the air
  Spread forth again his baffled pinion,
And hid his envy and despair,
  Self-tortured in his own dominion.

Then stepp'd a gloomy phantom up,
  Pale, cypress-crowned Night's awful daughter,
And proffer'd him a fearful cup
  Full to the brim of bitter water:
Poor Childhood bade her tell her name;
  And when the beldame mutter'd "Sorrow,"
He said—"Don't interrupt my game;
  I'll taste it, if I must, to-morrow."

The Muse of Pindus thither came,
  And woo'd him with the softest numbers
That ever scatter'd wealth and fame
  Upon a youthful poet's slumbers;
Though sweet the music of the lay,
  To Childhood it was all a riddle;
And "Oh!" he cried, "do send away
  That noisy woman with the fiddle!"

Then Wisdom stole his bat and ball,
  And taught him, with most sage endeavor,
Why bubbles rise and acorns fall,
  And why no toy may last forever;
She talk'd of all the wondrous laws
  Which Nature's open book discloses;
And Childhood, ere she made a pause,
  Was fast asleep among the roses.

Sleep on, sleep on!—Oh! manhood's dreams
  Are all of earthly pain or pleasure,
Of glory's toils, ambition's schemes,
  Of cherish'd love, or hoarded treasure:
But to the couch where Childhood lies
  A more delicious trance is given,
Lit up by rays from seraph-eyes,
  And glimpses of remember'd Heaven.    —PRAED.

## THE TSETSE.

A FEW remarks on the Tsetse, or *Glossina morsitans*, may here be appropriate. It is not much larger than the common house-fly, and is nearly of the same brown color as the common honey-bee; the after part of the body has three or four yellow bars across it; the wings project beyond this part considerably, and it is remarkably alert, avoiding most dexterously all attempts to capture it with the hand, at common temperatures; in the cool of the mornings and evenings it is less agile. Its peculiar buzz when once heard can never be forgotten by the traveller, whose means of locomotion are domestic animals; for it is well known that the bite of this poisonous insect is certain death to the ox, horse and dog. In this journey, though we were not aware of any great number having at any time lighted on our cattle, we lost forty-three fine oxen by its bite. We watched the animals carefully, and believe that not a score of flies were ever upon them.

A most remarkable feature in the bite of the tsetse is its perfect harmlessness in man and wild animals, and even calves, so long as they continue to suck the cows. We never experienced the slightest injury from them ourselves, personally, although we lived two months in their *habitat*, which was in this case as sharply defined as in many others, for the south bank of the Chobe was infested by them, and the northern bank, where our cattle were placed, only fifty yards distant, contained not a single specimen. This was the more remarkable, as we often saw natives carrying over raw meat to the opposite bank with many tsetse settled upon it.

The poison does not seem to be injected by a sting, or by ova placed beneath the skin, for, when one is allowed to feed freely on the hand, it is seen to insert the middle prong of three portions, into which the proboscis divides, somewhat deeply into the true skin; it then draws it out a little way, and it assumes a crimson color as the mandibles come into brisk operation. The previously shrunken belly swells out, and if left undisturbed, the fly quietly departs when it is full. A slight itching irritation follows, but not more than in the bite of a mosquito. In the ox this same bite produces no more immediate effects than in man. It does not startle him as the gad-fly does; but a few days afterwards the following symptoms supervene: the eye and nose begin to run, the coat stares as if the animal were cold, a swelling appears under the jaw, and sometimes at the navel; and though the animal continues to graze, emaciation commences, accompanied with a peculiar flaccidity of the muscles, and this proceeds unchecked until, perhaps months afterwards, purging comes on, and the animal, no longer able to graze, perishes in a state of extreme exhaustion. Those which are in good condition often perish soon after the bite is inflicted with staggering and blindness, as if the brain were affected by it. Sudden changes of temperature produced by falls of rain seem to hasten the progress of the complaint ; but in general the emaciation goes on uninterruptedly for months, and, do what we will, the poor animals perish miserably.

The mule, ass, and goat enjoy the same immunity from the tsetse as man and the game. Many large tribes on the Zambesi can keep no domestic animals except the goat, in consequence of the scourge existing in their country. Our children were frequently bitten, yet suffered no harm ; and we saw around us numbers of zebras, buffaloes, pigs, pallahs and other antelopes, feeding quietly in the very habitat of the tsetse, yet as undisturbed by its bite as oxen are when they first receive the fatal poison. There is not so much difference in the natures of the horse and zebra, the buffalo and ox, the sheep and antelope, as to afford any satisfactory explanation of the phenomenon. Is a man not as much a domestic animal as a dog ? The curious feature in the case, that dogs perish though fed on milk, whereas the calves escape so long as they continue sucking, made us imagine that the mischief might be produced by some plant in the locality, and not by tsetse ; but Major Vardon, of the Madras Army; settled that point by riding a horse up to a small hill infested by the insect without allowing him time to graze, and, though he only remained long enough to take a view of the country and catch some specimens of tsetse on the animal, in ten days afterwards the horse was dead.

—LIVINGSTONE.

## HOME—A DUET.

He. Dost thou love wandering ? whither wouldst thou go ?
    Dreamest thou, sweet daughter, of a land more fair ?
    Dost thou not love these aye-blue streams that flow ?
    These spicy forests ? and this golden air ?

She. Oh, yes ! I love the woods and streams so gay,
    And more than all, O father ! I love *thee;*
    Yet would I fain be wandering far away,
    Where such things never were, nor e'er shall be.

| | |
|---|---|
| HE. | Speak, mine own daughter, with the sun-bright locks, To what pale banished nation wouldst thou roam? |
| SHE. | O father, let us find our frozen rocks! Let's seek that country of all countries—Home! |
| HE. | See'st thou these orange flowers! this palm that rears Its head up tow'rd Heaven's blue and countless dome? |
| SHE. | I dream, I dream, mine eyes are hid in tears, My heart is wandering round our ancient home. |
| HE. | Why, then, we'll go. Farewell, ye tender skies, Who shelter'd us when we were forced to roam. |
| SHE. | On, on! Let's pass the swallow as he flies! Farewell, kind land! Now, father, *now* for Home! |

—BARRY CORNWALL (B. F. PROCTER).

# READING.

READING furnishes the mind only with materials of knowledge: it is thinking makes what we read ours. We are of the ruminating kind, and it is not enough to cram ourselves with a great load of collections; unless we chew them over again, they will not give us strength and nourishment. There are indeed in some writers visible instances of deep thought, close and acute reasoning, and ideas well pursued. The light these would give would be of great use, if their readers would observe and imitate them; all the rest at best are but particulars fit to be turned into knowledge; but that can be done only by our own meditation, and examining the reach, force and coherence of what is said; and then, as far as we apprehend and see the connection of ideas, so far it is ours; without that, it is but so much loose matter floating in our brain. The memory may be stored, but the judgment is little better, and the stock of knowledge not increased, by being able to repeat what others have said, or produce the arguments we have found in them. Such a knowledge as this is but a knowledge by hearsay, and the ostentation of it is at best but talking by rote, and very often upon weak and wrong principles. For all that is to be found in books is not built upon true foundations, nor always rightly deduced from the principles it is pretended to be built on. Such an examen as is requisite to discover that, every reader's mind is not forward to make, especially in those who have given themselves up to a party, and only hunt for what they can scrape together that may favor and support the tenets of it. Such men wilfully exclude themselves from truth, and from all true benefit to be received by reading.

Others, of more indifferency, often want attention and industry. The mind is backward in itself to be at the pains to trace every argument to its original, and to see upon what basis it stands, and how firmly; but yet it is this that gives so much the advantage to one man more than another in reading.  The mind should, by severe rules, be tied down to this, at first uneasy, task; use and exercise will give it facility.  So that those who are accustomed to it, readily, as it were with one cast of the eye, take a view of the argument, and presently, in most cases, see where it bottoms.  Those who have got this faculty, one may say, have got the true key of books, and the clue to lead them through the mizmaze of variety of opinions and authors to truth and certainty.  This, young beginners should be entered in and shown the use of, that they might profit by their reading.  Those who are strangers to it will be apt to think it too great a clog in the way of men's studies; and they will suspect they shall make but small progress, if, in the books they read, they must stand to examine and unravel every argument, and follow it step by step up to its original.

I answer, this is a good objection, and ought to weigh with those whose reading is designed for much talk and little knowledge, and I have nothing to say to it.  But I am here inquiring into the conduct of the understanding in its progress towards knowledge; and to those who aim at that, I may say, —that he who fair and softly goes steadily forward in a course that points right, will sooner be at his journey's end, than he that runs after every one he meets, though he gallop all day full speed.

To which let me add, that this way of thinking on, and profiting by, what we read, will be a clog and rub to any one only in the beginning; when custom and exercise have made it familiar, it will be dispatched, in most occasions, without resting or interruption in the course of our reading.  The motions and views of a mind exercised that way are wonderfully quick; and a man used to such sort of reflections sees as much at one glimpse as would require a long discourse to lay before another, and make out an entire and gradual deduction. Besides that, when the first difficulties are over, the delight and sensible advantage it brings mightily encourages and enlivens the mind in reading, which, without this, is very improperly called study. —LOCKE.

## LADY CLARE.

It was the time when lilies blow,
  And clouds are highest up in air,
Lord Ronald brought a lily-white doe
  To give to his cousin, Lady Clare.

I trow they did not part in scorn:
  Lovers long-betrothed were they:
They two will wed the morrow morn;
  God's blessing on the day!

He does not love me for my birth,
  Nor for my lands so broad and fair;
He loves me for my own true worth,
  And that is well," said Lady Clare.

In there came old Alice, the nurse,
  Said, "Who was this that went from thee?"
"It was my cousin," said Lady Clare,
  "To-morrow he weds with me."

"Oh! God be thanked!" said Alice, the nurse,
  "That all comes round so just and fair:
Lord Ronald is heir of all your lands,
  And you are not the Lady Clare."

"Are ye out of your mind, my nurse, my nurse?"
  Said Lady Clare, "that ye speak so wild?"
"As God's above," said Alice, the nurse,
  "I speak the truth: you are my child.

"The old Earl's daughter died at my breast—
  I speak the truth as I live by bread!
I buried her like my own sweet child,
  And put my child in her stead."

"Falsely, falsely have you done,
  Oh! mother," she said, "if this be true,
To keep the best man under the sun
  So many years from his due."

"Nay, now, my child," said Alice, the nurse,
  "But keep the secret for your life,
And all you have will be Lord Ronald's,
  When you are man and wife."

"If I'm a beggar born," she said,
  "I will speak out, for I dare not lie;
Pull off, pull off the brooch of gold,
  And fling the diamond necklace by."

"Nay, now, my child," said Alice, the nurse,
  "But keep the secret all ye can."
She said, "Not so: but I will know
  If there be any faith in man."

## LADY CLARE.

"Nay, now, what faith?" said Alice, the nurse,
  "The man will cleave unto his right."
"And he shall have it," the lady replied,
  "Though I should die to night."

"Yet give one kiss to your mother dear!
  Alas! my child, I sinned for thee."
"Oh! mother, mother, mother," she said,
  "So strange it seems to me.

"Yet here's a kiss for my mother dear,
  My mother dear, if this be so,
And lay your hand upon my head,
  And bless me, mother, ere I go."

She clad herself in a russet gown,
  She was no longer Lady Clare:
She went by dale, and she went by down,
  With a single rose in her hair.

The lily-white doe Lord Ronald had brought
  Leapt up from where she lay,
Dropt her head in the maiden's hand,
  And followed her all the way.

Down stept Lord Ronald from his tower:
  "Oh! Lady Clare, you shame your worth!
Why come you drest like a village maid,
  That are the flower of the earth?"

"If I come drest like a village maid,
  I am but as my fortunes are:
I am a beggar born," she said,
  "And not the Lady Clare."

"Play me no tricks," said Lord Ronald,
  "For I am your's in word and deed.
Play me no tricks," said Lord Ronald,
  "Your riddle is hard to read."

Oh! and proudly stood she up!
  Her heart within her did not fail!
She looked into Lord Ronald's eyes,
  And told him all her nurse's tale.

He laughed a laugh of merry scorn;
  He turned and kissed her where she stood:
"If you are not the heiress born,
  And I," said he, "the next in blood—

"If you are not the heiress born,
  And I," said he, "the lawful heir,
We two will wed to-morrow morn,
  And you shall still be Lady Clare."

—TENNYSON.

## JUSTICE.

JUSTICE is not a halt and miserable object ; it is not the ineffective bauble of an Indian pagod ; it is not the portentous phantom of despair ; it is not like any fabled monster formed in the eclipse of reason, and found in some unhallowed grove of superstitious darkness and political dismay ! No, my lords.

In the happy reverse of all these, I turn from this disgusting caricature, to the *real image—Justice !* I have now before me august and pure, the abstract idea of all that would be perfect in the spirits and the aspirings of men ;—where the mind rises ; where the heart expands ; where the countenance is ever placid and benign ; where her favorite attitude is—to stoop to the unfortunate ; to hear their cry, and to help them ; to rescue and relieve ; to succour and save ! Majestic from its mercy ; venerable from its utility ; uplifted, without pride ; firm, without obduracy ; beneficent in each preference ; lovely, though in her frown !

On that *justice* I rely, deliberate and sure ; abstracted from all party purposes and political speculation ; not in words, but in facts. You, my lords, who hear me, I conjure, by those rights it is your best privilege to preserve ; by that fame it is your best pleasure to inherit ; by all those feelings, which refer to the first term in the series of existence, the original compact of our nature, our controlling rank in the creation! This is the call on all to administer to truth and equity, as they would satisfy the laws and satisfy themselves, with the most exalted bliss possible or conceivable for our nature—the self-approving consciousness of virtue, when the condemnation we look for will be one of the most ample mercies accomplished for mankind since the creation of the world. —SHERIDAN.

## THE CONQUEROR'S GRAVE.

WITHIN this lowly grave a conqueror lies ;
And yet the monument proclaims it not,
Nor round the sleeper's name hath chisel wrought
The emblems of a fame that never dies—
Ivy and amaranth in a graceful sheaf
  Twined with the laurel's fair, imperial leaf.
    A simple name alone,
      To the great world unknown,
Is graven here, and wild flowers rising round,
Meek meadow-sweet and violets of the ground,
  Lean lovingly against the humble stone.

## THE CONQUEROR'S GRAVE.

Here, in the quiet earth, they laid apart
  No man of iron mould and bloody hands,
  Who sought to wreak upon the cowering lands
The passions that consumed his restless heart;
  But one of tender spirit and delicate frame,
      Gentlest in mien and mind
      Of gentle womankind,
Timidly shrinking from the breath of blame:
One in whose eyes the smile of kindness made
  Its haunt, like flowers by sunny brooks in May;
Yet, at the thought of others' pain, a shade
  Of sweeter sadness chased the smile away.

Nor deem that when the hand that moulders here
Was raised in menace, realms were chilled with fear,
  And armies mustered at the sign as when
Clouds rise on clouds before the rainy east,—
  Grey captains leading bands of veteran men
And fiery youths to be the vultures' feast.
Not thus were waged the mighty wars that gave
The victory to her who fills this grave:
      Alone her task was wrought;
      Alone the battle fought;
Through that long strife her constant hope was stayed
On God alone, nor looked for other aid.

She met the hosts of sorrow with a look
  That altered not beneath the frown they wore;
And soon the lowering brood were tamed, and took
  Meekly her gentle rule and frowned no more.
Her soft hand put aside the assaults of wrath,
      And calmly broke in twain
      The fiery shafts of pain,
And rent the nets of passion from her path.
By that victorious hand despair was slain.
With love she vanquished hate, and overcame
Evil with good in her great Master's name.

Her glory is not of this shadowy state,
  Glory that with the fleeting season dies;
But when she entered at the sapphire gate,
  What joy was radiant in celestial eyes!
How heaven's bright depths with sounding welcomes rung,
And flowers of heaven by shining hands were flung!
      And He who long before,
      Pain, scorn, and sorrow bore,
The mighty Sufferer, with aspect sweet,
Smiled on the timid stranger from his seat;
He who, returning glorious from the grave,
Dragged Death, disarmed, in chains, a crouching slave.

See, as I linger here, the sun grows low;
  Cool airs are murmuring that the night is near.
O gentle sleeper, from thy grave I go
  Consoled though sad, in hope and yet in fear.
      Brief is the time, I know,

> The warfare scarce begun,
> Yet all may win the triumphs thou hast won:
> Still flows the fount whose waters strengthened thee.
> The victors' names are yet too few to fill
> Heaven's mighty roll; the glorious armoury,
> That ministered to thee, is open still. —BRYANT.

---

# REFLECTIONS ON THE FRENCH REVOLUTION.

I HAVE often been astonished, considering that we are divided from you (in France) but by a slender dyke of about twenty-four miles, and that the mutual intercourse between the two countries has lately been very great, to find how little you seem to know of us. I suspect that this is owing to your forming a judgment of this nation from certain publications, which do, very erroneously, if they do at all, represent the opinions and dispositions generally prevalent in England. The vanity, restlessness, petulance, and spirit of intrigue, of several petty cabals, who attempt to hide their total want of consequence in bustle and noise, and puffing, and mutual quotation of each other, makes you imagine that our contemptuous neglect of their abilities is a general mark of acquiescence in their opinions. No such thing, I assure you. Because half a dozen grasshoppers under a fern make the field ring with their importunate chink, whilst thousands of great cattle, reposed beneath the shadow of the British oak, chew the cud and are silent, pray do not imagine that those who make the noise are the only inhabitants of the field; that of course, they are many in number; or that, after all, they are other than the little, shrivelled, meagre, hopping, though loud and troublesome, insects of the hour.

I venture to affirm that not one in a hundred amongst us participates in the "triumph" of the Revolution Society. If the king and queen of France, and their children, were to fall into our hands by the chance of war, in the most acrimonious of all hostilities, (I deprecate such an event, I deprecate such hostility,) they would be treated with another sort of triumphal entry into London. We formerly have had a king of France in that situation; you have read how he was treated by the victor in the field; and in what manner he was afterwards received in England. Four hundred years have gone over us; but I believe we are not materially changed since that period. Thanks to our sullen resistance to innovation, thanks to the cold sluggishness of our national character, we still bear the stamp of our forefathers. We have not (as I conceive) lost the generosity and dignity of thinking of the fourteenth century; nor as yet have we subtilized ourselves into savages. We are not the converts of Rousseau; we are not the disciples of Voltaire; Helvetius has made no progress amongst us. Atheists are not our preachers; madmen are not our lawgivers. We know that *we* have made no discoveries; and we think that no discoveries are to be made, in morality; nor many in the great principles of government, nor in the ideas of liberty, which were understood long before we were born, altogether as well as they will be after the grave has heaped its mould upon our presumption, and the silent tomb shall have imposed its law on our pert loquacity. In England we have not yet been completely embowelled of our natural entrails; we still feel within us, and we cherish and cultivate, those inbred sentiments which are the faithful guardians, the active monitors of our duty, the true supporters of all liberal and manly morals. We have not been drawn and trussed, in order that we may be filled, like stuffed birds in a museum, with chaff and rags, and paltry blurred shreds of paper about the rights of man; we preserve the whole of our feelings still native and entire, unsophisticated by pedantry and infidelity; we have real hearts of flesh and blood beating in our bosoms; we fear God; we honor the king. —BURKE.

## THE HUNTER.

Away to the Forests! the wilds of the West,
Where no foot save the step of the Hunter hath press'd,
Where no voice of the Earth on the echo floats back,
Save the wild cheer he gives on his arrowy track.
            Away!
O'er the hills of the West with the Hunters away!

Away to the Forests! the streams flash along,
With a murmur of gladness—a musical song,
And a fresh voice of wildness and freedom rings past,
When the green wood bends low to the sweep of the blast.
            Away!
Where the free winds sing welcome—Away! come away!

Away to the Forests! rough gladness is ours,
Mid the green Earth's wild treasures, her streams and her flowers,
Where the wolf claims a shelter—the strong elk may bound—
Blue wave—misty mountain—*our* footsteps are found.
            Away!
To the beautiful haunts of the Hunters away!

Away to the Forests! fair home for the brave—
Let the Mariner toss on the treacherous wave,
Let the Soldier exult in the storm of the fight—
But the Hunter's bold heart knows a purer delight.
Away!
Where the rifles are ringing—Away! come away!

Away to the Forests! kind eyes too have smiled
On the Hunter's rude hearth in the loneliest wild,
And a voice of affection—a love-lighted face,
Makes the homeward track sweet, as he turns from the chase
Away!
By the hearth of the Hunter there's welcome—Away!

Away to the Forests! true freedom is ours,
We look from afar on the city's dark towers—
And away to our kingdom—bright home for the brave,
The haunts of the Hunter—his cradle—his grave.
Away!
O'er the hills of the West with the Hunters away!
—Toronto Maple Leaf.

## THE BATTLE OF CRECI.
### (A. D. 1346.)

As soon as the troops had breakfasted, the marshals issued their orders, and each lord, under his own banner and pennon, marched to the ground which had been allotted to him on the preceding day. All were dismounted, to take away the temptation of pursuit or flight. The first division, under the nominal command of the prince, the real command of the Earls of Warwick and Oxford, consisted of eight hundred men at arms, a thousand Welsh infantry, and two thousand archers. At some distance behind them, but rather on their flank, was placed the second division of eight hundred men at arms, and twelve hundred archers. The third, under the command of the King, comprised seven hundred men at arms and two thousand archers, and was stationed as a reserve on the summit of the hill. The archers of each division formed in its front, in the shape of a portcullis; and orders were issued that no man should incumber himself with the charge of a prisoner, or quit his post to pursue a fugitive. Edward, on a small palfrey, with a marshal on each side, rode from company to company, speaking to all, exhorting them to defend his honor, and expressing his confidence of victory. About ten o'clock he ordered them to take refreshment. They sate in ranks on the ground, with their bows and helmets before them.

The King of France had marched from Abbeville about sunrise; but the multitude of his followers advanced in so disorderly a manner, that the knights who had reconnoitred the English army advised him to postpone the battle till the morrow, and employ the interval in marshalling his army. Two officers were immediately despatched, one to the van, the other to the rear, crying out, "Halt, banners, in the name of God and St. Denis." But these orders increased the confusion. By some they were obeyed, by many misunderstood, and by the greater part disregarded. Philip suffered himself to be carried forward by the stream; and as soon as he saw the English, he lost his temper, and ordered the Genoese to form, and begin the battle.

The Genoese were a body of six, or according to some writers, fifteen thousand Italians, who fought with cross-bows, under two celebrated leaders, Antonio Doria, and Carlo Grimaldi. They were supported by the King's brother, the Count d'Alençon, with a numerous cavalry superbly accoutred. The king himself followed with the rest of the army in four divisions: the amount of the combatants has been estimated by different writers at every intermediate number between sixty and one hundred and twenty thousand men.

Never perhaps were preparations for battle made under circumstances so truly awful. On that very day the sun suffered a partial eclipse; birds in clouds, the precursors of a storm, flew screaming over the two armies; and the rain fell in torrents, accompanied with incessant thunder and lightning. About five in the afternoon the weather cleared up, and the sun in full splendor darted his rays in the eyes of the enemy. The Genoese, setting up three shouts, discharged their quarrels. But they were no match for the English archers, who received the volley in silence, and returned their arrows in such numbers, and with such force that the cross-bow men began to waver. The Count d'Alençon, calling them cowards, ordered his men to cut down the runaways; but he only added to the disorder. Many of his knights were unhorsed by the archers, and as they lay on the ground were despatched by the Welshmen, who had armed themselves with long knives for the purpose.

At length the passage was cleared: the Count on one side, and his colleague the Earl of Flanders on the other, skirted the English archers, while a numerous body of French, Germans, and Savoyards, forced their way to the men at arms under the command of the prince. The second division immediately closed for his support: but the conflict grew fierce and doubtful, and Sir Thomas Norwich was sent to request a reinforcement. Edward, who from a windmill watched the chances of the battle, and the movements of the armies, inquired if his son were killed or wounded. The messenger replied, "No."—"Then," said he, "tell Warwick that he shall have no assistance. Let the boy win his spurs. He and those who have him in charge shall earn the whole glory of the day." This answer was hailed as a prediction of victory, and infused new courage into the combatants.

D'Alençon, unable to make any impression on the English in his front, attempted to turn their position by penetrating through a narrow pass on one side of the hill; but he found the outlet barricaded with carts and waggons from the camp, and was repulsed with great slaughter by a body of archers posted behind them. In the meantime Philip, who had hitherto been only a spectator of the action, grew impatient; he hastened with his force to the aid of his brother; and fought as if it had been his object to refute the taunt of cowardice so often applied to him by Edward. He was wounded in two places; his horse was killed under him; he retired till the blood was stanched, and then mounting another charger, rushed into the midst of the combatants. But the day was already lost: his brother, with the flower of the French chivalry, had fallen; and John of Hainault, seizing the king's bridle, and bidding him reserve himself for victory on some future occasion, led him by force out of the field. With a slender escort of five barons and sixty knights he escaped to the city of Amiens.

The flight of Philip did not terminate the contest. Many of the French continued in detached bodies to charge their adversaries; but as their efforts were made without concert, they generally ended in the destruction of the assailants. As the darkness increased the fighting gradually ceased; the voices of men, seeking the banners from which they had wandered, were no longer heard, and the English congratulated themselves on the repulse of the enemy. The King, ignorant of the extent of his victory, ordered fires to be kindled, and forbade his men to quit their posts. Eager to testify his approbation of the prince, he sprang to meet him, and clasping him in his arms, exclaimed, "Fair son, continue your career. You have behaved nobly. You have shown yourself worthy of me and the crown!" The young Edward sank on his knees, and modestly attributed all the merit to his father.

The darkness of the night was succeeded by a dense mist in the morning, which equally intercepted the view, and to gain information the King sent out before sunrise a detachment of three thousand men. They soon found themselves in the midst of a body of Militia from Beauvais and Amiens, which ignorant of the preceding events, had marched all night to overtake the army. These men, unsuspicious of danger, and unprepared for battle, were massacred almost without resistance. A similar mistake proved equally fatal to the Archbishop of Rouen, and the Grand Prior of France, with a numerous body of knights. As the day cleared, thousands of Frenchmen were discovered in the fields, who had passed the night under the trees and hedges, in the hope of finding their lords in the morning. These too were put to the sword by the English cavalry: so that the carnage of the second is asserted to have exceeded that of the former day.

At noon the King ordered the Lords Cobham and Stafford to examine the field of battle. They took with them three heralds, to ascertain from the surcoats of the knights, and two secretaries to record, the names and rank of those who had fallen. In the evening they presented to the King eighty banners, with a catalogue of eleven princes and twelve hundred knights. The slain of inferior note were not numbered. Report made them amount to thirty thousand. A truce of three days was proclaimed for the burial of the dead, and the King himself attended in mourning at the funeral service.

Among the slain the most distinguished was John, King of Bohemia. Age had not chilled in him the fire of youth: though blind, he placed himself in the first division of the French; and as the issue grew dubious, ordered the four knights, his attendants, to lead him into the hottest of the battle, "that I too," said he, "may have a stroke at the English." Placing him in the midst of them, and interlacing their bridles, they spurred forward their horses, and were almost immediately slain. The reader will probably consider the Bohemian monarch as foolishly prodigal of his life: by the writers of the age his conduct has been extolled as an instance of unparalleled heroism. His crest, three ostrich feathers, with the motto "Ich dien," I serve, was adopted by the prince of Wales, and has been always borne by his successors. —LINGARD.

## TEARS.

O TEARS, ye rivulets that flow profuse
Forth from the fountains of perennial love,
Love, sympathy, and sorrow, those pure springs
Welling in secret up from lower depths
Than couch beneath the everlasting hills:
Ye showers that from the cloud of mercy fall
In drops of tender grief,—you I invoke,
For in your gentleness there lies a spell
Mightier than arms or bolted chains of iron.
When floating by the reedy banks of Nile
A babe of more than human beauty wept,
Were not the innocent dews upon its cheeks
A link in God's great counsels? Who knows not
The loves of David and young Jonathan,
When in unwitting rivalry of hearts
The son of Jesse won a nobler wreath
Than garlands pluck'd in war and dipp'd in blood?
And haply she, who wash'd her Saviour's feet
With the soft silent rain of penitence,
And wiped them with her tangled tresses, gave
A costlier sacrifice than Solomon,
What time he slew myriads of sheep and kine,
And pour'd upon the brazen altar forth
Rivers of fragrant oil. In Peter's woe,
Bitterly weeping in the darken'd street,
Love veils his fall. The traitor shed no tear.
But Magdalene's gushing grief is fresh
In memory of us all, as when it drench'd
The cold stone of the sepulchre. Paul wept,
And by the droppings of his heart subdued
Strong men by all his massive arguments
Unvanquish'd. And the loved Evangelist
Wept, though in heaven, that none in heaven were found
Worthy to loose the Apocalyptic seals.
No holy tear is lost. None idly sinks
As water in the barren sand: for God,
Let David witness, puts His children's tears
Into His cruse and writes them in His book;—
David, that sweetest lyrist, not the less
Sweet that his plaintive pleading tones ofttimes
Are tremulous with grief. For he and all
God's nightingales have ever learn'd to sing
Pressing their bosom on some secret thorn.
In the world's morning it was thus: and, since
The evening shadows fell athwart mankind,
Thus hath it always been. Blind and bereft,
The minstrel of an Eden lost explored
Things all invisible to mortal eyes.
And he, who touch'd with a true poet's hand
The harp of prophecy, himself had learn'd
Its music in the school of mourners. But
Beyond all other sorrow stands enshrined
The imperishable record, - JESUS WEPT.

He wept beside the grave of Lazarus;
He wept lamenting lost Jerusalem;
He wept with agonizing groans beneath
The olives of Gethsemane. O tears,
For ever sacred, since in human grief
The Man of sorrows mingled healing drops
With the great ocean tides of human woe;
You I invoke to modulate my words
And chasten my ambition, while I search,
And by your aid with no unmoisten'd eye,
The early archives of the birth of time.
—BICKERSTETH.

## JERUSALEM.

JERUSALEM lies near the summit of a broad mountain ridge. This ridge or mountainous track extends, without interruption, from the plain of Esdraelon to a line drawn between the south end of the Dead Sea and the south-east corner of the Mediterranean: or more properly, perhaps, it may be regarded as extending as far as the southern desert, where, at Jebel Araif, it sinks down at once to the level of the great plateau. This tract, which is nowhere less than from twenty to twenty-five geographical miles in breadth, is, in fact, high, uneven table, land. The surface of this upper region is everywhere rocky, uneven, and mountainous, and is, moreover, cut up by deep valleys which run east or west on either side towards the Jordan or the Mediterranean.

From the great plain of Esdraelon onwards towards the south, the mountainous country rises gradually, forming the tract anciently known as the mountains of Ephraim and Judah; until, in the vicinity of Hebron, it attains an elevation of 3250 feet above the level of the Mediterranean Sea. Further north, on a line drawn from the north end of the Dead Sea towards the true west, the ridge has an elevation of only about 2710 feet; and here, close upon the watershed, lies the city of Jerusalem. Its mean geographical position is in lat. 31° 46' 43" N., and long. 35° 13' E. from Greenwich.

The traveller on his way from Ramleh to Jerusalem, at about an hour and a half distance therefrom, descends into and crosses the great Terebinth vale, or valley of Elah. On again reaching the high ground on its eastern side, he enters upon an open tract sloping gradually downwards towards the east, and sees before him, at the distance of about two miles, the walls and domes of the city, and beyond them the highest ridge of Olivet. The traveller now descends gradually towards the town along a broad swell of ground, having at some distance on his left the shallow northern part of the valley of Jehoshaphat, and close at hand on his right the basin which forms the beginning of the valley of Hinnom. Further down both these valleys become deep, narrow, and precipitous; that of Hinnom bends south, and again east, nearly at right angles, and unites with the other, which then continues its course to the Dead Sea. Upon the broad and elevated promontory within the fork of the two valleys of Jehoshaphat and of Hinnom, lies the holy city. All around are higher hills: on the east the Mount of Olives, on the south the Hill of Evil Counsel, so called, rising directly from the vale of Hinnom; on the west the ground rises gently, as above described, to the borders of the great valley; while, on the north, a bend of the ridge connected with the Mount of Olives bounds the prospect at a distance of more than a mile. Towards the south-west the view is somewhat more open; for here lies the plain of Rephaim, commencing just at the southern brink of the valley of Hinnom, and stretching off south-west, when it runs to the western sea. In the north-west, too, the eye reaches up along the upper part of the valley of Jehoshaphat, and from many points can discern the mosque of Neby Samwil (Prophet Samuel), situated on a lofty ridge beyond the great valley, at the distance of two hours.

The surface of the elevated promontory itself, on which the city stands, slopes somewhat steeply towards the east, terminating on the brink of the valley of Jehoshaphat. From the northern part, near the present Damascus gate, a depression or shallow valley runs in the southern direction, having on the west the ancient hills of Akra and Zion, and on the east the lower ones of Bezetha and Moriah. Between the hills of Akra and Zion another depression or shallow valley (still easy to be traced) comes down from near the Jaffa gate, and joins the former. It then continues obliquely down the slope, but with a deeper bed, in a southern direction, quite to the pool of Siloam and the valley of Jehoshaphat. This is the ancient Tyropœan. West of its lower part Zion rises loftily, lying mostly without the modern city; while on the east of the Tyropœan and the valley first mentioned lie Bezetha, Moriah, and Ophel, the last a long and comparatively narrow ridge, also outside of the modern city, and terminating in a rocky point over the pool of Siloam. These last three hills may srtictly be taken as only parts of one and the same ridge. The breadth of the whole site of Jerusalem from the brow of the valley of Hinnom, near the Jaffa gate, to the brink of the valley of Jehoshaphat, is about one thousand and twenty yards, or nearly half a geographical mile; of which distance three hundred and eighteen yards are occupied by the area of the great mosque of Omar, which occupies the site of Solomon's temple. North of the Jaffa gate the city wall sweeps round more to the west, and increases the breadth of the city in that part. The country around Jerusalem is all of limestone formation. The rocks everywhere come out above the surface, which in many parts is also thickly strewed with stones; and the aspect of the whole region is barren and dreary; yet the olive thrives here abundantly, and fields of grain are seen in the valleys and level places, but they are less productive than in the region of Hebron and Nabulus. Neither vineyards nor fig-trees flourish on the high ground around the city, though the latter are found in the gardens below Siloam, and very frequently in the vicinity of Bethlehem.

From the account of Josephus, as compared with those furnished by others, it appears that Jerusalem stood on three hills, Mount Zion, Mount Akra, and Mount Moriah, on which last the temple stood. Or we may consider them as two, after Mount Akra had been levelled, and the valley filled up which separated it from Mount Moriah. Of these hills Zion was the highest, and contained the upper city, "the city of David," with the citadel, the strength of which, and of the position on which it stood, enabled the Jebusites so long to retain it as their stronghold, and to maintain their command over the lower part of the city, even when they were obliged to allow the Israelites to share in its occupation. This Mount Zion (which we are only here noticing cursorily) formed the southern portion of the ancient city. It is almost excluded from the modern city, and is under partial cultivation. It is nearly a mile in circumference, is highest on the western side, and towards the east slopes down in broad terraces in the upper part of the mountain, and narrow ones on the side, toward the brook Kidron. This mount is considerably higher than the ground on which the ancient (lower) city stood, or that on the east leading to the valley of Jehosphaphat, but has very little relative height above the ground on the south and on the west, and must have owed its boasted strength principally to a deep ravine, by which it is encompassed on the east, south and west, and the strong high walls and towers by which it was enclosed and flanked completely round. The breadth of this ravine is about one hundred and fifty feet, and its depth, or the height of Mount Zion above the bottom of the ravine, above sixty feet. The bottom is rock, covered with a thin sprinkling of earth, and in the winter season is the natural channel for conveying off the water that falls into it from the higher ground. On both of its sides the rock is cut perpendicularly down; and it was probably the quarry from which much of the stone was taken for the building of the city.

The site, regarded *as a whole*, without further attending to the distinction of hills, is surrounded on the east, west and south by valleys of various depth and breadth, but to the north-west extends into the plain, which in this part is called, " the plain of Jeremiah," and is the best woody tract in the whole neighborhood. The progressive extension of the city was thus necessarily northward, as stated by Josephus. The town most probably, almost certainly, began at the southern, or Mount Zion, part of this site, and in its ultimate extension, according to Josephus, comprehended a circuit of thirty-three furlongs; whereas that of the modern town does not appear to exceed two miles and a half. The confining valleys are often mentioned in Scripture. Those on the east and south are very deep. The former is the valley of Jehoshaphat, through which flows the brook Kidron, and the latter is generally called the valley of Hinnom. This denomination is extended by some topographers also to the western and least deep valley, while others call it the valley of Gihon. On the opposite side of these valleys rise hills, which are mostly of superior elevation to that of the site of the city itself. That on the east, beyond the brook Kidron, is the Mount of Olives. That on the south is a broad and barren hill, loftier than the Mount of Olives, but without any of its picturesque beauty. On the west there is a rocky flat, which rises to a considerable elevation towards the north, and to which has been assigned the name of Mount Gihon. Even in the north-east, at Scopus, where the besieging Romans under Titus encamped, the ground is considerably more elevated than the immediate site of the town. Thus is explained the expression of David: " As the mountains are round about Jerusalem, so the Lord is round about his people." (Ps. cxxv. 2). The relative height of those surrounding hills gives to the city an apparent elevation inferior to that which it really possesses. The district for many miles round Jerusalem is now of a very barren and cheerless character, whatever may have been its ancient condition. Solomon must be considered as having permanently fixed its metropolitan character, by the erection of the temple and the royal establishment. But it was the temple, chiefly, which in all ages maintained Jerusalem as a metropolis of the country. Even after the destruction of that venerated fabric, the mere fact that it had existed there operated in preventing the selection of any new site, even when the opportunity occurred. The separation into two kingdoms, after the death of Solomon, did also necessarily prevent any intentions of change which might have arisen, had the whole country remained one kingdom, with a large choice for situations for a capital; and we are to remember that, although, after the erection of the temple, it always remained the *ecclesiastical* metropolis of the land, it was, in a civil sense, for a long series of years, the capital of only the smallest of the two kingdoms into which the land was divided. But under all disadvantages, many of which are perhaps the result of the wars, the desolations, and the neglect of many ages, the very situation of the town, on the brink of rugged hills, encircled by deep and wild valleys, bounded by eminences whose sides *were* covered with groves and gardens, added to its numerous towers and temples, must, as Carne remarks, have given it a singular and gloomy magnificence, scarcely possessed by any other city in the world.

Mr. Rae Williams says, the general view of this part of the country, as seen from the Mount of Olives, reminded him of many parts of the Highlands of Scotland—" A scene of hills, like an ocean, fixed at once into solidity when heaving in its wildest fury." —KITTO.

## PALESTINE.

Blest land of Judea! thrice hallowed of song,
Where the holiest of memories, pilgrim-like throng;
In the shade of thy palm, by the shores of thy sea,
On the hills of thy beauty, my heart is with thee!

With the eye of a spirit, I look on that shore,
Where the pilgrim and prophet have lingered before;
With the glide of a spirit, I traverse the sod
Made bright by the steps of the angels of God.

Blue sea of the hills! in my spirit I hear
Thy waters, Gennesaret, chime on my ear!
Where the Lowly and Just, with the people sat down,
And the spray on the dust of his sandals was thrown.

Beyond are Bethulia's mountains of green,
And the desolate hills of the wild Gadarene,
And I pause on the goat-crags of Tabor to see
The gleam of thy waters, oh! dark Galilee!

Hark, a sound in the valleys! Where swollen and strong,
Thy river, O Kishon, is sweeping along;
Where the Canaanite strove with Jehovah in vain,
And thy torrent grew dark with the blood of the slain.

There, down from his mountains stern Zebulon came,
And Naphtali's stag, with his eyeballs of flame,
And the chariots of Jabin rolled harmlessly on,
For the arm of the Lord was Abinoam's son!

There sleep the still rocks and the caverns which rang
To the song which the beautiful Prophetess sang,
When the Princess of Issachar stood by her side,
And the shout of a host in its triumph replied.

Lo! Bethlehem's hill side before me is seen,
With the mountains around, and the valleys between;
There rested the shepherds of Judah, and there
The song of the angels rose sweet on the air.

And Bethany's palm trees, in beauty still throw
Their shadows at noon, on the ruins below;
But where are the sisters who hastened to greet
The lowly Redeemer, and sit at his feet?

I tread with the TWELVE as they wayfaring trod;
I stand where they stood with the CHOSEN OF GOD!
Where his blessing was heard, and his lessons were taught,
Where the blind were restored, and the healing was wrought.

Oh! here with his flock the sad wanderer came,
These hills he toiled over in grief, are the same;
The founts where he drank by the way-side still flow,
And the same airs are blowing which breathed on his brow.

And throned on her hills, sits Jerusalem yet,
But with dust on her forehead, and chains on her feet;
For the crown of her pride to the mocker hath gone,
And the holy Shechinah is dark where it shone.

But wherefore this dream of the earthly abode
Of humanity clothed in the brightness of God?
Where my spirit but turned from the outward and dim!
It could gaze, even now, on the presence of Him!

Not in clouds and in terrors—but gentle as when
In love and in meekness He moved among men;
And the voice which breathed peace to the waves of the sea,
In the hush of my spirit would whisper to me!

And what if my feet may not tread where he stood,
Nor my ears hear the dashing of Galilee's flood,
Nor my eyes see the cross which he bowed Him to bear,
Nor my knees press Gethsemane's garden of prayer?

Yet, loved of the Father, thy spirit is near
To the meek and the lowly, and penitent here;
And the voice of thy love is the same even now,
As at Bethany's tomb, or on Olivet's brow.

Oh, the outward hath gone! but in glory and power,
The SPIRIT surviveth the things of an hour;
Unchanged, undecaying, its Pentecost flame
On the heart's secret altar, is burning the same!    —WHITTIER.

## PERILS OF BALLOONING.

ON the earth at 1h. 3m. the temperature of the air was 59°; at 1h. 13m., at the height of a mile, it was 39°; and shortly afterwards we entered a cloud, which was about 1100 feet in thickness, in which the temperature of the air fell to $36\frac{1}{2}$°, and the wet-bulb thermometer read the same, showing the air here was saturated with moisture. On emerging from the cloud at 1h. 17m. we came into a flood of light, with a beautiful blue sky without a cloud above us, and a magnificent sea of cloud below; its surface being varied with endless hills, hillocks, mountain chains, and many snow-white masses rising from it. I here tried to take a view with the camera, but we were rising too rapidly and revolving too rapidly for me to do so; the flood of light, however, was so great that all I should have needed would have been a momentary exposure, as Dr. Hill Norris had kindly furnished me with extremely sensitive dry plates for the purpose.

When we attained the height of two miles, at 1h. 21m., the temperature had fallen to the freezing point; we were three miles high at 1h. 28m. with a temperature of 18°; at 39m. we had reached four miles, and the temperature was 8°; in 10 minutes more we had reached the fifth mile, and the temperature of the air had passed below zero, and there read minus 2°; and at this point no dew was observed on Regnault's hygrometer when cooled down to minus 30°. Up to this time I had taken the observations with comfort. I had experienced no difficulty in breathing, while Mr. Coxwell, in consequence of the necessary exertion he had to make, had breathed with difficulty for some time. At 1h. 51m. the barometer read 11·05 inches, but which requires a subtractive correction of 0·25 inch, as found by comparison with Lord Wrottesley's standard barometer just before starting, both by his Lordship and myself, which would reduce it to 10·8 inches, or at a height of about 5¼ miles. I read the dry bulb as minus five degrees; in endeavoring to read the wet bulb I could not see the column of mercury. I rubbed my eyes, then took a lens, and also failed. I then tried to read the other instruments, and found I could not do so, nor could I see the hands of the watch. I asked Mr. Coxwell to help me, and he said he must go into the ring, and he would when he came down. I endeavored to reach some brandy which was lying on the table at about the distance of a foot from my hand, and found myself unable to do so. My sight became more dim; I looked at the barometer and saw it between 10 and 11 inches, and tried to record it, but I was unable to write. I then saw it at 10 inches, still decreasing fast, and just noted it in my book; its true reading therefore was at this time about 9¾ inches, implying a height of about 5¾ miles, as a change of an inch in the reading of the barometer at this elevation takes place on a change of height of about 2500 feet; I felt I was losing all power, and endeavored to rouse myself by struggling and shaking. I attempted to speak, and found I had lost the power. I attempted to look at the barometer; my head fell on one side. I struggled and got it right, and it fell on the other, and finally fell backwards. My arm, which had been resting on the table, fell down by my side. I saw Mr. Coxwell dimly in the ring. It became more misty, and finally dark, and I sunk unconsciously as in sleep; this must have been about 1h. 54m.

I then heard Mr. Coxwell say, "What is the temperature? Take an observation; now try." But I could neither see, move, nor speak. I then heard him speak more emphatically, "Take an observation; now do try." I shortly afterwards opened my eyes, saw the instruments and Mr. Coxwell very dimly, and soon saw clearly, and said to Mr. Coxwell, "I have been insensible;" and he replied, "You have, and I nearly." I recovered quickly, and Mr. Coxwell said, "I have lost the use of my hands; give me some brandy to bathe them." His hands were nearly black. I saw the temperature was still below zero, and the barometer reading 11 inches, but increasing quickly. I resumed my observations at 2h. 7m., recording the barometer reading 11.53 inches, and the temperature minus 2. I then found that the water in the vessel supplying the wet bulb thermometer, which I had by frequent disturbances kept from freezing, was one solid mass of ice. Mr. Coxwell then told me that while in the ring he felt it piercingly cold, that hoar frost was all round the neck of the balloon, and on attempting to leave the ring he found his hands frozen, and he got down how he could; that he found me motionless, with a quiet and placid expression on the countenance. He spoke to me without eliciting a reply, and found I was insensible. He then said he felt insensibility was coming over himself, that he became anxious to open the valve, that his hands failed him, and that he seized the line between his teeth and pulled the valve open until the balloon took a turn downwards. This act is quite characteristic of Mr. Coxwell. I have never yet seen him without a ready means of meeting every difficulty as it has arisen, with a cool self-possession that has always left my mind perfectly easy and given to me every confidence in his judgment in the management of so large a balloon.

On asking Mr. Coxwell whether he had noticed the temperature, he said he could not, as the faces of the instruments were all towards me; but that he had noticed that the centre of the aneroid barometer, its blue hand, and a rope attached to the car, were in the same straight line. If so, the reading must have been between 7 and 8 inches. A height of six miles and a half corresponds to 8 inches. A delicate self-registering *minimum* thermometer read minus 12°, but unfortunately I did not read it till I was out of the car, and I cannot say that its index was not disturbed.

On descending, when the temperature rose to 17°, it was remarked as warm, and at 24° it was noted as very warm.

The temperature then gradually increased to $57\frac{1}{2}°$ on reaching the earth. It was remarked that the sand was quite warm to the hand, and steam issued from it when it was discharged. Six pigeons were taken up. One was thrown out at the height of three miles; it extended its wings and dropped as a piece of paper. A second, at four miles, flew vigorously round and round, apparently taking a great dip each time. A third was thrown out between four and five miles, and it fell downwards. A fourth was thrown out at four miles when we were descending; it flew in a circle and shortly after alighted on the top of the balloon. The two remaining pigeons were brought down to the ground; one was found to be dead, and the other (a carrier) had attached to its neck a note. It would not however leave, and when jerked off the finger returned to the hand. After a quarter of an hour it began to peck a piece of riband encircling its neck, and I then jerked it off my finger, and it flew round two or three times with vigour, and finally towards Wolverhampton. Not one, however, had returned there when I left on the afternoon of the 6th.

Too much praise cannot be given to Mr. Proud, the engineer of the gas-works, for the production of gas of such a light specific gravity.

It would seem from this ascent that five miles from the earth is very nearly the limit of human existence. It is possible, as the effect of each high ascent upon myself has been different, that on another occasion I might be able to go higher, and it is possible that some persons may be able to exist with less air and bear a greater degree of cold; but still I think that prudence would say to all, whenever the barometer reading falls as low as 11 inches, open the valve at once: the increased information to be obtained is not commensurate with the increased risk: —GLAISHER.

## ONE BY ONE.

One by one the sands are flowing,
  One by one the moments fall;
Some are coming, some are going;
  Do not strive to grasp them all.

One by one thy duties wait thee,
　Let thy whole strength go to each,
Let no future dreams elate thee,
　Learn thou first what these can teach.

One by one (bright gifts from Heaven)
　Joys are sent thee here below ;
Take them readily when given,
　Ready be to let them go.

One by one thy griefs shall meet thee,
　Do not fear an armed band ;
One will fade as others greet thee,
　Shadows passing through the land.

Do not look at life's long sorrow ;
　See how small each moment's pain ;
God will help thee for to-morrow,
　So each day begin again.

Every hour that fleets so slowly,
　Has its task to do or bear ;
Luminous the crown, and holy,
　When each gem is set with care.

Do not linger with regretting,
　Or for passing hours despond ;
Nor, the daily toil forgetting,
　Look too eagerly beyond.

Hours are golden links, God's token,
　Reaching Heaven ; but one by one
Take them, lest the chain be broken
　Ere the pilgrimage be done.
　　　　　　　　—Adelaide Procter.

## WASHINGTON.

(A. D. 1732—1799.)

In this man we truly behold a marvellous contrast to almost every one of the endowments and vices which we have been contemplating, and which are so well fitted to excite a mingled admiration and sorrow and abhorrence. With none of that brilliant genius which dazzles ordinary minds ; with not even any remarkable quickness of apprehension ; with knowledge less than almost all persons in the middle ranks, and many well-educated of the humbler classes, possess—this eminent person is presented to our observation clothed in attributes as modest as unpretending ; as little calculated to strike or astonish as if he had passed unknown through some secluded region of private life. But he had a judgment sure and sound; a steadiness of mind which never suffered any passion, or even any feeling, to ruffle its calm; a strength of understanding which worked, rather than forced, its way through all obstacles —removing or avoiding rather than overleaping them. If profound sagacity, unshaken steadiness of purpose, the entire subjugation of all the passions which carry havoc through ordinary minds, and oftentimes lay waste the fairest prospects of greatness—nay, the discipline of those feelings which are wont to lull or seduce genius, and to mar and to cloud over the aspect of virtue herself—joined with, or rather leading to, the most absolute self-denial; the most habitual and exclusive devotion to principle—if these things can constitute a great character, without either quickness of apprehension, or resources of information, or inventive powers, or any brilliant quality that might dazzle the vulgar—then surely Washington was the greatest man that ever lived in the world, uninspired by Divine wisdom, and unsustained by supernatural virtue.

His courage, whether in battle or in council, was as perfect as might be expected from his pure and steady temper of soul. A perfectly just man, with a thoroughly firm resolution never to be misled by others any more than to be by others overawed; never to be seduced, or betrayed, or hurried away by his own weakness or self-delusions any more than by other men's arts; nor ever to be disheartened by the most complicated difficulties any more than to be spoilt in the giddy heights of fortune— such was this great man, great, pre-eminently great, whether we regard him sustaining alone the whole weight of campaigns, all but desperate, or gloriously terminating a just warfare by his resources and his courage—presiding over the jarring elements of his political council, alike deaf to the storm of all extremes, or directing the formation of a new government for a great people, the first time that so vast an experiment had ever been tried by man—or finally retiring from the supreme power to which his virtue had raised him over the nation he had created, and whose destinies he had guided as long as his aid was required—retiring with the veneration of all parties, of all nations, of all mankind, in order that the rights of men might be conserved, and that his example might never be appealed to by vulgar tyrants. This is the consummate glory of Washington—a triumphant warrior where the most sanguine had a right to despair; a successful ruler in all the difficulties of a course wholly untried, but a warrior whose sword only left its sheath when the first law of our nature commanded it to be drawn, and a ruler who, having tasted of supreme power, gently and unostentatiously desired that the cup might pass from him, nor would suffer more to wet his lips than the most solemn and most sacred duty to his country and his God required.

—Lord Brougham.

## NIGHT ON LAKE COUCHICHING.

### I.

The purple shadows dreamingly
Upon the dreaming waters lie,
And darken with the darkening sky.

Calmly across the lake we float,
I and thou, my little boat—
The lake, with its grey mist-capote.

We lost the moon an hour ago:
We saw it dip, and downward go,
Whilst all the west was still a-glow.

But in those blue depths, moon-forsaken,
A planet pale its place hath taken;
And one by one the stars awaken.

### II.

With noiseless paddle-dip we glide
Along the bay's dark-fringèd side,
Then out, amidst the waters wide!

With us there floated here last night
Wild threatening waves with foam-caps white,
But these have now spent all their might.

We knew they would not injure us,
Those tossing waves, so boisterous—
And where is now their fret and fuss

Only a ripple wrinkleth now
The summer lake—and plashes low
Against the boat, in fitful flow.

### III.

Still callest thou, thou Whip-poor-Will!
When dropped the moon behind the hill
I heard thee, and I hear thee still.

But mingled with thy plaintive cry
A wilder sound comes ebbing by,
Out of the pine-woods, solemnly.

It dies—and then from tree to tree
Deep breathings pass, and seem to be
The murmurs of a mighty sea.

But hark! The owl's cry comes anew—
Piercing the dark pine-forest through,
With its long too-hoo, too-hoo!

### IV.

Swifter and swifter, on we go;
For though the breeze but feigns to blow.
Its kisses greet us, soft and low.

But with us now, and side by side,
Striving awhile for place of pride,
A silent, dusky form doth glide.

Though, swift and light the birch-canoe,
It cannot take the palm from you,
My little boat, so trim and true.

Indian! where away to-night?"
Homewards I wend: yon beacon light
Shines out for me—good night!" "Good night

### V.

Shorewards again we glide—and go
Where the sumach shadows flow
Across the purple calm below.

There, hidden voices all night long
Keep up, the sedgy creeks among
The murmurs of their summer song—

A song most soft and musical—
Like the dulled voice of distant fall,
Or winds that through the pine-tops call.

And where the dusky swamp lies dreaming,
Shines the fire-flies' fitful gleaming
Through the cedars—dancing, streaming!

### VI.

Who hides in yonder dusky tree,
Where but the bats awake should be,
And with its whistling mocketh me?

Such quaint, quick pipings—two and two:
Half a whistle, half a coo:
Ah, Master Tree Frog, sure 'tis you:

The owls on noiseless wing gloom by
Beware, lest one a glimpse espy
Cf your grey coat and jewelled eye—

And so, good night!—We glide anew
Where shows the lake its softest blue,
With mirrored star-points sparkling through.

VII.

The lights upon the distant shore
That shone so redly, shine no more:
The Indian-fisher's toil is o'er.

And deepening in the eastern skies,
Where up and up new stars arise,
A pearly lustre softly lies.

Thy witchery waneth. Fare-thee-well,
O Summer Night! Thy tender spell
Within my dreams long time will dwell—

And paint, in many a distant scene,
The lake—the shore—the forest green,
"The marks of that which once hath been." —CHAPMAN.

## ROLLA'S ADDRESS TO THE PERUVIANS.

MY brave associates—partners of my toil, my feelings, and my fame!—Can Rolla's words add vigor to the virtuous energies which inspire your hearts?—No! you have judged as I have, the foulness of the crafty plea by which these bold invaders would delude you. Your generous spirit has compared, as mine has, the motives which, in a war like this, can animate their minds and ours. They, by a strange frenzy driven, fight for power, for plunder, and extended rule—we, for our country, our altars, and our homes. They follow an adventurer whom hey fear, and obey a power which they hate—we serve a monarch whom we love, a God whom we adore. Whene'er they move in anger, desolation tracks their progress! whene'er they pause in amity, affliction mourns their friendship. They boast they come but to improve our state, enlarge our thoughts, and free us from the yoke of error!—Yes; they will give enlightened freedom to our minds; who are themselves the slaves of passion, avarice, and pride!—They offer us their protection:—yes, such protection as vultures give to lambs—covering and devouring them. They call upon us to barter all the good we have inherited and proved, for the desperate chance of something better, which they promise. Be our plain answer this:—The throne we honor is the people's choice—the laws we reverence are our brave fathers' legacy—the faith we follow teaches us to live in bonds of charity with all mankind, and die with hopes of bliss beyond the grave. Tell your invaders this, and tell them too, we seek no change; and least of all such change as they would bring us.  —SHERIDAN.

## ON THE RIVER.

THE sun has gone down in liquid gold
On the Ottawa's gleaming breast;
And the silent Night has softly rolled
The clouds from her starry vest;
   Not a sound is heard,—
   Every warbling bird
Has silenced its tuneful note,
   As, with calm delight,
   In the moon's weird light,
I enter my little boat.

As down the river I dreamily glide,—
The sparkling and moonlit river,
Not a ripple disturbs the glassy tide,
Not a leaf is heard to quiver;
   The lamps of night
   Shed their trembling light,
With a tranquil and a silvery glory,
   Over river and dell,
   Where the Zephyrs tell
To the Night their plaintive story.

I softly time my gleaming oar,
To the music of joy-laden strains,
Which the silent woods, and the listening shore
Re-echo in soft refrains:
   Let holy thought,
   From this faery spot
Float up through the slumbering air;
   For who who would profane,
   With fancies vain,
A scene so unearthly fair?

Now dark-browed sorrowful Care retires,
And leaves the bright moments unclouded -
For why should I shade them with vain desires,
For hopes which the darkness has shrouded?
   Like phantoms grim,
   From the river's brim,

The trees stretch their shadows before me,
But no shadow mars—
For the blessed stars
Are tenderly beaming o'er me.

On the dark, and rapid stream of life
Are shadows of grief and sin,
But we reck not the gloom of the outer strife,
If no shadows obscure within;
Though darkness may lower,
It is reft of power
Over hearts that are tempered with love,—
There is fadeless light,
For life's darkest night,
With the bountiful Father above.
In holy thought, from this blissful hour—
While free from earth's darkling strife—
I may garner joy, and be nerved with power
To fight on in the battles of life. —E. H. DEWART.

## LOUIS XI. AND CHARLES, DUKE OF BURGUNDY

*(The scene is laid in the Duke's banqueting hall, at Peronne.)*

A BRIEF interval intervened, during which the Duke remained looking eagerly to the door, as if in a transport of impatience, whilst the guests sat with their eyes bent on the table, as if to conceal their curiosity and anxiety. Louis alone, maintaining perfect composure, continued his conversation alternately with the grand carver and with the jester.

At length Crevecœur entered, and was presently saluted by the hurried question of his master, "What news from Liege and Brabant, Sir Count?—the report of your arrival has chased mirth from our table—we hope your actual presence will bring it back to us."

"My liege and master," answered the Count, in a firm, but melancholy tone, "the news which I bring you are fitter for the council board than the feasting table."

"Out with them, man, whatever be your tidings!" said the Duke; "but I can guess them—the Liegois are again in mutiny."

"They are, my lord," said Crevecœur, very gravely.

"Look there, man," said the Duke, "I have hit at once on what you have been so much afraid to mention to me—the harebrained burghers are again in arms. It could not be in better time, for we may at present have the advice of our own

Suzerain," bowing to King Louis, with eyes which spoke the most bitter, though suppressed resentment, "to teach us how such mutineers should be dealt with.—Hast thou more news in thy packet? Out with them, and then answer for yourself why you went not forward to assist the Bishop."

"My lord, the farther tidings are heavy for me to tell, and will be afflicting to you to hear.—No aid of mine, or of living chivalry, could have availed the excellent Prelate. William de la Marck, united with the insurgent Liegeois, has taken his Castle of Schonwaldt, and murdered him in his own hall."

"*Murdered him !*" repeated the Duke, in a deep and low tone, but which nevertheless was heard from the one end of the hall in which they were assembled to the other; "thou hast been imposed upon, Crevecœur, by some wild report—it is impossible !"

"Alas! my Lord," said the Count, "I have it from an eye-witness, an archer of the King of France's Scottish Guard, who was in the hall when the murder was committed by William de la Marck's order."

"And who was doubtless aiding and abetting in the horrible sacrilege?" exclaimed the Duke, starting up and stamping with his foot with such fury, that he dashed in pieces the footstool which was placed before him. "Bar the doors of this hall, gentlemen—secure the windows—let no stranger stir from his seat, upon pain of instant death!—Gentlemen of my chamber, draw your swords." And turning upon Louis, he advanced his own hand slowly and deliberately to the hilt of his weapon, while the king, without either showing fear or assuming a defensive posture, only said,

"These news, fair cousin, have staggered your reason."

"No !" replied the Duke, in a terrible tone, "but they have awakened a just resentment, which I have too long suffered to be stilled by trivial consideration of circumstance and place. Murderer of thy brother !—rebel against thy parent !—tyrant over thy subjects !—treacherous ally !—perjured King !—dishonored gentleman !—thou art in my power, and I thank God for it."

"Rather thank my folly," said the King; "for when we met on equal terms at Montl'hery, methinks you wished yourself farther from me than we are now."

The Duke still held his hand on the hilt of his sword, but

refrained to draw his weapon, or to strike a foe, who offered no sort of resistance which could in any wise provoke violence.

Meanwhile, wild and general confusion spread itself through the hall.. The doors were now fastened and guarded by order of the Duke; but several of the French nobles, few as they were in number, started from their seats, and prepared for the defence of their Sovereign. Louis had spoken not a word either to Orleans or Dunois since they were liberated from restraint at the Castle of Loches, if it could be termed liberation, to be dragged in King Louis's train, objects of suspicion evidently, rather than of respect and regard; but, nevertheless, the voice of Dunois was first heard above the tumult, addressing himself to the Duke of Burgundy,—"Sir Duke, you have forgotten that you are a vassal of France, and that we, your guests, are Frenchmen. If you lift a hand against our Monarch, prepare to sustain the utmost effects of our despair; for, credit me, we shall feast as high with the blood of Burgundy as we have done with its wine,—Courage, my Lord of Orleans —and you, gentlemen of France, form yourselves round Dunois, and do as he does!"

It was in that moment when a King might see upon what tempers he could certainly rely. The few independent nobles and knights who attended Louis, most of whom had only received from him frowns of discountenance, unappalled by the display of infinitely superior force, and the certainty of destruction in case they came to blows, hastened to array themselves around Dunois, and, led by him, to press towards the head of the table where the contending Princes were seated.

On the contrary, the tools and agents whom Louis had dragged forward out of their fitting and natural places, into importance which was not due to them, showed cowardice and cold heart, and remaining still in their seats, seemed resolved not to provoke their fate by intermeddling, whatever might become of their benefactor.

The first of the more generous party was the venerable Lord Crawford, who, with an agility which no one would have expected at his years, forced his way through all opposition, (which was the less violent, as many of the Burgundians, either from a point of honor, or a secret inclination to prevent Louis's impending fate, gave way to him,) and threw himself boldly between the King and the Duke. He then placed his bonnet, from which his white hair escaped in dishevelled tresses, upon one side of his head—his pale cheek and withered brow coloured, and his aged eye lightened with all the fire of a gallant who is about to dare some desperate action. His cloak was flung over one shoulder, and his action intimated his readiness to wrap it about his left arm, while he unsheathed his sword with his right.

"I have fought for his father and his grandsire," that was all he said, "and, by Saint Andrew, end the matter as it will, I will not fail him at this pinch."

What has taken some time to narrate, happened, in fact, with the speed of light; for so soon as the Duke assumed his threatening posture, Crawford had thrown himself betwixt him and the object of his vengeance; and the French gentlemen, drawing together as fast as they could, were crowding to the same point.

The Duke of Burgundy still remained with his hand on his sword, and seemed in the act of giving the signal for a general onset, which must necessarily have ended in the massacre of the weaker party, when Crèvecœur rushed forward, and exclaimed, in a voice like a trumpet,—"My liege Lord of Burgundy, beware what you do! This is *your* hall—you are the King's vassal—do not spill the blood of your guest on your hearth, the blood of your Sovereign on the throne you have erected for him, and to which he came under your safeguard. For the sake of your house's honor, do not attempt to revenge one horrid murder by another yet worse!"

"Out of my road, Crèvecœur," answered the Duke, "and let my vengeance pass!—out of my path!—The wrath of kings is to be dreaded like that of Heaven."

"Only when, like that of Heaven, it is *just*," answered Crèvecœur, firmly—"Let me pray of you, my lord, to rein the violence of your temper, however justly offended.—and for you, my lords of France, where resistance is unavailing, let me recommend you to forbear whatever may lead towards bloodshed."

"He is right," said Louis, whose coolness forsook him not in that dreadful moment, and who easily foresaw, that if a brawl should commence, more violence would be dared and done in the heat of blood, than was likely to be attempted if peace were preserved.—My cousin Orleans— kind Dunois – and you, my trusty Crawford—bring not on ruin and bloodshed by taking offence too hastily. Our cousin the Duke is chafed at the tidings of the death of a near and loving friend, the venerable Bishop of Liege, whose slaughter we lament as he does. Ancient, and, unhappily, recent subjects of jealousy, lead him to suspect us of having abetted a crime which our bosom abhors. Should our host murder us on this spot—us, his King and his kinsman, under a false impression of our being accessory to this unhappy accident, our fate will be little lightened, but, on the contrary, greatly aggravated, by your stirring.—Therefore, stand back, Crawford.—Were it my last word, I speak as a King to his officer, and demand obedience—Stand back, and, if it is required, yield up your sword. I command you to do so, and your oath obliges you to obey."

"True, true, my lord," said Crawford, stepping back, and returning to the sheath the blade he had half drawn—"It may be all very true; but, by my honor, if I were at the head of three score and ten of my brave fellows, instead of being loaded with more than the like number of years, I would try whether I could have some reason out of these fine gallants, with their golden chains and looped-up bonnets, with brawwarld dyes and devices on them."

The Duke stood with his eyes fixed on the ground for a considerable space, and then said, with bitter irony, "Crèvecœur, you say well; and it concerns our honor that our obligations to this great King, our honored and loving guest, be not so hastily adjusted, as in our hasty anger we had at first proposed. We will so act, that all Europe shall acknowledge the justice of our proceedings.—Gentlemen of France, you must render up your arms to my officers! Your master has broken the truce, and has no title to take farther benefit of it. In compassion, however, to your sentiments of honor, and in respect to the rank which he hath disgraced, and the race from which he hath degenerated, we ask not our cousin Louis's sword."

"Not one of us," said Dunois, "will resign our weapon, or quit this hall, unless we are assured of at least our King's safety, in life and limb."

"Nor will a man of the Scottish Guard," exclaimed Crawford, "lay down his arms, save at the command of the King of France, or his High Constable."

"Brave Dunois," said Louis, "and you, my trusty Crawford,

your zeal will do me injury instead of benefit.—I trust," he added, with dignity, " in my rightful cause more than in a vain resistance, which would but cost the lives of my best and bravest.—Give up your swords—the noble Burgundians, who accept such honorable pledges, will be more able than you are to protect both you and me.—Give up your swords—It is I who command you."

It was thus that, in this dreadful emergency, Louis showed the promptitude of decision, and clearness of judgment, which alone could have saved his life. He was aware, that until actual blows were exchanged, he should have the assistance of most of the nobles present to moderate the fury of their Prince; but that were a *melée* once commenced, he himself and his few adherents must be instantly murdered. At the same time, his worst enemies confessed that his demeanor had in it nothing either of meanness or cowardice. He shunned to aggravate into frenzy the wrath of the Duke; but he neither deprecated nor seemed to fear it, and continued to look on him with the calm and fixed attention with which a brave man eyes the menacing gestures of a lunatic, whilst conscious that his own steadiness and composure operate as an insensible and powerful check on the rage even of insanity.

" Hold, gentlemen," said the Duke, in a broken voice, as one whom passion had almost deprived of utterance, " retain your swords; it is sufficient you promise not to use them.—And you, Louis of Valois, must regard yourself as my prisoner, until you are cleared of having abetted sacrilege and murder. Have him to the Castle—Have him to Earl Herbert's Tower. Let him have six gentlemen of his train to attend him, such as he shall choose.—My Lord of Crawford, your guard must leave the Castle, and shall be honorably quartered elsewhere. Up with every drawbridge, and down with every portcullis—Let the gates of the town be trebly guarded—Draw the floating-bridge to the right-hand side of the river—Bring round the Castle my band of Black Walloons, and treble the sentinels on every post!—You, d'Hymbercourt, look that patrols of horse and foot make the round of the town every half hour during the night, and every hour during the next day,—if, indeed, such ward shall be necessary after daybreak, for it is like we may be sudden in this matter—Look to the person of Louis, as you love your life!"

He started from the table in fierce and moody haste, darted a glance of mortal enmity at the King, and rushed out of the apartment.

"Sirs," said the King, looking with dignity around him, "grief for the death of his ally hath made your Prince frantic. I trust you know better your duty, as knights and noblemen, than to abet him in his treasonable violence against the person of his liege Lord."

At this moment was heard in the streets the sound of drums beating, and horns blowing, to call out the soldiery in every direction.

"We are," said Crèvecœur, who acted as the Marshal of the Duke's household, "subjects of Burgundy, and must do our duty as such: Our hopes and prayers, and our efforts, will not be wanting to bring about peace and union between your Majesty and our liege Lord. Meantime, we must obey his commands. These other lords and knights will be proud to contribute to the convenience of the illustrious Duke of Orleans, of the brave Dunois, and the stout Lord Crawford. I myself must be your Majesty's chamberlain, and bring you to your apartments in other guise than would be my desire, remembering the hospitality of Plessis."  —SCOTT.

## THE SOULS OF BOOKS.

Sit here and muse!—it is an antique room,
High-roofed, with casements through whose purple pane
Unwilling daylight steals amidst the gloom,
Shy as a fearful stranger.—There they reign
(In loftier pomp than waking life had known),
The Kings of Thought!—not crowned until the grave.—
When Agamemnon sinks into the tomb,
The beggar Homer mounts the monarch's throne!

Ye ever-living and imperial souls,
Who rule us from the page in which ye breathe!
What had ye been had Cadmus never taught
The art that fixes into form the thought,—
Had Plato never spoken from his cell,
Or his high harp blind Homer never strung?—
Kinder all earth hath grown since genial Shakespeare sung!

Lo! in their books, as from their graves, they rise,
Angels, that, side by side upon our way,
Walk with and warn us!—Hark! the world so loud,
And they, the movers of the world, so still!

From them how many a youthful Tully caught
The zest and ardor of the eager Bar;
By them each restless wing has been unfurled,
And their ghosts urge each rival's rushing car!
They made yon Preacher zealous for the truth;
They made yon Poet wistful for the star;
Gave Age its pastime, fired the cheek of Youth,
The unseen sires of all our beings are.

All books grow homilies by time; they are
Temples at once, and landmarks. In them, we,
Who, but for them, upon that inch of ground
We call "THE PRESENT," from the cell could see
No daylight trembling on the dungeon bar,
Turn, as we list, the globe's great axle round,
Traverse all space, and number every star,
And feel the Near less household than the Far!
There is no past, so long as Books shall live!
Rise up, ye walls, with gardens blooming o'er!
Ope but that page—lo! Babylon once more!

Books make the Past our heritage and home;
And is this all? No; by each prophet-sage—
No; by the herald souls that Greece and Rome
Sent forth, like hymns, to greet the Morning Star
That rose on Bethlehem—by thy golden page,
Melodious Plato—by thy solemn dreams,
World-wearied Tully!—and, above ye all,
By THIS, the Everlasting Monument
Of God to mortals, on whose front the beams
Flash glory-breathing day,—our lights they are
To the dark bourn beyond; in them are sent
The types of truths whose life is the To-COME;
In them soars up the Adam from the fall;
In them the Future as the Past is given—
Even in our death they bid us hail our birth;—
Unfold these pages, and behold the Heaven,
Without one gravestone left upon the Earth!

—LORD LYTTON.

## THE ORIGIN OF LANGUAGE.

THE opinions about the origin of language may be divided into three classes, as follows:—

*a.* The belief that man at his creation was endowed with a full, perfect, and copious language, and that, as his faculties were called forth by observation and experience, this language supplied him at every step with names for the various objects he encountered. In this view, which has found many able advocates, speech is separated from, and precedes, thought; for as there must have been a variety of phenomena both outward and in his mind, to which the first man was a stranger, until long experience gradually unfolded them, their names must have been entrusted to him long before the thoughts or images, which they were destined ultimately to represent, were excited in his mind.

*b.* The belief that the different families of men, impelled by necessity, invented and settled by agreement the names that should represent the ideas they possessed. In this view language is a human invention, grounded on convenience. But "to say that man has invented language, would be no better than to assert that he has invented law. To make laws, there must be a law obliging all to keep them; to form a compact to observe certain institutes, there must be already a government protecting this compact. To invent language presupposes language already, for how could men agree to name different objects without communicating by words their designs?" In proof of this opinion, appeal is made to the great diversity of languages. Here it is supposed again that thought and language were separate, and that the former had made some progress before the latter was annexed to it.

*c.* The third view is, that as the Divine Being did not give man at his creation actual knowledge, but the power to learn and to know, so He did not confer a language, but the power to name and describe. The gift of reason, once conveyed to man, was the common root from which both thought and speech proceeded, like the pith and the rind of the tree, to be developed in inseparable union. With the first inspection of each natural object, the first imposition of a name took place: "Out of the ground the Lord God formed every beast of the field, and every fowl of the air; and brought them unto Adam to see what he would call them; and whatsoever Adam called every living creature, that was the name thereof." (Gen. ii. 19.) In the fullest sense, language is a divine gift, but the power and not the results of its exercise, the germ and not the tree, was imparted. A man can teach names to another man, but nothing less than divine power can plant in another mind the far higher gift, the faculty of naming. From the first we have reason to believe that the functions of thought and language went together. A conception received a name; a name recalled a conception; and every accession to the knowledge of things expanded the treasures of expression. And we are entangled in absurdities by any theory which assumes that either element existed in a separate state, antecedently to the other.

It is impossible to trace the growth of language with certainty; but it is most probable that many of the *roots* of the primitive language were originally imitations of the various sounds emitted by things in the natural world. A bird or animal perhaps received a name derived from, and resembling, its own peculiar utterance. The cry of exclamation that man emitted instinctively under the pressure of some strong feeling, would be consciously reproduced to represent or recall the feeling on another occasion; and it then became a word, or vicarious sign. Where natural sounds failed, analogy would take the place of imitation; words harsh and difficult to pronounce would be preferred to stand for unpleasing objects, over those of a more bland and facile character, which would be appropriated to pleasant things and conceptions. Mere agreement among those who used the language, would be sufficient to stamp a vocal sound as the name of a certain object, where, neither imitation nor analogy suggested one. But these original roots, the simplest form of substantives, would gradually become less and less discernible as the language grew richer and more intricate. Wherever new arts are practised, we may easily find opportunities of watching the growth of new names for its instruments and processes, guided by these three principles, imitation, analogy, and mere convention.

The various parts of speech took their origin from the noun and verb, or possibly from the noun alone. Many instances can be found of adverbs and prepositions which are distinctly substantives, and of conjunctions which are but parts of verbs. Then the close connection between the verb and noun is indicated by the number of words which, in our own language, are both verb and noun, and only distinguished by mode of pronunciation. Inflexions perhaps originated in the addition of one word to another, so that the terminations of nouns and verbs are in reality distinct words incorporated with them. These are but slender hints of the direction in which profound and acute researches have been made. And I do not think that such attempts to dissect and analyze language, pursued with proper caution, tend at all to lower our estimate of the importance of the gift of speech, or of its marvellous nature. It is not more wonderful surely that the Giver of Good has endowed man with a complete language, than that he has endowed him with faculties which out of the shrieks of birds in the forest, the roar of beasts, the murmur of rushing waters, the sighing of the wind, and his own impulsive ejaculations, have constructed the great instrument that Demosthenes and Shakespeare and Massillon wielded, the instrument by which the laws of the universe are unfolded and the subtle workings of the human heart brought to light. But in no line of inquiry is caution more necessary, or deductions more likely to be fallacious. It does not follow that a word as we use it now bears a gross, narrow, or material sense, because the root to which we can refer it had a limited meaning, and was connected with matter. If *truth* according to its etymology means that which we *trow* or think, according to long usage it means that which is certain whether we think it or not; if spirit meant originally no more than breath, it has so far left that sense behind, that when the breath is exhaled the spirit remains immortal. —THOMSON.

## THE PRESENCE OF GOD.

O, THOU who fling'st so fair a robe
  Of clouds around the hills untrod -
Those mountain pillars of the globe
  Whose peaks sustain Thy throne, O God!
All glittering round the sunset skies,
  Their fleecy wings are lightly furl'd,
As if to shade from mortal eyes
  The glories of yon upper world;
There, while the evening star upholds
In one bright spot, their purple folds,
My spirit lifts its silent prayer,
For Thou, O God of love, art there.

The summer-flowers, the fair, the sweet,
  Up-springing freely from the sod,
In whose soft looks we seem to meet
  At every step, Thy smiles, O God!
The humblest soul their sweetness shares,
  They bloom in palace-hall, or cot,—
Give me, O Lord, a heart like theirs,
  Contented with my lowly lot;
Within their pure, ambrosial bells,
In odors sweet thy Spirit dwells.
Their breath may seem to scent the air
'Tis thine, O God! for Thou art there.

Hark! from yon casement, low and dim,
  What sounds are these that fill the breeze?

It is the peasant's evening hymn
 Arrests the fisher on the seas ;
The old man leans his silver hairs
 Upon his light suspended oar,
Until those soft, delicious airs
 Have died like ripples on the shore.
Why do his eyes in softness roll?
What melts the manhood from his soul?
His heart is fill'd with peace and prayer,
For Thou, O God, art with him there.

The birds among the summer blooms,
 Pour forth to Thee their hymns of love,
When, trembling on uplifted plumes,
 They leave the earth and soar above;
We hear their sweet, familiar airs,
 Where'er a sunny spot is found;
How lovely is a life like theirs,
 Diffusing sweetness all around !
From clime to clime, from pole to pole,
Their sweetest anthems softly roll;
Till, melting on the realms of air,
They reach Thy throne in grateful prayer.

The stars—those floating isles of light,
 Round which the clouds unfurl their sails,
Pure as a woman's robe of white
 That trembles round the form it veils,—
They touch the heart as with a spell,
 Yet set the soaring fancy free ;
And, O! how sweet the tales they tell
 Of faith, of peace, of love, and Thee.
Each raging storm that wildly blows,
Each balmy breeze that lifts the rose,
Sublimely grand, or softly fair—
They speak of Thee, for Thou art there.

The spirit, oft oppress'd with doubt,
 May strive to cast Thee from its thought
But who can shut Thy presence out,
 Thou mighty Guest that comest unsought
In spite of all our cold resolves?
 Magnetic like, where'er we be,
Still, still the thoughtful heart revolves,
 And points, all trembling, up to Thee.
We cannot shield a troubled breast
Beneath the confines of the blest—
Above, below, on earth, in air,
For Thou, the living God, art there.

Yet, far beyond the clouds outspread,
 Where soaring fancy oft hath been,
There is a land where Thou hast said
 The pure in heart shall enter in ;
There, in those realms so calmly bright,
 How many a loved and gentle one

Bathe their soft plumes in living light,
  That sparkles from Thy radiant throne!
There, souls once soft and sad as ours
Look up and sing mid fadeless flowers;
They dream no more of grief and care,
For Thou, the GOD of peace, art there.
                                —AMELIA B. WELBY.

# THE VASTNESS OF THE UNIVERSE.

IT is extremely difficult to devise any means of bringing before a common apprehension the scale on which the universe is constructed, the enormous proportion which the larger dimensions bear to the smaller, and the amazing number of steps from larger to smaller, or from small to larger, which the consideration of it offers. The following comparative representations may serve to give the reader to whom the subject is new some idea of these steps.

If we suppose the earth to be represented by a globe a foot in diameter, the distance of the sun from the earth will be about two miles; the diameter of the sun, on the same supposition, will be something above one hundred feet, and consequently his bulk such as might be made up of two hemispheres, each about the size of the dome of St. Paul's. The moon will be thirty feet from us, and her diameter three inches, about that of a cricket ball. Thus the sun would much more than occupy all the space within the moon's orbit. On the same scale, Jupiter would be above ten miles from the sun, and Uranus forty. We see then how thinly scattered through space are the heavenly bodies. The fixed stars would be at an unknown distance, but probably, if all distances were thus diminished, no star would be nearer to such a one-foot earth, than the moon now is to us.

On such a terrestrial globe the highest mountains would be about 1-80th of an inch high, and consequently only just distinguishable. We may imagine therefore how imperceptible would be the largest animal. The whole organized covering of such an earth would be quite undiscoverable by the eye, except perhaps by color, like the bloom on a plum.

In order to restore the earth and its inhabitants to their true dimensions, we must magnify the length, breadth, and thickness of every part of our supposed models forty millions of times; and to preserve the proportions, we must increase equally the distances of the sun and of the stars from us. They seem thus to pass off into infinity; yet each of them thus removed, has its system of mechanical and perhaps of organic processes going on upon its surface.

But the arrangements of organic life which we can see with the naked eye are few, compared with those which the microscope detects. We know that we may magnify objects thousands of times, and still discover fresh complexities of structure; if we suppose, therefore, that we thus magnify every member of the universe and every particle of matter of which it consists; we may imagine that we make perceptible to our senses the vast multitude of organised adaptions which lie hid on every side of us; and in this manner we approach towards an estimate of the extent through which we may trace the power and skill of the Creator, by scrutinising his work with the utmost subtlety of our faculties.

The other numerical quantities which we have to consider in the phenomena of the universe are on as gigantic a scale as the distances and sizes. By the rotation of the earth on its axis, the parts of the equator move at the rate of a thousand miles an hour, and the portions of the earth's surface which are in our latitude, at about six hundred. The former velocity is nearly that with which a cannon ball is discharged from the mouth of a gun; but, large as it is, it is inconsiderable compared with the velocity of the earth in its orbit about the sun. This latter velocity is sixty-five times the former. By the rotatory motion of the earth, a point of its surface is carried sometimes forwards and sometimes backwards with regard to the annual progression; but in consequence of the great predominance of the annual motion in amount, the diurnal scarcely affects it either way in any appreciable degree. And even the velocity of the earth in her orbit is inconsiderable compared with that of light; which comparison, however, we shall not make; since, according to the theory we have considered as most probable, the motion of light is not a transfer of matter but of motion from one part of space to another.

The extent of the scale of density of different substances has already been mentioned; gold is twenty times as heavy as water; air is eight hundred and thirty times lighter, steam eight thousand times lighter than water; the luminiferous ether is imcomparably rarer than steam: and this is true of the matter of light, whether we adopt the undulatory theory or any other.

The above estimates are vast in amount, and almost oppressive to our faculties. They belong to the measurement of the powers which are exerted in the universe, and of the spaces through which their efficacy reaches (for the most distant bodies are probably connected both by gravity and light). But these estimates cannot be said so much to give us any notion of the powers of the Deity, as to correct the errors we should fall into by supposing his powers to have any limits like those which belong to our faculties:—by supposing that numbers, and spaces, and forces, and combinations, which would overwhelm us, are any obstacle to the arrangements which his plan requires. We can easily understand that to an intelligence surpassing ours in degree only, that may be easy which is impossible to us. The child who cannot count beyond four, the savage who has no name for any number above five, cannot comprehend the possibility of dealing with thousands and millions: yet a little additional development of the intellect makes such numbers conceivable and manageable. The difficulty which appears to reside in numbers and magnitudes and stages of subordination, is one produced by judging from ourselves—by measuring with our own sounding line; when that reaches no bottom, the ocean appears unfathomable. Yet in fact how is a hundred millions of miles a *great* distance? how is a hundred million of times a *great* ratio? Not in itself; this *greatness* is no quality of the numbers which can be proved like their mathematical properties; on the contrary, all that absolutely belongs to number, space, and ratio, must, we know demonstrably, be equally true of the largest and the smallest. It is clear that the *greatness* of these expressions of measure has reference to *our* faculties only. Our astonishment and embarrassment take for granted the limits of our own nature. We have a tendency to treat a difference of degree and of addition, as if it were a difference of kind and of transformation. The existence of the attributes, design, power, goodness, is a matter depending on obvious grounds: about these qualities there can be no mistake: if we can know anything, we can know these attributes when we see them. But the extent, the limits of such attributes must be determined by their effects; our knowledge of their limits by what we can see of the effects. Nor is any extent, any amount of power and goodness improbable beforehand: we know that these must be great, we cannot tell how great. We should not expect beforehand to find them bounded; and therefore when the boundless prospect opens before us, we may be bewildered, but we have no reason to be shaken in our conviction of the reality of the cause from which their effects proceed; we may feel ourselves incapable of following the train of thought, and may stop, but we have no rational motive for quitting the point which we have thus attained in tracing the Divine Perfections.

On the contrary, those magnitudes and proportions which leave our powers of conception far behind;—that ever-expanding view which is brought before us, of the scale and mechanism, the riches and magnificence, the population and activity of the universe;—may reasonably serve, not to disturb, but to enlarge and elevate our conceptions of the Maker and Master of all; to feed an ever-growing admiration of his wonderful nature; and to excite a desire to be able to contemplate more steadily and conceive less inadequately the scheme of his government and the operation of his power. —WHEWELL.

## TWILIGHT.

THERE is an evening twilight of the heart,
  When its wild passion waves are lulled to rest
And the eye sees life's fairy scenes depart,
  As fade the day-beams in the rosy west.
'Tis with a nameless feeling of regret
  We gaze upon them as they melt away,
And fondly, we would bid them linger yet,
  But Hope is round us with her angel lay,
Hailing afar some happier moonlight hour;
Dear are her wishes still, though lost in early power.

In youth the cheek was crimsoned with her glow;
  Her smile was loveliest then; her native song
Was heaven's own music, and the note of woe
  Was all unheard her sunny bowers among.
Life's little world of bliss was newly born;
  We knew not, cared not, it was born to die.
Flushed with the cool breeze and the dews of morn,
  With dancing heart we gazed on the pure sky,
And mocked the passing clouds that dimmed its blue,
Like our own sorrows then— as fleeting and as few.

And manhood felt her sway too,—on the eye,
   Half realized, her early dreams burst bright,
Her promised bower of happiness seemed nigh,
   Its days of joy, its vigils of delight;
And though at times might lower the thunder storms,
   And the red lightnings threaten, still the air
Was balmy with her breath, and her loved form,
   The rainbow of the heart was hovering there.
'Tis in life's noontide she is nearest seen,
Her wreath the summer flower, her robe of summer green.

But though less dazzling in her twilight dress
   There's more of heaven's pure beam about her now,
That angel smile of tranquil loveliness,
   Which the heart worships, glowing on her brow;
That smile shall brighten the dim evening star
   That points our destined tomb, nor e'er depart
Till the faint light of life is fled afar.
   And hushed the last deep breathing of the heart,
The meteor bearer of one parting breath,
A moon-beam in the midnight cloud of death.   —HALLECK.

---

# THE DIGNITY OF LABOR.

THERE is dignity in toil—in toil of the hand as well as toil of the head—in toil to provide for the bodily wants of an individual life, as well as in toil to promote some enterprise of world wide fame. All labor that tends to supply man's wants, to increase man's happiness, to elevate man's nature—in a word, all labor that is honest, is honorable too.

What a concurrent testimony is given by the entire universe to the dignity of toil. Things inanimate and things irrational combine with men and angels to proclaim the law of Him who made them all. The restless atmosphere, the rolling rivers and the heaving ocean, nature's vast laboratory never at rest; countless agencies, in the heavens above and in the earth beneath, and in the waters under the earth; the unwearied sun coming forth from his chamber, and rejoicing as a strong man to run a race: the changeful moon, whose never slumbering influence the never resting tides obey; the planets, never pausing in the mighty sweep of their majestic march; the sparkling stars, never ceasing to show forth the handiwork of Him who bade them shine; the busy swarms of insect life; the ant providing her meat in the summer, and gathering her food in the harvest; the birds exuberant in their flight, pouring forth the melody of their song; the beasts of the forest rejoicing in the gladness of activity ; primeval man amid the bowers of Eden ; paradise untainted by sin, yet honored by toil ; fallen man, with labor still permitted him, an alleviation of his woe, and an earnest of his recovery ; redeemed man, divinely instructed, assisted, encouraged, honored in his toil ; the innumerable company of angels, never resting in their service, never wearied in their worship ; the glorious Creator of the universe, who never slumbereth or sleepeth : all, all, bear testimony to the dignity of labor !

The dignity of labor ! Consider its achievements ! Dismayed by no difficulty, shrinking from no exertion, exhausted by no struggle, ever eager for renewed efforts, in its persevering promotion of human happiness, "clamorous labor knocks with its hundred hands at the golden gate of the morning," obtaining each day, through succeeding centuries, fresh benefactions for the world ! Labor clears the forest, and drains the morass, and makes "the wilderness rejoice and blossom as the rose." Labor drives the plough and scatters the seeds, and reaps the harvest, and grinds the corn, and converts it into bread, the staff of life. Labor tending the pastures and sweeping the waters, as well as cultivating the soil, provides with daily sustenance the nine hundred millions of the family of man. Labor gathers the gossamer web of the caterpillar, the cotton from the field, and the fleece from the flock, and weaves it into raiment soft and warm, and beautiful—the purple robe of the prince, and the grey gown of the peasant, being alike its handiwork. Labor moulds the brick, and splits the slate, and quarries the stone, and shapes the column, and rears, not only the humble cottage, but the gorgeous palace, and the tapering spire, and the stately dome. Labor, diving deep into the solid earth, brings up its long-hidden stores of coal to feed ten thousand furnaces, and in millions of habitations to defy the winter's cold. Labor explores the rich veins of deeply buried rocks, extracting the gold and silver, the copper and tin. Labor smelts the iron, and moulds it into a thousand shapes for use and ornament, from the massive pillar to the tiniest needle, from the ponderous anchor to the wire gauze, from the mighty fly-wheel of the steam-engine to the polished purse-ring or the glittering bead. Labor hews down the gnarled oak, and shapes the timber, and builds the ship, and guides it over the deep, plunging through the billows, and wrestling with the tempest, to bear to our shores the produce of every clime. Labor, laughing at difficulties,. spans majestic rivers, carries viaducts over marshy swamps, suspends bridges over deep ravines, pierces the solid mountains with its dark tunnel, blasting rocks, and filling hollows, and while linking together with its iron but loving grasp all nations of the earth, verifying, in a literal sense, the ancient prophecy, "Every valley shall be exalted, and every mountain and hill shall be brought low ;" labor draws forth its delicate iron thread, and stretching it from city to city, from province to province, through mountains, and beneath the sea, realizes more than fancy ever fabled, while it constructs a chariot on which speech may outstrip the wind, compete with the lightning,—for the Telegraph flies as rapidly as thought itself. Labor, a mighty magician, walks forth into a region uninhabited and waste ; he looks earnestly at the scene, so quiet in its desolation ; then waving his wonder-working wand, those dreary valleys smile with golden harvests ; those barren mountains' slopes are clothed with foliage ; the furnace blazes ; the anvil rings ; the busy wheel whirls round ; the town appears ; the mart of commerce, the hall of science, the temple of religion, rear high their lofty fronts ; a forest of masts gay with varied pennons, rises from the harbor ; representatives of far-off regions make it their resort ; Science enlists the elements of earth and heaven in its service ; Art, awaking, clothes its strength with beauty ; Civilization smiles ; Liberty is glad ; Humanity rejoices ; Piety exults—for the voice of industry and gladness is heard on every side.

Working men ! walk worthy of your vocation ! You have a noble escutcheon ; disgrace it not ! There is nothing really mean and low but sin ! Stoop not from your lofty throne to defile yourselves by contamination with intemperance, licentiousness, or any form of evil. Labor allied with virtue, may look up to heaven and not blush, while all worldly dignities, prostituted to vice, will leave their owner without a corner of the universe in which to hide his shame. You will most successfully prove the honor of toil by illustrating in your own persons its alliance with a sober, righteous, and godly life. Be ye sure of this, that the man of toil who works in a spirit of obedient, loving homage to God, does no less than Cherubim and Seraphim in their loftiest flights and holiest songs !

Yes, in the search after true dignity, you may point me to

the sceptred prince, ruling over mighty empires; to the lord of broad acres, teeming with fertility; or the owner of coffers bursting with gold; you may tell me of them or of learning, of the historian or the philosopher, the poet or the artist; and while prompt to render such men all the honor which in varying degrees may be their due, I would emphatically declare that neither power nor nobility, nor wealth, nor learning, nor genius, nor benevolence, nor all combined, have a monopoly of dignity. I would take you to the dingy office, where day by day the pen plies its weary task, or to the shop, where from early morning till half the world have sunk to sleep, the necessities and luxuries of life are distributed, with scarce an interval for food, and none for thought—I would descend further—I would take you to the ploughman plodding along his furrows; to the mechanic throwing the swift shuttle, or tending the busy wheels; to the miner groping his darksome way in the deep caverns of earth; to the man of the trowel, the hammer, or the forge; and if, while he diligently prosecutes his humble toil, he looks up with a brave heart and loving eye to heaven—if in what he does he recognises his God, and expects his wages from on high—if, while thus laboring on earth, he anticipates the rest of heaven, and can say, as did a poor man once, who, when pitied on account of humble lot, said, taking off his hat, " Sir, I am the son of a King, I am a child of God, and when I die, angels will carry me from this Union Workhouse direct to the Court of Heaven." Oh! when I have shown you such a spectacle, I will ask—" Is there not dignity in labor?"

> Work! and pure slumbers shall wait on thy pillow—
> Work! thou shalt ride over care's coming billow—
> Lie not down wearied, 'neath woe's weeping willow,—
> But work with a stout heart and resolute will!
> Work for some good, be it ever so slowly—
> Work for some hope—be it ever so lowly—
> Work! for all labor is noble and holy!        —NEWMAN HALL.

## MY OWN FIRESIDE.

Let others seek for empty joys,
　At ball, or concert, rout or play;
Whilst, far from Fashion's idle noise,
　Her gilded domes and trappings gay,
I while the wintry eve away,
　'Twixt book and lute the hours divide;
And marvel how I e'er could stray
　From thee my own fireside!

## MY OWN FIRESIDE.

My own fireside! Those simple words
  Can bid the sweetest dreams arise;
Awaken feeling's tenderest chords,
  And fill with tears of joy mine eyes.
What is there my wild heart can prize,
  That doth not in thy sphere abide;
Haunt of my home-bred sympathies,
  My own—my own fireside!

A gentle form is near me now;
  A small, white hand is clasped in mine;
I gaze upon her placid brow,
  And ask, what joys can equal thine?
A babe, whose beauty's half divine,
  In sleep his mother's eyes doth hide;
Where may love seek a fitter shrine
  Than thou—my own fireside?

What care I for the sullen roar
  Of winds without, that ravage earth;
It doth but bid me prize the more
  The shelter of thy hallowed hearth;—
To thoughts of quiet bliss give birth;
  Then let the churlish tempest chide,
It cannot check the blameless mirth
  That glads my own fireside!

My refuge ever from the storm
  Of this world's passion, strife and care;
Though thunder-clouds the skies deform,
  Their fury cannot reach me there;
There all is cheerful, calm, and fair;
  Wrath, Envy, Malice, Strife, or Pride,
Hath never made its hated lair
  By thee—my own fireside!

Thy precincts are a charmed ring,
  Where no harsh feeling dares intrude;
Where life's vexations lose their sting;
  Where even grief is half subdued;
And Peace, the Halcyon, loves to brood.
  Then let the world's proud fool deride;
I'll pay my debt of gratitude
  To thee—my own fireside!

Shrine of my household deities;
  Bright scene of home's unsullied joys;
To thee my burdened spirit flies,
  When Fortune frowns, or Care annoys!
Thine is the bliss that never cloys;
  The smile whose truth hath oft been tried;—
What, then, are this world's tinsel toys,
  To thee—my own fireside!

Oh! may the yearnings, fond and sweet,
  That bid my thoughts be all of thee.
Thus ever guide my wandering feet
  To thy heart-soothing sanctuary!
Whate'er my future years may be,
  Let joy or grief my fate betide;
Be still an Eden bright to me,
  My own—my own fireside!

                    A. A. WATTS.

## BURNS.

To the ill-starred Burns was given the power of making man's life more venerable, but that of wisely guiding his own life was not given. Destiny—for so in our ignorance we must speak—his faults, the faults of others, proved too hard for him; and that spirit which might have soared, could it but have walked, soon sank to the dust, its glorious faculties trodden under foot in the blossom, and died, we may almost say, without ever having lived. And so kind and warm a soul, so full of inborn riches, of love to all living and lifeless things! How his heart flows out in sympathy over universal nature, and in her bleakest provinces discerns a beauty and a meaning! The daisy falls not unheeded under his ploughshare, nor the ruined nest of that "wee, cowering, timorous beastie," cast forth, after all its provident pains, "to thole the sleety dribble and cranreuch cauld." The "hoar visage" of winter delights him; he dwells with a sad and oft returning fondness in these scenes of solemn desolation; the voice of the tempest becomes an anthem to his ears; he loves to walk in the sounding woods, for "it raises his thoughts to Him that walketh on the wings of the wind." A true poet-soul, for it needs but to be struck, and the sound it yields will be music! But observe him chiefly as he mingles with his brother men. What warm, all-comprehending fellow-feeling, what trustful, boundless love, what generous exaggeration of the object loved! His rustic friend, his nut-brown maiden, are no longer mean and homely, but a hero and a queen, whom he prizes as the paragons of earth. The rough scenes of Scottish life, not seen by him in any Arcadian illusion, but in the rude contradiction, in the smoke and soil of a too harsh reality, are still lovely to him. Poverty is indeed his companion, but love also, and courage; the simple feelings, the worth, the nobleness that dwell under the straw roof, are dear and venerable to his heart; and thus over the lowest provinces of man's existence he pours the glory of his own soul, and they rise in shadow and sunshine, softened and brightened into a beauty which other eyes discern not in the highest.

He has a just self-consciousness which too often degenerates into pride ; yet it is a noble pride for defence, not for offence ; no cold suspicious feeling, but a frank and social one. The peasant-poet bears himself, we might say, like a king in exile : he is cast among the low, and feels himself equal to the highest ; yet he claims no rank, that none may be disputed to him. The forward he can repel ; the supercilious he can subdue ; pretensions of wealth or ancestry are of no avail with him ; there is a fire in that dark eye under which the " insolence of condescension" cannot thrive. In his abasement, in his extreme need, he forgets not for a moment the majesty of poetry and manhood. And yet, far as he feels himself above common men, he wanders not apart from them, but mixes warmly in their interests ; nay, throws himself into their arms, and, as it were, entreats them to love him. It is moving to see how, in his darkest despondency, this proud being still seeks relief from friendship, unbosoms himself often to the unworthy, and, amid tears, strains to his glowing heart a heart that knows only the name of friendship ; and yet "he was quick to learn," a man of keen vision, before whom common disguises afforded no concealment. His understanding saw through the hollowness even of accomplished deceivers, but there was a generous credulity in his heart. And so did our peasant show himself among us, "a soul like an Æolian harp, in whose strings the vulgar wind, as it passed through them, changed itself into articulate melody." And this was he for whom the world found no fitter business than quarrelling with smugglers and vintners, computing excise-dues upon tallow, and gauging ale-barrels. In such toils was that mighty spirit sorrowfully wasted ; and a hundred years may pass on, before another such is given us to waste. —CARLYLE.

## THE MOTHER.

A SOFTENING thought of other years,
A feeling link'd to hours
When Life was all too bright for tears,—
And Hope sang, wreath'd with flowers!

A memory of affections fled—
Of voices—heard no more!—
Stirred in my spirit when I read
That name of fondness o'er!

Oh Mother!—in that early word
What loves and joys combine;
What hopes—too oft, alas!—deferr'd;
What vigils—griefs—are thine!—
Yet, never, till the hour we roam,
By worldly thralls opprest,
Learn we to prize that truest home—
A watchful mother's breast!

The thousand prayers at midnight pour'd,
Beside our couch of woes;
The wasting weariness endured
To soften our repose!—
Whilst never murmur mark'd thy tongue—
Nor toils relax'd thy care—
How, Mother, is thy heart so strong
To pity and forbear?

What filial fondness e'er repaid,
Or could repay, tho past?—
Alas! for gratitude decay'd!
Regrets—that rarely last!—
'T is only when the dust is thrown
Thy lifeless bosom o'er,
We muse upon thy kindness shown—
And wish we'd loved thee more!

'T is only when thy lips are cold,
We mourn with late regret,
'Mid myriad memories of old,
The days for ever set!
And not an act—nor look—nor thought—
Against thy meek control,
But with a sad remembrance fraught
Wakes anguish in the soul!

On every land—in every clime—
True to her sacred cause,
Fill'd by that effluence sublime
From which her strength she draws,
Still is the Mother's heart the same—
The Mother's lot as tried;—
Then, oh! may Nations guard that name
With filial power and pride!

— SWAIN.

## THE SNOW STORM.

LITTLE Hannah Lee had left her master's house, soon as the rim of the great moon was seen by her eyes, that had been long anxiously watching it from the window, rising like a joyful dream, over the gloomy mountain-tops; and all by herself she tripped along beneath the beauty of the silent heaven. Still as she kept ascending and descending the knolls that lay in the bosom of the glen she sang to herself a song, a hymn, or a psalm, without the accompaniment of the streams, now all silent in the frost; and ever and anon she stopped to try to count the stars that lay in some more beautiful part of the sky, or gazed on the constellations that she knew, and called them, in her joy, by the names they bore among the shepherds. There were none to hear her voice, or see her smiles, but the ear and eye of Providence. As on she glided, and took her looks from heaven, she saw her own little fireside—her parents waiting for her arrival—the bible opened for worship—her own little room kept so neatly for her, with its mirror hanging by the window, in which to braid her hair by the morning light —her bed prepared for her by her mother's hand—the primroses in her garden peeping through the snow—old Tray, who ever welcomed her with his dim white eyes—the pony and the cow—friends all, and inmates of that happy household. So stepped she along, while the snow diamonds glittered around her feet, and the frost wove a wreath of lucid pearls round her forehead.

She had now reached the edge of the Black-moss, which lay half-way between her master's and her father's dwelling, when she heard a loud noise coming down Glen-Scrae, and in a few seconds she felt on her face some flakes of snow. She looked up the glen, and saw the snow-storm coming down fast as a flood. She felt no fears; but she ceased her song, and, had there been an human eye to look upon it there, it might have seen a shadow upon her face. She continued her course, and felt bolder and bolder every step that brought her nearer to her parents' house. But the snow-storm had now reached the Black-moss, and the broad line of light that had lain in the direction of her home was soon swallowed up, and the child was in utter darkness. She saw nothing but the flakes of snow, interminably intermingled, and furiously wafted in the air, close to her head; she heard nothing but one wild, fierce, fitful howl. The cold became intense, and her little feet and hands were fast being benumbed into insensibility.

"It is a fearful change," muttered the child to herself; but still she did not fear, for she had been born in a moorland cottage, and lived all her days among the hardships of the hills.

v

"What will become of the poor sheep!" thought she,—but still she scarcely thought of her own danger, for innocence, and youth, and joy, are slow to think of aught evil befalling themselves, and, thinking benignly of all living things, forget their own fear in their pity for others' sorrow. At last, she could no longer discern a single mark on the snow, either of human steps, or of the sheep-track, or the foot-print of the wild-fowl. Suddenly, too, she felt out of breath and exhausted—and, shedding tears for herself at last, sank down in the snow.

It was now that her heart began to quake with fear. She remembered stories of shepherds lost in the snow—of a mother and a child frozen to death on that very moor—and in a moment, she knew that she was to die. Bitterly did the poor child weep; for death was terrible to her, who, though poor, enjoyed the bright little world of youth and innocence. The skies of heaven were dearer than she knew to her, so were the flowers of earth. She had been happy at her work, happy in her sleep—happy in the kirk on Sabbath. A thousand thoughts had the solitary child—and in her own heart was a spring of happiness, pure and undisturbed as any fount that sparkles unseen all the year through, in some quiet nook among the pastoral hills. But now there was to be an end of all this—she was to be frozen to death, and lie there till the thaw might come; and then her father would find her body, and carry it away to be buried in the kirkyard.

The tears were frozen on her cheeks as soon as shed—and scarcely had her little hands strength to clasp themselves together, as the thought of an overruling and merciful Lord came across her heart. Then, indeed, the fears of this religious child were calmed, and she heard without terror the plover's wailing cry, and the deep boom of the bittern sounding in the moss. "I will repeat the Lord's Prayer;" and, drawing her plaid more closely around her, she whispered, beneath its ineffectual cover—"Our Father which art in Heaven, hallowed be Thy name—Thy kingdom come—Thy will be done on earth as it is in Heaven." Had human aid been within fifty yards, it could have been of no avail—eye could not see her ear could not hear her in that howling darkness. But that low prayer was heard in the centre of eternity—and that little sinless child was lying in the snow, beneath the all seeing eye of God.

The maiden, having prayed to her Father in Heaven—then

thought of her father on earth. Alas! they were not far separated! The father was lying but a short distance from his child; he too had sunk down in the drifting snow, after having, in less than an hour, exhausted all the strength of fear, pity, hope, despair, and resignation, that could rise in a father's heart blindly seeking to rescue his only child from death, thinking that one desperate exertion might enable them to perish in each other's arms. There they lay, within a stone's throw of each other, while a huge snow-drift was every moment piling itself up into a more insurmountable barrier between the dying parent and his dying child.

—CHRISTOPHER NORTH (JOHN WILSON).

## THE COMET OF 1811.

STRANGER of heaven! I bid thee hail!
   Shred from the pall of glory riven,
That flashest in celestial gale,
   Broad pennon of the King of Heaven!

Art thou the flag of woe and death,
   From angel's ensign staff unfurled?
Art thou the standard of his wrath,
   Waved o'er a sordid, sinful world?

No; from that pure, pellucid beam,
   That erst o'er plains of Bethlehem shone,
No latent evil we can deem,
   Bright herald of the eternal throne!

Whate'er portends thy front of fire,
   Thy streaming locks so lovely pale—
Or peace to man, or judgments dire,
   Stranger of heaven, I bid thee hail!

Where hast thou roamed these thousand years?
   Why sought these polar paths again,
From wilderness of glowing spheres,
   To fling thy vesture o'er the wain?

And when thou scal'st the Milky Way,
   And vanishest from human view,
A thousand worlds shall hail thy ray
   Through wilds of yon empyreal blue!

Oh, on thy rapid prow to glide!
   To sail the boundless skies with thee,
And plough the twinkling stars aside,
   Like foam-bells on a tranquil sea!

To brush the embers from the sun,
 The icicles from off the pole;
Then far to other systems run,
 Where other moons and planets roll!

Stranger of heaven! oh, let thine eye
 Smile on a rapt enthusiast's dream;
Eccentric as thy course on high,
 And airy as thine ambient beam!

And long, long may thy silver ray
 Our northern arch at eve adorn;
Then wheeling to the east away,
 Light the grey portals of the morn!  —HOGG.

## SHARKS AS FOOD.

As H.M.S. 'Wasp,' Captain Usherwood, was cruising in the Bight of Benin, near Lagos, on the 27th February, 1845, a strange sail was seen, and Lieutenant Stupart was immediately ordered in pursuit. At about eight o'clock in the evening he came up with her, and found her to be the 'Felicidade,' a Brazilian schooner, fitted for the slave trade, with a slave-deck of loose planks over the cargo, and a crew of twenty-eight men. With the exception of her captain and another man, they were transferred to the 'Wasp;' and Lieutenant Stupart, with Mr. Palmer, midshipman, and a crew of fifteen English seamen, remained in charge of the prize. On the 1st of March, the boats of the 'Felicidade,' under Mr. Palmer, captured a second prize, the 'Echo,' with 430 slaves on board, and a crew of twenty-eight men, leaving Mr. Palmer, with seven English seamen and two Kroomen, on board the 'Felicidade.' Several of the 'Echo's' crew were also got on board as prisoners, with their captain. The officer and prize crew were overpowered and murdered, and an unsuccessful attempt made to gain possession of the 'Echo.' The 'Felicidade' was seen and chased on the 6th March by H.M.S. 'Star,' Commander Dunlop. When she was boarded, no one was on her deck, the crew being concealed below; and on being found and questioned, they stated the vessel to be the 'Virginia,' and accounted for their wounds by the falling of a spar; but there were traces of a conflict, and many tokens which proved that English seamen had been on board. She was then sent to Sierra Leone, in charge of Lieutenant Wilson and nine men. While on the passage, during a heavy squall, the schooner went over, filled and sunk, so as only to leave part of her bow-rail above water. When the squall passed, the whole of the crew were found clinging to the bow rail. Some expert divers endeavored to extract provisions from the vessel, but without success; and nothing but death stared them in the face, as the schooner was gradually sinking. Lieutenant Wilson ascertained that there were three common knives among the party, and it was resolved to make a raft of the main-boom and gaff, and such other floating materials as remained above water. These they secured by such ropes as could be cut and unrove from the rigging, and a small quantity of cordage was retained to make good any defects they might sustain by the working of the spars; a small topgallant studding-sail was obtained for a sail; and upon this miserable float the ten persons made sail for the coast of Africa, distant 200 miles, without rudder, oar, compass, provisions, or water. Being almost naked, and washed by every wave, their sufferings were very great. Famished for food and drink, scorched by a burning sun during the day, and chilled with cold during the night, they thus remained twenty days. Delirium and death relieved the raft of part of its load of misery, two blacks being the first to sink under their sufferings. The question naturally suggests itself, How did the survivors support life? Some persons would be almost afraid to put the question, or hear the answer. There is nothing, however, to wound our feelings, but much to admire, in the admirable conduct of Lieutenant Wilson and his men during these melancholy and miserable twenty days. Showers of rain occasionally fell; they caught some water in their little sail, which they drank, and put some into a small keg, that had floated out of the vessel. The sea was almost always breaking over the spars of the raft, which was surrounded by voracious sharks. The famishing sailors actually caught with a bowling-knot a shark, eight feet in length, with their bare hands, and hauled it upon the raft; they killed it, drank the blood, and ate part of the flesh, husbanding the remainder. In this way three other sharks were taken, and upon these sharks the poor fellows managed to prolong their lives till picked up (in sight of land) in what may be termed the very zero of living misery. Lieutenant Wilson and four seamen survived, and recovered their strength. Order and discipline were maintained upon the raft; fortitude, fore-

thought, a reliance upon Divine Providence, and good conduct, enabled these Englishmen to surmount such hor ble sufferings, while the Kroomen and Portuguese sank under them.
—KINGSTON.

## THE OWL.

In the hollow tree in the gray old tower,
　The spectral owl doth dwell;
Dull, hated, despised in the sunshine
　But at dusk—he's abroad and well:
Not a bird of the forest e'er mates with him;
　All mock him outright by day;
But at night, when the woods grow still and dim,
　The boldest will shrink away;
　　Oh, when the night falls, and roosts the fowl,
　　Then, then is the reign of the horned owl!

And the owl hath a bride who is fond and bold,
　And loveth the wood's deep gloom;
And with eyes like the shine of the moonshine cold
　She awaiteth her ghastly groom!
Not a feather she moves, not a carol she sings,
　As she waits in her tree so still;
But when her heart heareth his flapping wings,
　She hoots out her welcome shrill!
　　Oh, when the moon shines, and the dogs do howl,
　　Then, then is the cry of the horned owl!

Mourn not for the owl nor his gloomy plight!
　The owl hath his share of good:
If a prisoner be he in the broad daylight,
　He is lord in the dark green wood!
Nor lonely the bird, nor his ghastly mate;
　They are each unto each a pride—
Thrice fonder, perhaps, since a strange dark fate
　Hath rent them from all beside!
　　So when the night falls, and dogs do howl,
　　Sing Ho! for the reign of the horned owl!
We know not alway who are kings by day,
　But the king of the night is the bold brown owl.
BARRY CORNWALL (B. F. PROCTER).

## GOLD LEAF.

OF all the substances on which man exercises his manufacturing ingenuity, gold is perhaps that which admits of being brought to the most extraordinary degree of fineness. Many of the productions in this department of industry are really "curiosities." Is not a solid, unbroken, uniform sheet of gold, less than one five-hundredth part the thickness of a sheet of ordinary printing paper, a curiosity; is it not a curiosity to know that one ounce of gold may be made to cover the floor of an ordinary sitting-room; that one grain of gold will gild thirty coat buttons; and that the covering of gold upon gold lace is very far thinner than even leaf gold? Let us glance a little at these remarkable productions.

And first for gold-leaf and the gold-beating processes whereby it is produced. Gold leaf, in strictness, it certainly is not: for it is found that a minute percentage of silver and of copper is necessary to give the gold a proper malleable quality—a percentage of perhaps one in seventy or eighty. The refiner manages this alloy, and brings the costly product to a certain stage of completion; he melts the gold and the cheaper alloys in a black-lead crucible; he pours the molten metal into an ingot mould, six or eight inches long; he removes the solidified and cooled ingot from its mould, and passes it repeatedly between two steel rollers until it assumes the thickness of a ribbon; and this ribbon, about one eight-hundredth of an inch in thickness, and presenting a surface of about five hundred square inches to an ounce, passes next into the hands of the gold-beater.

The working tools, the processes, and the products of a gold-beater, are all remarkable. That puzzling material, "gold-beaters' skin," is an indispensable aid to him: it is a membrane of extreme thinness and delicacy, but yet tough and strong, procured from the intestines of the ox; eight hundred pieces of this skin, four inches square, constitute a packet with which the gold-beater labors; and thus he proceeds:—A hundred and fifty bits of ribbon-gold, an inch square, are interleaved with as many vellum leaves four inches square; they are beaten for a long time with a ponderous hammer on a smooth marble slab, until the gold has thinned and expanded to the size of the vellum. How the workman manages so as to beat all the pieces equally, and yet beat none into holes, he alone can answer: it is one of the mysteries of his craft. The gold is liberated from its vellum prison, and each piece cut into four; the hundred and fifty have thus become six hundred, and these are interleaved with six hundred pieces of gold-beaters' skin, which are then packed into a compact mass. Another beating then takes place—more careful, more delicate, more precise than the former—until the gold, expanded like the silk worm, as far as its envelope will admit, requires to be again released. The leaves are again divided into four, by which the six hundred become twenty-four hundred; these are divided into three parcels of eight hundred each, and each parcel is subjected to a third beating. Heavy as the hammers are, there are yet degrees of heaviness: first, a sixteen-pounder gives its weighty thumps, then a twelve pounder, and in this last operation a hammer of ten pounds is employed.

Now if we exercise a little arithmetic, we shall find that the thin ribbon of gold has become thinner in an extraordinary degree; in fact it is reduced to about $\frac{1}{180}$th part of its thickness. A sheet of paper is equal in thickness to 800 gold-ribbons, but one gold-ribbon is equal to 180 gold-leaves; thus the little ingot of two ounces becomes spread out to a very large area. An apartment twelve feet square might be carpeted with gold for six or eight guineas: a thin carpet, it is true, but one of sound honest gold, purer than even standard gold.

The Great Exhibition has not failed to furnish illustrations of this remarkable product, and of the simple contrivances whereby it is produced. M. Bottier, from France, and Messrs. Vine and Ashmead, from the United States, exhibited machines intended to aid in the operations of the gold-beater; but in England these operations are wholly manipulative. Then the delicate membrane, the "gold-beaters' skin," was shown in specimens, not only from our own great metropolis, but from the far distant colony of Van Diemen's Land. In Mr. Marshall's collection, placed among the "precious metals" of the Crystal Palace, there was the packet of eight hundred films of gold-beaters' skin, just in the form in which the hammer is brought to bear upon it; and near this were specimens of all the various kinds of leaf-gold used in manufacturing operations, from the silvery white to the coppery red. These variations of tint are produced by varying the quantity of silver and of copper mixed with the gold; and there were also different thicknesses of leaf, applicable to different purposes. There was gold leaf from three English firms, from France, from the United States, from Turkey, and from Van Diemen's Land—the Old World and the New both displayed their knowledge of this art.

The applications of this exquisitely fine substance are

numerous and varied. In the edges of books, in picture-frames and looking-glasses, in the gorgeous decorations of the House of Lords and other sumptuous apartments, in gilt leather—we see some among the many applications of leaf-gold. In all these cases the gold is applied and secured by the aid of a particular kind of cement or gold size ; and this cement differs in character, according as the gold is or is not to be burnished with a smooth piece of agate or flint. —DODD.

## THE FOUNDING OF THE BELL.

HARK ! how the furnace pants and roars !
Hark ! how the molten metal pours,
As bursting from its iron doors
    It glitters in the sun !
Now through the ready mould it flows,
Seething and hissing as it goes,
And filling every crevice up,
As the red vintage fills the cup :
    *Hurrah! the work is done!*

Unswathe him now. Take off each stay
That binds him to his couch of clay,
And let him struggle into day ;
    Let chain and pulley run,
With yielding crank and steady rope,
Until he rise from rim to cope,
In rounded beauty, ribbed in strength,
Without a flaw in all his length :
    *Hurrah! the work is done!*

The clapper on his giant side
Shall ring no peal for blushing bride,
For birth, or death, or new-year tide,
    Or festival begun !
A nation's joy alone shall be
The signal for his revelry ;
And for a nation's woes alone
His melancholy tongue shall moan :
    *Hurrah! the work is done!*

Borne on the gale, deep-toned and clear,
His long, loud summons shall we hear,
When statesmen to their country dear,
    Their mortal race have run :
When mighty monarchs yield their breath,
And patriots sleep the sleep of death,
Then shall he raise his voice of gloom,
And peal a requiem o'er their tomb :
    *Hurrah! the work is done!*

Should foemen lift their haughty hand,
And dare invade us where we stand,
Fast by the altars of our land
    We'll gather every one :
And he shall ring the loud alarm,
To call the multitudes to arm,
From distant field and forest brown,
And teeming alleys of the town ;
    *Hurrah! the work is done!*

And as the solemn boom they hear,
Old men shall grasp the idle spear,
Laid by to rust for many a year,
    And to the struggle run ;
Young men shall leave their toils or books,
Or turn to swords their pruning-hooks ;
And maids have sweetest smiles for those
Who battle with their country's foes :
    *Hurrah! the work is done!*

And when the cannon's iron throat
Shall bear the news to dells remote,
And trumpet-blast resound the note,
    That victory is won ;
While down the wind the banner drops,
And bonfires blaze on mountain-tops,
His sides shall glow with fierce delight,
And ring glad peals from morn to night :
    *Hurrah! the work is done!*

But of such themes forbear to tell.
May never War awake this bell
To sound the tocsin or the knell!
    Hushed be the alarum gun!
Sheathed be the sword! and may his voice
Call up the nations to rejoice,
That War his tattered flag has furled,
And vanished from a wiser world!
    *Hurrah! the work is done!*

Still may he ring when struggles cease,
Still may he ring for joy's increase,
For progress in the arts of peace,
    And friendly trophies won!
When rival nations join their hands,
When plenty crowns the happy lands,
When knowledge gives new blessings birth,
And freedom reigns o'er all the earth!
    *Hurrah! the work is done!*

—McKay.

## A FOREST ON FIRE.

WE were sound asleep one night, when about two hours before day, the snorting of horses and lowing of our cattle which were ranging in the woods, suddenly awoke us. I took my rifle, and went to the door to see what beast had caused the hubbub, when I was struck by the glare of light reflected on all the trees before me, as far as I could see through the woods. My horses were leaping about, snorting loudly, and the cattle ran among them in great consternation.

On going to the back of the house, I plainly heard the crackling made by the burning brushwood, and saw the flames coming toward us in a far-extended line. I ran to the house, told my wife to dress herself and the child as quickly as possible, and take the little money we had, while I managed to catch and saddle two of the best horses. All this was done in a very short time, for I felt that every moment was precious to us.

We then mounted our horses and made off from the fire. My wife, who is an excellent rider, stuck close to me; and my daughter, who was then a small child, I took in one arm. When making off, I looked back and saw that the frightful blaze was close upon us, and had already laid hold of the house. By good luck there was a horn attached to my hunting clothes, and I blew it to bring after us, if possible, the remainder of my live stock, as well as the dogs. The cattle followed for a while; but before an hour had elapsed, they all ran, as if mad, through the woods, and that was the last of them. My dogs, too, although at all other times extremely tractable, ran after the deer, that in great numbers sprang before us, as if fully aware of the death that was so rapidly approaching.

We heard blasts from the horns of our neighbors, as we proceeded, and knew that they were in the same predicament. Intent on striving to the utmost, to preserve our lives, I thought of a large lake, some miles off, which might possibly check the flames; and, urging my wife to whip up her horse, we set off at full speed, making the best way we could over the fallen trees and the brush heaps, which lay like so many articles placed on purpose to keep up the terrific fires, that advanced with a broad front upon us.

By this time, we could feel the heat; and we were afraid

that our horses would drop down every instant. A singular kind of breeze was passing over our heads, and the glare of the atmosphere shone over the daylight. I was sensible of a slight faintness, and my wife looked pale. The heat had produced such a flush in the child's face, that when she turned toward either of us, our grief and perplexity were greatly increased. Ten miles, you know, are soon gone over on swift horses; but, notwithstanding this, when we reached the borders of the lake, covered with sweat and quite exhausted, our hearts failed us.

The heat of the smoke was insufferable, and sheets of blazing fire flew over us in a manner beyond belief. We reached the shore, however, coasted the lake for a while, and got round to the lee-side. There we gave up our horses, which we never saw again. Down among the rushes we plunged, by the edge of the water, and laid ourselves flat, to wait the chance of escaping from being burned or devoured. The water refreshed us, and we enjoyed the coolness.

On went the fire, rushing and crashing through the woods, such a night may we never again see! The heavens themselves, I thought, were frightened; for all above us was a red glare, mixed with clouds and smoke, rolling and sweeping away. Our bodies were cool enough, but our heads were scorching; and the child, who now seemed to understand the matter, cried so as nearly to break our hearts.

The day passed on, and we became hungry. Many wild beasts came plunging into the water beside us, and others swam across to our side, and stood still. Although faint and weary, I managed to shoot a porcupine, and we all tasted its flesh. The night passed, I cannot tell you how. Smouldering fires covered the ground, and the trees stood like pillars of fire, or fell across each other. The stifling and sickening smoke still rushed over us, and the burnt cinders and ashes fell thick about us. How we got through that night, I really cannot tell; for about some of it, I remember nothing.

When morning came, all was calm; but a dismal smoke still filled the air, and the smell seemed worse than ever. What was to become of us, I did not know. My wife hugged the child to her breast, and wept bitterly; but God had preserved us through the worst of the danger, and the flames had gone past, so I thought it would be both ungrateful to Him, and unmanly, to despair now. Hunger once more pressed upon us, but this was soon remedied. Several deer were standing in the water, up to the head, and I shot one of them. Some of its flesh was soon roasted, and after eating it, we felt wonderfully strengthened.

By this time, the blaze of the fire was beyond our sight, although the ground was burning in many places, and it was dangerous to go among the burnt trees. After resting awhile, we prepared to commence our march. Taking up the child, I led the way over the hot ground and rocks; and after two weary days and nights, during which we shifted in the best manner we could, we at last reached the hard woods, which had been free from the fire. Soon after we came to a house, where we were kindly treated. Since then, I have worked hard and constantly as a lumberman; and, thanks to God, we are safe, sound, and happy! —AUDUBON.

## THE BATTLE OF AGINCOURT.

(A. D. 1415.)

THE venerable Sir Thomas Erpingham, a Knight of the Garter, and a soldier of the highest reputation, was ordered to array the archers and place them in front, and he exhorted all in Henry's name to fight vigorously. Then, riding before the archers, he drew them up, and when this was done, threw his baton into the air, exclaiming, "Now strike!" and was answered by a loud cry, after which he dismounted and placed himself in the King's battalion, who was also on foot opposite his men, with his banner borne before him.

It was now between ten and eleven in the forenoon, and Henry finding that great part of the day had been wasted, and that the French would not approach, but were probably either waiting for reinforcements, or expecting to oblige him to surrender from the want of provisions, resolved to commence the attack. Having issued the command, "Banners advance," the soldiers immediately prostrated themselves on the ground, beseeching the protection of the Almighty, and each of them put a small piece of earth into his mouth, in remembrance, as has been conjectured, that they were mortal, and formed of dust. They then marched towards the enemy in three lines, with great firmness and intrepidity, uttering repeated shouts, and with their trumpets sounding.

The Constable on seeing them approach, after earnestly admonishing his men to confess their sins and to fight bravely, ordered his advanced guard to march towards the English, which they did, crying "Montjoye! Montjoye!"

The battle commenced by the English archers shooting their arrows as soon as they were within reach of the enemy, and much execution was done among them before the combatants closed. The French cavalry posted along the flanks, attacked the archers on each side; but the division commanded by Clignet de Brabant, Admiral of France, which consisted of eight hundred horse, and was intended to break through them, was reduced to about one hundred and fifty, who attempted it in vain, being compelled to retreat from the heavy volleys of arrows. Sir William de Saveuse, with three hundred men-at-arms likewise gallantly endeavored to accomplish this object, but he was immediately killed: his followers were repulsed by the archers placing their pointed stakes before them; and the horses being infuriated by wounds from the arrows, became unmanageable, great part of them, with their riders, rolling on the earth from pain, whilst the others fled at the utmost speed upon the van, threw it into confusion, and forced it back on some newly sown ground. Of this fortunate circumstance Henry took instant advantage, by causing his men to advance upon them with the greatest celerity, at which moment the flanks of both armies immerged into the woods on each side. When the French advanced guard, who had boldly marched towards them under the great disadvantage of having the sun in their eyes, came near, whether from the effect of the heavy discharges of arrows, which pierced through the sides and beavers of their basinets, or with the view of sooner penetrating the English lines, they suddenly formed themselves into three divisions and charged with so much impetuosity in the three places where the banners stood, that for a short period the English gave way; but, quickly rallying, they recovered their ground, and repulsed their assailants with tremendous loss. The conflict was then very severe, and as soon as the English archers had exhausted their arrows, they threw aside their bows, and fought with overwhelming impetuosity with the swords, bills, lances and hatchets, with which the field was covered, slaying all before them. A dreadful slaughter consequently took place in the van of the French army, and the assailants speedily reached the second line, which was posted in the rear of the first. For a time the English met with a spirited opposition, but the confusion which produced the defeat of the van now extended to this division, and those immense numbers upon which they placed such reliance became the chief cause of their destruction. Standing upon soft ground and heavily armed, without sufficient room to move, they necessarily impeded each other; and being thus unable to offer any material resistance, they fell victims, as much to the unfortunate situation and circumstances in which they were placed, as to the valor of their enemies. When the French lines gave way, the Duke of Alençon mounted his horse with the hope of rallying the fugitives; but finding it impossible, he returned to the scene of danger; and after performing prodigies of valor, was slain whilst in personal combat with the King of England. Duke Anthony of Brabant, whose anxiety to be present made him push forward with such rapidity that the greater part of his soldiers could not keep up with him, now joined the French. Finding that the battle had commenced he would not wait to equip himself, but seizing a banner which was attached to a trumpet, converted it into a surcoat of arms, threw himself with a small body of followers into the thickest of the fight, and nobly endeavored to resist the torrent; but he was speedily slain, and the fate of the second division was no longer doubtful.

The rear, seeing what had befallen their companions, took to flight, leaving only the chief leaders on the field; and such of them as survived were made prisoners. As a last effort, a gallant charge was made by the Counts of Marle and Fauquembergh at the head of about six hundred men-at-arms, whom with great difficulty they had kept firm, but without success, and they shared the fate of the bravest of their comrades.

An eye-witness says, though he is not candid enough to explain the reason, that there was no example in history of so fine a body of men having made so disorderly, so cowardly, or so unmanly a resistance; that they seemed seized with a panic; that many noblemen surrendered themselves more than ten times during the day, but as no one had leisure to make prisoners of them, they were all pressed to the ground and put to death without exception, either by those who had overcome, or by those who followed them.

Among the many instances of heroism which occurred during

the battle, Henry's conduct was particularly distinguished; and it is said that, even if he had been of the most inferior rank, the extraordinary valor which he displayed would have ensured to him greater renown than that of any other person. He fought on foot, and shared the dangers of the day in common with the humblest of his soldiers; but he more particularly signalized himself in preserving the life of his brother, the Duke of Gloucester. That prince having been wounded in the bowels with a dagger, and thrown senseless to the ground by the Duke of Alençon and his followers, with his feet towards his enemies, the King rushed between his legs, and defended him until he was removed from the field. This generous act nearly cost him his life, for whilst he was stooping to raise his brother, Alençon gave him a blow on his basinet which struck off a part of his crown. Being, however, soon surrounded by Henry's guards, Alençon found himself in the utmost peril, and lifting up his arm, exclaimed, "I am the Duke of Alençon, and I yield myself to you," but whilst the King was extending his hand to receive his pledge, the prince was slain. St. Remy relates, that the blow which struck off part of Henry's crown was given by one of a body of eighteen knights, belonging to the retinue of the Lord of Croy, led by Brunelet de Mausinguchen and Ganiot de Bournonville, who had sworn that they would force themselves sufficiently near to where the King of England fought to strike the royal diadem from his head, or that they would die in the attempt; a vow which was literally fulfilled, for though one of them with his axe struck a point from his crown, they were all cut to pieces. —Nicholas.

## THE PLEASANT DAYS OF OLD.

O! the pleasant days of old, which so often people praise!
True, they wanted all the luxuries that grace our modern days;
Bare floors were strewed with rushes, the walls let in the cold:
O, how they must have shivered in those pleasant days of old!

O, those ancient lords of old, how magnificent they were!
They threw down and imprisoned kings— to thwart them who might dare?
They ruled their serfs right sternly; they took from Jews their gold—
Above both law and equity were those great lords of old!

O, the gallant knights of old, for their valor so renowned!
With sword and lance, and armor strong, they scoured the country round;
And whenever aught to tempt them they met by wood or wold,
By right of sword they seized the prize—those gallant knights of old!

O, the gentle dames of old ! who, quite free from fear or pain,
Could gaze on joust or tournament, and see their champions slain ;
They lived on good beefsteaks and ale, which made them strong and bold,—
O, more like men than women were those gentle dames of old !

O, those mighty towers of old ! with their turrets, moat, and keep,
Their battlements. and bastions, their dungeons dark and deep ;
Full many a baron held his court within the castle hold ;
And many a captive languished there, in those strong towers of old.

O, the troubadours of old ! with their gentle minstrelsie,
Of hope and joy, or deep despair, whiche'er their lot might be—
For years they served their ladye-love ere they their passion told—
O, wondrous patience must have had those troubadours of old !

O, those blessed times of old ! with their chivalry and state ;
I love to read their chronicles, which such brave deeds relate ;
I love to sing their ancient rhymes, to hear their legends told—
But, Heaven be thanked ! I live not in those blessed times of old !
—FRANCES BROWN.

## CHARLES JAMES FOX.

MR. FOX united, in a most remarkable degree, the seemingly repugnant characters of the mildest of men and the most vehement of orators. In private life he was gentle, modest, placable, kind, of simple manners, and so averse from parade and dogmatism, as to be not only unostentatious, but even somewhat inactive in conversation. His superiority was never felt but in the instruction which he imparted, or in the attention which his generous preference usually directed to the more obscure members of the company. The simplicity of his manners was far from excluding that perfect urbanity and amenity which flowed still more from the mildness of his nature than from familiar intercourse with the most polished society of Europe.

His conversation, when it was not repressed by modesty or indolence, was delightful. The pleasantry, perhaps, of no man of wit had so unlabored an appearance. It seemed rather to escape from his mind than to be produced by it. He had lived on the most intimate terms with all contemporaries distinguished by wit, politeness, philosophy, learning, or the talents of public life. In the course of thirty years, he had known almost every man in Europe whose intercourse could strengthen, or enrich, or polish the mind. His own literature was various

W

and elegant. In classical erudition, which, by the custom of England, is more peculiarly called learning, he was inferior to few professed scholars. Like all men of genius, he delighted to take refuge in poetry from the vulgarity and irritation of business. His own verses were easy and pleasing; and the poetical character of his mind was displayed in his extraordinary partiality for the poetry of the two most poetical nations, or at least languages, of the west—those of the ancient Greeks and of the modern Italians. He disliked political conversation, and never willingly took any part in it.

To speak of him justly, as an orator, would require a long essay. Every where natural, he carried into public something of that simple and negligent exterior which belonged to him in private. When he began to speak, a common observer might have thought him awkward; and even a consummate judge could only have been struck with the exquisite justness of his ideas, and the transparent simplicity of his language. But no sooner had he spoken for some time than he was changed into another being. He forgot himself and every thing around him. He thought only of his subject. His genius warmed and kindled as he went on. He darted fire into his audience. Torrents of impetuous and irresistible eloquence swept along their feelings and conviction. He certainly possessed, above all moderns, that union of reason, simplicity, and vehemence, which formed the prince of orators. He was the most Demosthenean speaker since Demosthenes. "I knew him," says Mr. Burke, in a pamphlet written after their unhappy difference, "when he was nineteen; since which time he has risen, by slow degrees, to be the most brilliant and accomplished debater that the world ever saw." The quiet dignity of a mind roused only by great objects, the absence of petty bustle, the contempt of show, the abhorrence of intrigue, the plainness and downrightness, and the thorough good nature, which distinguished Mr. Fox, seem to render him no very unfit representative of that old English national character, which, if it ever changed, we should be sanguine, indeed, to expect to be succeeded by a better.

The simplicity of his character inspired confidence, the ardor of his eloquence roused enthusiasm, and the gentleness of his manners invited friendship. "I admired," says Mr. Gibbon, "the powers of a superior man, as they were blended in his attractive character with all the softness and simplicity of a child. No human being was ever more free from any taint of malignity, vanity, or falsehood."

From these qualities of his public and private character it probably arose that no English statesman ever preserved, during so long a period of adverse fortune, so many affectionate friends and so many zealous adherents. The union of ardor in public sentiment with mildness in social manners, was in Mr. Fox an inherent quality.

The same fascinating power over the attachment of all who came within his sphere is said to have belonged to his father; and those who know the survivors of another generation will feel that this delightful quality is not yet extinct in the race.

Perhaps nothing can more strongly prove the deep impression made by this part of Mr. Fox's character than the words of Mr. Burke, who, in January, 1797, six years after all intercourse between them had ceased, speaking to a person honored with some degree of Mr. Fox's friendship, said, "To be sure; he is a man made to be loved." And these emphatic words were uttered with a fervor of manner which left no doubt of their heartfelt sincerity.

These few hasty and honest sentences are sketched in a temper too sober and serious for intentional exaggeration, and with too pious an affection for the memory of Mr. Fox to profane it by intermixture with the factious brawls and wrangles of the day. His political conduct belongs to history. The measures which he supported or opposed may divide the opinions of posterity, as they have divided those of the present age; but he will most certainly command the unanimous reverence of future generations by his pure sentiments towards the commonwealth; by his zeal for the civil and religious rights of all men; by his liberal principles favorable to mild government, to the unfettered exercise of the human faculties, and to the progressive civilization of mankind; by his ardent love for a country of which the well-being and greatness were indeed inseparable from his own glory; and by his profound reverence for that free constitution which he was universally admitted to understand better than any other man of his age, both in an exactly legal and in a comprehensively philosophical sense.

—MACKINTOSH.

## THE CITY OF YEDDO.

OUR way lies, first, along the edge of the bay, under the bluff which skirts it, where the suburb of Sinagawa merges into the city, much as Kensington straggles into London. Along the ill-paved road (the worst bit for fifty miles in the country remarkable for the finest macadamised roads in the world) we pick our way. The bay, stretching to the right, is occasionally shut out by rows of houses—many of which are tea houses, and some only mere arbors for travellers coming from afar, to sit and rest in, while they sip their tea, and enjoy the fair prospect of the rippling waters and distant shores on the one side; —or the ways and manners of the Capital, if they turn to the great high road. This road forms, in fact, the main street here. So, as we pace gently along, not to incommode the never-failing stream of pedestrians,—of 'Norimons,' and 'Kangos,'—varied now and then by a group of Yakonins on horseback, or some Daimio's *cortége* of mixed horse and foot, with spear and halberd, crest and pennon, as in olden days in other lands—we have time to peer into the shops, open in front, and through the shops to the small back room, which generally forms the whole interior, and the region of domestic duties. The shops are of all kinds, but none in this quarter of the town are of very great size or importance. The common necessaries of life are on sale in many. There are booksellers';—shops of bronze and copper ware;—pawnbrokers', and old iron shops. Bath houses, coopers, and basket-makers, armorers and sword-makers, with here and there a stall for ready-made clothes, or a print shop, fill up the list. Every hundred steps, more or less, we pass a ward-gate, which at night they can close, if an alarm of thieves is given; or by day, if any disturbance should arise :— while a sort of decrepit municipal guard is kept in a lodge at each, supposed to be responsible for the peace of their wards, and to be ever vigilant! Some, as we pass, rush out with a long iron pole, to the top of which rings are attached, and make a distracting noise when the lower end is struck on the ground. This is considered an honor, but one to which my horses generally showed such a decided objection, that the warders in all my more usual beats learned at last to dispense with it on ordinary occasions: so now we pass unhonored— and unmolested; with a farther advantage of seeing how a

Japanese keeps vigilant guard. There they are, three in number—two old men and a boy—squatted on their knees, the eldest, half dozing,—the other two drawing, by long inhalation, the smoke out of their small copper-headed pipes,—and dreaming away their existence.

After a mile of the Tocado, our road turns off into a side street, narrower and more crowded. A Daimio's residence extends the greater part of its length on one side, with a large and imposing-looking gateway in the centre, from which stretches a long line of barred windows. Through these the faces of men, women, and children may be seen, eagerly or idly, as the case may be, looking at the passers-by. A small, narrow, and very muddy moat, little more than a gutter, keeps all intruders from too close prying. But these outbuildings are only the quarters of the numerous retainers attached, as in Europe in former times, to every baron and knight by a feudal tenure;—and constituting at once the chief sources of his expenditure, and the evidence of his rank or power. In many cases, these extend for a quarter of a mile on each side of the main entrance, and form in effect the best defence for their lord's apartments, which are at the back of the courtyard behind the gates, *entre cour et jardin*, as in the Faubourg St. Germain, and still to be seen there and elsewhere in Europe, as relics of a former age.

We soon emerge into an open space in front of the Tycoon's Cemetery, and through it a small river runs, fringed with fresh green banks, and a row of trees. A narrow strip next to the water, marking its tortuous course, has been taken possession of for cotters' cabbage-gardens. Here, in the open space above, forming a sort of boulevard, Matsuri, or public fairs, are often held, and, in their absence, story-tellers collect a little audience. A few noisy beggars generally take up their position by the wayside, and, although they receive gratefully a single cash from their own countrymen, they never condescend to ask a foreigner for less than a *tempo*,—equivalent to a hundred cash! Here a party of jugglers may often be seen too, collecting a crowd from the passers-by. Blondin and the Wizard of the North might both find formidable rivals here;—for the Japanese performers not only swallow portentously long swords, and poise themselves on bottles;—but out of their mouths come the most unimaginable things—flying horses, swarms of flies, ribbons by the mile, and paper shavings without end.

On crossing the bridge, we traverse one of the most densely populated of the commercial quarters, through which, indeed, we can only ride slowly, and in single file, amidst pedestrians and porters with their loads. Bullock-cars, Norimons, and Kangos are all here, jostling each other in contending currents. Over a gentle hill, then sharp round to the right, through a barrier-gate, we approach the official quarter, in the centre of which, within three moats of regal dimensions, the Tycoon himself resides. But we are not yet near to it. We pursue our way down some rather steep steps—a Daimio's residence on one side, and the wall and trees of the Tycoon's Cemetery, which we are skirting, on the other. As we emerge from this defile, we pass through a long line of booths, where a sort of daily bazaar is held for the sale of gaudily-colored prints, maps (many of them copies of European charts), story-books, swords, tobacco pouches, and pipes, for the humbler classes; and in the midst of which a fortune-teller may habitually be seen, seemingly finding plenty of credulous listeners, and the few cash necessary for his daily wants. Something very like the gambling table of our own fairs may also be seen in the same spot; but, judging by the stock-in-trade and the juvenile customers, the gambling, I suspect, is only for sweetmeats. Their serious gambling is reserved for tea-houses, and more private haunts, where the law may be better defied.

In all this there is little new, perhaps, except the mere outer lineaments and costume; for human nature is essentially the same under all skies and governments. And now we have arrived at our first halt. Through the gateway may be seen the double flight of steps, the one leading up to the top of the hill, in perpendicular and unbroken line; the other curving less abruptly upward. And, although the height is probably the same, the undulating flight *looks* so much less arduous, that we instinctively turn to the right, willing to believe in its gentler promise.

Many pedestrians—pilgrims from afar, and idle Yeddites from the neighboring thoroughfares—are passing up and down. And among all the strange and novel sights, few strike the stranger as more singular than a class of penitents, or disgraced officers, who move about habitually with their heads buried in a sort of basket mask, completely concealing the face. Lonins, outlaws, and great criminals, are said to adopt this mode of travelling when wishing to elude observation. Whether their incognito is always respected by the police, I cannot say. They recall the brothers of the Misericordia, and begging penitents —still to be seen in the towns of Italy—relics of mediæval times—and it is not a little singular to find their counterpart here.

Officers on horseback, wearing the badge either of the Tycoon or their feudal chief, are passing to and fro, preceded by one or more footmen or grooms, who always accompany their masters, and keep their pace, however rapid. Some of them have marvellous powers of running, in wind and limb. I had more than one who would run three or four leagues at a stretch by the side of the horse, and without distress;—or used to do so, before they got too fat and lazy in the foreigner's service.

Fair to look on is the capital of the Tycoon, even in winter, thus nestled in a broad valley, girdled with green woods and crowned by undulating hills, sloping with a gradual descent to the edge of a bay, into which the Pacific seeks in vain to pour its stormy waters. Nature has barred the entrance, twenty miles below, with a breakwater of volcanic islands and verdant headlands on either side. And, to make it more secure, she has shoaled the whole gulf, so that five miles from the city it is difficult to find anchorage for a vessel drawing twenty feet— the best of all defences against assault from without, whether the elements or a hostile fleet be the enemy! —ALCOCK.

## BABE CHRISTABEL.

    IN this dim world of clouding cares,
      We rarely know, till wildered eyes
        See white wings lessening up the skies,
    The Angels with us unawares.

    And thou hast stolen a jewel, Death!
      Shall light thy dark up like a Star,
        A Beacon kindling from afar
    Our light of love, and fainting faith.

    Thro' tears it gleams perpetually,
      And glitters thro' the thickest glooms,
        Till the eternal morning comes
    To light us o'er the Jasper Sea.

With our best branch, in tenderest leaf,
  We've strewn the way our Lord doth come;
  And, ready for the harvest home,
His Reapers bind our ripest sheaf.

Our beautiful Bird of light hath fled:
  Awhile she sat with folded wings—
  Sang round us a few hoverings—
Then straightway into glory sped.

And white-winged angels nurture her;
  With heaven's white radiance robed and crown'd,
  And all Love's purple glory round,
She summers on the Hills of Myrrh.

Thro' Childhood's morning-land serene
  She walkt betwixt us twain, like Love;
  While, in a robe of light above,
Her better Angel walkt unseen,

Till Life's highway broke bleak and wild;
  Then, lest her starry garments trail
  In mire, heart bleed, and courage fail,
The Angel's arms caught up the child.

Her wave of life hath backward roll'd
  To the great ocean, on whose shore
  We wander up and down, to store
Some treasures of the times of old:

And aye we seek and hunger on
  For precious pearls and relics rare,
  Strewn on the sands for us to wear
At heart, for love of her that's gone.

O weep no more! there yet is balm
  In Gilead! Love doth ever shed
  Rich healing where it nestles,—spread
O'er desert pillows some green palm!

God's ichor fills the hearts that bleed;
  The best fruit loads the broken-bough;
  And in the wounds our sufferings plough,
Immortal Love sows sovereign seed. —MASSEY.

## PREJUDICES AND OPINIONS.

PREJUDICES are notions or opinions which the mind entertains without knowing the grounds and reasons of them, and which are assented to without examination. The first notions which take possession of the minds of men, with regard to duties social, moral and civil, may therefore be justly styled prejudices. The mind of a young creature cannot remain empty; if you do not put into it that which is good, it will be sure to receive that which is bad.

Do what you can, there will still be a bias from education; and if so, is it not better this bias should lie towards things laudable and useful to society? This bias still operates, although it may not always prevail. The notions first instilled have the earliest influence, take the deepest root, and generally are found to give a colour and complexion to the subsequent lives of men, inasmuch as they are in truth the great source of human actions. It is not gold, or honor, or power, that moves men to act, but the opinions they entertain of those things. Hence it follows, that if a magistrate should say: "No matter what notions men embrace, I will take heed to their actions,' therein he shows his weakness; for, such as are men's notions, such will be their deeds.

For a man to do as he would be done by, to love his neighbor as himself, to honor his superiors, to believe that God scans all his actions, and will reward or punish them, and to think that he who is guilty of falsehood or injustice hurts himself more than any one else; are not these such notions and principles as every wise governor or legislator would covet above all things to have firmly rooted in the mind of every individual under his care? This is allowed even by the enemies of religion, who would fain have it thought the offspring of state policy, honoring its usefulness at the same time that they disparage its truth. What, therefore, cannot be acquired by every man's reasoning, must be introduced by precept, and riveted by custom; that is to say, the bulk of mankind must, in all civilized societies, have their minds, by timely instruction, well seasoned and furnished with proper notions, which, although the grounds or proofs thereof be unknown to them, will nevertheless influence their conduct, and so far render them useful members of the state. But if you strip men of these their notions, or, if you will, prejudices, with regard to modesty, decency, justice, charity, and the like, you will soon find them so many monsters utterly unfit for human society.

I desire it may be considered that most men want leisure, opportunity, or faculties, to derive conclusions from their principles, and establish morality on a foundation of human science. True it is—as St. Paul observes—that the "invisible things of God, from the creation of the world, are clearly seen;" and from thence the duties of natural religion may be discovered. But these things are seen and discovered by those alone who open their eyes and look narrowly for them. Now, if you look throughout the world, you shall find but few of these narrow inspectors and inquirers, very few who make it their business to analyse opinions, and pursue them to their rational source, to examine whence truths spring, and how they are inferred. In short, you shall find all men full of opinions, but knowledge only in a few.

It is impossible, from the nature and circumstances of human-kind, that the multitude should be philosophers, or that they should know things in their causes. We see every day that the rules, or conclusions alone, are sufficient for the shopkeeper to state his account, the sailor to navigate his ship, or the carpenter to measure his timber; none of which understand the theory, that is to say, the grounds and reasons either of arithmetic or geometry. Even so in moral, political and religious matters, it is manifest that the rules and opinions early imbibed at the first dawn of understanding, and without the least glimpse of science, may yet produce excellent effects, and be very useful to the world; and that, in fact, they are so, will be very visible to every one who shall observe what passeth round about him. —BERKELEY.

## THE COLOSSEUM BY MOONLIGHT.

The stars are forth, the moon above the tops
Of the snow-shining mountains.—Beautiful!
I linger yet with Nature, for the night
Hath been to me a more familiar face
Than that of man; and in her starry shade
Of dim and solitary loveliness,
I learn'd the language of another world.
I do remember me, that in my youth,
When I was wandering, upon such a night
I stood within the Coliseum's wall,
Midst the chief relics of almighty Rome;
The trees which grew along the broken arches
Waved dark in the blue midnight, and the stars
Shone through the rents of ruin; from afar
The watchdog bay'd beyond the Tiber; and
More near from out the Cæsar's palace came
The owl's long cry, and, interruptedly,

Of distant sentinels the fitful song
Began and died upon the gentle wind.
Some cypresses beyond the time-worn breach
Appear'd to skirt the horizon, yet they stood
Within a bowshot—Where the Cæsars dwelt,
And dwell the tuneless birds of night, amidst
A grove which springs through levell'd battlements,
And twines its roots with the imperial hearths,
Ivy usurps the laurel's place of growth;—
But the gladiators' bloody Circus stands,
A noble wreck in ruinous perfection!
While Cæsar's chambers, and the Augustan halls,
Grovel on earth in indistinct decay.—
And thou didst shine, thou rolling moon, upon
All this, and cast a wide and tender light,
Which soften'd down the hoar austerity
Of rugged desolation, and fill'd up,
As 'twere anew, the gaps of centuries;
Leaving that beautiful which still was so,
And making that which was not, till the place
Became religion, and the heart ran o'er
With silent worship of the great of old!—
The dead, but sceptred sovereigns, who still rule
Our spirits from their urns.—
    'Twas such a night!
'Tis strange that I recall it at this time;
But I have found our thoughts take wildest flight
Even at the moment when they should array
Themselves in pensive order.   —BYRON.

---

## COAL.

IT can scarcely be necessary to point out to the reader the vast importance of coal in all parts of the world, and the interest of every one to discover and make use of such stores of wealth, when they exist beneath the surface of the earth.

In a country like England, deprived of any large quantity of wood by the advance of civilization and the replacement of forests by corn fields, where should we obtain means for enduring the inclemency of the weather, or enjoying any comforts at our homes, if it were not for the supplies of this material, conveyed along our shores by numerous ships, and transported by every train on our railways?

But we must look farther. Where would be our manufactures—where would be our iron, the staple of all manufactures, if there were not abundant and cheap supplies of valuable fuel where the ores of these metals occur?

Without coal, could this country have advanced beyond its

condition many centuries ago—could there have been education—could there have been printed books available for the multitude—could there have been food and raiment for ourselves—or could science have advanced? Must not England have remained in the back-ground, its inhabitants unable to exercise that intellectual activity which they have exerted in placing their country in advance of the whole world?

Without coal there could have been no extensive use of steam, even if the vast power of that agent had been discovered. Without steam and iron, where should we now be in the advance of civilization over the world? Coal is indeed the indispensable food of all industry. It is a primary material, by whose aid we engender force, and obtain power sufficient for any purpose that has yet been imagined.

Marvellous indeed are the results obtained on considering the uses of those materials which form together the great carboniferous series of deposits as developed in the north of England. In a small strip of country, in an area of less than six or eight thousand square miles, which in some parts of Europe would be passed over almost without remark by the practical man, the politican, and the statistician—we find grouped together a multitude of large towns, a population of some millions of people, having, perhaps, more influence on the comforts of civilized man throughout the world than could elsewhere be found in a space of five, or even ten times that amount. Nor is this all. The other great manufacturing and commercial towns of England, with the exception of the capital, are similarly placed with reference to geological position. The coal and iron of the carboniferous rocks forms still the magnet towards which the other desirable things of this world are attracted, and they determine the growth and well-being of towns, not only in England, but elsewhere on the continent of Europe, and lately in America also. In France, Belgium and Germany, we everywhere see towns rising up into manufacturing importance, where fuel and iron exist beneath the soil; and rarely indeed has it been found possible to produce any great improvement in these respects, except where nature has pre-ordained ' by giving these sources of true riches. It is now well known that, however valuable in themselves other rarer natural products may be, there is no doubt of the enormously greater benefit to a people in the case of those materials which either enter into every manufacture, and are sources of power, or which are greatly increased in value by being subject t many processes to render them more generally useful, without, at the same time, causing them to be taken out of consumption.

Coal in this country is obtained at a serious expense and risk of human life. It often happens that, on taking up a newspaper, we see notice that another explosion from firedamp has taken place in some coal mine, and that ten, twenty, fifty, or a hundred of the workmen have been hurried unprepared into eternity. Some we read—and these are not the greatest sufferers—have been destroyed at once, burnt to death by the explosion itself, so that no human power, no system could, perhaps, have saved them. But a larger proportion have been found at a distance. They were performing their task some hundred yards off; they heard the shock; they felt that they were doomed men; they rushed at once to the pit bottom, but, cut off by the want of a direct communication, their only chance was to reach the main gallery, and try if, by any happy accident, they might escape. But the moment they arrived at this point, they found the effects of the explosion, the fearful after damp already on its way before them. They are stopped by this invisible, intangible, but fatal and impassable barrier. Some throw themselves upon the ground, and creep on for a few yards in the vain hope of escape. Some, in hopeless despair, await the advance of destruction. Such is a simple history of the whole event. One single inspiration of the after damp produces convulsions in the throat, and is the almost certain precursor of instant death, so that it rarely happens that any person escapes to tell the sad tale. It is not a question, then, worthy of consideration whether, by any method that could be adopted, these lives might be preserved? For whom do these men suffer? Their widows and orphans, their mothers, their sisters, and their friends have a right to call upon every one of us who benefit by their labors, but take no thought of their dangers and sufferings. They labor for our benefit. We induce them to run these risks, and are bound to weigh carefully the great social relations which impose it as a duty upon us to improve their condition. Each event of this kind concerns us all, and we are all, without exception, responsible in our degree; for if a sufficient interest was felt and expressed in this matter, it would not be allowed to go on as it does from accident to accident. That the subject is obscure and difficult, is not a sufficient reason that it should be neglected ; and because the sufferers are patient, the place of the accident far removed, and the objects of it beyond the sphere of our immediate exertions—because few amongst us have visited a coal mine, and know nothing of the danger personally, we are not therefore at liberty to let the matter take its course without an attempt to do good. Some pity should be felt and some sympathy also expressed for those whose lives are spent, and whose deaths may be caused ir providing us with the means of comfort and enjoyment. L us think seriously how much we owe to them—the comfort of the fireside, that essential requisite to home enjoyment—the luxuries that surround us—the facilities of travelling—the use of and interest in all machinery and manufactures—all these we owe to the coal miner ; and then think how little we do for him in return. He must daily descend some hundred yards into the bowels of the earth, traversing many miles of low subterranean passages, performing his task in the most inconvenient posture, in an atmosphere always impure and choked with dust, if not actually dangerous— lighted by a small candle, or by the yet fainter glimmer penetrating the meshes of a wire gauze—and then, from time to time, exposed to the chance of these accidents. He troubles not our repose—the tale of his distress hardly reaches our ears—he is poor—he is far away—he dies :—but he is our fellow-creature and our fellow-countryman. Each one amongst us is related to him by many bonds, and it is our duty to see that every practicable method is adopted to improve his condition. And if the dangers that surround him must still remain, in spite of all our exertions—if the terrible accidents from explosion must sometimes occur, still we have a duty to perform, for we are bound to use every means to diminish their frequency and extent, and to take away, if possible, from their frightful results. This duty is one, not only affecting the legislature, but every individual amongst us ; for all may in some way, either directly or indirectly, have influence with those upon whom ultimately the responsibility of so great an act of public justice must fall.

- -ANSTED,

## THE MINER.

They brought him from the dusky mine
　With kind but fruitless care ;
Yet few at first could hope resign,
　He lay so calm and fair.

Strange ! from beneath a mass of earth,
　So heavy and so deep,
The youth should thus be lifted forth
　Like living man asleep.

None knew the face, yet was it fair,
　Not twenty summers old ;
Around the snowy brow the hair
　Fell thick in curls of gold.

That earth from taint of all decay
　Mortality can screen ;
And who might guess how many a day
　The body there had been ?

The crowding miners gather'd round—
　Their garb the stripling wore—
But of them all could none be found
　Had seen that face before.

Soon every village wife and maid
　Amid the tumult press'd,
Each trembling lest the comely dead
　Were him she loved the best.

His was no form to be pass'd by,
　No face to be forgot,
Yet of that thronging company
　All own'd they knew him not.

"'The spirits of the mine with ease
　Can varying shapes assume ;
This form may harbor one of these—
　No tenant of the tomb."

All scatter'd back, a shapeless dread
　Turn'd every heart to stone ;
Mid a wide circle lay the dead,
　In beauty, all alone.

When, peering through the fearful crowd,
　A wrinkled woman old
Crept slowly forth, and scream'd aloud
　That visage to behold.

The grief in memory fondly nurs'd
　For threescore years in vain,
From its long numbing torpor burst
　To passion's thrill again,

She was his love! Oh, contrast strange
   In years, in form. in limb!
Life hath on her wrought drearier change
   Than death has brought on him.

The pitying crowd was moved to ruth,
   All felt the sight appalling,
The bitter burning tears of youth
   From such old eyelids falling.

"Is this the meeting," she exclaim'd,
   "I sought of Heaven so long?
The prayer that night and morn I framed?
   Oh, could the wish be wrong!

"For threescore years of living death
   I've held a fearful strife;
At times mistrusting of thy faith,
   At others of thy life.

"I have grown old 'mid woes and fears,
   Thou'st slept in youth the while;
My cheeks are seam'd with age and tears,
   Thou wear'st thine own sweet smile.

"I've borne the load of life alone,
   Alone, unwept, I'll die;
But in the grave, belovèd one,
   Thou'lt bear me company."

She totter'd—fell—around the dead
   Her wither'd arms were thrown;
Her long-toil'd soul its prison fled,
   And love with life was gone.
                    —MISS CLEPHANE.

---

## CLIVE.
### (A. D. 1725—1774.)

SOME lineaments of the character of the man were early discerned in the child. There remain letters written by his relations when he was in his seventh year; and from these letters it appears, that, even at that early age, his strong will and his fiery passions, sustained by a constitutional intrepidity, which sometimes seemed hardly compatible with soundness of mind, had begun to cause great uneasiness to his family. "Fighting," says one of his uncles, "to which he is out of measure addicted, gives his temper such a fierceness and imperiousness, that he flies out on every trifling occasion." The old people of the neighborhood still remember (1840) to have heard from their parents how Bob Clive climbed to the top of the lofty steeple of Market Drayton, and with what terror the inhabitants saw him seated on a stone spout near the summit. They also relate how he formed all the lads of the town into a kind of predatory army, and compelled the shopkeepers to submit to a tribute of apples and halfpence, in consideration of which he guaranteed the security of their windows. He was sent from school to school, making very little progress in his learning, and gaining for himself everywhere the character of being an exceeding naughty boy. One of his masters, it is said, was sagacious enough to prophecy that the idle lad would make a great figure in the world. But the general opinion seems to have been that poor Bob was a dunce, if not a reprobate. His family expected nothing good from such slender parts, and such a headstrong temper. It is not strange, therefore, that they gladly accepted for him, when in his eighteenth year, a writership in the service of the East India Company, and shipped him off to make a fortune, or die of a fever, at Madras.

From his first visit to India dates the renown of the English arms in the East. Till he appeared, his countrymen were despised as mere pedlars, while the French were revered as a people formed for victory and command. His courage and capacity dissolved the charm. With the defence of Arcot commences that long period of Oriental triumphs, which closes with the fall of Ghizni. Nor must we forget that he was only twenty-five years old when he approved himself ripe for military command. From his second visit to India dates the political ascendency of the English in that country. His dexterity and resolution realised, in the course of a few months, more than all the gorgeous visions which had floated before the imagination of Dupleix. Such an extent of cultivated territory, such an amount of revenue, such a multitude of subjects, was never added to the dominion of Rome by the most successful pro-consul; nor were such wealthy spoils ever borne under arches of triumph down the Sacred Way, and through the crowded forum, to the threshold of Tarpeian Jove. The fame of those who subdued Antiochus and Tigranes grows dim, when compared with the splendors of the exploits which the young English adventurer achieved, at the head of an army not equal in numbers to one-half of a Roman legion. From Clive's third visit to India dates the purity of the administration of our Eastern empire. When he landed in

x

Calcutta in 1765, Bengal was regarded as a place to which Englishmen were sent only to get rich, by any means, in the shortest possible time. He first made dauntless and unsparing war on that gigantic system of oppression, extortion, and corruption. In that war he manfully put to hazard his ease, his fame, and his splendid fortune. The same sense of justice, which forbids to conceal or extenuate the faults of his earlier days, compels us to admit that these faults were nobly repaired. If the reproach of the Company and its servants has been taken away—if in India the yoke of foreign masters, elsewhere the heaviest of all yokes, has been found lighter than that of any native dynasty—if to that gang of public robbers, which formerly spread terror through the whole plain of Bengal, has succeeded a body of functionaries not more highly distinguished by ability and diligence than by integrity and public spirit—if we now see such men as Munro, Elphinstone, and Metcalfe, after leading victorious armies, after making and deposing kings, return, proud of their honorable poverty, from a land which first held out to every greedy factor the hope of boundless wealth,—the praise is in no small measure due to Clive.

—MACAULAY.

## GLORY AND FAME.

THE warrior grasps the battle blade,
  Seeking the field of fight,
And madly lifts his daring hand
  Against all human right ;
He goeth with unholy wrath
To scatter death along his path,
  While nations mourn his might ;
And though he win the world's acclaim—
It is not Glory—'tis not Fame !

The roll of the arousing drum,
  The bugle's startling bray,
The thunder of the bursting bomb,
  The tumult of the fray ;
The oft-recurring hour of strife,
The blight of hope, the waste of life,
  The proud victorious day—
All this may be a splendid game,
But 'tis not Glory—'tis not Fame !

Can we subdue the widow's cries,
  The orphan's plaintive wail ;
Or turn from mute upbraiding eyes,
  And faces ghastly pale ?

Can we restore the mind gone dim,
    The broken heart !—the shattered limb !
By war's exulting tale ?
This is ambition, lust, and shame,
But 'tis not Glory—'tis not Fame !

There are who pour the light of truth
    Upon the glowing page,
To purify the soul of youth,
    And cheer the heart of age ;
There are whom God hath sent to show
The wonders of His power below—
    Such is the gifted sage :
And such have learned our love to claim,
For this is Glory—this is Fame !

There are—like Howard—who employ
    Their healthiest, happiest hours,
In shedding love, and hope, and joy
    Around this world of ours ;
Who free the captive—feed the poor,
And enter every humble door,
    Where sin or sorrow lowers,
Till nations breathe and bless their name ;
And this is Glory—this is Fame !

The poet, whose inspiring muse
    Waves her ecstatic wing,
Clothes thought and language with the hues
    Of every holy thing—
Of beauty in its thousand forms,
Of all that cheers, refines, and warms,
    He loves to dream and sing ;
And myriads feel his song of flame —
For this is Glory—this is Fame          —PRINCE.


## ANNE BOLEYN'S CORONATION PAGEANT.

(A-D. 1533.)

ON the morning of the 31st of May, the families of the London citizens were stirring early in all houses. From Temple-bar to the Tower, the streets were fresh strewed with gravel, the foot-paths were railed off along the whole distance, and occupied on one side by the guilds, their workmen, and apprentices, on the other by the City constables and officials in their gaudy uniforms, and ' with their staves in hand for to cause the people to keep good room and order.' Cornhill and Gracechurch street had dressed their fronts in scarlet and crimson, in arras and tapestry, and the rich carpet-work from Persia and the East ;

Cheapside, to outshine her rivals, was draped even more splendidly in cloth of gold, and tissue, and velvet. The sheriffs were pacing up and down on their great Flemish horses, hung with liveries, and all the windows were thronged with ladies crowding to see the procession pass. At length the Tower guns opened, the grim gates rolled back, and under the archway, in the bright May sunshine, the long column began slowly to defile. Two states only permitted their representatives to grace the scene with their presence,—Venice and France. It was, perhaps to make the most of this isolated countenance, that the French ambassador's train formed the van of the cavalcade. Twelve French knights came riding foremost in surcoats of blue velvet with sleeves of yellow silk, their horses trapped in blue, with white crosses powdered on their hangings. After them followed a troop of English gentlemen, two and two, and then the Knights of the Bath, 'in gowns of violet, with hoods purfled with miniver like doctors.' Next, perhaps, at a little interval, the abbots passed on, mitred in their robes; the barons followed in crimson velvet, the bishops then, and then the earls and marquises, the dresses of each order increasing in elaborate gorgeousness. All these rode on in pairs. Then came alone Audeley, lord-chancellor, and behind him the Venetian ambassador and the Archbishop of York; the Archbishop of Canterbury, and our old friend, Du Bellay, Bishop of Bayonne, not now with bugle and hunting frock, but solemn with stole and crozier. Next, the lord mayor, with the city mace in hand, and Garter in his coat of arms; and then Lord William Howard—Belted Will Howard, of the Scottish Border, Marshal of England. The officers of the Queen's household succeeded the marshal in scarlet and gold, and the van of the procession was closed by the Duke of Suffolk, as high constable, with his silver wand. It is no easy matter to picture to ourselves the blazing trail of splendor which in such a pageant must have drawn along the London streets, those streets which now we know so black and smoke-grimed, themselves then radiant with masses of color, gold, and crimson, and violet. Yet there it was, and there the sun could shine upon it, and tens of thousands of eyes were gazing on the scene out of the crowded lattices.

Glorious as this spectacle was, perhaps however, it passed unheeded. Those eyes were watching all for another object, which now drew near. In an open space behind the constable there was seen approaching 'a white chariot,' led by two palfreys in white damask which swept the ground, a golden canopy borne above it, making music with silver bells, and in the chariot sat the observed of all observers, the beautiful occasion of all this glittering homage, fortune's plaything of the hour, the Queen of England—queen at last—borne along upon the waves of this sea of glory, breathing the perfumed incense of greatness, which she had risked her fair name, her delicacy, her honor, her self-respect to win ; and she had won it.

There she sate, dressed in white tissue robes, her fair hair flowing loose over her shoulders, and her temples circled with a light coronet of gold and diamonds—most beautiful—loveliest—most favored perhaps, as she seemed at that hour, of all England's daughters. Alas ! 'within the hollow round' of that coronet—

> Kept death his court, and there the antick sate
> Scoffing her state and grinning at her pomp,
> Allowing her a little breath, a little scene
> To monarchize, be feared, and kill with looks,
> Infusing her with self and vain conceit,
> As if the flesh which walled about her life
> Were brass impregnable ; and humored thus,
> Bored through her castle walls ; and farewell, Queen.

Fatal gift of greatness! so dangerous ever ! so more than dangerous in those tremendous times when the fountains are broken loose of the great deeps of thought ; and nations are in the throes of revolution ; when ancient order and law and tradition are splitting in the social earthquake; and as the opposing forces wrestle to and fro, those unhappy ones who stand out above the crowd become the symbols of the struggle, and fall the victims of its alternating fortunes. And what if into an unsteady heart and brain, intoxicated with splendor, the outward chaos should find its way, converting the poor silly soul into an image of the same confusion,—if conscience should be deposed from her high place, and the Pandora box be broken loose of passions and sensualities and follies ; and at length there be nothing left of all which man or woman ought to value, save hope of God's forgiveness!

Three short years have yet to pass, and again, on a summer morning, Queen Anne Boleyn will leave the Tower of London—not radiant then with beauty on a gay errand of coronation,

but a poor wandering ghost, on a sad tragic errand, from whi[ch]
she will never more return, passing away out of an earth whe[re]
she may stay no longer, into a Presence where, neverthele[ss]
we know that all is well—for all of us—and therefore for h[er]
—FROUDE.

## CHIMES OF THE SEA.

BORN in the earliest dawn of Time,
  I shall be till Time is o'er;
I sing my songs in every clime,
  And compass every shore:
From North to South, from East to West,
  My giant waves are hurl'd;
Was there ever a monarch like me, possess'd
  Of more than half a world?

I'm grave, I'm gay, I shout or sing,
  As it suits my varying mind,
But, whatever my state, I wonder bring
  To the hearts of human kind:
And when first I show to stranger eyes,
  The majesty girding me,
How thrills his heart as he wildly cries
  "The sea! The sea! The sea!"

The broad Atlantic's my hall of pride
  A myriad serfs I own,
And at every ebb of my mighty tide,
  They gather about my throne;
They come, the near and the far away,
  From cave, and cliff, and tower,
From golden fields and gardens gay,
  And many a lady's bower.

In the fair Pacific I love to smile,
  And lull my waves to rest,
While many a glittering coral isle
  Gleams bright on my heaving breast:
But far away in the Northern seas,
  I am chill'd to the very soul,
For the icy winds my heart's blood freeze
  As I circle the silent Pole.

I bask beneath Italian skies,—
  I muse by classic Greece,
And scarce can an angry feeling rise
  'Mid scenes so full of peace;
And even I, over Glory's grave,
  A tear can almost shed,
As I flow, with bright and placid wave
  By the "city of the dead."

I wander among the Hebrides,
  Down Staffa's solemn aisles,
And dear to my soul is the passing breeze
  From Iona's sacred piles ;
For it whispers of ages dark and drear,
  Of a well-nigh pagan night,
When outcast Truth found a refuge here,
  And shone as a beacon bright.

Around Columbia's rocks I roar,
  And wealthy Hindostan ;
And many a bleak and barren shore,
  Untrod by the foot of man :
But Albion's isle I guard with awe,
  For I honor her bulwarks white,
And woe to the foe who defies her law,
  When she rules for truth and right !

Wherever my endless waters foam,
  Her red cross flag's unfurl'd,
As proudly she bears to her island home
  The wealth of a teeming world :
And scatters abroad, with bounteous hand,
  The blessings her God hath given,—
" The freedom of thought of her own free land,
  And the faith which lights to Heaven."

Spain, Venice, and Carthage, where are they?
  And where are the wreaths they won ?
They are silent all, in Fame's decay,—
  Their course of glory 's run ;
But a mightier monarch now wears my crown,
  For it graces Britannia's head,—
May her garments of state be Truth and Renown,
  Till her mission be nobly sped !         —DARNELL.

## THE LAW OF CAUSATION.

THE phenomena of nature exist in two distinct relations to one another ; that of simultaneity, and that of succession. Every phenomenon is related, in an uniform manner, to some phenomena that coexist with it, and to some that have preceded or will follow it.

Of the uniformities which exist among synchronous phenomena, the most important, on every account, are the laws of number ; and next to them those of space, or in other words, of extension and figure. The laws of number are common to synchronous and successive phenomena. That two and two make four, is equally true whether the second two follow the first two or accompany them. It is as true of days and years as of feet and inches. The laws of extension and figure, (in other words, the theorems of geometry, from its lowest to its highest branches,) are, on the contrary, laws of simultaneous phenomena only. The various parts of space, and of the objects which are said to fill space, coexist; and the unvarying laws which are the subject of the science of geometry, are an expression of the mode of their coexistence.

This is a class of laws, or in other words, of uniformities, for the comprehension and proof of which it is not necessary to suppose any lapse of time, any variety of facts or events succeeding one another. If all the objects in the universe were unchangeably fixed, and had remained in that condition from eternity, the propositions of geometry would still be true of those objects. All things which possess extension, or in other words, which fill space, are subject to geometrical laws. Possessing extension, they possess figure; possessing figure, they must possess some figure in particular, and have all the properties which geometry assigns to that figure. If one body be a sphere and the other a cylinder, of equal height and diameter, the one will be exactly two-thirds of the other, let the nature and quality of the material be what it will. Again, each body and each point of a body, must occupy some place or position among other bodies; and the position of two bodies relatively to each other, of whatever nature the bodies be, may be unerringly inferred from the position of each of them relatively to any third body.

In the laws of number, then, and in those of space, we recognise, in the most unqualified manner, the rigorous universality of which we are in quest. Those laws have been in all ages the type of certainty, the standard of comparison for all inferior degrees of evidence. Their invariability is so perfect, that we are unable even to conceive any exception to them; and philosophers have been led, although (as I have endeavored to show) erroneously, to consider their evidence as lying not in experience, but in the original constitution of the human intellect. If, therefore, from the laws of space and number, we were able to deduce uniformities of any other description, this would be conclusive evidence to us that those other uniformities possessed the same degree of rigorous certainty. But this we cannot do. From laws of space and number alone, nothing can be deduced but laws of space and number.

Of all truths relating to phenomena, the most valuable to us are those which relate to the order of their succession. On a knowledge of these is founded every reasonable anticipation of future facts, and whatever power we possess of influencing those facts to our advantage. Even the laws of geometry are chiefly of practical importance to us as being a portion of the premisses from which the order of the succession of phenomena may be inferred.

Inasmuch as the motion of bodies, the action of forces, and the propagation of influences of all sorts, take place in certain lines and over definite spaces, the properties of those lines and spaces are an important part of the laws to which those phenomena are themselves subject. Moreover, motions, forces or other influences, at times, are numerable quantities; and the properties of number are applicable to them as to all other things. But although the laws of number and space are important elements in the ascertainment of uniformities of succession, they can do nothing towards it when taken by themselves. They can only be made instrumental to that purpose whem we combine with them additional premisses, expressive of uniformities of succession already known. By taking, for instance, as premisses these propositions, that bodies acted upon by an instantaneous force move with uniform velocity in straight lines; that bodies acted upon by a continuous force move with accelerated velocity in straight lines; and that bodies acted upon by two forces in different directions move in the diagonal of a parallelogram, whose sides represent the direction and quantity of those forces; we may by combining these truths with propositions relating to the properties of straight lines and of parallelograms, (as that a triangle is half of a parallelogram of the same base and altitude,) deduce another important uniformity of succession, viz., that a body moving round a centre of force describes areas proportional to the times. But unless there had been laws of succession in our premisses, there could have been no truths of succession in our conclusions. A similar remark might be extended to every other class of phenomena really peculiar; and, had it been attended to, would have prevented many chimerical attempts at demonstrations of the indemonstrable, and explanations of what cannot be explained.

It is not, therefore, enough for us that the laws of space

which are only laws of simultaneous phenomena, and the laws of number, which though true of successive phenomena do not relate to their succession, possess that rigorous certainty and universality of which we are in search. We must endeavor to find some law of succession which has those same attributes, and is therefore fit to be made the foundation of processes for discovering, and of a test for verifying, all other uniformities of succession. This fundamental law must resemble the truths of geometry in their most remarkable peculiarity, that of never being, in any instance whatever, defeated or suspended by any change of circumstances.

' Now among all those uniformities in the succession of phenomena, which common observation is sufficient to bring to light, there are very few which have any, even apparent, pretension to this rigorous indefeasibility : and of those few, one only has been found capable of completely sustaining it. In that one, however, we recognise a law which is universal also in another sense ; it is coextensive with the entire field of successive phenomena, all instances whatever of succession being examples of it. This law is the Law of Causation. It is an universal truth that every fact which has a beginning has a cause.

This generalization may appear to some minds not to amount to much, since after all it asserts only this: "it is a law, that every event depends upon some law." We must not, however, conclude that the generality of the principle is merely verbal ; it will be found upon inspection to be no vague or unmeaning assertion, but a most important and really fundamental truth.
—MILL.

## LOSS OF THE ROYAL GEORGE.

(A.D. 1782.)

Toll for the Brave !
The brave that are no more !
All sunk beneath the wave
Fast by their native shore !

Eight hundred of the brave
Whose courage well was tried
Had made the vessel heel
And laid her on her side.

A land-breeze shook the shrouds
And she was overset;
Down went the Royal George,
With all her crew complete.

Toll for the brave!
Brave Kempenfelt is gone
His last sea-fight is fought,
His work of glory done.

It was not in the battle
No tempest gave the shock;
She sprang no fatal leak,
She ran upon no rock.

His sword was in its sheath,
His fingers held the pen,
When Kempenfelt went down
With twice four hundred men.

Weigh the vessel up
Once dreaded by our foes!
And mingle with our cup
The tear that England owes.

Her timbers yet are sound,
And she may float again
Full charged with England's thunder,
And plough the distant main!

But Kempenfelt is gone,
His victories are o'er;
And he and his eight hundred
Shall plough the wave no more. —COWPER.

---

## ELECTRO-PLATE.

How is an electro-silver vase, or candelabrum, or table ornament, or honorary trophy produced? The answer is full of interest. There is first the artist, the tasteful designer, employed; he exercises all the talent which he may have acquired by nature and education, to produce a design which shall combine fitness of adaptation with grace of form and decoration. Next comes the modeller: he places before him the design which has been laid down on paper, and proceeds to build up a realization of that design: he works upon a mass of smooth wax, which, by the aid of variously shaped tools in wood and bone, he fashions into an exact representation of the article to be produced. To the modeller succeeds the moulder, who makes a mould in lead or some other fusible metal; this would, of course present a reverse to the model—hollows instead of projections, and projections instead of hollows. Next to the moulder comes the pattern-maker, who, by a similar process of casting, makes a cast in brass from the lead mould; this brass pattern is carefully touched up and finished, and constitutes a more perfected edition of the wax model; and it serves as the type, as it were, of all the articles to be produced. Again and again does the casting proceed; for as there was a lead mould made from the wax model, so is there now a sand mould made from the brass pattern; and as this brass pattern was obtained from the lead mould, so lastly is there a white metal cast made from the sand mould. The white metal cast is the article to be produced and sold, though it has not yet received its silvery garment. The luxuriant ornament which we are here supposing to be under formation, may require other preparatory processes; it may have decorative details in thin metal, which require stamping; it may need the addition of thin pieces, made from sheets by brazing or hammering; or it may render necessary the soldering of many pieces together. But we will leap over these intermediate processes, and suppose the article to be completely formed, in a white metal, composed of zinc, copper, and nickel. It is dipped into a tank containing a chemical solution of silver, in which also a few sheets of pure silver are immersed. Then comes the mysterious agency of electro-chemistry. The vase or other article being placed in connection with the wires of a battery, a current is generated, the solution is decomposed, the atoms of silver leave it and cling to the vase, other atoms of silver leave the plates to re-invigorate the solution, and so the chain of operations proceeds, until the vase is coated with pure silver, atom by atom. These atoms cling together; and according to the intensity of the current, the strength of the solution, and the time of immersion, does the deposited coat become thicker. —Dodd.

## TO A FIELD MOUSE.

Wee, sleekit, cow'rin', tim'rous beastie,
O what a panic's in thy breastie!
Thou need na start awa sae hasty,
Wi' bickering brattle!
I wad be laith to rin and chase thee
Wi' murd'ring pattle!

## TO A FIELD MOUSE.

I'm truly sorry man's dominion
Has broken nature's social union,
And justifies that ill opinion
    Which makes thee startle
At me, thy poor earth-born companion
    And fellow-mortal!

I doubt na, whyles, but thou may thieve;
What then? poor beastie, thou maun live!
A daimen icker in a thrave
    'S a sma' request:
I'll get a blessin' wi' the lave,
    And never miss't!

Thy wee bit housie, too, in ruin!
Its silly wa's the win's are strewin':
And naething, now, to big a new ane,
    O' foggage green!
And bleak December's winds ensuin'
    Baith snell and keen!

Thou saw the fields laid bare and waste
And weary winter comin' fast
And cozie here, beneath the blast,
    Thou thought to dwell,
Till crash! the cruel coulter past,
    Out thro' thy cell.

That wee bit heap o' leaves and
Has cost thee mony a weary nibble!
Now thou's turn'd out, for a' thy trouble,
    But house or hald,
To thole the winter's sleety dribble
    And cranreuch cauld?

But Mousie, thou art no thy lane
In proving foresight may be vain:
The best laid schemes o' mice and men
    Gang aft a-gley,
And lea'e us nought but grief and pain,
    For promised joy.

Still thou art blest, compared wi' me!
The present only toucheth thee;
But och! I backward cast my e'e
    On prospects drear!
And forward, tho' I canna see,
    I guess and fear.

    —BURNS.

# THE STUDY OF THE CLASSICS.

I AM not one whose lot it has been to grow old in literary retirement, devoted to classical studies with an exclusiveness which might lead to an overweening estimate of these two noble languages. Few, I will not say evil, were the days allowed to me for such pursuits; and I was constrained, still young and an unripe scholar, to forego them for the duties of an active and laborious profession. They are now amusements only, however delightful and improving. Far am I from assuming to understand all their riches, all their beauty, or all their power; yet I can profoundly feel their immeasurable superiority in many important respects to all we call modern; and I would fain think that there are many even among my younger readers who can now, or will hereafter, sympathize with the expression of my ardent admiration. Greek—the shrine of the genius of the old world; as universal as our race, as individual as ourselves; of infinite flexibility, of indefatigable strength, with the complication and the distinctness of nature herself, to which nothing was vulgar, from which nothing was excluded; speaking to the ear like Italian, speaking to the mind like English; with words like pictures, with words like the gossamer film of the summer; at once the variety and the picturesqueness of Homer, the gloom and the intensity of Æschylus; not compressed to the closest by Thucydides, not fathomed to the bottom by Plato, not sounding with all its thunders, nor lit up with all its ardors even under the Promethean touch of Demosthenes! And Latin—the voice of empire and of war, of law and of the state; inferior to its half-parent and rival in the embodying of passion and in the distinguishing of thought, but equal to it in sustaining the measured march of history, and superior to it in the indignant declamation of moral satire; stamped with the mark of an imperial and despotizing republic; rigid in its construction, parsimonious in its synonyms; reluctantly yielding to the flowery yoke of Horace, although opening glimpses of Greek-like splendor in the occasional inspirations of Lucretius; proved indeed to the uttermost by Cicero, and by him found wanting; yet majestic in its bareness, impressive in its conciseness; the true language of history, instinct with the spirit of nations, and not with the passions of individuals; breathing the maxims of the world, and not the tenets of the schools ; one and uniform in its air and spirit, whether touched by the stern and haughty Sallust, by the open and discursive Livy, by the reserved and thoughtful Tacitus.

These inestimable advantages, which no modern skill can wholly counterpoise, are known and felt by the scholar alone. He has not failed, in the sweet and silent studies of his youth, to drink deep at those sacred fountains of all that is just and beautiful in human language. The thoughts and the words of the master-spirits of Greece and of Rome, are inseparably blended in his memory ; a sense of their marvellous harmonies, their exquisite fitness, their consummate polish, has sunken for ever in his heart, and thence throws out light and fragrancy upon the gloom and the annoyances of his maturer years. No avocations of professional labor will make him abandon their wholesome study ; in the midst of a thousand cares he will find an hour to recur to his boyish lessons—to re-peruse them in the pleasurable consciousness of old associations, and in the clearness of manly judgment, and to apply them to himself and to the world with superior profit. The more extended his sphere of learning in the literature of modern Europe, the more deeply, though the more wisely, will he reverence that of classical antiquity : and in declining age, when the appetite for magazines and reviews and the ten times repeated trash of the day has failed, he will retire, as it were, within a circle of school-fellow friends, and end his secular studies, as he began them, with his Homer, his Horace and his Shakspeare.

—H. N. COLERIDGE.

## YOUTHS AT AN EARLY AGE LEAVING COLLEGE.

LIFE is before ye ; and while now ye stand
Eager to spring upon the promised land,
Fair smiles the way, where yet your feet have trod
But few light steps upon a flowery sod.
Round ye are youth's green bowers, and to your eyes
The horizon-line joins earth to the bright skies.
Daring and triumph, pleasure, fame, and joy,
Friendship unwavering, love without alloy,
Brave thoughts of noble deeds, and glory won,
Like angels beckon ye to venture on.
And if o'er the bright scene some shadows rise,
Far off they seem—at hand the sunshine lies.
The distant clouds ! which of ye pause to fear?

May not a brightness gild them when more near?
Dismay and doubt ye know not, for the power
Of youth is strong within ye at this hour;
And the great mortal conflict seems to be
Not so much strife as certain victory—
A glory ending in eternity.
 Life is before ye : oh, could ye but look
Into the secrets of that sealed book!
Strong as ye are in youth, and hope, and faith,
Ye would sink down and falter, "Give us death."
If the dread Sphinx's lips might once unclose,
And utter but a whisper of the woes
Which overtake ye must in life's long doom,
Well might ye cry, "Our cradle be our tomb."
Could ye foresee your spirits' broken wings,
Fame's brightest triumphs what despised things,
Friendship how feeble, love how fierce a flame,
Your joy half-sorrow, half your glory shame,
Hollowness, weariness, and, worst of all,
Self-scorn that pities not its own deep fall,
Fast-waning brightness, and fast-gathering night;—
Oh, could ye see it all, ye might, ye might
Cower in the dust, unequal to the strife,
And die but in beholding what is life.
 Life is before ye : from the fated road
Ye cannot turn; then take ye up your load.
Not yours to tread or leave the unknown way,
Ye must go o'er it, meet ye what ye may.
Gird up your souls within ye to the deed,
Angels and fellow spirits bid ye speed!
What though the brightness dim, the pleasure fade,
The glory wane—oh, not of these is made
The awful life that to your trust is given,
Children of God! inheritors of heaven!
Mourn not the perishing of each fair toy;
Ye were ordain'd to do, not to enjoy—
To suffer, which is nobler than to dare;
A sacred burden is this life ye bear;
Look on it, lift it, bear it solemnly;
Stand up and walk beneath it steadfastly;
Fail not for sorrow, falter not for sin:
But onward, upward, till the goal ye win.
God guard ye, and God guide ye on your way,
Young pilgrim-warriors who set forth to-day!
—Mrs. Butler.

## THE REGATTA AT VENICE.

Venice, from her peculiar formation and the vast number of her watermen, had long been celebrated for this species of amusement. Families were known and celebrated in her traditions for dexterous skill with the oar, as they were known in

Rome for feats of a far less useful and of a more barbarous nature. It was usual to select from these races of watermen, the most vigorous and skilful; and, after invoking aid in prayer and arousing their pride and recollections by songs that recounted the feats of their ancestors, to start them from the goal with every incitement that pride and love of victory could awaken.

Most of these ancient usages were still observed. As soon as the Bucentaur was in its station, some thirty or forty gondoliers were brought forth, clad in their gayest habiliments, and surrounded and supported by crowds of anxious friends and relatives. The intended competitors were expected to sustain the long established reputations of their several names, and they were admonished of the disgrace of defeat. They were cheered by the men, and stimulated by the smiles and tears of the other sex. The rewards were recalled to their minds; they were fortified by prayers for success; and then they were dismissed amid the cries and wishes of the multitude to seek their allotted places beneath the stern of the galley of state.

The city of Venice is divided into two nearly equal parts by a channel much broader than the ordinary passages of the town. This dividing artery from its superior size and depth, and its greater importance, is called the Grand Canal. Its course is not unlike that of an undulating line, which greatly increases its length. As it is much used by the large boats of the bay—being in fact a sort of secondary port—and its width is so considerable, it has throughout the whole distance but one bridge—the celebrated Rialto. The regatta was to be held on this canal, which offered the requisites of length and space, and which, as it was lined with most of the palaces of the principal senators, afforded all the facilities necessary for viewing the struggle.

In passing from one end of this long course to the other, the men destined for the race were not permitted to make any exertion. Their eyes roamed over the gorgeous hangings, which, as is still wont throughout Italy on all days of festa, floated from every window, and on groups of females in rich attire, brilliant with the peculiar charms of the famed Venetian beauty, that clustered in the balconies. Those who were domestics rose and answered to the encouraging signals thrown from above, as they passed the palaces of their masters, while those who were watermen of the public, endeavored to gather hope among the sympathising faces of the multitude.

At length every formality had been duly observed, and the competitors assumed their places. The gondolas were much larger than those commonly used, and each was manned by three watermen in the centre, directed by a fourth, who, standing on a little deck in the stern, steered, while he aided to impel the boat. There were light, low staffs in the bows, with flags that bore the distinguishing colors of several noble families of the republic, or which had such other simple devices as had been suggested by the fancies of those to whom they belonged. A few flourishes of the oar, resembling the preparatory movements which the master of fence makes ere he begins to push and parry, were given; a whirling of the boats, like the prancing of curbed racers, succeeded; and then, at the report of a gun, the whole darted away as if the gondolas were impelled by volition. The start was followed by a shout which passed swiftly along the canal, and an eager agitation of heads that went from balcony to balcony, till the sympathetic movement was communicated to the grave load under which the Bucentaur labored.

For a few minutes the difference in force and skill was not very obvious. Each gondola glided along the element, apparently with that ease with which a light-winged swallow skims the lake, and with no visible advantage to either. Then, as more art in him who steered, or greater powers of endurance in those who rowed, or some of the latent properties of the boat itself came into service, the cluster of little barks which had come off like a closely united flock of birds taking flight together in alarm, began to open till they formed a broad and vacillating line in the centre of the passage. The whole train shot beneath the bridge so near to each other as to render it still doubtful which was to conquer, and the exciting strife came more in view of the principal personages of the city.

But here those radical qualities, which insure success in efforts of this nature, manifested themselves. The weaker began to yield, the train to lengthen, and hopes and fears to increase, until those in front presented the exhilarating spectacle of success, while those behind offered the still more noble sight of men struggling without hope. Gradually the dis tances between the boats increase, while that between them and the goal grew rapidly less, until three of those in advance came in, like glancing arrows, beneath the stern of the Bucentaur, with a length between them. The prize was won, the conquerors were rewarded, and the artillery gave forth the usual signals of rejoicing. Music answered to the roar of cannon and the peals of bells, while sympathy with success, that predominant and so often dangerous principle of our nature, drew shouts even from the disappointed.

—COOPER.

## "FROM THE EAST AND FROM THE WEST."

Not from Jerusalem alone,
  To heaven the path ascends;
    As near, as sure, as straight the way
    That leads to the celestial day,
  From farthest realms extends;
Frigid or torrid zone.

What matters how or whence we start?
  One is the crown to all;
    One is the hard but glorious race,
    Whatever be our starting-place;
  Rings round the earth the call
That says, Arise, depart!

From the balm-breathing, sun-loved isles
  Of the bright Southern Sea,
    From the dead North's cloud-shadowed pole,
    We gather to one gladsome goal,
  One common home in Thee,
City of sun and smiles!

The cold, rough billow hinders none;
  Nor helps the calm, fair main;
    The brown rock of Norwegian gloom,
    The verdure of Tahitian bloom,
  The sands of Mizraim's plain,
Or peaks of Lebanon.

As from the green lands of the vine,
  So from the snow-wastes pale,
    We find the ever open road
    To the dear city of our God;
  From Russian steppe, or Burman vale,
Or terraced Palestine.

Not from swift Jordan's sacred stream
  Alone we mount above;
    Indus or Danube, Thames or Rhone,
    Rivers unsainted or unknown;
  From each, the home of love
Beckons with heavenly gleam.

Not from grey Olivet alone
  We see the gates of light;
    From Morven's heather Jungfrau's snow,
  We welcome the descending glow
Of pearl and chrysolite,
And the unsetting sun.

Not from Jerusalem alone
  The church ascends to God;
    Strangers of every tongue and clime,
    Pilgrims of every land and time,
  Throng the well-trodden road
That leads up to the Throne.
          —BONAR.

---

## THE FARMER.

THE glory of the farmer is, that, in the division of labor, it is his part to create. All trade rests at last on his primitive authority. He stands close to nature; he obtains from the earth, the bread and the meat. The food which was not, he causes to be. The first farmer was the first man, and all historic nobility rests on possession and use of land. Men do not like hard work, but every man has an exceptional respect for tillage, and the feeling that this is the original calling of his race, that he himself is only excused from it by some circumstance which made him delegate it for a time to other hands. If he had not some skill which recommends him to the farmer, some product for which the farmer will give him corn, he must himself return into his due place among the planters. And the profession has in all eyes its ancient charm as standing nearest to God, the first cause. Then the beauty of nature, the tranquillity and innocence of the countryman, his independence and his pleasing arts—the care of bees, of poultry, of sheep, of cows, the dairy, the care of hay, of fruits, of orchards and forests, and the reaction of these on the workman in giving him a strength and plain dignity, like the face and manners of nature—all men acknowledge. All men keep the farm in reserve as an asylum, where, in case of mischance, to hide their property, or a solitude if they do not succeed in society. And who knows how many glances of remorse are turned this way from the bankrupts of trade, from mortified pleaders in courts and senates, or from the victims of idleness and pleasure! Poisoned by town life and town vices, the sufferer resolves :—' Well, my children, whom I have injured, shall go back to the land, to be recruited and cured by that which should have been my nursery, and now shall be their hospital.'

The farmer has grave trusts confided to him. In the great household of nature, the farmer stands at the door of the bread-room and weighs to each his load. Then he is the Board of Quarantine. The farmer is the hoarded capital of health, as he is also the capital of wealth, and it is from him that the health and the power, moral and intellectual, of the cities come. The city is always recruited from the country. The men in cities who are the centres of energy, the driving-wheels of trade, politics, or practical arts, and the women of beauty and genius, are the children or grandchildren of farmers, and are spending the energies which their fathers' hardy, silent life accumulated in frosty furrows, in poverty, necessity, and darkness. In English factories, the boy who watches the loom, to tie the threads when the wheel stops, to indicate that the thread is broken, is called a *minder*. And in this great factory of our Copernican globe, shifting its slides, rotating its constellations, times and tides ; bringing now the day of planting, then of watering, then of weeding, then of reaping, then of curing and storing—the farmer is the *minder*. His machine is of colossal proportions ; the diameter of the water-wheel, the arms of the levers, the power of the battery, are out of all mechanic measure ; and it takes him long to understand its parts and its working. This pump never 'sucks ;' these screws are never loose ; this machine is never out of gear ; the vat and piston-wheels and tires never wear out, but are self-repairing. We see the farmer with pleasure and respect, when we think what powers and utilities are so meekly worn. He knows every secret of labor. He changes the face of the landscape. Put him on a new planet and he would know where to begin ; yet there is no arrogance in his bearing, but a perfect gentleness. The farmer stands well on the world. Plain in manners as in dress, he would not shine in palaces; he is absolutely unknown and inadmissible therein. Living or dying he never shall be heard of in them. Yet the drawing-room heroes put down beside him would shrivel in his presence—the solid and unexpressive, they expressed to gold leaf. But he stands well on the world, as Adam did, as an Indian does, as Homer's heroes, Agamemnon and Achilles, do. He is a person whom a poet of any clime—Milton or Cervantes—would appreciate, as being really a piece of the old nature, comparable to sun and moon, rainbow and flood; because he is, as all natural persons are, representative of nature as much as these. That uncorrupted behaviour which we admire in animals and in young children belongs to him, to the hunter, the sailor—the man who lives in the presence of nature. Cities force growth, and make men talkative and entertaining, but they make them artificial. What possesses interest for us is the natural part of each, its constitutional excellence. This is for ever a surprise, engaging and lovely; we cannot be satiated with knowing it, and about it, and it is this which the conversation with nature cherishes and guards.

—*Country Gentleman's Magazine.*

## THE CANADIAN FARMER'S SONG.

LET the cities proud boast long and loud
   Of their palaces fair and grand;
In the country wide, spread on every side,
   Are the works of our Father's hand.
Though our fate may seem, to some idler's dream,
   A toilsome and weary lot,
Yet peace and health are the priceless wealth
   That are found in the settler's cot.
We are freemen good—not a slave ever stood
   On our loved Canadian soil—
No tyrant's power can withhold for an hour
   The fruits of our honest toil.

Though to Britain is due love loyal and true—
   Where the bones of our fathers rest
Yet the forest land, with its rivers grand,
   Is the land that we love the best.
Here our sons in pride grow side by side,
   The joy of our peaceful hours;
And our daughters fair as the wild-flowers rare
   That bloom in the forest bowers.

Tho' the son of the soil has a life of toil,
  Yet calm and sweet is his rest;
He wakes from his dreams, ere the Day King's beams
  Have shone on the blue-jay's nest.
He drinks of the rills that gush from the hills,
  And the soil he tills is his own;
And as happy and free as a king is he—
  Who bows but to God alone.

When the welcome Spring comes on golden wing,
  In the sugar-bush, blithe and free,
We gather with care the life-blood rare,
  That flows from the maple tree.
And we plough and sow in hope, for we know,
  If we waste the beautiful Spring,
Our regret will be vain, when in Winter's reign
  Gaunt Famine is on the wing.

When the Autumn yields the fruits of the fields,
  A reward for our toil is given:
We thankfully take her gifts, which bespeak
  The love of our Father in heaven.
When the wintry blast goes howling past,
  Spreading sorrow and want in its way,
By the bright maple fire, safe from rude Winter's ire,
  We sit at the close of the day.
And our songs of praise we joyfully raise,
  High over stern Nature's strife,
As to Heaven ascend thanks for home and friends,
  And the joys of a Farmer's life.

—DEWART.

## NATURAL PHILOSOPHY.

WIDE is the scope of Natural Philosophy. It leads to an acquaintance with the laws that keep the planets in their undeviating path; it treats of the phenomena of the earth, the air, and the ocean; of the simple principles of mechanism that man employs; of the falling of the silent dew or the rushing of the roaring cataract; of the heat of summer and the frost of winter; of the zephyr-breeze or the destructive tornado; of the swimming of fishes or the flying of birds; of the ripple of the placid lake or the mountain waves of the ocean; of the grace, motion and powers of the human form; of the mechanism of the voice, the ear, and the eye.

By an acquaintance with its first principles—the embellishments of a palace, the necessities of a cottage, the swinging of a carriage, and the management of a dray, are all better accomplished. The elasticity of air and steam, that drives the vessel despite of tide or wind, or sends tons of merchandize with surprising velocity to the extremes of a kingdom, are by its teaching comprehended. Knowing the cause of the awful voice of thunder, of the terrific destruction of lightning, and of the peaceful beauties of the rainbow, much ignorant teaching is dispelled. Man has so advanced in his comprehension of nature, that he chains one of the most fearful elements to his use, which he guides and directs as if it were possessed of the feebleness of a helpless babe; with it he sends his thoughts with a speed surpassing the rapid flight of time. No one can feel but abashed at not understanding the simple principles that produce such seemingly miraculous effects.

It is the duty of the natural philosopher, and the student in physics, to ascertain the nature and causes of the mysterious phenomena by which we are surrounded. Ultimate causes are certainly beyond our powers of analysis; we may approximate to a knowledge of some of them, but we cannot ascertain their nature, or the actual extent of their influence. Nearly all the appearances in nature may be resolved into the production of motion; and we are able to ascertain its laws, but cannot discover its origin.

The most important progress in Natural Philosophy by which the present century is distinguished, has been the discovery of a general law which embraces and rules all the various branches of physic and chemistry. This law is of as much importance for the highest speculations on the nature of forces, as for immediate and practical questions in the construction of machines. This law is now known by the name of "the principle of conservation of force." It might be better perhaps to call it, with Mr. Rankine, "the conservation of energy," because it does not relate to that which we call commonly *intensity of force*. It does not mean that the intensity of the natural force is constant; but it relates more to the whole amount of power which can be gained by any natural process, and by which a certain amount of work can be done. For example: if we apply this law to gravity, it does not mean, what is strictly and undoubtedly true, that the intensity of the gravity of any given body is the same as often as the body is brought back to the same distance from the centre of the earth. Or with regard to the other elementary forces of nature, *chemical force*: when two chemical elements come together, so that they influence each other either from a distance or by immediate contact, they will always exert the same force upon each other—the same force both in intensity, and in its direction, and in its quantity. This other law, indeed, is true; but it is not the same as the principle of conservation of force. We may express the meaning of the law of conservation of force by saying, that every force of nature, when it effects any alteration, loses and exhausts its faculty to effect the same alteration a second time. But while, by every alteration in nature, that force which has been the cause of this alteration is exhausted, there is always another force which gains as much power of producing new alterations in nature as the first has lost. Although, therefore, it is the nature of all inorganic forces to become exhausted by their own working, the power of the whole system in which these alterations take place, is neither exhausted nor increased by quantity, but only changed in form. Some special examples will enable us better to understand this law than any general theories. To begin with gravity,—that most general force, which not only exerts its influence over the whole universe, but which at the same time supplies the motive power to a very large number of our machines. Clocks and smaller machines are generally set in motion by a weight. The same is really the case with water-mills. Water-mills are driven by falling water, and it is the gravity, the weight of the falling water, which moves the mill. Now by water mills, or by a falling weight, any machine can be put in motion; and by such motive power every sort of work can be done which can be done at all by any machine. Therefore the weight of a heavy body, either solid or fluid, which descends from a higher place to a lower place is a motive power, and can do every sort of mechanical work. But if the weight has fallen down to the earth, then it has the same amount of gravity, the same intensity of gravity; and its power to move, its power to work, is exhausted; it must become again raised before it can work anew. In this sense, therefore, the faculty of producing a new work is exhausted—is lost; and this holds true of every power of nature, when this power has once produced alteration. —HOGG.

## CANADIAN CHRISTMAS CAROL.

No shepherds in the field to-night, no flocks upon the wold,
Thro' the shivering forest branches moans the north blast fierce and cold ;
But gloriously the white stars gleam as on that holy even
When the herald Angels' chorus swell'd through the soft Judean heaven.

Oh, Earth ! the white shrouds wraps thee now, in Death's cold grasp thou art,
Thy tears, thy music, bound alike in the ice-chain on thine heart :
So lay the darken'd world of sin, when the Angels spread abroad
The glorious tale of the Virgin-born—the birth of Incarnate God !

Melt, melt, oh cold and stony heart ! even as the ice-bonds shiver,
When Spring breathes soft on the frozen wood, when warm winds loose the river—
The Angel-vision sheds on thee its glory's softening ray—
The Angel-song is for thine ear, " A Saviour's born to-day !"

Morn on the sparkling wilds of snow—morn on the frozen West !
The holy chimes float musical o'er the deep wood's solemn breast ;
And the winter's sun plays cheerily on the wealth of bright green wreaths
Which thro' the lowly forest-shrine a spring-like freshness breathes.

Frail monitors ! your verdure speaks all eloquently bright,
Of a lustrous summer-morn to break on Life's long wintry night—
Of the waving palms—the crystal streams—the everlasting flowers,
Beyond the jasper battlement, by the Golden City's towers !

Let the wild wind sweep the snows without—within be joy and mirth ;
Let happy households cheerily meet around the Christmas hearth !
One welcome pledge must circle round—" Be happy hearts and smiles
To all we love in the forest land ! to all in our parent isles !"

The Christmas hearth ! Ah pleasant spot, where joyful kindred meet—
Kind eyes, with love and gladness lit, scarce mark the vacant seat ;
And if too-faithful Memory turn to mourn the loved, the fair—
Look up—the Shepherd's star's in heaven the lost one waits thee there !

Wake thy ten thousand voices, Earth ! outpour thy floods of praise
Up to the crystal gates of morn the deep hosannas raise !
Till heavenward wafted, seraph-wing'd, they pierce th' illumin'd zone
Where the Church-Triumphant's anthem floats round the Everlasting Throne !

—*Toronto Maple Leaf.*

# THE TELESCOPE AND THE MICROSCOPE.

It was the telescope that, by piercing the obscurity which lies between us and distant worlds, put Infidelity in possession of the argument against which we are now contending. But, about the time of its invention, another instrument was formed which laid open a scene no less wonderful, and rewarded the inquisitive spirit of man with a discovery which serves to neutralize the whole of this argument. This was the microscope. The one led me to see a system in every star. The other leads me to see a world in every atom. The one taught me, that this mighty globe, with the whole burden of its people and of its countries, is but a grain of sand on the high field of immensity. The other teaches me, that every grain of sand may harbor within it the tribes and the families of a busy population. The one told me of the insignificance of the world I tread upon. The other redeems it from all its insignificance; for it tells me that in the leaves of every forest, and in the flowers of every garden, and in the waters of every rivulet, there are worlds teeming with life, and numberless as are the glories of the firmament. The one has suggested to me, that beyond and above all that is visible to man, there may lie fields of creation which sweep immeasurably along, and carry the impress of the Almighty's hand to the remotest scenes of the universe. The other suggests to me, that within and beneath all that minuteness which the aided eye of man has been able to explore, there may lie a region of invisibles: and that, could we draw aside the mysterious curtain which shrouds it from our senses, we might there see a theatre of as many wonders as astronomy has unfolded, a universe within the compass of a point so small, as to elude all the powers of the microscope, but where the wonder-working God finds room for the exercise of all His attributes, where He can raise another mechanism of worlds, and fill and animate them all with the evidences of His glory.

Now, mark how all this may be made to meet the argument of our infidel astronomers. By the telescope, they have discovered that no magnitude, however vast, is beyond the grasp of the Divinity. But by the microscope we have also discovered that no minuteness, however shrunk from the notice of the human eye, is beneath the condescension of His regard. Every addition to the powers of the one instrument extends the limit of His visible dominions. But by every addition to the powers of the other instrument, we see each part of them more crowded than before with the wonders of His unwearying hand. The one is constantly widening the circle of his territory. The other is as constantly filling up its separate portions with all that is rich and various and exquisite. In a word, by the one I am told that the Almighty is now at work in regions more distant than geometry has ever measured, and among worlds more manifold than numbers have ever reached. But, by the other, I am also told, that with a mind to comprehend the whole, in the vast compass of its generality, He has also a mind to concentrate a close and a separate attention on each and on all of its particulars; and that the same God, who sends forth an upholding influence among the orbs and the movements of astronomy, can fill the recesses of every single atom with the intimacy of His presence, and travel, in all the greatness of His unimpaired attributes, upon every one spot and corner of the universe He has formed. They, therefore, who think that God will not put forth such a power, and such a goodness and such a condescension in behalf of this world, as are ascribed to him in the New Testament, because He has so many other worlds to attend to, think of Him as a man,—they confine their view to the informations of the telescope, and forget altogether the informations of the other instrument. They only find room in their minds for His one attribute of a large and general superintendence; and keep out of their remembrance the equally impressive proofs we have for His other attribute, of a minute and multiplied attention to all that diversity of operations, where it is He that worketh all in all. And when I think that as one of the instruments of philosophy has heightened our every impression of the first of these attributes, so another instrument has no less heightened our impression of the second of them—then I can no longer resist the conclusion, that it would be a transgression of sound argument, as well as a daring of impiety, to draw a limit around the doings of this unsearchable God—and should a professed revelation from heaven tell me of an act of condescension in behalf of some separate world, so wonderful that angels desired to look into it, and the Eternal Son had to move from His seat of glory to carry it into accomplishment, all I ask is the evidence of such a revelation; for, let it tell me as much as it may of God letting Himself down for the benefit of one single province of His dominions, this is no more than what I see lying scattered in numberless examples before me—and running through the whole line of my recollections—and meeting me in every walk of observation to which I can betake myself; and, now that the microscope has unveiled the wonders of another region, I see strewed around me, with a profusion which baffles my every attempt to comprehend it, the evidence that there is no one portion of the universe of God too minute for His notice, nor too humble for the visitations of His care.

As the end of all these illustrations, let me bestow a single paragraph on what I conceive to be the precise state of this argument.

It is a wonderful thing that God should be so unencumbered by the concerns of the whole universe, that he can give a constant attention to every moment of every individual in this world's population. But, wonderful as it is, you do not hesitate to admit it as true, on the evidence of your own recollections. It is a wonderful thing that He, whose eye is at every instant on so many worlds, should have peopled the world we inhabit with all the traces of the varied design and benevolence which abound in it. But, great as the wonder is, you do not allow so much as the shadow of improbability to darken it, for its reality is what you actually witness, and you never think of questioning the evidence of observation. It is wonderful, it is passing wonderful, that the same God, whose presence is diffused through immensity, and who spreads the ample canopy of His administration over all its dwelling-places, should, with an energy as fresh and as unexpended as if He had only begun the work of creation, turn Him to the neighborhood around us, and lavish on its every handbreadth all the exuberance of His goodness, and crowd it with the many thousand varieties of conscious existence. But, be the wonder incomprehensible as it may, you do not suffer in your mind the burden of a single doubt to lie upon it, because you do not question the report of the microscope. You do not refuse its information, nor turn away from it as an incompetent channel of evidence. But to bring it still nearer to the point at issue, there are many who never looked through a microscope, but who rest an implicit faith in all its revelations; and upon what evidence, I would ask? Upon the evidence of testimony—upon the credit they give to the authors of the books they have read, and the belief they put in the record of their observations. Now, at this point I make my stand. It is wonderful that God should be so interested in the redemption of a single world, as to send forth His well-beloved Son upon the errand; and He to accomplish it, should, mighty to save, put forth all His strength, and travail in the greatness of it. But such wonders as these have already multiplied upon you; and when evidence is given of their truth, you have resigned your every judgment of the unsearchable God, and rested in the faith of them. I demand, in the name of sound and consistent philosophy, that you do the same in the matter before us—and take it up as a question of evidence—and examine that medium of testimony through which the miracles and informations of the Gospel have come to your door—and go not to admit as argument here, what would not be admitted as argument in any of the analogies of nature and observation—and take along with you in this field of inquiry, a lesson which you should have learned upon other fields—even the depth of the riches both of the wisdom and the knowledge of God, that His judgments are unsearchable, and His ways are past finding out. —CHALMERS.

## CONTENTMENT.

SEE the soft green willow springing
   Where the waters gently pass,
Every way her free arms flinging
   O'er the moist and reedy grass.
Long ere winter blasts are fled,
See her tipp'd with vernal red,
And her kindly flower display'd
Ere her leaf can cast a shade.

Though the rudest hand assail her,
   Patiently she droops awhile,
But when showers and breezes hail her,
   Wears again her willing smile.
Thus I learn Contentment's power
From the slighted willow bower,
Ready to give thanks and live
On the least that Heaven may give. —KEBLE.

## LIGHT.

God said—" Let there be light !"
Grim darkness felt his might,
    And fled away ;
Then startled seas and mountains cold
Shone forth, all bright in blue and gold,
    And cried—" 'T is day ! 't is day !"
" Hail holy light !" exclaim'd
The thunderous cloud that flam'd
    O'er daisies white ;
And lo ! the rose, in crimson dress'd,
Lean'd sweetly on the lily's breast ;
    And blushing murmur'd—" Light !"
            —ELLIOTT.

## MUSIC.

MUSIC, though now a very complex and difficult art, is, in truth, a gift of the Author of Nature to the whole human race. Its existence and influence are to be traced in the records of every people from the earliest ages, and are perceptible, at the present time, in every quarter of the globe. It is a part of the benevolent order of Providence, that we are capable of receiving, from the objects around us, pleasures independent of the immediate purposes for which they have been created. Our eyes do not merely enable us to see external things, so as to avail ourselves of their useful properties ; they enable us also to enjoy the delight produced by the perception of *beauty*, a perception which (upon whatever principle it may be explained,) is something distinct from any consideration of the mere utility of an object. We could have had the most accurate perceptions of the form and position of everything that constitutes the most beautiful landscape, without receiving any idea of its beauty. We could have beheld the sun setting amid the glowing tints of a summer evening, without thinking of anything beyond the advantage of serene weather ; we might have contemplated the glassy expanse of the ocean reflecting the tranquil beams of the moon, without any other feeling than the comfort of a safe and easy navigation ; and the varieties of hill and dale, of shady woods and luxuriant verdure, might have been pleasant only in the eyes of farmers or graziers. We could, too, have listened to *sounds* with equal indifference to everything beyond the mere information they conveyed to us; and the sighing of the breeze, or the murmuring of the brook, while we learned from them nothing of which we could avail ourselves, might have been heard without pleasure. It is evident that the perception of external things, for the mere purpose of making use of them, has no connexion with the feeling of their beauty; and that our Creator, therefore, has bestowed on us this additional feeling, for the purpose of augmenting our happiness. Had he not had this design, he might have left us without the sense of beauty or deformity. "If God," says Paley, "had wished our misery, he might have made sure of his purpose by forming our senses to be as many sores and pains to us as they are now instruments of our gratification and enjoyment; or by placing us among objects so ill-suited to our perceptions, as to have continually offended us, instead of ministering to our refreshment and delight. He might have made, for instance, everything we saw loathsome, everything we touched a sting, and every sound a discord."

In place of every sound being a discord, the greater part of the sounds which we hear are more or less agreeable to us. The infinite variety of sounds produced by the winds and waters,—the cries of animals, the notes of birds,—and, above all, the tones of the human voice, all affect us with various kinds and degrees of pleasure; and, in general, it may be said, that it is such sounds as indicate something to be feared and avoided, such as the howling of wild beasts, or the hissing of serpents, that are positively painful to our ears. In this sense, all nature may be said to be full of music; the disagreeable and discordant sounds being (as in artificial music), in such proportion only as to heighten the pleasure derived from those which are agreeable. The human voice is that which pleases us chiefly, and affects us most powerfully. Its natural tones and accents are calculated to penetrate the heart of the listener; and the union of these to articulate speech, in every language, not only produces a melody which pleases the ear, but an effect on the feelings, of which the mere words would be incapable. These natural tones of the voice, either by themselves, or joined to articulate language, constitute music in its simplest state; and the pleasures and feelings derived from such music must necessarily have existed in every form of society.

The history of Music, therefore, is coeval with the history of our species. In the earlier ages of the world, of the music of which no remains have descended to the present times, its history must be gleaned from ancient literature ; and the scanty lights thus afforded, must be aided, (as far as possible,) by conjectures derived from the state of music in those rude and primitive stages of society which come under our own observation. Volumes upon volumes have been written upon the music of the ancients, full of learned research and ingenious speculation ; but the results have by no means repaid the labor. From these works, a good deal of information may be acquired respecting the customs and the manners of the ancients ; but they hardly contain a single fact which can be of any use to the practical musician of the present day, or to those *dilettanti* who prosecute musical inquiries from a love of the art as it now exists.

Without reference to historical details of any sort, it may be concluded, from the existence of music in every state of society at the present day, that it also existed in the earliest ages of the world. We find that the music of uncultivated tribes, and the music which, in civilized nations, has descended from their rude ancestors, though presenting many varieties, arising from the character of the people, the genius of their language, and other causes, has yet a strong general resemblance. By analysing the simple melodies found among the common people of Scotland, Ireland, France, and other parts of Europe, and in Hindostan, Persia, the Islands of the Indian Ocean, Africa, and even China, it is discovered that these melodies are formed upon a certain scale or series of sounds, which, therefore, is dictated and rendered agreeable to our ears by an original law of nature ; and this scale, too, is substantially the same as that on which the most artificial music of the present day is founded, the latter being only rendered more extensive and complete. It cannot, then, be doubted, that, in the most ancient time, there existed melodies founded on a similar scale, ánd possessing similar characters to the national music of the present day: and it may reasonably be supposed, that the strains, for example, of the shepherds and herdsmen of the patriarchal ages, whose manners are so beautifully described in Holy Writ, were nearly akin to the untutored lays which are found to express the loves and griefs of the present pastoral inhabitants of similar regions. —HOGARTH.

## THE VOICE OF THE WIND.

The wind, when first he rose and went abroad
Through the waste region, felt himself at fault,
Wanting a voice : and suddenly to earth
Descended with a wafture and a swoop,
Where, wandering volatile from kind to kind,
He wooed the several trees to give him one.
First he besought the ash ; the voice she lent
Fitfully with a free and lasting change,
Flung here and there its sad uncertainties :
The aspen next ; a fluttered frivolous twitter
Was her sole tribute : from the willow came,
So long as dainty summer dressed her out,
A whispering sweetness, but her winter note
Was hissing, dry, and reedy : lastly the pine
Did he solicit, and from her he drew
A voice so constant, soft, and lowly deep,
That there he rested, welcoming in her
A mild memorial of the ocean-cave
Where he was born.
—Taylor.

## THE SPRING.

Sweet daughter of a rough and stormy sire,
Hoar winter's blooming child, delightful spring!
   Whose unshorn locks with leaves
   And swelling buds are crowned;

From the green islands of eternal youth
(Crowned with fresh blooms, and ever-springing shade)
   Turn, hither turn thy step
   O thou, whose pow'rful voice

More sweet than softest touch of Doric reed,
Or Lydian flute, can soothe the madding winds,
   And thro' the stormy deep
   Breathe thy own tender calm.

Unlock thy copious stores ; those tender showers
That drop their sweetness on the infant buds ;
   And silent dews that swell
   The milky ear's green stem.
—Barbauld.

# SIEGE OF GIBRALTAR.
(A.D. 1782.)

FOR several months did the port of Algesiras resound with the stir and din of this great armament. Ten large ships were cut down as bases of the floating batteries; 200,000 cubic feet of timber were assigned for their construction; and they were mounted with 142 pieces of artillery, exclusive of those on the land side. Yet formidable as might seem such equipments, daily going on before his eyes, the Governor was in no degree dispirited. He continued with unremitting energy all his preparations for defence, placing especial hope in the system of red-hot balls, which were first devised and recommended by his Lieutenant-Governor, Boyd. To prepare them in sufficient numbers, there was a large distribution of furnaces and grates throughout the English troops. And so familiar did our soldiers grow, as was wished, with these new implements of death, that, in speaking of them to each other, their common phrase was "the roasted potatoes."

Early in September, the preparations of the Fre. - and Spaniards were almost completed, and in the second week their united fleet, so lately threatening the ·British Channel, sailed into Algesiras Bay. It was thought desirable to proceed at once to the grand attack, so as to anticipate the arrival of Lord Howe. On the morning of the 13th, accordingly, the signal was given; and while from all the lines on shore was maintained the tremendous fire which they had opened for some days, the ten floating batteries from Algesiras bore down in admirable order for their appointed stations. Before ten o'clock they were anchored at regular distances within six hundred yards of the English works. Then commenced a cannonade on both sides so fierce, so incessant, and from such a number of pieces of artillery, as it is alleged had never been seen since the discovery of gunpowder. During many hours the attack and the defence were steadily maintained; no superiority as yet being seen on either side. The English fire was not silenced, but, on the other hand, it could by no means prevail against the massy and strong-built sea-towers. The heaviest shells rebounded from their tops; the red-hot balls seemed to make no impression on their sides; or if by these last a momentary spark was kindled, it was at once subdued by the water-engines which they had on board. At length in the afternoon the discharges of their ordnance visibly slackened; and it became apparent that several of the last red-hot balls which had pierced their sides could not be extinguished. Before midnight the Talla Piedra, the strongest of the battering vessels, and the flag-ship, the Pastora, by her side, were in full flames, by the light of which the artillery of the garrison could resume its volleys and direct them with the surest aim. "The rock and neighboring objects," says an eye-witness, "were highly illuminated, forming with the constant flashes of our cannon a mingled scene of sublimity and terror." Six more of the battering ships caught fire, and the question to the French and Spaniards upon them was no longer of victory or conquest, but of life. Dismal shrieks were heard in the intervals of firing from the poor wretches who expired in the flames or in the waves: and numbers more were seen as they faintly clung to the sides of the burning vessels or floated on pieces of timber from the wrecks. More than sixteen hundred of the enemy are computed to have perished. Much greater still would have been the havoc, but for the humanity of our countrymen—above all, of Captain Curtis, with the sailors of the marine brigade, who no sooner saw the victory decided than they strained every nerve to save the vanquished. By their exertions between three and four hundred men were brought to shore. Eight of the floating batteries were already consuming or consumed; it was hoped to preserve the two that remained as trophies, but unexpectedly the one burst into flames and blew up, and it was deemed requisite, after a survey, to burn the other. Thus did the morrow's sun, instead of still beholding those vast sea towers which had so lately breasted the waves in all their pride, and "instinct with life and motion," shine only upon shattered hulls or stranded fragments from the wrecks. Thus did the Pillars of Hercules, so conspicuous as emblems on the device of the Emperor Charles the Fifth, with their ancient motto, NEC PLUS ULTRA; and borne by him upon his banners in the wars against King Francis the First, now in British hands baffle and beat back all the endeavors of the heirs of Charles the Fifth and Francis the First combined!

            · · Lord Mahon.

## FORE-KNOWLEDGE.

Too curious man, why dost thou seek to know
Events, which, good or ill, foreknown, are woe ;
Th' all-seeing power that made thee mortal, gave
Thee every thing a mortal state should have ;
Foreknowledge only is enjoy'd by heaven ;
And, for his peace of mind, to man forbidden:
Wretched were life, if he foreknew his doom ;
Even joys foreseen give pleasing hope no room,
And griefs assur'd are felt before they come.
—DRYDEN.

## THE USE OF ADVERSITY.

THE world had never taken so full note
Of what thou art, hadst thou not been undone ;
And only thy affliction hath begot
More fame, than thy best fortunes could have done:
For ever by adversity are wrought
The greatest works of admiration ;
And all the fair examples of renown,
Out of distress and misery are grown.

How could we know that thou couldst have endur'd,
With a reposed cheer, wrong and disgrace ;
And with a heart and countenance assur'd,
Have look'd stern Death and horror in the face !
How should we know thy soul had been secur'd,
In honest counsels, and in way unbase ;
Hadst thou not stood to show us what thou wert,
By thy affliction that descry'd thy heart !

It is not but the tempest that doth show
The seaman's cunning ; but the field that tries
The captain's courage : and we come to know
Best what men are, in their worst jeopardies.   —DANIEL.

## GOD'S CARE FOR MAN.

AND is there care in heaven ? And is there love
In heavenly spirits to these creatures base,
That may compassion of their evils move?
There is : else much more wretched were the case
Of men than beasts. But O th' exceeding grace
Of highest God, that loves his creatures so,
And all his workes with mercy doth embrace,
That blessed angels he sends to and fro,
To serve to wicked man, to serve his wicked foe.

How oft do they their silver bowers leave
To come to succour us, that succour want,
How oft do they with golden pineons cl
The flitting skyes, like flying pursuivant;
Against foule feendes to aide us militant:
They for us fight, they watch and dewly ward,
And their bright squadrons round about us plant
And all for love, and nothing for reward:
O, why should heavenly God to men have such regard?
—SPENSER.

## MACHINERY.

THE utility of machinery, in its application to manufatures, consists in the addition which it makes to human power, the economy of time, and in the conversion of substances apparently worthless into valuable products. The forces derived from wind, from water, and from steam are so many additions to human power, and the total inanimate force thus obtained in Great Britain (including the commercial and manufacturing) has been calculated, by Dupin, to be equivalent to that of 20,000,000 laborers. Experiments have shown that the force necessary to move a stone on the smoothed floor of its quarry is nearly two-thirds of its weight; on a wooden floor, three-fifths; if soaped, one-sixth; upon rollers on the quarry floor, one thirty-second; upon wood, one-fortieth. At each increase of knowledge, and on the contrivance of every new tool, human labor is abridged: the man who contrived rollers quintupled his power over brute matter. The next use of machinery is the economy of time, and this is too apparent to require illustration, and may result either from the increase of force, or from the improvement in the contrivance of tools, or from both united. Instances of the production of valuable substances from worthless materials, are constantly occurring in all the arts; and though this may appear to be merely the consequence of scientific knowledge, yet it is evident that science cannot exist, nor could its lessons be made productive by application, without machinery. In the history of every science, we find the improvements of its machinery, the invention of instruments, to constitute an important part. The chemist, the astronomer, the physician, the husbandman, the painter, the sculptor, is such only by the application of machinery. Applied science in all its forms, and the fine and useful arts, are the triumphs of the mind, indeed, but gained through the instrumentality of machinery. The difference between a tool and a machine is not capable of very precise distinction, nor is it necessary, in a popular examination of them, to make any distinction. A tool is usually a more simple machine, and generally used by the hand; a machine is a complex tool, a collection of tools, and frequently put in action by inanimate force. All machines are intended either to produce power, or merely to transmit power and execute work. Of the class of mechanical agents by which motion is transmitted,—the lever, the pully, the wedge,—it has been demonstrated that no power is gained by their use, however combined. Whatever force is applied at one part, can only be exerted at some other, diminished by friction and other incidental causes; and whatever is gained in the rapidity of execution, is compensated by the necessity of exerting additional force. These two principles should be constantly borne in mind, and teach us to limit our attempts to things which are possible.

1. *Accumulating Power.* When the work to be done requires more force for its execution than can be generated in the time necessary for its completion, recourse must be had to some mechanical method of preserving and condensing a part of the power exerted previously to the commencement of the process. This is most frequently accomplished by a fly-wheel, which is a wheel having a heavy rim, so that the greater part of the weight is near the circumference. It requires great power, applied for some time, to set this in rapid motion, and, when moving with considerable velocity, if its force is concentrated on a point, its effects are exceedingly powerful. Another method of accumulating power consists in raising a weight, and then allowing it to fall. A man, with a heavy hammer, may strike repeated blows on a head of a pile without any effect; but a heavy weight, raised by machinery to a greater height, though the blow is less frequently repeated, produces the desired effect.

2. *Regulating Power.* Uniformity and steadiness in the motion of machinery are essential both to its success and its duration. The governor in the steam-engine is a contrivance for this purpose. A vane or fly of little weight, but large surface, is also used. It revolves rapidly, and soon acquires a

uniform rate, which it cannot much exceed; because any addition to its velocity produces a greater addition to the resistance of the air. This kind of fly is generally used in small pieces of mechanism, and, unlike the heavy fly, it serves to destroy, instead of to preserve, force.

3. *Increase of Velocity.* Operations requiring a trifling exertion of force may become fatiguing by the rapidity of motion necessary, or a degree of rapidity may be desirable beyond the power of muscular action. Whenever the work itself is light, it becomes necessary to increase the velocity in order to economize time. Thus twisting the fibres of wool by the fingers would be a most tedious operation. In the common spinning-wheel, the velocity of the foot is moderate, but, by a simple contrivance, that of the thread is most rapid. A band, passing round a large wheel, and then round a small spindle, effects this change. This contrivance is a common one in machines.

4. *Diminution of Velocity.* This is commonly required for the purpose of overcoming great resistances with small power. Systems of pullies afford an example of this: in the smoke-jack, a greater velocity is produced than is required, and it is therefore moderated by transmission through a number of wheels.

5. *Spreading the Action of Force exerted for a few minutes over a large Time.* This is one of the most common and useful employments of machinery. The half minute which we spend daily in winding up our watches is an exertion of force which, by the aid of a few wheels, is spread over twenty-four hours. A great number of automata, moved by springs, may be classed under this division.

6. *Saving Time in natural Operations.* The process of tanning consists in combining the tanning principle with every particle of the skin, which, by the ordinary process of soaking it in a solution of tanning matter, requires from six months to two years. By enclosing the solution, with the hide, in a close vessel, and exhausting the air, the pores of the hide being deprived of air, exert a capillary attraction on the tan, which may be aided by pressure, so that the thickest hides may be tanned in six weeks. The operation of bleaching affords another example.

7. *Exerting Forces too large for human Power.* When the force of large bodies of men or animals is applied, it becomes

difficult to concentrate it simultaneously at a given point. The power of steam, air, or water is employed to overcome resistances which would require a great expense to surmount by animal labor. The twisting of the largest cables, the rolling, hammering, and cutting of large masses of iron, the draining of mines, require enormous exertions of physical force, continued for considerable periods. Other means are used when the force required is great, and the space through which it is to act is small. The hydraulic press can, by the exertion of one man, produce a pressure of 1500 atmospheres.

8. *Executing Operations too delicate for human Touch.* The same power which twists the stoutest cable, and weaves the coarsest canvas, may be employed to more advantage than human hands in spinning the gossamer thread of the cotton, and entwining with fairy fingers, the meshes of the most delicate fabric.

9. *Registering Operations.* Machinery affords a sure means of remedying the inattention of human agents, by instruments, for instance, for counting the strokes of an engine, or the number of coins struck in the press. The tell-tale, a piece of mechanism connected with a clock in an apartment to which a watchman has not access, reveals whether he has neglected, at any hour of his watch, to pull a string in token of his vigilance.

10. *Economy of Materials.* The precision with which all operations are executed by machinery, and the exact similarity of the articles made, produce a degree of economy in the consumption of the raw material which is sometimes of great importance. In reducing the trunk of a tree to planks, the axe was formerly used, with a loss of at least half the material. The saw produces thin boards, with a loss of not more than an eighth of the material.

11. *The Identity of the Result.* Nothing is more remarkable than the perfect similarity of things manufactured by the same tool. If the top of a box is to be made to fit over the lower part, it may be done by gradually advancing the tool of the sliding rest; after this adjustment, no additional care is requisite in making a thousand boxes. The same result appears in all the arts of printing: the impressions from the same block, or the same copperplate, have a similarity which no labor of the hand could produce.

12. *Accuracy of the Work.* The accuracy with which machinery executes its work is, perhaps, one of the most important advantages. It would hardly be possible for a very skilful workman, with files and polishing substances, to form a perfect cylinder out of a piece of steel. This process, by the aid of the lathe and the sliding rest, is the every day employment of hundreds of workmen. On these two last advantages of machinery depends the system of copying, by which pictures of the original may be multiplied, and thus almost unlimited pains may be bestowed in producing the model, which shall cost 10,000 times the price of each individual specimen of its perfections. Operations of copying take place, by printing, by casting, by moulding, by stamping, by punching, with elongation, with altered dimensions. A remarkable example of the arts of copying lies before the eye of the reader in these pages. 1. They are copies obtained by printing from stereotype plates. 2. Those plates are copies obtained (by casting) from moulds formed of plaster of Paris. 3. The moulds are copies obtained by pouring the plaster in a liquid state upon the moveable types. 4. The types are copies (by casting) from moulds of copper, called *matrices*. 5. The lower part of the matrices, bearing the impressions of the letters or characters are copies (by punching) from steel punches, on which the same characters exist in relief. 6. The cavities in these steel punches, as in the middle of the letters, *a*, *b*, &c., are produced from other steel punches in which those parts are in relief.

—*Popular Encyclopædia.*

## BERNARDO AND ALPHONSO.

With some good ten of his chosen men, Bernardo hath appear'd
Before them all in the palace hall, the lying king to beard ;
With cap in hand, and eye on ground, he came in reverend guise,
But ever and anon he frown'd, and flame broke from his eyes.

" A curse upon thee," cries the king, "who com'st unbid to me ;
But what from traitor's blood should spring, save traitors like to thee ?
His sire, Lords, had a traitor's heart ; perchance our champion brave
May think it were a pious part to share Don Sancho's grave."

" Whoever told this tale—the king hath rashness to repeat,"
Cries Bernard, " Here my gage I fling before Tur Liar's feet !
No treason was in Sancho's blood, no stain in mine doth lie—
Below the throne what knight will own the coward calumny ?

"The blood that I like water shed, when Roland did advance,
By secret traitors hired and led, to make us slaves of France;
The life of King Alphonso I saved at Roncesval,—
Your words, Lord King, are recompense abundant for it all.

"Your horse was down—your hope was flown—I saw the falchion shine,
That soon had drank your royal blood, had I not ventured mine;
But memory soon of service done deserteth the ingrate,
And ye've thank'd the son, for life and crown, by the father's bloody fate.

"Ye swore upon your kingly faith, to set Don Sancho free,
But, shame upon your paltering breath, the light he ne'er did see;
He died in dungeon cold and dim, by Alphonso's base decree,
And visage blind, and stiffen'd limb, were all they gave to me.

"The king that swerveth from his word hath stain'd his purple black,
No Spanish Lord will draw the sword behind a liar's back:
But noble vengeance shall be mine, an open hate I'll show—
The King hath injured Carpio's line, and Bernard is his foe."

"Seize—seize him!"—loud the king doth scream—"There are a thousand here—
Let his foul blood this instant stream—What, caitiffs, do you fear?
Seize—seize the traitor!"—But not one to move a finger dareth,—
Bernardo standeth by the throne, and calm his sword he bareth.

He drew the falchion from the sheath, and held it up on high,
And all the hall was still as death: cries Bernard, " Here am I,
And here is the sword that owns no lord, excepting Heaven and me;
Fain would I know who dares his point—King, Condé, or Grandee!"

Then to his mouth the horn he drew—(it hung below his cloak)—
His ten true men the signal knew—and through the ring they broke,
With helm on head, and blade in hand, the knights the circle brake,
And back the lordlings 'gan to stand, and the false king to quake.

"Ha! Bernard," quoth Alphonso, "what means this warlike guise?
Ye know full well I jested—ye know your worth I prize."
But Bernard turn'd upon his heel, and smiling pass'd away—
Long rued Alphonso and his realm the jesting of that day.
—LOCKHART.

## ALONZO DE AGUILAR.

IT was determined by the chiefs to strike at once into the heart of the Red Sierra, as it was called from the color of its rocks, rising to the east of Ronda, and the principal theatre of insurrection. On the 18th of March, 1501, the little army encamped before Monarda, on the skirts of a mountain, where the Moors were understood to have assembled in considerable force. They had not been long in these quarters before parties of the enemy were seen hovering along the slopes of the mountain, from which the Christian camp was divided by a narrow river, —the Rio Verde, probably, which has gained such mournful celebrity in Spanish song. Aguilar's troops, who occupied the van, were so much roused by the sight of the enemy, that a small party, seizing a banner, rushed across the stream without orders, in pursuit of them. The odds, however were so great, that they would have been severely handled, had not Aguilar, while he bitterly condemned their temerity, advanced promptly to their support with the remainder of his corps. The Count of Urena followed with the central division, leaving the Count of Cifuentes with the troops of Seville to protect the camp.

The Moors fell back as the Christians advanced, and retreating nimbly from point to point, led them up the rugged steep far into the recesses of the mountains. At length they reached an open level, encompassed on all sides by a natural rampart of rocks, where they had deposited their valuable effects, together with their wives and children. The latter, at sight of the invaders, uttered dismal cries, and fled into the remoter depths of the Sierra.

The Christians were too much attracted by the rich spoil before them to think of following, and dispersed in every direction in quest of plunder, with all the heedlessness and insubordination of raw, inexperienced levies. It was in vain that Alonzo de Aguilar reminded them that their wily enemy was still unconquered; or that he endeavored to force them into the ranks again, and restore order. No one heeded his call, or thought of anything beyond the present moment, and of securing as much booty to himself as he could carry.

The Moors, in the mean while, finding themselves no longer pursued, were aware of the occupation of the Christians, whom they not improbably had purposely decoyed into the snare. They resolved to return to the scene of action, and surprise their incautious enemy. Stealthily advancing, therefore, under the shadows of night, now falling thick around, they poured through the rocky defiles of the enclosure upon the astonished Spaniards. An unlucky explosion, at this crisis, of a cask of powder, into which a spark had accidentally fallen, threw a broad glare over the scene, and revealed for a moment the situation of the hostile parties—the Spaniards in the utmost disorder, many of them without arms, and staggering under the weight of their fatal booty; while their enemies were seen gliding, like so many demons of darkness, through every crevice and avenue of the enclosure, in the act of springing on their devoted victims. This appalling spectacle, vanishing almost as soon as seen, and followed by the hideous yells and war-cries of the assailants, struck a panic into the hearts of the soldiers, who fled, scarcely offering any resistance. The darkness of the night was as favorable to the Moors, familiar with all the intricacies of the ground, as it was fatal to the Christians, who, bewildered in the mazes of the Sierra, and losing their footing at every step, fell under the swords of their pursuers, or went down the dark gulfs and precipices which yawned all around.

Amidst this dreadful confusion, the Count de Urena succeeded in gaining a lower level of the Sierra, where he halted and endeavored to rally his panic-struck followers. His noble comrade, Alonzo de Aguilar, still maintained his position on the heights above, refusing all entreaties of his followers to attempt a retreat. "When," said he proudly, "was the banner of Aguilar ever known to fly from the field?" His eldest son, the heir of his house and honors, Don Pedro de Cordova, a youth of great promise, fought at his side. He had received a severe wound on the head from a stone, and a javelin had pierced quite through his leg. With one knee resting on the ground, however, he still made a brave defence with his sword. The sight was too much for his father, and he implored him to suffer himself to be removed from the field. "Let not the hopes of our house be crushed at a single blow," said he; "go, my son, live as becomes a Christian knight—live, and cherish your desolate mother." All his endeavors were fruitless, however, and the gallant boy refused to leave his father's side, till he was forcibly borne away by the attendants, who fortunately succeeded in bringing him in safety to the station occupied by the Count de Urena.

Meantime, the brave little band of cavaliers, who remained true to Aguilar, had fallen one after another; and the chief, left almost alone, retreated to a huge rock which rose in the middle of the plain, and placing his back against it, still made fight, though weakened by loss of blood, like a lion at bay, against his enemies. In this situation he was pressed so hard by a Moor of uncommon size and strength, that he was compelled to turn and close with him in single combat. The strife was long and desperate, till Don Alonzo, whose corselet had become unlaced in the previous struggle, having received a severe wound in the breast, followed by another on the head, grappled closely with his adversary, and they came rolling on the ground together. The Moor remained uppermost; but the spirit of the Spanish cavalier had not sunk with his strength, and he proudly exclaimed, as if to intimidate his enemy, "I am Don Alonzo de Aguilar,;" to which the other rejoined, "And I am the Feri de Ben Estepar," a well-known name of terror to the Christians. The sound of his detested name roused all the vengeance of the dying hero; and, grasping his foe in mortal agony, he rallied his strength for a final blow; but it was too late—his hand failed, and he was soon despatched by the dagger of his more vigorous rival.

Thus fell Alonzo Hernandez de Cordova, or Alonzo de Aguilar, as he is commonly called, from the land where his family estates lay. —Prescott.

## TIME.

Too late I've stayed :—forgive the crime—
Unheeded flew the hours :
How noiseless falls the foot of Time,
    That only treads on flowers!

What eye with clear account remarks
    The ebbings of the glass,
When all its sands are diamond sparks,
    That dazzle as they pass?

Ah, who to sober measurement
    Time's happy fleetness brings,
When Birds of Paradise have lent
    Their plumage for his wings? —Spencer.

Mark that swift arrow, how it cuts the air,
How it outruns thy following eye!
Use all persuasion now and try

If thou canst call it back or stay it there.
That way it went, but thou shalt find
No track it left behind.

Fool! 'tis thy life, and the fond archer thou:
Of all the time thou'st shot away,
I'll bid thee fetch but yesterday,
And it shall be too hard a task to do.
Beside repentance, what canst find
That it hath left behind?               COWLEY.

## THE INFIDEL AND THE ANGEL.

THERE are two kinds of minds of whose opinions we have been informed touching the relative importance of this world to other worlds, all being provinces in the same moral empire— the one is the mind of the infidel, the other is the mind of the angel. As a matter of course, they represent the extremes of sentiment, and are as widely apart from each other as might be the descriptions of the same landscape given by two men, the one of whom had dimly seen it for a moment, as he woke up from a slumber in a fast train; the other of whom, from some heathery slope or upland, had drunk in its beauty with ample leisure and with a broad sweep of vision. When the infidel thinks of this world, even if he is so much of a believer as to admit its fall, he looks at it with narrow sympathies; wrapt in his own selfishness, he cannot conceive of the nobility which would yearn with pity over some revolted province, and which would visit a scene of insurrection, not to destroy the rebels, but to pardon them; nay, he cannot even conceive of a vigilant tenderness, so comprehensive that it can govern a universe of worlds with as perfect a recognition of the minute as of the magnificent in each, and so unfailing that it is moved by no rebellion from its benevolent design. Hence the great facts of man's sin and ransom; of God's providence, caring for this world, the sickly, and the erring; and of God's grace stooping to replace it in its orbit; finding, as they do, no precedent in his own emotions, and evoking no response from the depths of his own consciousness, are treated by the sceptic as a delusion of fanaticism rather than as a reality of faith. He cannot believe that man, as insignificant in comparison with the planet whose surface he scarcely specks as the one crystal to the avalanche, or the one bubble, with its mimic rainbow, to the torrent waters of Niagara, can be even looked at in the administration of the great economy, much less that all his concerns and all his interests are noted as carefully as if there were no other on the earth beside him. He cannot believe that of all worlds which sun themselves in their Creator's smile, this reckling world which has strayed should be the object of especial graciousness, and that for its deliverance there should have been struck out of the heart of goodness a scheme of compassion unparalleled in the universe before. This is a knowledge altogether too wonderful, and a belief altogether too high, to have a home in an infidel's bosom. And yet these very facts are to the angels matters both of interest and of joy. These glorious beings, "full of eyes" to gather and observe all knowledge, and with large hearts of charity, vibrate, although of alien nature, to each chord of human struggle and conquest; to them it is but matter of higher praise that throughout the universe, and even into its very ravines and cells of being, there penetrate the glances of that eye whose brightness they must veil themselves to see; to them the grace which leaves the loyal worlds to condescend to the succor of the shrouded one, is the rarest grace of all; and to angelic eyes, in the wondrous scheme of earth's redemption by the offering of the Divine Substitute, there is a perpetual mystery, into which they still desire to look, and where to their enraptured study the whole Deity is known.

Not merely on the God-ward side do these facts excite their adoration, but on the man-ward side their sympathy. They have watched, you remember, over this our world from the beginning; they sang together at its birth; they revelled in the beauty of the young Eden, and strayed at dewy eve by the paths where its blest inhabitants wandered; they shuddered beneath sin's cold shadow, and grieved over the blight and the departure of the innocence they had loved so well. Hence they have known our world in all its fortunes; and just as an elder brother, of a benevolent heart, might heap caresses upon the infant born when he was old enough "to move about the house with joy, and with the certain step of man," finding endearment in its very helplessness; so those holy angels, bright in the radiance of their first estate, have quick sensibilities for all human welfare still ; and whenever the sinner is arrested in his course, or the penitent cry is heard, or the prodigal, in his far country, turns a homeward glance of soul ; there comes a hush upon their harping, only to be succeeded by a burst of more rapturous music, for "there is joy in the presence of the angels of God over one sinner that repenteth."—PUNSHON.

## THE PRAYER OF FESTUS.

The bells of time are ringing changes fast,
Grant, Lord ! that each fresh peal may usher in
An era of advancement, that each change
Prove an effectual, lasting, happy gain.
And we beseech Thee, overrule, O God !
All civil contests to the good of all ;
All party and religious difference
To honorable ends, whether secured
Or lost ; and let all strife, political
Or social, spring from conscientious aims,
And have a generous, self-ennobling end,
Man's good and Thine own glory in view always !
The best may then fail and the worst succeed
Alike with honor. We beseech Thee, Lord !
For bodily strength, but more especially
For the soul's health and safety. We entreat thee
In Thy great mercy to decrease our wants,
And add autumnal increase to the comforts
Which tend to keep men innocent, and load
Their hearts with thanks to thee as trees in bearing:—
The blessings of friends, families, and homes,
And kindnesses of kindred. And we pray
That men may rule themselves in faith in God,
In charity to each other, and in hope
Of their own souls' salvation :—that the mass,
The millions in all nations may be trained,
From their youth upwards in a nobler mode,
To loftier and more liberal ends. We pray
Above all things, Lord ! that all men be free
From bondage, whether of the mind or body ;—
Free as they ought to be in mind and soul
As well as by state-birthright ;—and that Mind,
Time's giant pupil. may right soon attain
Majority. and speak and act for himself.
Incline Thou to our prayers, and grant, O Lord !
That all may have enough, and some safe mean
Of worldly goods and honors, by degrees,
Take place, if practicable, in the fitness

And fulness of Thy time. And we beseech Thee,
That truth no more be gagged, nor conscience dungeoned,
Nor science be impeached of godlessness,
Nor faith be circumscribed, which as to Thee,
And the soul's self affairs is infinite;
But that all men may have due liberty
To speak an honest mind, in every land,
Encouragement to study, leave to act
As conscience orders. * —BAILEY.

## THE GIRONDISTS.

THE Girondists were the philosophers of the Revolution. Their ideas were often grand and generous, drawn from the heroes of Greece and Rome, or the more enlarged philanthropy of modern times; their language ever indulgent and seducing to the people; their principles those which gave its early popularity and its immense celebrity to the Revolution. But they judged of mankind by a false standard: their ruinous error consisted in supposing that the multitude could be regulated by the motives which influenced the austere patriots, whom they numbered among their own body. An abstract sense of justice, a passion for general equality, a repugnance for violent governments, distinguished their speeches but yet from their innovations has sprung the most oppressive tyranny of modern times, and they were at last found joining in many measures of the most flagrant iniquity. The dreadful war which ravaged Europe for twenty years was provoked by their declamations; the death of the King, the overthrow of the throne, the Reign of Terror, flowed from the principles which they promulgated. It is no apology for such conduct to allege that they were sincere in their desire for a Republic and the happiness of France: the common proverb, that "Hell is paved with good intentions," shows how generally perilous conduct, even when flowing from pure motives, is found to lead to the most disastrous consequences. They were too often, in their political career, reckless and inconsiderate; and thence their eloquence and genius only rendered them the more dangerous from the multitudes who were influenced by such alluring expressions. Powerful in raising the tempest, they were feeble and irresolute in allaying it; invincible in suffering, heroic in death, they were destitute of the energy and practical experience requisite to avert disaster. The democrats supported them as long as they urged forward the Revolution, and became their bitterest enemies as soon as they strove to allay its fury. They were constantly misled by expecting that intelligence was to be found among the lower orders; that reason and justice would prevail with the multitude; and as constantly disappointed by experiencing the invariable ascendant of passion or interest among their popular supporters ;—the usual error of elevated and generous minds, and which so frequently unfits them for the actual administration of affairs. Their tenets would have led them to support the constitutional throne, but they were unable to stem the torrent of democratical fury which they themselves had excited, and compelled, to avert still greater disasters, to concur in many cruel measures, alike contrary to their wishes and their principles. The leaders of this party were Vergniaud, Brissot, and Roland; men of powerful eloquence, generous philanthropy, and Roman firmness; who knew how to die, but not to live; who perished because they wanted the audacity and wickedness requisite for success in a Revolution.

The radical and inherent vice of this party was their irreligion ; and the dreadful misfortunes in which they involved their country proved how inadequate the most splendid talents are to the management of human affairs, or the right discharge of social duty, without that over-ruling principle. With all theit love of justice, they declared Louis guilty; with all their humanity they voted for his death. The peasants of La Vendée, who trusted only to the rule of duty prescribed in their religon, were never betrayed in the same manner into acts for which no apology can be found. Whenever statesmen abandon the plain rules of duty and justice, and base their conduct on the quicksands of supposed expediency, they are involved in a series of errors which quickly precipitate them into the most serious crimes. But the greatest efforts of human wisdom or virtue are unequal to direct or sustain the mind in the trying scenes which a Revolution induces : it is the belief of futurity, and a sense of religion alone, which can support humanity in such calamities ; and their want of such principles rendered all the genius and philanthropy of the Girondists of no practical avail in stemming the disasters of the Revolution. —ALISON.

## GO, DREAM NO MORE.

Go, dream no more of a sun-bright sky
  With never a cloud to dim!
Thou hast seen the storm in its robes of night,
Thou hast felt the rush of the whirlwind's night,
Thou hast shrunk from the lightning's arrowy flight,
  When the Spirit of Storms went by!

Go, dream no more of a crystal sea
  Where never a tempest sweeps!
For thy riven bark on a surf-beat shore,
Where the wild winds shriek and the billows roar,
A shattered wreck to be launched no more,
  Will mock at thy dream and thee '

Go, dream no more of a fadeless flower
  With never a cankering blight!
For the queenliest rose in thy garden bed,
The pride of the morn, ere the noon is fled,
With the worm at its heart, withers cold and dead
  In the Spoiler's fearful power!

Go, dream no more! for the cloud will rise,
  And the tempest will sweep the sea;
Yet grieve not thou, for beyond the strife,
The storm and the gloom with which earth is rife,
Gleam out the light of immortal life,
  And the glow of unchanging skies!

—Mrs. Yule.

## THE YOUNG MEN OF CANADA.

WHAT a large, wide, happy home is the land we live in! We have found it a goodly land, and have no sympathy with those who love it not! There is no piety, no genuine Christianity, in the heart of him who does not love his country, native or adopted! He cannot be a true, large, leal-hearted man, who looking through the vista of coming years, does not hope to see his own country grow greater and more glorious; and he is no true Canadian who does not cry, in the words emblazoned on my left, " Peace and Prosperity to Canada." There are those around me doubtless, who sympathise with the poet who wrote these lines a few years ago:

"They say thy hills are bleak,
  They say thy glens are bare—
But oh! they know not what fond hearts
  Are nurtured there.
"Scotland! I love thee well,
  Thy dust is dear to me—
This distant land is very fair
  But not like thee."

It matters not on what line of latitude or longitude it may be, one's native land should be the dearest, sweetest, and most hallowed spot on this side of heaven. Canada, our country! we love it; and because we love it, we wish you, young men, to be worthy of it. Our fathers have done much. They came from almost every country beneath the sun. They were a varied people; and we are, to some extent, varied still. Their national, educational, and ecclesiastical prejudices were varied. They had but one thing to bind them together; the deep fertile soil beneath their feet, and the clear canopy of the bright blue sky above their heads. Pioneers in this goodly land, some have found a home—many only a grave, and on the resting place of these we should tread lightly, doing reverence to their ashes, and living so as to honor them. With you, young men, I arm for the conflict, and gird myself for the coming struggle. We are the strength of the country. Upon us it depends whether, in twenty years, this country shall be progressive, and rise to assume its own just place in the heraldry of nations, and have the proud boast of possessing a God-fearing people; whether it shall become a dark spot in the geography of the world, and, by and by, vanish altogether, or whether intelligence and industry shall place Canada in the vanguard of nations.

—ORMISTON.

## THE JOYS OF HOME.

SWEET are the joys of home,
  And pure as sweet; for they,
Like dews of morn and evening, come
  To wake and close the day.

The world hath its delights,
  And its delusions too;
But home to calmer bliss invites,
  More tranquil and more true.

The mountain flood is strong,
  But fearful in its pride ;
While gently rolls the stream, along
  The peaceful valley's side.

Life's charities, like light,
  Spread smilingly afar ;
But stars approach'd become more bright,
  And home is life's own star.

The pilgrim's step in vain
  Seeks Eden's sacred ground!
But in home's holy joys, again
  An Eden may be found.

A glance of heaven to see,
  To none on earth is given ;
And yet a happy family
  Is but an earlier heaven.        — BOWRING.

## THE THREE SISTER ARTS.

OF all the arts, sculpture and architecture, from their durability and excellence, have the most powerful claims to the protection of a great nation. They afford the only means of shedding an enduring interest and a never-failing lustre over the history and achievements of a people. They are truly national arts. What imperishable fame and glory have they reflected on the nations of antiquity for a long succession of ages! Had the monuments of these arts not remained to us, ruined and defaced as they are, could we have formed so high an estimate of the national power and glory of Egypt, Greece, and Rome? The finest paintings, whether in fresco or oil, cannot retain their coloring beyond a certain lapse of time, should they even escape the numberless accidents to which they are hourly exposed. Yet a few revolving ages, and the greater number will no longer exist ; they will be known to posterity only by copies and engravings. But every painter cannot hope, like Raffael, to have a Marc Antonio Raimondi to hand down his works to posterity. When after a few fleeting centuries, the admired productions of the great masters shall have perished with those of antiquity, the works of the statuary and architect will continue to bloom in all their freshness and vigor ; and even when mutilated, defaced and in ruins, remain objects of interest and admiration to a distant posterity, rising, as it were, from their ashes into a second and more glorious *apotheosis*.

If Rome and the surrounding nations of antiquity were indebted to Greece for their knowledge of classic art, the moderns owe her a similar debt of gratitude. To the remains of Grecian sculpture we are solely indebted for the revival of modern art and the true principles of taste. From them Buonarotti and Raffael caught the spark of inspiration which was soon destined to blaze forth in the sublime works of the Sistine Chapel and Vatican Chambers. Without these remains we could neither have known nor appreciated the perfection of Grecian art and design, of which we might have remained as ignorant as we now are of their music and theatrical recitation. With the exception of the paintings preserved by a kind of miracle in Herculaneum and Pompeii, the imperfect remains in the baths of Titus and the palace of the Cæsars, and a few others, such as the Aldobrandini marriage—all the works of the greatest painters of antiquity have perished. What had we to guide us in the research but the vague descriptions, faint and contradictory allusions to art in ancient authors, not excepting the valuable, though often obscure, treatise of Pliny?

Architecture, sculpture, and painting, are truly and emphatically styled sister arts. Neither can attain its highest rank and grace, without the aid and co-operation of the other two. Sculpture and architecture are, however, more closely united; they are in a manner twin sisters. They are not so much separate arts, as branches of the same art. In Egypt, Greece and Rome, they rose and flourished together. In the decline of art, though corrupted and degraded, they are still found united. The same union is to be found in all the varieties of the Lombard, Norman, and Gothic, as well as the Italian and modern styles. Strip the Egyptian temple or palace, the Athenian Parthenon, the Roman triumphal arch, the Vatican Basilica, the Duomo of Florence or of Milan, the cathedrals of York or Lincoln, of their statuary, and you at once deprive them of their most beautiful and interesting attributes. Not only has sculpture strong claims to public patronage from its intrinsic excellence as a national art, and its indissoluble connexion with architecture—but from its powerful influence over the higher departments of painting and design. Like the three Graces, the three sister arts cannot be separated with impunity. We have seen that the greatest masters of antiquity excelled in all the three. Can we suppose that Phidias, Praxiteles, and Lysippus could have reached such perfection in statuary—Zeuxis, Parrhasius, and Apelles, in painting and design—Mnesicles, Callicrates, and Ictinus, in architecture, without the knowledge and aid of the sister arts? The same remark will apply to the great Italian masters. Who shall decide in which department Buonarotti was most pre-eminent—"the architect of the Cupola—the sculptor of the Moses—the painter of the Last Judgment?" Raffael, the prince of painters, was highly distinguished as an architect, besides being intimately acquainted with classical sculpture. Leonardo da Vinci, in addition to his fame as a painter, was distinguished for his skill in sculpture and modelling, as well as engineering and mechanics—Giulio Romano was at once painter, architect and modeller—Bernini, sculptor, architect, and painter—Brunelleschi and Ghiberti were equally famed for architecture as for sculpture. In our own times, Canova, besides sculpture, had a fine taste for architecture, and was eminently skilled in painting; in proof of which, it is only necessary to refer to his beautiful temple at Possagno, designed by himself, and its fine altar piece of the Descent from the Cross, painted with his own hand.

With regard to the cultivation of modern art, there can be but one opinion as to the inestimable benefit to be derived from antique sculpture and the ideal, provided it be conducted with judgment and discrimination, and accompanied by a constant reference to select nature, as a guide and corrective. In following this course we are treading in the footsteps of the great masters of Greece and modern Italy. Even had we possessed all the works of antiquity in perfect preservation, never could we have dispensed with the study of nature without becoming mere mannerists and copyists, destitute alike of originality and excellence. Among the various antique statues, busts, relievi, &c., now extent, with the exception of the sculptures of the Parthenon, and a few others of doubtful authenticity, we possess no works of the greatest masters of antiquity, or of the most flourishing periods of art. The *chefs-d'œuvres* of Grecian sculpture—the colossal statues of ivory and gold by Phidias—the great works of Praxiteles—the splendid bronze equestrian statues, quadrigæ, and groups of Lysippus,—all have perished in the wreck of ages. How excellent soever the existing specimens may be, some of the most celebrated, including the Apollo Belvidere and the Venus de Medici, have been suspected, not without reason, of being but good copies of former originals. Many must be copies, or copies of copies—many the works of secondary and inferior artists, who, it may be supposed, made a trade of their art, in repeating the same subjects in a cold and conventional manner, independently of any sentiment of beauty or study of nature. Such productions, and they form a considerable proportion of antique collections—have nothing of the style and taste of the great masters, but " a certain appearance of tradition more or less faithful." Moreover, all are mutilated and defaced, and what is even worse, many are patched, restored, or metamorphosed. Such considerations render it doubly imperative to beware of a blind, indiscriminate, and slavish admiration of the antique, to the exclusion of living nature. On the other hand, the sole and exclusive study of individual and ordinary nature will be apt to degenerate into the commonplace and vulgar. The highest department—the true epic of the heart, as already remarked, will be found in the union of select nature and the Grecian ideal.

—CLEGHORN.

## INSULT.

The purpose of an injury 'tis to vex
And trouble me ; now nothing can do that
To him that's valiant. He that is affected
With the least injury, is less than it.
It is but reasonable to conclude
That should be stronger still which hurts, than that
Which is hurt. Now no wickedness is stronger
Than what opposeth it ; not fortune's self,
When she encounters virtue, but comes off
Both lame and less ! why should a wise man then
Confess himself the weaker, by the feeling
Of a fool's wrong ? There may an injury
Be meant me. I may choose, if I will take it.
But we are now come to that delicacy
And tenderness of sense, we think an insolence
Worse than an injury, bare words worse than deeds ;
We are not so much troubled with the wrong,
As with the opinion of the wrong ; like children
We are made afraid of visors. —JONSON.

## THE BETTER LIFE.

WHAT is this life to me? not worth a thought:
Or, if it be esteem'd, 'tis that I lose it
To win a better: even thy malice serves
To me but as a ladder to mount up
To such a height of happiness, where I shall
Look down with scorn on thee and on the world;
Where, circled with true pleasures, plac'd above
The reach of death or time, 'twill be my glory
To think at what an easy price I bought it.
There's a perpetual spring, perpetual youth:
No joint-benumbing cold, or scorching heat,
Famine, nor age, have any being there.
Forget, for shame, your Tempe; bury in
Oblivion your feign'd Hesperian orchards;—
The golden fruit, kept by the watchful dragon,
Which did require a Hercules to get it,
Compared with what grows in all plenty there,
Deserves not to be named. —MASSINGER.

## THE TRUE KING.

'TIS not the bared pate, the bended knees,
Gilt tipstaff, Tyrian purple, chaires of state,
Troopes of pide butterflies, that flutter still
In greatnesse summer, that confirm a prince:
'Tis not the unsavoury breath of multitudes,
Showting and clapping with confused dinne,
That makes a prince. No, Lucio, he's a king,
A true right king, that dares doe ought, save wrong:
Feares nothing mortall, but to be unjust;
Who is not blowne up with the flattering puffes
Of spungy sycophants; who stands unmov'd,
Despight the justling of opinion:
Who can enjoy himselfe, maugre the throng
That strive to presse his quiet out of him:
Who sits upon Jove's footestoole as I doe,
Adoring, not affecting, majesty:
Whose brow is wreathed with the silver crown
Of cleare content: this, Lucio, is a king.
And of this empire, every man 's possest,
That 's worth his soule. —MARSTON.

## SOCIETY.

Why striv'st thou to be gone?
Why should'st thou so desire to be alone?
Thy cheek is never fair when none is by:
For what is red and white but to the eye?
And for that cause the heavens are dark at night,
Because all creatures close their weary sight;
For there's no mortal can so early rise,
But still the morning waits upon his eyes.
The early rising and soon-singing lark
Can never chant her sweet notes in the dark;
For sleep she ne'er so little or so long,
Yet still the morning will attend her song.
All creatures that beneath bright Cynthia be
Have appetite unto society;
The overflowing waves would have a bound
Within the confines of the spacious ground,
And all their shady currents would be placed
In hollow of the solitary vast,
But that they loathe to let their soft streams sing
Where none can hear their gentle murmuring.
—BEAUMONT.

## THE DEATH OF THEODORE.
### A.D. 1868.

AT first the King remained on foot, superintending the transport of the guns, but suddenly his eyes fired up, and he called for his favorite bay horse *Hamra*, and for his rifle sent him by M. Barroni, called the "elephant rifle." His friends asked him not to endanger his life; but he replied that he could not do better than die then and there. Six chiefs mounted at the same time. Theodore galloped furiously up and down, and in circles, firing off his rifle as a challenge; but no one came forward to fight him. Next to the Wakshum Teferri, whom he had immured in Magdala, the King was the best horseman, the best spearman, and the best shot in Abyssinia. Now for the last time he could display these qualities; and probably he then experienced a few short minutes of enjoyment for the last time in his life. He had barely four hours to live. More troops came up and opened fire, and at last he retreated up into Magdala, followed by the faithful few, and necessarily abandoning the two guns. After closing the doors of the Koket-bir, they set to work piling large stones against the inside, Theodore and

Ras Engeda setting the example. They then passed a weary time awaiting their fate, while the English were honoring them with a cannonade. The King was dressed in a magnificent *kinbob*, or shirt of gold and silk, with a lion-skin *lemd*, or tippet, and a belt containing sword and pistols. He took his seat on the rocks, between the first and second gates, surrounded by his friends, and watched the English guns with his glass. A shell burst a few feet above his head and killed two cows. He then changed his dress, believing that he made a conspicuous mark, and during the brief remainder of his life he had on a pair of cotton drawers, a fine muslin shirt, and a white *shama*, with a pistol-belt round his waist. He continued to watch the guns with his glass, ducking his head when he saw the flash and smoke. Soon his friends began to fall around him. His faithful minister, Ras Engeda, and his brother, were killed by one shell. Ras Engeda had sent his three little sons out of the *amba* for safety—fine young fellows, between twelve and fourteen, who stood amongst the English troops on Selassye, crying bitterly at the thought of their father's danger, and offering drinks of *tej* to the men if they would leave off firing.

When the firing began to get hot some of the chiefs and nearly all the soldiers deserted, and took refuge among the huts on Magdala. The chiefs who retired were Bitwaddad Hassane, Engeda Wark, and Agafari Mashesha. Thus when the assault commenced, and King Theodore came down into the Koket-bir to fire upon the overwhelming numbers of his assailants, many of his own little band were missing. The defenders of Magdala numbered about ten men, including Theodore himself. Basha Engeda, and the gun-bearer Amanyi were killed as they went down into the gateway. Walda Gabir, therefore, loaded the rifles and handed them up to the King, who fired through badly-constructed loop-holes in the wall. The others also kept up a feeble fire. When the English soldiers climbed over the hedge, and poured a volley into the heroic little band, most of the survivors were wounded. The bodies of the dying chiefs had, by the King's order been brought down from the rocks, and placed in a corner of the gateway, as the most sheltered spot. Even in this supreme moment of danger, Theodore took thought of his faithful comrades in arms. Bitwaddad Bakal, an old man, was seized, and afterwards half his head was blown out. His body was inside the gateway, by that of Ras Engeda, and he was still groaning in agony when we passed through. The rest fled up through the second gate, the King being last. He threw his arms in the air as a gesture of defiance from behind the last rock; and he was so placed as to look, from below, as if he was in a pulpit. Ras Baraku, Bitwaddad Damash, Bitwaddad Bahri, and Asalafee Kantiba were all wounded, the latter mortally. The King, Ras Tsaga, Ras B'sawur, Dadjatsh Abuye, and Walda Gabir were not touched. Another chief, named Basha Negusye, was killed at the door of his house, which was situated between the two gates, as the troops came in. He had been a good friend to the captives, and was a sincere Christian.

The English soldiers were now swarming through the Koketbir. Theodore reached some huts on the *amba*, about fifty yards from the second gate. Here he dismissed all his surviving followers, except his faithful valet Walda Gabir, telling them to leave him and save their own lives. "Flee," he said, "I release you from your allegiance; as for me, I shall never fall into the hands of the enemy." As soon as they were gone, he turned to Walda Gabir and said: "It is finished! Sooner than fall into their hands, I will kill myself." He put a pistol into his mouth, fired it, and fell dead; the ball passing through the roof of the mouth and out at the back of the head. This was, as nearly as possible, at ten minutes past four in the afternoon. The English soldiers were then running up between the first and second gates. Walda Gabir took the belt and *shama*, and with fifteen comrades ran across Magdala and out at the Kaffirbir gate, but the fugitives were confronted by some Galla thieves, so they hid in a cave and returned into Magdala the next day.

Even before the catastrophe, the old Afa Negus, a chief who had been ordered to guard the political prisoners, was overpowered and pushed aside. The captives broke out of their prisons, and came down the road clanking their irons. At this moment Sir Charles Staveley came through the second gate, and a man ran up to him saying that all the prisoners were declaring that a dead body lying near was that of the King. The body was put into a litter and brought to Sir Charles, and the prisoners, first glancing at the face, and then taking up one hand and looking at a finger that had been broken, one and all exclaimed "Teodoros!" —MARKHAM.

## A VOICE FOR THE TIMES.

Raise the hammer, strike the anvil,
　Let the wide earth feel the blow ;
Let her quake from zone to centre,
　Tropic, vale, and peak of snow.
Right, with sword drawn for the contest.
　Takes the field against the Wrong—
Sound aloud the deep-toned clarion,
　Let its notes be clear and long.

Human hearts with anguish bleeding,
　Human nature, held in thrall,
Myriads, waiting for redemption,
　Marshal at the trumpet's call.
Hold aloft your glorious 'banner,
　Let it float against the sky,
And with Truth's bright sword uplifted,
　Vow to conquer, though ye die.

Let no heart quail in the onset—
　From above, around, beneath,
Countless eyes the strife are watching,
　Through the war-cloud's dusky wreath,
Side by side all firm and valiant,
　In the God of Battles strong,
Grapple with each rampant error,
　In the serried ranks of Wrong.

Though the clouds, with thunder laden.
　Darken o'er the source of day—
Though the fork'd and fiery lightnings
　Flash and dart around your way ;-
Echoed loud above the thunder
　Let your watchword 'Victory,' sound ;
And, amid the jagged lightnings,
　Inch by inch maintain your ground.

Where intrenched in hoary bulwarks,
　Error and his chieftains dwell,
Scale the rampart, strike the ensign ;
　Track them to the gates of hell.
Not till then the waiting scabbard
　May receive the glitt'ring steel ;
Not till then, earth's groaning millions
　Freedom's bounding pulse may feel.

On the distant, dim horizon,
Faintly glimm'ring through the night,
Shines a star whose noon-tide glory
Truth's triumphal march shall light;
And e'en now, in far-off murm'rings
O'er the future's restless sea,
Faith may catch a premonition
Of the world's great jubilee. —MISS HAIGHT.

## PRECIOUS STONES.

BY precious gems are meant minerals remarkable for hardness, lustre, beauty of color, transparency, or for the extreme rarity of their occurrence in nature, which are used in personal ornaments, such as jewellery.

This definition excludes many gems so classed by mineralogists, but which have no commercial value, and many others that were prized by the ancients on account of the supernatural properties, and health-restoring charms they were supposed to possess, and which, if true, must have rendered them indeed precious and priceless to the possessor and wearer. The estimation in which these flowers of the mineral kingdom have been held from the very earliest ages, alike by the most refined and the most barbarous nations, is extraordinary, so that gems really seem to possess some occult charm which causes them to be coveted. The fixed, and, so to say, intrinsic value of jewels (coupled with their extreme portability), has always made them a favorite form of investment. In the French revolution of 1789, diamonds rose enormously in value, and, perhaps from the same causes, we observe a large increase in their price in the United States of America at the present time.

Precious stones are disseminated about the globe in profusion; they occur alike amid the torrid deserts of Africa and the icy steppes of Siberia; under the burning sun of India and Ceylon, and amidst the glaciers of Switzerland; in the beds of mighty rivers of South America; in Germany, Spain, and even in our own land; generally in the midst of some substance or deposit differing entirely from them. The tropical countries, however, are far more prolific in this respect than the other parts of the globe: it would seem as if the countries where the sun shines with most splendor produce gems in greater quantities; and perhaps the volcanic changes to which they are subject may have something to do with the matter. They are found most generally in the older formations, such as granite, gneiss, etc., in the beds of rivers, where they have been brought by torrents, generally accompanied by the precious metals; and often various kinds of gems are found together. When we consider the wonderful combination of seemingly fortuitous circumstances which are required for the formation of these beautiful crystals, to give them the required transparency, brilliancy, and lustre, the freedom from defects and flaws, and the presence of the exact quantity of coloring matter to furnish the desired tint, it will be no matter of astonishment that they occur so seldom; and the idea that one day precious stones may become as plentiful as marble may be dismissed as groundless, when the numerous qualifications which are necessary for a stone to enter into this aristocratic and exclusive family are considered; for there must not only exist the crystallization to give the required form, but the hardness to allow of the proper polish and lustre, and the coloring matter to produce the desired hue; and should one of these requisites be wanting, the gem loses its value in the eyes of the connoisseur.

The minerals which are the component parts of gems are plentiful throughout the globe; we can obtain magnesia, glucina, alumina, metallic oxides, etc., in profusion, and we can separate the gems themselves into their component parts; but, not all the researches of learned chemists, not all the accumulated science of the nineteenth century, has succeeded in wresting the secret from nature, or of producing them of any size or value by artificial means. The material of the diamond, for instance, "carbon," is found almost everywhere,—in the bread we eat, in the coal and wood we burn; uncrystallized, it is brittle and opaque, but when crystallized, is the hardest known substance, pure as the limpid stream, and shining with the greatest brilliancy when cut and polished; whilst the amorphous variety, *carbonate*, although of precisely the same composition, and of nearly equal specific gravity, is black and lustreless, and is degraded to the purpose of cutting and polishing other gems. Again, the emerald is composed of identically the same substances as the beryl, minus the required coloring matter; yet the emerald commands a large price, and the beryl is comparatively valueless. The amethyst and rock-crystal are exactly the same substance, except that one is white and the other colored; the amethyst, when of fine quality, has considerable value, rock-crystal very little. The oriental topaz and the ruby are the same stones, but different in color; yet the value of the ruby surpasses that of the topaz a hundredfold.

In fact, precious stones must not only have the desired color, but the exact hue and shade in demand to obtain the extreme value. No matter how brilliant the ruby, or how free from defects and flaws, it must have the precise pigeon's-blood-red to make it the gem which surpasses the diamond in value.

Almost all gems conceal their true beauties in a natural state. The diamond in the rough is most unattractive, and would be thrown away by a casual observer as a worthless pebble; its perfections are hidden under a hard crust, which can only be removed by its own powder. The deep velvety hue of the sapphire, the glowing brilliant red of the ruby, the soft clear green of the emerald, and the delicate strata of the onyx, alike only display themselves in their true character after the lapidary has exhausted his skill in cutting them into facets and polishing them; and on the perfection of this operation depends in a great measure the beauty of the gem. It may be here observed, that many pure and perfect jewels have been irretrievably spoilt by unskilful hands. —EMANUEL.

## THE SOUL'S ASPIRATIONS.

Who that, from Alpine heights, his laboring eye
Shoots round the wide horizon, to survey
Nilus or Ganges rolling his bright wave
Thro' mountains, plains, thro' empires black with shade,
And continents of sand; will turn his gaze
To mark the windings of a scanty rill
That murmurs at his feet? The high-born soul
Disdains to rest her heaven-aspiring wing
Beneath its native quarry. Tir'd of earth
And this diurnal scene, she springs aloft
Through fields of air: pursues the flying storm;
Rides on the vollied lightning through the heavens,
Or, yok'd with whirlwinds and the northern blast,
Sweeps the long tract of day. Then high she soars
The blue profound, and hovering round the sun
Beholds him pouring the redundant stream
Of light; beholds his unrelenting sway
Bend the reluctant planets to absolve
The fated rounds of Time. —AKENSIDE.

## MY MOTHER DEAR.

There was a place in childhood that I remember well,
And there a voice of sweetest tone bright fairy tales did tell,
And gentle words and fond embrace were giv'n with joy to me,
When I was in that happy place :—upon my Mother's knee.

When fairy tales were ended, " Good night," she softly said,
And kiss'd and laid me down to sleep, within my tiny bed;
And holy words she taught me there—methinks I yet can see
Her angel eyes, as close I knelt beside my Mother's knee.

In the sickness of my childhood ; the perils of my prime;
The sorrows of my riper years; the cares of ev'ry time;
When doubt and danger weigh'd me down—then pleading all for me,
It was a fervent pray'r to Heav'n that bent my Mother's knee.

—Lover.

## REFLECTIONS ON WAR.

*Though we must all die,* as the woman of Tekoa said, *and are as water spill upon the ground which cannot be gathered up,* yet it is impossible for a humane mind to contemplate the rapid extinction of innumerable lives without concern. To perish in a moment, to be hurried instantaneously, without preparation and without warning, into the presence of the Supreme Judge, has something in it inexpressibly awful and affecting. Since the commencement of these hostilities which are now so happily closed, it may be reasonably conjectured that not less than half a million of our fellow creatures have fallen a sacrifice. Half a million of beings, sharers of the same nature, warmed with the same hopes, and as fondly attached to life as ourselves, have been prematurely swept into the grave; each of whose deaths has pierced the heart of a wife, a parent, a brother, or a sister! How many of these scenes of complicated distress have occurred since the commencement of hostilities is known only to Omniscience: that they are innumerable cannot admit of a doubt. In some parts of Europe, perhaps, there is scarcely a family exempt.

Though the whole race of man is doomed to dissolution, and we are all hastening to our long home; yet, at each successive moment, life and death seem to divide betwixt them the dominion of mankind, and life to have the largest share. It is otherwse in war: death reigns there without a rival, and without control. War is the work, the element, or rather the sport and triumph, of death, who glories, not only in the extent of his conquest, but in the richness of his spoil. In the other methods of attack, in the other forms which death assumes, the feeble and the aged, who at the best can live but a short time, are usually the victims; here it is the vigorous and the strong. It is remarked by an ancient historian, that in peace children bury their parents, in war parents bury their children: nor is the difference small. Children lament their parents, sincerely indeed, but with that moderate and tranquil sorrow, which it is natural for those to feel who are conscious of retaining many tender ties, many animated prospects. Parents mourn for their children with the bitterness of despair; the aged parent, the widowed mother, loses, when she is deprived of her children, everything but the capacity of suffering; her heart, withered and desolate, admits no other object, cherishes no other hope. *It is Rachel weeping for her children, and refusing to be comforted, because they are not.*

But to confine our attention to the number of the slain would give us a very inadequate idea of the ravages of the sword. The lot of those who perish instantaneously may be considered, apart from religious prospects, as comparatively happy, since they are exempt from those lingering diseases and slow torments to which others are liable. We cannot see an individual expire, though a stranger or an enemy, without being sensibly moved, and prompted by compassion to lend him every assistance in our power. Every trace of resentment vanishes in a moment: every other emotion gives way to pity and terror. In these last extremities, we remember nothing but the respect and tenderness due to our common nature. What a scene, then, must a field of battle present, where thousands are left without assistance, and without pity, with their wounds exposed to the piercing air, while their blood, freezing as it flows, binds them to earth, amidst the trampling of horses, and the insults of an enraged foe! If they are spared by the humanity of the enemy, and carried from the field, it is but a prolongation of torment. Conveyed in uneasy vehicles, often to a remote distance, through roads almost impassable, they are lodged in ill-prepared receptacles for the wounded and the sick, where the variety of distress baffles all the efforts of humanity and skill, and renders it impossible to give to each the attention he demands. Far from their native home, no tender assiduities of friendship, no well-known voice, no wife, or mother, or sister, is near to soothe their sorrows, relieve their thirst, or close their eyes in death. Unhappy man! and must you be swept into the grave unnoticed and unnumbered, and no friendly tear be shed for your suffering, or mingled with your dust?

We must remember, however, that as a very small proportion of a military life is spent in actual combat, so it is a very small part of its miseries which must be ascribed to this source. More are consumed by the rust of inactivity than by the edge of the sword; confined to a scanty or unwholesome diet, exposed in sickly climates, harassed with tiresome marches and perpetual alarms, their life is a continual scene of hardships and dangers. They grow familiar with hunger, cold, and watchfulness. Crowded into hospitals and prisons, contagion spreads among their ranks, till the ravages of disease exceed those of the enemy.

We have hitherto only adverted to the sufferings of those who are engaged in the profession of arms, without taking into our account the situation of the countries which are the scene of hostilities. How dreadful to hold everything at the mercy of an enemy, and to receive life itself as a boon dependant on the sword! How boundless the fears which such a situation must inspire, where the issues of life and death are determined by no known laws, principles, or customs, and no conception can be formed of our destiny except as far as it is dimly deciphered in characters of blood, in the dictates of revenge, and the caprices of power! Conceive, but for a moment, the consternation which the approach of an invading army would impress on the peaceful villages in this neighborhood. When you have placed yourself for an instant in that situation, you will learn to sympathize with those unhappy countries which have sustained the ravages of arms. But how is it possible to give you an idea of these horrors? Here you behold rich harvests, the bounty of heaven and the reward of industry, consumed in a moment, or trampled under foot, while famine and pestilence follow the steps of desolation. There the cottages of peasants given up to the flames, mothers expiring through fear, not for themselves but for their infants; the inhabitants flying with their helpless babes in all directions, miserable fugitives on their native soil. In another part, you witness opulent cities taken by storm; the streets, where no sounds were heard but those of peaceful industry, filled on a sudden with slaughter and blood, resounding with the cries of the pursuing and the pursued; and every age, sex, and rank, mingled in promiscuous massacre and ruin.   —HALL.

## FAME.

Ah! who can tell how hard it is to climb
The steep where Fame's proud temple shines afar:
Ah! who can tell how many a soul sublime
Has felt the influence of malignant star,
And wag'd with fortune an unequal war;
Checked by the scoff of pride, by envy's frown,
And poverty's unconquerable bar,
In life's low vale remote has pined alone,
Then dropt into the grave, unpitied and unknown!

And yet the languor of inglorious days
Not equally oppressive is to all:
Him, who ne'er listen'd to the voice of praise,
The silence of neglect can ne'er appal.
There are, who deaf to mad Ambition's call,
Would shrink to hear th' obstreperous trump of fame;
Supremely blest, if to their portion fall
Health, competence, and peace.
                                             —BEATTIE.

## REPOSE.

      Sure I am, 'tis madness,
Inhuman madness, thus from half the world
To drain its blood and treasure, to neglect
Each art of peace, each care of government;
And all for what? By spreading desolation,
Rapine, and slaughter o'er the other half,
To gain a conquest we can never hold.
I venerate this land. Those sacred hills,
Those vales, those cities, trod by saints and prophets,
By God himself, the scenes of heavenly wonders
Inspire me with a certain awful joy.
But the same God, my friend, pervades, sustains,
Surrounds and fills this universal frame;
And every land, where spreads his vital presence,
His all-onlivening breath, to me is holy.
                                             —THOMSON.

## THE SURRENDER OF THE EMPEROR NAPOLEON III.
### SEPTEMBER 1ST, 1870.

THE Bavarians of Von der Tann's corps, on whom devolved the difficult task of carrying the village or town of Bazeilles and Balan (a suburb of Sedan, outside the fortifications), suffered enormously. They were exposed to a fire of infantry in the houses, and to the guns of the works, and the musketry from the parapets. The inhabitants joined in the defence, and as soon as the Bavarians had crossed the Meuse by their pontoons and by the railway bridge they could receive but little protection from their artillery placed on the heights. The French made the most strenuous attempts to repulse them, in which the Marines were particularly distinguished; and three divisions of Bavarians, which began to fight at four o'clock, were exposed to three distinct onslaughts from the town and from the corps under the walls. At one time it appeared as if they would be overpowered, although it seems as if success against them would scarcely have secured the French army from its ultimate fate. It is believed by the Bavarians that Mac Mahon himself was wounded very early in the day, when directing his troops in an offensive movement against Bazeilles. General Ducrot then took command of the whole army, but General de Wimpffen, producing a sealed letter, showed that he was authorized to assume the control of the operations of the army in case of any accident to Marshal MacMahon. The Marshal was wounded early in the morning, and according to the reports of the French officers, prisoners to the Bavarians, there was a difference of opinion between General Ducrot and General Wimpffen respecting the plan of attack which the French adopted at one period of the day as the best means of defence. Having beaten the Bavarians out of Balan at one time, the French made a rush in the direction of Illy, as if determined to cut their way through on the flank of the Saxon army, and pass towards Metz. But the Crown Prince of Saxony had by that time resumed the offensive, and had brought an overwhelming force to block their way. They were driven back, delivering the Bavarians from the stress to which they had been exposed. Their divisions advanced once more, and Bazeilles, or as much as remained of it, was firmly occupied; but the fight about Balan lasted much later. Here i, was, according to Bavarian reports, that the Emperor, declaring that he only served as a private soldier, went with an attacking column, composed of the remnants of various regiments, to drive out the Bavarians. But the artillery on the heights above the river and the cross fire from the heights above the road were too much for troops shaken by incessant fighting and frightful losses. Shell and shot rained fast about the Emperor, one of the former bursting close to his person and enveloping him in its smoke. The officers around entreated him to retire, and the Bavarians quickly following occupied Balan and engaged the French on the glacis of the fort. I cannot say whether this was previous to the period referred to by General Wimpffen in his address to the army. He speaks therein of a supreme moment when it was necessary to make a final effort and cut their way through the masses of the enemy at any hazard. But of all the great host of 90,000 men, there were only 2,000, he says, left who answered to the appeal. Of the remainder there were probably 20,000 in the hands of the Prussians, but 60,000 men, deducting killed and wounded, had by this time become an utterly disorganized mass, without cohesion "willing to wound, but yet afraid to strike," and crushed out of all semblage and military vitality by an overwhelming and most murderous artillery, of which the moral effect was at least as great as the physical. The bitterness of recrimination between officers and men shows that long before the battle a radical element of force was wanting. There was not only a deficiency of cordial relations in their kind between the officer and the soldier, but a worse evil still—an actual apprehension on the part of the officers of those whom they were to command—a fear to enforce the ordinary rules of discipline, lest the soldier should become unmanageable altogether. The scene can neither be imagined or described which occurred when the army, or that uniformed rabble, had been fairly driven in by the beaters, to be shot down at will. The French artillery had practically ceased to exist as a protecting arm. The guns on the works are ridiculously small ordnance of the date of 1815, with a few heavy pieces here and there, and Sedan, commanded completely from the south bank of the Meuse, was to all intents and purposes an open town, with the inconvenience of having a walled *enceinte* to embarrass the movements of the troops. The Emperor retired, I believe, within the place, but not, surely, for safety, but rather to escape from the surging mass of impotent soldiery. There was a rain of Prussian and Bavarian bombs upon the town, filled with terrified citizens, who had had no time to escape. The troops outside had been fighting without food since the morning, and there were no resources within the city to meet their wants. They were in an angry and terrible mood, upbraiding their officers, mutinous, and every shell that fell increased the evil of their spirit. To one of the many missiles was now reserved a great mission. A shell fell into a warehouse or manufactory in which was stored some inflammable material. A vast volume of flame rushed for a moment into the air, a volume of thick white smoke which towered and spread out so as to overshadow half the city gave a rise to the apprehension on one side and expectation on the other that some central magazine had gone up. But no noise ensued. Still, at the moment the resolve was taken that Sedan and all that it contained should be placed in the power of the victor, in the belief that it was impossible to resist with any prospect but that of ruin, complete, however lingering.

The Emperor could not oppose counsels dictated by obvious prudence, nor could he encourage the despair of brave men. A white flag was called for, but none was forthcoming. A Lancer's flag was raised aloft. General Lauriston stood upon the battlements and waved it, while a trumpeter sounded, but in that infernal din neither sight nor sound attracted the besiegers, and it was only when the gate was opened, after attempts in which officers and men were killed and wounded, that the Prussians recognised the first omen of their stupendous victory. The firing suddenly ceased after the discharge of a few dropping shots, and then, as all along the bloodstained hills and valleys in which the smoke of battle had been hanging, the news, or rather the instinct, prevailed that the enemy had asked for terms, there rose, I am told, cheers such as only can be given by a triumphant soldiery. Shakos, thousands of helmets and caps, thousands of bayonets and sabres rose in the air. What an additional pang of agony that must have been to the wounded French, who felt that they had given their blood in vain, while the Prussians beside them, maimed as they were, tried to swell with their feeble voices the chorus of joy! An officer related to me that he saw a huge Prussian who had been lying with his hand to his side in mortal agony rise suddenly to his feet as he comprehended the reason of the ringing voices, utter a loud Hurrah, wave his hands on high, and then, as the blood rushed from his wound, fall dead across a Frenchman. The officer who came out eventually and met General Moltke in consultation was, I believe, General Reille, who was the officer in attendance on the King when he was at Compeigne. He was the bearer of an autograph letter from the Emperor addres ed to His Majesty, and written in no agitated hand. You already know the terms :—" *Mon Frère,—N'ayant pu mourir à la tête de mon armée, Je dépose mon épée aux pieds de votre Majesté.*" This letter was immediately conveyed to the King, who, with Count Bismark, General Moltke, and his staff, was looking down from a height above Wadelincourt on the extinction of an Empire His Majesty's answer was courteous and firm, and meantime General Wimpffen was informed that the terms offered to the army was the surrender of the whole force, guns, horses, and material, to the Prussians. I do not know whether the officers were then exempted from the general surrender, but, any way, the French commander declared he would sooner perish in the field than sign such a disgraceful capitulation ; and so the sun went down in the west, lighting the path of the King to Vendresse, through the most enthusiastic ovation from all the soldiery along the road south of the Meuse. * * *

The hesitation to sign the capitulation did not signify much, for a night's reflection, strengthened and matured by the sight of the preparations for maintaining possession of what remained of the French army by force, would, it was felt, render a positive refusal out of the question. Orders were sent to the various corps to close up round the town, and when the watchfires were alight Sedan seemed a black spot in a broad belt of fire, which lighted up the heavens. What a night it must have been for the wounded cannot be imagined by those who have not seen how great are the sufferings which kind nature, however, appeases generally as time wears on, and life ebbs away.

At 10 o'clock the town was to be bombarded, and the French army around it to be shelled, unless the capitulations were signed. It is stated that the scene inside of the walls and out was, to use a strong expression, " Hell broke loose." When the Emperor, who had passed weary hours, looked out in the early morning he beheld a forest of steel and iron on valley and hilltop, batteries posted on every eminence, cavalry in all the plains, as far as his eye could reach the hosts of embattled Germans. His decision was taken at last. He would see the King, and seek to obtain from him some mitigation of the terms. Attended by a few of his staff on horseback, His Majesty proceeded along the road from Sedan in a brougham.

\*   \*   \*   \*   \*   \*   \*   \*

At 11.30 the capitulations were signed, as agreed upon by General Wimpffen and General Von Moltke, and the Emperor remained as a prisoner of war of the King of Prussia.
—RUSSELL.

## AUFIDIUS AND CORIOLANUS.

*Cor.* Hail, lords ! I am return'd your soldier;
No more infected with my country's love
Than when I parted hence, but still subsisting
Under your great command. You are to know,
That prosperously I have attempted, and,
With bloody passage, led your wars even to
The gates of Rome. Our spoils we have brought home
Do more than counterpoise, a full third part
The charges of the action. We have made peace,
With no less honor to the Antiates,
Than shame to the Romans ; and we here deliver,
Subscribed by the consul and patricians,
Together with the seal o' the senate, what
We have compounded on.
   *Auf.* Read it not, noble lords ;
But tell the traitor, in the highest degree
He hath abused your powers.
   *Cor.* Traitor !—How now ?
   *Auf.* Ay, traitor, Marcius.
   *Cor.* Marcius !
   *Auf.* Ay, Marcius, Caius Marcius ; dost thou think
I'll grace thee with that robbery, thy stolen name
Coriolanus in Corioli ?
You lords and heads of the state, perfidiously
He has betray'd your business, and given up,
For certain drops of salt, your city Rome
(I say your city) to his wife and mother:
Breaking his oath and resolution, like
A twist of rotten silk ; never admitting
Counsel o' the war ; but at his nurse's tears
He whined and roar'd away your victory ;
That pages blush'd at him, and men of heart
Look'd wondering each at other.
   *Cor.* Hear'st thou, Mars ?
   *Auf.* Name not the god, thou boy of tears
   *Cor.* Ha !

*Auf.* No more.
　　*Cor.* Measureless liar, thou hast made my heart
Too great for what contains it. Boy! Oh slave!—
Pardon me, lords, 'tis the first time that ever
I was forced to scold. Your judgments, my grave lords,
Must give this cur the lie: and his own notion
(Who wears my stripes impress'd on him; that must bear
My beating to his grave) shall join to thrust
The lie unto him.
　　1 *Lord.* Peace, both, and hear me speak.
　　*Cor.* Cut me to pieces, Volsces; men and lads,
Stain all your edges on me.—Boy! False hound!
If you have writ your annals true, 'tis there,
That, like an eagle in a dove-cote, I
Flutter'd your Volsces in Corioli:
Alone I did it—Boy!
　　*Auf.* Why, noble lords,
Will you be put in mind of his blind fortune,
Which was your shame, by this unholy braggart,
'Fore your own eyes and ears?
　　*Con.* [*Several speak at once.*] Let him die for 't.
　　*Citizens.* [*Speaking promiscuously.*] Tear him to pieces, do it presently. He killed my son; my daughter;—he killed my cousin Marcus; he killed my father,—
　　2. *Lord.* Peace, ho!—no outrage!—peace!
The man is noble, and his fame folds in
This orb o' the earth. His last offence to us
Shall have judicious hearing.—Stand, Aufidius,
And trouble not the peace.
　　*Cor.* O that I had him,
With six Aufidiuses, or more, his tribe,
To use my lawful sword!
　　*Auf.* Insolent villain!
　　*Con.* Kill, kill, kill, kill, kill him!

[AUFIDIUS *and the* Conspirators *draw, and kill* CORIOLANUS, *who falls, and* AUFIDIUS *stands on him.*]

---

## SAMSON'S DEATH.

*Messenger.* OH, whither shall I run, or which way fly
　　　　The sight of this so horrid spectacle,
　　　　Which erst my eyes beheld, and yet behold?
　　　　For dire imagination still pursues me.
　　　　But providence or instinct of nature seems,
　　　　Or reason, though disturbed and scarce consulted,
　　　　To have guided me aright, I know not how,
　　　　To thee first, reverend Manoa, and to these
　　　　My countrymen, whom here I knew remaining,
　　　　As at some distance from the place of horror,
　　　　So in the sad event too much concerned.
*Manoa.* 　The accident was loud, and here before thee
　　　　With rueful cry, yet what it was we hear not.
　　　　No preface needs, thou seest we long to know.

*Mess.* It would burst forth : but I recover breath
And sense distract, to know well what I utter.
*Man.* Tell us the sum, the circumstance defer.
*Mess.* Gaza yet stands, but all her sons are fallen,
All in a moment overwhelmed and fallen.
*Man.* Sad ; but thou knowest to Israelites not saddest
The desolation of a hostile city.
*Mess.* Feed on that first, there may in grief be surfeit.
*Man.* Relate by whom.
*Mess.*           By Samson.
*Man.*                   That still lessens
The sorrow, and converts it nigh to joy.
*Mess.* Ah ! Manoa, I refrain too suddenly
To utter what will come at last too soon ;
Lest evil tidings with too rude irruption
Hitting thy aged ear should pierce too deep.
*Man.* Suspense in news is torture, speak them out.
*Mess.* Take then the worst in brief, Samson is dead.
*Man.* All by him fell thou say'st, by whom fell he ?
What glorious hand gave Samson his death's wound ?
*Mess.* Unwounded of his enemies he fell.
*Man.* Wearied with slaughter then, or how ? explain.
*Mess.* By his own hands.
*Man.*           Self-violence ! what cause
Brought him so soon at variance with himself
Among his foes ?
*Mess.*          Inevitable cause,
At once both to destroy and be destroyed.
The edifice where all were met to see him,
Upon their heads and on his own he pulled.
*Man.* Oh, lastly over-strong against thyself !
A dreadful way thou tookest to thy revenge.
More than enough we know : but, while things yet
Are in confusion, give us, if thou can'st
Eye-witness of what first or last was done,
Relation more particular and distinct.
*Mess.* Occasions drew me early to this city,
And as the gates I entered with sun-rise,
The morning trumpets festival proclaimed
Through each high street. Little I had dispatched
When all abroad was rumored that this day
Samson should be brought forth to show the people
Proof of his mighty strength in feats and games.
I sorrowed at his captive state, but minded
Not to be absent at that spectacle.
The building was a spacious theatre,
Half-round, on two main pillars vaulted high,
With seats where all the lords and each degree
Of sort might sit in order to behold ;
The other side was open, where the throng
On banks and scaffolds under sky might stand ;

## SAMSON'S DEATH.

I among these aloof obscurely stood.
The feast and noon grew high, and sacrifice
Had filled their hearts with mirth, high cheer, and wine,
When to their sports they turned. Immediately
Was Samson as a public servant brought,
In their state livery clad ; before him pipes
And timbrels ; on each side went armed guards,
Both horse and foot, before him and behind.
Archers and slingers, cataphracts and spears.
At sight of him the people with a shout
Rifted the air, clamoring their god with praise,
Who had made their dreadful enemy their thrall.
He patient, but undaunted, where they led him
Came to the place, and what was set before him,
Which without help of eye might be assayed,
To heave, pull, draw, or break, he still performed,
All with incredible, stupendous force,
None daring to appear antagonist.
At length for intermission sake they led him
Between the pillars ; he his guide requested
—For so from such as nearer stood we heard,—
As over-tired to let him lean awhile
With both his arms on those two massy pillars,
That to the arched roof gave main support.
He unsuspicious led him ; which when Samson
Felt in his arms, with head awhile inclined,
And eyes fast fixt he stood, as one who prayed,
Or some great matter in his mind revolved.
At last with head erect thus cried aloud :
"Hitherto, Lords, what your commands imposed
I have performed, as reason was, obeying,
Not without wonder or delight beheld :
Now of my own accord such other trial
I mean to show you of my strength, yet greater
As with amaze shall strike all who behold."
This uttered, straining all his nerves he bowed,
As, with the force of winds and waters pent,
When mountains tremble, those two massy pillars
With horrible confusion to and fro
He tugged, he shook, till down they came and drew
The whole roof after them with burst of thunder
Upon the heads of all who sat beneath,
Lords, ladies, captains, counsellors, or priests,
Their choice nobility and flower, not only
Of this but each Philistian city round,
Met from all parts to solemnize this feast.
Samson, with these immixed, inevitably
Pulled down the same destruction on himself ;
The vulgar only 'scaped who stood without.

—MILTON.

## MAXIMILIAN AND OCTAVIO.

*Max.* HE is possessed by a commanding spirit,
And his, too, is the station of command,
And well for us it is so!
Well for the whole, if there be found a man
Stands fixed and stately, like a firm-built column,
Where all may press with joy and confidence.
Now, such a man is Wallenstein.
The oracle within him, that which lives,
He must invoke and question—not dead books,
Not ordinances, not mould-rotted papers.
  *Octavio.* My son, of those old narrow ordinances
Let us not hold too lightly.
The way of ancient ordinance, though it winds,
Is yet no devious way.   Straight forward goes
The lightning's path, and straight the fearful path
Of the cannon-ball.   Direct it flies and rapid,
Shattering that it may reach, and shattering what it reaches.
My son, the road the human being travels,
That on which blessing comes and goes, doth follow
The river's course, the valley's playful windings,
Curves round the cornfield and the hill of vines,
Honoring the holy bounds of property;
And thus secure, though late, loads to its end.
  *Questenburg.* O, hear your father, noble youth! hear him,
Who is at once the hero and the man.
  *Oct.* My son, the nursling of the camp spoke in thee.
A war of fifteen years
Hath been thy education and thy school.
Peace hast thou never witnessed!   There exists
A higher than the warrior's excellence.
In war itself war is no ultimate purpose.
The vast and sudden deeds of violence,
Adventures wild, and wonders of the moment,
These are not they, my son, that generate
The Calm, the Blissful, the enduring mighty!
Lo there! the soldier, rapid architect,
Builds his light town of canvas, and at once
The whole scene moves and bustles momently
With arms and neighing steeds; and mirth and quarrel
The motley market fill; the roads, the streams,
Are crowded with new freights; trade stirs and hurried!
But on some morrow morn all suddenly
The tents drop down, the horde renews its march.—
Dreary and solitary as a church-yard
The meadow and down-trodden seed-plot lie:
And the year's harvest is gone utterly.
  *Max.* O, let the emperor make peace, my father!
Most gladly would I give the blood-stained laurel

For the first violet of the leafless spring,
Plucked in those quiet fields where I have journeyed!
  *Oct.* What ails thee? What so moves thee, all at once?
  *Max.* Peace have I ne'er beheld? I have beheld it.
From thence am I come hither: O! that sight,
It glimmers still before me, like some landscape
Left in the distance,—some delicious landscape!
My road conducted me through countries where
The war has not yet reached. Life, life, my father—
My venerable father, life has charms
Which we have ne'er experienced. We have been
But voyaging along its barren coasts.
Like some poor, ever-roaming horde of pirates,
That, crowded in the rank and narrow ship,
House on the wild sea with wild usages,
Nor know aught of the mainland, but the bays
Where safeliest they may venture a thieves' landing.
Whate'er in the inland dales the land conceals
Of fair and exquisite,—O! nothing, noth ng
Do we behold of that in our rude voyage.
  *Oct.* And so your journey has revealed this to you?
  *Max.* 'T was the first leisure of my life. O, tell me,
What is the meed and purpose of the toil,
The painful toil, which robbed me of my youth,
Left me a heart unsouled and solitary,
A spirit uninformed, unornamented!
For the camp's stir, and crowd, and ceaseless 'larum,
The neighing war-horse, the air shattering trumpet,
The unvaried, still returning hour of duty,
Word of command, and exercise of arms—
There's nothing here, there's nothing in all this
To satisfy the heart, the gasping heart!
Mere bustling nothingness, where the soul is not—
This cannot be the sole felicity,
These cannot be man's best and only pleasures!
  *Oct.* Much hast thou learnt, my son, in this short journey.
  *Max.* O! day thrice lovely! when at length the soldier
Returns home into life; when he becomes
A fellow-man among his fellow-men.
The colors are unfurled, the cavalcade
Marshals, and now the buzz is hushed, and, hark!
Now the soft peace-march beats, Home, brothers, home!
The caps and helmets are all garlanded
With green boughs, the last plundering of the fields.
The city gates fly open of themselves;
They need no longer the petard to tear them.
The ramparts are all filled with men and women,
With peaceful men and women, that send onwards
Kisses and welcomings upon the air,
Which they make breezy with affectionate gestures.
From all the towers rings out the merry peal,

The joyous vespers of a bloody day.
O, happy man, O, fortunate! for whom
The well-known door, the faithful arms are open,
The faithful tender arms with mute embracing!
           SCHILLER, *translated by* COLERIDGE

## ADRASTUS CRYTHES, AND ION.

*Cry.* The king!
*Ad.* Stranger, I bid thee welcome;
We are about to tread the same dark passage,
Thou almost on the instant.—Is the sword (*to* CRYTHES)
Of justice sharpen'd, and the headsman ready?
*Cry.* Thou may'st behold them plainly in the court;
Even now the solemn soldiers line the ground,
The steel gleams on the altar, and the slave
Disrobes himself for duty.
*Ad.* (*to* ION)          Dost thou see them?
*Ion.* I do.
*Ad.*     He sees and yet he does not change!
If, even now, thou wilt depart, and leave
Thy traitorous thoughts unspoken, thou art free.
*Ion.* I thank thee for thy offer; but I stand
Before thee for the lives of thousands, rich
In all that makes life precious to the brave;
Who perish not alone, but in their fall
Break the far-spreading tendrils that they feed,
And leave them nurtureless. If thou wilt hear me
For them, I am content to speak no more.
*Ad.* Thou hast thy wish, then. Crythes! till yon dial
Casts its thin shadow on the approaching hour,
I hear this gallant traitor. On the instant,
Come without word, and lead him to his doom.
Now leave us.
*Cry.*      What, alone?
*Ad.*                Yes, slave, alone:
He is no assassin!          (*Exit* CRYTHES.)
          Tell me who thou art.
What generous source owns that heroic blood,
Which holds its course thus bravely? What great wars
Have nursed the courage that can look on death—
Certain and speedy death—with placid eye!
*Ion.* I am a simple youth, who never bore
The weight of armor—one who may not boast
Of noble birth, or valor of his own.
Deem not the powers which nerve me thus to speak
In thy great presence, and have made my heart
Upon the verge of bloody death, as calm,
As equal in its beatings, as when sleep

Approach'd me nestling from the sportive toils
Of thoughtless childhood, and celestial forms
Began to glimmer through the deepening shadows
Of soft oblivion—to belong to me!
These are the strengths of Heaven ; to thee they speak,
Bid thee to hearken to thy people's cry,
Or warn thee that thy hour must shortly come!
   *Ad.* I know it must ; so may'st thou spare thy warnings.
The envious gods in me have doom'd a race,
Whose glories stream from the same cloud-girt founts,
Whence their own dawn upon the infant world ;
And I shall sit on my ancestral throne
To meet their vengeance ; but till then I rule
As I have ever ruled, and thou wilt feel.
   *Ion.* I will not further urge thy safety to thee ;
It may be, as thou say'st, too late ; nor seek
To make thee tremble at the gathering curse
Which shall burst forth in mockery at thy fall ;
But thou art gifted with a nobler sense—
I know thou art my sovereign!—sense of pain
Endured by myriad Argives, in whose souls,
And in whose fathers' souls, thou and thy fathers
Have kept their cherish'd state ; whose heartstrings, still
The living fibres of thy rooted power,
Quiver with agonies thy crimes have drawn
From Heavenly justice on them.
   *Ad.*                         How! my crimes?
   *Ion.* Yes ; 'tis the eternal law, that where guilt is,
Sorrow shall answer it ; and thou hast not
A poor man's privilege to bear alone,
Or in the narrow circle of his kinsmen,
The penalties of evil ; for in thine,
A nation's fate lies circled. King Adrastus !
Steel'd as thy heart is with the usages
Of pomp and power, a few short summers since
Thou wert a child, and canst not be relentless.
Oh, if maternal love embraced thee then,
Think of the mothers who with eyes unwet
Glare o'er their perishing children · hast thou shared
The glow of a first friendship which is born
'Midst the rude sports of boyhood, think of youth
Smitten amidst its playthings ;—let the spirit
Of thy own innocent childhood whisper pity !
                                              —TALFOURD.

# APPENDIX,

ILLUSTRATING THE

ORIGIN AND PROGRESS OF THE ENGLISH LANGUAGE.

## I. ANGLO-SAXON PERIOD.—A.D. 449—1066.*

*From* THE CREATION.

| | |
|---|---|
| Nu we sceolan herian | Now we shall praise |
| heofon rices weard, | the guardian of heaven, |
| metodes mihte, | the might of the creator, |
| and his mod-ge-thonc, | and his counsel, |
| wera wuldor fæder! | the glory-father of men! |
| swa he wundra ge-hwœs, | how he of all wonders, |
| ece dryhten, | the eternal lord, |
| oord onstealde. | formed the beginning. |
| He ærest ge-sceóp | He first created |

---

* "The reader will do well to keep in mind, or under his eye, the four following Schemes, or Synoptical Views, according to which the history of the English language in its entire extent may be methodized:—

### I.

1. Original, Pure, Simple, or First English (commonly called Saxon, or Anglo-Saxon); Synthetic, or Inflectional, in its Grammar, and Homogeneous in its Vocabulary;
2. Broken, or Second English (commonly called Semi-Saxon).—from soon after the middle of the eleventh century to about the middle of the thirteenth:—when its ancient Grammatical system had been destroyed, and it had bee  converted from an Inflectional into a Non-Inflectional and Analytic Language, by the *first* action upon it of the Norman Conquest;
3. Mixed, or Compound, or Composite, or Third English,—since the middle of the thirteenth century—about which date its Vocabulary also began to be changed by the combination of its original Gothic with a French (Romance or Neo-Latin) element, under the *second* action upon it of the Norman Conquest.

### II.

1. The Original form, in which the three vowel-endings *a*, *e*, and *u* are employed in the declension of nouns and the conjugation of verbs;
2. The Second form, in which the single termination *e* represents indiscriminately the three ancient vowel-endings, but still constitutes a distinct syllable;
3. The Third form, in which this termination *e* of nouns and verbs, though still written, is no longer syllabically pronounced.

### III.

1. *Saxon*, or *Anglo-Saxon*; throughout the period before the Norman Conquest;
2. *Semi-Saxon*; from about the middle of the eleventh to the middle of the thirteenth century; the period of the Infancy and Childhood of our existing national speech;
3. *Old*, or rather *Early*, *English*; from the middle of the thirteenth to the middle of the fourteenth century; the period of the Boyhood of our existing speech,

| | |
|---|---|
| ylda bearnum | for the children of men |
| heofon to hrofe, | heaven as a roof, |
| halig scyppend! | the holy creator! |
| tha middan-geard | then the world |
| mon-cynnes weard, | the guardian of mankind, |
| ece dryhten, | the eternal lord, |
| æfter teode, | produced afterwards, |
| firum foldan, | the earth for men, |
| frea ælmihtig! | the almighty master! |

—CÆDMON (died A. D. 680).

*From his translation of Boethius's work* ON THE CONSOLATION OF PHILOSOPHY.

| | |
|---|---|
| Fela spella him sædon tha Beormas, ægther ge of hyra agenum lande ge of thæm lande the ymb hy utan wæron; ac he nyste hwæt thæs sothes wær, for-thæm he hit sylf no gesceah. Tha Finnas him | Many things him told the Beormas, both of their own land and of the land that around them about were; but he wist-not what (of-the sooth was, for-that he it self not saw. The Finns him thought, and |

---

4. *Middle English;* from the middle of the fourteenth to the middle of the sixteenth century; the youth, or Adolescence of our existing speech;
5. *Modern English;* since the middle of the sixteenth century; the Manhood of our existing speech.

### IV.

**A.D.**
450. Commencement of the conquest and occupation of South Britain by the Angles and Saxons, bringing with them their ancestral Gothic speech;
1066. Conquest of England by the Normans; Establishment of French as the courtly and literary language of the country; Commencement of the reduction of the ancient vernacular tongue to the condition of a patois, and of its conversion from a synthetic to an analytic tongue;
1154. End of the reign of the four Norman kings and accession of the Plantagenet dynasty; Beginning of the connexion with Southern France through the marriage of Henry II. with Eleanor of Poitou; Termination of the National Chronicle, the latest considerable composition in the regular form of the ancient language; Full commencement of the intermixture of the two races;
1272. New age of the Edwards; Commencement of the connexion of the English royal family with that of France by the second marriage of Edward I. with a daughter of Philip III.; Employment, at first occasionally, afterwards habitually, of French instead of Latin as the Language of the Statutes; Commencement of its active intermixture with the vernacular tongue;
1362. Trials at law in the King's Courts directed by the statute of 36 Edward III. to be conducted no longer in French but in English; Victory of the native tongue in its new composite form over its foreign rival, and recovery of its old position as the literary language of the country, under the impulse of the war with France, and of the genius of Minot, Langland, and Chaucer.
1455. Outbreak of the desolating War of the Roses, and complete extinction for a time of the light of literature in England;
1558. Accession of Elizabeth; Commencement of a new literary era, with the native language in sole dominion;
1660. Restoration of the Stuarts; Noonday of the Gallican age of English literature;
1760. Accession of George III.; Complete association in the national literature of Scottish and Irish writers with those of England."- *Craik.*

thuhte, and tha Beormas spræcon neah an getheode. Swithost he for thyder, to-eacan thæs landes scea-wunge, for thæm hors-hwælum, for-thæm hi habbath swythe ætheic ban on hyra tothum, tha teth hy broh-ton sume thæm cyninege : and hyra hyd bith swythe god to scip-rapum. Se hwæl bith micle læssa thonne othre hwalas, ne bith he lengra thonne syfan elna lang ; ac on his agnum lande is se betsta hwæl-huntath, tha beoth eahta and feo-wertiges elna lange, and tha mæstan fiftiges elna lange ; thara he sæde thæt he syxa sum ofsloge syxtig on twam dagum. He was swythe spe-dig man on thæm æhtum the heora speda on beoth, thæt is on wild-deorum.

the Beormas spoke nigh one lan-guage. Chiefliest he fared thither, besides the land's seeing, for the horse-whales, for-that they have very noble bones in their teeth, these teeth they brought some (to-) tho the king : and their hide is very good for ship-ropes. This whale is much less than other whales, not is he longer than seven ells long ; but in his own land is the best whale-hunting, they are eight and forty ells long, and the largest fifty ells long ; (of-) these he said that he (of-) six some slew sixty in two days. He was (a) very wealthy man in the ownings that their wealth in is, that is in wild-deer.

—KING ALFRED. (849-901.)

## II. SEMI-SAXON PERIOD.—A.D. 1066—1250.

## KING ARTHUR'S DREAM.

To niht a mine slepe,
Ther ich laei on bure,
Me imaette a sweuen ;
Ther uore ich ful sari aem.
Me imette that mon me hof
Uppen are halle.
Tha halle ich gon bestriden,
Swule ich wolde riden
Alle tha lond tha ich ah
Alle ich ther ouer sah.
And Walwain sat biuoren me ;
Mi sweord he bar an honde
Tha com Moddred faren ther

Mid unimete uolke.

He bar an his honde
Ane wiax stronge.
He bigon to hewene
Hardliche swithe,
And tha postes for-heoualle

To night in my sleep,
Where I lay in bower (chamber),
I dreamt *a* a dream ;
Therefore I full sorry am.
I dreamt *b* that men raised me
Upon a hall.
The hall I gan bestride,
So as I would ride
All the land that I owned
All I there over-saw.
And Walwain sat before me ;
My sword he bare in hand.
Then came Modred to fare (go) there
With unmeasured (unnumbered) folk.
He bare in his hand
An axe strong.
He began to hew
Hardly exceedingly,
And the posts thoroughly-hewed all

*a* Rather, There met me, there occurred to me ?   *b* It occurred to me ?

## KING ARTHUR'S DREAM.

| | |
|---|---|
| Tha heolden up the halle. | That held up the hall. |
| Ther ich isey Wenheuer eke, | There I saw Wenhever (Guinever, the Queen) eke |
| Wimmonen leofuest me : | Of women loveliest to me ; |
| Al there muche halle rof | All the great (mickle) hall roof |
| Mid hire honden heo to-droh. | With her hands she drew (down). |
| Tha halle gon to haelden, | The hall gan to tumble, |
| And ich haeld to grunden, | And I tumbled to ground, |
| That mi riht aerm to-brac, | That my right arm broke. |
| Tha seide Modred, Haue that! | Then said Modred, Have that! |
| Adun neol tha halle | Adown fell the hall, |
| And Walwain gon to ualle, | And Walwain gan to fall, |
| And feol a there eorthe ; | And fell on the earth ; |
| His aermes brekeen beine. | His arms brake both. |
| And ich igrap mi sweord leofe | And I grasped my dear sword, |
| Mid mire leoft honde, | With my left hand, |
| And smaet of Modred is haft, | And smote off Modred his head, |
| That hit wond a theno ueld ; | That it rolled (wended) on the field ; |
| And tha queno ich al to-snathde, | And the queen I all cut to pieces (snedded), |
| Mid deore mine sweorde, | With my dear sword, |
| And seodthen ich heo adun sette | And then I her adown set |
| In ane swarte putte. | In a black pit. |
| And al mi uole riche | And all my rich (great) people |
| Sette to fleme, | Set to flight, |
| That nuste ich under Criste | That I wist not under Christ |
| Whar heo bicomen weoren. | Where they were become (gone). |
| Buten mi scolf ich gond atstonden | But myself I gan stand |
| Uppen ane wolden | Upon a wold (or weald) |
| And ich ther wondrien agon | And I there gan to wander |
| Wide yeond than moren. | Wide over the moors. |
| Ther ich isah gripes | There I saw gripes (griffons), |
| And grisliche fugheles. | And grisly fowls (birds). |
| Tha com an guldene leo | Then came a golden lion |
| Lithen ouer dune. | To glide over *the* down. |
| Deoren switho hende, | A beast (deer) very handsome, |
| Tha ure Drihten make. | That our Lord made. |
| Tha leo me orn foren to, | The lion ran forward to me, |
| And iueng me bi than midle, | And took me by the middle, |
| And forth hire gun yeongen | And forth her*self* gan move |
| And to there sae wende. | And to the sea went. |
| And ich isaeh thae vthen | And I saw the waves |
| I there sae driuen ; | In the sea drive ; |
| And the leo i than ulode | And the lion in the flood |
| Iwende with me seolue. | Went with myself. |
| Tha wit i sae comen, | When we in sea came, |
| Tha ythen me hire binomen. | The waves *from* me her took. |
| Com ther an flsc litho, | Came there a fish to glide *a* |

*a* That is, A fish approached. Unless we should understand *litho* to be an epithet of the fish. But the later text, " Com thar a fisc swimme" is against that.

| | |
|---|---|
| And fereden me to londe. | And brought me to land. |
| Tha wes ich al wet, | Then was I all wet, |
| And weri of soryen, and seoc. | And weary from sorrow, and sick. |
| Tha gon ich iwakien | When I gan to awake |
| Swithe ich gon to quakien; | Greatly I gan to quake; |
| Tha gon ich to binien | Then gan I to tremble |
| Swulc ich al for burne. | As *if* I all *with* fire burned. |
| And swa ich habbe al niht | And so I have all night |
| Of mine sweuene swithe ithoht; | Of my dream much thought; |
| For ich what to iwisse | For I wot to certainty |
| Agan is al mi blisse; | Agone is all my bliss; |
| For a to mine liue | For aye to (throughout) my life |
| Soryen ich mot driye. | Sorrow I must endure. |
| Wale that ich nabbe here | Welaway (alas) that I have not here |
| Wenhauer mine quene! | Wenhaver, my queen! |

—LAYAMON (between 1155 and 1200.)

## III. OLD ENGLISH PERIOD.—A.D. 1250—1558.

## FROM PIERS PLOUGHMAN'S VISION.

In a summer season,
  When soft was the sun,
I shoop me into shrowds *a*
  As I a sheep *b* were;
In habit as an hermit
  Unholy of werkes, *c*
Went wide in this world
  Wonders to hear;
Ac *d* on a May morwening
  On Malvern hills
Me befel a ferly, *e*
  Of fairy me thought.
I was weary for-wandered, *f*
  And went me to rest
Under a brood bank,
  By a burn's *h* side;
And as I lay and leaned,
  And looked on the waters,
I slombered into a sleeping,

*a* I put myse into clothes.    *b* A shepherd.
*c* Whitaker's interpretation is "In habit, not like an anchorite who keeps his cell, but like one of those unholy hermits who wander about the world to see and hear wonders." He reads, "That went forth in the world," &c.   *d* And.    *e* Wonder.
*f* Worn out with wandering.    *g* Broad.    *h* Stream's.

It swayed so mury. *a*
Then gan I meten *b*
A marvellous sweven, *c*
That I was in a wilderness,
   Wist I never where;
And, as I beheld into the east
   On high to the sun,
I seigh *d* a tower on a toft *e*
   Frieliche ymaked, *f*
A deep dale beneath,
   A donjon therein,
With deep ditches and darke,
   And dreadful of sight.
A fair field full of folk
   Found I there between,
Of all manner of men,
   The mean and the rich,
Werking *g* and wandering
   As the world asketh.
Some putten hem *h* to the plough,
   Playden full seld, *i*
In setting and sowing
   Swonken *j* full hard,
And wonnen that wasters
   With gluttony destroyeth. *k*
And some putten hem to pride,
   Apparelled hem thereafter,
In countenance of clothing
   Comen deguised, *l*
In prayers and penances
   Putten hem many, *m*
All for the love of our Lord
   Liveden full strait, *n*
In hope to have alter
   Heaven-riche bliss; *o*
As anchors and heremites *p*
   That holden hem in hir *q* cells,
And coveten nought in coun
   To carryen about,
For no likerous liflode
   Hir likame to please. *r*
And some chosen chaffer: *s*

*a* It sounded so pleasant.   *b* Meet.   *c* Dream.
*d* Saw.   *e* An elevated ground.   *f* Handsomely built.
*g* Working.   *h* Put them.   *i* Played full seldom.
*j* Labored.   *k* Won that which wasters with gluttony destroy.
*l* Came disguised. Whitaker reads, "In countenance and in clothing."
*m* Many put them, applied themselves to, engaged in.   *n* Lived full strictly.
*o* The bliss of the kingdom of heaven.   *p* Anchorites and eromites, or hermits.
*q* Hold them in their.   *r* By no likerous living their body to please   chandise

· They cheveden *a* the better,
As it seemeth to our sight
That swich me thriveth. *b*
And some murths to make
As minstralles con,*c*
And geten gold with hir glee,*d*
Guiltless, I lieve.*e*
Ac japers and jaugellers *f*
Judas' children,
Feignen hem fantasies
And fools hem maketh,
And han hir *g* wit at will
To werken if they wold.
That Poul preacheth of hem
I wol nat preve *h* it here :
But *qui loquitur turpiloquium i*
Is Jupiter's hine. *j*

—LANGLANDE (about 1360.)

## THE TEMPLE OF MARS.

WHY should I not as well eke tell you all
The portraiture that was upon the wall
Within the Temple of mighty Mars the Red?
All painted was the wall in length and bred *k*
Like to the estres *l* of the grisley place
That hight *m* the great Temple of Mars in Trace, *n*
In thilke *o* cold and frosty region
There as Mars hath his sovereign mansion.
  First on the wall was painted a forest,
In which there wonneth *p* neither man ne beast ;
With knotty knarry barren trees old,
Of stubbes sharp and hidous to behold,
In which there ran a rumble and a swough,*q*
As though a storm should bresten *r* every bough ;
And downward from an hill under a bent *s*
There stood the Temple of Mars Armipotent,
Wrought all of burned *t* steel, of which the entree
Was long, and strait, and ghastly for to see ;
And thereout came a rage and swich a vise *u*
That it made all the gates for to rise.

*a* Achieved their end.  *b* That such men thrive.
*c* And some are skilled to make mirths, or amusements, as minstrels.
*d* And get gold with their minstrelsy.  *e* Believe.  *f* But jesters and jugglers.
*g* Have their.  *h* Will not prove.  *i* Whoso speaketh ribaldry.
  *j* Our modern hind, or servant.
*k* Breadth.  *l* The interior.  *m* Is called.  *n* Thrace.  *o* That same.  *p* Dwelleth.
*q* A long sighing noise, such as in Scotland is called a *sugh*.  *r* Was going to break.
*s* A declivity.  *t* Burnished.  *u* A violent blast ?

The northern light in at the dore shone;
For window on the wall ne was there none
Through which men mighten any light discern.
The door was all of athamant *a* etern,
Yclenched overthwart and endelong *b*
With iron tough, and, for to make it strong,
Every pillar the temple to sustene
Was tonne-great, *c* of iron bright and shene.
There saw I first the dark imagining
Of Felony, and all the compassing;
The cruel Ire, red as any gled; *d*
The Picke-purse, and eke the pale Dread;
The Smiler with the knife under the cloak;
The shepen *e* brenning *f* with the blake smoke;
The treason of the murdering in the bed;
The open wer, *g* with woundes al bebled;
Contek *h* with bloody knife and sharp menace;
All full of chirking *i* was that sorry place.
The sleer *j* of himself yet saw I there;
His hearte-blood hath bathed all his hair;
The nail ydriven in the shod *k* or hight;
The colde death, with mouth gaping upright.
Amiddes of the Temple sat Mischance,
With discomfort and sorry countenance.
Yet saw I Woodness *l* laughing in his rage,
Armed Complaint, Outhees, *m* and fierce Outrage
The carrain *n* in the bush, with throat ycorven;;
A thousand slain, and not of qualm ystorven; *p*
The tyrant, with the prey by force yraft; *q*
The town destroyed;—there was nothing laft. *r*

—CHAUCER (1328—1400.)

## CAIUS FABRICIUS.

In a Croniq I fynde thus,
How that Caius Fabricius
Wich whilome was consul of Rome,
By whome the lawes yede and come, *s*
Whan the Sampnitees to him brouht
A somme of golde, and hym by souht
To done hem fauoure in the lawe,
Towarde the golde he gan hym drawe:
Whereof, in alle mennes loke,
A parte into his honde he tooke,

*a* Adamant.   *b* Across and lengthwise.   *c* Of the circumference of a tun.
*d* Burning coal.   *e* Stable.   *f* Burning.   *g* War.   *h* Contention.
*i* Disagreeable sound.   *j* Slayer.   *k* Hilt of the head.   *l* Madness.   *m* Outcry.
*n* Carrion.   *o* Cut.   *p* Dead (starved).   *q* Reft.   *r* Left.
*s* Went and came.

Wich to his mouthe in alle haste
He put hit for to smelle and taste,
And to his ihe and to his ere,
Bot he ne fonde no comfort there :
And thanne he be gan it to despise,
And tolde vnto hem in this wise:
" I not what is with golde to thryve,
Whan none of alle my wittes fyve
Fynt savour ne delite ther inne ;
So is it bot a nyce sinne
Of golde so ben to coveitous.
Bot he is riche an glorious
Wich hath in his subieccion
The men wich in possession
Ben riche of gold, and by this skille, *a*
For he may alday whan he wille,
Or be him leef or be him loth,
Justice don vppon hem bothe."
Lo thus he seide, and with that worde
He threwe to fore hem on the borde
The golde oute of his honde anon,
And seide hem that he wolde none,
So that he kepte his liberte,
To do justice and equite,
Without lucre of such richesse.
There be nowe fewe of such I gesse,
For it was thilke tymes used
That every juge was refused,
Wich was not frende to commoun riht ;
Bot thei that wolden stonde vpriht
For trouth only to do justice
Preferred were in thilke office,
To deme and juge common lawe,
Wich nowe men seyn is alle withdrawe.
To set a lawe and keep it nouht
There is no common profit souht,
But, above alle, natheless,
The lawe wich is made for pees
Is good to kepe for the beste,
For that set alle men in reste. —GOWER (1325-1408 )

---

## FREEDOM.

A ! fredome is a nobill thing !        Ah ! Freedom is a noble thing !
Fredome mayse man to haiff liking !    Freedom makes man to have liking!
Fredome all solace to man giffis :     Freedom all solace to man gives :
He levys at ese that frely levys !     He lives at ease that freely lives !

A noble hart may haiff naue ese, | A noble heart may have none ease,
Na ellys nocht that may him plese, | Nor else nought that may him please
Gyff fredome failythe : for fre liking | If freedom faileth : for free liking
Is yearnyt our all othir thing. | Is yearned over all other thing.
Na he, that ay hase levyt fre, | Nor he, that aye has lived free,
May nocht knaw weill the propyrte, | May not know well the property,
The angyr, na the wrechyt dome, | The anger, nor the wretched doom,
That is cowplyt to foule thyrldome. | That is coupled to soul thraldom.
Bot gyff he had assayit it, | But if he had assayed it,
Than all perquer he suld it wyt ; | Then all perquer[a] he should it wit ;[b]
And suld think fredome mar to pryse | And should think freedom more to prize
Than all the gold in warld that is. | Than all the gold in world that is.

—BARBOUR. (died 1395.)

## MAHOMET.

AND zee schull vnderstonde that Machamete was born in Arabyc, that was first a pore knaue that kept cameles that wenten with marchantes for marchandise, and so befell that he wente with the marchandes in to Egipt, and they were thanne cristene in thoo partyes. And at the desartes of Arabyc he wente in to a chapell wher a Eremyte duelte. And whan he entred in to the chapell, that was but a lytill and a low thing, and had but a lytil dor' and a low, than the entree began to wexe so gret and so large, and so high, as though it had be of a gret mynstr, or the zate of a paleys. And this was the first myracle the Sarazins seyn that Machomete dide in his zouthe. After began he for to wexe wyse and riche ; and he was a gret Astronomer ; and, after, he was gouernour and prince of the lond of Corrodane, and he gouerned it full wisely, in such manere, that whan the Prince was ded, he toke the lady to wyfe that highte[d] Gadrige. And Machomete fell often in the grete sikeness that men calle the fallynge euyll. Wherfore the lady was full sory that euere scho toke him to husbonde. But Machomete made hire to beleeue that all tymes when he fell so, Gabriel the angel cam for to speke with him, and for the grete light and brightnesse of the angell, he myghte not susteyne him fro fallynge. And therefore the Sarazines seyn that Gabriel cam often to speke with him. This Machomete regned in Arabye, the zeer of our Lord Jhesu Crist sixe hundred and ten, and was of the generacion of Ysmael. * * * And also Machomete loued wel a godo heremyte that duelled in the desertes, a myle from Mount Synay in the weye that men gon fro Arabye toward Caldee, and toward Ynde, o[e] day iorney fro the See wher the Marchaunts of Venyse comen often for merchandize. And so often wente Machomete to this heremyte that all his men were wrothe, for he wolde gladly here this heremyte preche, and make his men wake all nyght ; and therefore his men thoughten to putte the heremyte to deth ; and so befell vpon a nyght that Machomete was

a Perfectly.   b Know.   c Those.   d Was called.   e One.

dronken of god wyn and he fell on slepe, and his men toke Machomete's swerd out of his schethe, whils he slepte, and there with thei slowgh this heremyte and putte his swerd al blody in his schethe azen. And at morwe whan he found the heremeyte ded, he was fully sory and wroth, and wolde haue don his men to deth, but thei all with on accord (said) that he him self had slayn him whan he was dronken and schewed him his swerd all blody, and he trowed that thei hadden seyd soth.*a* And than he cursed the wyn, and all tho that dryuken it. And therefore Sarrazines that be douout drynken neuer no wyn, but sum drynken it priuyly, for zif thei dronken it openly thei sholde ben reproued. But thei drynken gode beuerage, and swete and noryfshynge, that is made of Galamell, and that is that men maken sugr' of that is of right gode sauor, and it is gode for the breest. Also it befalleth sumtyme that cristene men become Sarazines outher for pouertee or for sympleness, or elles for her owne wykkedness. And therefore the Archiflamyn or the Flamyn, os *b* our Echobisshopp or Bisshopp, whan he resceyueth hem seyth thus : *La ellec olla syla Machomet rores alla,* that is to seye, " There is no God but on and Machomete his messager." —MANDEVIL (1300-1372.)

## BE MERRY.

BE merry, man, and tak not sair in mind
 The wavering of this wretched world of sorrow :
To God be humble, to thy friend be kind,
 And with thy neighbours gladly lend and borrow ;
 His chance to-night, it may be thine to-morrow ;
Be blyth in hearte for my aventure,
 For oft with wise men it has been said aforow,
Without Gladness availes no Treasure.

Make thee gude cheer of it that God thee sends,
 For warld's wrak but welfare *b*nought avails ;
Nae gude is thine save only that thou spends,
 Remanant all thou bruikes but with bails ; *c*
 Seek to solace, when sadness thee assails ;
*In dolour lang thy life may not endure,*
 Wherefore of comfort set up all thy sails ;
Without Gladness availes no Treasure.

Follow on pity, flee trouble and debate,
 With famous folkis hald thy company :
Be charitable and hum'le in thine estate,
 For warldly honour lastes but a cry.
 For trouble in earth tak no melancholy
Be rich in patience, if thou in gudes be poor
 Who lives merrily he lives mightily ;
Without Gladness availes no Treasure.
                                —DUNBAR (1465-1520.)

*a* Truth.    *b* As.    *c* World's trash without health.    *d* Injuries.

## SIR LANCELOT.

Oh! ye mighty and pompous lords, winning in the glorious transitory of this unstable life, as in reigning over great realms and mighty great countries, fortified with strong castles and towers, edified with many a rich city; yea also, ye fierce and mighty knights, so valiant in adventurous deeds of arms, behold! behold! see how this mighty conqueror, King Arthur, whom in his human life all the world doubted,*a* yea also the noble Queen Guenever, which sometime sat in her chair adorned with gold, pearls, and precious stones, now lie full low in obscure foss, or pit, covered with clods of earth and clay! Behold also this mighty champion, Sir Lancelot, peerless of all knighthood; see now how he lieth grovelling upon the cold mould; now being so feeble and faint, that sometime was so terrible : how, and in what manner, ought ye to be so desirous of worldly honour so dangerous? Therefore, me thinketh this present book is right necessary to be often read; for in all *b* ye find the most gracious, knightly, and virtuous war, of the most noble knights of the world, whereby they got praising continually; also me seemeth, by the oft reading thereof, ye shall greatly desire to accustom yourself in following of those gracious knightly deeds; that is to say, to dread God and to love righteousness, faithfully and courageously to serve your sovereign prince; and, the more that God hath given you the triumphal honour, the meeker ought ye to be, ever fearing the unstableness of this deceitful world.

And so, within fifteen days, they came to Joyous Guard, and there they laid his corpse in the body of the quire, and sung and read many psalters and prayers over him and about him, and even his visage was laid open and naked, that all folk might behold him. For such was the custom in those days, that all men of worship should so lie with open visage, till that they were buried. And right thus as they were at their service, there came Sir Ector de Maris, that had sought seven years all England, Scotland, and Wales, seeking his brother Sir Lancelot. . . .

And then Sir Ector threw his shield, his sword, and his helm from him; and when he beheld Sir Lancelot's visage, he fell down in a swoon; and, when he awoke, it were hard for any tongue to tell the doleful complaints that he made for his brother. "Ah! Sir Lancelot," said he, "thou wert head of all Christian knights."—"And now, I dare say," said Sir Bors, "that Sir Lancelot, there thou liest, thou wert never matched of none earthly knight's hands. And thou wert the courtliest knight that ever bare shield : and thou wert the truest friend to thy lover that ever bestrode horse ; and thou wert the truest lover, of a sinful man, that ever loved woman; and thou wert the kindest man that ever stroke with sword ; and thou wert the goodliest person that ever came among press of knights ; and thou wert the meekest man, and the gentlest, that ever eat in hall among ladies ; and thou wert the sternest knight to thy mortal foe that ever put spear in rest."

—MALORY (1485.)

*a* Dreaded, held as redoubtable. *b* It?

# LETTER OF SIR THOMAS MORE TO HIS WIFE.

MAISTRES ALYCE, in my most harty wise I recommend me to you; and whereas I am enfourmed by my son Heron of the losse of our barnes and of our neighbours also, with all the corn that was therein, albeit, (saving God's pleasure) it is gret'pitie of so much good corne lost, yet sith it hath liked hym to sende us such a chaunce, we must and are bounden, not only to be content, but also to be glad of his visitacion. He sente us all that we have loste: and sith he hath by such a chaunce taken it away againe, his pleasure be fulfilled. ' Let us never grudge ther at, but take it in good worth, and hartely thank him, as well for adversitie as for prosperitie. And peradventure we have more cause to thank him for our losse, then for our winning; for his wisdome better seeth what is good for vs then we do our selves. Therfore I pray you be of good chere, and take all the howsold with you to church, and there thanke God, both for that he hath given us, and for that he hath taken from us, and for that he hath left us, which if it please hym he can encrease when he will. And if it please hym to leave us yet lesse, at his pleasure be it.

I pray you to make some good ensearche what my poore neighbours have loste, and bid them take no thought therfore : for aud I shold not leave myself a spone, there shal no pore neighbour of mine bere no losse by any chaunce happened in my house. I pray you be with my children and your household merry in God. And devise somewhat with your frendes, what waye wer best to take, for provision to be made for corne for our household, and for sede thys yere comming, if ye thinke it good that we kepe the ground stil in our handes. And whether ye think it good that we so shall do or not, yet I think it were not best sodenlye thus to leave it all up, and to put away our folk of our farme till we have somwhat advised us thereon. How beit if we have more nowe than ye shall nede, and which can get them other maisters, ye may then discharge us of them. But I would not that any man were sodenly sent away, he wote nere wether.

. At my comming hither I perceived none other but that I shold tary still with the Kinges Grace. But now I shal (I think) because of this chance, get leave this next weke to come home and se you ; and then shall we further devyse together uppon all thinges, what order shal be best to take. And thus as hartely fare you well with all our children as ye can wishe. At Woodestok the thirde daye of Septembre by the hand of

your louing husbande,
THOMAS MORE, Knight (1480-1535.)

## THE SHEPHERDS OF BETHLEHEM.

But I pray you to whome was the nativitie of Christ first opened, to the Bishoppes or great Lordes which were at that time at Bethleem ? or to those iolly damsels with their fardingales, with their round aboutes, or with their bracelets ? No, no, they had so many lettes to trimme and dresse theselves so that they coulde have no time to heare of the nativitie of Chryst, theyr myndes were so occupyed otherwise that they were not allowed to heare of them. But his nativitie was revealed first to the shepheardes, and it was revealed vnto them in the night time when everybody was at rest, the they heard this ioyfull tidinges of the Saviour of the World ; for these shepheardes were keeping theyr sheep in the night season from the wolfe or other beastes, and from the foxe : for the sheepe in that countrey do lambe two tymes in the yeare, and therefore it was needefull for the sheep to have a shepheard to keep the. And here note the diligence of these shepheardes ; for whether the sheepe were theyr owne, or whether they were servaunts, I cannot tell : for it is not expressed in the booke, but it is most lyke they were servauntes, and theyr maysters had put them in trust to keepe theyr sheepe. Now if these shepheardes hadde bene deceitfull fellowes, that when theyr maysters had put them in trust to keepe theyr sheepe, they had bene drinking in yᵉ alehouse all night as some of our servaunts do now a dayes, surely the Aungell had not appeared vnto them to have tolde them this great ioy and good tidinges. And here all servaunts may learn by these shepheards to serve truely and diligently vnto their maisters ; in what busines soever they are set to doo let them be paynefull and diligent, like as Jacob was vnto his maister Laban. O what a paynefull, faythfull, and trustye man was he : he was day and night at his worke, keeping his sheep truely, as he was put in trust to doo ; and when any chance happened that any thing was lost, he made it good and restored it agayne of his owne. So likewise was Eleazarus a paynful man, a faythfull and trustye servaunt. Suche a servaunt was Joseph in Egipt to his mayster Potiphar. So likewise was Daniell vnto hys maister the King. But I pray you where are these servauntes now a dayes ? In deede I feare me there bee but very few of such faythfull servauntes. —Latimer (died 1555.)

## BLAME NOT MY LUTE.

Blame not my Lute ! for he must sound
Of this or that as liketh me ;
For lack of wit the Lute is bound
  To give such tunes as pleaseth me ;
Though my songs be somewhat strange,
And speak such words as touch my change,
    Blame not my Lute !

## BLAME NOT MY LUTE.

My Lute, alas! doth not offend
Though that per force he must agree
To sound such tunes as I intend,
　To sing to them that heareth me;
Then though my songs be somewhat plain,
And toucheth some that use to feign,
　　　　Blame not my Lute!

My Lute and strings may not deny,
　But as I strike they must obey;
Break not them then so wrongfully,
　But wreak thyself some other way;
And though the songs which I indite,
Do quit thy change with rightful spite,
　　　　Blame not my Lute!

Spite asketh spite, and changing change,
　And falsed faith, must needs be known;
The faults so great, the case so strange:
　Of right it must abroad be blown:
Then since that by thine own desert
My songs do tell how true thou art,
　　　　Blame not my Lute!

Blame but thyself that hast misdone,
　And well deserved to have blame;
Change thou thy way, so evil begone,
　And then my Lute shall sound that same;
But if till then my fingers play,
By thy desert their wonted way,
　　　　Blame not my Lute!

Farewell! unknown; for though thou break
　My strings in spite with great disdain,
Yet have I found out for thy sake,
　Strings for to string my Lute again:
And if perchance this silly rhyme,
Do make thee blush at any time,
　　　　Blame not my Lute.

　　　　　　　　　—WYATT (1503-1541.)

# THE FIRST FIFTEEN VERSES OF THE EIGHTH CHAPTER OF MATTHEW.

1. The Anglo-Saxon version.
2. A word for word translation of the Anglo-Saxon text.
3. Wycliffe's Translation (about 1380.)
4. Purvey's revision (about 1390.)
5. Tyndale's translation (1526.)
6. Cheke's translation (about 1550.)

*(From Marsh's Origin and History of the English Language.)*

### I.

1. Soðlice þa se Hælend of þam munte nyðer-astah, þa
2. (For-)sooth when the Saviour from the mount came down, there
3. Forsothe when Jhesus hadde comen doun fro tho hil,
4. But whanno Jhesus was come doun fro tho hil,
5. When Jesus was come downe from the mountayne,
6. And when he cãm from y⁰ hil y͏ͬ

1. fyligdon him mycle mænio.
2. followed him great multitudes.
3. many cumpanyes folewiden hym.
4. mych puple suede hym.
5. moch people folowed him.
6. folowd him a greet companj of men.

### II.

1. Da genealæhte án hreofla to him and hine to him
2. Then nighed a leper to him and him(-self) to him
3. And loo! a leprouse man cummyngo worshipide
4. And loo! a leprouse man cam and worschipide
5. And lo, there cam a lepre and worsheped
6. And lo á leper stood, and bowd himself

1. ge-eaðmedde, and þus cwæð; Drihten, gyf þu wylt, þu
2. humbled and thus spake; Lord, if thou wilt, thou
3. hym, sayinge; Lord, yf thou wolt, thou
4. hym. and seide; Lord, if thou wolt, thou
5. him saynge, Master, if thou wylt, thou
6. to him and said L., if yow wilt yow

1. miht        mé   geclænsian.
2. canst       me   cleanse.
3. maist make  me   clene.
4. maist make  me   clene.
5. canst make  me   clene.
6. maist            clens me.

### III.

1. Ða     astrehte       se     Hælend   hys hand,   and hrepode hyne
2. Then outstretched     the    Saviour  his hand,   and touched him
3. And Jhesus holdynge forthe           the hond,           touchide hym
4. And Jhesus helde    forth            the hoond,   and touchide hym,
5.          He   putt   forthe          his hond    and touched him
6. And Jesus stretched forth            his hand    and touched him

1. and þus cwæð,    Ic wylle;       beo geclænsod.   And hys
2. and thus spake,  I  will;        be  cleansed.   And his
3.     sayinge,     I  wole; be thou maad clene.    And anoon
4.     and seide,   Y  wole; be thou maad cleene.   And anoon
5.     saynge:      I  will, be          clene, and immediatly
6. and said.        J  wil.  be thow     clensed.   And bí and bí

1. hreofla wæs      hrædlice          geclænsod.
2. leprosy was      immediately       cleansed.
3. the lepre of hym         was      clensid.
4. the lepre of him         was      clensid.
5. his    leprosy           was      clensed.
6. his    lepernes          was      clensed.

### IV.

1. Ða  cwæð  sé Hælend to him,  Warna þe þæt þu hyt nænegum
2. Then said the Saviour to him,   See      that thou it   (to) no
3. And Jhesus saith   to hym;     See,     say thou      to no
4. And Jhesus seide   to hym;     Se,      seie thou     to no
5. And  Jesus  said vnto him.     Se            thou    tell no
6. And  Jesus  said vnto him,     Look          yow     tel no

1. men ne seege; ac gang, ætcowde þe þam sacerde, and bring hym
2. man     tell;  but go,    show thee (to) the priest, and bring him
3. man;           but go,    shewe thee to     prestis, and offre
4. man;           but go,    shewe thee to the prestis, and offre
5. man,           but go and shewe thysilf to the preste, and offer
6. man            But go y ways schew yself to yᵉ priest. And offer

1. a þlac þe Moyses bebead      on hyra   gecyðnesse.
2. the gift that Moses bad,     for their  information.
3. that ȝifte that Moyses comaundide,  into witnessing to hem.
4. the ȝift that Moyses comaundide,    in  witnessyng to hem.
5. the gyfte, that Moses commaunded to be offred, in witnes to them.
6. yᵉ gift which Moses cōmanded to be given yᵗ yᵉⁱ might beer witness
[yccrof.

V.

1. Soðlice      þa    se Hælend     ineode    on Capharnaum, þa
2. (For-)sooth when   the Saviour   went-in   to Capernaum, there
3. Sothely    when    he   hadde entride in to Capharnaum,
4. And        whanne  he   hadde entrid  in to Cafarnaum,
5.            When    Jesus was entred in to Capernaum, there
6.            As      Jesus     cam     into Capernaum, yeer

1. genealæhte . hym   an hundredes caldor,  hyne biddende,
2. nighed (to) him    a hundred's captain,  him praying,
3. centurio            neiȝido               to hym preyinge him,
4. the centurien       neiȝede               to him and preiede him,
5. cam    vnto him a certayne Centurion,    besechyng him,
6. cam            an hunderder vnto him and sued vnto him

VI.

1. And þus cweðende, Drihten,  min cnapa lið on mīnum huse
2. And thus saying,  Lord,     my knave lieth in  my  house
3. And       said,   Lord,     my child lyeth in  the hous
4. And       seide,  Lord,     my childe lijth in the hous
5. And       saynge: Master,   my servaunt lyeth sicke att home
6. on this sort.     Sir,      mi servant lieth sick in mi house

1.       lama,         and mid    yflo   gebread.
2.       lame,         and with   evil   afflicted.
3. sike on the palsie, and  is    yuel   tourmentid.
4. sijk on the palesie, and is    yuel   turmentid.
5. . off the palsyo, and     is   grevously payned.
6.   of yᵉ palscj,          grevousli tormented.

VII.

1. Da cwæð se Hælend to him, Ic cume  and hine gehæle.
2. Then said the Saviour to him, I come and him  heal.
3. And  Jhesus saith to hym,  I shal cume, and shal hele hym.
4. And  Jhesus seide to him,  Y schal come, and schal heele him.
5. And  Jesus  sayd vnto him. I will come and     cure   him.
6. And  Jesus  said vnto him. I wil come and      heel   him.

## VIII.

1. Ða andswarode se hundredes caldor . and þus cwæð, Drihten,
2. Then answered the hundred's captain and thus said, Lord,
3. And centurio answerynge saith to hym, Lord,
4. And the centurien answeride, and seide to hym, Lord,
5. The Conturion answered and saide : Syr
6. And yᵉ hunderder answerd him with yᵉˢ wordes. Sir

1. ne com ic wyrðe þæt þu ingange under mine þecene ;
2. not am I worthy that thou in-go under my roof ;
3. I am not worthi, that thou entre vndir my roof ;
4. Y am not worthi, that thou entre vndur my roof ;
5. I am not worthy that thou shuldest com vnder the rofe of my housse ;
6. J am not á fit man, whoos house ye schold enter.

1. ac cwæð þin an word, and min cnapa bið gehæled.
2. but speak thy one word, and my knave will-be healed.
3. but oonly say bi word, and my child shall be helid.
4. but oonli seie thou bi word, and my childe shal be heelid.
5. but speake the worde only, and mo servaunt shal be healed.
6. Sai ye onli yᵉ word, and mi servant schal be heeled.

## IX.

1. Soðlice ic com man under anwealde gesett, and ic
2. (For-)sooth I am (a) man under authority set, and I
3. For whi and I am a man ordeynd vnder power,
4. For whi Y am a man ordeyned vndur power, and
5. For y also myselfe am a man vndre power, and
4. For I am a man vnder yᵉ power of oyer, and

1. hæbbe þegnas under me; and ic cweðe to þysum, Gang, and
2. have soldiers under me; and I say to this, Go, and
3. hauynge vndir me kniȝtis; and I say to this, Go, and
4. haue knyȝtis vndir me : and Y seie to this, Go, and
5. have sowdeeres vndre me, and y saye to one, go, and
6. have soldiers vnderneth me, and J sai to yᵉ soldier go, and

1. he gæð ; and ic cweðe to oþrum, Cum, and he cymð ;
2. he goeth ; and I say to (an-)other, Come, and he cometh ;
3. he goth ; and to an other, Come thou, and he cometh ;
4. he goith ; and to another, Come, and he cometh ;
5. he goeth ; and to anothre, come, and he cometh :
6. he goeth, and to an other com, and he cometh,

1. to minum þeowe,      Wyrc þis,              and hé wyrcð.
2. to my servant,       Do this,               and he doeth.
3. and to my seruaunt,  Do thou this thing,    and he doth.
4. and to my seruaunt,  Do this,               and he doith it.
5. and to my servaunt,  do this,               and he doeth it.
6. and to mi servant    do yᵉ,                 and he doth it.

## X.

1. Witodlice þa      se Hælend   þis     gehyrde,   þa   wundrode he,
2. Now      when     the Saviour this    heard,     then wondered he,
3. Sothely  Jhesus,  heerynge these      thingis,        wondrido,
4. And      Jhesus   herde   these       thingis, and    wondride,
5. When     Jesus    herde   these       sayngcs,       he marveyled,
6.          Jesus    heering             yᵗ             marvelled

1. and cwæð to þam   þe him fyligdon :   Soð ic secge cow no
2. and said  to them that him followed : Sooth I say (to) you not
3. and saide to men       suynge hym :   Trewly I sayo to jou
4. and seide to men  that sueden him :   Treuli I seie to jou
5. and said  to them that folowed him :  Verely y say vnto you,
6. and said  to yᵐ        yᵗ folowed him. Truli J sai vnto yow,

1. gemette ic  swa  mycelne geleafan on Israhel.
2. met     I   so   much    belief   in Israel.
3. I   fond    nat  so grete feith    in Ysrael.
4. Y   foond        not so greete feith in Israel.
5. I have not founde so great fayth : no, not in Israell.
6. J have not found  so greet faith,  no not in Jsrl.

## XI.

1. To soðum     ic secge cow,   Ðæt manigo           cumað fram
2. In sooth     I  say (to) you, That many (shall)   come  from
3. Sothely      Y  say to jou,  that manye shulen    come  fro
4. And          Y  seie to jou, that many schulen    come  fro
5. I say therfore  vnto you,    that many shall      come  from
6. But J sai       vnto yow,    yᵗ  mani schal       cóm   from

1. east dæle   and  west dæle,  and wuniað       mid Abrahame
2. (the) east-deal and (the) we-t-deal, and dwell with Abraham
3. the eat     and  west,       and shulen rest  with Abraham
4. the est     and the west,    and schulen reste with Abraham
5. the est     and  weest,      and shall rest   with Abraham
6. yᵉ Est      and yᵉ West,     and schal be set with Abraham

1. and Isaace and Jacobe,  on     heofena     rice ;
2. and Isaac and Jacob    in     heaven's    realm ;
3. and Ysaac and Jacob    in the kyngdam of heuenes :
4. and Ysaac and Jacob    in the kyngdom of heuenes ;
5.     Ysaac and Jacob,   in the kyngdom of heven ;
6.     Jsaak and Jacob    in y⁰ kingdoom of heaven,

## XII.

1. Witodlice þises rices bearn     beoð aworpene on þa ytemestan
2. Verily this realm's children (shall) be out-cast in(to) the outermost
3. forsothe the sonys of the rewme shulen be cast out into vttremest
4. but    the sones of the rewme schulen be cast out in to vtmer
5. And the children of the kingdom shalbe cast out in to the vtmoost
6. but yᵉ childern of yᵉ kingdoom schal be thrown in to outward

1. þystro :   þær   bið   wóp,   and    toþa   gristbitung.
2. darkness :   there (shall) be weeping, and (of) teeth grinding.
3. derknessis ; there  shal be weepynge, and beetynge togidre of teeth.
4. derknessis ; there schal be wepyng,  and   grynting    of teeth.
5. dercknes,    there  shalbe wepinge  and   gnasshing    of tethe.
6. darknes,    yeer  schal be weping  and   gnasching    of teth.

## XIII.

1. And se Hælend cwæð to þam hundrydes caldre, Ga ; and gewurðe
2. And the Saviour said to the hundred's captain, Go ; and bo (it)
3. And Jhesus   saide to       centurio,    Go ; and as thou
4. And Jhesus   seide to the   conturioun,  Go ; and as thou
5. Then Jesus  said vnto the Centurion, go thy waye, and as thou hast
6. And Jesus    said to y. hunderder, go y  wais, and as yow

1. þé swa swa þu gelyfdest. And se cnapa wæs gehæled on þære tide.
2. (to) theeso as thou believedst. And the knave was healed in that hour.
3. hast biloened be it don to thee. And the child was helid fro that houre.
4. hast bileuyd be it doon to thee. And the child was heelid fro that hour.
5. believed so be it vnto the. And his servaunt was healed that same houre.
6. belevedst, so be it vnto yᵉ. And his servant was heeled even in yᵉ saam
[howr.

## XIV.

1. Ða   se Hælend    com on      Petres   huse,    þa
2. When   the Saviour   came in(to)   Peter's  house,   then
3. And when   Jhesus hadde comen in to the hous of Symond Petre,
4. And whanne Jhesus was   comun in to the hous of Symount Petre,
5. And        Jesus  went    into       Peters   housse,   and
6. And        Jesus  cam    in to       Peters   hous,    and

1. geseah he hys    swegre     licgende, and      hriðgende.
2. saw   he his    mother-in-law lying  and       feverish.
3. he say    his wyues moder liggynge, and shakun with feueris.
4. he say    his wyues modir liggynge, and shakun with fcueris.
5. saw       his wyves mother lyinge      sicke of a fevre.
6. saw       his moother in law laid down and sick of y⁰ aXess,

## XV.

1. And he æðrán hyre     hand,  and  se fefor hig fortlet:
2. And he touched her    hand,  and  the fever her  left:
3. And he touchide hir   hond,  and  the feuer lefte . hir:
4. And he touchide hir   hoond, and  the feuer lefte   hir:
5. And he thouched her   hande, and  the fevre leeft  her;
6. and he touched her bi y⁰ hand  and  y⁰ aXes left   her,

1. þa aras heo,   and þenode      him.
2. then arose she and served      them.
3. and  she roose, and seruyde    hom.
4. and  she roos,  and seruede    hem.
5. and  she arose, and ministred vnto them.
6. and scho roos  and served    · them.

———

# INDEX OF AUTHORS

IN THE

## FOURTH, FIFTH AND ADVANCED READING BOOKS,

With dates of birth (and death if deceased), and mention
of their chief works.

NOTE.—*The names of the Authors marked * are those of natives of the United States
of America ; those marked † of natives of Canada, or of those who are or have
been residents in this country.*

| | | |
|---|---|---|
| Addison, Joseph (1672-1719) - | "*The Spectator*" & *Poems.* | VI., 152. |
| Aikin, Dr. (1747-1822) - | "*Evenings at Home.*" | V., 66, 108. |
| Akenside, Mark (1721-1770) - | "*Pleasures of Imagination.*" | V., 427; VI., 433. |
| Albert, Prince (1819-1861) - | *Speeches.* | V., 347. |
| Alcock, Sir Rutherford, (1808-....) | "*Three Years in Japan.*" | VI., 356. |
| Alexander, Mrs. C. F. - | "*Poems on Old Testament Subjects.*" | IV., 321. |
| Alford, Dean (1810-1870) - | *Sermons and Poems* - | VI., 4. |
| Alfred, King (849-901) - | *Translation of Boethius.* - | VI., 452. |
| Alison, Sir Archibald (1792-1867) | *History of Europe.* - | V., 215, 208, 30 450; VI., 418. |
| *Allston, Washington (1779-1843) | *Poems.* - | IV., 113. |
| Anderson, James - | | V., 200. |
| Angus, George F. - | "*Scenes in Australia.*" | IV., 310. |
| Ansted, D. T. (1814-....) - | "*Picturesque Sketches of the Ancient World.*" | VI., 185, 363. |
| Arnold, Dr. Thomas (1795-1842) | *History of Rome.* - | V., 61 : VI.,122. |
| †Ascher, Isidoro G. - | | VI., 267. |
| Atherstone, Edwin (1788-....) - | "*The Fall of Nineveh.*" | V., 87; VI., 11. |
| *Audubon, J. J. (1780-1851) | *American Ornithology.* | VI., 347. |
| Aytoun, W. E. (1813-1865) | "*Lays of the Scottish Cavaliers.*" | V., 152: VI., 177. |
| Bacon, Lord (1561-1626) - | *Essays & "Novum Organum."* | V., 367. |
| Bailey, Philip James (1816-....) | "*Festus" and other Poems.* | VI., 417. |
| Baillie, Joanna (1762-1851) - | "*Plays of the Passions.*" | V., 146. |
| Baker, Sir Samuel W. (1821-....) | "*The Albert N'Yanza.*" - | V., 8; VI., 29. |
| †Ballantyne, R. M. - | "*The Coral Island,*" and other *Tales.* - | Iv., 7, 83; V., 176; VI., 49, 172. |

474      INDEX OF AUTHORS.

| Barbauld, Mrs. (1743-1825) | "*Hymns for Children*," &c., | V., 60; VI., 402. |
| Barbour, John (1316-1396) | "*The Bruce.*" | VI., 459. |
| Beattie, James (1735-1803) | "*The Minstrel" and Essays.* | IV., 360; VI., 437. |
| Beaumont, Francis (1586-1616) | *Dramas.* | VI., 427. |
| Bell, Henry Glasford | *Life of Mary, Queen of Scots.* | V., 195. |
| Berkeley, Bishop (1684-1753) | *Principles of Human Knowledge.* | VI., 360. |
| Bickersteth, E, H. (1825-....) | "*Yesterday, To-Day and Forever.*" | VI., 296. |
| Boethius, (455-526) | *Consolations of Philosophy.* | VI., 452. |
| Bonar, Dr. Horatius | "*Hymns of Faith and Hope.*" | VI., 387. |
| Bossuet, J. B. (1627-1704) | "*Oraisons Funèbres*" &c. | V., 215. |
| Bowles, W. Lisle (1762-1850) | *Sonnets and other Poems.* | V., 443. |
| Bowring, Sir John (1792-....) | "*Matins and Vespers," and Travels.* | V., 377; VI., 421. |
| *Brainard, John G. C. (1796-1828) | *Poems.* | IV., 114. |
| Brewster, Sir David (1781-1868) | *Biographies and Scientific Treatises.* | V., 313. |
| Brougham, Lord (1778-1868) | *Speeches and Essays.* | V., 18, 33, 285; VI., 145, 307. |
| Brown, Miss Frances (1816-....) | *Lyrics and Autobiography.* | VI., 352. |
| Browning, Robert (1812-....) | "*Men and Women," Dramatic Lyrics.* | IV., 211. |
| *Bryant, W. C. (1794-....) | *Poems and Travels* | IV., 49, 73, 124; V., 72; VI., 193, 288. |
| Bulwer, Sir E. L. (see *Lord Lytton*) | | |
| Burke, Edmund (1730-1797) | *Speeches and Essays.* | V., 250, 255; VI., 290. |
| Burn, R. Scott | "*Modern Farming," &c.* | V., 400. |
| Burns, Robert (1759-1796) | *Poems and Songs.* | IV., 375; V., 97; VI., 380. |
| Burritt, Elihu (1811-....) | "*Sparks from the Anvil," &c.* | IV., 131. |
| Butler, Mrs (Fanny Kemble) (ab. 1811-) | "*Year of Consolation," &c.* | VI., 383. |
| Byron, Lord (1788-1824) | "*Childe Harold," and other Poems.* | IV., 252, 291, 365; V., 110, 276; VI., 154, 368. |
| Cædmon, (.. -680) | "*Hymn to the Creator.*" | VI., 451. |
| Campbell, Thomas (1777-1844) | "*Pleasures of Hope," "Gertrude of Wyoming," &c.* | IV., 105, 212, 226; V., 142, 508; VI., 196. |
| Canning, George (1770-1827) | *Anti-Jacobin and Speeches.* | V., 282; VI., 270. |
| *Carey, Alice (1822-1871) | "*Clovernook" and Poems.* | VI., 196. |
| Carlisle, Earl of (1802-1864) | *Travels and Lectures.* | IV., 107. |
| Carlyle, Thomas (1795-....) | *Essays, Life of Cromwell, &c.* | VI., 270, 394. |
| Carpenter, J. E. | *Poems and Songs.* | IV., 381. |
| Chalmers, Dr. Thomas (1780-1847) | "*Astronomical Discourses," Sermons, &c.* | V., 270; VI., 395. |

Chambers, William (1800-....) — "Journal," Information for the People, Encyclopædia, &c. — IV., 174, 220; VI., 189.
Chambers, Robert (1802-1871) —
Cheadle, Dr. W. B. — North-West Passage by Land. IV., 24.
*Channing, W. E. (1780-1842) — Sermons and Essays. — V., 288; VI., 72.
†Chapman, Prof E. J. ‡ — "Songs of Charity" and other Poems. — VI., 309.
Chateaubriand, F. A. de (1769-1848) — Genie du Christianisme, &c. IV., 343.
Chatterton, Thomas (1752-1770) — Poems. — VI., 95.
Chaucer, Geoffrey (1328-1400) — "Canterbury Tales." — VI., 457.
Cheke, Sir John (1514-1557) — Translation of New Testament. — VI. 46C.
Cicero, M. Tullius (B. C. 106-43) — "Orations." — V., 02.
Clarendon, Lord (1608-1674) — "History of the Great Rebellion." — VI. 140.
*Clay, Henry (1777-1852) — Speeches. — V, 321.
Cleghorn, George — "Ancient and Modern Art." VI., 422.
Clephane, Miss — VI., 307.
†Clive, Mrs. (1820-....) — "Paul Ferrol" and Poems. V., 526.
Coleridge, S. T. (1772-1834) — Poems, Table-Talk, &c. — V.,328; VI., 114, 440.
Coleridge, H. N. (1800-1843) — Introduction to the Study of the Greek Classic Poets. VI., 382.
Collier, W. F. — Great Events of History, &c. V., 129; IV., 287.
Collins, William (1720-1756) — "Odes" and other Poems. V., 504; VI., 41.
Cook, Eliza (ab. 1818-....) — Poems. — IV., 188.
*Cooper, J. Fenimore (1789-1851) — "The Spy," "The Prairie, &c. V., 400; VI., 384.
Cormack — Journey Across Newfoundland. — IV., 38.
Cowley, Abraham (1618-1667) — "Anacreontics" and other Poems. — VI., 414.
Cowper, William (1731-1800) — "The Task" and other Poems. IV., 253; V., 83, 394; VI., 80, 378.
Crabbe, George (1754-1832) — "The Village" and other Poems. — V., 371; VI., 109.
Craik, George L. (1709-1866) — History of Literature and Learning in England. VI., 451.
Creasy, Sir E. S. (1812-....) — Decisive Battles of the World. V., 98; VI., 44.
Croly, George (ab. 1786-1860) — "Salathiel" and other Poems. V., 27; VI., 146.
Daniel, Samuel (1562-1619) — Poems and Plays. — VI., 405.
†Darnell, Rev. H. F. — IV., 86; VI.,374.
Davy, Rev. Charles (fl. 1755) — "Letters on Literary Subjects." — VI., 61.
Demosthenes, (B. C. 382-322) — "Orations." — V., 33.
DeQuincey, Thomas (1786-1859) — "Confessions of an Opium Eater." — V., 403; VI., 208.
†Dewart, Rev. E. H. — Poems. — VI., 312, 390.
Dickens, Charles (1812-1870) — "Pickwick Papers," "David Copperfield," &c. — IV., 176; V., 399; VI., 218.

# 476  INDEX OF AUTHORS.

| Author | Work | Reference |
|---|---|---|
| Disraeli, Isaac, (1766–1848) | "Curiosities of Literature." | V., 458, 461. |
| Disraeli, Benjamin (1805–....) | "Coningsby" and other Novels. | VI., 230. |
| Dobell, Sydney (1824–....) | "The Roman" and other Poems. | V., 521. |
| Dodd, George | "Curiosities of Industry." | VI., 342, 379. |
| Dryden, John (1631–1700) | Satires and Fables. | V., 421, 501; VI., 405. |
| 'DuChaillu, P. B. (ab. 1820–....) | "Explorations in Equatorial Africa." | IV., 258. |
| Dufferin, Lord (1826–....) | Letters from High Latitudes. | IV., 222. |
| Dunbar, William (ab. 1460–1520) | Poems. | VI., 461. |
| Duncan, Rev. Henry | "Sacred Philosophy of the Seasons." | V., 430. |
| Elliott, Ebenezer (1781–1849) | Poems. | VI., 399. |
| Emanuel, H. | History of Diamonds and Precious Stones. | VI., 431. |
| Erskine, (Thomas) Lord (1750–1823) | Speeches. | V., 302. |
| 'Everett, Edward (1794–1865) | Orations and Essays. | V., 470. |
| Ewald, | (From the German.) | IV., 231. |
| Ferguson, Samuel | "Lays of the Western Gael." | V., 23. |
| Finlay, George (ab. 1801–....) | "History of the Byzantine and Greek Empires." | VI., 182. |
| Forbes, Edward (1815–1854) | "History of British Mollusca," &c. | IV., 280. |
| Foster, John (1770–1843) | Essays and Letters. | VI., 264. |
| Fownes, George (1815–....) | "Manual of Chemistry," &c. | V., 64, 118. |
| Francis, Sir Philip (1740–1818) | "Junius's Letters." | V., 418. |
| Froude, Rev. J. A. (1818–....) | "History of England." | VI., 371. |
| Fyfe, J. H. | Triumphs of Invention and Discovery. | IV., 173, 174; VI., 147. |
| Gibbon, Edward (1737–1794) | Decline and Fall of the Roman Empire. | V., 30, 143; VI., 128, 150. |
| Gladstone, W. E. (1809–....) | "Homer and the Homeric Age." | V., 301. |
| Glaisher, James | Meteorology. | VI., 303. |
| Goldsmith, Oliver (1728–1774) | "Vicar of Wakefield" and Poems. | IV., 90, 364; V., 386; VI., 217. |
| 'Goodrich, F. B. (1826–....) | The Sea and her Famous Sailors. | IV., 144, 270, 300; V., 20, 315. |
| Gordon, Hon. Arthur | Journeys in New Brunswick. | IV., 74. |
| 'Gould, Miss Hannah F. (ab. 1805–....) | Poems. | IV., 57; VI., 220. |
| Gower, John (ab. 1325–1408) | "Confessio Amantis." | VI., 458. |
| Grattan, Henry (1746–1820) | Speeches. | V., 208. |
| 'Gray, Asa (1810– ...) | "Flora of North America." | V., 09. |
| Gray, Thomas (1716–1771) | Odes and Elegy. | IV., 356, V., 503. VI., 130. |

## INDEX OF AUTHORS. 477

| | | |
|---|---|---|
| Greenwell, Dora (1821-....) | *"Patience of Hope,"* and other *Poems.* | IV., 160. |
| Griffin, Gerald (1803-1840) | *" The Colleen Bawn,"* &c. | VI., 263. |
| Grote, George (1794-1871) | *History of Greece.* | VI., 23. |
| Guizot, F. P. G. (1787-....) | *History of Civilization in Europe.* | V., 330. |
| Hack, Mrs. Maria | *Stories of the Olden Time.* | V., 324. |
| †Haight, Miss | | VI., 430. |
| *Hale, Mrs. S. J. (1795-....) | *" Woman's Record,"* &c. | VI., 151. |
| †Haliburton, T. C. (1796-1865) | *Sam Slick, The Attaché,* &c. | V., 401. |
| Hall, Captain Basil (1788-1844) | *Voyages and Travels.* | VI., 170. |
| Hall, Rev. Newman (1816-.....) | *Sermons and Tracts.* | VI., 329. |
| Hall, Rev. Robert (1764-1831) | *Sermons.* | V., 271; VI.,434. |
| Hallam, Henry (1777-1859) | *History of the Middle Ages,*&c. | V.,101; VI., 242. |
| *Halleck, Fitzgreene (1795-1867) | *Poems.* | V., 515; VI.,328. |
| Hardy, Lieut. Campbell | *Sporting Adventures in the New World* | IV., 60. |
| Harris, Major W. C. | *Wild Sports of South Africa.* | IV., 267. |
| †Hawkins, | *" Picture of Quebec."* | IV., 88, 93. |
| Head, Sir F. B. (1792-....) | *"The Emigrant,"* &c. | IV., 105, 167; VI., 77. |
| Heber, Bishop (1783-1826) | *"Journey Through India,"* and *Poems.* | IV., 339, 347;VI. 15. |
| Hemans, Mrs. (1793-1835) | *"Songs of the Affections,"* and other *Poems.* | IV., 122,242,332. 353, 360, 365; V., 491; VI., 245. |
| Herschel, Sir John (1792-1871) | *"Outlines of Astronomy,"*&c. | V., 325. |
| Hinckley, | | V., 456. |
| Hogg, Jabez | *Experimental and Natural Philosophy.* | VI., 391. |
| Hogg, James (1772-1835) | *"Queen's Wake,"* and other *Poems.* | VI., 339. |
| Hogarth, George (....-1870) | *History of the Musical Drama* | VI., 390. |
| Hood, Thomas (1798-1845) | *Poems of Wit and Humor.* | VI., 185. |
| Hooker, Richard (ab. 1553-1600) | *"Ecclesiastical Polity."* | VI., 136. |
| Howitt, Mary (ab.1804-....) | *Poems and Translations.* | IV.,157; VI.,135. |
| Humboldt, Alex. Von (1769-1859) | *Cosmos, Travels in America.* | IV., 151. |
| Hume, David (1711-1776) | *History of England.* | V.,108; VI.,149. |
| *Irving, Washington (1783-1859) | *Tales of a Traveller, Sketch Book,* &c. | V., 390; VI., 234. |
| Jeffrey, Francis (1773-1850) | *Contributions to Edinburgh Review.* | V., 205. |
| Jerrer, | *(From the German.)* | IV., 204. |
| Jewsbury, Miss (ab. 1820-....) | *" Zoë," and other Tales.* | V., 29. |
| Johnson, Dr. Samuel (1709-1784) | *Rasselas, Lives of the Poets,* &c. | V., 417, 42... f., 121. |

| | | |
|---|---|---|
| Jones, Sir William (1746-1794) | Poems and Translations. | VI., 344. |
| Jonson, Ben (1574-1637) | Plays and Poems. | VI., 425. |
| Junius, (see Sir Philip Francis,) | | |
| *Kane, Dr. E. K. (1820-1857) | Arctic Explorations. | IV., 3. |
| †Kane, Paul (....-1871) | Wanderings among the Indians of North America.. | IV., 16. |
| Kearley, George | Curiosities of Animal Life | V., 73. |
| Keble, Rev. John (1792-1866) | "Christian Year," &c. | IV., 351; V., 384; VI., 398. |
| Keightley, Thomas (1789-....) | Histories of Greece & Rome. | V., 46. |
| Kingston, W. H. G. | "Old Jack" and other Tales. | VI., 115, 340. |
| Kitto, Dr. John (1804-1854) | Daily Bible Readings. | VI., 297. |
| Knowles, J. Sheridan (1784-1862) | "Virginius" and other Plays. | V., 404. |
| Landon, L. E. (Mrs. MacLean), (1802-1838) | Poems and Tales | VI., 250. |
| Langlande, Robert (fl. 1300) | Vision of Piers Ploughman. | VI., 455. |
| *Lanman, Charles (1819-....) | Adventures in the Wilds of North America. | IV., 99. |
| Latimer, Bishop (ab. 1475-1555) | Sermons. | VI., 464. |
| Layamon, (fl. 1190) | Metrical Romance. | VI., 453. |
| Layard, A. H., (1817-....) | "Nineveh and its Remains." | IV., 290; VI., 5 |
| Lever, Charles, (1809-....) | "Charles O'Malley," and other Novels. | IV., 76. |
| Liddell, Dean (1811-....) | History of Rome. | VI., 94. |
| Lingard, Dr. John (ab. 1771-1851) | History of England. | V., 213; VI., 292. |
| Livingstone, Dr. David (1817-....) | Travels in South and Central Africa. | IV., 272 ; VI., 95, 281. |
| Locke, John (1632-1704) | Essay on the Human Understanding. | VI.. 284. |
| Lockhart, J. G., (1794-1854) | Spanish Ballads, Life of Scott. | V., 522; VI., 410. |
| *Longfellow, H. W., (1807-....) | Evangeline, Hiawatha, &c. | IV., 27, 37, 202, 342; V., 523; VI., 172, 213. |
| Lover, Samuel (1797-1868) | "Handy Andy," &c. | IV., 194; VI., 434. |
| Lushington, H., | Poems. | IV., 234. |
| Lyons, J. G. | | V., 421. |
| Lytton, Lord (1805-....) | Novels, Poems, and Plays. | V., 25, 113, 428, 499; VI., 41, 280, 319. |
| Macaulay, Lord (1800-1859) | History of England and Lays of Ancient Rome. | V., 32, 55, 140 ; VI., 102, 130, 174, 368. |
| *McCartee, Jesse G., | Poems. | VI., 21. |
| †McCaul, Rev. Dr. John | Britanno-Roman Inscriptions. | V., 382. |
| †McGee, T D'Arcy( 1825-1868) | "Canadian Ballads," &c. | V., 164. |

# INDEX OF AUTHORS. 479

| | | |
|---|---|---|
| †McGeorge, Rev. R. J., | *Tales and Sketches.* | V., 221. |
| McGregor, J., | *History of the British Empire.* | V., 160. |
| Mackay, Charles (ab. 1812-....) | "*Voices from the Crowd,*" and other *Poems.* | IV.. 317; V., 51. VI., 345. |
| Mackintosh, Sir James (1765-1832) | *History of England and Essays.* | 355. V., 297, 334; VI., |
| MacLeod, Dr. Norman (1812-....) | "*Earnest Student,*" "*Parish Papers,*" &c. | IV., 69. |
| †McLachlan, Alexander | *Poems.* | VI , 254. |
| *McLellan, Isaac | *Poems.* | V., 183. |
| Maginn, Dr. Wm. (1795-1842) | "*Pictures, Grave and Gay.*" | VI., 162. |
| Mahon, Lord (see *Earl Stanhope*) | | |
| Malory, Sir Thomas (fl. 1485) | "*La Mort d'Arthur.*" | VI., 462. |
| Mandeville, Sir John (1300-1372) | *Voyages and Travels.* | VI., 460. |
| Mansfield, Earl of (1705-1793) | *Speeches.* | V., 275. |
| Markham, | "*Abyssinian Campaign.*" | VI., 427. |
| Marlowe, Christopher (ab. 1563-1593) | *Plays.* | V., 475. |
| Marsden, | | IV., 363. |
| *Marsh, Geo. P. (1801-....) | "*Lectures on the English Language.*" | VI., 466. |
| Marston, John (fl. 1600) | *Poems and Tragedies.* | VI., 426. |
| Martin, R. Montgomery (ab. 1800) | *History of the British Colonies.* | IV., 42. |
| Marvell, Andrew (1620-1678) | *Poems.* | IV., 143. |
| Massey, Gerald (1828-....) | *Poems.* | VI., 359. |
| Massillon, J. B. (1663-1742) | *Sermons.* | V., 239. |
| Massinger, Philip (1584-1640) | *Plays* | VI., 426. |
| *Maury, M. F. (1806-....) | *Physical Geography of the Sea* | [III. V., 125, 344; VI., |
| Melvill, Rev. Henry (1798-1871) | *Sermons and Lectures* | V., 332; VI., 247. |
| Merivale, Rev. Charles (1800-....) | *History of the Romans under the Empire.* | V., 81; VI., 107. |
| Mill, John Stuart (1806-....) | *System of Logic.* | VI., 375. |
| Miller, Hugh (1802-1856) | *Footprints of the Creator.* | VI, 267. |
| Milman, Dean (1791-1868) | "*History of the Jews,*" &c. | IV., 338, 354; V., 12, 84; VI., 145. |
| Milner, Rev. Thomas | *Gallery of Nature.* | IV., 256, 302; V., 138; VI., 83, 110. |
| Milton, John (1608-1674) | "*Paradise Lost*" and *Sonnets.* | IV., 374 ;V., 220, 380 ; VI., 60, 443. |
| Milton, Lord | *North West Passage by Land* | IV., 24. |
| Mitford, Miss (1786-1855) | "*Our Village,*" and other *Tales.* | VI., 222. |
| Mitford, William (1744-1827) | *History of Greece.* | VI., 12. |
| Moir, D. M. (1798-1851) | "*Domestic Verses,*" and other *Poems.* | IV., 196 ; V., 514. |
| Montgomery, James (1771-1854) | "*Pelican Island,*" and other *Poems.* | IV.,149, 340, 366; V., 369 |

†Moodie, Mrs. (1805-....) - - - "Roughing it in the Bush." IV., 103.
Moore, Thomas (1779-1852) - - Lalla Rookh, Irish Melodies,
&c. - - - - IV.,135, 277, 325,
339; V., 382, 518;
VI., 241.
More, Hannah (1745-1833) - - - Sacred Dramas and Tales. VI., 18.
More, Sir Thomas (1480-1535) - - Utopia, or the Happy Republic. - - - - VI., 463.
*Motley, J. L. (1814-....) - - - Rise of the Dutch Republic. VI., 259.
Neale, F. A. - - - - - Narrative of Residence in
Siam. - - - - IV., 208.
Nicolas, Sir Harris (1799-1848) - - Historic Peerage of England. VI., 349.
*Norton, Andrews (1786-1853) - - Sermons and Poems. - VI., 269.

Ogilvie, Rev. John (1733-1814) - - Sermons and Poems. - IV., 347.
†Ormiston, Rev. Dr. - - - - Sermons and Addresses. - VI., 420.
*Orne, Caroline F. - - - - Poems - - - - V., 355.

Page, David - - - - - Text Book of Geology. - V., 41.
†Page, Miss( Mrs. Faulkner) - - V., 223.
Paley, Archdeacon (1743-1805) - - Evidences of Christianity. VI., 227.
Palmerston, Lord (1784-1865) - - Speeches. - - - V., 371 ; VI.,271.
*Parkman, Francis (1823-....) - - Conspiracy of Pontiac. - V., 242.
*Peabody, E. (1807-1856) - - - Christian Days and Thoughts IV., 126.
*Peabody, W. B. O. (1799-1848) - - Literary Remains. - - V., 300.
†Pedley, C. - - - - - History of Newfoundland. IV., 30.
Pepys, Samuel (1633-1703) - - Diary. - - - - V., 226.
*Percival, J. O. (1795-1856) - - Poems. - - - - IV. 312.
Percy, Bishop (1728-1811) - - Reliques of Ancient Poetry. VI., 34.
Pfeiffer, Ida (1797-1858) - - - Woman's Journey round the
World. - - - IV., 158.
*Poe, Edgar Allan (1811-1849) - - Poems and Tales. - V., 237.
Pope, Alexander (1688-1744) - - "Rape of the Lock," and
Translation of Homer. V., 528 ; VI., 82.
Praed, W. M. (1802-1839) - - - Poems and Charades. - VI., 280.
*Prescott, W. H. (1796-1850) - - "Conquest of Mexico," &c. V., 140; VI., 411.
Prince, J. C. - - - - - Autumn Leaves. - - VI., 370.
Pringle, Thomas (1788-1834) - - "African Sketches," &c. IV., 254.
Procter, B. W. (Barry Cornwall) (ab.
1790-....) - - - - "Dramatic Scenes," and {342.
other Poems. - V., 108; VI.,283
Procter, Adelaide A. (1835-1864) - Legends and Lyrics. - VI., 300.
†Punshon, Rev. W. M. (1828-....) - Sermons and Lectures. - VI., 415.
Purvey, (fl. 1300-....) - - - Revision of Wycliffe's New
Testament - - - VI., 400.

Raleigh, Sir Walter (1552-1618) - "History of the World," and
Poems - - - - IV., 235.
Rawlinson, Rev. George (ab. 1815) - "Five Great Ancient Monarchies." - - - VI., 8.

## INDEX OF AUTHORS. 481

| Reade, Charles (1814–....) | *Novels and Dramas* | IV., 304. |
| †Reid, Hugo | "*Elements of Physical Geography.*" | V., 293. |
| Robertson, Dr. Wm. (1721–1793) | "*History of Charles V*," &c. | IV., 46 ; V., 192 ; VI., 213. |
| Rogers, Samuel (1763–1855) | "*Pleasures of Memory.*" | IV., 362; V., 506. |
| 'Rogers, W. B. | | VI., 252. |
| Roscoe, William (1753–1831) | "*Life of Lorenzo de Medici.*" | IV., 281. |
| †Ross, Alexander | "*Red River Settlement.*" | IV., 20. |
| Rowe, Mrs. E. | "*Exercises of the Heart.*" | VI., 192. |
| Ruskin, John (1819–....) | "*Modern Painters*," &c. | V.,425 ; VI., 194. |
| Russell, Dr. W. H. (1821–....) | "*Letters from the Crimea,*" &c. | V.,329 ; VI.,438 |
| †Ryerson, Rev. Dr. (1803–....) | *Speeches and Lectures.* | V., 388. |
| St. John, Horace (1830–....) | "*British Conquests in India.*" | IV., 200. |
| Sandwith, Dr. | "*Siege of Kars.*" | V., 336. |
| †Sangster, Charles (1822–....) | "*The Saguenay,*" and other *Poems.* | IV.,97 ; V., 172. |
| Schiller, F. (1759–1805) | "*Thirty Years' War,*" and *Plays* | VI., 440. |
| Schmitz, Dr. L. (1807–....) | "*Manuals of Ancient Geography and History.*" | V., 8. |
| Scoresby, Captain (1789–1857) | "*Arctic Regions, and Whale Fishery.*" | IV., 1. |
| Scott, Sir Walter (1771–1832) | "*Waverley Novels*" and *Poems.* | IV., 181, 186; V., 133, 302, 510; VI. 19, 163, 313. |
| Segur, Count de (1780–....) | "*Napoleon and the Grand Army.*" | IV., 228. |
| Shakespeare, Wm. (1564–1616) | *Plays and Poems.* | V., 460, 476, 480 ; V., 484, 485, 437, 488; VI., 43, 201, 202, 442. |
| Shelley, Percy B. (1792–1822) | "*Prometheus,*" "*The Cenci,*" &c. | V., 123. |
| Sheridan, R. B. (1751–1816) | *Plays and Speeches.* | V., 253. 489; VI., 283, 311. |
| Shirley, James (ab. 1594–1666) | *Plays* | VI., 72. |
| 'Sigourney, Lydia H. (1791–1865) | "*Pocahontas,*" and other *Poems.* | V., 75; VI., 188. |
| Skinner, James | "*Way of the Wilderness.*" | VI., 50. |
| Smiles, Samuel (1816–....) | "*Self-Help*," &c. | IV., 294; VI., 274. |
| Smith, Adam (1723–1790) | "*Wealth of Nations.*" | V., 353. |
| Smith, Horace (1779–1849) | "*Rejected Addresses.*" | V., 6. |
| Smith, Rev. Sydney (1771–1845) | "*Peter Plymley's Letters,*" &c. | [369. IV., 290; V., 304, |
| Smith, Dr. Wm. (1814–....) | *Classical and Bible Dictionaries.* | V., 1, 11, 444. |
| Southey, Caroline (1787–1854) | "*Solitary Hours,*" &c. | V., 387. |

# INDEX OF AUTHORS.

| | | |
|---|---|---|
| Southey, Robert (1774-1843) | "Joan of Arc," and other Poems; "Life of Nelson," | [VI., 98. IV., 179; V.,256; |
| Spencer, Hon. W. R. (1770-1834) | Poems. | VI., 414. |
| Spenser, Edmund (1553-1599) | "Faery Queen." | VI., 405. |
| *Sprague, Charles (1791-....) | Poems. | VI., 181. |
| Spratt, Lieut. T. | "Travels in Lycia, Syria, &c." | IV., 280. |
| Stanhope, Earl (1805-...) | History of England. | V., 246; VI. 403- |
| Stanley, Bishop (1779-1849) | "Familiar History of Birds." | VI., 203. |
| Stanley, Dean (1815-....) | "Life of Dr. Arnold," &c. | VI., 19. |
| Sterne, Lawrence (1713-1768) | "Tristram Shandy," &c. | IV., 368; V.,394. |
| Stevenson, David | "Civil Engineering of N. America." | IV., 111. |
| Stewart, Dugald (1753-1828) | "Philosophy of the Human Mind." | VI., 180. |
| *Street, A. B. (1811-....) | "Frontenac," and other Poems. | IV., 17. |
| Swain, Charles (1803-....) | Poems and Songs. | V., 460; VI., 335. |
| Swift, Dean (1667-1745) | "Gulliver's Travels;" "Tale of a Tub," &c. | V., 376. |
| Talfourd, Sir T. N. (1795-1854) | "Plays;" "Memorials of Charles Lamb." | IV.,240; VI.,448. |
| Taylor, Henry (ab. 1800) | "Philip van Artevelde," &c. | VI.., 402. |
| Taylor Dr. W. C. (1800-1849) | Manuals of Ancient and Modern History. | V., 16. |
| Tennyson, Alfred (1810-....) | "Maud;" "Idylls of the King," &c. | [520; VI., 280. V., 311,332, 525, |
| Thackeray, W. M. (1811-1863) | "Vanity Fair," "Pendennis," &c. | V., 278. VI.,255. |
| Thirlwall, Bishop (1797- ...) | History of Greece. | VI., 39. |
| Thompson, | | IV., 340. |
| Thomson, James (1700-1748) | "The Seasons." | VI., 437. |
| *Thomson, Rev. Wm. | "The Land and the Book." | IV., 278. |
| Thomson, Archbishop (1810-....) | "Laws of Thought." | VI., 320. |
| Thorne | | V., 207. |
| Thurlow, Lord (1732-1820) | Speeches. | V., 252. |
| Toplady, Rev. Augustus (1740-1776) | Sermons and Hymns. | IV., 346. |
| †Traill, Mrs. | "Backwoods of Canada." | IV., 101. |
| Trench, Archbishop (1807-....) | Notes on the Parables and Miracles. | [VI., 93, 160. IV., 270; V., 411; |
| *Tucker, Professor | Money and Banks. | VI., 80. |
| Tupper, Martin F. (1810....) | "Proverbial Philosophy." | IV., 352; V.,465. |
| Tweedie, Rev. W. K. | Jerusalem and its Environs. | VI., 78. |
| Tynedale, William (ab. 1476-1536) | New Testament in English. | VI., 466. |
| Tyndall, John (1820-....) | "Glaciers of the Alps," &c. | V., 220, 264. |
| Varley, Mrs. | Rudimentary Mineralogy. | V. 68. |

## INDEX OF AUTHORS.

| | | |
|---|---|---|
| Warburton, Eliot (1810-1852) | "Conquest of Canada," Hochelaga, &c. | IV., 240; V., 15. 163, 166, 178; VI. 198. |
| Watts, Alaric A. (1799-1864) | Lyrics of the Heart | VI., 332. |
| *Wayland, Francis (1796-1865) | Elements of Moral Science. | V., 356. |
| *Webster, Daniel (1782-1852) | Speeches. | V., 320. |
| *Welby, Amelia B. (1821-1852) | Poems. | VI., 323. |
| Whewell, Dr. Wm. (1795-1866) | History of the Inductive Sciences. | VI., 210, 325. |
| White, Henry Kirke (1785-1806) | Poetical Remains. | VI., 205. |
| White, Rev. Hugh | Sermons and Addresses. | V., 379. |
| White, Rev. James (1804-1865) | "Landmarks of History." | IV., 183. |
| Whitehead, | | IV., 115. |
| *Whittier, J. G. (1808....) | "Songs of Labor," and other Poems. | IV., 67; VI., 302. |
| †Wilkins, Miss | | VI., 258. |
| Wilkinson, Sir J. G. (1797....) | History of Ancient Egyptians | VI., 1. |
| *Willis, N. P. (1807-1867) | "People I have met, &c." | IV., 255; V.,447; VI., 277. |
| †Wilson, Dr. Daniel | Pre-historic Annals of Scotland. | V. 53. |
| Wilson, Dr. George (1818-1859) | "Religio Chemici." | V., 290, 334. |
| Wilson, Prof. John (1785-1854). | "Recreations of Christopher North." | V., 228, 519; VI., 336. |
| Wilson, Rev. J. M. | Wonders of Creation. | V., 217, 309. |
| Wood, Rev. J. G. (1827-....) | Illustrated Natural History. | IV., 136. |
| Wordsworth, Wm. (1770-1850) | "The Excursion" and "Lyrical Ballads." | IV ; 200; V., 338; VI., 207, 229. |
| Wotton, Sir Henry (1568-1639) | Essays and Poems. | VI., 71. |
| Wyatt, Sir Thomas (1503-1542) | Poems. | VI., 464. |
| Wycliffe, John (ab. 1324-1384) | New Testament in English. | VI., 466. |
| Yonge, Miss C. M. (1823-....) | "Heir of Redclyffe," &c. | V., 114. |
| Young, Edward (1681-1765) | "Night Thoughts." | V., 393. |
| †Yule, Mrs. (Miss Vining) | | VI., 420. |

www.ingramcontent.com/pod-product-compliance
Lightning Source LLC
Chambersburg PA
CBHW021426300426
44114CB00010B/663